东莞统计年鉴

DONGGUAN STATISTICAL YEARBOOK

2017

(总第27期 NO.27)

东莞市统计局
国家统计局东莞调查队 编

Compiled by
Dongguan Municipal Bureau of Statistics
Survey Office of the National Bureau of Statistics in Dongguan

中国统计出版社
China Statistics Press

图书在版编目（CIP）数据

东莞统计年鉴. 2017 / 东莞市统计局, 国家统计局东莞调查队编.
-- 北京：中国统计出版社, 2017.8
ISBN 978-7-5037-8176-6

Ⅰ. ①东…
Ⅱ. ①东… ②国…
Ⅲ. ①统计资料-东莞-2017-年鉴
Ⅳ. ①C832.653-54

中国版本图书馆 CIP 数据核字 (2017) 第 158560 号

东莞统计年鉴-2017

作　　者/ 东莞市统计局　国家统计局东莞调查队
责任编辑/ 陈越月
装帧设计/ 钟锦漩
出版发行/ 中国统计出版社
地　　址/ 北京市丰台区西三环南路甲 6 号
邮政编码/ 100073
电　　话/ 邮购（010）63376909　书店（010）68783171
网　　址/ http://csp.stats.gov.cn
印　　刷/ 东莞市本色印刷有限公司
经　　销/ 新华书店
开　　本/ 890mm×1240mm　1/16
字　　数/ 1200 千字
印　　张/ 33 印张
版　　别/ 2017 年 8 月第 1 版
版　　次/ 2017 年 8 月第 1 次印刷
定　　价/ 450.00 元

如有印装差错，由本社发行部调换。

编者说明

一、《东莞统计年鉴—2017》（以下简称年鉴）是一部反映东莞国民经济和社会发展情况的资料性年刊，本年鉴收录了东莞2016年经济社会各方面的统计数据以及历年主要指标数据，旨在全面系统地反映东莞经济和社会发展变化情况。

二、本年鉴主要内容分为三部分，具体为：第一部分概述，包括中英文统计公报和政府工作报告；第二部分统计资料，具体分为综合、人口与劳动力、农业、工业、固定资产投资与建筑业、运输邮电、国内贸易、价格指数、对外经济贸易与旅游、财政、金融与保险、人民生活、社会事业、能源、镇街主要指标、村（居）委会主要指标、历年国民经济和社会发展主要指标、东莞与全国、全省、三角洲城市及港澳台主要指标比较等17个篇章；第三部分基本单位情况。

三、本年鉴资料大部分来自东莞市统计局和国家统计局东莞调查队，部分来自中央省属单位和市直属各部门的统计资料。

四、本年鉴统计表中的符号说明："#"表示其中主要项；"空格"表示该项统计指标数据不详或无该项数据。

五、与2016年版《东莞统计年鉴》相比，本年鉴在内容上主要作了如下修订：第二部分中"人口与劳动力"篇增加了"全社会从业人员"分行业情况；"国内贸易"篇增加了"限额以上批发和零售业商品购进、销售、库存总额"；"社会事业"篇增加了"规模以上服务业企业R&D活动及相关情况"；"财政、金融与保险"篇增加了"历年本外币存、贷款余额"情况；另根据新的部门报表制度对个别专业内容及相关统计指标进行了调整。

本年鉴在编辑出版过程中，得到省统计局、市有关部门和镇街（园区）的大力支持，在此我们表示衷心感谢。鉴于我们的水平有限，本年鉴难免有疏漏之处，敬请批评指正，以帮助我们进一步改进年鉴编辑工作，更好地为广大读者服务。

《东莞统计年鉴—2017》
编委会和编辑出版人员

目　　录

CONTENTS

第一部分　概　述

Part One　Outline

第二部分　统计资料

Part Two　Statistics

一、综　合

General Survey

二、人口与劳动力
Population and Labor Force

三、农 业
Agriculture

四、工　业

Industry

五、固定资产投资与建筑业
Investment in Fixed Assets and Construction

六、运输邮电

Transport, Postal and Telecommunication Services

七、国内贸易
Domestic Trade

八、价格指数
Price Indices

九、对外经济贸易与旅游
Foreign Trade and Tourism

十、财政、金融与保险
Finance, Banking and Insurance

十一、人民生活
People's Living Conditions

十二、社会事业
Social Undertakings

十三、能源
Energy

十四、镇街主要指标
Main Indicators of Towns

十五、村（居）委会主要指标
Main Indicators of Villagers' (Neighborhood) Committees

十六、历年国民经济和社会发展主要指标
Main Indicators of National Economy and Social Development over Years

十七、东莞与全国、全省、三角洲城市及港澳台主要指标比较
Comparison of Main Indicators between Dongguan and China, Guangdong Province, the Cities of the Pearl River Delta Hong Kong Macao Taiwan

第三部分　基本单位情况
Part Three　Basic Units

生产总值

地区生产总值（亿元）

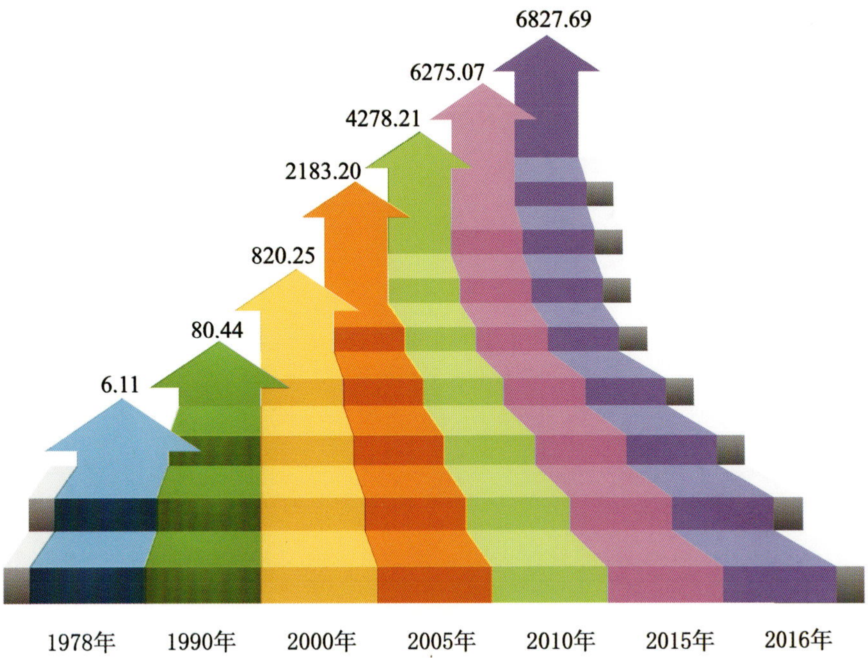

地区生产总值构成（%）

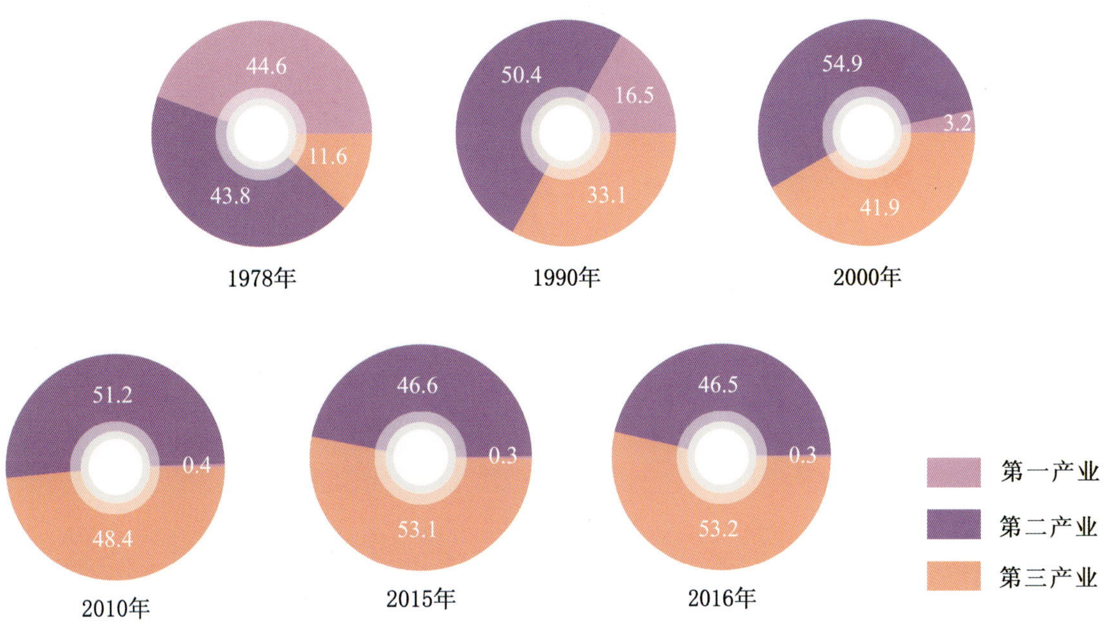

人口与劳动力

人口（万人）

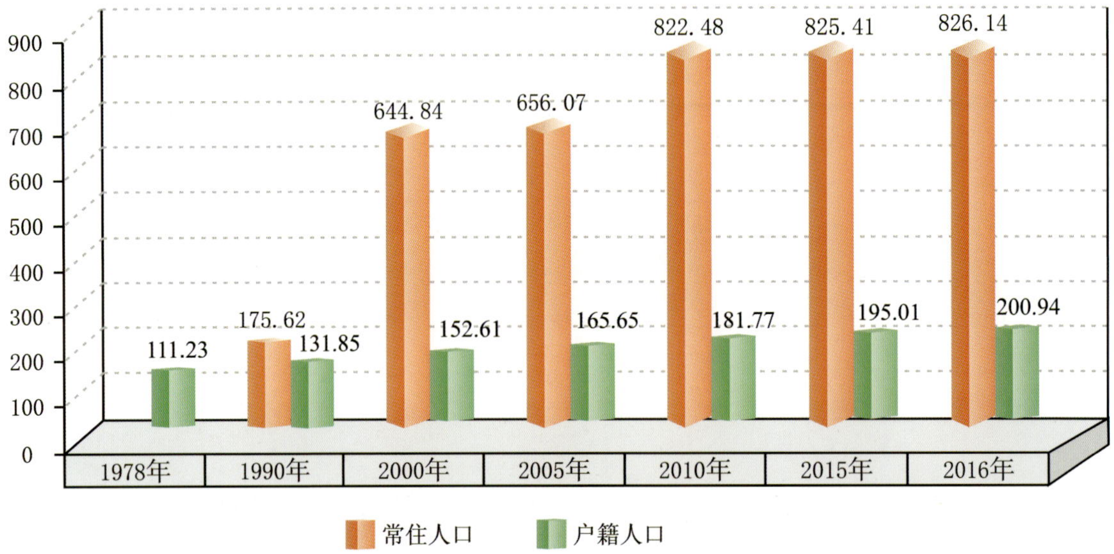

全社会从业人员（万人）

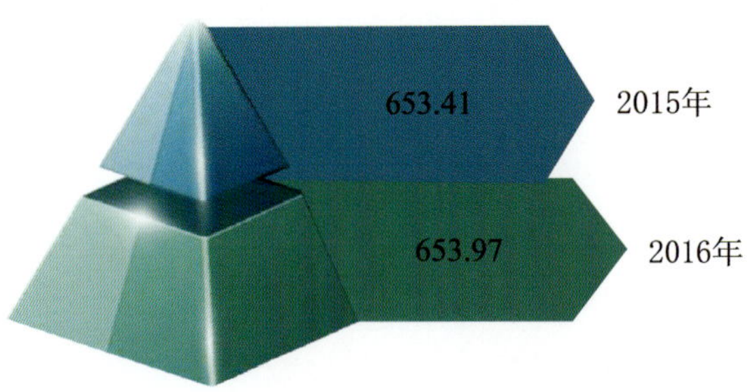

城镇非私营单位在岗职工年平均工资（元）

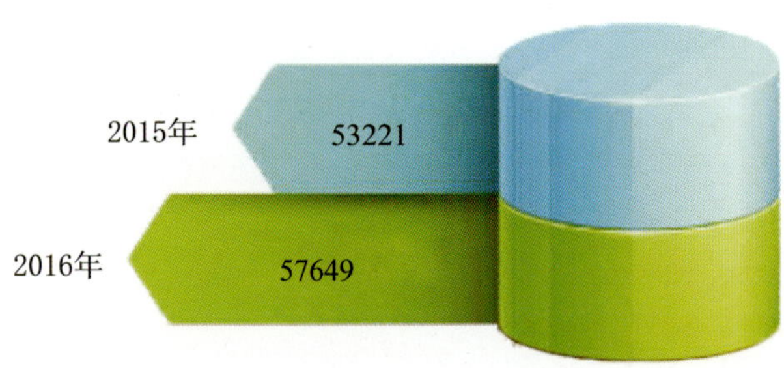

农业

农、林、牧、渔业总产值（亿元）

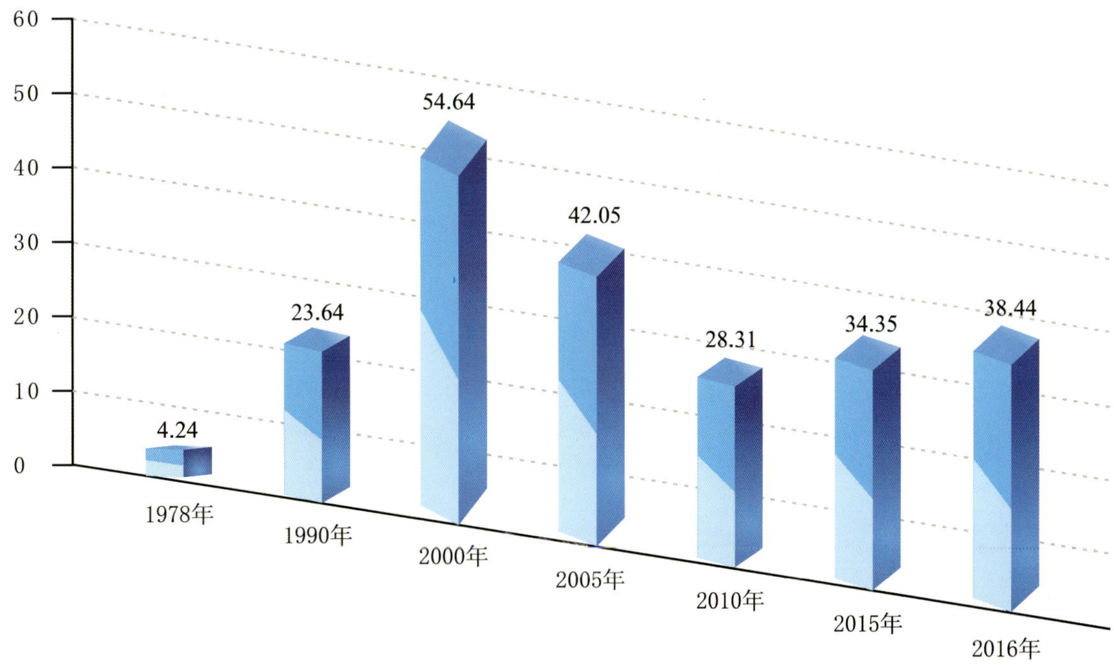

农、林、牧、渔业增加值（亿元）

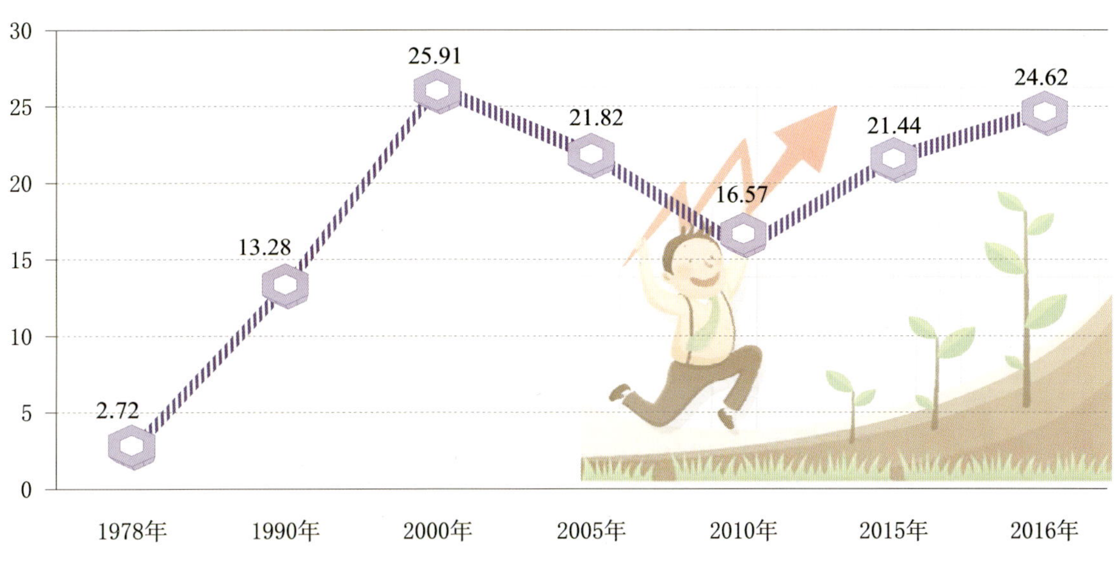

工业

规模以上工业增加值（亿元）

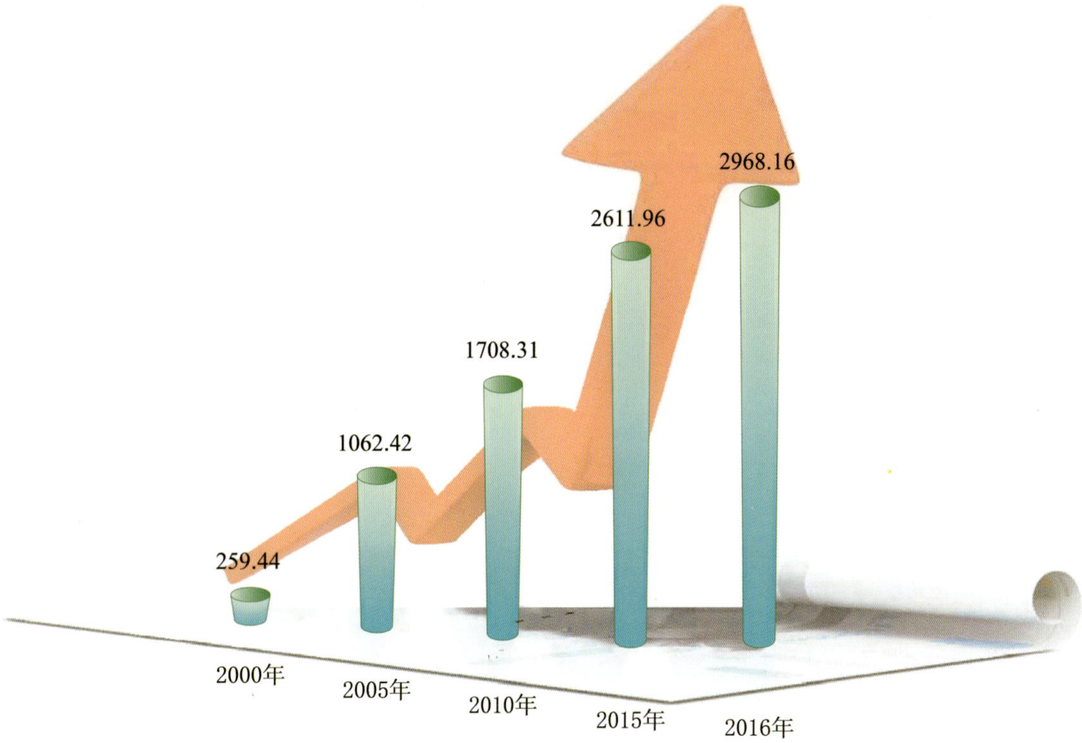

规模以上工业增加值构成（%）

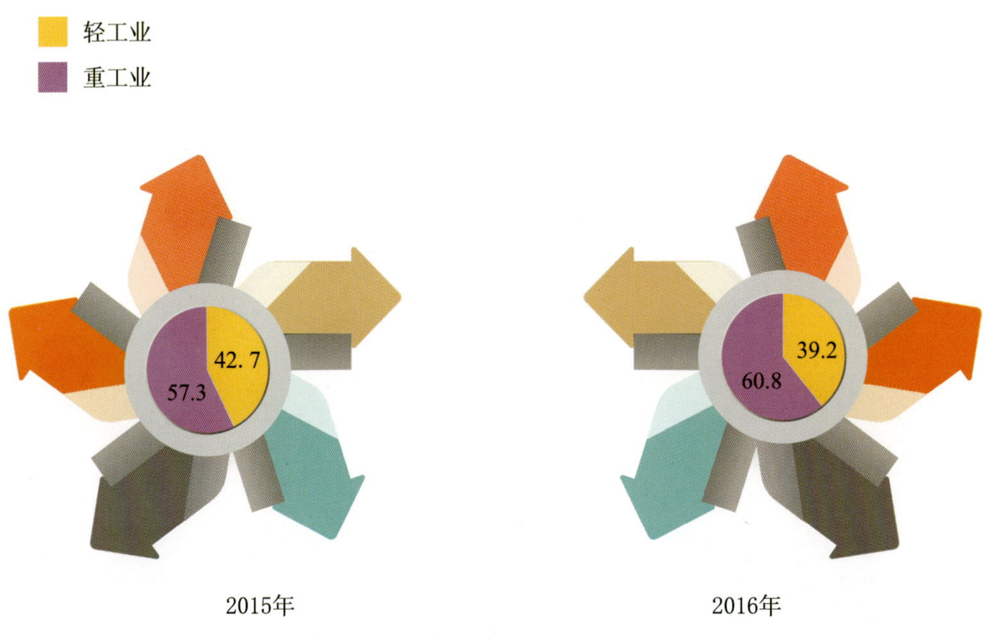

固定资产投资

固定资产投资总额（亿元）

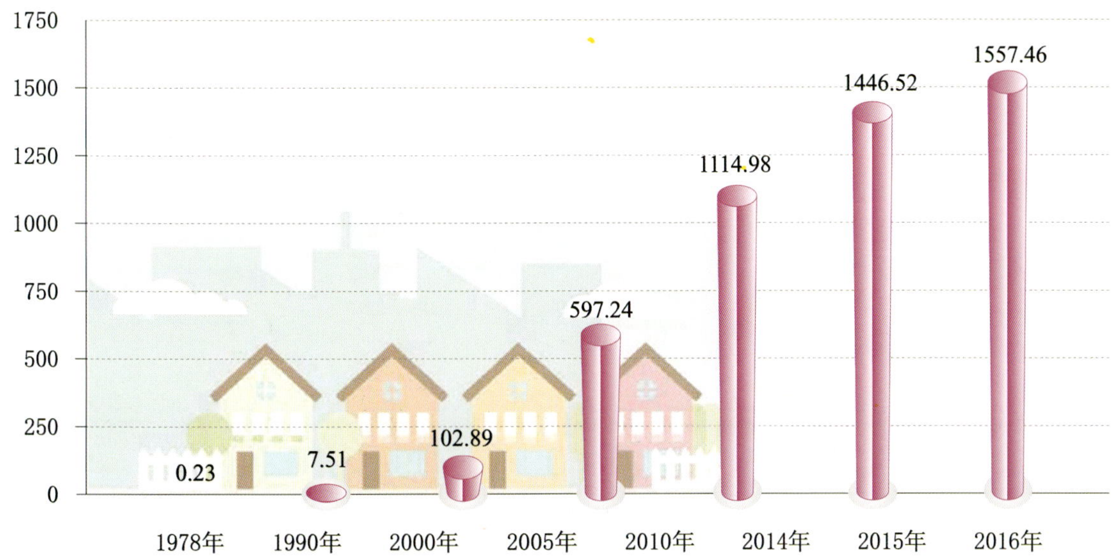

房地产开发投资总额（亿元）

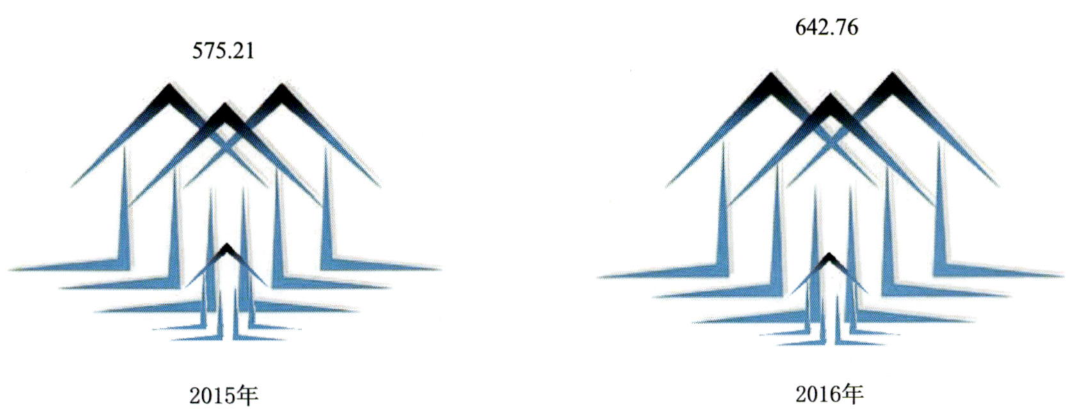

运输邮电

货物、旅客运输量

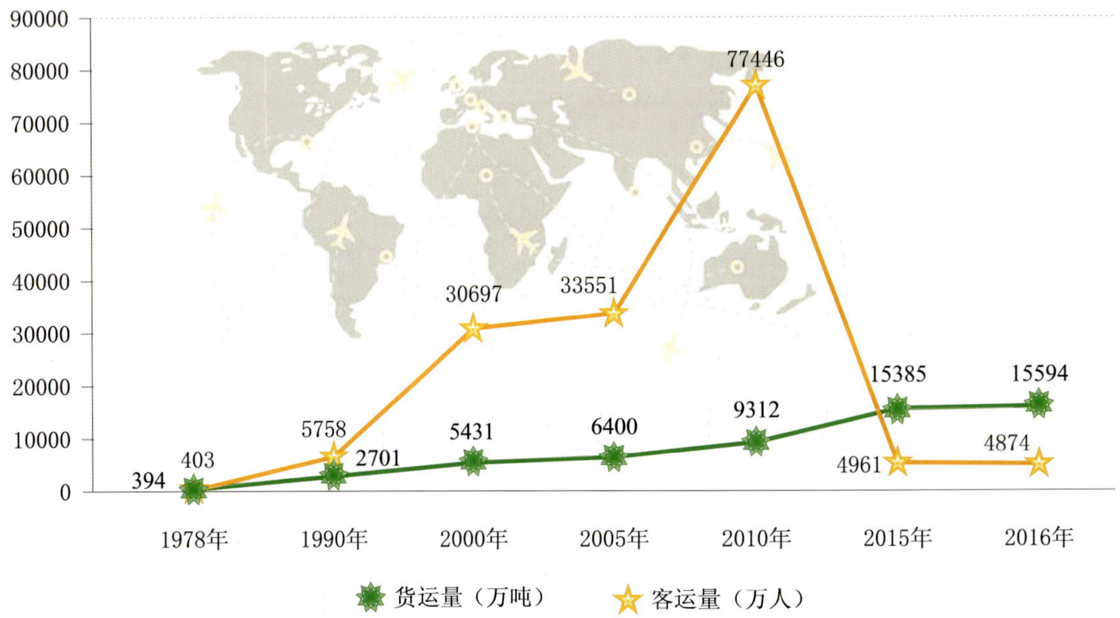

注：2014年起，客运量和旅客周转量不含城市客运量，数据与往年不可比。

本地电话用户、移动电话用户（万户）

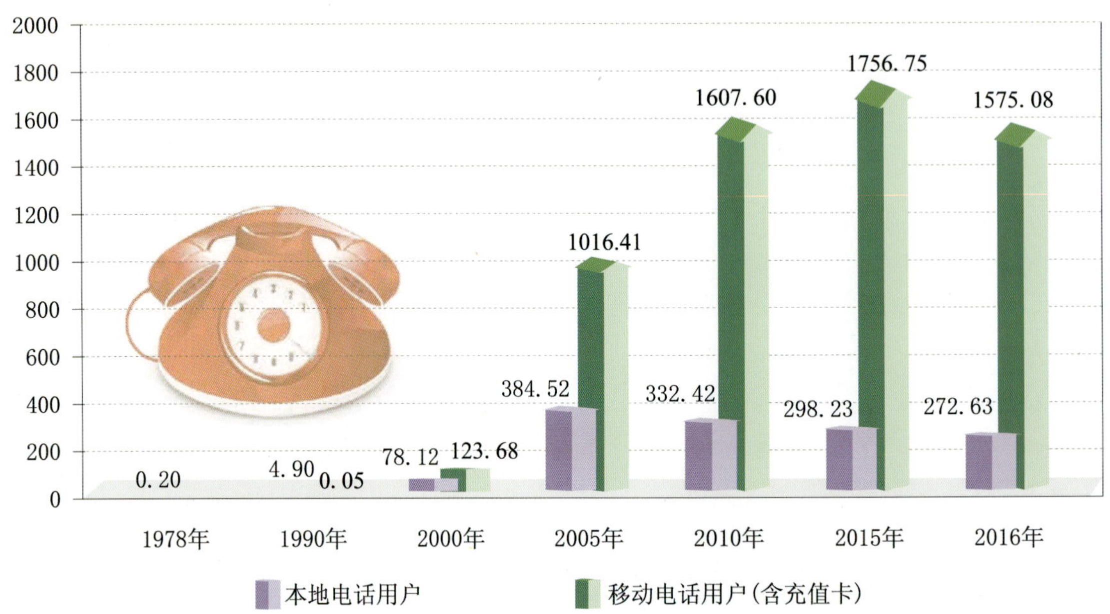

注：2015年起，本地电话用户取消小灵通。

国内贸易

社会消费品零售总额（亿元）

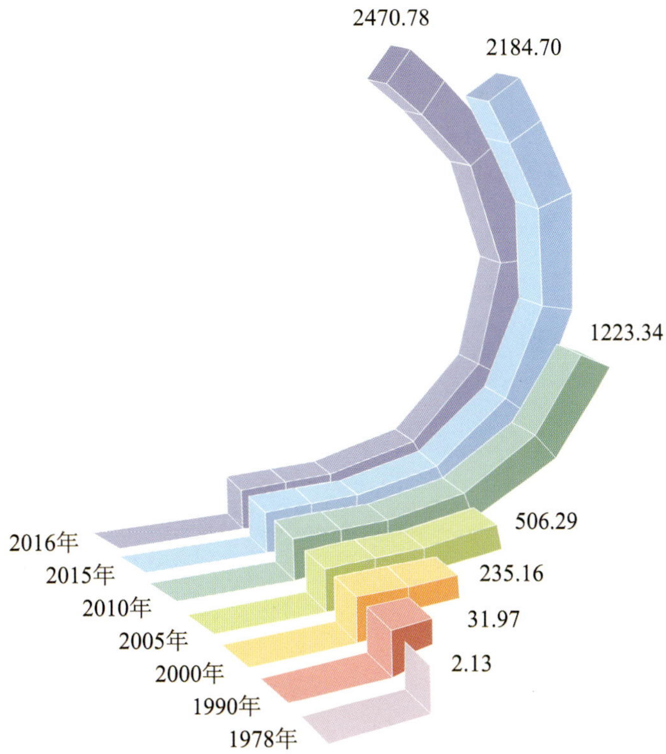

批发和零售、住宿和餐饮

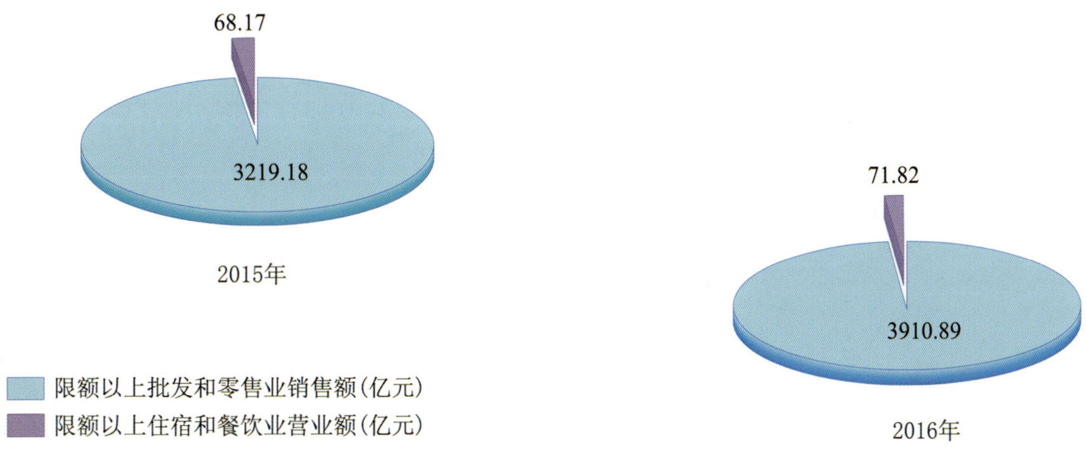

价格指数

居民消费价格总指数(以上年为100)

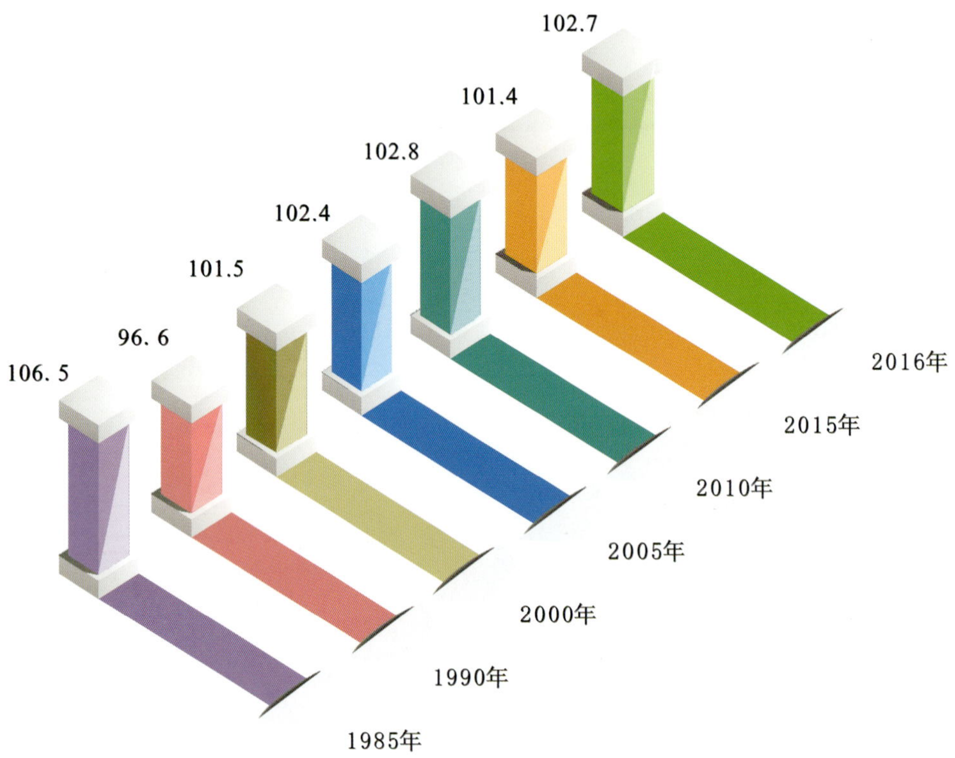

工业生产者出厂价格指数(以上年为100)

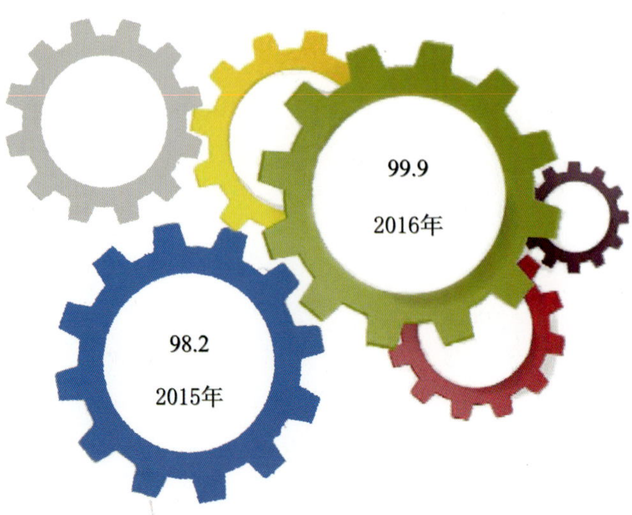

对外经济贸易与旅游

进口总额(亿元)

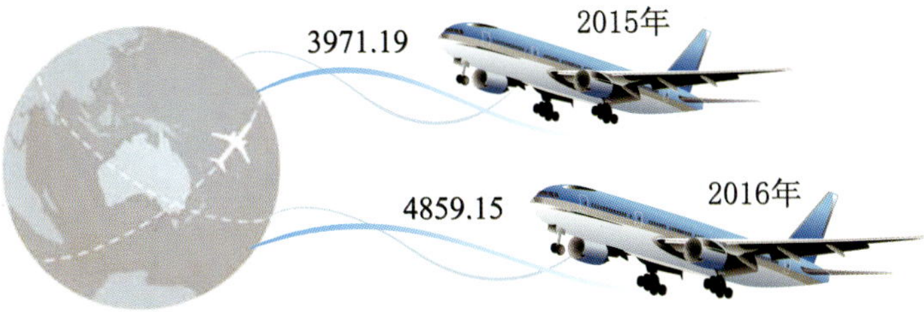

出口总额(亿元)

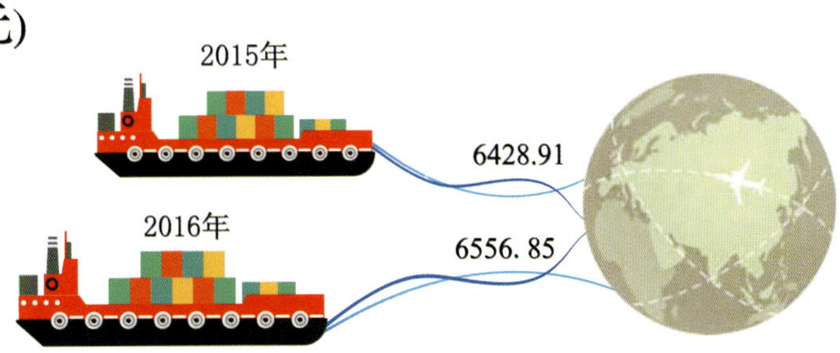

当年实际利用外资(亿美元)

全年接待国内外旅游人数(万人次)

财政、金融

来源于东莞的财政收入 (亿元)

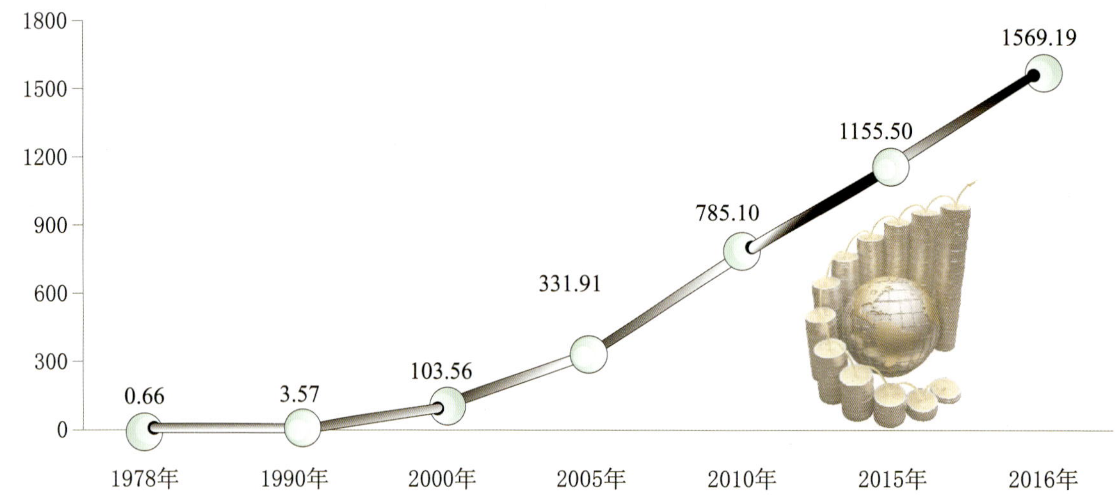

各项人民币存、贷款余额 (亿元)

人民生活

2015年人民生活 (元)

38651 全体居民人均可支配收入

39793 城镇常住居民人均可支配收入

24225 农村常住居民人均可支配收入

2016年人民生活 (元)

全体居民人均可支配收入 41902

城镇常住居民人均可支配收入 43096

农村常住居民人均可支配收入 26526

社会事业

建城区绿地面积（万平方米）

专利申请量（件）

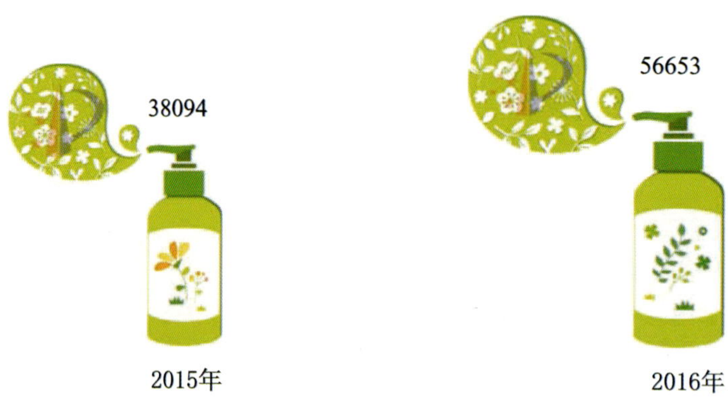

专利授权量（件）

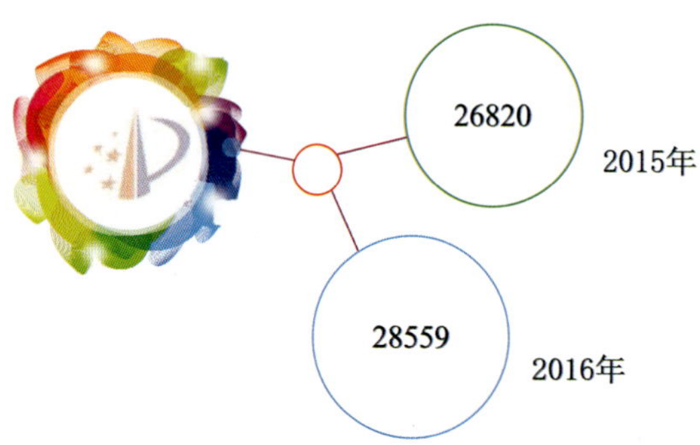

卫生事业机构床位数（张）

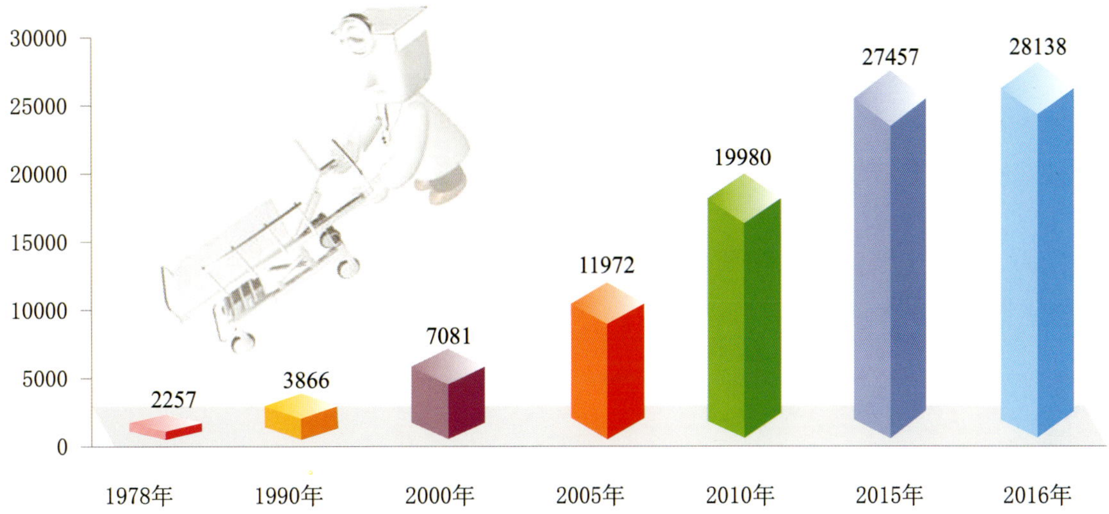

执业（助理）医师（人）

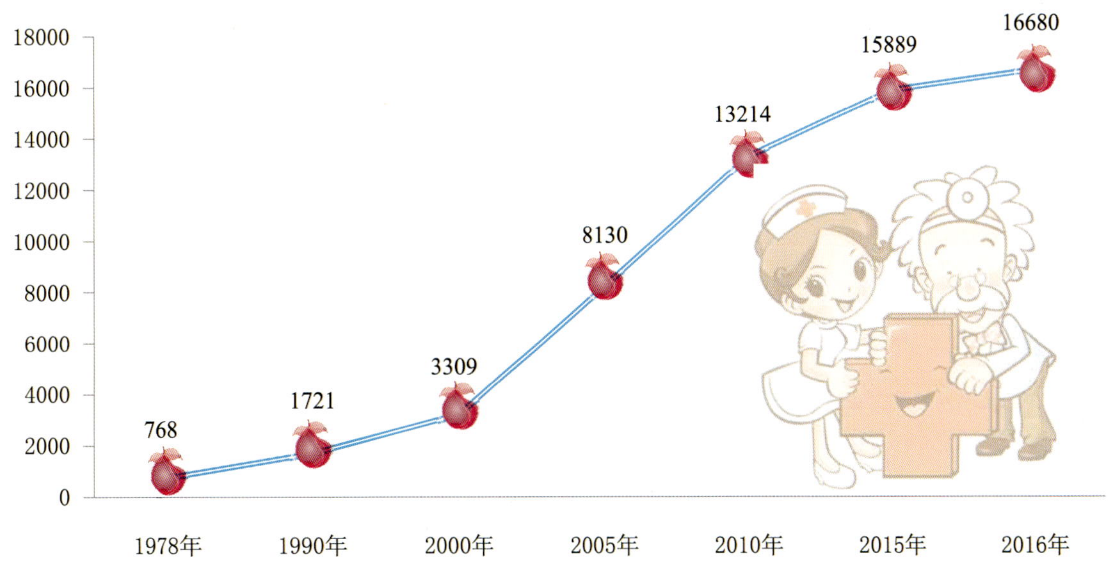

各类学校 (所)

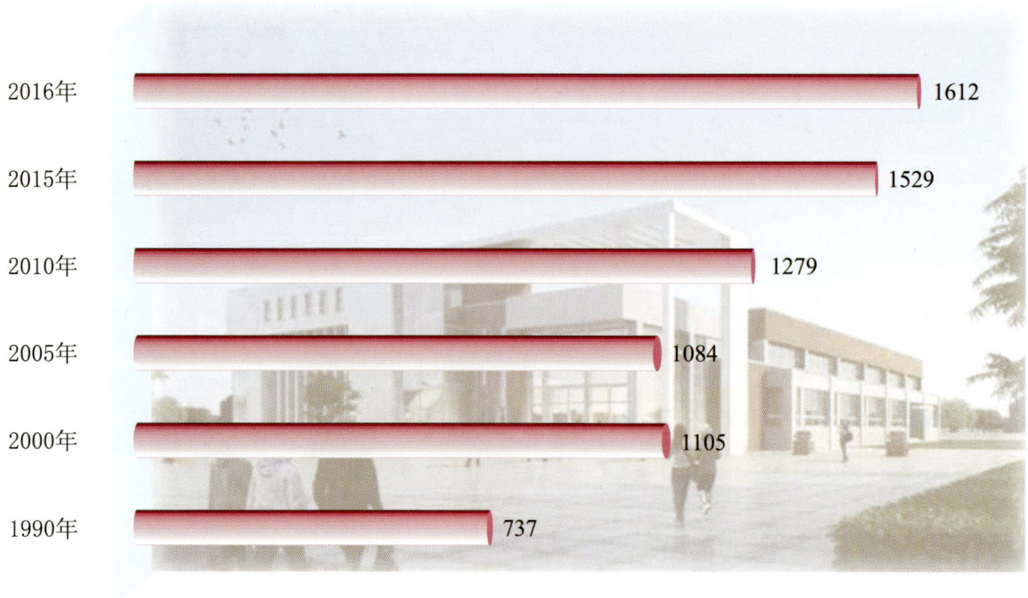

各类学校在校学生 (万人)

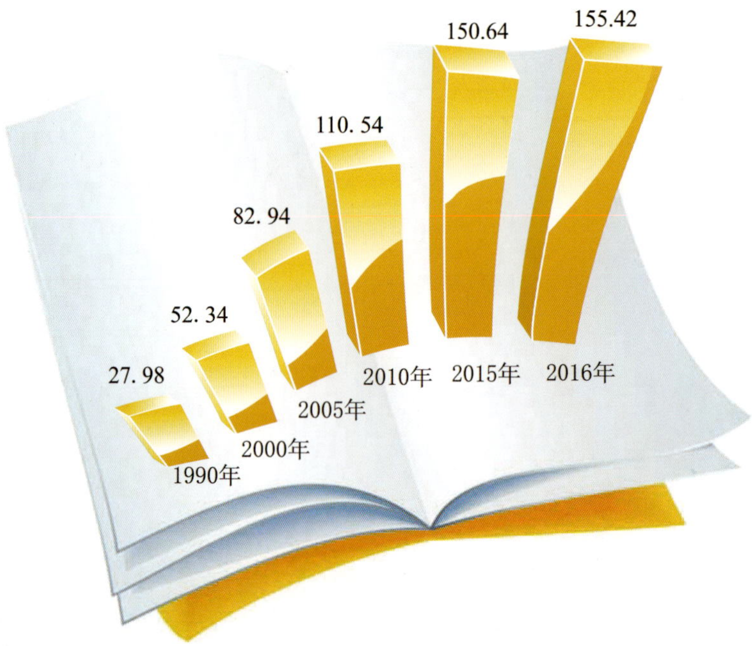

能源

单位生产总值能耗上升率或下降率(%)

规模以上工业综合能源消费量(万吨标准煤)

第一部分　概　述

Part One　Outline

2016 年东莞市国民经济和社会发展统计公报

2016 年，面对严峻复杂的宏观形势和改革发展稳定的艰巨任务，全市上下在市委、市政府的正确领导下，认真贯彻党的十八届三中、四中、五中、六中全会和习近平总书记系列重要讲话精神，紧紧围绕“三个走在前列”目标，主动适应经济发展新常态，以供给侧结构性改革为统领，以构建开放型经济新体制为契机，凝心聚力，克难奋进，深入实施创新驱动战略，着力提高经济发展质量和效益，努力稳增长、促改革、调结构、惠民生，实现了“十三五”的良好开局。全市经济呈现出稳中有进、进中向好的良好态势，经济社会发展取得了新成绩。

一、综　合

初步核算，2016 年东莞生产总值（GDP）6827.67 亿元，比上年增长 8.1%。分产业看，第一产业增加值 22.80 亿元，下降 0.3%；第二产业增加值 3172.50 亿元，增长 7.2%；第三产业增加值 3632.37 亿元，增长 8.9%。三次产业比例为 0.3：46.5：53.2。人均地区生产总值 82682 元，增长 8.6%。

在现代产业中，规模以上先进制造业增加值 1435.17 亿元，增长 15.2%；现代服务业增加值 2180.84 亿元，增长 10.3%。

在第三产业中，交通运输、仓储和邮政业增长 1.1%，批发和零售业增长 7.7%，住宿和餐饮业增长 0.4%，金融业增长 8.2%，房地产业增长 3.5%，其他服务业增长 14.4%。

图一　2011－2016 年地区生产总值及增长速度

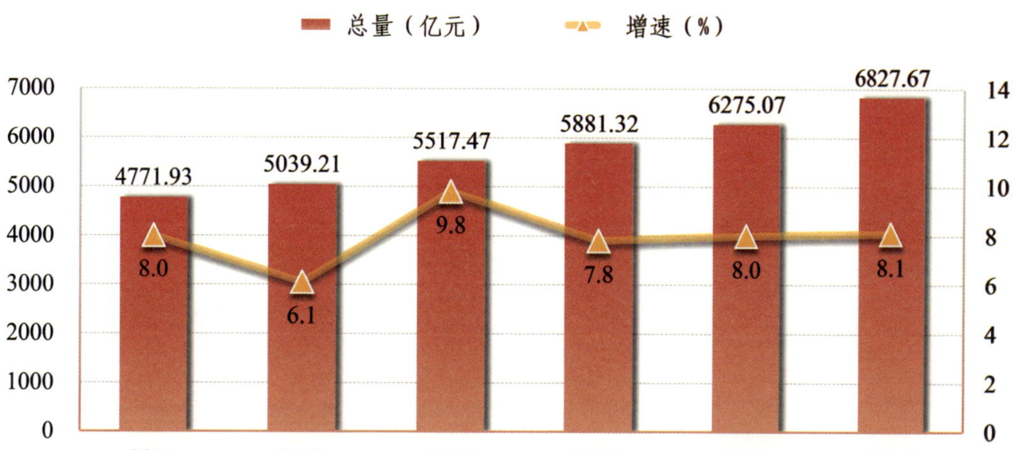

年末，全市工商登记总数 84.04 万户，同比增长 17.8%。其中企业工商登记 32.89 万户，增长 28.3%；个体户登记 51.08 万户，增长 12.0%。私营企业登记户数增长较快，增长 30.7%。从新登记注册情况看，2016 年，全市工商新登记 17.39 万户，增长 41.3%；新登记企业 8.22 万家，增长 49.7%。

全年居民消费价格总水平比上年上涨 2.7%。其中食品烟酒类上涨 6.3%，衣着类上涨 1.2%，居住类上涨 0.8%，生活用品及服务类上涨 2.0%，交通和通信类下降 1.4%，教育文化和娱乐类上涨 1.3%，医疗保健类上涨 7.5%，其他用品和服务类上涨 0.5%。此外，全年商品零售价格总指数上涨 0.9%。工业生产者出厂价格指数下降 0.1%。

图二 2011—2016 年居民消费价格总指数（上年=100）

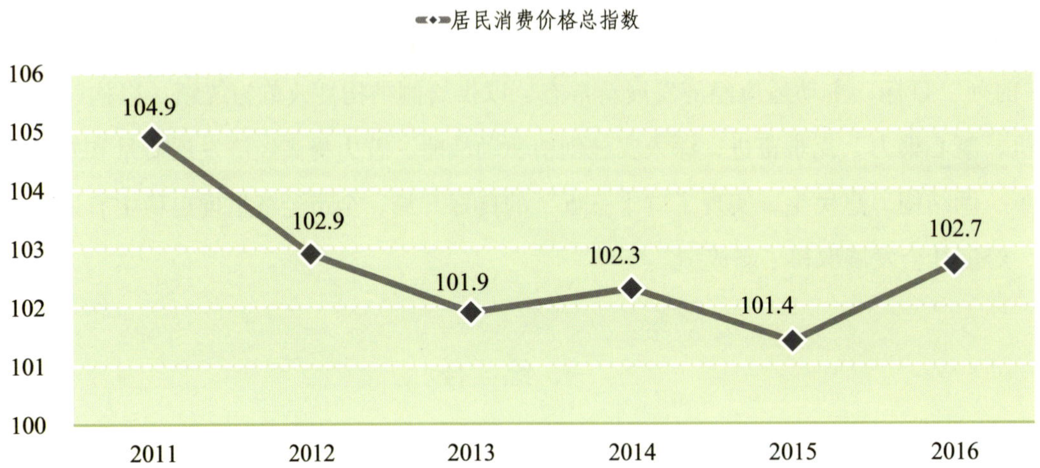

表一 2016 年价格变动情况

类别	价格指数（上年=100）
居民消费价格总指数	102.7
食品烟酒	106.3
其中：粮食	104.2
畜肉类	109.7
食用油	98.7
蛋类	94.2
菜	111.8
水产品	109.2
衣着	101.2
居住	100.8
生活用品及服务	102.0
交通和通信	98.6
教育文化和娱乐	101.3
医疗保健	107.5
其他用品和服务	100.5
商品零售价格总指数	100.9
工业生产者出厂价格指数	99.9

全年来源于东莞的财政收入1569.19亿元，比上年增长35.8%。市一般公共预算收入544.75亿元，增长8.2%。市一般公共预算支出599.29亿元，增长3.1%。其中，一般公共服务支出63.67亿元，公共安全支出81.54亿元，教育支出142.95亿元，社会保障和就业支出35.29亿元。全年全市税收总额1704.96亿元，增长20.7%。

年末城镇实有登记失业人数1.38万人，全年失业人员安置就业人数1.01万人，城镇登记失业率为2.26%。

二、农　业

2016年全市农林牧渔业总产值38.44亿元，比上年增长3.1%。其中农业产值27.01亿元，增长12.4%，占农林牧渔业总产值的70.3%；林业产值0.39亿元，增长3.6%，占1.0%；牧业产值3.50亿元，下降15.2%，占16.9%；渔业产值6.51亿元，下降15.5%，占16.9%。全年农作物总播种面积37.65万亩，其中水果种植面积19.89万亩。全年粮食产量1.26万吨；水产品总产量5.66万吨；蔬菜产量40.43万吨，增长0.7%；生猪出栏11.49万头，下降15.8%；家禽出栏398.27万只，下降1.7%。

2016年新增20家农民专业合作社。目前，全市共有农民专业合作社190家、农业龙头企业43家（其中省级以上11家，国家级3家）、有效期内的省级农业类名牌产品达52个（含林业、渔业）。

三、工业和建筑业

全年全市规模以上工业实现增加值2878.23亿元，比上年增长7.0%。在规模以上工业中，重工业增加值1750.98亿元，增长13.5%，占60.8%；轻工业增加值1127.25亿元，下降1.5%，占39.2%。

全年全市规模以上工业五大支柱产业完成增加值1952.24亿元，增长8.5%；工业四个特色产业完成增加值281.47亿元，增长0.3%。

全年高技术制造业增加值增长17.6%，其中，医药制造业增长7.5%，电子及通信设备制造业增长20.9%，电子计算机及办公设备制造业下降4.0%，医疗设备及仪器仪表制造业增长17.8%。

全年先进制造业增加值增长15.2%，其中，装备制造业增长16.0%，钢铁冶炼及加工业下降4.2%，石油及化学制造业增长1.7%。装备制造业中，金属制造业增长7.5%，通用设备制造业增长8.0%，专用设备制造业增长13.1%，汽车制造业增长19.5%，铁路、船舶、航空航天和其他运输设备制造业下降30.5%，电气机械和器材制造业增长0.7%，计算机、通信和其他电子设备制造业增长20.4%，仪器仪表制造业增长19.5%；钢铁冶炼及加工业中，钢压延加工下降4.2%；石油及化学行业中，石油加工、炼焦及核燃料加工业下降16.0%，化学原料及化学制品制造业增长3.8%，橡胶制品业下降3.2%。

全年优势传统产业增加值下降0.1%，其中，纺织服装业下降6.8%，食品饮料业增长1.0%，家具制造业下降0.5%，建筑材料增长3.2%，金属制品业增长8.3%，家用电力器具制造业增长3.5%。

规模以上工业综合经济效益指数为160.5%，实现利润总额472.12亿元。

表二　2016 年规模以上工业主要产品产量

产品名称	计量单位	产量	增长（%）
移动通信手持机（手机）	万台	35909.47	58.0
数字激光音、视盘机	万台	4591.87	−19.2
集成电路	万块	72539.49	53.6
光电子器件	万只（万片、万套）	1314191.01	33.8
电子元件	亿只	12319.20	8.7
汽车仪器仪表	万台	96.45	17.4
光学仪器	万台（万个）	94.80	−17.0
眼镜成镜	万副	6496.96	1.3
自来水生产量	亿立方米	15.87	−4.2
大米	吨	277980.61	−10.8
糖果	吨	237158.81	−0.7
服装	万件	137783.07	−6.8
轻革	万平方米	193.20	−27.7
人造板	万立方米	21.33	−17.6
纸制品	万吨	204.71	−3.9
家具	万件	3748.92	−30.0
机制纸及纸板（外购原纸加工除外）	万吨	1507.86	6.0
塑料制品	万吨	117.96	3.4
化学试剂	吨	129957.92	−8.4
瓷质砖	万平方米	3335.11	20.2
金属集装箱	万立方米	361.29	−47.9
电动手提式工具	万台	2689.52	5.5
数码照相机	万台	43.42	69.7
模具	万套	6.43	1.4
锂离子电池	万只（万自然只）	32845.83	−24.3
灯具及照明装置	万套（万台、万个）	24307.97	−7.9
电子计算机整机	万台	125.65	15.8
打印机	万台	59.89	−38.5
电话单机	万部	3158.54	−5.0

全年全市建筑业实现增加值 91.21 亿元，比上年增长 1.9%。总承包和专业承包建筑企业完成总产值 245.18 亿元，增长 15.5%；施工面积 914.05 万平方米，下降 14.8%；竣工面积 349.06 万平方米，下降 23.0%。总承包和专业承包建筑企业按施工产值计算的全员劳动生产率为 34.07 万元 / 人，增长 16.4%。

四、固定资产投资

全年固定资产投资 1557.46 亿元，比上年增长 7.7%。按投资主体分，国有经济投资 120.66 亿元，下降 32.3%；民营经济投资 1061.05 亿元，增长 12.0%；外商及港澳台商投资 293.14 亿元，增长 9.4%。

图三 2011—2016 年固定资产投资增长速度

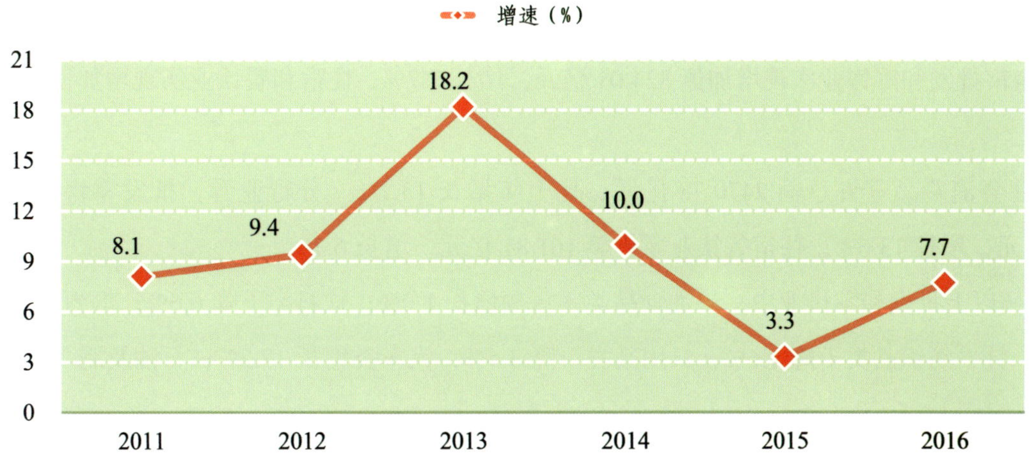

从产业投向看，投资集中在第二、三产业。第二产业投资 566.06 亿元，其中制造业投资 503.74 亿元；第三产业投资 990.23 亿元。

表三 2016 年分行业固定资产投资情况

行 业	投资额（万元）	增长（%）
总 计	15574580	7.7
农、林、牧、渔业	13345	55.7
制造业	5037401	16.4
电力、热力、燃气及水生产和供应业	617045	−11.8
建筑业	10000	28.5
交通运输、仓储和邮政业	1333819	−8.6
信息传输、软件和信息技术服务业	172826	−10.0
批发和零售业	178852	−7.4
住宿和餐饮业	28047	−56.3
金融业	55934	39.0
房地产业	7092286	10.6
租赁和商务服务业	21262	−42.3
科学研究和技术服务业	173136	−23.3
水利、环境和公共设施管理业	453295	3.7
居民服务、修理和其他服务业	5100	−44.3
教育	251368	4.8
卫生和社会工作	65507	−10.0
文化、体育和娱乐业	37400	84.3
公共管理、社会保障和社会组织	27957	60.0

全年完成房地产开发投资 642.76 亿元，增长 11.7%。商品房屋施工面积 4408.65 万平方米，增长 12.4%；竣工面积 232.68 万平方米，下降 28.5%；新建商品房网上签约销售面积 1061.88 万平方米，下降 1.4%，其中商品住宅销售面积 887.71 万平方米，下降 9.2%。全年新建商品房网上签约销售额 1459.43 亿元，增长 35.6%，其中商品住宅销售额 1221.79 亿元，增长 27.3%。

五、国内贸易

全年全市批发和零售业实现增加值 824.01 亿元，增长 7.7%；住宿和餐饮业实现增加值 158.61 亿元，增长 0.4%。

全年社会消费品零售总额 2470.78 亿元，比上年增长 13.1%。分行业看，批发零售贸易业零售额 2308.97 亿元，增长 13.6%；住宿餐饮业零售额 161.81 亿元，增长 6.7%。

在限额以上批发和零售业中，粮油食品类零售额增长 1.0%；饮料类下降 6.6%；烟酒类下降 0.5%；服装鞋帽、针、纺织品类下降 1.6%；日用品类下降 3.5%；汽车类增长 17.2%；石油及制品类增长 2.7%。

图四 2011—2016 年社会消费品零售总额及增长速度

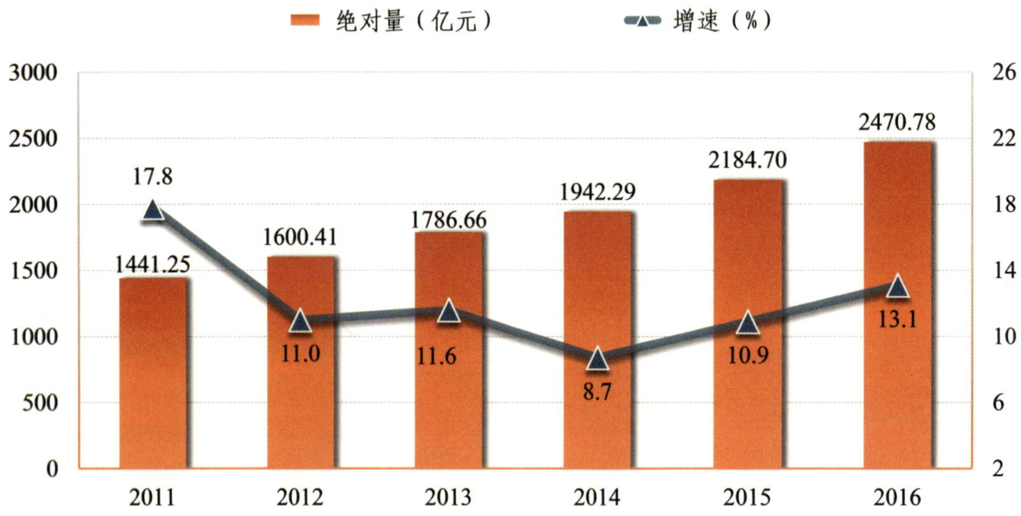

六、对外经济

全年全市进出口总额 11415.99 亿元，增长 9.8%。其中进口 4859.15 亿元，增长 22.4%；出口 6556.85 亿元，增长 2.0%。

按贸易方式分，一般贸易出口 2360.95 亿元，增长 0.6%；加工贸易出口 3794.46 亿元，下降 1.7%；其他出口 401.4 亿元，增长 81.8%。

按出口的地区分，对亚洲出口 3548.91 亿元，增长 6.0%；对北美洲出口 1532.11 亿元，下降 5.4%；对欧洲出口 1102.57 亿元，增长 5.1%；对拉丁美洲出口 200.78 亿元，下降 5.5%；对大洋洲出口 80.96 亿元，下降 5.0%。

全年机电产品出口 4659.17 亿元，增长 6.3%，占出口总额的 71.1%；高新技术产品出口 2586.40 亿元，增长 17.7%，占 39.4%。

全年全市新签外商直接投资项目 446 宗，合同外资金额 47.32 亿美元，下降 6.5%。实际利用外资 39.26 亿美元，下降 26.2%。其中通信设备、计算机及其他电子设备制造业实际利用外资 2.66 亿美元，下降 59.7%；专用设备制造业实际利用外资 1.48 亿美元，下降 40.2%。

表四　2016年主要商品出口情况

商品名称	金额（万元）	增长（%）
机电产品（包括本目录已具体列名的机电产品）	46591748	6.3
高新技术产品	25863984	17.7
自动数据处理设备及其部件	4108710	−8.5
服装及衣着附件	3547696	−17.4
电话机	6575345	63.6
家具及其零件	2913072	−8.5
鞋类	1647909	−17.3
自动数据处理设备的零件	1725291	−12.1
静止式变流器	1959852	2.1
灯具、照明装置及类似品	1504777	−14.9
箱包及类似容器	1411831	−12.9
玩具	1757329	13.9
电线和电缆	1375527	−1.6
塑料制品	1275546	−8.2
通断保护电路装置及零件	1442230	4.9
纺织纱线、织物及制品	1024553	−9.5
打印机（包括多功能一体机）	717632	−32.8
电视、收音机及无线电讯设备的零附件	972333	26.5
贵金属或包贵金属的首饰	1644500	116.4
印刷电路	582453	−0.8
文化产品	5581884	15.9
眼镜及其零件	669281	15.4

表五　2016年分行业利用外资情况

行业名称	合同外资金额（万美元）	增长（%）	实际利用外资（万美元）	增长（%）
总　计	473173	−6.5	392617	−26.2
制造业	187106	−17.5	169649	−17.5
纺织业	11948	1.6	9200	−46.4
纺织服装、鞋、帽制造业	5890	−61.9	2301	−91.7
家具制造业	1876	37.7	1107	−74.6
通用设备制造业	2472	−65.2	5017	−76.3
专用设备制造业	15785	9.0	14762	−40.2
电气机械及器材制造业	17712	−28.0	12402	−52.8
通信设备、计算机及其他电子设备制造业	27960	−45.8	26625	−59.7
金属制品业	17611	−32.9	19087	−54.1
塑料制品业	11380	10.0	6830	−70.8
文教体育用品制造业	3376	−58.4	5214	−56.2
造纸及纸制品业	28044	39.4	33584	350.9
其他制造业	43052	21.3	33520	−52.8
交通运输、仓储和邮政业	12763	−22.7	6904	−22.7
批发和零售业	27463	−51.6	23529	−23.2

七、交通、邮电和旅游

全年全市交通运输、仓储和邮政业实现增加值 209.60 亿元，增长 1.1%。

全年全市公路通车里程 5266.25 公里，公路密度 213.64 公里 / 百平方公里，继续位居全省前列。年末全市机动车保有量（民用）225.11 万辆，增长 19.7%。其中汽车保有量 224.62 万辆，增长 21.8%。

全年公路货物运输量 10325 万吨，货物周转量 71.67 亿吨公里；水路货物运输量 5268.67 万吨，货物周转量 383.56 亿吨公里。全年公路运输完成客运量 4847.42 万人，旅客周转量 77.14 亿人公里；水路运输完成客运量 27.04 万人，旅客周转量 1757.07 万人公里。全年港口旅客吞吐量 26.67 万人次，货物吞吐量 14583.72 万吨。

表六　2016 年客（货）运量、周转量

指　　标	单 位	数 值	增长（%）
客运量	万人	4874	−1.8
# 公路	万人	4847	−1.6
旅客周转量	亿人公里	77.32	0.2
# 公路	亿人公里	77.14	0.3
货运量	万吨	15593	1.4
# 公路	万吨	10325	−1.4
货物周转量	亿吨公里	455.23	−9.8
# 公路	亿吨公里	71.67	−0.03

全年完成邮电业务（含快递）收入 295.13 亿元，比上年增长 18.5%。邮政发送信函 9201 万件，邮政快递包裹 975 万件，邮政汇款金额 66 亿元。年末全市固定电话用户 280.54 万户；移动电话用户 1575.08 万户，减少 181.67 万户。年末互联网用户 185.27 万户，比上年减少 16.47 万户；宽带接入用户 181.01 万户，减少 154339 户。

图五 2011—2016 年移动电话用户数

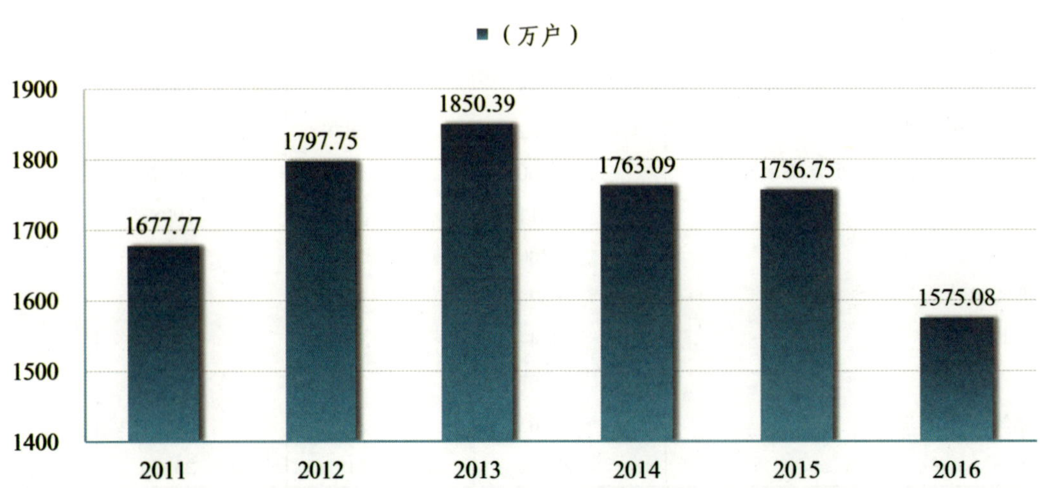

年末全市有星级酒店 38 家，其中五星级酒店 16 家。全市有旅行社 112 家，全年接待国际及港澳台游客 399.54 万人次，增长 7.0%。其中接待外国游客 110.62 万人次，增长 5.3%；接待港澳台游客 288.92 万人次，增长 7.7%。国际旅游外汇收入 15.31 亿美元，下降 2.9%。全年接待国内游客 3392.43 万人次，增长 20.1%。旅游总收入 445.40 亿元，增长 12.7%。全年东莞组团外出旅游 148.04 万人次，增长 3.6%。其中，国内旅游 131.31 万人次，增长 5.4%；出境旅游 16.72 万人次，下降 8.3%。

八、金　融

全年全市金融业实现增加值 441.64 亿元，增长 8.2%。

年末全市有各类金融机构 129 家，其中银行类机构 38 家（含 1 家代表处），保险类机构 56 家，证券期货类机构 35 家。年末全市金融机构各项本外币存款余额 11545.10 亿元，同比增长 15.8%。其中住户存款余额 4943.56 亿元，增长 6.8%。各项本外币贷款余额 6545.66 亿元，增长 9.4%。在个人消费贷款余额中，个人住房按揭贷款余额 2347.74 亿元，增长 48.2%；个人汽车消费贷款余额 3.64 亿元，下降 19.6%。

图六 2011—2016 年各项本外币存、贷款余额

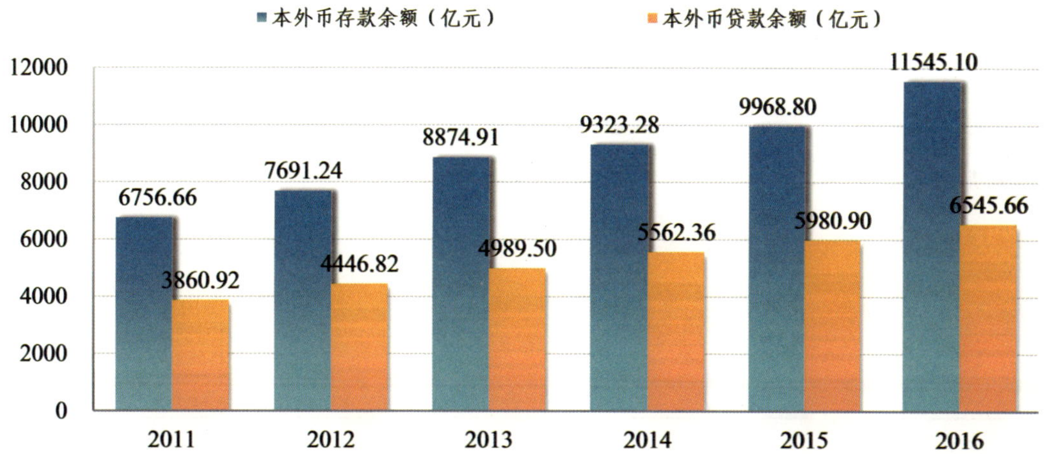

全年股票总成交额 12981.50 亿元，同比下降 65.5%。年末保证金余额 152.27 亿元，下降 26.2%。

全年全市各类保险保费收入 472.69 亿元，同比增长 54.8%。其中财产险保费收入 107.61 亿元，增长 8.6%；人寿险保费收入 365.08 亿元，增长 77.0%。

九、科技和教育

2016 年全年新增国家高新技术企业 1042 家，总数达 2028 家，位居省内地级市首位。全市专利申请量和授权量分别为 56653 件和 28559 件，其中，发明专利申请量为 17024 件，同比增长 52.46%，占专利申请总量的 30.05%，数量排全省第四位；发明专利授权量为 3682 件，同比增长 31.74%，数量排全省第三位；PCT 国际专利申请量为 876 件，同比增长 160.71%，排全省第三位。科技资源加快集聚，全市新

增创新型研发机构 1 家，总数达 32 家，科技企业孵化载体达到 59 家，其中国家级 11 家；成功举办 2016 中国（东莞）国际科技合作周；全市目前引进省创新科研团队立项总数达到 26 个，居全省第三；新引进 11 个市级创新科研团队，总数达到 27 个；国家自主创新示范区、国家可持续发展实验区建设工作稳步推进。科技金融结合得到加强，大力推进科技信贷、科技保险等工作，推动 12 家签约银行为我市 655 家企业发放贷款 1017 笔，贷款金额达 44.62 亿元，推动 39 家企业购买科技保险，保额 34 亿元，保费 399.49 万元，申请保费补贴共 114.56 万元，专利质押融资累计贷款 1.22 亿元。

年末，全市有幼儿园 1016 所，比上年增加 67 所，其中，省、市一级幼儿园 499 所，比上年增加 49 所。全市有小学 328 所，在校学生 73.87 万人，本市户籍学龄儿童入学率达 100%，小学毕业生升学率达 100%。全市有初中 191 所（不含完全中学），在校学生 21.59 万人，本市户籍适龄少年初中入学率 100%，初中毕业生升学率 98.4%。全市高中阶段学校共有 62 所，其中普通高中（含完中和多层次学校高中部）40 所，在校生 7.99 万人，中职学校 26 所（含技工学校 4 所），在校生 7.47 万人。全市有普通高等院校 9 所，在校学生 11.26 万人。全年普通高等院校共招收本科、专科学生 3.14 万人，毕业生 2.30 万人。

表七　教育情况

指　　标	招生（万人）	增　长（%）	在校生（万人）	增　长（%）	毕业生（万人）	增　长（%）
普通本专科	3.14	−5.9	11.26	−1.8	2.30	−4.0
成人本专科	0.91	−36.8	2.23	−49.2	0.55	−54.2
中等职业技术教育	2.91	11.8	7.47	7.1	2.05	20.3
普通高中	2.72	1.6	7.99	1.2	2.57	1.4
初中	8.35	9.0	21.59	3.5	5.99	1.1
小学	13.82	−1.4	73.87	2.7	9.88	10.3
学前教育	13.47	1.3	33.17	5.5	11.56	6.1

十、文化、卫生和体育

年末全市有市民艺术中心 1 个，文化站 33 个，公共图书馆 641 个，公共电子阅览室 589 个，公办博物馆 18 个，民办博物馆 31 个，文化广场 769 个，电影放映单位 96 个。全市有公共广播节目 10 套，公共电视节目 65 套。全年共发行报纸 7953.44 万份，其中《东莞日报》5690.82 万份；电影放映 104 万场次，观众 1802 万人次。

年末全市有医疗机构 2304 个，其中，三级甲等医院 8 所（含 1 所妇幼保健院），门诊部、诊所、医务室、卫生站、社区卫生服务机构等基层医疗机构 2213 个。全市卫生技术人员 4.8 万人，医疗机构的实有病床 2.81 万张。全市门诊量 6482 万人次，同比增长 3.8%，住院量 91.9 万人次，同比增长 4.1%。

全年全市运动员共获得 175 枚金牌、159 枚银牌、178 枚铜牌。其中夺得全国赛金牌 42 枚；广东省赛金牌 122 枚、银牌 120 枚、铜牌 141 枚。全年举办全市全民健身活动 417 次，参加人数 41.8 万人次。全市有各类体育运动场地 14451 个（座），其中体育场 526 个，体育馆 169 座，灯光篮球场 5625 个，健身路径 1319 条，室外游泳池 419 个，室内游泳池 63 个，室外羽毛球场 1409 个。全市有体育彩票发行网点 1250 个，销售总额 16.56 亿元，体彩公益金 12484 万元。

十一、人民生活

2016 年东莞居民收入稳步增长，全年居民人均可支配收入 41902 元，同比增长 8.4%。其中，城镇常住居民人均可支配收入 43096 元，增长 8.3%，农村常住居民人均可支配收入 26526 元，增长 9.5%，城乡收入差距进一步缩小。

从收入构成上看，居民人均工资性收入 31466 元，占人均可支配收入的 75.1%，是居民收入的首要来源；其次是人均财产净收入，达 7053 元，占人均可支配收入的 16.8%。

居民生活消费呈现多样性，2016 年居民生活消费支出 29906 元，同比增长 5.8%。其中人均食品烟酒支出 9837 元，占生活消费支出 32.9%，比上年减少 0.6 个百分点。在八大类生活消费支出中，居住、教育文化娱乐、衣着及交通通讯消费支出增幅较大。

十二、社会保障

全市参加各类社会保险总人次为 2558.79 万人次，比上年下降 3.8%。基本医疗保险 574.57 万人次，失业保险 409.11 万人次，工伤保险 445.07 万人次。全年社会保险基金总收入 476.38 亿元，保险基金总支出 195.53 亿元，年末保险基金累计余额 1431.1 亿元。

年末全市有收养类福利事业单位 37 个，其中社会福利院 1 个，社会福利中心 1 个，敬老院 34 个，敬老院供养老人 1688 人。社会福利事业单位收养 2810 人，全年社会救济 1.26 万人。全市居民最低生活保障支出 7826.5 万元，自然灾害生活救助支出 687.1 万元，慈善基金结余 2.23 亿元。全市纳入“五保户”对象有 824 人，“五保户”费用支出 1371.1 万元。

十三、人口、资源和环境

年末全市户籍人口 200.94 万人。全年出生人口 2.76 万人，出生率为 13.92‰；死亡人口 1.05 万人，死亡率为 5.28‰；人口自然增长率为 8.64‰。年末全市常住人口 826.14 万人，其中城镇常住人口 736.42 万人。人口城镇化率为 89.14%。

全年雨日天数 203 天，日照时数 1641.6 小时，平均气温 22.8 摄氏度，相对湿度 82%，降水量 2612 毫米。

年末全市森林公园达 22 个，新增森林公园配套设施一批。林业用地面积 87.32 万亩，生态公益林

32.91 万亩，林木积蓄量 374.26 万立方米，林木总生长量 12.78 万立方米。

年末全市建成区土地面积 956.54 平方公里，公共管理与公共服务用地面积 48.12 平方公里。森林覆盖率为 37.4%。城市建成区绿地率为 43.68%，绿化覆盖率为 47.71%，人均公园绿地面积 22.87 平方米；全市已建成公园 1510 个，面积 2.08 万公顷。

注：1. 本公报中 2016 年数据为初步统计数，统计图中 2011–2015 年数据为年报数，最后统计数据以《东莞统计年鉴–2017》为准。

2. 地区生产总值、各行业增加值、农业总产值绝对数按当年价格计算，增长速度按可比价格计算。

3. 从 2011 年起，规模以上工业统计口径由年主营业务收入 500 万元调整为 2000 万元及以上的工业法人企业;固定资产投资项目统计起点由计划总投资 50 万元提高到 500 万元，增速为可比口径。

4. 五大支柱产业包括电子信息制造业、电气机械及设备制造业（包括电气机械及器材制造业，仪器仪表制造业，通用设备制造业，专用设备制造业，铁路、船舶、航空航天和其他运输设备制造业以及汽车制造业）、纺织服装鞋帽制造业（包括纺织业，纺织服装、服饰制造业，皮革、毛皮、羽毛及其制品和制鞋业）、食品饮料加工制造业（包括食品制造业，酒、饮料和精制茶制造业，农副产品加工业）、造纸及纸制品业。

四个特色产业包括玩具及文体用品制造业、家具制造业、化工制品制造业（包括化学原料及化学制品制造业，石油加工、炼焦业及核燃业）、包装印刷业。

先进制造业包括装备制造业、钢铁冶炼及加工制造业、石油及化学制造业。

高技术制造业包括医药制造业、航空、航天器及设备制造业、电子及通信设备制造业、医疗仪器设备及仪器仪表制造业、信息化学品制造业。

5. 2012 年四季度，国家统计局实施了城乡一体化住户调查改革。2014 年起按照新的调查口径对外发布城乡一体的居民人均可支配收入和分城镇、农村常住居民人均可支配收入数据。由于新老调查方案在调查范围、调查对象、城乡划分标准、样本抽选、计算和汇总方式、指标口径等方面变化较大，改革后新口径数据和旧口径数据存在不可比的差异。

6. 阅读本公报时，请注意统计指标的时间、口径和计算方法等。

7. 资料来源:本公报中城镇实有登记失业人数及失业人员安置就业人数、城镇登记失业率数据来自市人力资源局；新增农民专业合作社、龙头企业及省级农业类名牌产品数来自市农业局；进出口、利用外资数据来自市商务局；公路通车里程、交通运输、公路、水路相关数据来自市交通运输局；邮电业务收入、邮政发送信函、电话用户等数据来自市邮政、电信、移动等相关运营商；星级酒店及旅游情况来自市旅游局；年末各类金融机构数据来自金融工作局；本外币存贷款余额来自市人民银行；股票总成交额及年末保证金余额数据来自证券期货业协会；保险保费及赔款与给付来自市保险行业协会；国家高新技术企业家数、专利申请和授权量以及科研成果奖等数据来自市科学技术局；教育数据来自市教育局；市民艺术中心、文化站、公共图书馆、公共电子阅览室、博物馆、文化广场、公共广播节目、报纸等数据来自市文化广电新闻出版局；卫生医疗机构等数据来自市卫生局；运动员获得奖牌、健身活动、体育彩票发行情况来自市体育局；社会保障数据来自市社会保障局；福利单位、敬老院等数据来自市民政局；户籍人口数据来自市公安局；出生和死亡人口等相关数据来自市卫生和计划生育局；气象数据来自市气象局；森林公园、林业用地、生态公益林、林木积蓄量等数据来自市林业局；建成区及公共管理与公共服务用地面积来自市城乡规划局；建成区绿地率、绿化覆盖率、人均公园绿地面积及公园数据来自市城市综合管理局。

Statistical Communique on Economic and Social Development of Dongguan in 2016

In 2016, faced with the severe and complicated macro situation, and the arduous tasks of reform, development and stability, Dongguan under the correct leadership ofthe Municipal CPC and the Municipal Government, conscientiously implemented the spirit of the third, the fourth, the fifth, and the sixth Plenary Session of the 18th CPC Central Committee and General Secretary Xi Jinping's important speeches, focused on "three forefront", and actively adapted to the new normal economic development. By taking the structural reform of supply side as a guide, building a new system of open economy as an opportunity, the whole city has worked to overcome obstacles and has pressed ahead with a pioneering spirit, further implemented the strategy of innovation driven, and strived to improve the quality and efficiency of economic development, made efforts to stabilize growth, promote reform, adjust structure, and improve people's livelihood. As a result, progress has been achieved and stability ensured in economic and social development. The main tasks and targets for the year have been fulfilled, and good start has been achieved in 13th Five-Year Plan.

I. Outlook

According to preliminary accounting, in 2016 Dongguan's GDP increased to 682.77 billion yuan, up by 8.1% over the previous year. From the perspective of three industries, the added value of the primary industry was 2.28 billion yuan, down by 0.3%. In contrast, the secondary and tertiary industries increased to 317.25 billion and 363.24 billion yuan, up by 7.2% and 8.9% respectively. The proportion of the three major industries is 0.3:46.5:53.2. The per capita GDP realized 82.68 thousand yuan, up by 8.6% over the previous year.

In the modern industry, the added value of advanced manufacturing industry above the designated size was 143.52 billion yuan, up by 15.2%, and that of the modern service industry rose by 10.3%, reaching 218.08 billion yuan.

In tertiary industry, the growth rate of added-value in transport, storage and post is 1.1%, 7.7% in wholesale and retail trade, 0.4% in lodging and catering services, 8.2% in financial service, 3.5% in real estate development, and 14.4% in other services.

Figure 1: Dongguan GDP & Growth Rates 2011-2016

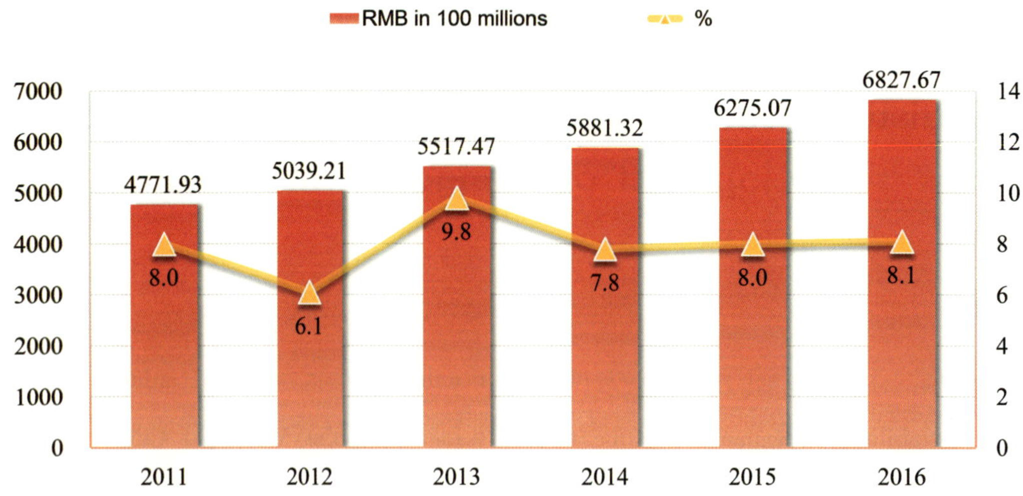

At the end of the year, the city's total number of industrial and commercial registrations reached 840.4 thousand, up by 17.8%, including 328.9 thousand enterprises and 510.8 thousand sole proprietors which increased by 28.3% and 12.0% respectively. Particularly, private-own enterprises had a rapid growth of 30.7%. From the new registrations, in 2016 there were 173.9 thousand new industrial and commercial registrations, up by 41.3%, of which 82.2 thousand were enterprises, up by 49.7%.

The overall Consumer Price Index (CPI) of Dongguan increased by 2.7% throughout last year. In detail, food, tobacco and alcohol index rose by 6.3%, apparel index rose by 1.2% and housing index rose by 0.8%. Daily necessities and services index increased by 2.0%. Transportation and communication index decreased by 1.4%. Educational, cultural and recreational goods index rose by 1.3% while medical care index increased by 7.5%. The other goods and services index rose by 0.5%. Moreover, Retail Price Index (RPI) increased by 0.9%, and Producer Price Index (PPI) declined by 0.1%.

Figure 2: Dongguan yearly Changes of CPI in 2011-2016

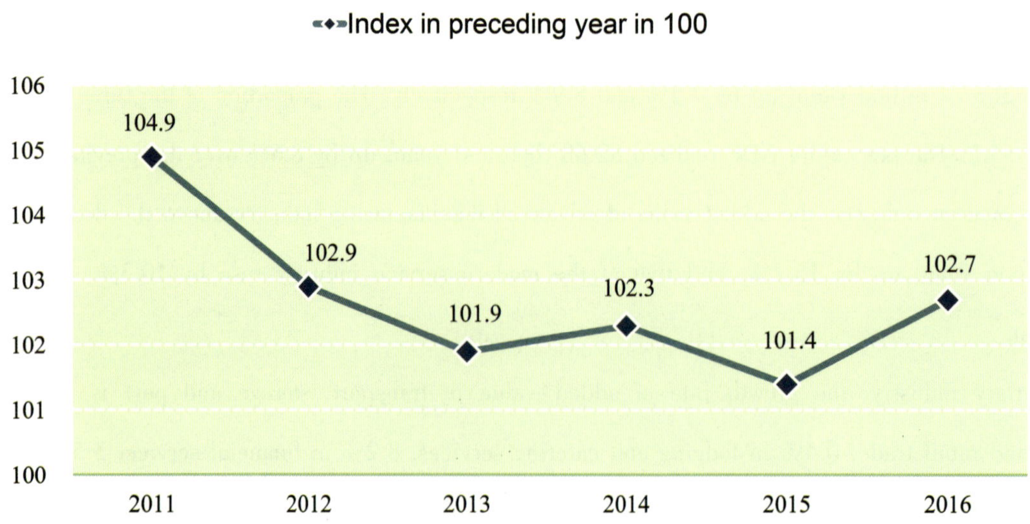

Table 1: CPI Changes in 2016

Item	CPI (Index in preceding year is 100)
General CPI level	102.7
Food, tobacco and alcohol	106.3
-Grain	104.2
-Meat poultry	109.7
-Oil	98.7
-Eggs	94.2
-Vegetables	111.8
-Aquatic products	109.2
Clothing	101.2
Housing	100.8
Daily necessities and services	102.0
Transportation and telecommunications	98.6
Education, culture and recreation	101.3
Medical care	107.5
Other goods and services	100.5
Retail price index	100.9
Producer price index	99.9

In 2016, Dongguan's fiscal revenue reached 156.92 billion yuan, up by 35.8% over the previous year. The general public budget revenue was 54.48 billion yuan, up by 8.2%. The general public budget expenditure amounted to 59.93 billion yuan, up by 3.1%, of which 6.37 billion yuan was appropriated for general public services, 8.15 billion yuan for public security, 14.30 billion yuan for education, as well as 3.53 billion yuan for social insurances and employment. Overall, the taxes collected in the whole year were 170.50 billion yuan, up by 20.7%.

By the end of 2016, the urban unemployed had amounted to 13.8 thousand, while 10.1 thousand job placements had been created. The urban registered unemployment rate was kept at 2.26%.

Ⅱ. Agriculture

In 2016, the gross output value of farming, forestry, animal husbandry and fishery reached 3.84 billion yuan, up by 3.1% over the previous year. In detail, the output value of farming accounted for 70.3%, (2.70 billion yuan, up by 12.4%) . Forestry constituted 1.0% (39 million yuan, up by 3.6%) . Animal husbandry accounted for 16.9% (350 million yuan, down by 15.2%) . Fishery constituted 16.9% (651 million yuan, down by 15.5%) . The total planted areas for agriculture reached 25.1 thousand hectares, including 13.26 thousand hectares for planting fruit. The crop's annual output was total 12.6 thousand tons. The production of fishery was 56.6 thousand tons, and the vegetable production was 404.3 thousand tons up by 0.7%. Besides,

114.9 thousand heads of hogs and 3.98 million heads of poultry were slaughtered, down by 15.8% and 1.7% respectively. During 2016, Dongguan added 20 new farmer cooperatives. So far, there were 190 farmer cooperatives, 43 leading agricultural enterprises (including 11 provincial level and 3 national level corporations) , and 52 provincial agricultural brand products within the term of validity.

Ⅲ. Industry and Construction

In 2016, the added value of industrial enterprises above designated size reached a total of 287.82 billion yuan, up by 7.0% over the previous year. Among which, heavy industry created an added value of 175.10 billion yuan, which contributed 60.8% to the total, up by 13.5%, while the other 112.73 billion yuan was generated by light industry, accounted for 39.2%, down by 1.5%.

The added value of five pillar industries above designated size in Dongguan economy reached 195.22 billion yuan, up by 8.5%, while the added value of four characteristic industries reached 28.15 billion yuan, up by 0.3%. The added value of high-tech manufacturing industries increased by 17.6%, of which that of manufacture of medicines increased by 7.5%, manufacture of electronic and communications equipment increased by 20.9%, manufacture of electronic computer and office equipment decreased by 4.0%, manufacture of medical equipment and instruments increased by 17.8%.

The added value of advanced manufacturing industry increased by 15.2%, of which that of manufacture of equipment increased by 16.0%, iron and steel smelting and processing decreased by 4.2%, manufacture of petroleum and chemical increased by 1.7%. Of the manufacture of equipment, the added value of manufacture of metal increased by 7.5%, manufacture of general-purpose machinery increased by 8.0%, manufacture of special-purpose machinery increased by 13.1%, manufacture of automobile increased by 19.5%, manufacture of railway, ship, aeronautics and other transport equipment decreased by 30.5%, manufacture of electrical machinery and equipment increased by 0.7%, manufacture of communication equipment, computers and other electronic equipment increased by 20.4%, manufacture of instruments and meters increased by 19.5%. Of iron and steel smelting and processing, the added value of smelting and pressing of steel decreased by 4.2%. Of petroleum and chemical industry, the added value of petroleum refining, coking and nuclear-fuel processing decreased by 16.0%, manufacture of raw chemical materials and chemical products increased by 3.8%, rubber and plastic products decreased by 3.2%.

The added value of traditional advantageous industries decreased by 0.1%. Of which that of manufacture of textile garments decreased by 6.8%, manufacture of food and beverage increased by 1.0%, manufacture of furniture decreased by 0.5%, manufacture of building materials increased by 3.2%, manufacture of metal products increased by 8.3%, and the household electric appliances industry increased by 3.5%.

The comprehensive economic efficiency index of industrial enterprises above designated size was 160.5%, while the total profits were 47.21 billion yuan.

Table 2: Output and Growth Rates of Major Products by Industrial Enterprises above Designated Size in 2016

Items	Unit	Quantity	Increase over 2015 (%)
Mobile phones	10000 Sets	35,909.47	58.0
DVD players	10000 Sets	4,591.87	−19.2
Integrated circuits	10000 Sets	72,539.49	53.6
Opto-electronic devices	10000 Pcs	1,314,191.01	33.8
Electronic components	1 billion Pcs	1,231.92	8.7
Automobile instruments	10000 Sets	96.45	17.4
Optical instruments	10000 Sets	94.80	−17.0
Glasses	10000 Sets	6,496.96	1.3
Tap water	1 million Cbm	1587	−4.2
Rice	Ton	277,980.61	−10.8
Candy	Ton	237,158.81	−0.7
Garments	10000 Pcs	137,783.07	−6.8
Light leathers	10000 Sqm	193.20	−27.7
Wood-based panels	10000 Cbm	21.33	−17.6
Paper products	10000Tons	204.71	−3.9
Furniture	10000 Pcs	3,748.92	−30.0
Machine-made paper & paperboards	10000 Tons	1,507.86	6.0
Plastic products	10000 Tons	117.96	3.4
Chemical reagents	Ton	129,957.92	−8.4
Porcelains	10000 Sqm	3,335.11	20.2
Metal containers	10000 Cbm	361.29	−47.9
Electric portable tools	10000 Sets	2,689.52	5.5
Digital cameras	10000 Sets	43.42	69.7
Moulds	10000 Sets	6.43	1.4
Lithium-ion battery	10000 Sets	32,845.83	−24.3
Lighting equipment	10000 Sets	24,307.97	−7.9
Computers	10000 Sets	125.65	15.8
Printers	10000 Sets	59.89	−38.5
Fixed phones	10000 Sets	3,158.54	−5.0

In 2016, the added value of construction enterprises was 9.12 billion yuan, up by 1.9%. The gross output value of general contracting and specialized contracting construction enterprises was 24.52 billion yuan, up by 15.5%; The floor space of buildings under construction was 9.14 million square meters, down by 14.8%; The completion area was 3.49 million square meters, down by 23.0%. Labor productivity based on the total output value of general contracting and specialized contracting construction enterprises was 340.70 thousand yuan/person, up by 16.4%.

IV. Investment in Fixed Assets

The total investment in fixed assets reached 155.75 billion yuan in 2016, an increase of 7.7% over the previous year. According to the investment subjects, the state-owned enterprises reached 12.07 billion yuan, down by 32.3%. The private investment was 106.11 billion yuan, up by 12.0%. Foreign businessmen and Hong Kong, Macao and Taiwan businessmen invested 29.31 billion yuan, an increase of 9.4%.

Figure 3: Investment in Fixed Assets and Its Growth 2011-2016

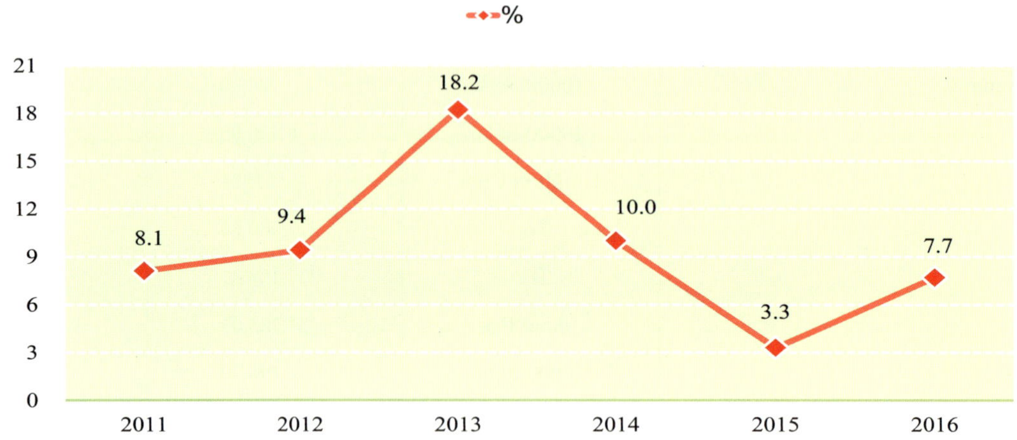

From the investment direction, the capital mainly flew into the secondary and tertiary industries. The fixed asset investment in secondary industry was 56.61 billion yuan, including 50.37 billion yuan in manufacturing, and that in tertiary industry was 99.02 billion yuan.

Table 3: Fixed Assets Investments in Sectors in 2016

Sectors	Capital (in ten-thousand yuan)	Increase over 2015 (%)
Total	15,574,580	7.7
Farming, forestry, animal husbandry and fishery	13,345	55.7
Manufacturing	5,037,401	16.4
Production and supply of electric power, heat, gas and water	617,045	−11.8
Construction industry	10,000	28.5
Transport, storage and postal services	1,333,819	−8.6
Information transmission, computer services and software	172,826	−10.0
Wholesale and retail trade	178,852	−7.4
Hotel and catering services	28,047	−56.3
Finance	55,934	39.0
Real estate	7,092,286	10.6
Leasing and business services	21,262	−42.3
Scientific research and technical services	173,136	−23.3
Water conservancy, environment and public facilities Management	453,295	3.7
Resident services, repairing and other services	5,100	−44.3
Education	251,368	4.8
Health care and social work	65,507	−10.0
Culture, sports and recreation	37,400	84.3
Public administration, social security and social Organization	27,957	60.0

The investment in real estate development reached 64.28 billion yuan in 2016, up by 11.7%. The gross floor area of condominiums under construction was 44.09 million square meters, up by 12.4%, and that of completed condominiums was 2.33 million square meters, down by 28.5%. The sale area of newly-built condominium after online sign-up registration was 10.62 million square meters, down by 1.4%, of which residential condominium was 8.88 million square meters, down by 9.2%. The sales value in total was 145.94 billion yuan, up by 35.6%, including 122.18 billion yuan from residential condominium which was 27.3% more than that of last year.

Ⅴ. Domestic Trade

The total added value of wholesale and retail trade was 82.40 billion yuan in 2016, up by 7.7% over the previous year, and that of lodging and catering sector reached 15.86 billion yuan, up by 0.4%.

The gross retail sales of Dongguan reached 247.08 billion yuan, up by 13.1%. In terms of sectors, the retail sales of the wholesale and retail trade was total 230.90 billion yuan, up by 13.6%, and that of the lodging and catering amounted to 16.18 billion yuan, up by 6.7%.

Among enterprises above designated size in wholesale and retail trades, in terms of retail sales value, cereal, oil and food increased by 1.0%. Beverages decreased by 6.6%. Tobacco and liquor decreased by 0.5%. Clothing, shoes, hats and textiles decreased by 1.6%. Daily necessities decreased by 3.5%. Automobiles increased by 17.2%. Petroleum and related products increased by 2.7%.

Figure 4: Retail Sales of Consumer Goods and Its Growth 2011-2016

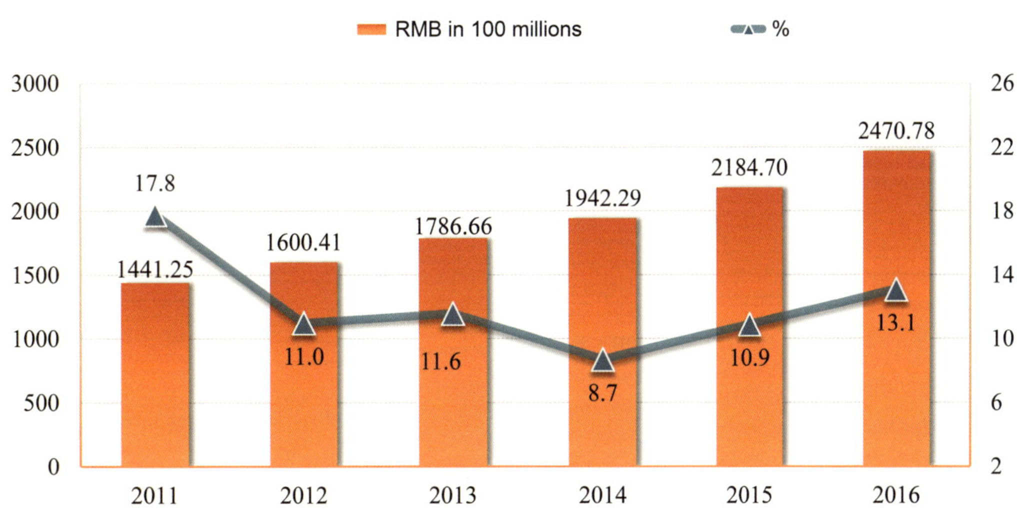

Ⅵ. Foreign Trade

The total value of imports and exports in 2016 reached 1,141.60 billion yuan, up by 9.8% over the previous year. The import value was 485.92 billion yuan, up by 22.4%. The export value was 655.69 billion yuan, up by 2.0%.

From the angle of category, the export value of general merchandises reached 236.10 billion yuan, up by 0.6% while the export value of labor-intensive products decreased by 1.7% to 379.45 billion yuan. In addition, the export value of other trading goods increased by 81.8% to 40.14 billion yuan.

According to the export area, exports to Asian were 354.89 billion yuan, an increase of 6.0%. Exports to North America were 153.21 billion yuan, down by 5.4%. Exports to Europe were 110.26 billion yuan, up by 5.1%. Exports to Latin American were 20.08 billion yuan, down by 5.5%. Exports to Oceania were 8.10 billion yuan, down by 5.0%.

Electromechanical products took up 71.1% of the gross export value and reached 465.92 billion yuan, up by 6.3% . The hi-tech products occupied 39.4% of the gross export and increased by 17.7% to 258.64 billion yuan.

Table 4: Values and Growth Rates of Major Export Merchandises in 2016

Numbers in 10, 000 RMB

Commodities	Value	Increase over 2015 (%)
Electromechanical products (including relevant products listed as below)	46,591,748	6.3
Hi-tech products	25,863,984	17.7
Automatic data processing machines and components	4,108,710	−8.5
Garments and relevant accessories	3,547,696	−17.4
Telephones	6,575,345	63.6
Furniture and components	2,913,072	−8.5
Shoes	1,647,909	−17.3
Parts of automatic data processing machines	1,725,291	−12.1
Static converters	1,959,852	2.1
Lamps,lighting fixtures and similar products	1,504,777	−14.9
Traveling supplies and cases	1,411,831	−12.9
Toys	1,757,329	13.9
Wires or cables	1,375,527	−1.6
Plastic products	1,275,546	−8.2
Electric apparatus for switching or protecting electrical circuits	1,442,230	4.9
Spinning yarn, fabric and products	1,024,553	−9.5
Printers (including the MFP)	717,632	−32.8
Parts of televisions, radios and wireless telecommunication equipments	972,333	26.5
Precious metal and jewelries with precious metal	1,644,500	116.4
Printed circuit	582,453	−0.8
Cultural products	5,581,884	15.9
Glasses and parts	669,281	15.4

There were 446 newly-added foreign direct investment projects in 2016. The total capital on contracts of foreign investment saw a 6.5% decrease to 4.73 billion. The actual utilized capital decreased by 26.2% to 3.93

billion, of which the capital of communicational equipments, computers and other electronic equipment manufacturing decreased by 59.7% to 266 million, and that of specialized machinery manufacturing decreased by 40.2% to 148 million.

Table 5: Utilized Foreign Capitals in Sectors, 2016

Numbers in 10, 000 USD

Sectors	Capital on contrasts	Increase over 2015 (%)	Capital Utilized	Increase over 2015 (%)
In total	473,173	−6.5	392,617	−26.2
Manufacturing	187,106	−17.5	169,649	−17.5
Textile	11,948	1.6	9,200	−46.4
Garments, shoes and hats	5,890	−61.9	2,301	−91.7
Furniture	1,876	37.7	1,107	−74.6
General-purpose machineries	2,472	−65.2	5,017	−76.3
Special-purpose machineries	15,785	9.0	14,762	−40.2
Electric machineries and equipments	17,712	−28.0	12,402	−52.8
Communication equipments, computers and other electronic equipments	27,960	−45.8	26,625	−59.7
Metal products	17,611	−32.9	19,087	−54.1
Plastics products	11,380	10.0	6,830	−70.8
Stationery and sport commodities	3,376	−58.4	5,214	−56.2
Papers and paper-made products	28,044	39.4	33,584	350.9
Others	43,052	21.3	33,520	−52.8
Transportation,storage and postal industry	12,763	−22.7	6,904	−22.7
Wholesale and retail trade	27,463	−51.6	23,529	−23.2

Ⅶ. Transportation, Post, Telecommunication and Tourism

The added value of the transport, storage and post sectors amounted to 20.96 billion yuan last year, up by 1.1%.

By the end of 2016, the total length of highway and expressway in Dongguan had reached 5,266.25 kilometers. The highway density was 213.64 kilometers per hundred $kilometers^2$, ranking top among cities in Guangdong Province. The total number of vehicles (for civil use) in Dongguan had increased to 2.25 million, up by 19.7%, including 2.25 million cars with 21.8% growth by the end of 2016. Over the same period, the freight volume by land was 103.25 million tons, and the freight turnover was equaled to 7.17 billion ton -

kilometers. The freight volume by water was 52.69 million tons, and the turnover was 38.36 billion ton-kilometers. The total volume of passengers by land was 48.47 million person-times, with a turnover of 7.71 billion person-kilometers. The total volume of passengers by water was 270.4 thousand person-times, with a turnover of 17.57 million person-kilometers. The seaports in Dongguan handled 266.7 thousand passengers and 145.84 million tons of cargo in total.

Table 6: Volume and Turnover of Handled Cargo and Passengers in 2016

Indicators	Unit	Volume	Increase over 2015 (%)
Passengers	million	48.74	−1.8
# by land	million	48.47	−1.6
Turnover	billion person-km	7.73	0.2
# by land	billion person-km	7.71	0.3
Cargos	million tons	155.93	1.4
# by land	million tons	103.25	−1.4
Turnover	billion ton-km	45.52	−9.8
# by land	billion ton-km	7.17	−0.03

Last year, the revenue of post and telecommunication industries reached 29.51 billion yuan, up by 18.5%. In postal industry, 92.01 million single mails were delivered, including 9.75 million express mails. The wire transfer through Dongguan Post Office reached 6.6 billion yuan in total. At the end of 2016, there were 2.81 million landline subscribers and the mobile phone users reduced 1.82 million to 15.75 million. The number of internet users reduced 164.7 thousand to 1.85 million, and the wideband subscribers were 1.81 million, 154.34 thousand less than those of 2015 .

Figure 5: Number of Mobile Phone Subscribers 2011-2016

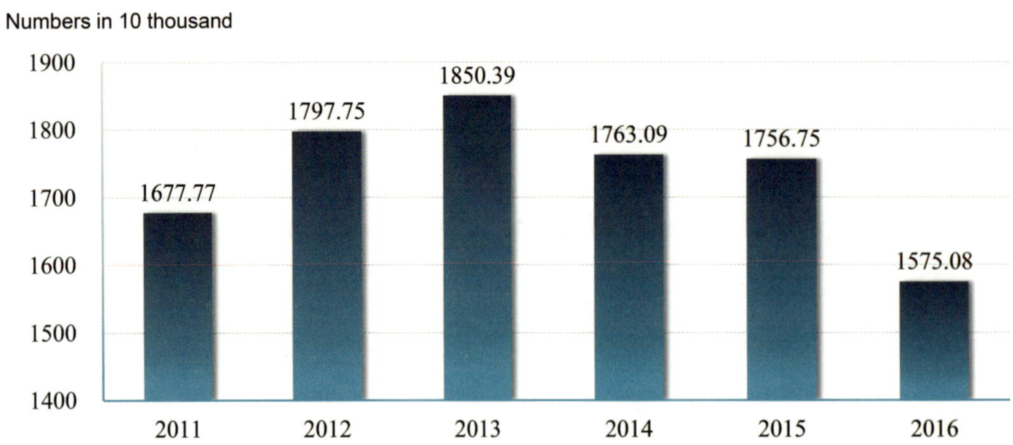

At the end of 2016, Dongguan processed 38 star-rated hotels, among which 16 hotels were five-star ranking. There were 112 travel agencies, receiving 4.0 million visitors from abroad, up by 7.0%, of which 2.89 million passengers came from Hong Kong, Macao and Taiwan, up by 7.7%, and the other 1.11 million tourists were from foreign countries worldwide, up by 5.3%. The international tourists generated revenue of $1.53

billion, down by 2.9%. The number of domestic tourists reached 33.92 million, up by 20.1%. Tourists in total contributed 44.54 billion yuan, an increase of 12.7% on year. The passengers travelling in groups from Dongguan increased by 3.6%, equivalent to 1.48 million, of which 1.31 million passengers having a tour in mainland, up by 5.4%, and 167.2 thousand travelling overseas, down by 8.3%.

Ⅷ. Financial Service

In 2016, the added value of finance was 44.16 billion yuan, up by 8.2%.

At the end of 2016, Dongguan had 129 financial institutions, including 38 depositary institutions (including 1 representative office) , 56 insurance institutions, and 35 securities and futures institutions. The total savings deposit in Renminbi and foreign currencies in all financial institutions in Dongguan reached 1,154.51 billion yuan, up by 15.8%, of which 494.36 billion yuan was contributed by households, up by 6.8%. The total number of loans in Renminbi and foreign currencies in all financial institutions reached 654.57 billion yuan, up by 9.4%. Of individual consumer loans, the individual housing mortgage loans rose by 48.2% to 234.77 billion yuan, while individual car loans decreased by 19.6% to 364 million yuan.

Figure 6: Deposits and Loans in Renminbi and Foreign Currencies 2011-2016

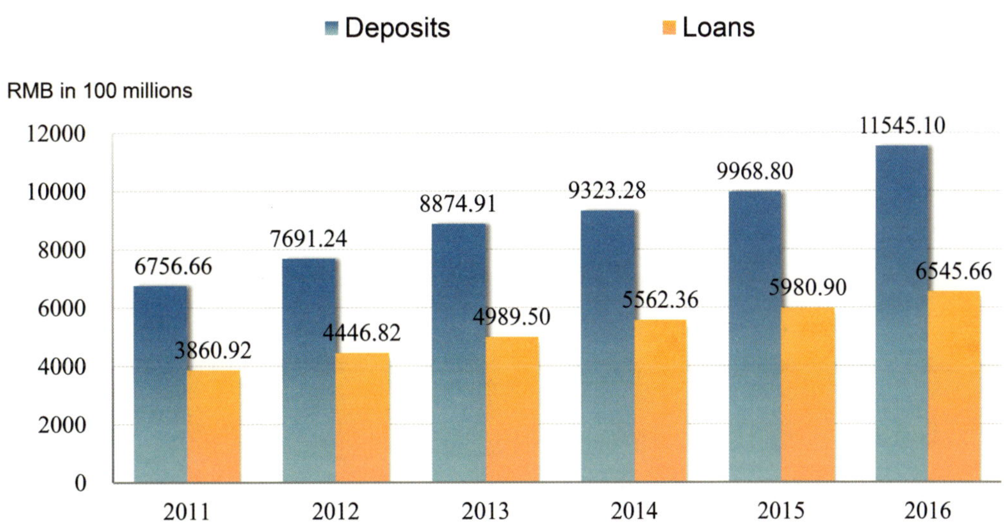

The total turnover of the stock market was 1,298.15 billion yuan, down by 65.5%. The balance of guarantee fund totalled 15.23 billion yuan, down by 26.2%.

The revenue of insurance companies in Dongguan amounted to 47.27 billion yuan, up by 54.8%. Of which 10.76 billion yuan was contributed by property insurance, reaching up by 8.6%, and the other 36.51 billion yuan by life insurance, up by 77.0%.

Ⅸ.Technology and Education

With 1,042 newly added enterprises, the total number of National High-Tech Enterprises reached 2,028 in

2016, ranked the top among the prefecture-level cities of Guangdong. There were 56,653 patent applications and 28,559 were licensed in 2016. Among them 17,024 were inventory patent applications, an increase of 52.46% compared with 2015, accounting for 30.05% of the total applications, ranked 4th in Guangdong. And 3,682 inventory patents were licensed, with an increase of 31.74%, ranked 3rd in Guangdong. The number of PCT applications was 876, up by 160.71%, ranked 3rd in Guangdong. Scientific and technological resources were gathering at a fast pace. 1 new innovative research and development institution was established, bringing the total to 32. The amount of science and technology enterprise incubation carriers rose up to 59, among which 11 reached national level. China (Dongguan) International Science and Technology Cooperation Week 2016 had been successfully held. 26 provincial-level innovation and scientific-research team projects had been approved, ranked 3rd in Guangdong. 11 city-level innovation and scientific-research teams were newly introduced and the amount added up to 27. The process of applying for National Sustainable Development Experimental Area was moving on steadily. Cooperation between technology and finance was strengthened. Technology credits and insurances were vigorously promoted. 12 contracting banks offered 1017 fiduciary loans to nearly 655 technological companies with over 4.46 billion yuan. 39 companies had bought technology insurance, with the coverage of 3.4 billion yuan, and the premium of 3.99 million yuan, while a premium subsidy of 1.15 million yuan of the total premium was applied. The patent backed loans added up to 122 million yuan.

At the end of the year, there were 1,016 kindergartens, 67 more than that of 2015. Of these 499 were first-level in Dongguan and even Guangdong, an increase of 49 over last year. And there were 328 primary schools with 738.7 thousand pupils in Dongguan, with 100% school-aged children (local residents) enrollment rate and primary school graduation rate. Also, there were 191 middle schools (schools that combine middle and high school were not included) with 215.9 thousand students, with 100% school-aged students (local residents) enrollment rate and 98.4% graduation rate. And there were 62 high schools as a whole in Dongguan, including 40 traditional schools (including comprehensive schools that combine middle and high school, as well as multi-level schools with high school department) with 79.9 thousand students and 26 vocational schools (including 4 technical schools) with 74.7 thousand students. In terms of higher education, 112.6 thousand students were studying in 9 universities or colleges in Dongguan. In 2016, 31.4 thousand students were enrolled in these colleges or universities while 23 thousand graduated with diplomas.

Table 7: Education Situation in 2016

Indicators	Enrollment (in thousands)	Increase over 2015 (%)	Total students (in thousands)	Increase over 2015 (%)	Graduates (in thousands)	Increase over 2015 (%)
Higher education, full time	31.4	−5.9	112.6	−1.8	23.0	−4.0
Higher education, remote	9.1	−36.8	22.3	−49.2	5.5	−54.2
Vocational middle schools	29.1	11.8	74.7	7.1	20.5	20.3
Senior middle schools	27.2	1.6	79.9	1.2	25.7	1.4
Junior middle schools	83.5	9.0	215.9	3.5	59.9	1.1
Primary schools	138.2	−1.4	738.7	2.7	98.8	10.3
Kindergartens	134.7	1.3	331.7	5.5	115.6	6.1

X. Culture, Health and Sports

At the end of 2016, there was 1 public art center, 33 cultural stations, 641 libraries, 589 public electronic reading rooms, 18 public museums, 31 private museums, 769 cultural squares and 96 theatres around Dongguan. In addition, 10 public radio programs and 65 television programs were available for the citizens. Last year, 79.53 million newspapers had been printed and distributed, including Dongguan Daily of 56.91 million publications for a whole year. Furthermore, movies had been broadcasted by 1.04 million times in theatres with 18.02 million audiences in total as well.

Moreover, there were 2,304 medical care institutions, including 8 AAA hospitals (Including 1 maternal and child health care hospital) , and 2,213 primary health care facilities, such as outpatient departments, clinics, dispensary, health stations, infirmaries and community medical care institutions, with 48 thousand medical staffs and 28.1 thousand hospital beds. The number of outpatients was 64.82 million person-time, up by 3.8%, and that of inpatients reached 919 thousand person-time, up by 4.1%.

In the past calendar year, athletes registered in Dongguan won 175 gold, 159 silver and 178 bronze medals, including 42 gold medals in national competitions, 122 gold medals, 120 silver medals and 141 bronze medals in provincial games. 417 sport activities for fitness were held, attracting 418 thousand participants totally. There were 14.45 thousand sports venues, including 526 stadiums, 169 gymnasiums, 5,625 floodlit basketball courts, 1,319 fitness trails, 419 outdoor and 63 indoor swimming pools, and 1,409 outdoor badminton courts. There were 1,250 sport lottery retailers in Dongguan which generated 1.66 billion yuan in sales and raised prize fund over 124.84 million yuan.

XI. Living Conditions

In 2016, the income of Dongguan citizens maintained a stable growth rate. The average annual disposable income per citizen was 41,902 yuan, a growth of 8.4%. The average annual disposable income per urban resident was 43,096 yuan with a growth of 8.3%, while the average annual disposable income per rural resident was 26,526 yuan, with a growth of 9.5%, further minimizing income disparity between urban and rural.

From the perspective of income structure, the average salary income of Dongguan citizens was 31,466 yuan, accounting for 75.1% of total disposable income, which became the main source of resident income. Average property income, the second major source of income, was 7,053 yuan, accounting for 16.8% of the total.

The residents' living consumption had become diverse. In 2016, residents' living expenditure was 29,906 yuan, up by 5.8% compared with last year. Among these, the average expenditure on food, tobacco and alcohol was 9,837 yuan, taking up 32.9% of living consumption, down by 0.6% over last year. In the 8 categories of living expenditure, that on housing, education, culture, leisure, clothing, and telecommunication had increased considerably.

Ⅻ. Social security

The total number of people participating in various social insurance was 25.59 million person-times, down by 3.8%.In detail, 5.75 million people bought basic medical insurance, 4.09 million people chose unemployment insurance, and 4.45 million people purchased injury insurance. The total revenue of social insurance fund was 47.64 billion yuan, and the total expenditures were 19.55 billion yuan. By the end of 2016, accumulative balance of the insurance fund had reached 143.11 billion yuan.

At the end of 2016, there were 37 welfare institutions for adoption in Dongguan, including 1 social welfare institute, 1 social welfare center, and 34 nursing homes receiving 1,688 elderly residents. In 2016, 2,810 people were adopted and 12.6 thousand people got social assistance by social welfare institutions.The expenditures of residents' lowest-level living allowance were 78.27 million yuan, and the social relief spending for natural disasters was 6.87 million yuan. The balance of charity fund was 223 million yuan. There were 824 people registered in the list of "Five-Guaranteed Households", which cost 13.71 million yuan of public budget last year.

XIII. Demographics, Resource and Environment

At the end of 2016, there were 2.01 million Dongguan registered permanent residents. The birth rate was 13.92‰, equivalent to 27.6 thousand infants born, meanwhile the death rate was 5.28‰ with 10.5 thousand deaths. Thus, the growth rate of population was 8.64‰. The inhabitants of Dongguan reached 8.26 million, of whom 7.36 million were urban residents. The urbanization rate of population is 89.14%.

There were 203 rainy days and 1,641.6 hours of sunshine over the year. The average temperature was 22.8℃, and the average relative humidity was 82% throughout the year with the average rainfall of 2,612 millimeters.

By the end of 2016, the number of forest parks amounted to 22, in which the facilities had been greatly added. Furthermore, the forest planning areas covered 582.13 square kilometers with 219.4 square kilometers of natural woods which supplied with 3.74 million cubic meters of timber in potential, and 127.8 thousand cubic meters of wood increment.

At the end of 2016, urban areas in Dongguan covered 956.54 km^2, which contained 48.12 square kilometers for public administration and public services. The forest coverage rate was 37.4%. The radio of greening land of built-up areas was 43.68%, and the green coverage rate was 47.71%, with an average of 22.87 square kilometers per person in terms of greening land. There were 1,510 parks in Dongguan covering an area of 2.08 square hectares as a whole.

政府工作报告

REPORT ON THE WORK OF THE GOVERNMENT

——2017年1月10日在东莞市第十六届人民代表大会第一次会议上

东莞市人民政府市长　梁维东

各位代表：

我代表市人民政府，向大会报告政府工作，请予审议，并请市政协委员和其他列席人员提出意见。

过去五年回顾及2016年主要工作

市第十五届人民代表大会第一次会议以来的五年，是我市加快转型升级、建设幸福东莞、实现高水平崛起的五年，是东莞加快建设国际制造名城、现代生态都市的五年。五年来，面对严峻复杂的宏观形势和改革发展稳定的艰巨任务，全市政府系统和社会各界一道，在上级和市委的坚强领导下，强化“三个走在前列”的使命担当，凝心聚力，砥砺奋进，较好地完成了市十五届人大历次会议确定的目标任务。

这五年，是东莞主动适应经济发展新常态、推动高水平崛起、综合实力稳步提升的五年。紧紧扭住发展第一要务，积极应对经济下行压力，全力推动东莞经济行稳致远。经济实力稳中有进。全市生产总值相继突破5000亿元和6000亿元，预计达到6770亿元，比2011年增长46.6%，年均增长8%。来源于东莞的财政总收入、市一般公共预算收入、金融机构各项存款余额分别达1569亿元、545亿元和11500亿元，是五年前的1.87倍、1.74倍和1.77倍。三次产业比例从0.4∶50.7∶48.9调整为0.3∶46.5∶53.2。东莞经济总量名列全国大中城市第21位。在中国社科院与联合国人居署联合发布的报告中，东莞城市竞争力排全球第154位、全国第10位（含港澳台）、广东第3位。园区实力持续提升。松山湖纳入珠三角国家自主创新示范区，在全国国家高新区综合排名由第53位升至第29位。东莞港吞吐量从58万标箱增长到350万标箱，成为全国第十一大沿海港口、珠三角第二大内贸港口。松山湖与生态园、沙田镇与东莞港、长安镇与滨海湾开发区统筹整合，水乡经济区、大学创新城、银瓶创新区等“三大增长极”初具雏形。镇村实力继续壮大。镇街平均生产总值突破200亿元。300亿元以上镇街由1个增至7个，3个镇街进入400亿元俱乐部。村组两级总资产和经营纯收入分别达到1508亿元和124亿元，比2011年增长22.2%和57%；资产负债率17.4%，五年下降5.3个百分点。企业实力稳步增强。“三重”建设扎实推进，五年来累计引进重大产业项目268宗、完成投资1015亿元。全市市场主体增至84万户。主营收入1000亿元企业实现零的突破，500亿元、100亿元、50亿元企业分别增至3家、11家和31家，超10亿元企业数位居全省地级市首位，拥有境内外上市企业33家。新三板挂牌企业168家，总量居全省地级市首位、全国地级市第三。“星月同辉”的格局逐步形成。城市影响力不断提升。东莞先后实现全国文明城市“三连冠”、全国双拥模范城“八连冠”，蝉联全国创新社会治理优秀城市、全国社会治安综合治理优秀市，荣获全国质量强市示范城市、国家知识产权示范城市、国家电子商务示范城市、国家森林城市、国家节能减排财政政策综合示范城市、国家公共文化服务体系示范区等称号。

这五年，是东莞打造创新型经济、转型升级步伐加快、发展质量效益提高的五年。深入实施创新驱动发展战略，科技金融产业融合步伐加快，产业转型升级取得扎实成效。创新能力有效提升。全市R&D比重预计达2.4%，增速连续五年排全省第一位。国家高新技术企业从413家增加到1500家，省级创新科研团队从9个增加到26个，总数均居全省地级市首位。新增新型研发机构17个、科技孵化器42个、博士后科研工作平台44个，总数分别达到32个、48个和68个。制造业转型升级加快。率先对接国家战略实施“东莞制造2025”战略，智能制造等“六大工程”全面推进，“机器换人”深入实施。先进制造业、高技术制造业增加值分别占规模以上工业增加值的48.5%和38%，比2011年提高6.6和9.3个百分点。服装、家具、五金模具等传统产业加速向“微笑”曲线两端延伸。新增全国知名品牌创建示范区2个。省级专业镇达34个。省级以上企业工程（技术）中心、名牌名标达到247个和558个，分别增长165.6%和62.7%。“四新”经济蓬勃发展。智能手机产业成为经济新增长点，2016年出货量达到2.55亿台，约占全球20%。机器人及智能装备、电子商务、现代物流、文化创意等产业加快发展，为产业升级注入了新动力。内外源经济协调发展。预计全市进出口总额、出口总额分别达11000亿元和6500亿元，稳居全国大中城市第5位和第4位。“一带一路”战略扎实推进。加工贸易自主性、根植性增强。外资企业新设立研发机构1265个，总数达到1712个。规模以上工业企业内销比重超过外销，民营工业占比提高17.8个百分点，民营经济税收与增加值贡献率逐年提高。

这五年，是东莞推进重要领域改革、体制机制活力增强、各项改革全面深化的五年。稳步推进国家和省50多项改革试点任务，全面推进330多项莞版改革措施，努力向改革要动力要红利，打造法治化国际化营商环境。行政审批改革深化提速。项目审批流程再造和直接落地改革成效凸显。水陆口岸“三互”大通关改革减少企业一半以上手续和时间。“放管服”改革积极推进。五年精简行政审批项目512项，向镇街（园区）下放经济社会管理权限546项，复制推广自贸区改革政策63项。市场活力有效激发。商事制度改革全面铺开，东莞商改模式成为全国样本，企业注册时间平均缩短60%以上，市场主体比2012年改革前增加29.9万户，增长55.2%。五年取消、下调或免征停征涉企行政事业性收费260多项。通过各种途径累计为企业减负近280亿元。东莞营商环境“加一”、综合成本“减一”的努力得到广泛认可。与此同时，土地生态利用制度、农村综合改革、基层社会治理创新、社区网格化管理和微治理等一大批特色改革扎实推进，为经济社会发展带来了更多改革红利。

这五年，是东莞践行以人为本理念、城乡面貌不断改善、社会民生事业长足进步的五年。加快国家新型城镇化综合试点步伐，加强公共安全管理，推进幸福东莞建设，让人民群众享有更宜居的城市环境、更安定的社会环境、更优质的公共服务。城市功能日趋完善。东莞新火车站、地铁2号线、莞惠城际轨道常平至惠州段、沿江高速、博深高速等一批交通基础设施建成，市篮球中心、市民艺术中心等一批公共服务设施投入使用。生态环境持续优化。完成江库联网一期工程。茅洲河等跨界河和内河涌污染治理全面加强。空气质量明显改善。水乡地区“两高一低”企业加快退出。19.6万辆黄标车和老旧车顺利淘汰。推广应用新能源汽车2800辆。超额完成“十二五”节能减排任务，单位生产总值能耗降幅及二氧化硫、氮氧化物减排量位居全省第一。新建森林公园、湿地公园17个，建成绿道956公里、休闲绿地1287处。社会治理水平提升。社会建设全面加强，创建全省创新社会管理引领区成效明显。“黄赌毒”现象得到铁腕整治，规模化、组织化“涉黄”犯罪强力清除，“两抢一盗”等违法犯罪行为逐步下降，全市破案数上升34.2%，命案数压减32.7%。安全生产、食品药品安全等得到切实加强，劳资纠纷、群众信访等得到妥善处置，市民法治意识显著增强，社会文明程度持续提高。社会民生事业全面发展。坚持每年办好十件实事。城乡居民人均可支配收入达到41782元，比2011年增加65.4%。文化名城战略扎实推进，公共文化服务体系日益完善，一大批艺术精品获国家级大奖，“音乐剧之都”的品牌更加响亮。连续五年提高基本养老金，城乡救助及福利水平逐步提高，在全国率先建立起城乡一体化的社会养老和医疗保险体系。成功创建广东省推进教育现代化先进市。体育、医疗、就业、住房保障、住房公积金、武装和民兵预备役等工作全面加强，基本公共服务均等化扎实推进，市内外对口帮扶任务进展顺利，群众在发展中得到更多实惠。

这五年，是东莞加强政府自身建设、依法行政全面推进、工作作风持续改进的五年。切实转变政府职能，加强民主法治和廉政建设，打造为民务实清廉政府。机关作风进一步优化。在政府系统相继开展群众路线教育实践活动和“三严三实”、“两学一做”等专题教育，撤并72.7%的考核检查评比表彰活动，压减47%的节庆、论坛、展会活动，“四风”问题、“不严不实”问题得到积极整改。政府职能进一步转变。物价、商贸、卫生、计生等职能调整理顺。编制市镇两级政府权责清单，开展行政审批标准化建设，梳理分类行政许可和公共服务事项1812项。市网上办事大厅初步建成，各镇街及园区办事站建设实现全覆盖，建成593个社区综合服务管理中心。12345政府服务热线开通。行政机关负责人出庭应诉制度不断完善。依法行政水平进一步提升。法治政府建设深入推进。东莞正式获得地方立法权，城管、环保、交通、文化等领域地方立法工作有序铺开。“六五”普法顺利完成。在全省率先实现一村（社区）一法律顾问全覆盖。主动接受人大法律监督、政协民主监督和社会舆论监督。在中国政法大学近年发布的法治政府评估报告中，东莞总分均位居全国地级市前列。

刚刚过去的2016年，是实施“十三五”规划的开局之年，全市政府系统认真贯彻落实上级和市委的决策部署，较好地完成了年度目标，205项具体任务高效落实，十件实事圆满完成，实现了“十三五”的良好开局。刚刚过去的2016年，也是东莞承前启后、深化改革发展的一年，全市政府系统按照市委的统一部署，以供给侧结构性改革为统领，以构建开放型经济新体制综合试点试验为契机，开展八大专题调研，摸清了现状，找准了短板，理清了思路，不少调研成果正逐步转化为指导政府工作开展的系统方案。李克强总理莅莞考察时，对东莞在动能转换过程中保持较快发展速度、经济结构和动能不断优化表示了肯定，指出这一走势很好地说明新旧动能正在加速转换，希望东莞保持发展势头，让新动能逐步挑起大梁，旧动能不断焕发生机。一年来，我们突出抓了以下工作：

——着力保障经济稳中向好，扎实推进供给侧结构性改革。预计全市生产总值增长8.1%左右，快于全国、全省增速。进出口总额增长10%左右，增速在全国五大进出口城市中位居第一，其中出口增长2%左右。东莞成为全国第2个国税突破1000亿元的地级市。落实“三去一降一补”。全年为企业减负超200亿元。产业供给结构进一步优化，先进制造业、高技术制造业增加值分别增长15.1%和17.8%。新增主营收入超10亿元企业17家，总数达243家。新增500亿元企业2家。华为终端率先突破千亿元。全力抓好重大项目建设。全年完成投资439.4亿元，超过计划18.7个百分点，同比增长10.5%，完成情况近年最好。总投资99亿元的19个重大产业项目建成投产。加快战略性新兴产业发展。智能手机主营收入近3000亿元，增长40%以上。华为、OPPO、VIVO手机出货量均进入全球前六、稳居全国前三。在智能终端产业的带动下，电子信息制造业规上工业增加值增长20%左右。全市新登记新兴产业市场主体6207户，增长113%。

——**着力强化创新驱动，加快集聚创新要素**。抓好高企培育"育苗造林"计划和孵化体系建设。全市新增高企761家、高企后备企业819家，总量均居全省地级市第一。用好相关政策，为高企减免税款32.3亿元，增长54.5%。新增新型研发机构6个、科技孵化器12个、国家级众创空间9个。促进科技金融产业紧密融合，新增上市企业2家、新三板挂牌企业105家。实施"机器换人"带动智能制造。全市申报"机器换人"项目577个，总投资72亿元，其中莞产设备占16%。项目数和总投资额均居全省第一，带动全市工业技改投资增长35%。加快国家自主创新示范区建设。松山湖生产总值、税收分别增长16%和24.3%，综合实力在全省国家高新区中排名第三。全国智能制造试点示范经验交流会、全省推进珠三角创新驱动发展培育高新技术企业工作现场会、专业镇协同创新工作现场会在莞召开，东莞相关经验得到肯定和推广。

——**着力优化对企服务，促进外资和民营经济协调发展**。高规格召开非公经济工作会议，制定实施提升外经贸水平45条和民营"亲企清政"36条。扎实推进外贸稳增长调结构。推动加工贸易企业提质增效，加快广东（石龙）铁路国际物流基地和中俄贸易产业园建设，成功举办海丝博览会、加博会、智博会、台博会等展会。对"一带一路"国家出口超过1350亿元。跨境电商贸易增长迅速，国际邮包出口量突破7000万件，跃居全国第四。国际邮件互换局兼交换站落户东莞。实施"亲企清政"工程。建成"千干扶千企"网络平台，开展"问暖企业总部"系列活动。民营规上工业增加值增长18.3%，占全市比重达38.6%。民间投资增长13%，占固定资产投资总额的70%。新登记非公经济市场主体17.1万户，增长41%。毫不松懈加强招商引资。主动加强与周边城市产业合作。组团赴欧美、日韩及全国各地招商。全市合同外资47.3亿美元、实际外资39.3亿美元，扣除不可比因素分别增长8.8%和3.1%。协议内资1174亿元。实际内资662亿元，增长20%。

——**着力促进区域协作，积极推动优势互补、密切合作**。主动对接广东自贸区，深莞惠3+2经济圈合作日益紧密，莞深产业合作不断强化。实施新一轮市内帮扶工作，落实帮扶专项资金1.8亿元，支持次发达村加快发展。对口帮扶韶关工作在全省考核中排名第三。推进韶关、揭阳精准扶贫精准脱贫工作，完成到村帮扶项目1026个，到户项目36218个。启动对口帮扶云南昭通工作。援疆工作进展顺利，兵团草湖广东纺织产业园首期30万锭项目建成投产。援藏援川工作成效明显。

——**着力优化城市环境，加速推进重大基础设施和生态环境建设**。加快轨道交通等建设。地铁2号线开通运营，累计客流量2160多万人次。莞惠城际轨道常平至惠州段通车。启动地铁1号线工程前期工作。与深圳、广州加快研究地铁对接规划。从莞高速主线、粤晖大桥等项目建成。虎门二桥、深圳外环高速东莞段、莞番高速扎实推进。打通了南丫大桥等5条断头路。实施信息基础建设大会战和电网大会战，WIFI接入点建设规模全省第一，建成110千伏及以上电网工程项目15个。深入推进污水和固废治理。全面打响新一轮水污染治理攻坚战。加强茅洲河、石马河污染整治。建成260公里截污管网，完成4家污水处理厂扩建，新增污水处理能力17万吨/日。试点推进麻涌、清溪的分散式污水处理项目建设。综合整治桥头大东洲等3个生活垃圾填埋场。完成厚街环保热电厂二期扩建工程，一批环保热电厂扩建工程扎实推进。农村生活垃圾处理连续两年全省考核第一。抓好节能减排和大气污染治理。全面完成国家节能减排财政政策综合示范城市建设任务，推动水乡地区101家污染企业整治和退出，主要污染物排放量持续下降。单位地区生产总值能耗下降5%以上。空气优良天数达到318天，同比增加11天。

——着力开展文明创建，全面实施“四大提升工程”和“十大专项行动”。深入开展城市文明“补短板促提升”工作，集中整治户外广告、城市“牛皮癣”、环境卫生、交通秩序，大力实施核心价值观融入提升、市民素质提升等行动，广泛开展“东莞好人”评选活动，着力打造“友善之城”，市、镇、村一体化文明创建取得阶段性成效。全市增设核心价值观等公益广告17.3万块，公益广告比例达到30%以上。实施文明创建工程项目311个、总投资额超过9.5亿元。镇容村貌更加整洁有序，清理卫生死角超过52万处、关停处理“牛皮癣”号码近1.3万个，签约“门前三包”责任书150多万份。城市精细化管理进一步加强，处理占道经营超过33万宗、违章建筑超过1万处。城市品位和城市形象有效提升。

——着力维护安定和谐，以“智网工程”等为抓手提升社会服务管理水平。全面启动“智网工程”。划分基础网格3201个，配置管理员9177人，首批推动公安等七个部门77个事项入格，在所有镇街（园区）全面铺开。全市实有人口公共基础信息平台上线试运行。努力提升群众安全感。深入开展“飓风2016”等专项行动，严厉打击各类突出违法犯罪，强化命案防范打击，开展“以案说防”活动，提升“全民创安”参与度。狠抓安全生产、消防和信访工作。严格履行安全生产责任，深入开展危险化学品和易燃易爆物品安全、火灾隐患重点地区“百村挂牌”督办、“三小”场所和出租屋消防安全、建筑施工安全等领域的专项整治，整改各类风险隐患20多万处。加强信访源头防控和积案化解，妥善处置劳资纠纷、非法集资等引发的群体性事件，社会大局保持和谐稳定。

——着力加强民生保障，全面发展文教体卫等社会事业。实施文化惠民工程。推进国家公共文化服务标准化、基层综合性文化服务中心和国家数字文化馆试点建设。开展“寻找最美家庭”活动。加强文艺精品创作。推出首部本土题材音乐剧《虎门销烟》，完成大型电视剧《袁崇焕》现场拍摄。提升教育公共服务水平。注重民办教育发展，新设6.5亿元民办教育专项资金，新创建义务教育阶段优质民办学校39所。重视解决随迁子女教育问题，铺开向民办学校购买学位政策，为随迁子女提供学位3.5万个，增长23.8%。在22所学校实施托管改革，推进莞式“慕课”教学试点。高考各项指标位居全省前列。东莞被认定为全国义务教育发展基本均衡市。扎实推动卫生、体育等社会事业发展。推进公立医院医疗服务价格改革，推行分级诊疗制度，方便群众就医。对8家市属公立医院给予2.05亿元补助，减轻医院负担。基本医疗保险年度最高支付限额由20万元增加到30万元。有序实施“全面两孩”政策。建立危重症孕产妇和新生儿急救网络。市社会福利中心改扩建项目投入使用。发放就业创业补贴3.68亿元。成功举办国际马拉松赛和亚欧男子乒乓球全明星对抗赛。出台住房限购政策，促进房地产市场平稳健康发展。认真做好台风“妮妲”、“海马”防御工作。国防动员、统计审计、外事侨务、工青妇幼、民族宗教、档案方志、残疾人、红十字会、打私等工作有效推进。在2016中国地级市民生发展100强城市中，东莞名列第3位。

各位代表，过去五年，我们攻坚克难，锐意进取，迈出了转型升级的新步伐，谱写了改革发展的新篇章。这离不开上级和市委的正确领导，离不开历届党委政府打下的坚实基础，是全市人民共同奋斗的结果。在此，我代表东莞市人民政府，向全市干部群众，向人大代表和政协委员，向各民主党派、各人民团体、社会各界人士，向各驻莞单位、驻莞部队和武警官兵，向所有参与和支持东莞建设发展的港澳台同胞、海外侨胞和国际友人，表示衷心的感谢和崇高的敬意！

与此同时，我们也清醒地看到，全市发展仍然存在不少困难和问题，需要引起我们高度重视：一是经济下行压力仍然较大。外部市场环境复杂严峻，高端制造回流和低端市场分流同时并存，引进的重大项目建成释放产能尚需时日，新的经济增长点仍较单一，稳增长的基础有待加强。二是新旧动能转换还处于胶着状态。传统的路径依赖尚未根本转变，集约发展水平有待提高，扩大优质供给和有效需求难度较大，一些企业和行业仍缺乏核心竞争力，转型升级任重道远。三是利益固化的藩篱制约了深层次改革的推进。随着改革步入深水区，一些深层次矛盾和长期积累问题亟待攻坚破解。进一步解放思想的观念束缚、局部碎片化的土地利用状况、固化胶着的利益格局等，制约了全市改革向纵深推进，统筹发展、征地拆迁、城市更新、“两违”整治等工作仍需加大力度突破。四是环境污染治理任务艰巨。大气、土壤等污染治理以及垃圾处理问题亟待解决，特别是水环境整治历史欠账较多，深度治理刻不容缓。五是城市品质和内涵有待进一步提升。与优质企业和高端人才的需求相比，基础设施和城市配套还需完善，精细化管理需要进一步加强，化解社会矛盾和消除安全隐患的能力有待提升，文化、教育、医疗、交通等公共服务仍待优化。六是作风建设和履职水平仍需改进。一些干部存在“顺其自然”的工作心态，攻坚克难的锐气和韧劲不够，甚至消极对待、无所作为，影响工作推进。对此，我们必须高度警醒，尽最大努力予以解决。

今后五年的奋斗目标和主要任务

今后五年，是东莞加快经济转型、实现动能转换的决胜时期，也是我市加速城市升级、促进和谐善治的关键时期。市第十四次党代会明确了“**在更高起点上实现更高水平发展**”的价值追求，提出了全市发展的主要目标：一是率先全面建成小康社会，率先迈上基本实现社会主义现代化新征程；二是跨越生产总值万亿元；三是跨越“中等收入陷阱”；四是动能转换与经济转型取得根本性突破；五是社会和谐善治水平得到根本性提升。发展蓝图已经绘就，全市政府系统必须紧紧围绕市委决策部署，紧密结合东莞实际，以清晰的思路、有力的措施抓好工作落实，促进全市经济结构更优、发展动力更足、体制机制更活、城市环境更美、人民生活更好，奋力谱写东莞改革发展的新篇章。

今后五年，要在更高起点上实现更高水平发展，必须练好内功，率先突围，促进城市综合实力再上新台阶。从当前态势综合判断，今后几年总需求低迷和产能过剩并存的格局难以根本改变。国家正大力推进供给侧结构性改革，主动摆脱“粗放发展”，努力实现“内涵增长”。实践证明，这是适应新常态、应对下行压力的最佳途径。无论对一个企业、还是一座城市，今后几年都是练好内功、加快转型、提升核心竞争力的关键时期。我们必须保持定力，坚定转型，毫不动摇地强化创新驱动发展，加快转型升级步伐，切实优化产业供给结构，不断增强东莞先进制造业的核心竞争力；必须造好环境、打好基础，以提升城市品质和内涵为核心，沉下心来，更高水平地推进新一轮规划建设，加强精细化管理，增强综合承载力，把东莞打造成创新创业热土和宜居生态城市。力争未来五年，随着转型成效的逐步显现和新动能的逐步释放，全市地区生产总值年均增速达到8.3%以上，到2021年超过万亿元，东莞的综合实力与城市地位进一步提升，继续处在全国地级市前列。

今后五年，要在更高起点上实现更高水平发展，必须以最积极主动的态度集聚高端资源，强化创新驱动，实现新旧动能的转换和转型升级的突破。随着粤港澳大湾区一体化进程的加快，珠三角城市群正处于区域分工格局调整的关键时期。周边中心城市作为产业高地和创新中心，辐射带动能力日益增强。东莞依托优越的区位优势和坚实的产业集群优势，正日益成为高端产业加速和产能扩张的首选之地，迎来了新一轮产业大发展的重大历史机遇。我们必须正视港珠澳大桥、深中通道开通后发展格局的变化，以强烈的使命感和紧迫感，抓住这3—5年的窗口期，努力在新一轮产业发展中占据先机、赢得主动。在产业增量上，以最积极主动的态度，腾挪发展空间，狠抓招商引资，集聚高端资源，引进一批支撑城市未来发展的重大优质项目和先进产业集群。同时，推动已列入“十三五”规划、总投资5779亿元的317项重大项目落地，最快速度释放产能。在产业存量上，出台实施倍增计划，市镇两级集中力量扶持一批存量优势企业规模与效益倍增，形成市镇联动、以点带面的良好态势，促进全市产业总量扩张和集约发展。在产业动力上，深入实施创新驱动发展战略，加快建设珠三角国家自主创新示范区，培育高企2500家以上，新型研发机构50家以上，科技孵化器加速器100家以上，让东莞制造插上科技与金融两大翅膀。深入实施“东莞制造2025”战略，加快“机器换人”和智能化改造，不断提高东莞制造的自动化、智能化、绿色化水平。深入推进构建开放型经济新体制综合试点试验，促进传统产业加快转型、加工贸易创新发展、民营经济提质增效，推动一般贸易占比提高到40%以上，规上工业企业内销比例55%以上。力争用五年左右时间，先进制造业、高技术制造业增加值占比分别达到52%和50%，初步建成国内领先的创新型城市，在全省建设国家科技产业创新中心中走在前列，动能转换与经济转型取得根本性突破，实现东莞制造向东莞智造、东莞速度向东莞质量的跨越。市场主体超过100万户，其中既有3—5家超千亿的大型企业、500多家上市企业和新三板挂牌企业，也有大量创新型、高成长性的中小企业。智能手机、机器人及智能装备等超千亿元的新产业、新动能挑起大梁；新一代电子信息、半导体、新能源、高端装备、生物医药等产业形成气候；服装、家具、鞋业等传统制造业占据高端、不断焕发生机。先进制造业与现代服务业“双轮驱动”、外资和民营“比翼齐飞”、出口和内销“两分天下”的格局全面形成，东莞作为国际制造名城的地位得到进一步巩固和提升。

今后五年，要在更高起点上实现更高水平发展，必须大力实施城市品质提升计划，全面提高城市承载力与核心竞争力。东莞是一个组团式的现代化城市，在后工业化时代，这种特殊格局很好地顺应了高端产业和人才向往魅力小城和美丽乡村的追求，是我们参与区域竞争的重要优势和基础。但东莞也是一个地处穗港深经济走廊的典型通道城市，只有把城市品质和承载力提升上来，才能发挥自身优势，产生先进制造业“洼地效应”，与周边中心城市形成分工明确、联动发展的良好格局。否则，高端产业和人才过境而不留，优质要素反倒因周边中心城市“虹吸效应”而流失。我们必须强化“有什么样的城市、就有什么样的产业、就有什么样的人才”的理念，坚定“产城人”融合的方向，力争通过三五年时间的努力，实现城市品质内涵的跨越，全面提升城市承载力和竞争力。首先是推动城市总体格局大优化。完善一中心多组团的城市结构。通过功能轴线打造、重点单元建设提升和城市更新改造，适度强化城市中心和组团中心的集聚度，提升城市集约发展水平。因地制宜推动各组团片区打造一批以“产城人”融合为特征的魅力小城。推动一大批村（社区）打造成为设施完善、整洁有序、和谐宜居的美丽幸福村居。其次是促进城市基础设施大提升。抓紧推进地铁 1 号、2 号等线路新建续建工程规划建设，配合推进穗莞深、佛莞惠等城际轨道以及赣深、深茂等铁路的规划建设，全面对接深圳、广州等城市的轨道交通，力争尽快形成网络。加快虎门二桥、深圳外环高速东莞段、莞番高速等建设，进一步完善“五纵四横六连”的高速路网。加快环莞快速路、桑茶快线等建设，形成“8”字形环城路网 + 多条放射状的市域快速路格局。加快打通与深圳、广州等城市及市内各镇街（园区）之间的断头路，大力推动东莞港建设，进一步强化内畅外联的交通网络。全面完善水、电、气、通信等基础设施网络。基本完成珠三角水资源配置工程东莞项目建设，科学推进江库联网工程，初步形成双水源保障新格局。第三是打好环境污染治理攻坚战。突出以水环境治理为核心，“十三五”完成不少于 200 条内河涌以及 6 公里海岸线的污染整治和生态修复，累计建成 4500 公里左右的截污管网，新建扩建 15 家集中污水处理厂及上百家分散式污水处理设施，基本形成厂网一体化运营管理的截污治水格局。主要河流基本消除劣五类水体，力争四个国考断面水质达到考核要求。空气优良天数比例达 92%以上，土壤污染得到有效控制。新增生活垃圾实现无害化全焚烧零填埋处理，存量垃圾逐步消化处理，垃圾分类处理稳步推进。第四是再造宜居生态环境新品质。从满足市民高品质生活的需求出发，充分发挥生态本底好的优势，着力加强森林公园、湿地公园、体育公园、农业公园、滨海公园及现代渔港等建设，大力发展都市农业，切实完善城市配套，进一步彰显宜居生态之城的特色。力争经过三五年努力，体现东莞都市形象的大市区、体现魅力特色的各组团、体现基层活力的村容村貌都得到质的提升，“环莞一小时生活圈”基本实现，深莞惠 3+2 经济圈合作更加密切，东莞与穗港深一体化、同城化的态势更加明显。全市天更蓝、水更清，国际化、法治化、市场化的营商环境更加优越，对优质企业和高端人才的吸引力不断增强，东莞成为珠三角乃至全省全国最适宜创新创业的城市之一。

今后五年，要在更高起点上实现更高水平发展，必须坚持民生优先导向，让人民群众有更多的安全感、获得感和幸福感。把执政为民作为一切工作的出发点和落脚点，努力建设更加平安和谐、更加幸福美好的东莞。社会服务管理方面，突出以“智网工程”为主抓手，促进社会服务管理模式实现根本性变革，将网格化管理延伸到市域各个片区、拓展到社会治理各个层面，做到精准服务、精准管理、精准执法。加强社会治安综合治理，推进友善之城和平安文化建设，进一步提升群众安全感。强化公共安全和应急管理，全面排查整改各类安全隐患，妥善解决好群众的利益诉求，营造安定和谐的良好环境。公共服务配置方面，按照适度超前、循序渐进、实事求是的理念，提升优化公共服务的供给结构和质量，并根据组团格局优化资源配置，加大对次发达镇的扶持力度。建立健全非户籍常住人口与居住年限等条件相挂钩享受基本公共服务的机制，稳步推进基本公共服务均等化。民生事业发展方面，坚持每年办好十件实事，带动民生事业全面发展。着力打造东莞“慧教育”，提升各类教育优质均衡发展水平，加快高等教育发展，推动职业教育创新发展，打造教育现代化强市。深入推进“健康东莞”建设，积极构建与居民健康需求相匹配的医疗卫生服务体系。健全全民参保机制，建立更加完善的社保体系。构建轨道交通、常规公交、慢行交通一体化的公共交通体系，让市民出行更加便捷。提升城市文明方面，践行社会主义核心价值观，弘扬东莞城市精神，推进文化名城建设，全面提升市民素质和社会文明程度。把发展群众文化、群众体育作为基本方向，建设城市“十分钟健身圈”、镇村“十里文化圈”，承办好男篮世界杯、亚洲马拉松锦标赛，进一步打响篮球、莞香、音乐剧等品牌。深入改进作风，加强法治政府建设和廉政建设，营造风清气正、政通人和的良好环境。力争用五年时间，全市社会服务管理水平再上新台阶，“学有所教、劳有所得、病有所医、老有所养、住有所居”得到更好体现，在东莞工作生活的广大市民群众感到更加安全、舒适、开心和幸福。

2017 年工作安排

2017 年是实施“十三五”规划的重要一年，是推进供给侧结构性改革的深化之年，做好各项工作意义重大。今年政府工作的**指导思想**是：全面贯彻党的十八大和十八届三中、四中、五中、六中全会及中央经济工作会议精神，深入学习贯彻习近平总书记系列重要讲话精神，统筹推进“五位一体”总体布局，协调推进“四个全面”战略布局，自觉践行“五大发展理念”，按照省委十一届七次、八次全会和省委经济工作会议的要求，认真贯彻落实市第十四次党代会和市委经济工作会议的决策部署，坚持稳中求进工作总基调，以供给侧结构性改革为统领，以加速新旧动能转换为方向，以构建开放型经济新体制综合试点试验为契机，以“十大行动计划”为抓手，深化创新驱动，加快转型升级，强化执行落实，突出抓好实施倍增计划、加强招商引资、提升城市品质、优化民生保障等重点工作，促进经济平稳健康发展与社会和谐稳定，努力推动东莞在更高起点上实现更高水平发展。

今年全市经济社会发展的**主要预期目标**为：生产总值增长 8—8.5%，人均生产总值增长 8%左右，市一般公共预算收入增长 9.5%，固定资产投资总额增长 10%左右，社会消费品零售总额增长 10%，进出口总额增长 3%。先进制造业、高技术制造业增加值占比分别达到 50%和 40%，R&D 比重提高至 2.5%。全面完成年度节能减排目标任务。

围绕上述目标和要求，突出抓好以下工作：

一、加快创新驱动和转型升级步伐，打造智能制造新高地

以倍增计划带动集约化水平提升。按照“选好选优、培优培强”的原则，选取 200 家存量优势企业进行重点培育。支持企业通过科技创新、发展总部经济、推进兼并重组、加强产业链整合、强化资本运作等提升综合竞争力，力争用 3—5 年时间，推动试点企业实现规模和效益的倍增。同时，示范带动各镇街（园区）实施镇级倍增计划，引导全市存量优势企业全面提升产业集约、资源集约、空间集约水平。

实施精准服务企业行动。按“一企一策”方针，对龙头企业提供个性化服务方案，系统解决企业用地、人才保障房、员工子女入学、配套工厂落地及扩张等问题。深化“千干扶千企”服务，探索建立“企业十件实事”工作机制，帮助中小企业解决融资、引才等共性问题。积极探索解决市属转制企业历史遗留问题。清理规范行政审批中介服务事项。实行涉企收费目录清单管理制度，进一步减轻企业负担。

着力加强高企培育和创新平台建设。落实珠三角国家自主创新示范区总体实施方案。深入实施高企“育苗造林”行动计划，力争年内高企达 2000 家，高企后备企业 1000 家。鼓励高企组建重点实验室和工程中心，引导规上企业设立研发机构。以发展科技产业为重点，加大产业加速器环节的培育扶持力度，推动科研成果加速成为产能。加强新型研发机构绩效评估考核，加快大学创新城和高水平理工科大学建设。推进散裂中子源建设，力争 9 月出第一束试验束。启动建设先进高端材料研发实验基地。加快筹建名校研究生院，启动研究生实践基地建设。打造国家知识产权强市。

推进“机器换人”和智能化改造。实施智能制造示范工程，完成 100 条示范线建设。完善“机器换人”资金管理，用好省市融资租赁资金，撬动技改融资 20 亿元以上。集聚一批智能化改造系统集成商和服务商。引进培育一批龙头企业，推动机器人及智能装备产业产值增长 20%以上。办好智博会与科技合作周。积极创建“中国制造 2025”试点示范城市。

培育壮大智能终端等高端产业和新兴产业。构建完整的智能终端产业生态系统，力争成为全球智能终端产业最重要的研发设计、生产配套、品牌聚集基地之一。扶持新一代信息技术、新能源、生物医药、激光等产业加快发展。为 1000 家企业提供两化融合服务。大力推进“互联网 + 创新创业”。建设科技“四众”平台。支持企业利用互联网、大数据等创新商业模式，开展个性化定制、柔性化生产。大力发展研发设计、会展物流、文化创意和新型旅游等现代服务业。

促进科技金融产业深度融合。发挥产业投资母基金作用，形成“1+N”产业投资基金体系。推动企业上市和挂牌新三板融资，推动东莞上市板块扩容。支持企业通过发行公司债券、中期票据等筹集资金。支持金融机构拓宽业务领域，积极申报各类金融牌照。探索创建贸易金融创新示范基地，在松山湖等条件成熟的园区和镇街大力引进和发展基金业，促进股权投资基金、融资租赁、消费金融等新型经济金融组织集聚发展。力争私募投资基金突破 250 家。

大力弘扬企业家精神和工匠精神。强化“优秀企业家是经济发展脊梁”的理念，弘扬“厚德务实、敢为人先”的莞商精神，在全社会营造支持企业发展和推崇企业家精神的良好氛围。支持各大商协会及世界莞商联合会发展，推动企业家抱团发展。办好莞商学院，实施万名民营企业家培训计划。加强“创二代”的培养。鼓励有条件的民企引入现代管理模式。依法保护企业和企业家的合法权益。弘扬精益求精的工匠精神，实施技能人才培养行动计划，提升东莞制造品质。

二、加强重大产业项目建设招商，增强经济发展后劲

抓好年度 225 个重大项目建设。坚持市政府主要领导每月督导协调制度。完善重大项目全链条服务管理机制。推动项目审批提速，着力破解征地拆迁、管线迁改等难题。力争年内完成重大项目投资 430 亿元，其中重大产业项目 290 亿元。推动 23 个重大产业项目建成投产，新开工 43 个、总投资 337 亿元的重大项目。

主动到位加强产业精准招商。加强全市产业布局的统筹规划和引导，完善重大项目招商引资统筹流转和利益分享机制。实行引资、引智、引技有机结合，实施面向广深港澳台和欧美先进地区（国家）招商合作计划，瞄准 100 家左右高端制造项目开展精准招商。打造专业化招商团队，推动国际经贸合作网点建设，与投资促进机构、商协会建立常态化合作机制。对重点增资项目实行市镇领导挂钩督导，支持企业通过“工改工”扩建扩产。推动外地企业将在莞分支机构转为法人企业，鼓励企业在莞设立总部。力争引进超亿元内资项目 100 宗、超千万美元外资项目 90 宗。

强化产业用地统筹保障。做好基本农田与耕地调整工作，解决一批涉农土地历史遗留问题。分期用好新增建设用地指标，优先保障重大平台、重大项目、倍增计划、TOD 开发的用地需求。加大对供而未

用土地的处置力度，收回一批过期不动的项目用地指标。加强对镇街用地进度和产出效益的评估考核。处置闲置用地3000亩。探索农村集体土地使用制度改革，改进征地和拆迁补偿制度。完善镇村土地统筹利益分享机制。研究创新建筑工程招投标方式。开展被征地农民补偿款、征地留用地安置、农村土地“三乱”问题专项治理。加强土地收储整合，力争整合1000亩以上连片地块2—3块。

三、积极探索对外经贸合作新模式、新业态、新体制，促进开放型经济发展水平提升

加快构建开放型经济新体制综合试点试验工作。制定年度行动计划。在探索对接国际经济管理新模式等六大方面，推进20项重点任务，力争年底前取得阶段性突破。在经济管理服务改革等五大方面，推进32项具体改革措施，力争形成一批可复制推广的改革经验。积极向上争取第一批19项支持政策。

大力推动加工贸易创新发展。制定加工贸易转型升级评价体系。建立鼓励加工贸易企业技术创新、品牌推广、营销培育、质量提升的四大机制。扶持港台企业转型升级。办好加博会和台博会。鼓励加工贸易企业在莞设立地区总部或与民营企业融合发展。推广以企业为单元的加工贸易监管模式。搭建“东莞制造”品牌推广服务平台，推动优势企业联合“走出去”。

深度对接国家“一带一路”战略。加快建设广东（石龙）铁路国际物流基地，常态化开通中亚、中欧国际班列。推动华南火车邮件物流枢纽建设。推进中俄贸易产业园先行启动区建设。实施“一港一铁”、“多式联运”工程，推动东莞港与日韩和东南亚国家沿线港口建立直航航线。探索创建滨海湾“一带一路”国际合作示范区。办好海丝博览会。推进广东海丝跨境商品展示交易中心、南非商品中国（东莞）展示交易中心、巴西中国经济贸易促进会总部基地、广东（东莞）珠宝玉石交易中心等建设。

大力发展跨境电商和保税物流。实施电子商务企业50强清单行动计划，抓好物流标准化等四大服务平台建设。加快建设电子商务统计系统。积极推动跨境电商通关模式改革。加快东莞跨境电商中心园区、京东现代服务业产业园、珠三角汽车博览中心等项目建设。建成东莞国际邮件互换局兼交换站。对接香港“超级中国干线”业务，为企业提供空陆多式联运服务。推进全国外贸综合服务企业试点。力争综合保税区早日获批。

积极参与粤港澳大湾区建设，加强区域协作与对口帮扶。主动对接广东自贸区，推广出口退税无纸化等37项改革经验。推进深莞惠3+2经济圈建设，加强与深圳、广州在交通对接、产业互动、协同创新、环境治理等层面的全方位合作。打造莞港澳台创新创业基地。积极争取将水乡经济区、滨海湾开发区和东莞港纳入粤港澳大湾区核心区域重大平台。扎实推进对韶关、揭阳帮扶工作。落实援藏援疆任务，抓好巴宜区富民兴藏工作，推进兵团草湖工业园示范项目。深入开展与昭通市的扶贫协作。加强与四川雅江县、九龙县和重庆巫山县的对口联系。

四、构建园镇统筹发展新格局，推动区域协调发展

推动松山湖、水乡管委会与周边镇联动协同发展。用好松山湖珠三角国家自主创新示范区政策，加速集聚创新要素，增强松山湖辐射带动能力。进一步明确水乡管委会职能定位，支持设立控股平台和开发基金，加快水乡新城和重大基础设施建设。加大松山湖、水乡管委会与周边镇的统筹发展力度，实施市级行政审批事项服务前移，高标准开发建设片区重点区域，探索建立园镇统筹发展的决策、规划、招商、投融资、项目布局等机制。启动一批一体化的交通、环境工程建设。

创新园区开发模式，“一园一策”加快园区发展。明确市与园区及相关统筹发展镇街的事权划分，加大市级权限下放园区力度。着力解决制约园区发展的行政管理、土地开发、投融资、交通连通等共性问题。理顺银瓶创新区政企合作关系，抓好基础设施和公共服务项目建设，加快粤海产业园和银山科技园建设与招商。推动东莞港发展，加快疏港交通快速通道建设，打造立沙岛、主港区、新沙南三大临港产业板块。加快滨海湾开发区建设，科学谋划发展定位，完成5000亩以上滩涂填土，加快围填海和基础设施建设，探索推进土地1.5级开发。启动原东部工业园企石辖区开发，解决土地遗留问题，建立利益平衡和投融资机制。

扶持镇村经济发展。推动专业镇从“一镇一品”向“一镇一品一特色服务”提升，促进五金模具、纺织服装等产业集群向价值链高端延伸。推进特色小镇建设。设立10亿元的扶持次发达镇产业发展资金池。用好三年6.4亿元市内帮扶资金，力争年内70%的次发达村经营性纯收入达到300万元。探索搭建集体经济与实业投资、金融信托等机构的合作平台，推动集体经济从单一的物业租赁向物业型、服务型和投资型多元化发展转变，探索建立“效益决定分配、盈利共享、风险共担、可增可减”的股东分红机制。

五、全面启动新一轮基础设施及城市配套规划建设，进一步提升城市品质和内涵

以强化中心城区功能为先导，统筹推进市域顶层设计。抓住土地利用总体规划调整完善、国家住建部城市总体规划改革试点等契机，推进“多规融合”，力争中心城区土规、城规重合率达90%以上。探索组团规划编制和控规编制改革，开展城市密度分区和容积率专题研究，加强对中心城区、松山湖核心片区等开发强度的控制和引导。推进南城国际商务区等重点单元规划建设，探索对同沙生态公园周边片区、东江大桥至环城西路的滨水片区实施综合规划开发，研究推动东莞水道、厚街水道、汾溪河的综合改造。研究松山湖大道、环城路、东部快速路、新城大道、生态园大道等道路连接体系的综合改造提升。启动市中心主干道交通改造工程，新建和打通支线道路，研究缓解市区交通拥堵的系统改造和治理方案。

加快轨道交通等重大基础设施建设。推进赣深客专东莞段建设。加快穗莞深、佛莞惠等城际轨道和地铁1号线建设。加快1号线南延线（对接深圳6号线支线）、西延线（对接广州5号线），2号线三期及南延线（对接深圳20号线），以及深圳13号线北延至松山湖的前期工作。优化协调莞番高速线位，加快虎门二桥、莞番高速、深圳外环高速东莞段、常虎高速虎门港支线二期、桑茶快线及延长线、中洪支线等建设改造。建成松山湖大道大朗段。推进环莞快速路建设，力争年内二期建成通车，加快推进三期建设。研究推动市区至松山湖第二通道的规划建设。加快疏港大道延长线建设，启动望沙路升级改造、水乡地区横向通道工程建设。推进东莞站配套工程、新沙港区二期工程等建设。试点推进海绵城市和地下综合管廊建设。推进信息基础设施建设大会战。启动电网升级行动。

实施打通断头路行动计划。建成梨川大桥、东宝河新安大桥。加强穗深莞惠交通对接，加快东平东江大桥、龙江东江大桥、金龙路、恒心路、黄江生态路等建设。加快市内道路连通，抓好石龙南岸二桥改建、道滘大桥重建等工程。系统研究市际、市内、镇村等一批断头路的贯通方案，逐步启动实施。

加快城市更新连片改造和TOD开发建设。完善统筹协调城市更新工作的体制机制。出台连片改造专项政策。建立城市更新成效与新增用地指标分配挂钩制度。加快东城黄旗南、万江龙湾滨江等5个共约1.4万亩的片区改造。新启动南城东华、长安科技商务区等8个共约3万亩的片区改造。支持东城“33小镇”、鳒鱼洲、常平科技加速园、黄江裕元灵狮小镇等旧工业区活化更新。探索推进挂影洲围的统筹开发。每个次发达镇至少实施1个城市更新项目，其他镇街实施2—3个。启动虎门站、东莞西站、

东莞火车站、东莞东站、松山湖北站、黄江北站等TOD开发试点，示范带动全市TOD开发。

推进魅力小城和美丽幸福村居建设。出台实施魅力小城建设三年行动计划，选择若干片区重点单元作为示范试点，切实加强产业指引、空间规划和资金支持，推进一批规划建设有品质、产业发展有特色的魅力小城建设。启动美丽乡村特色连片示范建设。力争完成100个村（社区）美丽幸福村居建设。推动麻涌、樟木头、清溪等镇创建省级全域旅游示范区。

按照“建管结合、重在管理”的思路，大力整治交通拥堵问题。完善多部门联动的交通工作机制。优先发展公共交通。完善提升枢纽站、换乘站的规划建设。做好轨道交通站点与公交的衔接。优化公交线路、班次和服务水平。试行政府购买公交服务运营模式。出台网约车管理细则。研究通过增设掉头立交等微治理手段，对交通拥堵路段实施系统改造。建设智能交通管理系统，提高交通管理信息化水平。

加强城市精细化管理。深入推进城市执法体制改革。建立城乡环境“六整治”长效机制。出台户外广告设置、市容环境卫生管理等法规规章，建全城市管理考核评价机制。严格控制新增“两违”。对历史遗留违法建筑摸清底数、建立台账，探索实施分类处理，修订产权补办手续办法，逐步消化存量违法建筑。

深化投融资体制改革。编制中长期政府投融资规划。完善政府债务管理。推广应用PPP模式，探索政府购买服务。创新交通、环保、园区开发、民生项目的投融资模式。优化整合市属金融企业股权。进一步增强市属国有企业的融资能力。梳理盘活各类国有和集体闲置资产。深化市属国资国企改革，推进国有资产重组，增强在公益性、战略性领域的支撑保障作用。

六、加强污染治理和生态绿化，提升生态文明建设水平

全面打响水环境污染治理攻坚战。年内新建不少于500公里、两年新建1800公里截污次支管网，年内新建扩建10家集中污水处理厂。启动分散式污水处理设施建设。落实四大重点流域河长制。加快茅洲河、石马河等跨界河流的综合治理。“一河一策”加快内河涌整治，确保两年内完成不少于100条内河涌污染整治和生态修复。完成年度黑臭水体达标整治任务。推进饮用水源保护工程建设。

加强固废、大气、土壤污染治理。完成麻涌、横沥、市区环保热电厂新建扩建工程，将日处理能力提升到1.2万吨，实现新增生活垃圾全部无害化焚烧处理。建成麻涌餐厨垃圾处理项目和谢岗飞灰填埋场项目。加快海心沙循环经济产业园和建筑垃圾堆场建设。做好绿色供应链环境管理试点工作。全面淘汰黄标车。加强臭氧污染防治，开展重点行业挥发性有机物污染整治。推进燃煤工业锅炉整治和沙角电厂排放改造。加快中堂造纸基地等一批集中供热项目建设。开展土壤环境质量调查，推进3个土壤污染修复治理试点，形成经验推广至全市。

实施森林公园分类提升工程。对大岭山等森林公园进行升级改造，启动银瓶山三期建设，完成清溪湖森林通道等项目。做好城市森林公园周边空间的开发利用、郊野森林公园周边旅游设施的规划建设。加强“小山小湖”保护与开发。推进同沙湿地公园、黄江农业公园等建设，建成植物园一期工程。推进水源涵养林、生物防火林带等改造和营建。加快森林小镇建设。

七、推进社会治理现代化，营造安全稳定的社会环境

全面推开“智网工程”。完成网格员队伍整编和指挥调度中心建设，加强队伍培训，建立科学的日常管理、考核奖惩制度。全面启用“智网工程”信息系统。推动基层市场网格化监管等更多服务管理事项入格，推动大数据在社会治理中的创新运用，做到横向打破信息孤岛、纵向联动政府社会，实现精准管理。

全面强化社会治安管理。重拳打击电信诈骗、网络金融犯罪、“两抢一盗”、黑恶势力等违法犯罪行为，加快建设立体化社会治安防控体系，推动社会治安实现更加明显的好转。深入开展“以案说防”活动，大力推动“全民创安”。加快公安情报指挥中心升级改造。加强和改进公安派出所工作。推动出租屋管理地方立法。完善通过法定途径分类处理信访投诉的机制。创新基层劳资治理机制，实行兼职仲裁员办案制度。加强第三方调解组织建设，完善诉前联调机制，更好地发挥社会力量在管理社会事务中的作用。

全面加强安全生产、消防安全、食品安全等工作。推动“智慧安监”二期建设，加强基层专职安全员队伍建设。狠抓危化行业安全监管，推进立沙岛整岛封闭式管理，加快建设危化品应急救援基地。深入开展城市风险点、危险源排查整治行动和建筑、轨道交通施工安全大检查。实施部门“分镇包干”督导消防工作制度，加强消防安全专项治理，抓好省市挂牌督办重点镇村的集中整治。加强灾害性天气安全防范。打造 50 家食品安全示范市场，新建 150 家农贸市场快速检测室，建成市食品药品检测中心，铁腕查处食品药品安全违法行为。落实粮食保障任务。建设以企业信用管理为核心的科学市场监管体系。加强应急预案管理和演练，提升突发事件应对能力。

八、优化公共服务供给，切实增进民生福祉

努力提供更多的优质教育资源。编制各镇街、园区公办学校建设规划，制定居住区配套教育设施规划建设管理办法，新建扩建 21 所公办学校。实现民办义务教育标准化学校基本全覆盖、优质学校比例提升到 60%。大力发展公益普惠性幼儿园。推进高等教育发展。优化积分制入学办法。完善企业人才子女入学机制。购买民办义务教育学位同比增加 20%。创新和推广委托管理等办学模式，完善学校绩效管理机制。推进教育信息化和“慕课”试点。引进德国、台湾等优秀职教教学团队，提升办学水平。争取成功创建省现代职业教育综合改革示范市。

全面推进卫生强市建设。优化整合医疗资源，推动区域医疗中心建设。加快“一中心三平台”信息化建设。提升社区卫生服务机构水平，完善分级诊疗制度，力争基层诊疗服务量占 65%以上。建设市第九人民医院。鼓励市镇医院联合办医，推动部分公立医院向专科医院、医养结合机构或社区卫生服务中心转型。引进一批高层次医疗卫生人才，加强“东莞名医”和省名中医药专家培养，推进中医药强市建设。

促进房地产平稳健康发展，建立健全住房保障体系。落实房地产调控和住房限购政策。稳定房地产市场土地供应。加快非住宅商品房去库存。探索建立房地产用地招拍挂的创新机制。研究出台有利于长远发展包括保障房、人才房在内的、购租并举的住房保障体系政策。研究改善刚需部分村（居）民居住条件的政策。推进不动产统一登记，建立完善产权保护制度。出台物业管理办法。稳步扩大住房公积金缴存覆盖面。

着力加强文化体育建设和民生保障。推进基层综合性文化服务中心试点建设。实施“文物保护与利用”和“城市历史文化特色与价值强化”两大工程。挖掘工业遗产资源，推进文化创意改造。争取成功申报国家历史文化名城。争创全国版权示范城市。推动全民健身运动，办好亚洲马拉松锦标赛和市运会。继续办好十件实事。将低保标准从每人每月 610 元提高到 720 元。推广电子社保建设。新建 25 个社区综合服务中心。落实“8+1”社会救助制度。发展志愿服务、慈善、老龄和残疾人事业，新增养老床位 500 张以上，开展医养结合试点。加快市老年大学新校区建设。做好关心下一代工作，积极帮助青少年成长成才。开展新一轮双拥模范城创建。扩大法律援助范围。实施“巾帼关爱行动”。落实就业创业扶持政策。

九、强化法治意识和担当意识，提升与更高水平发展相适应的行政服务和履职能力

加强法治政府和廉洁政府建设。依法接受人大及其常委会的监督，自觉接受政协的民主监督，接受社会和舆论监督。完善政府法律顾问、经济顾问和决策咨询机制。全面公开部门预决算和“三公”经费支出信息，推动镇街公开财政预决算信息。加强地方立法工作，实施“七五”普法规划，深入开展法治创建活动。扎实推进反腐倡廉建设。

深化“一门式一网式”改革。组建市政务服务办和镇街（园区）政务服务中心。加快市镇实体办事大厅和网上统一申办受理平台建设，实现“一窗通办”、“一网通办”。深化项目投资管理体制改革，推进以承诺制为核心的项目直接落地改革。完善商改“宽进严管”体系。加快行政审批标准化建设，优化办事流程，推进数据共享和信息互认，让市民逐渐从“排队办事”变为“手机办事”、从“群众跑腿”变为“数据跑腿”。

提振敢于担当、主动作为的精气神。摒弃小富即安、“顺其自然”的工作心态，增强干事创业、克难奋进的攻坚锐气。加强工作督促考核，宽容改革创新失误，营造鼓励干事、支持改革、奖优罚劣的良好政风环境，进一步提振干部勇于担责、主动作为的精气神，务求高质高效完成全年目标任务。

各位代表！新的征程已经开启，新的目标催人奋进。让我们紧密团结在以习近平同志为核心的党中央周围，在省委、省政府的正确领导下，在市委的坚强领导下，与全市人民一道，务实创新、真抓实干、团结奋进，为推动东莞在更高起点上实现更高水平发展而不懈努力，以优异成绩迎接党的十九大胜利召开！

名词注解：

三个走在前列：深入推进创新驱动发展走在前列、对外开放合作走在前列、重点改革突破走在前列。

智能制造等“六大工程”：智能制造、服务型制造、创新制造、优质制造、集群制造、绿色制造“六大工程”。

四新经济：由“新技术、新业态、新模式、新产业”构成的新型经济形态。

直接落地改革：东莞开展的以企业依法承诺制、备案制和事后监管制为主要内容，实行“先建后验、宽进严管”模式的投资项目审批改革。

“三互”大通关：强化跨部门、跨区域的内陆沿海沿边通关协作，完善口岸工作机制，实现口岸管理相关部门信息互换、监管互认、执法互助，提高通关效率。

“放管服”改革：全国统一推进的简政放权、放管结合、优化服务改革。

营商环境“加一”、综合成本“减一”：“加一”指提高政府服务水平，使东莞的营商环境比其他地区更胜一筹。“减一”指努力降低企业综合经营成本，使其享受到更为低廉的成本优势。

智能终端：具有多媒体、通讯、网络、数据管理等功能的智能设备，如智能手机。

智网工程：把辖区分成一个个“网格”，依托统一的信息系统，通过网格员每日巡查反馈工商信息、城市管理、公共安全等情况，实现精准执法、精准管理。

以案说防：公安等部门以分析典型案例为主题在社区开展的普法活动，旨在提高群众的法律意识和安全防范技能。

民办教育专项资金：为支持我市民办教育各项事业发展，由市财政安排的、具有专项用途和绩效目标的公共预算资金。从2016年起至2020年，预计共投入6.5亿元。

托管改革：将部分公办、民办学校交由优质学校托管办学，进一步提升全市教育优质均衡发展水平。

慕课：英文“MOOC”的音译，指运用网络开放课程，进行大规模远程授课的教育模式。

分级诊疗制度：按照疾病的轻重缓急及治疗的难易程度进行分级，不同级别的医疗机构承担不同疾病的治疗，实现基层首诊和双向转诊。

两违：违法用地、违章建筑。

中等收入陷阱：指当一个国家或地区的人均收入达到中等水平后，由于不能顺利实现经济发展方式的转变，导致经济增长动力不足，最终出现经济停滞的一种状态。

粤港澳大湾区：国家为深化泛珠三角区域合作，要求充分发挥广州、深圳在管理创新、科技进步、产业升级、绿色发展等方面的辐射带动和示范作用，携手港澳共同打造粤港澳大湾区，建设世界级城市群。

深中通道：连接深圳市和中山市的大桥，全长 24 千米。计划 2023 年底或 2024 年上半年建成通车。

洼地效应：增创城市环境的比较优势，形成对各类生产要素的较强吸引力，促进外来资源向本地区汇聚。

虹吸效应：区域中心城市利用自身优势产生的强大吸引力，将其他地区的投资、消费或资源吸引过来，被吸引地区的发展因此而减缓。

五纵四横六连：我市"十三五"规划建设的高速公路网络。"五纵"指广深沿江高速、广深高速、增莞深高速、从莞高速、博深高速；"四横"指莞番高速—河惠莞高速、虎岗高速—惠常高速、龙林高速—从莞高速清溪支线、深圳外环高速；"六连"指莲花山通道、虎岗高速虎门港支线二期、虎门大桥、深茂铁路公路通道、龙大高速、清平高速。

"8"字形环城路网：指环莞快速路建成后与环城路形成的"8"字形路网。

双水源保障：指东江、西江双水源的东莞供水保障体系。

国考断面：指《广东省水污染防治目标责任书》中，国家对省地表水水质考核的断面。

慧教育：以引领学生智慧成长、促进教师生成教育智慧、引导家长智慧养育为根本目标，以智慧校园、智慧德育、智慧管理、智慧课堂、智慧评价等为重要内容，努力实现智慧育人、育智慧人。

十大行动计划：市委、市政府以党代会精神为指导，以八大调研成果转化为重点，出台了以供给侧结构性改革为统领、推动在更高起点上实现更高水平发展的十大行动计划。

产业加速器：以高成长企业为主要服务对象，通过服务模式创新充分满足高成长企业对于空间、管理、服务、合作等方面个性化需求的新型平台载体。

融资租赁：指企业购买设备等实物时，由第三方出资，企业向第三方支付租金的新型融资方式。

个性化定制、柔性化生产：用易编程、易修改、易扩展的数控设备、软件控制代替刚性的生产设备和工序过程，使刚性生产线实现柔性化、个性化，快速响应市场需求，多快好省地完成多品种、中小批量的生产任务。

中期票据：指具有法人资格的非金融企业在银行间债券市场按照计划分期发行的、约定在一定期限还本付息的债务融资工具。

股权投资基金：指以非公开方式向特定对象募集资金设立，对非公开交易的企业股权进行投资并提供增值服务的非证券类投资企业。

TOD 开发：Transit-Oriented-Development，以公共交通为导向的开发。

一港一铁：东莞港与广东（石龙）铁路国际物流基地。

多式联运：由两种及以上的交通工具相互衔接、转运而共同完成的运输过程。

超级中国干线：是向来往香港与东莞的国际物流提供班次式的空、陆联运服务和保税仓服务的一种国际物流仓储服务。

土地 1.5 级开发：根据基础设施建设情况和土地开发时序，通过租赁或短期土地使用，建设可移动、可生长的建筑和设施，开展品牌推广，挖掘土地价值，形成滚动开发。

多规融合：将国民经济和社会发展规划、城乡规划、土地利用规划、生态环境保护规划等融合到可以明确边界线的市县域图上，实现一个市县一本规划、一张蓝图，解决现有各类规划自成体系、内容冲突、缺乏衔接协调等突出问题。

海绵城市：新一代城市雨洪管理概念，是指在适应环境变化和应对雨水带来的自然灾害等方面具有良好"弹性"的城市。

城乡环境"六整治"：城乡环境卫生、道路设施、违章户外广告、违法建筑、城市"六乱"和打击"黑煤气"专项整治。

PPP 模式：即政府和社会资本的合作模式。

"一中心三平台"信息化建设：一中心指全市卫生计生数据中心，三平台指基本医疗、公共卫生、计生服务信息平台。

"8+1"社会救助制度：包括低保救助、特困人员供养、受灾人员救助、医疗救助、教育救助、住房救助、就业救助、临时救助、社会力量参与等九方面的社会救助制度。

第二部分　统计资料

Part Two　Statistics

一、综　合

General Survey

1-1 东莞行政区划（2016年）

Divisions of Administrative Areas in Dongguan (2016)

镇 街	村（居）委会		
	个 数		名 称
合 计	村委会	350	
	社区居委会	243	
莞 城	社区居委会	8	东正 市桥 北隅 西隅 罗沙 博厦 兴塘 创业
石 龙	村委会	7	西湖 忠维 林屋 蒲溪 新维 王屋洲 黄家山
	社区居委会	3	中山东 中山西 兴龙
虎 门	社区居委会	30	虎门寨 东方 则徐 大宁 树田 白沙 沙角 怀德 博涌 镇口 村头 新联 九门寨 居岐 金洲 南面 北栅 小捷滘 北面 陈村 东风 武山沙 黄村 南栅 龙眼 宴岗 赤岗 路东 新湾 民泰
东 城	社区居委会	23	岗贝 花园新村 东泰 温塘 桑园 周屋 余屋 鳌峙塘 峡口 柏洲边 上桥 下桥 樟村 梨川 堑头 主山 石井 同沙 光明 牛山 立新 火炼树 星城
万 江	社区居委会	28	万江墟 万江 石美 莫屋 拔蛟窝 黄粘洲 蚬涌 谷涌 小享 滘联 上甲 新村 新谷涌 共联 水蛇涌 大莲塘 牌楼基 严屋 大汾 流涌尾 金泰 曲海 坝头 胜利 官桥滘 简沙洲 新和 新城
南 城	社区居委会	18	鸿福 宏远 胜和 元美 亨美 三元里 篁村 新基 周溪 袁屋边 白马 石鼓 蛤地 西平 雅园 水濂 新城 宏图
中 堂	村委会	15	潢涌 三涌 湛翠 凤冲 袁家涌 吴家涌 鹤田 中堂 一村 东向 蕉利 槎滘 下芦 马沥 四乡
	社区居委会	5	中心 斗朗 红锋 东泊 江南
望牛墩	村委会	21	李屋 望东 扶涌 赤滘 五涌 下漕 上合 聚龙江 望联 洲湾 洲涡 杜屋 寮厦 芙蓉沙 官桥涌 横沥 福安 石排 官洲 朱平沙 锦涡
	社区居委会	1	望牛墩
麻 涌	村委会	13	麻一 麻三 麻四 大步 东太 新基 川槎 鸥涌 华阳 南洲 大盛 漳澎 黎滘
	社区居委会	2	麻涌 麻二
石 碣	村委会	14	石碣 唐洪 黄泗围 西南 单屋 梁家村 沙腰 刘屋 水南 四甲 鹤田厦 涌口 横滘 桔洲
	社区居委会	1	城中
高 埗	村委会	18	冼沙 卢溪 宝莲 塘厦 草墩 护安围 保安围 三联 横滘头 低涌 朱磡 新联 欧邓 芦村 高埗 凌屋 上江城 下江城
	社区居委会	1	新创
道 滘	村委会	13	南城 南丫 闸口 大鱼沙 小河 永庆 北永 昌平 厚德 九曲 大罗沙 大岭丫 蔡白
	社区居委会	1	兴隆
洪 梅	村委会	9	洪屋涡 新庄 梅沙 氹涌 黎洲角 夏汇 尧均 乌沙 金鳌沙
	社区居委会	1	洪梅
沙 田	村委会	16	中围 和安 大流 泥洲 杨公洲 福禄沙 阇西 民田 先锋 西大坦 穗丰年 大泥 齐沙 稔洲 义沙 西太隆
	社区居委会	2	横流 滨港
厚 街	社区居委会	24	竹溪 厚街 珊美 宝屯 三屯 陈屋 赤岭 河田 寮厦 汀山 环冈 大迳 新围 桥头 南五 新塘 涌口 双岗 溪头 沙塘 宝塘 下汴 白濠 湖景
长 安	社区居委会	13	长盛 涌头 霄边 咸西 锦厦 新安 乌沙 新民 沙头 上沙 厦岗 厦边 上角

1-1 续表

(2016年)

镇 街	村（居）委会		
	个 数		名 称
寮 步	村委会	20	西溪 凫山 石龙坑 石步 良边 富竹山 塘唇 向西 霞边 上屯 下岭贝 竹园 上底 药勒 刘屋巷 浮竹山 陈家埔 井巷 小坑 长坑
	社区居委会	10	寮步 塘边 横坑 岭厦 新旧围 缪边 牛杨 泉塘 坑口 良平
大岭山	村委会	21	太公岭 大塘朗 下高田 连平 鸡翅岭 马蹄岗 金桔 大沙 百花洞 大塘 水朗 杨屋 矮岭冚 颜屋 大片美 梅林 元岭 大岭 新塘 旧飞鹅 大环
	社区居委会	2	大岭山 农场
大 朗	村委会	16	高英 洋乌 洋坑塘 松柏朗 黎贝岭 松木山 犀牛陂 水平 宝陂 石厦 杨涌 沙步 新马莲 佛子凹 蔡边 水口
	社区居委会	12	大朗 佛新 巷头 巷尾 大井头 屏山 竹山 求富路 长塘 黄草朗 圣堂 长富
黄 江	社区居委会	7	新市 田美 三新 梅塘 宝山 北岸 长龙
樟木头	社区居委会	10	圩镇 樟罗 百果洞 樟洋 石新 柏地 官仓 裕丰 金河 樟新
清 溪	村委会	20	浮岗 上元 清厦 铁松 铁场 谢坑 青皇 大埔 长山头 三中 九乡 三星 渔樑围 厦坭 大利 土桥 重河 松岗 罗马 荔横
	社区居委会	1	清溪
塘 厦	社区居委会	22	塘厦 三局 林村 石潭埔 四村 振兴围 大坪 莆心湖 平山 诸佛岭 桥陇 龙背岭 石鼓 田心 横塘 蛟乙塘 凤凰岗 莲湖 沙湖 石马 清湖头 塘新
凤 岗	村委会	11	雁田 官井头 油甘埔 凤德岭 塘沥 黄洞 竹塘 竹尾田 三联 五联 天堂围
	社区居委会	1	凤岗
谢 岗	村委会	11	黎村 窑山 南面 大龙 大厚 赵林 稔子园 五星 曹乐 谢岗 谢山
	社区居委会	1	泰园
常 平	村委会	31	岗梓 塘角 苏坑 袁山贝 金美 还珠沥 朗贝 桥沥 卢屋 九江水 朗洲 陈屋贝 司马 霞坑 漱旧 漱新 黄泥塘 元江元 横江厦 沙湖口 白石岗 松柏塘 上坑 木棆 下墟 板石 田尾 白花沥 桥梓 麦元 土塘
	社区居委会	2	常平 新民
桥 头	村委会	11	田头角 李屋 朗厦 岗头 屋厦 禾坑 邓屋 邵岗头 东江 山和 石水口
	社区居委会	6	莲城 田新 桥头 大洲 迳联 岭头
横 沥	村委会	16	石涌 隔坑 半仙山 田头 田坑 横沥 村头 长巷 田饶步 六甲 村尾 水边 新四 山厦 月塘 张坑
	社区居委会	1	恒泉
东 坑	村委会	14	东坑 坑美 角社 塔岗 黄麻岭 初坑 凤大 黄屋 寮边头 长安塘 新门楼 井美 彭屋 丁屋
	社区居委会	2	草塘 骏达
企 石	村委会	19	铁岗 深巷 湖美 博夏 上洞 江边 旧围 清湖 东平 上截 下截 东山 莫屋 杨屋 新南 南坑 铁炉坑 企石 霞朗
	社区居委会	1	宝石
石 排	村委会	18	石排 下沙 福隆 庙边王 沙角 黄家壆 赤坎 向西 水贝 田寮 横山 埔心 谷吓 塘尾 李家坊 田边 中坑 燕窝
	社区居委会	1	太和
茶 山	村委会	16	上元 茶山 下朗 横江 增埗 卢边 寒溪水 南社 塘角 博头 冲美 粟边 孙屋 超朗 京山 刘黄
	社区居委会	2	茶山圩 茶溪
松山湖 (生态园)	社区居委会	1	松山湖

1-2 历年东莞行政区划

Divisions of Administrative Areas in Dongguan over Years

单位：个

年 份	镇 街	村（居）委会		
			村委会	社区居委会
1978	33	526	496	30
1979	33	531	501	30
1980	33	545	515	30
1981	34	554	524	30
1982	34	561	531	30
1983	34	561	531	30
1984	34	542	512	30
1985	33	546	516	30
1986	33	560	530	30
1987	34	580	537	43
1988	33	582	542	40
1989	33	583	544	39
1990	33	583	543	40
1991	33	586	546	40
1992	33	590	549	41
1993	33	590	549	41
1994	33	592	551	41
1995	33	592	551	41
1996	33	593	552	41
1997	33	594	551	43
1998	32	594	551	43
1999	32	593	546	47
2000	32	675	546	129
2001	32	678	546	132
2002	32	678	546	132
2003	32	616	487	129
2004	32	596	440	156
2005	32	596	404	192
2006	32	596	394	202
2007	32	591	386	205
2008	32	591	383	208
2009	32	598	383	215
2010	32	599	383	216
2011	32	594	350	244
2012	32	595	350	245
2013	32	597	350	247
2014	32	597	350	247
2015	32	597	350	247
2016	32	593	350	243

注：2013年起，虎门港社区居委会并入沙田镇；2015年起，生态园并入松山湖。

1-3 主要年份户数、人口与自然资源

Number of Households, Population and Natural Resources in Main Years

项　目	单 位	1978年	1990年	1995年	2000年	2005年	2010年	2015年	2016年
户　数									
年末户籍总户数	万户	24.82	32.73	36.43	41.40	46.50	53.05	56.72	58.26
#城镇户数	万户	4.37	8.91	10.06	11.44	18.90	27.08	50.39	51.88
人口与劳动力									
年末常住人口	万人		175.62	336.45	644.84	656.07	822.48	825.41	826.14
年末户籍人口	万人	111.23	131.85	143.65	152.61	165.65	181.77	195.01	200.94
#城镇人口	万人	18.49	30.87	35.38	39.61	65.84	92.09	172.65	178.20
人口密度（常住人口）	人/平方公里		712	1365	2616	2662	3343	3355	3358
人口密度（户籍人口）	人/平方公里	451	535	583	619	672	739	793	817
全社会从业人员	万人					388.13	626.25	653.41	653.97
第一产业	万人					13.65	6.05	6.08	5.89
第二产业	万人					250.04	476.94	445.81	446.32
第三产业	万人					124.45	143.26	201.52	201.76
城镇登记失业率	%				0.60	1.29	1.70	2.26	2.26
土　地									
土地面积	平方公里	2465	2465	2465	2465	2465	2460	2460	2460
年末耕地面积	万亩	118.39	88.26	70.86	66.33	50.29	57.69	55.05	54.62
人均耕地面积	亩	1.06	0.67	0.49	0.43	0.30	0.32	0.28	0.27
建成区面积	平方公里			82.48	147.68	620.31	798.48	928.87	956.54
#市区建成区面积	平方公里				28.13	108.10	91.65	119.18	119.97
气　候									
年降水量	毫米	1748.3	1602.9	1664.8	2019.3	1837.6	2165.9	2137.9	2612.0
年平均气温	摄氏度	21.9	22.8	22.4	23.2	22.7	22.4	23.5	22.8
极端最高气温	摄氏度	35.7	37.8	36.2	37.0	37.4	36.1	36.5	37.1
极端最低气温	摄氏度	2.7	4.3	6.7	5.6	1.8	1.9	7.5	2.0
年日照时数	小时	1958.8	1910.2	1935.7	2059.5	1736.3	1699.7	1787.2	1641.6
森　林									
有林地面积	万亩		83.48	91.48	92.16	89.23	87.30	77.32	86.42
林木蓄积量	万立方米		167.18	123.02	136.11	175.38	255.82	352.00	374.26
森林覆盖率	%		31.4	29.7	30.6	33.1	36.7	37.4	37.4
水资源									
大陆海岸线总长度	公里	61.4	61.4	61.4	115.9	92.1	97.2	112.2	112.2
海水养殖可养面积	万亩	5.0	5.0	5.5	2.6	16.9	2.0	0.9	0.4
淡水养殖可养面积	万亩	30.0	30.0	28.0	14.3	30.7	10.0	12.0	10.2

注：1．土地面积数据来源于市国土局，不包括海域面积。
2．人均耕地面积按户籍人口计算。
3．大陆海岸线从2000年起以咸水为界定。
4．常住人口2006-2010年数据，根据东莞市第六次全国人口普查数据结果重新修订，下同。
5．按建立城乡统一的户口登记制度要求，2015年起户籍户数和人口数按城镇和乡村划分，取消原来的农业和非农业的登记统计，数据与往年不可比，下同。

1-4 历年土地与自然资源

Land and Natural Resources over Years

年份	土地面积（平方公里）	气候				
		年降水量（毫米）	年平均气温（摄氏度）	极端最高气温（摄氏度）	极端最低气温（摄氏度）	年日照时数（小时）
1978	2465	1748.3	21.9	35.7	2.7	1958.8
1979	2465	2007.1	21.9	36.5	2.9	1991.4
1980	2465	1434.7	22.3	37.7	3.3	2157.1
1981	2465	2394.9	22.1	35.6	3.2	1792.2
1982	2465	1454.1	22.1	37.5	3.8	1754.1
1983	2465	1947.1	21.8	35.8	3.3	1909.7
1984	2465	1444.5	21.5	35.9	3.1	1749.2
1985	2465	1678.0	21.8	35.8	4.2	1671.7
1986	2465	1665.2	22.2	35.9	3.0	2098.1
1987	2465	1908.8	22.9	37.0	4.3	1816.6
1988	2465	1735.0	22.0	37.0	7.0	1836.5
1989	2465	1567.2	22.5	37.6	5.2	1926.0
1990	2465	1602.9	22.8	37.8	4.3	1910.2
1991	2465	1219.6	23.0	36.6	1.2	1968.8
1992	2465	1827.1	22.3	37.0	4.5	1854.5
1993	2465	2393.6	22.5	35.6	3.0	1965.7
1994	2465	1809.1	23.0	38.2	5.4	1828.6
1995	2465	1664.8	22.4	36.2	6.7	1935.7
1996	2465	1547.4	22.7	37.1	3.4	2036.0
1997	2465	2074.0	22.8	36.3	6.1	1558.1
1998	2465	1844.5	23.6	36.5	5.6	1699.0
1999	2465	1614.5	23.3	37.8	3.1	2015.8
2000	2465	2019.3	23.2	37.0	5.6	2059.5
2001	2465	2042.6	23.3	36.6	6.6	1978.2
2002	2465	1557.4	23.6	36.7	4.5	2046.9
2003	2465	1416.7	23.0	36.1	3.8	2268.7
2004	2465	1705.8	22.8	38.0	3.5	2192.9
2005	2465	1837.6	22.7	37.4	1.8	1736.3
2006	2465	2412.0	22.7	36.8	4.7	1616.4
2007	2465	1806.9	22.9	35.9	6.7	1876.7
2008	2465	2710.9	22.2	36.8	4.8	1879.3
2009	2465	1881.6	22.8	36.3	5.3	1967.8
2010	2460	2165.9	22.4	36.1	1.9	1699.7
2011	2460	1298.6	22.1	36.2	3.2	2120.1
2012	2460	1838.6	22.6	36.7	4.1	1708.7
2013	2460	2087.2	22.8	36.4	6.1	1830.0
2014	2460	1935.6	22.9	36.8	3.9	1958.8
2015	2460	2137.9	23.5	36.5	7.5	1787.2
2016	2460	2612.0	22.8	37.1	2.0	1641.6

注：土地面积数据由市国土资源局提供，不包括海域面积，下同。

1-4 续表

年份	森林			水资源		
	有林地面积(万亩)	林木蓄积量(万立方米)	森林覆盖率(%)	大陆海岸线总长度(公里)	海水养殖可养面积(万亩)	淡水养殖可养面积(万亩)
1978				61.4	5.0	30.0
1979	44.4	110.3	14.7	61.4	5.0	30.0
1980				61.4	5.0	30.0
1981				61.4	5.0	30.0
1982				61.4	5.0	30.0
1983				61.4	5.0	30.0
1984	76.6	160.5	21.9	61.4	5.0	30.0
1985	78.3	156.0	28.6	61.4	5.0	30.0
1986	82.4	157.8	30.0	61.4	5.0	30.0
1987	83.9	183.9	34.5	61.4	5.0	30.0
1988	84.3	169.1	34.7	61.4	5.0	30.0
1989	80.9	164.8	31.1	61.4	5.0	30.0
1990	83.5	167.2	31.4	61.4	5.0	30.0
1991	85.0	169.2	31.6	61.4	5.0	29.0
1992	86.3	169.8	31.3	61.4	5.5	29.0
1993	87.3	168.9	31.9	61.4	5.5	28.0
1994	86.1	116.8	28.3	61.4	5.5	28.0
1995	91.5	123.0	29.7	61.4	5.5	28.0
1996	91.9	115.7	29.9	61.4	5.5	28.5
1997	93.5	121.1	29.9	61.4	5.7	28.7
1998	93.4	126.0	30.1	61.4	5.7	28.7
1999	92.2	120.4	30.1	115.9	4.8	28.7
2000	92.2	136.1	30.6	115.9	2.6	14.3
2001	93.3	146.0	31.2	116.0	2.8	12.9
2002	93.8	155.0	31.7	115.9	4.1	11.7
2003	93.3	165.1	32.2	92.1	4.2	10.4
2004	93.3	165.1	33.0	92.1	4.0	10.0
2005	89.2	175.4	33.1	92.1	16.9	30.7
2006	88.9	194.4	33.5	92.1	16.6	30.5
2007	89.1	215.1	35.5	92.1	16.9	30.7
2008	88.6	227.9	36.2	97.2	2.5	15.0
2009	90.1	241.4	36.5	97.2	2.0	10.0
2010	87.3	255.8	36.7	97.2	2.0	10.0
2011	87.4	273.0	36.9	97.2	1.1	10.0
2012	87.6	291.0	37.1	97.2	1.1	10.0
2013	79.3	262.8	37.3	97.2	0.9	8.5
2014	79.8	282.9	37.4	97.2	0.9	12.9
2015	77.3	352.0	37.4	112.2	0.9	12.0
2016	86.4	374.3	37.4	112.2	0.4	10.2

1-5 主要年份国民经济主要指标

Main Indicators on National Economy in Main Years

项目	单位	1978年	1990年	1995年	2000年	2005年	2010年	2015年	2016年
国民经济核算									
地区生产总值	亿元	6.11	80.44	296.29	820.25	2183.20	4278.21	6275.07	6827.69
第一产业	亿元	2.72	13.28	21.43	25.91	20.55	16.57	21.03	24.20
第二产业	亿元	2.68	40.53	166.97	450.71	1227.86	2191.78	2922.05	3173.24
第三产业	亿元	0.71	26.63	107.89	343.64	934.78	2069.86	3332.00	3630.25
农村经济									
农林牧渔业总产值	亿元	4.24	23.64	42.69	54.64	42.05	28.31	34.35	38.44
农村集体经营总收入	亿元		7.18	41.23	77.50	120.57	143.38	180.43	190.35
年末耕地面积	万亩		88.26	70.86	66.33	50.29	57.69	55.05	54.62
工　业									
规模以上工业企业指标									
工业增加值	亿元		12.25	64.99	259.44	1062.42	1708.31	2611.96	2968.16
主营业务收入	亿元	2.69	47.27	275.84	988.91	3912.15	7708.17	12454.22	14889.63
年末固定资产原值	亿元	0.78	14.29	60.14	728.85	1856.09	3216.25	4355.07	4701.29
年末固定资产净值	亿元	0.51	11.95	46.26	470.19	1105.26	1783.69	2158.12	2303.51
流动资产合计	亿元	0.26	1.74	21.28	529.82	1873.28	3788.83	6189.26	7445.44
资产总额	亿元		13.51	52.98	1122.60	3345.33	6001.71	9134.65	10676.05
负债总额	亿元				563.04	1858.09	3525.30	5369.92	6435.49
资产负债率	%				50.2	55.5	58.7	58.8	60.3
利润总额	亿元				50.36	124.35	352.36	407.50	502.73
综合效益指数	%				114.0	119.9	130.3	148.7	159.8
能源消费									
单位GDP能耗上升率或下降率	±%						-2.02	-7.90	-4.65
规模以上工业综合能源消费量	万吨标准煤					1203.77	1496.06	1329.38	1388.87

注：1. 2005年以前地区生产总值采用全国第一次经济普查资料修订的数据；2005—2008年采用第二次经济普查资料修订的数据；2009—2013年采用第三次经济普查资料修订的数据；2013年起，三次产业分类依据国家统计局2012年制定的《三次产业划分规定》，下同。

2. 规模以上工业企业1997年及以前为独立核算企业口径，1998—2005年为全部国有及年销售收入500万元以上非国有企业口径，2006—2010年为年主营业务收入500万元及以上口径，2011年起为年主营业务收入2000万元及以上口径，下同。

3. 2005年以前工业相关数据采用第一次经济普查资料修订的数据，2008年采用第二次经济普查资料修订的数据，下同。

1-5 续表 1

项　　目	单 位	1978年	1990年	1995年	2000年	2005年	2010年	2015年	2016年
运输邮电									
公路通车里程	公里	1259	1325	2327	2518	2871	4751	5165	5266
#高速公路	公里				89	154	217	335	388
旅客周转量	亿人公里	0.94	32.22	44.62	100.19	118.53	129.07	77.13	77.32
水　运	亿人公里	0.43	0.15	0.19	0.14	0.33	0.20	0.21	0.18
公　路	亿人公里	0.51	32.07	44.43	100.05	118.20	128.87	76.92	77.14
货物周转量	亿吨公里	1.51	18.47	26.46	40.47	42.48	109.03	504.85	455.23
水　运	亿吨公里	1.42	11.25	13.66	15.86	15.23	57.95	433.16	383.56
公　路	亿吨公里	0.09	7.22	12.80	24.60	27.25	51.08	71.69	71.67
港口货物吞吐量	万吨	293	233	201	746	2280	5657	13149	14584
邮政业务收入(含快递)	亿元						6.32	99.25	139.55
电信业务收入	亿元						149.02	149.73	155.58
局用交换机容量	万门		6.98	52.29	103.13	286.25	365.02	358.00	358.00
年末移动电话交换机总容量	万户			4.80	154.20	1059.10	1657.00	2033.00	2424.00
本地电话用户	万户	0.20	4.90	31.58	78.12	384.52	332.42	298.23	272.63
移动电话用户(含充值卡)	万户		0.05	4.77	123.68	1016.41	1607.60	1756.75	1575.08
#充值卡	万户				42.71	839.58	1433.56	1004.69	787.65
互联网用户	万户			0.05	13.78	52.90	153.92	201.74	185.27
供用电									
总供电量	亿千瓦时	1.64	18.01	68.00	178.03	415.66	556.89	661.26	695.59
#网供	亿千瓦时	1.64	11.18	38.48	134.91	342.26	547.33	648.27	681.39
全社会用电量	亿千瓦时		18.01	68.00	179.66	419.83	562.00	666.84	702.01
#工业用电	亿千瓦时				136.79	337.43	159.37	483.31	506.00
固定资产投资									
固定资产投资总额	亿元	0.23	7.51	63.14	102.89	597.24	1114.98	1446.52	1557.46
#房地产开发	亿元			8.52	11.25	144.43	298.99	575.21	642.76
房地产开发当年房屋施工面积	万平方米					1160.20	2060.54	3921.20	4408.65
房地产开发当年房屋竣工面积	万平方米					132.90	296.59	325.43	232.68
商品房销售面积	万平方米					321.90	511.25	1040.65	1024.25
商品房销售额	亿元					119.40	373.77	1019.11	1418.17
新增固定资产	亿元					173.30	577.86	726.94	742.60
固定资产交付使用率	%					29.0	51.8	50.3	47.7
国内贸易									
限额以上批发和零售业销售额	亿元				135.46	568.35	1427.14	3219.18	3910.89
社会消费品零售总额	亿元	2.13	31.97	113.01	235.16	506.29	1223.34	2184.70	2470.78
城　镇	亿元						1129.10	2011.67	2204.93
乡　村	亿元						94.24	173.03	265.85

注：1．2006年起公路通车里程含专用公路和村道，与往年数据不可比，下同。
2．2014年客运量和旅客周转量不含城市客运量，数据与往年不可比，下同。
3．2005年以前国内贸易相关数据采用第一次经济普查资料修订的数据，2005—2008年采用第二次经济普查资料修订的数据，2009—2013年采用第三次经济普查资料修订的数据，下同。
4．2015年起邮政业务收入采用邮管局数据，含快递业务，数据与往年不可比，下同。
5．2015年起本地电话取消小灵通用户，下同。

1-5 续表 2

项目	单位	1978年	1990年	1995年	2000年	2005年	2010年	2015年	2016年
物价指数（以上年价格为100）									
商品零售物价总指数	%	100.4	94.9	109.7	100.1	103.0	103.2	99.4	100.9
居民消费价格总指数	%		96.6	113.9	101.5	102.4	102.8	101.4	102.7
消费品价格指数	%		94.9	109.7	100.1	103.0	102.8	101.2	103.1
服务项目价格指数	%		111.0	128.9	112.8	100.4	102.6	101.9	102.1
对外经济贸易、旅游									
进出口总额（海关口径）	亿美元（亿元）		10.82	153.91	320.45	743.72	1213.38	1676.73	11415.99
进口总额	亿美元（亿元）		5.14	75.92	148.86	334.42	517.40	639.55	4859.15
出口总额	亿美元（亿元）		5.68	77.99	171.59	409.29	695.98	1037.19	6556.85
#一般贸易	亿美元（亿元）			2.32	2.09	17.55	95.41	379.63	2360.95
来料加工装配	亿美元（亿元）			43.46	83.43	161.17	195.54	105.40	559.69
进料加工	亿美元（亿元）			32.02	85.84	230.43	394.62	516.77	3234.77
新签利用外资协议（合同）数	宗					773	869	440	446
合同外资金额（新口径）	亿美元					29.80	25.97	50.59	47.32
实际利用外资（新口径）	亿美元					14.68	27.32	53.20	39.26
全年接待旅游人数	万人次		125	89	291	1156	2251	3199	3792
#国际及港澳台旅游者	万人次		27	27	106	169	327	373	400
国际旅游外汇收入	万美元				7617	28189	67592	157743	153117
财政、金融									
来源于东莞的财政收入	亿元	0.66	3.57	18.01	103.56	331.91	785.10	1155.50	1569.19
一般公共预算收入	亿元			11.56	30.47	103.97	277.84	517.97	544.75
一般公共预算支出	亿元	0.18	2.28	12.42	33.61	117.04	289.83	581.24	599.29
金融机构各项人民币存款余额	亿元	1.05	68.07	383.68	1228.67	2933.40	5943.39	9736.24	11198.43
#住户存款余额	亿元	0.54	45.51	232.97	672.07	1728.28	3386.85	4591.38	4882.91
金融机构各项人民币贷款余额	亿元	1.96	63.04	254.85	630.84	1500.52	3329.82	5816.04	6402.48
人民生活									
全市职工年平均工资	元						16108	41864	46242
城镇在岗职工年平均工资	元	474	3552	9682	14051	28253	46576	53221	57649
城镇常住居民人均可支配收入	元		2508	9588	14142	22882	35690	39793	43096
城镇常住居民人均消费性支出	元		2038	9220	12529	21768	25733	29001	30688
农村常住居民人均可支配收入	元	149	1542	4769	8484	13076	20486	24225	26526
科技									
全社会R&D人员	人						38330	68211	73113
全社会R&D经费支出	亿元						51.67	147.88	164.83
R&D占GDP比重	%						1.22	2.36	2.41

注：1．2013年起，将原属于乡镇企业且符合城镇非私营单位条件的“四上”企业纳入城镇单位从业人员及工资统计的范围，下同。

2．全年接待旅游人数和旅游外汇收入2002年起是旅游局口径，与往年数不可比。

3．按照国家统计局的统一部署，自2012年12月起正式启动城乡住户调查一体化改革工作。2014年起正式发布全体居民人均可支配收入和消费性支出指标。新口径指标将城市居民人均可支配收入和人均消费性支出改为城镇常住居民人均可支配收入和人均消费性支出，农民人均纯收入改为农村常住居民人均可支配收入，与往年数不可比，下同。

4．2015年起，“城乡居民储蓄存款余额”改名为“住户存款”，口径有变，数据与往年不可比。

5．2016年起，进出口相关数据采用人民币口径。

1-6 主要年份国民经济和社会发展主要比例与效益指标

Main Indicators on National Economy and Social Development in Main Years

项　　目	单 位	1990年	1995年	2000年	2005年	2010年	2015年	2016年
户籍人口								
出生率	‰	17.07	17.59	12.11	10.62	10.90	11.34	13.92
死亡率	‰	4.76	4.84	4.59	4.60	4.68	4.93	5.28
自然增长率	‰	12.31	12.75	7.52	6.02	6.23	6.41	8.64
人口性别比（男/女）	%	97.1	100.4	102.4	103.1	103.1	102.5	102.0
地区生产总值中三次产业比重								
第一产业	%	16.5	7.2	3.2	0.9	0.4	0.3	0.3
第二产业	%	50.4	56.4	54.9	56.2	51.2	46.6	46.5
第三产业	%	33.1	36.4	41.9	42.8	48.4	53.1	53.2
全员劳动生产率	元/人				59743	71440	95520	104448
(按全社会从业人员、增加值计算)								
第一产业	元/人				14238	24017	35795	40433
第二产业	元/人				50634	51883	65170	71139
第三产业	元/人				86154	122110	164392	180034
农　业								
农林牧渔业总产值结构								
农　业	%	54.9	45.7	39.6	25.5	52.3	64.0	70.3
林　业	%	1.8	2.1	0.7	0.4	1.0	1.1	1.0
牧　业	%	19.2	30.0	41.4	57.7	19.6	10.7	9.1
渔　业	%	13.3	16.1	14.9	14.9	24.0	21.3	16.9
农林牧渔服务业	%				1.5	3.0	2.9	2.7
工　业								
规模以上工业企业效益								
固定资产利税率	%	8.5	10.7	11.5	9.9	26.3	30.0	35.9

1-6　续表 1

项　　目	单 位	1990年	1995年	2000年	2005年	2010年	2015年	2016年
资金利税率	%	6.3	7.7	7.5	5.5	7.8	7.8	8.5
产值利税率	%	5.4	10.0	9.2	4.6	6.1	5.1	5.6
固定资产投资								
固定资产投资相当于地区生产总值比例	%	9.3	17.0	12.5	27.4	26.3	23.1	22.8
全社会房屋建筑面积竣工率	%	45.2	34.1	60.7	22.5	20.7	9.4	5.6
财　政								
来源于东莞的财政收入相当于地区生产总值比例	%	4.4	6.1	12.6	15.2	18.5	18.4	23.0
一般公共预算支出相当于地区生产总值比例	%	2.8	4.2	4.1	5.4	6.5	9.3	8.8
外经外贸								
利用外资结构								
外商直接投资	%	41.2	63.6	66.0	75.2	86.4	97.3	98.6
外商其他投资	%	58.8	36.4	34.0	24.8	13.6	2.7	1.4
实际利用外资额相当于协议规定外商投资额比例	%	80.6	31.9	89.7	78.9	103.0	107.2	83.0
进出口总额比例								
进口总额	%	47.5	49.3	46.5	45.0	42.6	38.1	42.6
出口总额	%	52.5	50.7	53.6	55.0	57.4	61.9	57.4
#一般贸易	%		3.0	1.2	4.3	13.7	36.6	36.0
来料加工装配	%		55.7	48.6	39.4	28.1	10.2	8.5
进料加工	%		41.1	50.0	56.3	56.7	49.8	49.3
保税物流	%						3.4	4.0
其他	%		0.2	0.2		1.5	0.02	2.1

1-6 续表 2

项　　目	单 位	1990年	1995年	2000年	2005年	2010年	2015年	2016年
交通运输								
货运量中各种运输方式比例								
公　路	%	58.2	55.7	63.3	71.7	82.0	68.0	66.2
水　运	%	41.8	44.3	36.7	28.3	18.0	32.0	33.8
金　融								
各项人民币存款相当于生产总值比例	%	84.6	129.5	149.8	134.5	140.0	155.2	164.0
各项人民币贷款相当于生产总值比例	%	78.4	86.0	76.9	68.8	78.4	92.7	93.8
人民币住户存款占人民币存款比例	%	66.9	60.7	54.7	58.9	57.0	47.2	43.6
科技、教育、文化、卫生								
科教文卫事业费占财政支出比例	%	28.7	24.5	25.8	17.8	27.9	33.5	36.3
学龄儿童入学率	%	99.9	100.0	100.0	100.0	100.0	100.0	100.0
小学毕业生升学率	%	95.4	99.2	99.8	99.9	100.0	100.0	100.0
初中毕业生升学率	%	44.1	85.4	90.3	94.1	97.9	98.5	98.4
普通高中毕业生升学率	%	31.2	64.9	70.5	96.5	95.1	98.0	98.9
每一教师负担学生数								
普通高等学校	人		13.7	20.1	15.4	17.6	17.4	24.2
职业技术学校	人	20.6	21.8	19.0	18.2	20.3	23.5	22.9
普通中学	人	20.7	21.1	22.4	19.8	17.7	16.2	15.7
小学	人	24.0	24.2	34.3	27.5	23.3	23.8	22.9
人民生活								
城镇常住居民消费结构								
食品类	%	63.5	39.5	32.3	27.7	33.9	33.2	32.5
衣着类	%	4.7	6.6	3.9	5.9	6.6	5.6	6.0
其　他	%	31.8	53.9	63.8	66.4	59.5	61.2	61.5

1-7 国民经济主要指标分月变化情况（2016年，累计绝对数）

Main Indicators on National Economy by Month (2016, Accumulative Figures in Value Terms)

项　　目	单位	1 月	1-2 月	1-3 月	1-4 月	1-5 月	1-6 月
规模以上工业增加值	亿元		400.85	617.82	846.75	1037.19	1278.34
#内资企业	亿元		170.87	263.04	365.29	436.09	550.87
外资企业	亿元		229.98	354.78	481.46	601.11	727.47
#民营企业	亿元		150.28	234.40	325.87	382.46	483.66
#五大支柱产业	亿元		279.51	431.74	591.71	708.38	871.63
#四个特色产业	亿元		34.66	55.25	75.58	95.86	119.10
#先进制造业	亿元		204.41	308.41	426.25	503.64	619.54
#高技术制造业	亿元		159.57	241.07	332.63	384.40	471.78
规模以上工业销售产值	亿元		1893.06	2861.02	3924.80	5014.94	6187.04
规模以上工业产品出口交货值	亿元		741.17	1177.05	1607.26	2044.34	2512.90
规模以上工业产品产销率	%		99.8	97.9	97.6	97.0	97.2
规模以上工业企业主营业务收入	亿元		1794.82	2818.35	3988.07	5090.68	6276.02
规模以上工业企业利润总额	亿元		24.52	51.82	87.15	119.71	154.77
固定资产投资总额	亿元		154.52	262.54	381.86	517.18	669.23
#房地产开发	亿元		72.32	121.20	179.21	241.96	296.25
来源于东莞的财政收入	亿元	194.47	280.33	366.76	528.25	661.74	768.70
一般公共预算收入	亿元	58.49	98.27	142.79	195.53	243.20	283.13
一般公共预算支出	亿元	34.50	95.20	124.14	165.41	248.76	277.64
金融机构各项本外币存款余额	亿元	10315.54	10208.49	10502.89	10522.57	10573.32	10726.04
#住户存款	亿元	4639.11	4544.93	4650.78	4609.09	4653.28	4732.87
金融机构各项本外币贷款余额	亿元	6176.32	6257.20	6345.85	6317.91	6368.86	6400.91
进出口总额（海关口径）	亿元	828.7	1357.6	2131.1	2970.0	3792.8	4648.0
#进口总额	亿元	322.8	556.2	879.3	1235.1	1585.5	1945.7
出口总额	亿元	505.9	801.5	1251.8	1734.9	2207.3	2702.3
新签项目宗数	宗	33	58	93	135	165	200
合同规定外商投资额	亿美元	1.18	4.01	6.68	7.72	9.95	22.47
实际利用外资	亿美元	1.79	2.69	4.06	5.19	6.33	7.87
社会消费品零售总额	亿元		372.94	570.47	764.11	965.53	1174.32
居民消费价格总指数	%	102.1	102.6	102.6	102.8	102.8	102.8
全社会用电量	亿千瓦时	49.41	78.07	131.62	184.28	246.72	314.13
#工业用电	亿千瓦时	38.42	60.14	94.60	135.47	182.02	231.67
工商注册登记户数	户	718904	721301	729403	739130	749364	760957
#企业	户	260346	262176	267239	273465	279814	287413
邮政业务总量（含快递）	亿元	15.87	24.49	42.17	60.13	79.16	98.53

注：物价指数以上年同期为100；各项指标1-12月累计不等于年报数。

1-7 续表

(2016年，累计绝对数)

项　　目	单位	1-7 月	1-8 月	1-9 月	1-10 月	1-11 月	1-12 月
规模以上工业增加值	亿元	1517.58	1774.00	2069.48	2322.44	2591.25	2878.23
#内资企业	亿元	659.80	773.05	898.17	1015.93	1136.10	1270.80
外资企业	亿元	857.78	1000.95	1171.31	1306.51	1455.15	1607.43
#民营企业	亿元	577.70	676.24	788.93	893.30	999.16	1118.97
#五大支柱产业	亿元	1033.96	1209.02	1403.13	1574.20	1759.35	1952.24
#四个特色产业	亿元	141.36	166.47	197.80	224.51	250.50	281.47
#先进制造业	亿元	738.07	869.12	1012.87	1142.89	1285.91	1435.17
#高技术制造业	亿元	563.04	662.37	771.25	873.28	986.13	1100.76
规模以上工业销售产值	亿元	7384.68	8660.85	10068.74	11350.84	12712.67	14197.51
规模以上工业产品出口交货值	亿元	2973.04	3551.40	4150.32	4705.18	5287.59	5879.86
规模以上工业产品产销率	%	97.3	97.4	97.2	97.2	97.3	97.6
规模以上工业企业主营业务收入	亿元	7497.09	8783.74	10185.61	11480.91	12883.07	14518.46
规模以上工业企业利润总额	亿元	201.80	259.00	326.71	373.42	429.28	472.12
固定资产投资总额	亿元	798.91	943.62	1140.99	1246.09	1372.04	1557.46
#房地产开发	亿元	356.86	416.66	481.88	526.78	582.76	642.76
来源于东莞的财政收入	亿元	906.58	992.54	1088.94	1286.90	1447.91	1569.19
一般公共预算收入	亿元	324.84	360.68	408.77	464.23	503.67	544.75
一般公共预算支出	亿元	345.33	371.75	445.88	538.31	585.02	601.23
金融机构各项本外币存款余额	亿元	10867.05	11076.49	11124.65	11432.38	11566.31	11545.10
#住户存款	亿元	4748.88	4790.77	4865.29	4876.68	4936.05	4943.56
金融机构各项本外币贷款余额	亿元	6451.76	6395.99	6487.30	6603.21	6632.93	6545.66
进出口总额（海关口径）	亿元	5562.68	6569.61	7687.36	8884.84	10300.52	11415.99
#进口总额	亿元	2326.23	2767.90	3246.59	3762.41	4372.82	4859.15
出口总额	亿元	3236.45	3801.71	4440.77	5122.43	5927.70	6556.85
新签项目宗数	宗	237	272	310	325	379	446
合同规定外商投资额	亿美元	26.15	32.20	33.64	36.19	40.58	47.32
实际利用外资	亿美元	9.36	14.23	26.62	29.30	32.35	39.26
社会消费品零售总额	亿元	1375.57	1577.95	1792.17	2019.45	2240.37	2470.78
居民消费价格总指数	%	102.7	102.7	102.7	102.7	102.7	102.7
全社会用电量	亿千瓦时	387.87	459.54	526.02	587.25	644.90	702.01
#工业用电	亿千瓦时	282.46	332.21	377.57	421.05	462.38	506.00
工商注册登记户数	户	774855	790841	804121	814867	828703	840367
#企业	户	294876	301602	307109	313117	321095	328859
邮政业务总量（含快递）	亿元	118.11	137.88	159.02	180.60	205.64	229.21

1-8 国民经济主要指标分月变化情况（2016年，比上年同期增长）

Main Indicators on National Economy by Month (2016, Compare with Same Period of Preceding Year %)

项　　目	单位	1 月	1-2 月	1-3 月	1-4 月	1-5 月	1-6 月
规模以上工业增加值	%		6.2	6.4	6.3	6.4	5.5
#内资企业	%		24.8	19.3	18.2	17.8	18.4
外资企业	%		-4.5	-1.2	-1.0	-0.4	-2.5
#民营企业	%		29.8	23.2	21.6	21.4	21.3
#五大支柱产业	%		10.0	8.2	8.3	8.7	8.0
#四个特色产业	%		-4.7	0.5	-2.3	-2.4	-4.1
#先进制造业	%		17.3	13.3	13.5	14.4	13.8
#高技术制造业	%		23.3	17.0	17.3	18.8	17.8
规模以上工业销售产值	%		13.9	8.3	10.5	10.8	9.5
规模以上工业产品出口交货值	%		-1.2	-1.2	-1.5	-0.5	-1.0
规模以上工业产品产销率	%		2.0	0.4	-	-0.2	0.5
规模以上工业企业主营业务收入	%		8.5	9.7	12.7	12.2	11.9
规模以上工业企业利润总额	%		-29.9	-11.8	0.6	-5.6	-6.7
固定资产投资总额	%		5.4	4.0	6.7	13.4	13.7
#房地产开发	%		4.3	11.9	18.1	27.0	19.5
来源于东莞的财政收入	%	48.2	50.6	38.0	49.2	57.7	44.0
一般公共预算收入	%	30.8	16.0	11.5	19.2	22.6	11.5
一般公共预算支出	%	35.6	24.2	25.7	20.0	41.0	15.2
金融机构各项本外币存款余额	%	8.3	10.2	9.6	11.7	9.1	7.6
#住户存款	%	-0.1	0.5	1.1	2.5	3.7	2.5
金融机构各项本外币贷款余额	%	9.4	10.1	10.8	10.2	9.8	7.7
进出口总额（海关口径）	%	-0.2	-3.3	1.9	2.5	1.3	-0.8
#进口总额	%	0.3	2.9	4.5	7.2	8.9	8.7
出口总额	%	-0.5	-7.3	0.2	-0.6	-3.6	-6.7
新签项目宗数	%	-5.7	11.5	4.5	8.9	9.3	2.0
合同规定外商投资额	%	-63.3	6.9	-24.5	-31.6	-66.6	-27.8
实际利用外资	%	-45.6	-54.2	-54.7	-55.4	-59.1	-67.3
社会消费品零售总额	%		7.1	10.0	10.4	11.1	12.1
居民消费价格总指数	%	2.1	2.6	2.6	2.8	2.8	2.8
全社会用电量	%	-2.5	1.2	4.5	2.8	3.5	3.5
#工业用电	%	-3.2	-0.04	2.4	1.2	1.9	2.1
工商注册登记户数	%	12.9	12.7	13.3	13.5	13.7	14.2
#企业	%	22.0	21.5	22.6	22.8	23.2	24.1
邮政业务总量（含快递）	%	14.7	15.5	22.0	24.8	27.2	29.2

1-8 续表

(2016年，比上年同期增长)

项　　目	单位	1-7 月	1-8 月	1-9 月	1-10 月	1-11 月	1-12 月
规模以上工业增加值	%	5.5	5.6	6.5	6.7	6.8	7.0
#内资企业	%	18.5	17.5	17.6	17.6	16.4	17.2
外资企业	%	-2.6	-2.0	-0.5	-0.2	0.7	0.4
#民营企业	%	21.2	20.1	20.1	19.9	18.3	18.6
#五大支柱产业	%	8.3	8.4	8.6	8.6	8.6	8.5
#四个特色产业	%	-6.1	-6.3	-4.0	-1.5	-	0.3
#先进制造业	%	15.5	15.6	16.0	15.6	15.1	15.2
#高技术制造业	%	19.2	18.8	18.6	18.4	17.8	17.6
规模以上工业销售产值	%	9.5	9.4	11.2	12.4	10.1	10.6
规模以上工业产品出口交货值	%	-1.9	0.2	1.9	3.5	3.9	4.9
规模以上工业产品产销率	%	0.4	0.4	0.3	-	-0.1	0.1
规模以上工业企业主营业务收入	%	12.0	12.0	13.4	14.1	15.4	17.2
规模以上工业企业利润总额	%	-4.5	3.3	13.0	12.6	14.4	17.3
固定资产投资总额	%	11.1	8.7	6.9	7.2	6.8	7.7
#房地产开发	%	16.4	13.7	12.9	12.9	12.3	11.7
来源于东莞的财政收入	%	35.9	34.2	33.4	33.0	38.2	35.8
一般公共预算收入	%	9.7	12.1	11.6	10.4	10.7	8.2
一般公共预算支出	%	27.0	16.2	11.0	19.1	16.7	4.7
金融机构各项本外币存款余额	%	7.9	8.8	9.1	13.0	14.4	15.8
#住户存款	%	2.9	3.0	2.4	3.1	7.2	6.8
金融机构各项本外币贷款余额	%	7.2	5.3	6.9	9.3	9.6	9.4
进出口总额（海关口径）	%	-4.0	-2.7	-0.2	4.2	9.7	9.8
#进口总额	%	6.1	8.6	11.5	17.1	23.1	22.4
出口总额	%	-10.2	-9.6	-7.3	-3.6	1.6	2.0
新签项目宗数	%	-1.7	-2.9	-1.0	3.8	-4.8	1.4
合同规定外商投资额	%	-21.2	-12.5	-12.7	-11.1	-4.9	-6.5
实际利用外资	%	-69.3	-58.8	-29.8	-27.6	-24.2	-26.2
社会消费品零售总额	%	12.0	12.1	12.6	12.7	12.8	13.1
居民消费价格总指数	%	2.7	2.7	2.7	2.7	2.7	2.7
全社会用电量	%	4.0	3.9	4.3	4.8	5.1	5.3
#工业用电	%	2.8	2.6	3.1	3.8	4.1	4.7
工商注册登记户数	%	15.2	16.1	16.4	16.9	17.4	17.8
#企业	%	25.4	25.8	25.7	26.5	27.4	28.3
邮政业务总量（含快递）	%	30.4	31.9	33.3	36.0	32.2	33.6

1-9 历年地区生产总值

Gross Domestic Product over Years

年 份	地区生产总值（万元）	第一产业	第二产业	第三产业	人均地区生产总值（元）
1978	61122	27235	26781	7106	553
1979	66233	26460	29244	10528	593
1980	72199	26323	33290	12586	643
1981	91131	32772	42980	15379	802
1982	114322	37257	58137	18927	991
1983	130340	39847	68962	21531	1115
1984	159632	45671	78091	35869	1350
1985	226033	61475	116584	47973	1885
1986	300167	81416	135735	83016	2462
1987	392859	98236	177249	117373	3170
1988	554583	118888	282771	152924	4408
1989	609202	126568	279724	202910	4768
1990	804401	132787	405290	266325	6173
1991	959073	134523	503220	321330	5095
1992	1108922	144115	592701	372106	5038
1993	1570491	143953	873114	553424	5850
1994	2170341	174796	1194928	800616	6357
1995	2962892	214306	1669723	1078863	7421
1996	3617502	248645	1994826	1374031	8444
1997	4485981	256388	2432816	1796777	9747
1998	5579964	259437	3056779	2263749	11265
1999	6672386	257863	3670519	2744004	12494
2000	8202530	259087	4507072	3436372	13679
2001	9918905	260968	5405092	4252845	15268
2002	11869374	248791	6488109	5132474	18131
2003	14525186	228165	7981954	6315068	22174
2004	18060258	227087	10160382	7672789	27554
2005	21831961	205546	12278624	9347791	33287
2006	26279791	120089	15065985	11093717	39173
2007	31600489	118991	17546573	13934924	45057
2008	37036004	148251	19016068	17871685	50471
2009	37858259	147877	18360096	19350286	49273
2010	42782106	165719	21917828	20698558	53193
2011	47719336	178776	24175357	23365203	57913
2012	50392120	187556	24446097	25758468	60907
2013	55174708	195518	26226700	28752490	66440
2014	58813173	203493	27944169	30665510	70605
2015	62750737	210250	29220473	33320014	75616
2016	68276868	241986	31732421	36302461	82682

注：人均地区生产总值1990年及以前按户籍人口计算，1991年起按常住人口计算，与以前年份不可比。

1-10 历年地区生产总值指数

Indices of Gross Domestic Product over Years

年 份	地区生产总值指数(上年=100)	第一产业	第二产业	第三产业	人均地区生产总值指数(上年=100)	人均地区生产总值指数与地区生产总值指数之比
1979	99.5	86.5	107.0	146.4	98.6	0.991
1980	102.7	90.3	117.3	113.9	102.0	0.993
1981	116.6	115.0	122.1	110.8	115.4	0.989
1982	116.9	105.3	131.0	117.6	115.1	0.985
1983	110.4	104.8	115.7	111.3	108.9	0.987
1984	114.2	109.0	107.0	140.9	112.9	0.988
1985	132.3	118.9	144.5	132.7	130.5	0.986
1986	126.1	111.9	110.3	174.7	124.0	0.983
1987	122.5	111.6	127.7	126.0	120.5	0.984
1988	115.7	90.6	143.7	103.0	114.0	0.985
1989	107.1	99.8	106.2	113.7	105.5	0.985
1990	123.2	104.4	127.6	128.0	120.8	0.980
1991	117.5	103.1	121.5	118.6	108.8	0.926
1992	108.3	100.0	112.6	105.1	92.6	0.855
1993	127.9	79.4	139.2	129.0	104.8	0.820
1994	122.5	107.2	124.7	122.3	96.3	0.786
1995	127.4	110.5	135.1	116.8	108.9	0.855
1996	117.5	109.4	115.5	123.5	109.5	0.932
1997	119.6	104.5	119.8	121.8	111.3	0.931
1998	121.8	100.9	122.1	124.5	113.1	0.929
1999	119.7	102.3	120.6	120.3	111.0	0.928
2000	119.7	99.8	120.7	120.0	106.6	0.891
2001	119.9	103.0	121.6	118.9	110.7	0.923
2002	120.5	97.6	122.6	119.1	119.6	0.992
2003	120.5	90.2	122.3	119.7	120.4	0.999
2004	121.0	90.0	125.6	115.8	120.9	0.999
2005	119.5	102.3	120.0	119.3	119.4	0.999
2006	119.2	58.9	121.9	117.1	116.6	0.978
2007	118.3	89.9	114.8	123.3	113.1	0.957
2008	114.0	110.6	106.1	124.0	109.0	0.956
2009	105.3	102.3	100.3	110.8	100.6	0.955
2010	110.3	101.6	117.1	103.7	105.4	0.956
2011	108.0	100.5	107.4	108.7	105.4	0.976
2012	106.1	100.0	106.1	106.2	105.7	0.996
2013	109.8	100.1	111.9	107.7	109.4	0.996
2014	107.8	102.8	109.1	106.3	107.4	0.996
2015	108.0	101.9	106.1	110.2	108.4	1.004
2016	108.1	105.6	108.7	107.6	108.6	1.005

1-11 历年地区生产总值产业构成

Composition of Gross Domestic Product over Years

单位：%

年 份	地区生产总值	第一产业	第二产业	第三产业
1978	100.0	44.6	43.8	11.6
1979	100.0	40.0	44.2	15.9
1980	100.0	36.5	46.1	17.4
1981	100.0	36.0	47.2	16.9
1982	100.0	32.6	50.9	16.6
1983	100.0	30.6	52.9	16.5
1984	100.0	28.6	48.9	22.5
1985	100.0	27.2	51.6	21.2
1986	100.0	27.1	45.2	27.7
1987	100.0	25.0	45.1	29.9
1988	100.0	21.4	51.0	27.6
1989	100.0	20.8	45.9	33.3
1990	100.0	16.5	50.4	33.1
1991	100.0	14.0	52.5	33.5
1992	100.0	13.0	53.5	33.6
1993	100.0	9.2	55.6	35.2
1994	100.0	8.1	55.1	36.9
1995	100.0	7.2	56.4	36.4
1996	100.0	6.9	55.1	38.0
1997	100.0	5.7	54.2	40.1
1998	100.0	4.7	54.8	40.6
1999	100.0	3.9	55.0	41.1
2000	100.0	3.2	54.9	41.9
2001	100.0	2.6	54.5	42.9
2002	100.0	2.1	54.7	43.2
2003	100.0	1.6	55.0	43.5
2004	100.0	1.3	56.3	42.5
2005	100.0	0.9	56.2	42.8
2006	100.0	0.5	57.3	42.2
2007	100.0	0.4	55.5	44.1
2008	100.0	0.4	51.3	48.3
2009	100.0	0.4	48.5	51.1
2010	100.0	0.4	51.2	48.4
2011	100.0	0.4	50.7	48.9
2012	100.0	0.4	48.5	51.1
2013	100.0	0.4	47.5	52.1
2014	100.0	0.4	47.5	52.1
2015	100.0	0.3	46.6	53.1
2016	100.0	0.3	46.5	53.2

1-12 各行业增加值项目（2016年）

Composition of Value-added by Industry (2016)

单位:万元

项　　目	增加值	劳动者报酬	生产税净额	固定资产折旧	营业盈余
地区生产总值	68276868	33215692	10283662	10102123	14675392
#农林牧渔业	246214	233567		12647	
工业	30892562	17426133	4390966	3525107	5550356
建筑业	913683	620678	124180	49739	119086
交通运输、仓储和邮政业	2104604	1255747	46262	442429	360166
交通运输和仓储业	1930163	1119380	41428	434666	334689
邮政业	174441	136367	4834	7762	25477
信息传输、软件和信息技术服务业	2535801	349077	273106	402371	1511246
批发和零售业	8541383	3634757	3566536	173160	1166930
住宿和餐饮业	1511161	1103545	99456	211428	96732
金融业	4417682	1247237	555740	98988	2515718
#货币金融服务	3201676	849661	320726	80646	1950642
房地产业	4889136	544717	873789	2563087	907543
房地产开发经营业	1847190	177054	819974	28412	821749
物业管理业	302799	230473	26271	11784	34271
房地产中介服务业	106745	70255	8738	1036	26716
自有房地产经营活动	2602950	45262	15207	2519992	22489
其他房地产业	29453	21674	3600	1862	2318
租赁和商务服务业	4484492	1032500	183845	1379969	1888179
科学研究和技术服务业	939739	387018	52032	87806	412883
水利、环境和公共设施管理业	282227	157728	15148	67648	41703
居民服务、修理和其他服务业	1148429	950890	43110	51883	102546
教育	1795132	1441914	5003	311620	36596
卫生和社会工作	1144846	853745	16023	122220	152858
文化、体育和娱乐业	496030	560541	37179	85460	-187150
#娱乐业	91509	62763	11478	11300	5969
公共管理、社会保障和社会组织	1933746	1415899	1287	516560	
#第一产业	241986	229339		12647	
第二产业	31732421	17995947	4510067	3565335	5661072
第三产业	36302461	14990406	5773595	6524141	9014319

1-13 主要年份支出法地区生产总值

Gross Domestic Product by Expenditure Approach in Main Years

项　　目	1995年	2000年	2005年	2010年	2015年	2016年
支出法地区生产总值（万元）	2962892	8202530	21831961	42782106	62750737	68276868
最终消费	1502524	4342481	11201390	22984391	34479829	38380049
资本形成总额	1210079	2369818	7148513	12757774	18527476	23102252
货物和服务净出口	250290	1490232	3482058	7039941	9743432	6794567
资本形成率（投资率）(%)	40.8	28.9	32.7	29.8	29.5	33.8
最终消费率（消费率）(%)	50.7	52.9	51.3	53.7	54.9	56.2

1-14 主要年份资本形成总额及构成

Gross Capital Formation and Its Composition in Main Years

项　　目	1995年	2000年	2005年	2010年	2015年	2016年
资本形成总额（万元）	1210079	2369818	7148513	12757774	18527476	23102252
固定资产形成总额	884671	1775228	6115306	10513989	15893330	17922567
存货增加	325407	594590	1033207	2243785	2634146	5179685
比重（资本形成总额=100）						
固定资产形成总额	73.1	74.9	85.5	82.4	85.8	77.6
存货增加	26.9	25.1	14.5	17.6	14.2	22.4

1-15 主要年份最终消费支出及构成

Final Consumption Expenditure and Its Composition in Main Years

项　　目	1995年	2000年	2005年	2010年	2015年	2016年
最终消费（万元）	1502524	4342481	11201390	22984391	34479829	38380049
居民消费	1262972	3752814	9798031	19852461	29347377	31333711
政府消费	239552	589666	1403359	3131930	5132452	7046337
比重（最终消费=100）						
居民消费	84.1	86.4	87.5	86.4	85.1	81.6
政府消费	15.9	13.6	12.5	13.6	14.9	18.4

1-16 主要年份全市企业和个体工商户登记注册年末实有数量

Enterprises and Self-employed Individuals Registered in Main Years

单位：户

项　　目	2005年	2010年	2014年	2015年	2016年
工商登记户数合计	353266	518544	629333	713298	840367
#内资企业	13898	12439	14424	16096	18854
#国有	1977	1058	890	815	831
集体	6478	2180	1549	1471	1398
有限责任公司	1606	7649	10239	11764	14461
外商投资企业	7675	10113	11932	12279	12614
#中外合资	1013	1120	449	476	522
中外合作	482	179	99	91	87
“三来一补”企业	9552	4906	1715	1535	1386
私营企业	29017	88650	180829	226499	296005
个体工商户	293124	402405	419584	456055	510754

注：本表数据来源于市工商局。

1-17 个体工商户情况（2016年）

Statistics on Self-employed Individuals (2016)

项　　目	户　数（户）	从　业人　员（人）	资　金数　额（万元）	其中城镇		
				户　数（户）	从业人员（人）	资金数额（万元）
合　　计	510754	1129437	1471722	243778	506920	663532
农、林、牧、渔业	595	1829	9486.37	157	372	2504.33
工　业	78633	288488	356521.88	25243	91589	108722.47
建筑业	552	1351	2469.49	258	645	1033.98
交通运输、仓储和邮政业	2783	6847	11582.86	1272	3153	4792.85
信息传输、软件和信息技术服务业	994	1558	1425.09	601	918	757.12
批发和零售业	334526	601147	763213.96	170358	293624	376041.82
住宿和餐饮业	50345	129986	187429.54	23927	65211	95266.14
房地产业	34	65	75.7	23	42	44.4
租赁和商务服务业	5202	10754	17486.6	2856	5937	9050.59
居民服务、修理和其他服务业	33035	78167	98447.08	16894	40109	48774.39
卫生和社会工作	200	912	9031.68	162	813	8449.7
文化、体育和娱乐业	727	2243	7445.43	391	1288	4262.83
其他行业	3128	6090	7105.87	1636	3219	3831.65

注：本表数据来源于市工商局。

1-18 私营工商企业基本情况（2016年）

Basic Statistics on Private Industrial & Commercial Enterprises (2016)

项目	户数（户）	投资者人数（人）	雇工人数（人）	注册资本（万元）	其中：1. 独资企业			
					户数（户）	投资者人数（人）	雇工人数（人）	注册资本（万元）
合　计	296005	497198	1622976	66699226	9924	9771	68328	301880
农、林、牧、渔业	893	1515	8802	553202	222	222	4870	18677
工　业	109295	187839	636808	18938329	4011	4004	33912	104074
建筑业	13601	21327	73707	4933335	24	24	90	257
交通运输、仓储和邮政业	5330	8453	26376	1242423	53	52	119	380
信息传输、软件和信息技术服务业	6517	10711	33148	1542072	1323	1314	6148	60862
批发和零售业	96021	150981	507932	14878808	1804	1762	5572	19561
住宿和餐饮业	3770	5996	23036	493652	571	543	5440	41976
房地产业	5630	9219	27699	1692046	5	5	19	75
租赁和商务服务业	30921	59631	158712	15447091	326	309	956	3653
居民服务、修理和其他服务业	7390	11148	39515	881945	773	734	5793	18221
卫生和社会工作	99	150	744	61598	3	3	15	700
文化、体育和娱乐业	4082	6758	22315	676063	746	742	5159	31437
其他行业	12456	23470	64182	5358664	63	57	235	2009

1-18 续表

项目	2. 合伙企业				3. 有限责任公司			
	户数（户）	合伙人数（人）	雇工人数（人）	注册资本（万元）	户数（户）	投资者人数（人）	雇工人数（人）	注册资本（万元）
合　计	1606	8323	8044	5358071	283714	476081	1542082	58832092
农、林、牧、渔业	60	148	975	4628	608	1115	2947	392664
工　业	279	669	2202	19863	104792	182066	599052	17937708
建筑业	1	3	5	25	13541	21267	73426	4898754
交通运输、仓储和邮政业	3	8	12	95	5267	8387	26207	1237648
信息传输、软件和信息技术服务业	140	300	834	68092	5015	8964	25971	1305096
批发和零售业	83	178	330	6530	94003	148408	501479	14541239
住宿和餐饮业	83	222	739	21578	3114	5226	16854	429098
房地产业	5	19	10	334	5612	9179	27634	1669899
租赁和商务服务业	741	5701	2134	5135245	29748	53089	155181	10017070
居民服务、修理和其他服务业	71	276	457	5061	6531	10114	33236	856054
卫生和社会工作					96	147	729	60898
文化、体育和娱乐业	41	94	149	5025	3288	5896	16980	631492
其他行业	99	705	197	91595	12099	22223	62386	4854472

注：本表数据来源于市工商局。

1-19 历年总供用电

Gross Electricity Supply over Years

单位：万千瓦时

年份	总供电量	#网供	全社会用电量	#工业用电	照明用电
1978	16375	16376			1741
1979	19271	19271			2338
1980	21659	21569			3372
1981	22247	22247			4650
1982	26871	26351			6272
1983	31527	31527			8052
1984	32617	28566			9484
1985	38183	33907			9934
1986	39305	35100			10204
1987	64258	45129			16657
1988	94842	66295			22347
1989	120861	76762			26139
1990	180142	111800	180142		39677
1991	240471	139841	240471		56504
1992	320003	180902	320003		25578
1993	436231	242205	436231		103583
1994	585763	393312	585763		110357
1995	680030	384764	680004		125135
1996	800300	506062	800300		153093
1997	949296	612907	948296		180583
1998	1094816	724758	1094818		221750
1999	1327788	973427	1343746	1017261	261629
2000	1780290	1349134	1796578	1367883	337044
2001	2077248	1649458	2091668	1616179	584700
2002	2585474	2219054	2598555	2004227	392879
2003	3216468	2846679	3235342	2499705	424869
2004	3728441	3196454	3758498	2822014	527332
2005	4156629	3422603	4198289	3374306	652514
2006	4644506	3676492	4720112	3735651	759384
2007	5078933	4167125	5154025	4061784	859851
2008	5073489	4423085	5141578	3962669	935510
2009	4888467	4318868	4955750	3673716	1011494
2010	5568902	5473261	5619996	4262339	1070692
2011	5793482	5699321	5860652	4351290	1196914
2012	6005828	5911793	6042842	4429317	1274923
2013	6172030	6061530	6225139	4537990	1338917
2014	6557176	6450483	6609853	4829488	1473307
2015	6612570	6482740	6668438	4833053	1530443
2016	6955925	6813874	7020063	5060048	1618277

1-20 历年国民经济主要指标人均水平

The Per Capita Level of Main National Economic Indicators over Years

年 份	人均地区生产总值（元）	人均一般公共预算收入（元）	人均出口总额美元（元）	人均消费品零售额（元）	人均固定资产投资额（元）	人均用电量（千瓦时）	年末人均住户存款余额（元）
1978	553	60	36	192	21		49
1979	593	59	48	224	15		64
1980	643	60	69	281	21		104
1981	802	60	81	354	33		178
1982	991	70	94	417	157		238
1983	1115	73	102	447	157		328
1984	1350	72	110	625	254		520
1985	1885	93	146	781	589		761
1986	2462	132	191	1004	945		1068
1987	3170	163	216	1214	1145		1519
1988	4408	215	253	1959	1315		1965
1989	4768	250	273	2116	392		2529
1990	6173	274	436	2454	576		2592
1991	5095	236	879	1943	732	1280	3074
1992	5038	263	1217	2073	883	1496	3580
1993	5850	385	1318	2615	1345	1791	4131
1994	6357	277	1548	3070	5074	2111	5130
1995	7421	366	2468	3577	1998	2152	6924
1996	8444	268	2553	3489	1879	2224	8300
1997	9747	278	2774	3564	1608	2314	9758
1998	11265	324	2799	3753	1650	2509	10740
1999	12494	344	2851	3806	1662	2528	10890
2000	13679	503	2834	3884	1700	2968	10422
2001	15268	693	2923	4244	1932	3220	12212
2002	18131	845	3626	4907	2926	3971	15297
2003	22174	1030	4275	5645	4876	4939	18788
2004	27554	1261	5369	6506	6940	5734	21836
2005	33287	1585	6240	7719	9106	6401	26343
2006	39173	1922	7062	8934	10516	7036	29364
2007	45057	2658	8588	10301	11994	7349	29577
2008	50471	2851	8931	12008	12869	7007	35146
2009	48988	3009	7180	13393	14239	6450	36950
2010	52798	3455	8653	15210	13863	6988	41179
2011	57470	3799	9506	17491	13099	7113	44956
2012	60557	4307	10282	19344	14267	7304	50700
2013	66109	4929	10942	21514	16665	7496	53825
2014	70604	5465	11653	23317	17132	7935	55217
2015	75616	6242	12498	26326	17431	8036	55626
2016	82682	6597	79402	29921	18861	8501	59105

注：1. 人均指标1991年以前按户籍人口计算，1991年起按常住人口计算；时点数按年末人口计算，时期数按年平均人口计算。
2. 人均指标2006—2010年数据，根据东莞市第六次全国人口普查数据结果重新修订，下同。
3. 2016年起，出口数据按人民币计算，数据与往年不可比。

主要统计指标解释

Explanatory Notes on Main Statistical Indicators

国内（地区）生产总值 指按市场价格计算的一个国家（或地区）所有常住单位在一定时期内生产活动的最终成果。国内（地区）生产总值有三种计算方法，即生产法、收入法和支出法。三种方法分别从不同的方面反映国内（地区）生产总值及其构成。

增加值 指常住单位生产过程创造的新增价值和固定资产的转移价值。它可以按生产法计算，也可以按收入法计算，按生产法计算，它等于总产出减去中间投入；按收入法计算，它等于劳动者报酬、生产税净额、固定资产折旧和营业盈余之和。

劳动者报酬 指劳动者因从事生产活动所获得的全部报酬，包括劳动者获得的各种形式的工资、奖金和津贴，既包括货币形式的，也包括实物形式的，还包括劳动者所享受的公费医疗和医药卫生费、上下班交通补贴和单位支付的社会保险费、住房公积金等。对于个体经济来说，其所有者所获得的劳动报酬和经营利润不易区分，这两部分统一作为劳动者报酬处理。

生产税净额 指生产税减生产补贴后的差额。生产税指政府对生产单位从事生产、销售和经营活动以及因从事生产活动使用某些生产要素（如固定资产、土地、劳动力）所征收的各种税、附加费和规费。生产补贴与生产税相反，指政府对生产单位的单方面转移支付，因此视为负生产税，包括政策性亏损补贴、价格补贴等。

固定资产折旧 指一定时期内为弥补固定资产损耗按照规定的固定资产折旧率提取的固定资产折旧，或按国民经济核算统一规定的折旧率虚拟计算的固定资产折旧。它反映了固定资产在当期生产中的转移价值。各类企业和企业化管理的事业单位的固定资产折旧是指实际计提的折旧费；不计提折旧的政府机关、非企业化管理的事业单位和居民住房的固定资产折旧是按照统一规定的折旧率和固定资产原值计算的虚拟折旧。

营业盈余 指常住单位创造的增加值扣除劳动者报酬、固定资产折旧和生产税净额后的余额。它相当于企业的营业利润加上生产补贴，但要扣除从利润中开支的工资和福利等。

三次产业 三次产业的划分是世界上较为常用的产业结构分类，但各国的划分不尽一致。根据《国民经济行业分类》（GB/T 4754—2011），我国的三产产业划分是：

第一产业：指农、林、牧、渔业（不含农、林、牧、渔服务业）；

第二产业：指采矿业（不含开采辅助活动），制造业（不含金属制品、机械和设备修理业），电力、热力、燃气及水生产和供应业，建筑业；

第三产业：指服务业，是指除第一产业、第二产业以外的其他行业。第三产业包括：批发和零售业，交通运输、仓储和邮政业，住宿和餐饮业，信息传输、软件和信息技术服务业，金融业，房地产业，租赁和商务服务业，科学研究和技术服务业，水利、环境和公共设施管理业，居民服务、修理和其他服务业，教育，卫生和社会工作，文化、体育和娱乐业，公共管理、社会保障和社会组织，国际组织，以及农、林、牧、渔业中的农、林、牧、渔服务业，采矿业中的开采辅助活动，制造业中的金属制品、机械和设备修理业。

支出法国内（地区）生产总值 是从最终使用的角度反映一个国家（或地区）一定时期内生产活动最终成果的一种方法，包括最终消费支出、资本形成总额及货物和服务净出口三部分。计算公式为：

支出法国内（地区）生产总值=最终消费支出+资本形成总额+货物和服务净出口

最终消费支出 指常住单位为满足物质、文化和精神生活的需要，从本国经济领土和国外购买的货物和服务的支出。不包括非常住单位在本国经济领土内的消费支出。最终消费支出分为居民消费支出和政府消费支出。

居民消费支出 指常住住户在一定时期内对于货物和服务的全部最终消费支出。居民消费支出除了直接以货币形式购买的货物和服务的消费之外，还包括以其他方式获得的货物和服务的消费，即所谓的虚拟消费支出。居民虚拟消费支出包括如下几种类型：单位以实物报酬及实物转移的形式提供给劳动者的货物和服务；住户生产并由本住户消费发的货物和服务，其中的服务仅指住户的自有住房服务和付酬的家庭雇员提供的家庭和个人服务；金融机构提供的金融媒介服务等。

政府消费支出 指政府部门为全社会提供公共服务的消费支出和免费或以较低价格向住户提供的货物和服务的净支出。前者等于政府服务的产出价值减去政府单位所获得的经营收入后的价值，后者等于政府部门免费或以较低价格向住户提供的货物和服务的市场价值减去向住户收取的价值。

资本形成总额 指常住单位在一定时期内获得的减去处置的固定资产和存货的净额，包括固定资本形成总额和存货变动两部分。

固定资本形成总额 指生产者在一定时期内获得的固定资产减处置的固定资产的价值总额。固定资产是通过生产活动生产出来的，且其使用年限在一年以上、单位价值在规定标准以上的资产，不包括自然资产。可分为有形固定资本形成总额和无形固定资本形成总额。有形固定资本形成总额包括一定时期内完成的建筑工程、安装工程、设备工器具购置（减处置）价值，以及土地改良、新增役、种、奶、毛、娱乐用牲畜和新增经济林木价值。无形固定资本形成总额包括矿藏的勘探、计算机软件等获得减处置的价值。

存货变动 指常住单位存货实物量变动的市场价值，即期末价值减期初价值的差额，再扣除当期由于价格变动而产生的持有收益。存货增加可以是正值，也可以是负值；正值表示存货上升，负值表示存货下降。存货包括生产单位购进的原材料、燃料和储备物资等存货，以及生产单位生产的产成品、在制品和半成品等存货。

货物和服务净出口 指货物和服务出口减货物和服务进口的差额。出口包括常住单位向非常住单位出售或无偿转让的各种货物和服务的价值；进口包括常住单位从非常住单位购买或无偿得到的各种货物和服务价值。由于服务活动的提供与使用同时发生，一般把常住单位从非常住单位得到的服务作为进口，非常住单位从常住单位得到的服务作为出口。货物的出口和进口都按离岸价格计算。

发展速度 用以反映社会经济发展程度的相对指标，根据两个时期发展水平的对比而得。由于比较的标准时期不同，发展速度可分为定基发展速度和环比发展速度两种。

增长速度 发展速度 - 1（或 100%）就是增长速度。即增长速度=发展速度 - 1（或 100%）。

平均每年增长速度 我国计算平均增长速度有两种方法，一种是习惯上经常使用的“水平法”，又称几何平均法，是以间隔最后一年的水平同基期水平对比来计算平均每年增长（或下降）的速度；另一种是“累计法”又称代数平均法或方程法，是以间隔年内各年水平的总和同基期水平对比来计算平均每年增长（或下降）的速度。具体计算方法，可参照中国财经出版社出版的《平均增长速度查对表》。

在一般正常情况下，两种方法计算的平均每年增长速度比较接近，但在经济发展不平衡出现大起大落时，两种方法计算的结果差别较大。

本《年鉴》内所列的平均每年增长速度都是用水平法计算的。从某年到某年平均增长速度的年份，均不包基期年在内。如 1981-2016 年平均每年增长速度，是以 1980 年为基期，2016 年为报告期，年份从 1981 年算起，共 36 年。

二、人口与劳动力

Population and Labor Force

2-1 历年总人口数与人口密度

Total Population and Density over Years

单位：万人

年 份	户籍人口	按性别分		按城镇、乡村分		外来暂住人口	常住人口	人口密度(人/平方公里)
		男	女	城镇人口	乡村人口			
1949	68.24	32.87	35.37	11.95	56.29			
1952	71.68	34.53	37.15	12.99	58.69			
1957	77.48	37.50	39.98	14.96	62.52			
1962	79.64	38.07	41.57	15.22	64.42			
1965	86.46	41.83	44.63	16.18	70.28			
1970	98.56	47.91	50.65	17.30	81.26			
1975	107.94	52.70	55.24	17.57	90.37			
1978	111.23	54.34	56.89	18.29	92.74			451
1979	112.04	54.45	57.59	19.18	92.86			455
1980	112.70	54.43	58.27	19.83	92.87			457
1981	114.46	55.36	59.10	20.38	94.08			464
1982	116.19	56.28	59.91	20.87	95.32			471
1983	117.59	57.05	60.54	21.23	96.36			477
1984	118.95	57.80	61.15	22.48	96.47			483
1985	120.85	58.84	62.01	25.49	95.36			490
1986	123.01	59.95	63.06	26.48	96.53	15.62		499
1987	124.86	61.02	63.84	27.66	97.20	25.29		507
1988	126.76	62.09	64.67	28.80	97.96	36.89		514
1989	128.76	63.27	65.49	29.94	98.82	47.19		522
1990	131.85	64.96	66.89	30.86	100.99	65.59	175.62	712
1991	133.65	66.10	67.55	31.86	101.79	80.58	200.01	811
1992	136.06	67.55	68.51	32.71	103.35	114.48	227.78	924
1993	138.92	69.20	69.72	33.74	105.18	121.70	259.41	1052
1994	141.40	70.64	70.76	34.55	106.85	139.09	295.43	1198
1995	143.65	71.97	71.68	35.38	108.27	142.18	336.45	1365
1996	145.25	72.92	72.33	36.14	109.11	143.32	383.17	1554
1997	147.12	74.04	73.08	36.97	110.15	144.68	436.38	1770
1998	148.77	74.99	73.78	37.84	110.93	199.11	496.97	2016
1999	150.82	76.18	74.64	38.73	112.09	244.81	565.98	2296
2000	152.61	77.22	75.39	39.61	113.00	254.72	644.84	2616
2001	153.89	77.94	75.95	40.37	113.52	457.82	654.43	2655
2002	156.19	79.14	77.05	41.02	115.17	433.65	654.84	2657
2003	158.96	80.65	78.31	56.87	102.09	440.45	655.25	2658
2004	161.97	82.25	79.72	61.48	100.49	486.95	655.66	2660
2005	165.65	84.07	81.58	65.84	99.81	584.98	656.07	2662
2006	168.31	85.43	82.88	70.42	97.89	586.76	685.66	2782
2007	171.26	87.00	84.26	73.67	97.59	557.80	717.02	2909
2008	174.86	88.88	85.98	76.80	98.06	552.50	750.60	3045
2009	178.73	90.78	87.95	81.46	97.27	429.96	786.08	3189
2010	181.77	92.27	89.50	92.09	89.68	411.47	822.48	3343
2011	184.77	93.76	91.01	94.46	90.31	413.62	825.48	3356
2012	187.02	94.92	92.10	95.96	91.05	416.74	829.23	3371
2013	188.93	95.83	93.10	97.34	91.59	434.68	831.66	3381
2014	191.39	97.02	94.37	99.17	92.21	415.86	834.31	3392
2015	195.01	98.71	96.30	172.65	22.36	400.81	825.41	3355
2016	200.94	101.47	99.47	178.20	22.74	428.39	826.14	3358

注：1.人口密度1990年以前户籍人口计算，1990年起按常住人口计算。
2.常住人口2006—2010年数据，根据东莞市第六次全国人口普查数据结果重新修订，下同。
3.按建立城乡统一的户口登记制度要求，2015年起户籍户数和人口数按城镇和乡村划分，取消原来的农业和非农业的登记统计，数据与往年不可比，下同。

2-2 主要年份户籍人口与劳动力指标

Main Indicators of Household Population and Labor in Main Years

指　　标	单 位	1990年	1995年	2000年	2005年	2010年	2015年	2016年
年末户籍人口	人	1318526	1436525	1526090	1656541	1817709	1950089	2009352
#乡村人口	人	1009857	1082703	1130002	998159	896789	223575	227379
人口性别比（女性人口=100）	%	97.1	100.4	102.4	103.1	103.1	102.5	102.0
人口密度	人/平方公里	535	583	619	672	739	793	817
人口出生率	‰	17.1	17.6	12.1	10.6	10.9	11.3	13.9
人口死亡率	‰	4.8	4.8	4.6	4.6	4.7	4.9	5.3
人口自然增长率	‰	12.3	12.8	7.5	6.0	6.2	6.4	8.6
人口净迁移率	‰	1.9	1.9	2.2	16.4	12.0	7.8	18.5
城镇本年新登记的失业人员人数	人		6536	6524	7080	3207	10143	11065
城镇失业人员安置就业人数	人			5683	6088	3796	9276	10136

2-3 历年户籍人口自然变动情况

Changes of Household Population over Years

年 份	出 生		死 亡		自然增长	
	人 数 (人)	出生率 (‰)	人 数 (人)	死亡率 (‰)	人 数 (人)	自然增长率 (‰)
1978	20728	18.73	5451	4.92	15277	13.81
1979	26931	24.13	5755	5.13	21176	19.00
1980	27428	24.41	5747	5.10	21681	19.31
1981	24828	21.86	6016	5.29	18812	16.57
1982	21991	19.07	5681	4.93	16310	14.14
1983	19573	16.74	6100	5.21	13473	11.53
1984	18380	15.54	5841	4.94	12539	10.60
1985	18432	15.37	5439	4.54	12993	10.83
1986	20049	16.44	5955	4.88	14094	11.56
1987	19962	16.11	5502	4.44	14459	11.67
1988	21077	16.75	5863	4.66	15214	12.09
1989	23457	17.06	5966	4.67	17491	12.39
1990	22238	17.07	6208	4.76	16030	12.31
1991	23771	17.91	6070	4.57	17701	13.34
1992	26040	19.31	6485	4.81	19555	14.50
1993	25270	18.38	6833	4.97	18437	13.41
1994	24152	17.88	6319	4.51	17833	13.37
1995	25312	17.59	6898	4.84	18414	12.75
1996	24635	17.05	7333	5.08	17302	11.97
1997	24106	16.50	6448	4.41	17658	12.09
1998	22563	15.31	6553	4.45	16010	10.86
1999	21673	14.55	6460	4.34	15213	10.22
2000	18260	12.11	6923	4.59	11337	7.52
2001	17083	11.16	6344	4.14	10739	7.01
2002	16029	10.35	6873	4.44	9156	5.91
2003	16204	10.34	7346	4.69	8858	5.65
2004	17312	10.86	7814	4.90	9498	5.96
2005	17301	10.62	7497	4.60	9804	6.02
2006	16819	10.14	7103	4.28	9716	5.86
2007	17482	10.39	7418	4.41	10064	5.98
2008	18382	10.77	7752	4.54	10630	6.23
2009	18584	10.67	7587	4.36	10997	6.31
2010	19509	10.90	8367	4.68	11142	6.23
2011	19884	10.92	8728	4.79	11156	6.13
2012	24712	13.32	9684	5.22	15028	8.10
2013	22222	11.79	8693	4.61	13529	7.18
2014	21383	11.20	10253	5.37	11130	5.83
2015	21951	11.34	9545	4.93	12406	6.41
2016	27613	13.92	10475	5.28	17138	8.64

2-4 历年户籍人口迁移变动情况

Changes of Household Migration over Years

年 份	迁 入		迁 出		总迁移		净迁移	
	人 数（人）	迁入率（‰）	人 数（人）	迁出率（‰）	人 数（人）	总迁移率（‰）	人 数（人）	净迁移率（‰）
1978	10148	9.2	13179	11.9	23327	21.1	-3031	-2.7
1980	13345	11.9	28624	25.5	41969	37.4	-15279	-13.6
1985	19205	16.0	15636	13.0	34841	29.1	3569	3.0
1990	13485	10.4	11061	8.5	24546	18.8	2424	1.9
1991	12628	9.5	12531	9.4	25159	19.0	97	0.1
1992	14622	10.8	11168	8.3	25790	19.1	3454	2.5
1993	10801	7.9	4886	3.6	15687	11.4	5915	4.3
1994	10127	7.2	6406	4.6	16533	11.8	3721	2.7
1995	10312	7.2	7675	5.4	17987	12.6	2637	1.9
1996	9273	6.4	11508	8.0	20781	14.4	-2235	-1.6
1997	10284	7.0	9469	6.5	19753	13.5	815	0.6
1998	12400	8.4	11253	7.6	23653	16.0	1147	0.8
1999	15049	10.0	11497	7.6	26546	17.6	3552	2.4
2000	15618	10.2	12314	8.1	27932	18.3	3304	2.2
2001	15968	10.4	11099	7.2	27067	17.6	4869	3.2
2002	20214	12.9	8033	5.1	28247	18.1	12181	7.8
2003	27143	17.1	7173	4.5	34316	21.6	19970	12.6
2004	29621	18.3	7618	4.7	37239	23.0	22003	13.6
2005	43026	26.0	15798	9.5	58824	35.5	27228	16.4
2006	30710	18.2	11442	6.8	42152	25.0	19268	11.4
2007	26940	15.7	4847	2.8	31787	18.6	22093	12.9
2008	33595	19.2	5974	3.4	39569	22.6	27621	15.8
2009	36387	20.4	7381	4.1	43768	24.5	29006	16.2
2010	28534	15.7	6651	3.7	35185	19.4	21883	12.0
2011	28623	15.5	7425	4.0	36048	19.5	21198	11.5
2012	20698	11.1	8326	4.5	29024	15.5	12372	6.6
2013	18812	10.0	11035	5.8	29847	15.8	7777	4.1
2014	25530	13.3	10748	5.6	36278	19.0	14782	7.7
2015	21654	11.1	6480	3.3	28134	14.4	15174	7.8
2016	43738	21.8	6630	3.3	50368	25.1	37108	18.5

2-5 历年外来暂住人口与外来劳动力

Temporary Residents and Labor over Years

单位：人

年份	外来暂住人口总计	按性别分		按省内省外分						
		男性	女性	本省	外省	#湖南省	四川省	广西自治区	湖北省	江西省
1986	156222									
1987	252895									
1988	368913									
1989	481850									
1990	655902			333180	322722					
1991	805790			360379	445411					
1992	1144753	440500	704253	494278	650475					
1993	1217010	529096	687914	370770	846240					
1994	1390884	547435	843449	380790	1010094	257348	227793	139137	66189	60638
1995	1421754	581304	840450	371816	1023510	253574	223727	149478	84727	67562
1996	1433157	606524	826633	305821	1106749	232329	223315	137933	90528	79730
1997	1446830	554193	892637	298510	1130981	243384	227077	140483	89140	83272
1998	1991122	850266	1140856	402267	1569963	330241	294149	183734	143662	118685
1999	2448134	1084492	1363642	504722	1921206	391491	387730	236936	173787	149000
2000	2547221	1155277	1391944	485889	2041959	377257	319039	240923	196697	157323
2001	4578163	2138218	2439945	731931	3826830	718295	622166	442904	359872	294740
2002	4336453	1973316	2363137	722894	3593034	685311	555569	394088	389735	294086
2003	4404467	2198324	2206143	665549	3720408	663487	591145	432738	443603	339518
2004	4869462	2347115	2522347	747804	4096599	812976	581272	483329	490063	329715
2005	5849785	2746833	3102952	1036417	4747692	844053	642170	574634	514760	376526
2006	5867555	2775718	3091837	1012637	4807064	875904	617644	556961	531987	367094
2007	5577988	2666292	2911696	986062	4551507	816688	553907	497438	521529	355798
2008	5525022	2657712	2867310	1012341	4468505	828779	533496	488226	517519	353738
2009	4299615	2093055	2206560	889160	3367565	604891	441758	396425	391650	269133
2010	4114745	2010869	2103876	791665	3275768	587153	411005	405051	353414	252936
2011	4136177	2054179	2081998	900560	3194930	571601	370717	387198	350490	264965
2012	4167396	2072592	2094804	940956	3183488	587921	387226	398858	352191	236544
2013	4346839	2186786	2160053	949443	3356719	629746	387979	438718	380395	258666
2014	4158580	2103624	2054956	927905	3189809	570631	350809	441886	356586	252054
2015	4008120	2047374	1960746	867677	3099936	549724	330102	430882	334220	233460
2016	4283923	2274363	2009560	1112539	3171384	561944	319526	446556	334267	235517

2-5 续表

单位：人

年份	外来劳动力	工业	农业	商业	服务业
1986	104091	87154	9849	2509	4579
1987	180285	154842	13110	4181	8152
1988	292499	260237	16911	5797	9554
1989	405287	365840	19893	7763	11791
1990	572044	518971	25576	10793	16704
1991	701982	633400	25838	17945	24799
1992	1071048	874149	62324	88087	46488
1993	1126813	933147	40177	88524	64965
1994	1241814	1069478	52146	39869	80321
1995	1265368	1084860	54714	52965	72829
1996	1276626	1084330	64732	61092	66472
1997	1307279	1114235	57214	67242	68588
1998	1831939	1577922	68143	100041	85833
1999	2161487	1609539	113324	282938	155686
2000	2448415	2043270	88195	187015	129935
2001	4496771	3681099	174936	283277	357459
2002	4260142	3573355	127584	300642	258561
2003	4327312	3753904	85109	278632	209667
2004	4733903	4078400	98272	315021	242210
2005	5534248	4676454	107933	420810	329051
2006	5669798	4820388	124942	412180	312288
2007	5389490	4480800	102519	460114	346057
2008	5303008	4227211	97597	560345	417855
2009	4134581	3361306	74982	430183	268110
2010	3912274	3191436	92451	402786	225601
2011	3947135	3277984	82025	358941	228185
2012	3979414	3278448	85557	390327	225082
2013	4127952	3431195	93051	397091	206615
2014	3893258	3243831	63386	377854	208187
2015	3765415	3147707	55658	365507	196543
2016	3953862	3016145	65948	352141	259544

2-6 全社会从业人员

Number of Employed Persons of the Whole City by Sector

单位：人

指　　标	2010年	2014年	2015年	2016年
全社会从业人员	6262527	6604575	6534121	6539724
#农、林、牧、渔业	60497	56786	60857	59010
采矿业	830			35
制造业	4650613	4384904	4334996	4339951
电力、热力、燃气及水的生产和供应业	20937	13084	12935	12950
建筑业	97018	111476	110207	110334
交通运输、仓储和邮政业	78872	136555	135001	135156
信息传输、软件和信息技术服务业	26167	49664	49099	49155
批发和零售业	630398	465602	460303	460832
住宿和餐饮业	215599	158826	157018	157199
金融业	36628	26611	26308	26338
房地产业	47851	131421	129925	130075
租赁和商务服务业	32401	304049	300588	300934
科学研究和技术服务	6515	66587	65829	65905
水利、环境和公共设施管理业	15898	23289	23024	23050
居民服务、修理和其他服务业	89676	76947	76071	76159
教育	65895	186495	184372	184585
卫生和社会工作	39119	83584	82633	82728
文化、体育和娱乐业	21732	41027	40560	40607
公共管理、社会保障和社会组织	125881	287668	284394	284721
国际组织				
#第一产业	60497	56704	60772	58925
第二产业	4769398	4509365	4458138	4463158
第三产业	1432632	2038506	2015210	2017641

注：全社会从业人员统计范围为东莞市辖区内城乡各类法人单位、城乡个体从业人员及农村从事农林牧渔业的从业人员。

2−7 主要年份城镇在岗职工年末人数

Number of Employed Persons in Urban Areas at Year-end in Main Years

单位：人

项　　目	1985年	1990年	1995年	2000年	2005年	2010年	2015年	2016年
合　　计	122951	131631	178724	164080	188579	226268	2267844	2269355
第一产业	2432	2053	620	476	483	625		
第二产业	64525	72993	110885	76153	80596	87136	1882650	1871092
工　业	60571	68508	105782	68354	79359	84992	1840487	1830149
采矿业			130	62	59	52	35	35
制造业			99194	62790	71569	77544	1831287	1821209
电力、热力、燃气及水的生产和供应业			6458	5502	7731	7396	9165	8905
建筑业			5103	7799	1237	2144	42163	41055
第三产业	55994	56585	67219	87451	107500	138507	385194	398263
交通运输、仓储和邮政业						6427	28719	28436
信息传输、软件和信息技术服务业						2535	8406	11091
批发和零售业						6215	56306	59023
住宿和餐饮业						739	27861	26247
金融业	2270	4291	9487	13945	16584	20706	27169	23821
房地产业	1551	2529	73	387	427	488	22879	26297
租赁和商务服务业						2270	39146	47380
科学研究和技术服务						1984	13991	13041
水利、环境和公共设施管理业						654	2764	4051
居民服务、修理和其他服务业						105	12471	12270
教育						26138	35671	37782
卫生和社会工作						26859	45983	46304
文化、体育和娱乐业						1711	6812	6632
公共管理、社会保障和社会组织	5854	7887	9711	15733	28542	41676	56670	55520
国际组织								

注：1.2012年起城镇在岗职工含劳务派遣人员。
　　2.2013年起，将原属于乡镇企业且符合城镇非私营单位条件的“四上”企业纳入城镇单位从业人员及工资统计的范围，下同。

2-8 历年分行业城镇在岗职工人数

Numbers of Employers by Sector in Urban Areas over Years

单位：人

年 份	年末城镇在岗职工人数合计	第一产业	第二产业	#工业	第三产业
1978	81971	2875	41179	38729	37917
1979	96807	3051	44905	42251	48851
1980	98587	2637	47374	44737	48576
1981	106626	2897	52638	50370	51091
1982	114119	2133	56391	52418	55595
1983	115926	1978	58139	53246	55809
1984	117627	1933	59129	54916	56565
1985	122951	2432	64525	60571	55994
1986	132744	2252	73922	65674	56570
1987	136666	2359	76393	69985	57914
1988	127098	2702	69385	64631	55011
1989	131039	2397	73042	68738	55600
1990	131631	2053	72993	68508	56585
1991	145873	2083	84992	79389	58798
1992	154712	2043	89713	82611	62956
1993	176578	1933	107296	92212	67349
1994	160872	621	95378	83322	64873
1995	178724	620	110885	105782	67219
1996	174964	497	98061	91228	76406
1997	164987	616	82513	76619	81858
1998	164047	779	80510	70499	82758
1999	163917	583	76905	68860	86429
2000	164080	476	76153	68354	87451
2001	164226	444	76181	69260	87601
2002	164209	431	75384	68348	88394
2003	165978	522	73357	72118	92099
2004	175415	565	78003	76786	96847
2005	188579	483	80596	79359	107500
2006	199878	483	84618	83328	114777
2007	205640	487	81448	79949	123705
2008	207234	459	77982	76563	128793
2009	225990	477	94365	92943	131148
2010	226268	625	87136	84992	138507
2011	246083	966	82164	80648	162953
2012	250225	925	85582	82647	163718
2013	2398215	575	2001324	1968085	396316
2014	2342549	28	1956590	1922112	385931
2015	2267844		1882650	1840487	385194
2016	2269355		1871092	1830149	398263

2-9 主要年份国有单位分行业年末城镇在岗职工人数

Number of Employed Persons in Urban State-owned Units at Year-end by Sector in Main Years

单位：人

指标	1985年	1990年	1995年	2000年	2005年	2010年	2015年	2016年
合计	56534	63469	71165	78216	94902	121690	141037	139412
按企业、事业、机关单位分								
企业	40201	43538	38022	31988	20401	20348	15922	14738
事业	11362	13072	23147	31506	46382	60310	69850	70504
机关	4971	6859	9996	14722	28119	41032	55265	54170
按国民经济行业分								
第一产业	2264	1956	712	476	483	625		
第二产业	22373	22877	17363	11658	4442	4888	653	632
工　业	20919	19390	14610	10119	3471	3638	615	540
采矿业	423	72	130	62	59	52		
制造业	19625	16912	12908	6611	1217	981	615	519
电力、热力、燃气及水的生产和供应业	871	2406	1572	3446	2195	2605		21
建筑业	1454	3487	2753	1539	971	1250	38	92
第三产业	31897	38571	53090	66082	89977	116177	140384	138780
交通运输、仓储和邮政业					3381	2182	5166	4153
信息传输、软件和信息技术服务业					2243	2275	243	129
批发和零售业					1582	1790	128	133
住宿和餐饮业								
金融业	943	2215	5634	7343	9401	9319	10231	10010
房地产业	138	149	44	98	244	329	17	15
租赁和商务服务业					676	1437	442	747
科学研究和技术服务					1496	1928	1001	1058
水利、环境和公共设施管理业					484	542	693	465
居民服务、修理和其他服务业					95	105	119	125
教育					23301	26138	26795	27641
卫生和社会工作					17134	26795	37102	36992
文化、体育和娱乐业					1398	1661	1566	1573
公共管理、社会保障和社会组织	4971	6859	9563	15372	28542	41676	56670	55520
国际组织								

2-10 主要年份集体单位分行业年末城镇在岗职工人数

Number of Employed Persons in Urban Collective-owned Units at Year-end by Sector in Main Years

单位：人

指 标	1985年	1990年	1995年	2000年	2005年	2010年	2015年	2016年
合 计	63383	58749	64923	50592	44251	35106	39317	31884
按企业、事业、机关单位分								
企业	58258	54671	63194	49257	43200	34245	35833	28072
事业	4062	3050	1581	974	1051	861	236	210
机关	1063	1028	148	361				
按国民经济行业分								
第一产业	168	97	33					
第二产业	39858	41795	52334	34958	32778	23765	18850	13486
工 业	37358	40979	49984	28698	32527	22879	13825	9681
采矿业		433						
制造业		40458	48600	27268	30772	21497	11624	7731
电力、热力、燃气及水的生产和供应业		88	1384	1430	1755	1382	2201	1950
建筑业	2500	998	2350	6260	251	886	5025	3805
第三产业	23357	16857	12556	15634	11473	11341	20467	18398
交通运输、仓储和邮政业					3446	3543	464	93
信息传输、软件和信息技术服务业					45	40		
批发和零售业					2078	1818	1376	1415
住宿和餐饮业					307	289	663	424
金融业	1327	2076	3844	3437	4184	4533	5932	5986
房地产业			29	289	183	159	743	705
租赁和商务服务业					843	677	7126	6731
科学研究和技术服务					16	56	1467	303
水利、环境和公共设施管理业					237	112	109	131
居民服务、修理和其他服务业							5	5
教育								30
卫生和社会工作					92	64	2485	2493
文化、体育和娱乐业					42	50	97	82
公共管理、社会保障和社会组织	1063	1028	148	361				
国际组织								

2-11 主要年份其他所有制单位分行业年末城镇在岗职工人数

Number of Employed Persons in Urban Other Ownership Units at Year-end by Sector in Main Years

单位：人

指　　标	1985年	1990年	1995年	2000年	2005年	2010年	2015年	2016年
合　　计	3034	9413	42636	35272	49426	69472	2087490	2098059
按企业、事业、机关单位分								
企业	2312	9413	42597	35272	49426	69472	2080290	2090782
事业	722		39				320	305
机关								
其他							6880	6972
按国民经济行业分								
第一产业								
第二产业	2294	8321	41188	29537	43376	58483	1863147	1856974
工　业	2294	8321	41188	29537	43361	58475	1826047	1819928
采矿业		48					35	35
制造业		8273	37686	28911	39580	55066	1819048	1812959
电力、热力、燃气及水的生产和供应业			3502	626	3781	3409	6964	6934
建筑业					15	8	37100	37158
第三产业	740	1092	1448	5735	6050	10989	224343	241085
交通运输、仓储和邮政业					412	702	23089	24190
信息传输、软件和信息技术服务业					240	220	8163	10962
批发和零售业					1530	2607	54802	57475
住宿和餐饮业					678	450	27198	25823
金融业			9	3165	2999	6854	11006	7825
房地产业	722						22119	25577
租赁和商务服务业					191	156	31578	39902
科学研究、技术服务业							11523	11680
水利、环境和公共设施管理业							1962	3455
居民服务、修理和其他服务业							12347	12140
教育							8876	10111
卫生和社会工作							6396	6819
文化、体育和娱乐业							5149	4977
公共管理、社会保障和社会组织								
国际组织								

2-12 工业、建筑业企业年末城镇在岗职工人数（2015-2016年）

Number of Urban Employed Persons in Industrial and Construction Enterprises at Year-end (2015-2016)

单位：人

指　　标	2015年	2016年
工业总计	1840487	1830149
按经济类型分		
国有经济单位	615	540
城镇集体经济单位	13825	9681
其他各种经济单位	1826047	1819928
按工业行业分（大类）		
非金属矿采选业	35	35
农副食品加工业	5086	5288
食品制造业	13178	18234
酒、饮料和精制茶制造业	6462	4975
烟草制品业		
纺织业	30307	26098
纺织服装、服饰业	95983	83368
皮革、毛皮、羽毛及其制品和制鞋业	174416	128369
木材加工和木、竹、藤、棕、草制品业	1594	1682
家具制造业	53676	52754
造纸和纸制品业	40530	37867
印刷和记录媒介复制业	36396	39455
文教、工美、体育和娱乐用品制造业	132980	133986
石油加工、炼焦和核燃料加工业	230	232
化学原料和化学制品制造业	15765	16433
医药制造业	2718	2822
化学纤维制造业	1456	1335
橡胶和塑料制品业	143685	142613
非金属矿物制品业	16355	19932
黑色金属冶炼和压延加工业	5432	2808
有色金属冶炼和压延加工业	6072	6023
金属制品业	92595	100579
通用设备制造业	69757	79877
专用设备制造业	51093	66807
汽车制造业	19027	19287
铁路、船舶、航空航天和其他运输设备制造业	8024	6597
电气机械和器材制造业	184014	184981
计算机、通信和其他电子设备制造业	564126	580372
仪器仪表制造业	48194	48031
其他制造业	12082	10246
废弃资源综合利用业	54	46
电力、热力生产和供应业	3710	3660
燃气生产和供应业	940	850
水的生产和供应业	4515	4395
建筑业总计	42163	41055
国有经济单位	38	92
城镇集体经济单位	5025	3805
其他各种经济单位	37100	37158

2–13 按经济类型分行业城镇在岗职工人数及构成（2016年）

Employed Persons in Urban Areas by Registration Status and Sector (2016)

项目	合计	国有经济单位	城镇集体经济单位	其他经济单位
合计（人）	2269355	139412	31884	2098059
第一产业				
第二产业	1871092	632	13486	1856974
工业	1830149	540	9681	1819928
采矿业	35			35
制造业	1821209	519	7731	1812959
电力、热力、燃气及水的生产和供应业	8905	21	1950	6934
建筑业	41055	92	3805	37158
第三产业	398263	138780	18398	241085
交通运输、仓储和邮政业	28436	4153	93	24190
信息传输、软件和信息技术服务业	11091	129		10962
批发和零售业	59023	133	1415	57475
住宿和餐饮业	26247		424	25823
金融业	23821	10010	5986	7825
房地产业	26297	15	705	25577
租赁和商务服务业	47380	747	6731	39902
科学研究和技术服务	13041	1058	303	11680
水利、环境和公共设施管理业	4051	465	131	3455
居民服务、修理和其他服务业	12270	125	5	12140
教育	37782	27641	30	10111
卫生和社会工作	46304	36992	2493	6819
文化、体育和娱乐业	6632	1573	82	4977
公共管理、社会保障和社会组织	55520	55520		
国际组织				
各项比重（%）				
第一产业				
第二产业	82.45	0.45	42.30	88.51
工业	80.65	0.39	30.36	86.74
采矿业				0.002
制造业	80.25	0.37	24.25	86.41
电力、燃气及水的生产和供应业	0.39	0.02	6.12	0.33
建筑业	1.81	0.07	11.93	1.77
第三产业	17.55	99.55	57.70	11.49
交通运输、仓储和邮政业	1.25	2.98	0.29	1.15
信息传输、软件和信息技术服务业	0.49	0.09		0.52
批发和零售业	2.60	0.10	4.44	2.74
住宿和餐饮业	1.16		1.33	1.23
金融业	1.05	7.18	18.77	0.37
房地产业	1.16	0.01	2.21	1.22
租赁和商务服务业	2.09	0.54	21.11	1.90
科学研究和技术服务	0.57	0.76	0.95	0.56
水利、环境和公共设施管理业	0.18	0.33	0.41	0.16
居民服务、修理和其他服务业	0.54	0.09	0.02	0.58
教育	1.66	19.83	0.09	0.48
卫生和社会工作	2.04	26.53	7.82	0.33
文化、体育和娱乐业	0.29	1.13	0.26	0.24
公共管理、社会保障和社会组织	2.45	39.82		
国际组织				

主要统计指标解释

Explanatory Notes on Main Statistical Indicators

总人口数 指一定时点、一定地区范围内的有生命的个人的总和。按不同的统计范围可分为常住人口和户籍人口；统计时点通常为每年12月31日24时。

常住人口 指实际居住在某地区半年以上的人口，应抱括：1.居住在本乡、镇、街道，并已在本乡、镇街道办理常住户口登记的人；2.已在本乡、镇 、街道居住半年以上，常住户口在本乡、镇 、街道以外的人；3.在本乡、镇 、街道居住不满半年，但已离开常住户口登记地半年以上的人；4.居住在本乡、镇 、街道，常住户口待定的人；5.原住本乡、镇、街道，人口统计（或登记）时在国外工作或学习的人。

户籍人口 指公民依照《中华人民共和国户口登记条例》在公安户籍管理机关登记了常住户口的人。这类人口不管其是否外出，也不管外出时间长短，只要在某地注册有常住户口，则为该地区的户籍人口。

外来暂住人口 指户口登记地在外县、市，目前在本市暂住的人口。

性别比 反映两性人口之间比例的指标。指在总人口中或在各年龄人口中，男性人数与女性人数之比。通常用每100个女性人口相应有多少男性人口表示。

出生率（又称粗出生率） 指在一定时期（通常为一年）内活产婴儿数与同期总人口的生存人口数（或同期平均总人口、年中人口数）之比，一般用千分率表示。

死亡率（又称粗死亡率） 指在一定时期内（通常为一年）一定地区的死亡人数与同期平均人数（或期中人数）之比，一般用千分率表示。

人口自然增长率 指在一定时期内（通常为一年）人口自然增加数（出生人数减死亡人数）与该时期内平均人口数（或期中人数）之比，一般用千分率表示。

总迁移率 是反映人口迁移变动总规模的相对指标，是某地区一定时期内（通常为一年）迁入人数及迁出人数之和与同时期平均人口数之比，一般用千分率表示。

净迁移率 是反映人口迁移变动的相对指标之一，是某地区一定时期内（通常为一年）迁入与迁出相抵销后（迁入人口减迁出人口）与同时期平均总人口数之比，一般用千分率表示。

在岗职工 指在本单位工作且与本单位签订劳动合同，并由单位支付各项工资和社会保险、住房公积金的人员，以及上述人员中由于学习、病伤、产假等原因暂未工作仍由单位支付工资的人员。在岗职工还包括：

(1)应订立劳动合同而未订立劳动合同人员（如使用的农村户籍人员）；

(2)处于试用期人员；

(3)编制外招用的人员；

(4)派往外单位工作，但工资仍由本单位发放的人员（如挂职锻炼、外派工作等情况）。

三、农 业

Agriculture

3-1 主要年份农业指标

Main Indicators of Agriculture in Main Years

指　　标	单　位	1978年	1980年	1985年	1990年	1995年	2000年
乡镇从业人员	人	467757	478599	544734	598911	639985	727328
第一产业	人	390585	368322	283425	269460	202138	189349
第二产业	人	51422	94576	167116	228114	283050	362666
第三产业	人	25750	15701	94193	101337	154797	175313
年末耕地面积	亩	1183926	1177400	966725	882602	708595	663304
农业机械总动力	千瓦	248760	354250	667750	1003980	795120	586063
水利建设总投资	万元	413	927	886	5428	16900	35550
化肥施用量（实物量）	吨	113296	100776	150083	235836	124263	103570
农药施用量	吨	4276	3382	2951	3453	1924	1836
农村用电量	万千瓦时	5667	7355	14365	82545	406327	1312931
农林牧渔业总产值	万元	42394	41943	91244	236412	426901	546383
主要农产品产量							
粮　食	吨	532308	529381	488705	494259	227441	204136
糖　蔗	吨	508976	447318	526033	538712	233803	49359
花　生	吨	14157	29015	20963	13411	3724	1960
水　果	吨	26457	23688	189350	282410	243231	129367
水产品	吨	30900	25471	32641	68508	74778	95076
肉　类	吨	26920	27652	33298	62191	97572	179032
#猪　肉	吨	22790	23461	25759	40130	68649	149648
禽　蛋	吨	425	398	2424	6906	5431	4367
森林覆盖率	%			28.6	31.4	29.2	30.6

注：本表乡镇从业人员含部分外来从业人员，下同。

3-1 续表

指　　标	单　位	2005年	2010年	2015年	2016年
乡镇从业人员	人	830705	878912	963509	970192
#从事农业人员	人	110612	72856	60857	59460
年末耕地面积	亩	502937	576883	550482	546163
农业机械总动力	千瓦	229297	367988	450375	463104
水利建设总投资	万元	59437	78308	90322	90746
化肥施用量(实物量)	吨	52749	41445	28149	23498
农药施用量	吨	1090	819	757	711
农村用电量	万千瓦时	2970738	3950486	4765174	5000900
农林牧渔业总产值	万元	420496	283092	343471	384373
主要农产品产量					
粮　食	吨	20004	12482	12675	12577
花　生	吨	114	115	202	161
水　果	吨	151255	75540	62981	59410
水产品	吨	67381	76268	68946	56623
肉　类	吨	171737	28830	15168	12936
#猪　肉	吨	159169	22339	9907	8326
禽　蛋	吨	1355	386	573	312
森林覆盖率	%	33.1	36.7	37.4	37.4

注：1. 2010年起，农业机械总动力数据采用农业局统计口径，下同。
2. 2011年起，农村用电量数据采用供电局统计口径，下同。

3-2 主要年份农村经济比例和效益指标

Main Indicators of Proportions and Efficiency in Rural Economy in Main Years

指　　标	单　位	1990年	1995年	2000年	2005年	2010年	2015年	2016年
农村基层组织								
镇街政府	个	33	33	32	32	32	32	32
社区居委会、村委会	个	583	594	593	596	599	597	593
镇街户籍总户数	户	327344	364273	414007	465008	530497	567171	582644
#乡村户	户	238221	263669	299576	275988	259691	63280	63812
镇街户籍总人口	人	1318526	1436525	1526090	1656541	1817709	1950089	2009352
#乡村人口	人	1009857	1082703	1130002	998159	896789	223575	227379
乡镇从业人员	人	598911	639985	727328	830705	878912	963509	970192
按性别分								
男性	人	289258	315892	364866	427840	475996	512145	515985
女性	人	309653	324093	362462	402865	402916	451364	454207
劳动生产条件								
平均每一农业人口用电量	千瓦时	826	3778	11666	29762	44051	213135	219937
每亩耕地农业机械总动力	瓦特	1138	1122	884	455	638	818	848
平均每亩耕地化肥施用量	公斤	267	175	156	105	72	51	43
平均每亩耕地农药施用量	公斤	3.91	2.72	2.77	2.17	1.42	1.38	1.30
农林牧渔业增加值率	%		57.8	56.9	51.9	58.5	62.4	64.1
劳动生产率								
人均农林牧渔业总产值	元/人	3977	6737	7828	5062	3221	3565	3962
人均农林牧渔业增加值	元/人		3892	4453	2627	1886	2225	2538
人均粮食产量	吨/人	0.83	0.36	0.29	0.02	0.01	0.01	0.01
人均蔬菜（含菜用瓜）产量	吨/人	0.75	0.88	0.94	0.55	0.45	0.42	0.42
人均水果产量	吨/人	0.48	0.38	0.19	0.18	0.09	0.07	0.06
人均畜牧总肉产量	吨/人	0.10	0.15	0.26	0.21	0.03	0.02	0.01
#猪　肉	吨/人	0.07	0.11	0.21	0.19	0.03	0.01	0.01
人均水产品产量	吨/人	0.12	0.12	0.14	0.08	0.09	0.07	0.06

注：1.平均每亩耕地化肥施用量按化肥施用实物量计算。
　　2.按建立城乡统一的户口登记制度要求，2015年起户籍户数和人口数按城镇和乡村划分，取消原来的农业和非农业的登记统计，数据与往年不可比，下同。

3-3 主要年份农村集体(经联社、经济社两级)资产负债及收益分配

Assets, Liabilities and Income Distribution of Rural Collective Economy in Main Years

单位：亿元

指　　标	2005年	2010年	2015年	2016年
资产负债情况				
资产总额	929.60	1228.20	1436.83	1522.07
负债总额	221.56	292.15	253.69	266.06
资产负债率(%)	23.83	23.79	17.66	17.48
净资产	708.04	936.05	1183.14	1256.01
收益分配情况				
经营总收入	120.57	143.38	180.43	190.35
#销售收入	12.83	14.39	6.17	6.58
出租收入	77.02	91.65	130.21	136.28
#协作服务款	13.07	7.51	7.41	6.96
农业发包及上交收入	3.17	2.09	2.29	2.45
投资收益	5.07	7.07	15.90	17.59
其他收入	9.40	17.15	22.44	23.28
经营总费用	48.05	66.45	66.70	67.36
#销售成本	6.46	8.59	5.97	6.00
出租成本	24.05	32.62	36.78	37.80
经营税金		1.90	2.84	2.57
管理费用	9.34	12.46	11.90	12.73
其他支出	7.92	10.89	6.72	5.75
经营纯收入	72.52	76.93	113.73	122.98
收益分配总额	64.57	92.79	110.71	116.82
可弥补分配的收益总额	3.29	15.79	20.19	20.10

3-4 历年莞产农产品户籍人口人均拥有量

Per Capita Possession of Agricultural Products over Years

单位：公斤/人

年 份	粮 食		#稻 谷		蔬 菜（含菜用瓜）	
	按总人口	按乡村人口	按总人口	按乡村人口	按总人口	按乡村人口
1949	312	378	304	368		
1952	379	463	364	444		
1957	373	463	337	419		
1962	414	514	392	486		
1965	513	632	502	618		
1970	463	562	451	546		
1975	473	565	452	539		
1980	471	570	462	558	111	134
1985	408	510	397	497	260	330
1990	379	495	368	480	337	440
1995	160	211	148	196	388	515
1996	168	224	155	207	411	548
1997	169	225	155	207	436	582
1998	167	224	151	203	450	603
1999	165	222	149	200	443	597
2000	135	181	121	163	431	582
2001	83	113	71	97	459	623
2002	34	54	27	43	418	653
2003	19	30	13	20	352	549
2004	19	30	8	12	329	530
2005	12	20	7	12	278	461
2006	6	10	4	8	212	364
2007	6	10	4	7	200	351
2008	7	12	3	6	224	399
2009	7	12	4	7	224	412
2010	7	14	5	10	216	438
2011	7	14	5	10	211	431
2012	7	14	4	9	207	425
2013	7	14	3	7	203	418
2014	6	13	3	5	204	423
2015	6	57	2	18	206	1796
2016	6	55	2	15	201	1778

注：本表按户籍人口计算。按建立城乡统一的户口登记制度要求，2015年起户籍户数和人口数按城镇和乡村划分，取消原来的农业和非农业的登记统计，数据与往年不可比，下同。

3-4 续表

单位：公斤/人

年份	水果		猪肉		水产品	
	按总人口	按乡村人口	按总人口	按乡村人口	按总人口	按乡村人口
1949					5	6
1952					5	6
1957					5	7
1962					8	10
1965	53	66			12	14
1970	71	87			17	20
1975	34	41			20	24
1980	21	26	21	25	23	27
1985	158	197	21	27	27	34
1990	218	283	31	40	53	69
1995	171	226	48	64	52	70
1996	143	190	58	77	56	76
1997	113	151	68	91	63	84
1998	77	103	84	112	65	88
1999	91	122	87	117	63	84
2000	85	115	97	131	61	82
2001	98	132	109	148	58	79
2002	121	190	106	165	53	82
2003	92	143	85	133	48	74
2004	108	175	79	128	44	71
2005	91	152	96	159	41	68
2006	83	143	18	31	28	48
2007	77	135	9	15	28	48
2008	58	104	10	18	41	74
2009	51	94	11	20	41	75
2010	42	84	12	25	42	85
2011	40	82	10	21	42	87
2012	35	71	10	21	41	85
2013	32	67	9	19	39	81
2014	33	68	8	16	38	79
2015	32	282	5	44	35	308
2016	30	261	4	37	28	249

3-5 历年耕地面积

Area of Cultivated Land over Years

单位：亩

年 份	年末实有 耕地面积	当 年 新增面积	当 年 减少面积	粮食占用 耕地面积
1949	1398338			1260357
1952	1445016			1283151
1957	1435861			1199575
1962	1214417	15405	75905	1053985
1965	1199611	4142	11473	956906
1970	1203350	11359	8818	944903
1975	1193180	1246	6402	922916
1978	1183926	288	6515	874967
1979	1182292	120	1754	896347
1980	1177400	177	5069	856824
1981	1159963	279	17716	824166
1982	1146458	1086	14591	834028
1983	1121311	216	25363	837642
1984	1077659	664	44316	784763
1985	966725	1655	112589	691895
1986	889780	2350	79295	624471
1987	887369	1986	22271	618066
1988	877308	12374	22435	609332
1989	885694	13885	5499	626334
1990	882602	6991	10083	621564
1991	878980	962	4584	614994
1992	845159	100	33921	532296
1993	753746	6319	97732	391736
1994	718144	11169	46771	382238
1995	708595	12227	21776	394913
1996	674588	6270	40277	391610
1997	663013	6350	17925	382890
1998	663045	156	124	376133
1999	663122	1684	1607	381933
2000	663304	1632	1450	354980
2001	643648	4410	24066	255771
2002	500694		150	116989
2003	492433	1922	10183	81939
2004	489448	625	3610	85988
2005	502937	291	4302	76037
2006	491535		11403	34366
2007	483740		7795	32314
2008	479260	375	4855	40795
2009	516623	9	1212	41561
2010	576883	65649	5362	41922
2011	571850		5033	41461
2012	564267	12181	19621	41282
2013	560884	67	3421	41115
2014	554163	5	6326	41263
2015	550482	42	3702	42089
2016	546163	17	4336	41664

3-6 历年耕地面积变动情况

Changes of Cultivated Land over Years

单位：亩

年　份	当年增加耕地面积	#新开荒	围海造田	当年减少耕地面积	#国家基建占用	种果占用	鱼塘占用
“六五”时期累计	3900	1152		214575	6687	148244	33462
1981	279	91		17716	1275	7577	4507
1982	1086	215		14591	505	3345	8073
1983	216	135		25363	788	19590	2152
1984	664	148		44316	1122	31072	7694
1985	1655	563		112589	2997	86660	11036
“七五”时期累计	33250	2507	600	38017	9587	9138	2698
1986							
1987							
1988	12374	1199		22435	6971	5379	1871
1989	13885	651	100	5499	1433	330	151
1990	6991	657	500	10083	1183	3429	676
“八五”时期累计	30777	569	150	204784	5339	101880	44542
1991	962	95	150	4584	1463	430	57
1992	100	5		33921	1090	17435	3154
1993	6319	270		97732	808	64790	19032
1994	11169	139		46771	645	16031	16162
1995	12227	60		21776	1333	3194	6137
“九五”时期累计	16092	443	175	61383	2824	26550	9637
1996	6270	194	19	40277	532	16382	5597
1997	6350			17925	797	10168	4027
1998	156		156	124	85		
1999	1684	148		1607	128		
2000	1632	101		1450	1282		13
“十五”时期累计	7248			42311	3114	14531	5704
2001	4410			24066	1406	14434	5704
2002				150			
2003	1922			10183	1587		
2004	625			3610	121		
2005	291			4302		97	
“十一五”时期累计	66033	23627		30627			
2006				11403			
2007				7795			
2008	375			4855			
2009	9			1212			
2010	65649	23627		5362			
“十二五”时期累计	12295	251		38103			
2011				5033			
2012	12181	138		19621			
2013	67	67		3421			
2014	5	4		6326			
2015	42	42		3702			
“十三五”时期累计							
2016	17	17		4336			

3-7 历年乡镇从业人员

Towmship Employees over Years

单位：人

年 份	合 计	#从事农业人员	#男	女
1978	467757	390585		
1979	468059	373438		
1980	478599	368322	227496	251103
1981	484346	367225	231033	253313
1982	502066	360387	239398	262668
1983	512240	305715	262608	249632
1984	526766	248406	253922	272844
1985	544734	283425	260439	284295
1986	557048	277085	265132	291916
1987	571077	269984	272044	299033
1988	582425	270357	281299	301126
1989	589920	273377	281420	308500
1990	598911	269460	289258	309653
1991	601467	261271	286328	315139
1992	612142	239845	298997	313145
1993	625571	219230	311208	314363
1994	627366	200833	313942	313424
1995	639985	202138	315892	324093
1996	639492	206543	316928	322564
1997	643671	208030	320844	322827
1998	661604	205300	329713	331891
1999	668473	207432	333136	335337
2000	727328	189349	364866	362462
2001	743662	174786	377491	366171
2002	754294	151487	384417	369877
2003	851484	130930	439406	412078
2004	798954	119347	412687	386267
2005	830705	110612	427840	402865
2006	847361	92819	445915	401446
2007	837283	85246	446755	390528
2008	842933	82059	451325	390608
2009	870156	77502	468137	402019
2010	878912	72856	475996	402916
2011	913251	58767	490951	422300
2012	944317	60062	506083	438234
2013	951610	59340	509024	442586
2014	927522	56786	496671	430851
2015	963509	60857	512145	451364
2016	970192	59460	515985	454207

注：本表乡镇从业人员包含部分外来从业人员，下同。

3−8 历年农林牧渔业总产值及指数

Gross Output Value and Indices of Agriculture over Years

年　　份	农林牧渔业总产值(万元)	农业	林业	牧业	渔业	农林牧渔服务业
1978	42394	29425	312	5665	3149	
1980	41943	28054	238	6313	2878	
1985	91244	57684	759	12652	6219	
1986	122988	79251	2425	18078	8940	
1987	148414	90502	2330	23324	11930	
1988	203685	109531	4732	36915	26500	
1989	221079	117464	4316	45313	28495	
1990	236412	129032	4324	45405	31449	
1991	242587	130986	4038	47839	32640	
1992	271293	148412	5307	57163	38026	
1993	284539	130666	5489	78919	46737	
1994	347451	158315	6735	101117	60263	
1995	426901	194921	8850	128089	68547	
1996	497161	213018	9149	155112	86992	
1997	514373	232721	4383	176254	81573	
1998	536047	220614	5472	193404	93090	
1999	537442	236429	5640	197474	75495	
2000	546383	216318	3649	226293	81118	
2001	559280	228740	5309	245444	72132	
2002	536729	224452	2346	242928	67003	
2003	490206	209739	1414	203477	67276	8300
2004	441912	163246	2247	199912	67272	9235
2005	420496	107174	1746	242534	62639	6403
2006	212632	116110	3101	50638	31968	10815
2007	199782	114389	3238	38354	33562	10239
2008	255307	129962	3585	53221	60296	8243
2009	253077	131924	2232	49982	60642	8297
2010	283092	148151	2937	55499	67958	8547
2011	306621	160161	2109	63758	71450	9143
2012	320083	169305	1675	63278	76427	9398
2013	331545	189296	3626	52378	76620	9625
2014	339364	203503	3579	45138	77288	9856
2015	343471	219725	3651	36912	73180	10003
2016	384373	270134	3889	34976	65124	10250

注：绝对值按当年价格计算，指数按可比价格计算；从2003年起新增农林牧渔服务业，下同。

3-8 续表

年　份	农林牧渔业总产值(%)	农业	林业	牧业	渔业	农林牧渔服务业
指数（1978=100）						
1978	100.0	100.0	100.0	100.0	100.0	
1980	98.0	100.3	65.6	81.4	88.3	
1985	138.9	131.3	154.2	130.7	127.5	
1986	174.6	158.0	677.2	183.5	166.7	
1987	186.4	160.1	416.9	194.9	241.0	
1988	182.1	143.5	476.4	215.1	262.2	
1989	181.9	138.0	372.4	225.4	288.4	
1990	195.3	150.6	320.6	238.5	316.2	
1991	199.5	149.4	286.4	262.1	335.9	
1992	211.3	163.7	325.7	289.3	356.7	
1993	175.5	115.7	281.8	320.1	332.3	
1994	188.4	123.9	235.5	364.3	382.1	
1995	207.8	132.8	337.0	410.4	407.0	
1996	216.3	122.6	312.7	465.1	467.4	
1997	225.0	129.1	167.7	532.0	540.4	
1998	227.3	103.6	225.3	612.8	659.7	
1999	242.8	140.2	297.4	616.2	686.0	
2000	243.3	111.5	214.9	697.5	769.6	
2001	246.3	111.8	233.4	750.0	766.0	
2002	263.2	150.9	124.5	730.2	652.5	
2003	209.7	105.7	62.1	600.5	666.2	100.0
2004	213.5	118.0	123.9	563.1	647.9	108.0
2005	222.2	107.7	171.4	662.2	653.8	72.9
2006	121.0	108.3	246.6	155.2	590.7	121.2
2007	105.6	102.7	261.7	93.6	584.9	111.5
2008	118.3	106.0	286.3	109.5	899.5	84.2
2009	122.2	109.4	178.9	116.9	929.2	84.8
2010	126.2	107.6	205.2	132.2	982.2	84.8
2011	126.1	111.2	144.5	121.1	983.2	86.1
2012	126.9	108.8	111.7	125.1	1034.3	86.1
2013	125.1	111.2	240.5	107.2	1022.9	86.1
2014	126.4	118.5	236.7	94.8	981.0	86.1
2015	126.1	126.1	242.9	73.9	931.0	86.1
2016	130.0	141.7	251.6	62.7	786.7	86.3

3–9 历年农林牧渔业增加值

Added Value of Agriculture over Years

单位：万元

年　份	农林牧渔　业增加值	农业	林业	牧业	渔业	农林牧渔服务业
1978	27235	18903	200	3639	2023	
1980	26323	17606	149	3962	1806	
1985	61475	38864	511	8524	4190	
1986	81416	52463	1605	11967	5918	
1987	98236	59904	1542	15438	7897	
1988	118888	63932	2762	21547	15468	
1989	126568	67248	2471	25942	16313	
1990	132787	72474	2429	25503	17664	
1991	134523	72636	2239	26528	18100	
1992	144115	78839	2819	30366	20200	
1993	143953	66106	2777	39926	23645	
1994	174796	79645	3388	50870	30317	
1995	214306	97851	4443	64301	34411	
1996	248645	106537	4576	77576	43507	
1997	256388	115999	2185	87853	40660	
1998	259437	106773	2648	93604	45054	
1999	257863	113438	2706	94747	36222	
2000	259087	102575	1730	107305	38465	
2001	260968	106733	2477	114528	33658	
2002	248791	104041	1087	112605	31058	
2003	228165	96676	658	94708	31313	4810
2004	227087	84939	1155	102730	34569	3694
2005	218212	82306	1162	97864	34412	2468
2006	123936	83612	1913	17938	16011	4462
2007	118991	82374	1997	13586	16810	4224
2008	148250	93585	2212	18851	30202	3400
2009	147877	94998	1378	17703	30375	3423
2010	165719	106684	1812	19658	34040	3525
2011	178777	115332	1301	22583	35789	3772
2012	187556	121950	1033	22413	38282	3878
2013	199488	136350	2237	18552	38379	3970
2014	207558	146584	2208	15988	38714	4065
2015	214377	158268	2252	13074	36656	4126
2016	246214	194578	2399	12388	32621	4228

注：绝对值按当年价格计算。

3-10 历年农作物播种面积

Total Sown Area of Farm Crops over Years

单位：亩

年 份	农作物总播种面积	#粮食	#稻谷	薯类	大豆	甘蔗	花生	蔬菜(含菜用瓜)
1978	2859494	2072184	1715230	66400	36764	131200	155021	68743
1979	2585334	1937441	1676936	62537	37993	110580	185434	63959
1980	2436118	1756854	1624873	49665	39261	92397	232541	58550
1981	2267521	1606926	1525072	48999	32143	131453	264903	63768
1982	2204381	1600137	1511345	57188	35450	125787	217612	82982
1983	2193087	1635344	1530918	71430	32029	110684	152335	119370
1984	2165276	1576777	1468801	77105	31718	98449	173198	153636
1985	1950081	1395692	1293847	70997	28982	96627	159918	139795
1986	1791221	1257126	1174464	54993	31469	67920	152214	159100
1987	1795990	1250934	1165554	57850	28471	63655	130292	184744
1988	1792952	1236359	1151493	55368	27929	69694	113882	208930
1989	1834039	1284184	1199979	55964	26200	85238	101077	211217
1990	1848814	1286028	1194153	61281	26444	85977	97808	229532
1991	1791266	1226573	1138043	60107	22785	90137	85537	238418
1992	1561497	963947	889074	51273	20688	76184	67897	318193
1993	1068053	551155	499223	34449	12843	43720	39062	361826
1994	1009468	536191	482051	32615	7542	36346	25344	367122
1995	1078363	598547	527594	43346	7058	28521	24779	379362
1996	1083418	628347	559499	37989	8276	32620	20805	363331
1997	1082610	624091	560506	32629	8190	41427	18490	369113
1998	1101826	624383	558668	34799	7028	48602	16824	385151
1999	1088854	626481	558508	36329	5597	31641	14305	388173
2000	986022	527689	465616	31754	5290	7566	11969	407304
2001	854229	338467	283351	31214	3947	4610	9405	465659
2002	634205	148184	112388	18265	1983	3193	4746	445447
2003	509504	84782	54970	11154	1550	1879	2823	380252
2004	462244	81207	31108	24683	816	868	1544	350412
2005	410648	62084	34356	9390	1006	950	574	315537
2006	333854	34366	25159	4100	183	575	556	241070
2007	320500	32314	19534	5330	253	1676	340	236490
2008	352222	40352	18781	4381	443	2330	586	287618
2009	370740	41421	18629	5047	140	4144	838	306270
2010	369257	41922	26124	3192		2944	713	300622
2011	366840	41461	26412	4247	418	2395	456	297537
2012	372455	41282	23675	8044	901	2434	930	303778
2013	367808	41115	17974	12484	1088	1733	1025	303783
2014	366082	41263	13713	17035	1242	1050	1152	304555
2015	374491	42089	11056	21177	2122	1301	922	313509
2016	376451	41664	9250	23702	1903	775	764	313071

注：2010年及以前年份，粮食数据不含大豆，下同。

3-11　历年农作物产量

Total Output of Farm Crops over Years

单位：吨

年　份	粮食	#稻谷	薯类	大豆	甘蔗	花生	蔬菜（含菜用瓜）
1978	532308	501074	6458	1948	511492	14157	135603
1979	535342	516263	6568	1982	366424	19100	127918
1980	529381	518591	5432	2245	449907	29015	124859
1981	447540	439534	6318	1722	678160	35506	132846
1982	543349	532998	8430	2162	707764	29930	123117
1983	561246	548073	11345	1875	553174	19662	168878
1984	558216	545548	10946	1980	569225	23076	230454
1985	488705	476399	10304	1771	556983	20963	314539
1986	455243	443760	9422	2050	382608	20056	427138
1987	462830	451032	10058	1920	378094	17019	414261
1988	460929	448923	9950	1965	420391	15119	412436
1989	487648	474476	11052	2023	528463	13746	410879
1990	494259	479350	12452	2184	557102	13411	444377
1991	473663	458425	12998	1838	619884	11510	446204
1992	368083	354298	11070	1763	543657	9323	523806
1993	202097	192018	7366	1035	343133	5594	572376
1994	202356	189688	7929	668	313851	3678	537442
1995	227441	210876	10758	647	246707	3724	557807
1996	243204	224469	11271	806	285732	3120	597732
1997	246901	227163	11487	811	354420	2879	641403
1998	247194	223938	13916	758	411555	2588	668753
1999	247287	223403	14580	566	242773	2204	668822
2000	204136	183485	9730	610	54095	1960	658196
2001	128366	109881	9920	426	33387	1556	706775
2002	53732	42508	5420	244	20224	865	653272
2003	30500	20423	3415	215	8019	395	560523
2004	30374	12230	9803	138	4763	216	532116
2005	20004	11941	2733	147	4433	114	460204
2006	10040	7548	1314	31	3167	99	356347
2007	9864	6467	1732	48	10834	73	342703
2008	11902	6007	1381	95	15286	130	391192
2009	11912	6560	1437	19	23044	113	400335
2010	12482	8768	668		15952	115	392904
2011	12890	9137	888	53	14239	78	389014
2012	12476	8357	1609	162	13032	281	386603
2013	12435	6450	3171	145	9452	241	382619
2014	12406	4965	4674	186	5369	211	390484
2015	12675	4106	6030	325	6982	202	401640
2016	12577	3430	6871	307	4091	161	404297

3-12 主要年份农作物播种面积、亩产及总产量

Sown Area, Yield Per Acreage and Total Output of Farm Crops in Main Years

单位：亩、公斤/亩、吨

指　标	1978年			1985年			1990年		
	播种面积	亩产	总产量	播种面积	亩产	总产量	播种面积	亩产	总产量
粮食作物	2072184	257	532308	1395692	350	488705	1286028	384	494259
按品种分									
稻谷	1715230	292	501074	1293847	368	476399	1194153	401	479350
旱粮	290554	85	24776	30848	65	2002	30594	80	2457
薯类	66400	97	6458	70997	145	10304	61281	203	12452
大豆	36764	53	1948	28982	61	1771	26444	83	2184
按季节分									
春收				30978	131	4042	33352	174	5790
夏收	1127790	248	279552	649856	377	244755	614059	399	244890
#早稻	814852	309	251907	620409	389	241413	587821	410	241018
秋收	944394	268	252757	714858	336	239907	638617	381	243579
#晚稻	900378	277	249167	673438	349	234985	606332	393	238332
经济作物				306406			209120		
#甘蔗	131200	3899	511492	96627	5765	556983	85977	6480	557102
糖蔗	130676	3895	508976	91884	5725	526033	83246	6471	538712
果蔗	524	4802	2516	4743	6525	30950	2731	6734	18390
油料作物				160186	131	20974	97808	137	13411
#花生	155021	91	14157	159918	131	20963	97808	137	13411
其他作物				219001			327222		
#蔬菜（含菜用瓜）	68743	1973	135603	139795	2250	314539	229532	1936	444377

3-12 续表 1

单位：亩、公斤/亩、吨

指 标	1995年			2000年			2005年		
	播种面积	亩产	总产量	播种面积	亩产	总产量	播种面积	亩产	总产量
粮食作物	598547	380	227441	527689	387	204136	62084	322	20004
按品种分									
稻谷	527594	400	210876	465616	394	183485	34356	348	11941
旱粮	27607	210	5807	30319	360	10921	18338	291	5330
薯类	43346	248	10758	31754	306	9730	9390	291	2733
大豆	7058	92	647	5290	115	610	1006	146	147
按季节分									
春收	17880	224	4008	20787	287	5966	9665	312	3019
夏收	282978	388	109914	245110	392	96015	23286	306	7136
#早稻	255886	405	103592	225985	397	89729	14713	351	5164
秋收	297689	381	113519	261792	390	102155	29133	338	9850
#晚稻	271708	395	107284	239631	391	93756	19643	345	6777
经济作物	62092			35221			18011		
#甘蔗	28521	8650	246707	7566	7150	54095	950	4666	4433
糖蔗	26488	8827	233803	6775	7285	49359	55	8182	450
果蔗	2033	6347	12904	791	5987	4736	895	4450	3983
油料作物	24779	150	3724	11969	164	1960	574	199	114
#花生	24779	150	3724	11969	164	1960	574	199	114
其他作物	410666			417822			329547		
#蔬菜（含菜用瓜）	379362	1470	557807	407304	1616	658196	315537	1458	460204

3-12 续表 2

单位：亩、公斤/亩、吨

指　　标	2010年			2015年			2016年		
	播种面积	亩产	总产量	播种面积	亩产	总产量	播种面积	亩产	总产量
粮食作物	41922	298	12482	42089	301	12675	41664	302	12577
按品种分									
稻谷	26124	336	8768	11056	371	4106	9250	371	3430
旱粮	12606	242	3046	7734	286	2214	6764	290	1960
薯类	3192	209	668	21177	285	6030	23702	290	6871
大豆				2122	153	325	1903	161	307
按季节分									
春收	5202	221	1150	6740	266	1794	7818	275	2153
夏收	17948	306	5501	17296	295	5104	16863	307	5180
#早稻	12017	330	3965	5574	372	2073	4498	372	1673
秋收	18772	311	5831	18575	316	5864	16983	309	5244
#晚稻	14107	340	4803	5482	371	2033	4752	370	1757
经济作物	14084			15545					
#甘蔗	2944	5418	15952	1301	5367	6982	775	5279	4091
果蔗	2844	5328	15152	1301	5367	6982	775	5279	4091
油料作物	713	161	115	922	219	202	764	211	161
#花生	713	161	115	922	219	202	764	211	161
其他作物	313251			316857			315648		
#蔬菜（含菜用瓜）	300622	1307	392904	313509	1281	401640	313071	1291	404297

3-13 主要年份农机总动力、水利、化肥、农药及农村用电量

Basic Statistics on Total Power of Agricultural Machinery, Water Conservancy, Consumption of Chemical Fertilizers and Pesticides, and Electricity Consumed in Rural Areas in Main Years

指　　标	单 位	1978年	1990年	1995年	2000年	2005年	2010年	2015年	2016年
农业机械总动力	千瓦	248760	1003980	795120	586063	229297	367988	450375	463104
#耕作机械	千瓦	42550	157910	83482	51848	16386	24079	25863	25446
排灌机械	千瓦	104050	178280	112392	91745	36251	99716	124388	124412
收获机械	千瓦	6180	84130	54722	51084	969	2280	766	766
运输机械	千瓦	16930	322950	397735	184949	41678	12463	20806	18146
水利建设总投资	万元	413	5428	16900	35550	59437	78308	90322	90746
化肥施用实物量	吨	113296	235836	124263	103570	52749	41445	28149	23498
氮肥	吨	86371	84642	43441	30214	14439	10214	6336	5775
磷肥	吨	23164	52483	28939	23939	10967	8055	5842	4169
钾肥	吨	3761	26131	16915	14606	6403	5030	3466	3057
复合肥	吨		39098	34968	34811	20940	18146	12505	10497
农药施用量	吨	4276	3453	1924	1836	1090	819	757	711
农村用电量	万千瓦时	5667	82545	406327	1312931	2970738	3950486	4765174	5000900
平均每一农业人口用电量	千瓦时		826	3778	11666	29762	44051	213135	219937

注：农业机械总动力数据从2010年起采用农业局统计口径，数据与往年不可比，下同。

3-14 历年水果面积及产量

Planted Area and Output of Fruits over Years

年份	年末种植水果面积(亩)	#香(大)蕉	荔枝	水果总产量(吨)	#香(大)蕉	荔枝
1978	93245	18828	46678	26457	18867	4959
1979	91021	17977	46697	23346	12165	8667
1980	88444	15582	46743	23688	10894	7884
1981	97468	18042	48230	46909	25513	15599
1982	114730	28439	50669	58196	40872	7042
1983	159260	39749	63349	77225	42079	20724
1984	235311	66506	84183	105851	69186	14714
1985	407416	125998	115428	189350	133503	19304
1986	609347	171168	168820	307743	210439	18577
1987	609569	158874	175366	363085	222826	17439
1988	548482	99256	176979	263710	126655	7699
1989	476598	54867	164782	221418	69410	6165
1990	452729	54185	160355	282410	73555	16994
1991	440442	56481	154456	343155	85702	6201
1992	420661	81331	139584	344751	97986	22972
1993	360130	86299	117557	271346	80982	717
1994	325336	67595	121236	264875	92072	12703
1995	322876	62351	142370	243231	86466	23324
1996	326291	59822	159403	206276	77768	14804
1997	319556	57583	188220	165016	80355	22572
1998	310873	46377	208899	114106	78978	2885
1999	285514	48975	198144	136317	82169	35218
2000	297618	71454	189862	129367	108913	9107
2001	275428	86578	156019	150115	132292	7059
2002	209924	76764	109948	189343	135209	45339
2003	199634	82024	95812	146414	130688	9012
2004	183375	84812	80115	175389	150669	18312
2005	176845	75452	83357	151255	123986	21026
2006	173470	73493	81395	139582	124601	8615
2007	163448	66904	80313	131571	116833	10107
2008	178337	64141	94953	101541	86817	8498
2009	177281	52761	103364	91544	75341	10240
2010	170536	47420	100136	75540	60236	8266
2011	167667	42874	101458	73866	55291	11032
2012	178746	36661	118158	64916	51883	6333
2013	194327	34951	133793	61144	46701	7910
2014	198288	31704	140915	62475	43439	11500
2015	195885	31038	138273	62981	43019	11280
2016	198870	31085	138981	59410	43123	5492

3-15 历年林业生产

Basic Statistics on Forestry Production over Years

年 份	林业用地面积（亩）	#杉	松	桉	当年育苗面积（亩）	当年幼林抚育面积（亩）	当年四旁植树（万株）
1978	700570	63994	541492	49008	485	32900	44
1979	705764	67104	543210	50439	880	14900	30
1980	740052	70665	568729	56272	316	9500	15
1981	743697	67236	584674	49994	133	12500	12
1982	698715	63730	535072	52925	500	11945	19
1983	769893	67423	574171	56724	361	40464	17
1984	739402	66107	552721	58092	501	106982	16
1985	761460				801	120000	150
1986	706823	61438	510042	60581	33231	210540	22
1987	714664	57824	526254	75498	1728	53759	35
1988	729896	59351	512451	90998	3667	70275	37
1989	691944	53293	490370	103887	2101	64950	58
1990	709240	47054	484397	133706	3464	56647	54
1991	709306	44432	459015	148127	609	53827	63
1992	662919	39326	422527	149944	762	60764	49
1993	628612	36213	400816	144346	677	28511	57
1994	1016138	43815	382482	129473	2492	28127	34
1995	1015223	43661	360591	125133	4273	25130	48
1996	1014972	9654	248288	115878	699	21000	133
1997	1014954	8843	235410	113928	823	23745	218
1998	1014876	8367	222147	112005	387	36000	417
1999	1009965	10890	221585	133500	506	29863	522
2000	1009037	29940	526797	280618	625	47145	425
2001	1007298	9678	189930	133464	705	45000	357
2002	900335	8265	187665	138525	516	46500	98
2003	890877	6540	66206	105666	420	38910	147
2004	980942				255	60000	625
2005	934700	3086	2860	100145	195	61005	253
2006	930162	3716	60890	162125	15	25320	480
2007	926760	3870	62363	149440	255	43320	600
2008	923097	3873	59864	145340	255	49571	610
2009	921000	3719	58375	143690	610	56545	60
2010	909900	3719	56987	142971	285	37278	18
2011	905370	3719	56801	141945	345	41085	22
2012	902927	2934	41480	99353	360	35790	19
2013	902148	3719	56433	144674	390	39920	309
2014	803735	1091	10821	101783	885	39810	316
2015	803735	1091	10821	101783	906	31403	320
2016	733000	323	7915	40172	456	31021	344

3-16 历年畜牧业生产及产品产量

Production of Animal Husbandry and Output of Livestock Products over Years

年 份	牛年末存栏量（头）	羊年末存栏量（头）	生 猪饲养量（头）	生 猪存栏量（头）	生 猪出栏量（头）	三 鸟饲养量（万只）	三 鸟出栏量（万只）	畜 牧总肉量（吨）	#猪肉	禽 蛋总产量（吨）
1978	53004		1018060	672919	345141	428	219	26920	22790	425
1979	50595		995408	626435	368973	379	187	29209	25647	367
1980	53385		799568	501380	298188	420	209	27652	23461	444
1981	58619		703659	449638	254021	476	252	28011	23387	1284
1982	64067		791518	526106	265412	568	309	33037	27374	679
1983	69117		842198	489887	352311	630	370	35695	28872	1256
1984	70992		784473	458804	325669	652	369	33260	26301	1899
1985	62763		790505	471268	319237	832	414	33298	25759	2424
1986	62874		812102	428545	383557	940	655	43302	30920	5159
1987	58577		781957	396082	385875	1235	862	46120	32588	5478
1988	54723		811945	402035	409910	1400	1020	56125	35067	6734
1989	52713		846598	407317	439281	1565	1136	58563	38270	7109
1990	48760	1559	870782	410875	459907	1592	1188	62191	40130	6906
1991	44121	1396	930377	420919	509458	1806	1336	68844	44702	5924
1992	32259	1068	981698	448586	533112	1889	1419	67983	45492	5845
1993	18688	783	982084	404352	577732	2185	1647	76562	49470	4990
1994	14219	863	1089793	434904	654889	2334	1730	85448	57920	5521
1995	12207	1593	1250597	469355	781242	2501	1881	97572	68649	5431
1996	12945	1806	1407080	490161	916919	2418	1851	116058	83404	5862
1997	12675	2391	1772892	619114	1153778	2608	1863	128992	99300	6295
1998	10522	2159	2217247	776851	1440396	2291	1742	153513	123874	4738
1999	6811	1508	2573310	900285	1673025	2228	1667	159889	130494	4742
2000	5550	1675	2894126	967056	1927070	2362	1784	179032	149648	4367
2001	4618	1851	3255780	1079397	2176383	2226	1683	198423	168353	4441
2002	2919	1931	3075523	927477	2148046	1962	1557	188774	165344	4052
2003	1727	1789	2525252	742101	1783151	1652	1282	154615	135344	3597
2004	1024	1936	2444990	785289	1659701	1396	1048	146184	128286	3435
2005	827	998	2487962	214120	2273842	1314	1072	171737	159169	1355
2006	82	242	530959	110396	420563	485	312	34891	30199	371
2007	399	415	292234	88648	203586	525	341	20257	14862	361
2008	55		454117	195016	259101	758	574	24052	17946	106
2009	94		464727	183904	280823	767	576	25457	19095	515
2010	224	60	511356	174933	336423	761	591	28830	22339	386
2011	200	50	455875	176805	279070	706	547	26010	19074	643
2012	28	80	428781	142454	286327	733	577	26726	19570	842
2013	25	30	298476	65977	232499	576	448	22829	16965	1057
2014	25	1335	285531	77291	208240	528	408	20068	14844	1130
2015	1164	853	199573	63005	136568	488	376	15168	9907	573
2016	769	889	177402	62463	114939	434	355	12936	8326	312

注：牛年末存栏量1978年至2014年为耕牛数量，2015年起为“肉牛年末存栏量”。

3-17 历年水产品产量及养殖面积

Output and Cultured Area of Aquatic Products over Years

年 份	水产品产量(吨)	海水产量	海水捕捞	海水养殖	淡水产量	淡水捕捞	淡水养殖	养殖面积(亩)	海水养殖	淡水养殖
1978	30900	23307	23307		7593		7593	89040		89040
1979	22309	13878	13878		8431		8431	94916		94916
1980	25471	17069	17069		8402		8402	95549		95549
1981	24905	15669	15669		9236		9236	104069		104069
1982	27695	16120	16120		11575		11575	112586		112586
1983	30292	17330	17330		12962		12962	116943		116943
1984	32465	18025	18025		14440		14440	119456		119456
1985	32641	15422	15214	208	17219		17219	131350	5301	126049
1986	46534	28439	25918	2521	18095		18095	138651	16078	122573
1987	65679	45214	42793	2421	20465		20465	163225	15036	148189
1988	68087	44111	42926	1185	23976	182	23794	137966	9670	128296
1989	62306	37189	35372	1817	25117	1194	23923	123090	10350	112740
1990	68508	41002	38423	2579	27506	2177	25329	136174	19286	116888
1991	69025	39906	37209	2697	29119	2147	26972	131849	18446	113403
1992	73164	42429	38033	4396	30735	2590	28145	134558	20400	114158
1993	64973	33745	28192	5553	31228	3120	28108	143696	25855	117841
1994	67420	31284	24059	7225	36136	2565	33571	144869	26583	118286
1995	74778	32132	24637	7495	42646	2084	40562	162609	27795	134814
1996	81067	33363	25471	7892	47704	1940	45764	172656	27791	144865
1997	91901	35407	26704	8703	56494	5157	51337	184889	30326	154563
1998	96872	33618	24319	9299	63254	3146	60108	192381	29223	163158
1999	94023	31332	24257	7075	62691	2747	59944	167880	19440	148440
2000	95076	33234	24180	9054	61842	3135	58707	167841	25695	142146
2001	89599	30877	23726	7151	58722	2285	56437	155720	27928	127792
2002	82361	30800	23474	7326	51561	2762	48799	142167	26696	115471
2003	75756	30151	22826	7325	45605	2121	43484	126660	27097	99563
2004	71526	29289	22382	6907	42237	3078	39159	125116	25652	99464
2005	67381	28319	21622	6697	39062	1783	37279	102023	23530	78493
2006	47059	21152	15256	5897	25907	1062	24845	71745	6345	65400
2007	47292	21637	15992	5645	25655	857	24797	71100	5925	65175
2008	72282	21297	14322	6975	50985	512	50473	137718	17559	120159
2009	73323	19034	13205	5829	54289		54289	129136	4197	124939
2010	76268	19300	13257	6043	56968	1563	55405	132960	4147	128813
2011	78229	17816	12255	5561	60413	1801	58612	118676	3473	115203
2012	76967	17131	11664	5467	59836	1513	58323	131640	10175	121465
2013	74526	14672	10783	3889	59854	1494	58360	144005	9395	134610
2014	72660	13838	9386	4452	58822	1442	57380	137818	9114	128704
2015	68946	12662	8375	4287	56284	1560	54724	128550	8850	119700
2016	56623	7817	6422	1395	48806	1392	47414	7056	258	6797

3-18 主要农产品产量与最高年份比较（2016年）

Output of Main Agricultural Products in Comparison with Peak Year (2016)

指　　标	单位	2016年	建国以来最高年份		
			年　份	产　量	2016年为最高年份的(%)
粮食总产量	吨	12577	1977	563463	2.2
#稻　谷	吨	3430	1973	548073	0.6
#早　稻	吨	1673	1983	279723	0.6
晚　稻	吨	1757	1984	279898	0.6
大　豆	吨	307	1954	2790	11.0
经济作物					
#甘　蔗	吨	4091	1982	707764	0.6
花　生	吨	161	1981	35506	0.5
其他作物					
#蔬　菜（含菜用瓜）	吨	404297	2001	706775	57.2
水果总产量	吨	59410	1987	363085	16.4
#香（大）蕉	吨	43123	1987	222826	19.4
荔　枝	吨	5492	2002	45339	12.1
水产品	吨	56623	1998	96872	58.5
生猪年末存栏量	头	62463	2001	1079397	5.8
生猪年出栏头数	头	114939	2005	2273842	5.1
猪肉产量	吨	8326	2001	168353	5.0
三鸟饲养量	万只	434	2000	2362	18.4
三鸟出栏量	万只	355	2000	1784	19.9
禽蛋产量	吨	312	1989	7109	4.4

主要统计指标解释

Explanatory Notes on Main Statistical Indicators

耕地面积 指可以用来种植农作物、经常进行耕锄的田地，包括熟地、当年新开荒地、连续撂荒未满三年的耕地和当年的休闲地(轮歇地)，还包括以种植农作物为主并附带种植桑树、茶树、果树和其他林木的土地，以及沿海、沿湖地区已围垦利用的“海涂”、“湖田”等面积。不包括属于专业性的桑园、茶园、果园、果木苗圃、林地、芦苇地、天然或人工草地面积。

农作物播种面积 指实际播种或移植有农作物的面积。凡是实际种植有农作物的面积，不论种植在耕地上还是种植在非耕地上，均包括在农作物播种面积中。在播种季节基本结束后，因遭灾而重新改种和补种的农作物面积，也包括在内。

粮食产量 指全社会的产量。包括国有经济经营的、集体统一经营的和农民家庭经营的粮食产量，还包括工矿企业办的农场和其他生产单位的产量。粮食除包括稻谷、小麦、玉米、高粱、谷子及其他杂粮外，还包括薯类和豆类。其产量计算方法，豆类按去豆荚后的干豆计算；薯类(包括甘薯和马铃薯，不包括芋头和木薯)1963年以前按每4公斤鲜薯折1公斤粮食计算，从1964年开始改为按5公斤鲜薯折1公斤粮食计算。城市郊区作为蔬菜的薯类(如马铃薯等)按鲜品计算，并且不作粮食统计。其他粮食一律按脱粒后的原粮计算。

水产品产量 指人工养殖的水产品和天然生长的水产品的捕捞量。包括海水的鱼类、虾蟹类、贝类和藻类以及内陆水域的鱼类、虾蟹类和贝类，不包括淡水生植物。

猪、牛、羊肉产量 指当年出栏并已屠宰、除去头蹄下水后带骨肉(即胴体重)的重量。

期初(末)畜禽存栏头(只)数 指报告期初(末)农村各种合作经济组织和国营农场、农民个人、机关、团体、学校、工矿企业、部队等单位以及城镇居民饲养的大牲畜、猪、羊、家禽等畜禽的存栏数。

农林牧渔业总产值 指以货币表现的农、林、牧、渔业全部产品的总量，它反映一定时期内农业生产总规模和总成果。农业总产值的计算方法通常是按农林牧渔业产品及其副产品的产量分别乘以各自单位产品价格求得；少数生产周期较长，当年没有产品或产品产量不易统计的，则采用间接方法匡算其产值；然后将四业产品产值相加即为农业总产值。

农业机械总动力 指主要用于农、林、牧、渔业的各种动力机械的动力总和。包括耕作机械、排灌机械、收获机械、农用运输机械、植物保护机械、牧业机械、林业机械、渔业机械和其他农业机械〔内燃机按引擎马力折成瓦(特)计算、电动机按功率折成瓦(特)计算〕。不包括专门用于乡、镇、村、组办工业、基本建设、非农业运输、科学试验和教学等非农业生产方面用的动力机械与作业机械。

四、工 业

Industry

4-1 主要年份工业主要指标

Main Indicators of Industry in Main Years

指　　　标	单位	1998年	2000年	2005年	2010年	2015年	2016年
全市工业企业单位数	个	16406	16975	21868	38273	97944	121762
全市工业增加值	万元	2906904	4304525	11732288	21094155	28403504	30892562
规模以上工业：							
企业单位数	个	1500	1663	4505	5899	5688	5869
年末固定资产原值合计	万元	6257040	7288486	18560858	32162507	43550738	47012949
年末固定资产	万元	4392164	4701886	11052566	17836928	22538217	23833905
年末流动资产	万元	3798813	5298239	18732801	37888251	61892638	74454397
年末资产总额	万元	9267121	11225950	33453291	60017098	91346482	106760526
年末负债总额	万元	4752964	5630399	18580908	35252952	53699190	64354878
所有者权益	万元	4514157	5595551	14872383	24750103	37005020	42437530
工业增加值	万元	1687134	2594352	10624190	17083110	26119633	29681560
主营业务收入	万元	6399088	9889058	39121487	77081695	124542179	148896282
利润总额	万元	255715	503589	1243516	3523632	4075012	5027329
全员劳动生产率（按增加值计算）	元/人	26688	36101	53340	60854	102756	118291
综合效益指数	%	94.1	114.0	119.9	130.3	148.7	159.8

注：1. 2005年以前数据根据东莞市第一次经济普查取得，2008年数据根据第二次经济普查取得，下同。
2. 规模以上工业企业1997年及以前年份为独立核算工业企业口径，1998—2005年为全部国有工业及年销售收入500万元以上非国有工业企业口径，2006—2010年为年主营业务收入500万元及以上工业企业口径，2011年起为年主营业务收入2000万元及以上的工业企业口径,下同。

4-2 历年工业企业单位数（按经济成份分）

Number of Industrial Enterprises over Years (by Ownership)

单位：个

年 份	全市工业企业单位数	国有	集体企业	外商企业	其他类型企业
1949	1	1			
1952	23	20	3		
1957	262	76	186		
1962	280	57	223		
1965	260	61	199		
1970	220	57	163		
1975	324	61	263		
1978	1290	64	1226		
1979	1250	63	1187		
1980	1293	64	1229		
1981	1479	64	1415		
1982	1862	66	1796		
1983	1964	68	1896		
1984	2329	69	2109		151
1985	4187	73	2990	79	1045
1986	5949	81	4263	89	1516
1987	8106	74	5123	175	2734
1988	8408	72	5424	241	2671
1989	8757	76	5835	323	2523
1990	9892	78	6165	525	3124
1991	10094	77	6404	758	2855
1992	11639	72	6400	936	4231
1993	12449	75	7129	1412	3833
1994	14086	45	7185	2193	4663
1995	15215	70	9345	2841	2959
1996	15326	40	8958	2381	3947
1997	16857	41	9949	2379	4488
1998	16406	29	8814	2511	5052
1999	16877	29	10325	3358	3165
2000	16975	23	10184	3610	3158
2001	18094	20	9978	4791	3305
2002	21313	19	198	11737	9359
2003	21935	19	200	11927	9789
2004	22156	13	211	10872	11060
2005	21868	10	220	12234	9404
2006	22447	10	211	12461	9765
2007	22587	16	151	12569	9851
2008	26372	35	484	7611	18242
2009	31160	26	313	7580	23241
2010	38273	21	262	7864	30126
2011	46413	20	215	8676	37502
2012	57808	20	254	8965	48569
2013	67332	17	222	9151	57942
2014	80567	16	194	8911	71446
2015	97944	15	138	8978	88813
2016	121762	14	170	8987	112591

注：本表来源于市工商局,2002年起集体企业不包括“三来一补”企业。

4-3 主要年份工业企业单位数（按不同类型分）

Number of Industrial Enterprises in Main Years (by Ownership)

单位：个

指　　标	1998年	2000年	2005年	2010年	2015年	2016年
全市企业单位数	16406	16975	21868	38273	97944	121762
轻工业	14389	14440	12651	20651	50091	60663
重工业	2017	2535	9217	17622	47853	61099
在总计中：						
（一）规模以上工业企业	1500	1663	4505	5899	5688	5869
按轻重工业分						
轻工业	1082	1124	2569	3183	2909	2924
重工业	418	539	1936	2716	2779	2945
按登记注册类型分						
国有	29	16	5	10	2	2
集体	204	248	162	151	31	27
私营	24	44	621	1159	1434	1566
联营	5	6	2	5		
股份合作	9	6	1	2		
股份有限公司	6	3	18	20	84	116
外商投资	134	201	820	1321	1057	991
港澳台商投资	1082	1119	2481	2564	1918	1889
其他	7	20	395	667	1162	1278
按企业规模分						
大型企业	16	28	39	84	240	266
中型企业	27	19	579	1327	1701	1638
小型企业	1457	1616	3887	4488	3557	3760
微型企业					190	205
（二）规模以下工业企业	14906	15312	17363	32374	92256	115893

注：2011年起采用新的企业规模划分标准，共分大型、中型、小型、微型四类企业规模，下同。

4-4 历年工业增加值

Value-added of Industry over Years

年 份	工业增加值	
	绝对值（万元）	增速（%）
1986	105398	
1987	142357	25.8
1988	250456	51.4
1989	272185	6.4
1990	391840	30.6
1991	483441	21.8
1992	566316	13.7
1993	828934	38.5
1994	1107729	24.3
1995	1541922	35.3
1996	1878517	16.2
1997	2307863	20.1
1998	2906904	22.2
1999	3495304	20.7
2000	4304525	20.9
2001	5170314	22.0
2002	6218553	23.0
2003	7571849	21.4
2004	9680128	26.5
2005	11732288	20.2
2006	14416864	22.0
2007	16818293	15.0
2008	18192243	6.4
2009	17544607	0.1
2010	21094155	18.0
2011	23397456	8.1
2012	23664869	6.4
2013	25426000	12.1
2014	27089969	9.3
2015	28403504	6.3
2016	30892562	8.9

注：本表工业增加值绝对值为当年价，增速按可比价计算。

4-5 规模以上工业企业单位数（2016年）

Number of Industrial Enterprises above Designated Size (2016)

单位：个

项　　目	工业单位数	按登记注册类型分		
		内资企业	港澳台商投资企业	外商投资企业
总　　计	5869	2989	1889	991
按轻重工业分				
轻工业	2924	1477	1028	419
重工业	2945	1512	861	572
按企业规模分				
大型企业	266	70	130	66
中型企业	1638	529	741	368
小型企业	3760	2260	975	525
微型企业	205	130	43	32
按工业行业分（大类）				
煤炭开采和洗选业				
石油和天然气开采业				
黑色金属矿采选业				
有色金属矿采选业				
非金属矿采选业	1	1		
开采辅助活动				
其他采矿业				
农副食品加工业	53	38	5	10
食品制造业	44	27	14	3
酒、饮料和精制茶制造业	14	7	4	3
烟草制品业				
纺织业	112	49	54	9
纺织服装、服饰业	380	246	113	21
皮革、毛皮、羽毛及其制品和制鞋业	323	138	118	67
木材加工和木、竹、藤、棕、草制品业	31	20	7	4
家具制造业	298	204	56	38
造纸和纸制品业	202	138	55	9
印刷和记录媒介复制业	120	51	53	16
文教、工美、体育和娱乐用品制造业	271	86	139	46
石油加工、炼焦和核燃料加工业	4	1	3	
化学原料和化学制品制造业	205	129	43	33
医药制造业	12	8	2	2
化学纤维制造业	14	5	6	3
橡胶和塑料制品业	631	281	246	104
非金属矿物制品业	125	81	29	15
黑色金属冶炼和压延加工业	27	13	8	6
有色金属冶炼和压延加工业	69	37	16	16
金属制品业	383	202	128	53
通用设备制造业	260	149	69	42
专用设备制造业	278	162	74	42
汽车制造业	58	21	14	23
铁路、船舶、航空航天和其他运输设备制造业	32	17	5	10
电气机械和器材制造业	642	305	218	119
计算机、通信和其他电子设备制造业	1064	468	337	259
仪器仪表制造业	98	39	39	20
其他制造业	52	17	22	13
废弃资源综合利用业	2	2		
金属制品、机械和设备修理业	3	2	1	
电力、热力生产和供应业	17	5	10	2
燃气生产和供应业	6	2	1	3
水的生产和供应业	38	38		

4-6 规模以上工业增加值（2016年）

Value-added of Industrial Enterprises above Designated Size (2016)

单位：万元

项　　目	工业增加值	按登记注册类型分		
		内资企业	港澳台商投资企业	外商投资企业
总　计	29681560	12889889	10642678	6148993
按轻重工业分				
轻工业	11625350	4280755	5245233	2099362
重工业	18056210	8609135	5397445	4049631
按企业规模分				
大型企业	14083746	6470838	4911219	2701689
中型企业	9047990	2927746	3798297	2321946
小型企业	6149127	3328097	1722149	1098881
微型企业	400697	163208	211013	26476
按工业行业分（大类）				
煤炭开采和洗选业				
石油和天然气开采业				
黑色金属矿采选业				
有色金属矿采选业				
非金属矿采选业	1064	1064		
开采辅助活动				
其他采矿业				
农副食品加工业	332801	194278	51636	86887
食品制造业	356848	70368	275002	11478
酒、饮料和精制茶制造业	154114	32465	15051	106597
烟草制品业				
纺织业	425009	79443	244515	101051
纺织服装、服饰业	1227205	683892	469268	74046
皮革、毛皮、羽毛及其制品和制鞋业	1113079	283685	516373	313021
木材加工和木、竹、藤、棕、草制品业	61984	36756	6765	18464
家具制造业	702653	389332	195083	118238
造纸和纸制品业	1358548	515503	798401	44644
印刷和记录媒介复制业	511372	143382	261073	106916
文教、工美、体育和娱乐用品制造业	1086306	241472	691342	153492
石油加工、炼焦和核燃料加工业	24157	2834	21323	
化学原料和化学制品制造业	602866	229376	192416	181074
医药制造业	78729	83705	-9078	4102
化学纤维制造业	20261	9377	8626	2259
橡胶和塑料制品业	1798561	625718	849939	322905
非金属矿物制品业	526032	216062	254339	55631
黑色金属冶炼和压延加工业	108577	51550	36055	20973
有色金属冶炼和压延加工业	115769	54072	39038	22659
金属制品业	1510960	613362	684809	212788
通用设备制造业	1055046	403832	369201	282014
专用设备制造业	972592	496604	356757	119232
汽车制造业	468539	93258	52527	322754
铁路、船舶、航空航天和其他运输设备制造业	137006	33187	48389	55430
电气机械和器材制造业	2424343	853769	1018190	552385
计算机、通信和其他电子设备制造业	9887848	4840678	2600335	2446834
仪器仪表制造业	511988	91763	205948	214277
其他制造业	100154	29094	54282	16778
废弃资源综合利用业	1459	1459		
金属制品、机械和设备修理业	5481	3796	1686	
电力、热力生产和供应业	1789319	1356698	329369	103252
燃气生产和供应业	87163	4332	4020	78811
水的生产和供应业	123725	123725		

4-7 规模以上工业企业主要财务指标（2016年）

Main Financial Indicators of Industrial Enterprises above Designated Size (2016)

单位：万元

指标	全市总计	按登记注册类型分			按轻重工业分	
		内资企业	港澳台商投资企业	外商投资企业	轻工业	重工业
企业单位数（个）	5869	2989	1889	991	2924	2945
年末资产						
流动资产合计	74454397	37569848	23323940	13560610	26395023	48059374
#产成品存货	5519184	2761375	1741257	1016552	2259730	3259454
固定资产净值	23035106	10033368	8675896	4325843	8307128	14727977
年末资产总额	106760526	52334305	35219928	19206293	38359577	68400949
年末负债及所有者权益						
年末负债总额	64354878	37250197	17531244	9573437	21057887	43296991
所有者权益合计	42437530	14953831	17770013	9713685	17252140	25185390
损益及分配						
主营业务收入	148896282	79165656	41394064	28336562	46150157	102746124
主营业务成本	131097348	69818393	36201956	25076999	39736575	91360773
主营业务税金及附加	476901	213900	155970	107031	194344	282556
主营业务利润	17322034	9133363	5036138	3152532	6219238	11102795
销售费用	3403971	1982317	895742	525911	1534775	1869196
管理费用	8166344	3917566	2694085	1554694	3007569	5158775
财务费用	397436	334827	58215	4394	156072	241364
#利息支出	555999	309391	157219	89388	208700	347299
利润总额	5027329	2318972	1609275	1099082	1685254	3342075
亏损企业亏损总额	605300	135999	256317	212985	275494	329806

4-8 规模以上工业企业主要指标（2016年）

Main Indicators of Industrial Enterprises above Designated Size (2016)

单位：万元

项　　目	企业单位数（个）	#亏损企业	工业销售产值	工　业增加值
总　　计	5869	804	143507573	29681560
按轻重工业分				
轻工业	2924	416	45396501	11625350
重工业	2945	388	98111072	18056210
按企业规模分				
大型企业	266	26	80198406	14083746
中型企业	1638	208	34502697	9047990
小型企业	3760	487	27135905	6149127
微型企业	205	83	1670566	400697
按工业行业分（大类）				
煤炭开采和洗选业				
石油和天然气开采业				
黑色金属矿采选业				
有色金属矿采选业				
非金属矿采选业	1		3965	1064
开采辅助活动				
其他采矿业				
农副食品加工业	53	10	3542719	332801
食品制造业	44	7	1105202	356848
酒、饮料和精制茶制造业	14	3	804100	154114
烟草制品业				
纺织业	112	16	1416607	425009
纺织服装、服饰业	380	55	4587657	1227205
皮革、毛皮、羽毛及其制品和制鞋业	323	54	3072307	1113079
木材加工和木、竹、藤、棕、草制品业	31	8	227529	61984
家具制造业	298	29	2753434	702653
造纸和纸制品业	202	19	6082398	1358548
印刷和记录媒介复制业	120	15	1539531	511372
文教、工美、体育和娱乐用品制造业	271	44	3710404	1086306
石油加工、炼焦和核燃料加工业	4		64376	24157
化学原料和化学制品制造业	205	24	2970620	602866
医药制造业	12	2	236082	78729
化学纤维制造业	14		112900	20261
橡胶和塑料制品业	631	80	6536509	1798561
非金属矿物制品业	125	16	1876066	526032
黑色金属冶炼和压延加工业	27	5	508398	108577
有色金属冶炼和压延加工业	69	14	1018834	115769
金属制品业	383	41	4261998	1510960
通用设备制造业	260	32	5745697	1055046
专用设备制造业	278	29	3229664	972592
汽车制造业	58	4	1593641	468539
铁路、船舶、航空航天和其他运输设备制造业	32	7	517947	137006
电气机械和器材制造业	642	77	10006781	2424343
计算机、通信和其他电子设备制造业	1064	175	67046980	9887848
仪器仪表制造业	98	18	1388644	511988
其他制造业	52	8	352848	100154
废弃资源综合利用业	2	1	6859	1459
金属制品、机械和设备修理业	3		9416	5481
电力、热力生产和供应业	17	4	6492331	1789319
燃气生产和供应业	6		348977	87163
水的生产和供应业	38	7	336154	123725

4-8 续表 1

(2016年)

单位：万元

项目	年末资产合计	#流动资产合计	#产成品	固定资产合计	年末负债合计
总计	106760526	74454397	5519184	23833905	64354878
按轻重工业分					
轻工业	38359577	26395023	2259730	8659251	21057887
重工业	68400949	48059374	3259454	15174654	43296991
按企业规模分					
大型企业	52001080	35701408	2255199	12333707	32747115
中型企业	29605159	20437739	1862317	6657856	16106889
小型企业	23569450	17161032	1347597	4629019	14565940
微型企业	1584836	1154218	54072	213323	934934
按工业行业分（大类）					
煤炭开采和洗选业					
石油和天然气开采业					
黑色金属矿采选业					
有色金属矿采选业					
非金属矿采选业	4277	1515		2762	745
开采辅助活动					
其他采矿业					
农副食品加工业	2325111	1627317	172813	477896	1669517
食品制造业	1148620	754979	47910	320527	609820
酒、饮料和精制茶制造业	676477	339263	16945	229434	403351
烟草制品业					
纺织业	1637594	1192452	105002	389124	592925
纺织服装、服饰业	4173751	3327420	323669	438406	2370460
皮革、毛皮、羽毛及其制品和制鞋业	2134699	1664614	169747	330717	1354696
木材加工和木、竹、藤、棕、草制品业	207157	146364	13101	33246	154727
家具制造业	1922722	1512266	161078	270074	1133523
造纸和纸制品业	5948401	2886351	182256	2445768	2821975
印刷和记录媒介复制业	1653263	1193600	57081	363091	757181
文教、工美、体育和娱乐用品制造业	2499795	1900147	261194	422340	1441102
石油加工、炼焦和核燃料加工业	74704	64426	9012	4373	43543
化学原料和化学制品制造业	2571147	1903346	149251	397481	1301197
医药制造业	675137	261602	8293	96038	276561
化学纤维制造业	81439	54146	4337	23279	43505
橡胶和塑料制品业	5544914	3798834	328825	1121646	3006143
非金属矿物制品业	2287629	1295430	74509	733784	1187557
黑色金属冶炼和压延加工业	361628	276366	35960	71098	211840
有色金属冶炼和压延加工业	648584	545713	44801	75390	415962
金属制品业	4335188	2775009	202241	1337308	2249378
通用设备制造业	4042525	3071310	269880	706010	2531778
专用设备制造业	3159972	2295436	247767	612253	1644205
汽车制造业	1445620	936074	47892	339398	714148
铁路、船舶、航空航天和其他运输设备制造业	804480	569055	37843	180259	572867
电气机械和器材制造业	9151472	6974944	550329	1464089	4786390
计算机、通信和其他电子设备制造业	37523160	30277322	1902913	5340788	27137201
仪器仪表制造业	1169162	697998	56990	310145	450835
其他制造业	305753	200970	17959	81992	143671
废弃资源综合利用业	17257	10429	693	6339	6857
金属制品、机械和设备修理业	21010	8993	1503	11497	14761
电力、热力生产和供应业	6790061	1433795	16349	4518025	3345581
燃气生产和供应业	311113	76633		198347	148033
水的生产和供应业	1106705	380278	1041	480983	812844

4-8 续表 2

(2016年)

单位：万元

项　　目	主营业务收入	主营业务税金及附加	成本费用总额	本年应交增值税
总　计	148896282	476901	146053231	2758748
按轻重工业分				
轻工业	46150157	194344	44864201	881599
重工业	102746124	282556	101189030	1877149
按企业规模分				
大型企业	84557788	216660	83375058	1666972
中型企业	34478119	151961	33462438	550937
小型企业	28291264	100733	27552242	506905
微型企业	1569111	7546	1663492	33933
按工业行业分（大类）				
煤炭开采和洗选业				
石油和天然气开采业				
黑色金属矿采选业				
有色金属矿采选业				
非金属矿采选业	3389	167	1489	508
开采辅助活动				
其他采矿业				
农副食品加工业	4502763	1758	4667708	19870
食品制造业	1123668	9349	1035154	60490
酒、饮料和精制茶制造业	792231	14747	781517	40320
烟草制品业				
纺织业	1418822	6382	1385736	16336
纺织服装、服饰业	4372448	19128	4172757	118059
皮革、毛皮、羽毛及其制品和制鞋业	3051383	16443	3055389	32033
木材加工和木、竹、藤、棕、草制品业	231985	942	226166	6674
家具制造业	2802221	12915	2737767	51663
造纸和纸制品业	6063912	20879	5801125	213178
印刷和记录媒介复制业	1547238	6790	1464272	30795
文教、工美、体育和娱乐用品制造业	3690209	15560	3605096	22309
石油加工、炼焦和核燃料加工业	61079	1092	59724	1554
化学原料和化学制品制造业	2946117	12234	2749804	73883
医药制造业	238915	2360	213591	12229
化学纤维制造业	116514	429	113057	2643
橡胶和塑料制品业	6627186	26879	6449874	126428
非金属矿物制品业	1864668	9127	1772190	48359
黑色金属冶炼和压延加工业	504476	1337	493859	9904
有色金属冶炼和压延加工业	957596	1557	977742	8095
金属制品业	4307274	19579	4173936	90221
通用设备制造业	5731257	16734	5565493	51780
专用设备制造业	3237782	15944	3058635	81641
汽车制造业	1598233	8268	1459541	48848
铁路、船舶、航空航天和其他运输设备制造业	529835	2470	512498	7960
电气机械和器材制造业	9957840	42538	9537023	132375
计算机、通信和其他电子设备制造业	71608357	146989	71351453	1117672
仪器仪表制造业	1376043	6070	1322847	12072
其他制造业	361800	1731	359224	2373
废弃资源综合利用业	6859	71	8121	25
金属制品、机械和设备修理业	12206	66	12053	546
电力、热力生产和供应业	6576850	33453	6322532	296440
燃气生产和供应业	345522	1260	293166	9759
水的生产和供应业	329604	1656	312697	11708

4-8 续表 3

(2016年)

项　　目	亏损企业亏损总额（万元）	全部从业人员平均人数（人）	利润总额（万元）	人均利润（元）
总　计	605300	2509208	5027329	20036
按轻重工业分				
轻工业	275494	1199882	1685254	14045
重工业	329806	1309326	3342075	25525
按企业规模分				
大型企业	151166	929517	2732290	29395
中型企业	201205	1048716	1352355	12895
小型企业	188491	527951	866013	16403
微型企业	64438	3024	76671	253543
按工业行业分（大类）				
煤炭开采和洗选业				
石油和天然气开采业				
黑色金属矿采选业				
有色金属矿采选业				
非金属矿采选业		35	1733	495229
开采辅助活动				
其他采矿业				
农副食品加工业	35658	8804	55567	63116
食品制造业	13406	19474	73217	37597
酒、饮料和精制茶制造业	48284	7365	12079	16401
烟草制品业				
纺织业	7237	39942	58138	14556
纺织服装、服饰业	13735	152110	188418	12387
皮革、毛皮、羽毛及其制品和制鞋业	45776	176873	1400	79
木材加工和木、竹、藤、棕、草制品业	615	4761	6941	14579
家具制造业	13957	83621	69506	8312
造纸和纸制品业	3973	59407	346151	58268
印刷和记录媒介复制业	6035	49995	97148	19432
文教、工美、体育和娱乐用品制造业	24031	167241	68217	4079
石油加工、炼焦和核燃料加工业		243	2537	104403
化学原料和化学制品制造业	5682	27057	198453	73346
医药制造业	282	3399	41372	121719
化学纤维制造业		2852	4234	14845
橡胶和塑料制品业	43204	187447	207412	11065
非金属矿物制品业	16743	36064	103957	28826
黑色金属冶炼和压延加工业	1168	7117	14754	20731
有色金属冶炼和压延加工业	5255	9384	14870	15846
金属制品业	18014	131260	187267	14267
通用设备制造业	14302	95283	233901	24548
专用设备制造业	16062	87031	192064	22068
汽车制造业	2494	24821	146948	59203
铁路、船舶、航空航天和其他运输设备制造业	2826	10846	27025	24917
电气机械和器材制造业	24965	257861	465581	18056
计算机、通信和其他电子设备制造业	189855	763761	1612564	21113
仪器仪表制造业	19302	52313	56422	10786
其他制造业	4585	12670	2451	1934
废弃资源综合利用业	918	123	-776	-63106
金属制品、机械和设备修理业		251	660	26307
电力、热力生产和供应业	22799	23716	452641	190859
燃气生产和供应业		871	62766	720618
水的生产和供应业	4139	5210	21712	41673

4–9 规模以上工业企业主要经济效益指标（2016年）

Main Indicators on Economic Benefit of Industrial Enterprises above Designated Size (2016)

项　　目	工业增加值率(%)	总资产贡献率(%)	资　产负债率(%)	流动资产周转率(次/年)	成本费用利润率(%)	全员劳动生产率(元/人)	产　品销售率(%)
总　　计	20.2	8.1	60.3	2.0	3.4	118291	97.7
按轻重工业分							
轻工业	24.9	7.6	54.9	1.8	3.8	96887	97.2
重工业	18.0	8.3	63.3	2.2	3.3	137905	97.9
按企业规模分							
大型企业	17.2	9.1	63.0	2.4	3.3	151517	97.8
中型企业	25.6	7.4	54.4	1.7	4.0	86277	97.5
小型企业	22.1	6.7	61.8	1.7	3.1	116472	97.4
微型企业	24.7	7.5	59.0	1.5	4.6	1325056	103.0
按工业行业分（大类）							
煤炭开采和洗选业							
石油和天然气开采业							
黑色金属矿采选业							
有色金属矿采选业							
非金属矿采选业	26.8	56.3	17.4	2.2	116.4	303969	100.0
开采辅助活动							
其他采矿业							
农副食品加工业	9.3	3.9	71.8	2.9	1.2	378011	99.4
食品制造业	31.0	13.1	53.1	1.5	7.1	183243	96.0
酒、饮料和精制茶制造业	18.7	10.6	59.6	2.4	1.6	209252	97.4
烟草制品业							
纺织业	29.1	5.1	36.2	1.2	4.2	106406	96.9
纺织服装、服饰业	24.2	8.3	56.8	1.3	4.5	80679	90.4
皮革、毛皮、羽毛及其制品和制鞋业	35.5	2.5	63.5	1.8	0.1	62931	97.9
木材加工和木、竹、藤、棕、草制品业	26.6	7.9	74.7	1.6	3.1	130191	97.7
家具制造业	25.1	7.1	59.0	1.9	2.5	84028	98.5
造纸和纸制品业	22.0	10.5	47.4	2.1	6.0	228685	98.6
印刷和记录媒介复制业	33.1	8.4	45.8	1.3	6.6	102285	99.7
文教、工美、体育和娱乐用品制造业	29.0	5.0	57.7	2.0	1.9	64955	99.0
石油加工、炼焦和核燃料加工业	38.3	8.7	58.3	1.0	4.3	994132	102.0
化学原料和化学制品制造业	19.8	11.5	50.6	1.6	7.2	222813	97.4
医药制造业	32.2	8.4	41.0	0.9	19.4	231624	96.4
化学纤维制造业	17.2	9.4	53.4	2.2	3.7	71043	95.6
橡胶和塑料制品业	26.6	6.7	54.2	1.8	3.2	95950	96.5
非金属矿物制品业	27.8	7.6	51.9	1.5	5.9	145861	99.0
黑色金属冶炼和压延加工业	21.2	7.6	58.6	1.9	3.0	152561	99.4
有色金属冶炼和压延加工业	11.2	4.2	64.1	1.8	1.5	123369	98.8
金属制品业	34.0	7.3	51.9	1.6	4.5	115112	95.8
通用设备制造业	18.1	7.7	62.6	1.9	4.2	110728	98.6
专用设备制造业	29.3	9.4	52.0	1.4	6.3	111752	97.1
汽车制造业	28.7	14.5	49.4	1.7	10.1	188767	97.6
铁路、船舶、航空航天和其他运输设备制造业	26.4	5.6	71.2	1.0	5.3	126319	99.8
电气机械和器材制造业	23.5	7.1	52.3	1.4	4.9	94017	96.8
计算机、通信和其他电子设备制造业	14.5	7.7	72.3	2.4	2.3	129463	98.1
仪器仪表制造业	36.5	6.6	38.6	2.0	4.3	97870	99.0
其他制造业	27.2	2.2	47.0	1.8	0.7	79048	95.7
废弃资源综合利用业	21.6	-3.2	39.7	0.7	-9.6	118615	101.6
金属制品、机械和设备修理业	41.2	6.8	70.3	1.4	5.5	218386	70.7
电力、热力生产和供应业	27.1	12.6	49.3	4.7	7.2	754478	98.2
燃气生产和供应业	24.8	24.1	47.6	4.6	21.4	1000719	99.4
水的生产和供应业	36.1	5.1	73.5	0.9	6.9	237475	98.0

4-10 规模以上国有及国有控股工业企业主要经济指标（2016年）

Main Indicators of State-owned and State-holding Industrial Enterprises above Designated Size (2016)

项　　目	企业单位数（个）	#亏损企业	工业增加值（万元）	主营业务收入（万元）
总　计	35	5	1916731	7852728
按轻重工业分				
轻工业	18	2	258251	1593392
重工业	17	3	1658479	6259337
按企业规模分				
大型企业	4	1	1447859	5784717
中型企业	11		199708	898176
小型企业	18	4	88620	770579
微型企业	2		180544	399256
按销售收入分				
10亿元以上	7	1	1646601	7044342
5-10亿元	8		201563	558322
1-5亿元	9	1	62049	198076
1亿元以下	11	3	6518	51988
按工业行业分（大类）				
煤炭开采和洗选业				
石油和天然气开采业				
黑色金属矿采选业				
有色金属矿采选业				
非金属矿采选业				
开采辅助活动				
其他采矿业				
农副食品加工业	3		49636	947375
食品制造业	1	1	-5810	1402
酒、饮料和精制茶制造业	2		7055	57493
烟草制品业				
纺织业				
纺织服装、服饰业	1		4749	14163
皮革、毛皮、羽毛及其制品和制鞋业				
木材加工和木、竹、藤、棕、草制品业				
家具制造业				
造纸和纸制品业				
印刷和记录媒介复制业	1		964	6266
文教、工美、体育和娱乐用品制造业	2		2416	17705
石油加工、炼焦和核燃料加工业				
化学原料和化学制品制造业	1		425	4380
医药制造业				
化学纤维制造业				
橡胶和塑料制品业	1		1365	5444
非金属矿物制品业				
黑色金属冶炼和压延加工业	1		7347	48243
有色金属冶炼和压延加工业	1	1	429	3728
金属制品业	2	1	21567	74512
通用设备制造业	2	1	128441	385855
专用设备制造业				
汽车制造业				
铁路、船舶、航空航天和其他运输设备制造业	1		32810	106872
电气机械和器材制造业	2		7750	27155
计算机、通信和其他电子设备制造业	2		45098	128955
仪器仪表制造业				
其他制造业				
废弃资源综合利用业				
金属制品、机械和设备修理业				
电力、热力生产和供应业	6	1	1547053	5870336
燃气生产和供应业				
水的生产和供应业	6		65434	152846

4−10 续表

(2016年)

项　　目	亏损企业亏损总额(万元)	利润总额(万元)	人均利润(元)
总　计	18729	416725	100244
按轻重工业分			
轻工业	12622	31471	19381
重工业	6107	385254	152076
按企业规模分			
大型企业	1311	256107	80309
中型企业		33814	47280
小型企业	17417	1363	6821
微型企业		125441	2362362
按销售收入分			
10亿元以上	1311	359169	115887
5−10亿元		56802	96866
1−5亿元	5683	5113	18847
1亿元以下	11734	-4359	-21783
按工业行业分（大类）			
煤炭开采和洗选业			
石油和天然气开采业			
黑色金属矿采选业			
有色金属矿采选业			
非金属矿采选业			
开采辅助活动			
其他采矿业			
农副食品加工业		7459	112510
食品制造业	11311	-11311	-280658
酒、饮料和精制茶制造业		1114	26336
烟草制品业			
纺织业			
纺织服装、服饰业		1953	44086
皮革、毛皮、羽毛及其制品和制鞋业			
木材加工和木、竹、藤、棕、草制品业			
家具制造业			
造纸和纸制品业			
印刷和记录媒介复制业		603	67011
文教、工美、体育和娱乐用品制造业		4153	84574
石油加工、炼焦和核燃料加工业			
化学原料和化学制品制造业		632	191606
医药制造业			
化学纤维制造业			
橡胶和塑料制品业		417	69433
非金属矿物制品业			
黑色金属冶炼和压延加工业		431	74259
有色金属冶炼和压延加工业	202	-202	-12374
金属制品业	222	4837	267260
通用设备制造业	1311	5608	5634
专用设备制造业			
汽车制造业			
铁路、船舶、航空航天和其他运输设备制造业		1028	9187
电气机械和器材制造业		225	1593
计算机、通信和其他电子设备制造业		25808	80674
仪器仪表制造业			
其他制造业			
废弃资源综合利用业			
金属制品、机械和设备修理业			
电力、热力生产和供应业	5683	360596	173380
燃气生产和供应业			
水的生产和供应业		13374	64205

4-11 规模以上国有及国有控股工业企业主要经济效益指标（2016年）

Main Indicators on Economic Benefit of State-owned and State-holding Industrial Enterprises above Designated Size (2016)

项目	工业增加值率(%)	总资产贡献率(%)	资产负债率(%)	流动资产周转率(次/年)	成本费用利润率(%)	全员劳动生产率(元/人)	产品销售率(%)
总计	25.8	10.8	54.1	3.4	5.6	461074	98.6
按轻重工业分							
轻工业	22.7	4.4	71.1	1.9	2.0	159041	100.9
重工业	26.3	12.4	50.0	4.3	6.5	654672	98.2
按企业规模分							
大型企业	25.1	11.5	52.6	7.3	4.6	454017	99.5
中型企业	22.8	5.4	62.0	1.0	3.9	279234	102.1
小型企业	23.6	3.2	61.1	2.6	0.2	443542	75.4
微型企业	44.0	36.5	30.4	1.2	46.2	3400069	100.0
按工业行业分（大类）							
煤炭开采和洗选业							
石油和天然气开采业							
黑色金属矿采选业							
有色金属矿采选业							
非金属矿采选业							
开采辅助活动							
其他采矿业							
农副食品加工业	10.2	2.7	71.5	3.2	0.8	748659	105.2
食品制造业	-74.1	-29.4	87.7	0.3	-81.7	-144165	19.9
酒、饮料和精制茶制造业	12.7	9.3	31.0	4.6	2.0	166787	99.8
烟草制品业							
纺织业							
纺织服装、服饰业	31.9	11.4	34.1	1.1	16.0	107207	95.0
皮革、毛皮、羽毛及其制品和制鞋业							
木材加工和木、竹、藤、棕、草制品业							
家具制造业							
造纸和纸制品业							
印刷和记录媒介复制业	15.9	10.8	23.8	1.6	10.2	107134	98.0
文教、工美、体育和娱乐用品制造业	15.2	52.9	15.8	1.8	31.0	49216	102.2
石油加工、炼焦和核燃料加工业							
化学原料和化学制品制造业	21.2	50.3	31.2	4.5	16.6	128667	140.0
医药制造业							
化学纤维制造业							
橡胶和塑料制品业	26.1	13.3	21.1	1.4	8.2	227573	103.9
非金属矿物制品业							
黑色金属冶炼和压延加工业	15.2	7.4	73.8	3.5	0.9	1266784	100.0
有色金属冶炼和压延加工业	10.9	-0.5	59.0	0.8	-5.1	26334	94.6
金属制品业	25.2	-1.7	93.8	1.3	6.9	1191533	88.8
通用设备制造业	34.4	2.5	85.2	1.2	1.5	129034	100.6
专用设备制造业							
汽车制造业							
铁路、船舶、航空航天和其他运输设备制造业	30.6	2.8	80.2	0.3	1.0	293208	98.8
电气机械和器材制造业	24.5	3.4	61.2	0.9	0.8	54965	88.0
计算机、通信和其他电子设备制造业	28.7	18.9	56.7	1.8	20.3	140977	82.1
仪器仪表制造业							
其他制造业							
废弃资源综合利用业							
金属制品、机械和设备修理业							
电力、热力生产和供应业	26.3	13.4	45.5	6.0	6.5	743847	98.7
燃气生产和供应业							
水的生产和供应业	40.1	7.1	71.1	1.2	9.4	314133	97.5

4-12 规模以上集体工业企业主要经济指标（2016年）

Main Indicators of Collective-owned Industrial Enterprises above Designated Size (2016)

项目	企业单位数(个)	#亏损企业	工业增加值(万元)	主营业务收入(万元)
总计	27	6	79814	180341
按轻重工业分				
轻工业	26	6	79659	177665
重工业	1		154	2676
按企业规模分				
大型企业	1		23549	41051
中型企业	2		13983	16917
小型企业	24	6	42282	122373
微型企业				
按销售收入分				
10亿元以上				
5-10亿元				
1-5亿元	5		46621	88325
1亿元以下	22	6	33193	92015
按工业行业分（大类）				
煤炭开采和洗选业				
石油和天然气开采业				
黑色金属矿采选业				
有色金属矿采选业				
非金属矿采选业				
开采辅助活动				
其他采矿业				
农副食品加工业				
食品制造业				
酒、饮料和精制茶制造业				
烟草制品业				
纺织业				
纺织服装、服饰业				
皮革、毛皮、羽毛及其制品和制鞋业	1		3045	5421
木材加工和木、竹、藤、棕、草制品业				
家具制造业				
造纸和纸制品业				
印刷和记录媒介复制业	1		960	2587
文教、工美、体育和娱乐用品制造业	2		34487	52547
石油加工、炼焦和核燃料加工业				
化学原料和化学制品制造业	1		154	2676
医药制造业				
化学纤维制造业				
橡胶和塑料制品业				
非金属矿物制品业				
黑色金属冶炼和压延加工业				
有色金属冶炼和压延加工业				
金属制品业				
通用设备制造业				
专用设备制造业				
汽车制造业				
铁路、船舶、航空航天和其他运输设备制造业				
电气机械和器材制造业				
计算机、通信和其他电子设备制造业				
仪器仪表制造业				
其他制造业				
废弃资源综合利用业				
金属制品、机械和设备修理业				
电力、热力生产和供应业				
燃气生产和供应业				
水的生产和供应业	22	6	41168	117110

4-12 续表

(2016年)

项　　目	亏损企业亏损总额（万元）	利润总额（万元）	人均利润（元）
总　计	1063	11627	11194
按轻重工业分			
轻工业	1063	11588	11244
重工业		39	4778
按企业规模分			
大型企业		1088	1997
中型企业		3787	14190
小型企业	1063	6752	29769
微型企业			
按销售收入分			
10亿元以上			
5-10亿元			
1-5亿元		9128	11014
1亿元以下	1063	2499	11901
按工业行业分（大类）			
煤炭开采和洗选业			
石油和天然气开采业			
黑色金属矿采选业			
有色金属矿采选业			
非金属矿采选业			
开采辅助活动			
其他采矿业			
农副食品加工业			
食品制造业			
酒、饮料和精制茶制造业			
烟草制品业			
纺织业			
纺织服装、服饰业			
皮革、毛皮、羽毛及其制品和制鞋业		116	3061
木材加工和木、竹、藤、棕、草制品业			
家具制造业			
造纸和纸制品业			
印刷和记录媒介复制业		470	111929
文教、工美、体育和娱乐用品制造业		4759	6150
石油加工、炼焦和核燃料加工业			
化学原料和化学制品制造业		39	4778
医药制造业			
化学纤维制造业			
橡胶和塑料制品业			
非金属矿物制品业			
黑色金属冶炼和压延加工业			
有色金属冶炼和压延加工业			
金属制品业			
通用设备制造业			
专用设备制造业			
汽车制造业			
铁路、船舶、航空航天和其他运输设备制造业			
电气机械和器材制造业			
计算机、通信和其他电子设备制造业			
仪器仪表制造业			
其他制造业			
废弃资源综合利用业			
金属制品、机械和设备修理业			
电力、热力生产和供应业			
燃气生产和供应业			
水的生产和供应业	1063	6243	29103

4−13 规模以上集体工业企业主要经济效益指标（2016年）

Main Indicators on Economic Benefit of Collective-owned Industrial Enterprises above Designated Size (2016)

项　　目	工业增加值率(%)	总资产贡献率(%)	资　产负债率(%)	流动资产周转率(次/年)	成本费用利润率(%)	全员劳动生产率(元/人)	产　品销售率(%)
总　　计	44.6	4.3	73.1	0.9	6.8	76840	98.9
按轻重工业分							
轻工业	45.2	4.3	73.2	0.9	6.9	77294	98.9
重工业	5.8	10.2	54.6	2.3	1.5	19060	100.0
按企业规模分							
大型企业	57.4	6.2	95.6	13.2	2.7	43209	100.0
中型企业	82.3	35.2	18.9	1.7	28.6	52391	100.0
小型企业	34.9	3.4	73.6	0.7	5.8	186428	98.4
微型企业							
按工业行业分（大类）							
煤炭开采和洗选业							
石油和天然气开采业							
黑色金属矿采选业							
有色金属矿采选业							
非金属矿采选业							
开采辅助活动							
其他采矿业							
农副食品加工业							
食品制造业							
酒、饮料和精制茶制造业							
烟草制品业							
纺织业							
纺织服装、服饰业							
皮革、毛皮、羽毛及其制品和制鞋业	55.4	5.2	71.6	4.2	2.2	80129	100.0
木材加工和木、竹、藤、棕、草制品业							
家具制造业							
造纸和纸制品业							
印刷和记录媒介复制业	32.8	12.7	5.8	0.9	18.8	228459	100.0
文教、工美、体育和娱乐用品制造业	65.6	18.3	66.0	4.6	10.0	44562	100.0
石油加工、炼焦和核燃料加工业							
化学原料和化学制品制造业	5.8	10.2	54.6	2.3	1.5	19060	100.0
医药制造业							
化学纤维制造业							
橡胶和塑料制品业							
非金属矿物制品业							
黑色金属冶炼和压延加工业							
有色金属冶炼和压延加工业							
金属制品业							
通用设备制造业							
专用设备制造业							
汽车制造业							
铁路、船舶、航空航天和其他运输设备制造业							
电气机械和器材制造业							
计算机、通信和其他电子设备制造业							
仪器仪表制造业							
其他制造业							
废弃资源综合利用业							
金属制品、机械和设备修理业							
电力、热力生产和供应业							
燃气生产和供应业							
水的生产和供应业	35.7	3.2	74.4	0.7	5.6	191926	98.4

4-14 规模以上外商投资工业企业主要经济指标（2016年）

Main Indicators of Industrial Enterprises above Designated Size with Foreign Funds (2016)

项目	企业单位数（个）	#亏损企业	工业增加值（万元）	主营业务收入（万元）
总计	991	181	6148993	28336562
按轻重工业分				
轻工业	419	85	2099362	9127141
重工业	572	96	4049631	19209421
按企业规模分				
大型企业	66	7	2701689	13419180
中型企业	368	65	2321946	9374621
小型企业	525	92	1098881	5357416
微型企业	32	17	26476	185345
按销售收入分				
10亿元以上	49	5	2601872	15019980
5-10亿元	42	6	779663	2863805
1-5亿元	345	56	1965719	7506258
1亿元以下	555	114	801739	2946520
按工业行业分（大类）				
煤炭开采和洗选业				
石油和天然气开采业				
黑色金属矿采选业				
有色金属矿采选业				
非金属矿采选业				
开采辅助活动				
其他采矿业				
农副食品加工业	10	5	86887	1371580
食品制造业	3	1	11478	27314
酒、饮料和精制茶制造业	3		106597	360787
烟草制品业				
纺织业	9	1	101051	352945
纺织服装、服饰业	21	4	74046	222036
皮革、毛皮、羽毛及其制品和制鞋业	67	11	313021	901343
木材加工和木、竹、藤、棕、草制品业	4	1	18464	62605
家具制造业	38	5	118238	500935
造纸和纸制品业	9	3	44644	135784
印刷和记录媒介复制业	16	4	106916	271988
文教、工美、体育和娱乐用品制造业	46	11	153492	456365
石油加工、炼焦和核燃料加工业				
化学原料和化学制品制造业	33	3	181074	978316
医药制造业	2	1	4102	12880
化学纤维制造业	3		2259	13562
橡胶和塑料制品业	104	21	322905	1427650
非金属矿物制品业	15	4	55631	185883
黑色金属冶炼和压延加工业	6	1	20973	129458
有色金属冶炼和压延加工业	16	5	22659	167941
金属制品业	53	6	212788	661263
通用设备制造业	42	8	282014	1772544
专用设备制造业	42	4	119232	344213
汽车制造业	23	1	322754	1131592
铁路、船舶、航空航天和其他运输设备制造业	10	2	55430	190581
电气机械和器材制造业	119	13	552385	2131254
计算机、通信和其他电子设备制造业	259	60	2446834	13193490
仪器仪表制造业	20	4	214277	665274
其他制造业	13	2	16778	57005
废弃资源综合利用业				
金属制品、机械和设备修理业				
电力、热力生产和供应业	2		103252	298601
燃气生产和供应业	3		78811	311374
水的生产和供应业				

4-14 续表

(2016年)

项目	亏损企业亏损总额(万元)	利润总额(万元)	人均利润(元)
总计	212985	1099082	19517
按轻重工业分			
轻工业	99041	262530	11367
重工业	113944	836552	25184
按企业规模分			
大型企业	51609	527412	22545
中型企业	85919	360927	14762
小型企业	56483	224934	26707
微型企业	18974	-14191	-296263
按销售收入分			
10亿元以上	45066	678286	38923
5-10亿元	21077	155643	26010
1-5亿元	94251	236003	11049
1亿元以下	52591	29151	2525
按工业行业分(大类)			
煤炭开采和洗选业			
石油和天然气开采业			
黑色金属矿采选业			
有色金属矿采选业			
非金属矿采选业			
开采辅助活动			
其他采矿业			
农副食品加工业	29149	7995	41816
食品制造业	1213	3633	43199
酒、饮料和精制茶制造业		53058	416791
烟草制品业			
纺织业	2	20579	22378
纺织服装、服饰业	794	4620	3968
皮革、毛皮、羽毛及其制品和制鞋业	16026	713	119
木材加工和木、竹、藤、棕、草制品业	40	4756	37445
家具制造业	10200	-1243	-738
造纸和纸制品业	962	6939	26038
印刷和记录媒介复制业	4108	16955	17881
文教、工美、体育和娱乐用品制造业	12684	-1602	-661
石油加工、炼焦和核燃料加工业			
化学原料和化学制品制造业	543	63457	99681
医药制造业	166	211	13245
化学纤维制造业		1019	20264
橡胶和塑料制品业	17191	43966	12950
非金属矿物制品业	7624	2776	6546
黑色金属冶炼和压延加工业	383	4228	54690
有色金属冶炼和压延加工业	1855	-176	-774
金属制品业	824	31133	20739
通用设备制造业	3444	60700	23787
专用设备制造业	2913	31083	33767
汽车制造业	1461	116692	77004
铁路、船舶、航空航天和其他运输设备制造业	715	19336	38819
电气机械和器材制造业	6070	95388	15464
计算机、通信和其他电子设备制造业	91803	359131	16038
仪器仪表制造业	2742	38807	23090
其他制造业	73	644	2533
废弃资源综合利用业			
金属制品、机械和设备修理业			
电力、热力生产和供应业		56628	3852224
燃气生产和供应业		57659	733578
水的生产和供应业			

4−15 规模以上外商投资工业企业主要经济效益指标（2016年）

Main Indicators on Economic Benefit of Industrial Enterprises above Designated Size with Foreign Funds (2016)

项　　目	工业增加值率 (%)	总资产贡献率 (%)	资　产负债率 (%)	流动资产周转率 (次/年)	成本费用利润率 (%)	全员劳动生产率 (元/人)	产　品销售率 (%)
总　　计	21.5	7.9	49.9	2.1	4.0	109193	98.2
按轻重工业分							
轻工业	23.2	6.8	49.7	2.1	2.9	90898	98.1
重工业	20.7	8.4	49.9	2.1	4.5	121913	98.3
按企业规模分							
大型企业	19.8	8.1	51.1	2.4	4.1	115487	98.3
中型企业	24.2	8.1	47.9	2.1	3.9	94971	98.0
小型企业	21.4	7.6	50.3	1.8	4.4	130474	97.8
微型企业	14.2	-4.1	54.8	1.4	-6.3	552735	114.5
按工业行业分（大类）							
煤炭开采和洗选业							
石油和天然气开采业							
黑色金属矿采选业							
有色金属矿采选业							
非金属矿采选业							
开采辅助活动							
其他采矿业							
农副食品加工业	8.7	3.6	62.7	4.6	0.5	454431	110.1
食品制造业	48.1	17.4	32.1	2.2	16.9	136484	103.5
酒、饮料和精制茶制造业	25.1	31.2	45.7	2.2	17.0	837368	87.7
烟草制品业							
纺织业	28.5	4.1	26.7	0.8	6.0	109886	98.2
纺织服装、服饰业	32.0	6.8	52.5	1.8	2.1	63597	97.4
皮革、毛皮、羽毛及其制品和制鞋业	34.3	1.4	55.1	1.6	0.1	52369	97.6
木材加工和木、竹、藤、棕、草制品业	27.9	13.8	69.6	1.5	8.1	145384	95.2
家具制造业	23.5	1.4	48.9	1.8	-0.3	70267	99.2
造纸和纸制品业	26.5	10.3	31.8	1.9	5.4	167520	79.2
印刷和记录媒介复制业	39.0	9.9	45.1	1.5	6.7	112757	99.9
文教、工美、体育和娱乐用品制造业	33.3	0.8	45.9	1.7	-0.4	63372	98.6
石油加工、炼焦和核燃料加工业							
化学原料和化学制品制造业	18.2	12.5	45.2	1.8	7.0	284440	98.4
医药制造业	42.5	4.2	77.1	1.5	1.7	258015	99.4
化学纤维制造业	15.9	14.9	36.7	1.9	7.9	44912	100.0
橡胶和塑料制品业	21.5	6.7	51.1	1.8	3.1	95109	97.4
非金属矿物制品业	30.8	4.6	43.2	2.1	1.5	131173	100.5
黑色金属冶炼和压延加工业	15.9	4.7	50.4	1.4	3.3	271314	97.5
有色金属冶炼和压延加工业	11.4	1.1	58.2	1.4	-0.1	99643	99.2
金属制品业	31.5	7.7	42.8	1.6	4.9	141745	97.9
通用设备制造业	15.6	7.9	55.0	2.5	3.5	110516	97.2
专用设备制造业	33.4	10.4	37.3	1.2	9.9	129530	97.1
汽车制造业	28.3	18.1	41.9	2.0	11.5	212983	98.9
铁路、船舶、航空航天和其他运输设备制造业	28.9	13.7	46.9	2.0	11.3	111284	99.5
电气机械和器材制造业	24.3	7.1	46.1	1.8	4.7	89548	93.1
计算机、通信和其他电子设备制造业	18.4	6.4	53.7	2.4	2.8	109270	99.3
仪器仪表制造业	32.4	9.2	36.5	2.6	6.2	127493	100.4
其他制造业	29.1	1.7	39.0	1.8	1.2	66056	99.6
废弃资源综合利用业							
金属制品、机械和设备修理业							
电力、热力生产和供应业	32.0	14.2	59.3	2.1	21.7	7023941	76.3
燃气生产和供应业	25.2	24.5	48.4	4.7	22.0	1002689	100.0
水的生产和供应业							

4-16 规模以上港澳台商投资工业企业主要经济指标（2016年）

Main Indicators of Industrial Enterprises above Designated Size with Hong Kong, Macao and Taiwan Funds (2016)

项目	企业单位数（个）	#亏损企业	工业增加值（万元）	主营业务收入（万元）
总计	1889	301	10642678	41394064
按轻重工业分				
轻工业	1028	174	5245233	17890482
重工业	861	127	5397445	23503582
按企业规模分				
大型企业	130	10	4911219	21096855
中型企业	741	103	3798297	12502036
小型企业	975	166	1722149	7225126
微型企业	43	22	211013	570046
按销售收入分				
10亿元以上	66	5	3862557	18718804
5-10亿元	68	2	1422596	4677490
1-5亿元	588	64	3537929	12066639
1亿元以下	1167	230	1819597	5931131
按工业行业分（大类）				
煤炭开采和洗选业				
石油和天然气开采业				
黑色金属矿采选业				
有色金属矿采选业				
非金属矿采选业				
开采辅助活动				
其他采矿业				
农副食品加工业	5	2	51636	408657
食品制造业	14	3	275002	746705
酒、饮料和精制茶制造业	4	2	15051	245096
烟草制品业				
纺织业	54	9	244515	808316
纺织服装、服饰业	113	22	469268	1704196
皮革、毛皮、羽毛及其制品和制鞋业	118	28	516373	1235593
木材加工和木、竹、藤、棕、草制品业	7	3	6765	27668
家具制造业	56	7	195083	587431
造纸和纸制品业	55	6	798401	3289548
印刷和记录媒介复制业	53	5	261073	773719
文教、工美、体育和娱乐用品制造业	139	26	691342	1793208
石油加工、炼焦和核燃料加工业	3		21323	53810
化学原料和化学制品制造业	43	7	192416	773173
医药制造业	2	1	-9078	47062
化学纤维制造业	6		8626	40955
橡胶和塑料制品业	246	38	849939	2983905
非金属矿物制品业	29	2	254339	860831
黑色金属冶炼和压延加工业	8	2	36055	150195
有色金属冶炼和压延加工业	16	5	39038	461071
金属制品业	128	16	684809	1771608
通用设备制造业	69	11	369201	2284105
专用设备制造业	74	10	356757	1334966
汽车制造业	14	1	52527	156997
铁路、船舶、航空航天和其他运输设备制造业	5		48389	161335
电气机械和器材制造业	218	25	1018190	3862144
计算机、通信和其他电子设备制造业	337	53	2600335	13437615
仪器仪表制造业	39	10	205948	472293
其他制造业	22	3	54282	181260
废弃资源综合利用业				
金属制品、机械和设备修理业	1		1686	4288
电力、热力生产和供应业	10	4	329369	721352
燃气生产和供应业	1		4020	14964
水的生产和供应业				

4-16 续表

(2016年)

项　　目	亏损企业亏损总额(万元)	利　润总　额(万元)	人　均利　润(元)
总　计	256317	1609275	14703
按轻重工业分			
轻工业	131020	741363	12534
重工业	125297	867912	17252
按企业规模分			
大型企业	79368	891868	21227
中型企业	76705	382503	7462
小型企业	68760	241818	15032
微型企业	31485	93087	992394
按销售收入分			
10亿元以上	62886	923097	37000
5-10亿元	16868	290271	21924
1-5亿元	73714	367696	8451
1亿元以下	102849	28210	1016
按工业行业分（大类）			
煤炭开采和洗选业			
石油和天然气开采业			
黑色金属矿采选业			
有色金属矿采选业			
非金属矿采选业			
开采辅助活动			
其他采矿业			
农副食品加工业	6087	-4430	-47588
食品制造业	581	67888	54046
酒、饮料和精制茶制造业	47039	-45449	-108522
烟草制品业			
纺织业	4501	35990	14320
纺织服装、服饰业	8290	33246	4620
皮革、毛皮、羽毛及其制品和制鞋业	27588	-12845	-1562
木材加工和木、竹、藤、棕、草制品业	351	-209	-2751
家具制造业	1933	21789	9624
造纸和纸制品业	1146	265719	106530
印刷和记录媒介复制业	1215	60738	22868
文教、工美、体育和娱乐用品制造业	10469	32547	2814
石油加工、炼焦和核燃料加工业		1597	75340
化学原料和化学制品制造业	2312	86257	109436
医药制造业	116	256	4245
化学纤维制造业		1894	13803
橡胶和塑料制品业	19899	83144	8455
非金属矿物制品业	1000	70865	58019
黑色金属冶炼和压延加工业	721	6974	35492
有色金属冶炼和压延加工业	2947	7292	29547
金属制品业	3996	86548	14283
通用设备制造业	8106	92999	28902
专用设备制造业	10398	51832	14193
汽车制造业	164	6201	12819
铁路、船舶、航空航天和其他运输设备制造业		4396	14637
电气机械和器材制造业	11103	166839	13694
计算机、通信和其他电子设备制造业	47733	331760	11670
仪器仪表制造业	13653	2643	930
其他制造业	2172	3292	4741
废弃资源综合利用业			
金属制品、机械和设备修理业		605	104345
电力、热力生产和供应业	22799	146558	454724
燃气生产和供应业		2340	570829
水的生产和供应业			

4-17 规模以上港澳台商投资工业企业主要经济效益指标（2016年）

Main Indicators on Economic Benefit of Industrial Enterprises above Designated Size with Hong Kong, Macao and Taiwan Funds (2016)

项目	工业增加值率(%)	总资产贡献率(%)	资产负债率(%)	流动资产周转率(次/年)	成本费用利润率(%)	全员劳动生产率(元/人)	产品销售率(%)
总计	24.9	6.9	49.8	1.8	4.0	97233	98.4
按轻重工业分							
轻工业	28.4	7.2	46.5	1.7	4.3	88680	98.7
重工业	22.2	6.7	52.6	1.9	3.8	107290	98.1
按企业规模分							
大型企业	22.4	8.1	47.5	2.1	4.4	116889	98.8
中型企业	29.3	5.2	51.9	1.6	3.1	74102	97.9
小型企业	23.3	6.0	52.8	1.5	3.4	107052	98.1
微型企业	36.4	17.3	40.6	1.5	15.3	2249605	99.4
按工业行业分（大类）							
煤炭开采和洗选业							
石油和天然气开采业							
黑色金属矿采选业							
有色金属矿采选业							
非金属矿采选业							
开采辅助活动							
其他采矿业							
农副食品加工业	12.7	-1.2	75.8	3.4	-1.1	554627	99.7
食品制造业	35.5	16.0	45.8	1.5	10.2	218933	96.2
酒、饮料和精制茶制造业	7.1	-11.4	72.6	2.1	-15.9	35939	115.0
烟草制品业							
纺织业	29.0	6.0	30.9	1.5	4.6	97288	97.0
纺织服装、服饰业	24.0	5.4	54.2	1.7	2.0	65210	95.7
皮革、毛皮、羽毛及其制品和制鞋业	39.6	0.4	66.4	1.9	-1.0	62795	98.2
木材加工和木、竹、藤、棕、草制品业	24.7	1.3	77.4	0.7	-0.7	89126	91.8
家具制造业	31.7	7.1	41.2	1.6	3.8	86167	99.2
造纸和纸制品业	24.2	10.1	39.3	2.0	8.6	320090	100.6
印刷和记录媒介复制业	33.7	8.0	39.6	1.1	8.4	98296	99.8
文教、工美、体育和娱乐用品制造业	38.9	4.0	54.7	1.8	1.9	59784	98.7
石油加工、炼焦和核燃料加工业	38.3	6.3	61.2	0.9	3.0	1005811	102.5
化学原料和化学制品制造业	23.7	15.6	41.3	1.4	12.4	244120	96.5
医药制造业	-16.9	-4.4	79.6	1.4	0.5	-150302	87.8
化学纤维制造业	22.6	7.2	44.1	1.8	4.9	62868	97.4
橡胶和塑料制品业	27.8	5.1	46.0	1.7	2.9	86433	96.3
非金属矿物制品业	29.3	8.8	47.8	1.5	8.9	208236	99.1
黑色金属冶炼和压延加工业	23.9	10.3	49.1	1.7	4.9	183487	98.1
有色金属冶炼和压延加工业	8.0	3.2	67.9	1.9	1.6	158178	98.4
金属制品业	37.0	7.1	42.2	1.6	5.0	113012	95.3
通用设备制造业	15.7	8.6	56.4	2.3	4.2	114741	99.1
专用设备制造业	25.9	7.4	47.7	1.7	4.0	97691	97.2
汽车制造业	34.8	6.1	30.9	1.9	4.1	108594	103.5
铁路、船舶、航空航天和其他运输设备制造业	31.2	3.4	76.7	0.4	2.9	161135	100.1
电气机械和器材制造业	25.9	6.5	47.3	1.5	4.5	83571	99.0
计算机、通信和其他电子设备制造业	18.5	5.5	56.3	2.2	2.5	91468	98.9
仪器仪表制造业	42.2	2.4	46.8	1.8	0.6	72456	97.4
其他制造业	29.1	3.0	43.9	1.7	1.8	78171	97.2
废弃资源综合利用业							
金属制品、机械和设备修理业	40.1	18.1	13.4	1.2	16.5	290668	10.0
电力、热力生产和供应业	45.3	15.7	50.9	1.6	20.1	1021933	97.8
燃气生产和供应业	22.0	21.6	37.7	5.3	16.9	980421	89.2
水的生产和供应业							

4-18 规模以上私营工业企业主要经济指标（2016年）

Main Indicators of Private Industrial Enterprises above Designated Size (2016)

项 目	企 业 单位数 (个)	#亏 损 企 业	工 业 增加值 (万元)	主营业 务收入 (万元)
总 计	1566	158	5769908	41463819
按轻重工业分				
轻工业	759	80	1797538	7444132
重工业	807	78	3972371	34019686
按企业规模分				
大型企业	20	3	2694460	28293076
中型企业	250	19	1246724	4856165
小型企业	1232	118	1761903	7936886
微型企业	64	18	66821	377691
按销售收入分				
10亿元以上	13	1	2546006	28226632
5-10亿元	23	2	337783	1600008
1-5亿元	304	18	1347013	5727115
1亿元以下	1226	137	1539106	5910065
按工业行业分（大类）				
煤炭开采和洗选业				
石油和天然气开采业				
黑色金属矿采选业				
有色金属矿采选业				
非金属矿采选业				
开采辅助活动				
其他采矿业				
农副食品加工业	14	2	61647	622221
食品制造业	13		20946	93204
酒、饮料和精制茶制造业	3		19452	102943
烟草制品业				
纺织业	20	2	27386	94098
纺织服装、服饰业	178	20	558914	1870313
皮革、毛皮、羽毛及其制品和制鞋业	54	5	127696	412919
木材加工和木、竹、藤、棕、草制品业	8	2	10382	39274
家具制造业	105	10	153214	671281
造纸和纸制品业	73	2	179780	996701
印刷和记录媒介复制业	30	5	75970	259544
文教、工美、体育和娱乐用品制造业	43	3	90768	383564
石油加工、炼焦和核燃料加工业				
化学原料和化学制品制造业	61	4	108523	475497
医药制造业	3		6502	16078
化学纤维制造业	4		8357	56299
橡胶和塑料制品业	139	11	295431	1099406
非金属矿物制品业	38	4	75576	283351
黑色金属冶炼和压延加工业	8	1	9840	53735
有色金属冶炼和压延加工业	19	1	32279	186521
金属制品业	104	13	235879	697319
通用设备制造业	87	8	139339	598845
专用设备制造业	87	6	227663	755398
汽车制造业	6		46730	150663
铁路、船舶、航空航天和其他运输设备制造业	9	2	13569	93690
电气机械和器材制造业	174	21	490933	2467545
计算机、通信和其他电子设备制造业	252	30	2689956	28796447
仪器仪表制造业	20	2	45715	122667
其他制造业	8	2	9216	36066
废弃资源综合利用业	1	1	783	3712
金属制品、机械和设备修理业	1		2009	5462
电力、热力生产和供应业				
燃气生产和供应业				
水的生产和供应业	4	1	5453	19056

4-18 续表

(2016年)

项　　目	亏损企业亏损总额(万元)	利　润总　额(万元)	人　均利　润(元)
总　　计	74602	1057188	26776
按轻重工业分			
轻工业	15127	290824	16955
重工业	59475	766364	34321
按企业规模分			
大型企业	11188	656754	66229
中型企业	23320	214521	15468
小型企业	30158	193018	12379
微型企业	9935	-7105	-68580
按销售收入分			
10亿元以上	33	651335	83622
5-10亿元	3044	76287	29817
1-5亿元	28722	257280	20610
1亿元以下	42802	72286	4341
按工业行业分（大类）			
煤炭开采和洗选业			
石油和天然气开采业			
黑色金属矿采选业			
有色金属矿采选业			
非金属矿采选业			
开采辅助活动			
其他采矿业			
农副食品加工业	118	30495	136566
食品制造业		3285	16822
酒、饮料和精制茶制造业		4091	37396
烟草制品业			
纺织业	1018	997	4699
纺织服装、服饰业	2458	143617	27251
皮革、毛皮、羽毛及其制品和制鞋业	693	10557	7070
木材加工和木、竹、藤、棕、草制品业	69	287	3156
家具制造业	1350	8649	4727
造纸和纸制品业	303	23689	18517
印刷和记录媒介复制业	621	5666	6898
文教、工美、体育和娱乐用品制造业	446	5328	6264
石油加工、炼焦和核燃料加工业			
化学原料和化学制品制造业	120	17679	26650
医药制造业		310	5484
化学纤维制造业		1247	13872
橡胶和塑料制品业	3980	36132	12707
非金属矿物制品业	538	8678	11800
黑色金属冶炼和压延加工业	60	2329	22898
有色金属冶炼和压延加工业	48	3930	16120
金属制品业	12493	5419	2335
通用设备制造业	1287	41979	34610
专用设备制造业	1174	48468	26693
汽车制造业		15135	91616
铁路、船舶、航空航天和其他运输设备制造业	1645	-343	-2239
电气机械和器材制造业	4399	121618	30236
计算机、通信和其他电子设备制造业	37651	510967	42010
仪器仪表制造业	76	7674	22840
其他制造业	64	362	3012
废弃资源综合利用业	918	-918	-116139
金属制品、机械和设备修理业		26	1778
电力、热力生产和供应业			
燃气生产和供应业			
水的生产和供应业	3076	-167	-4096

4-19 规模以上私营工业企业主要经济效益指标（2016年）

Main Indicators on Economic Benefit of Private Industrial Enterprises above Designated Size (2016)

项目	工业增加值率(%)	总资产贡献率(%)	资产负债率(%)	流动资产周转率(次/年)	成本费用利润率(%)	全员劳动生产率(元/人)	产品销售率(%)
总计	14.8	9.0	77.2	2.1	2.6	146140	96.8
按轻重工业分							
轻工业	23.1	9.5	64.3	1.7	4.1	104794	94.2
重工业	12.7	8.9	81.0	2.2	2.2	177902	97.4
按企业规模分							
大型企业	10.4	10.0	84.2	2.3	2.3	271718	96.3
中型企业	24.8	9.1	58.6	1.7	4.6	89892	97.4
小型企业	22.5	7.0	73.6	1.7	2.5	112993	97.8
微型企业	15.3	0.6	77.4	1.6	-1.8	644991	100.9
按工业行业分（大类）							
煤炭开采和洗选业							
石油和天然气开采业							
黑色金属矿采选业							
有色金属矿采选业							
非金属矿采选业							
开采辅助活动							
其他采矿业							
农副食品加工业	13.8	11.0	68.0	2.7	5.1	276074	100.3
食品制造业	23.0	11.3	61.9	2.3	3.7	107252	99.0
酒、饮料和精制茶制造业	18.8	20.7	56.2	3.1	4.2	177808	99.2
烟草制品业							
纺织业	29.5	3.9	68.7	0.9	1.1	129057	98.1
纺织服装、服饰业	24.5	11.7	51.2	1.2	8.4	106052	84.6
皮革、毛皮、羽毛及其制品和制鞋业	30.4	8.8	60.4	2.3	2.6	85512	97.1
木材加工和木、竹、藤、棕、草制品业	25.5	2.2	77.0	2.0	0.7	114091	93.8
家具制造业	22.9	4.8	74.1	1.5	1.3	83742	97.4
造纸和纸制品业	18.0	11.3	72.2	3.1	2.4	140530	98.7
印刷和记录媒介复制业	30.8	7.4	77.6	2.1	2.2	92488	100.1
文教、工美、体育和娱乐用品制造业	19.6	9.2	84.8	3.9	1.4	106711	100.2
石油加工、炼焦和核燃料加工业							
化学原料和化学制品制造业	20.8	7.6	61.2	1.5	3.8	163586	93.1
医药制造业	39.8	10.0	79.4	1.3	2.0	114882	103.8
化学纤维制造业	14.1	12.6	64.2	3.1	2.3	92961	92.9
橡胶和塑料制品业	27.2	9.0	71.4	1.9	3.4	103901	96.8
非金属矿物制品业	27.0	6.2	75.3	1.3	3.2	102769	101.2
黑色金属冶炼和压延加工业	17.3	11.8	58.5	1.9	4.5	96757	99.1
有色金属冶炼和压延加工业	17.1	8.9	62.6	2.2	2.1	132399	99.8
金属制品业	33.3	4.8	78.3	1.8	0.8	101650	95.9
通用设备制造业	22.5	10.3	63.4	1.3	7.5	114881	98.0
专用设备制造业	29.3	10.7	57.7	1.4	6.9	125379	96.5
汽车制造业	25.0	13.6	80.4	0.9	11.0	282866	79.4
铁路、船舶、航空航天和其他运输设备制造业	15.4	2.5	77.8	1.6	-0.3	88514	98.8
电气机械和器材制造业	18.9	7.4	62.2	1.2	5.2	122053	97.1
计算机、通信和其他电子设备制造业	10.4	9.2	88.1	2.4	1.7	221157	97.7
仪器仪表制造业	32.2	6.8	22.7	1.3	6.5	136055	98.1
其他制造业	24.4	5.0	52.6	1.6	1.0	76671	95.2
废弃资源综合利用业	21.1	-14.2	65.4	1.1	-19.2	99143	100.0
金属制品、机械和设备修理业	31.7	3.2	88.7	1.8	0.4	139548	95.2
电力、热力生产和供应业							
燃气生产和供应业							
水的生产和供应业	33.5	1.3	90.8	0.4	-0.9	133968	95.7

4-20 大中型工业企业主要经济指标（2016年）

Main Indicators of Large and Medium-sized Industrial Enterprises (2016)

项目	企业单位数（个）	#亏损企业	工业增加值（万元）	主营业务收入（万元）
总计	1904	234	23131736	119035907
按轻重工业分				
轻工业	1007	126	8677169	32063035
重工业	897	108	14454567	86972872
按企业规模分				
大型企业	266	26	14083746	84557788
中型企业	1638	208	9047990	34478119
按工业行业分（大类）				
煤炭开采和洗选业				
石油和天然气开采业				
黑色金属矿采选业				
有色金属矿采选业				
非金属矿采选业				
开采辅助活动				
其他采矿业				
农副食品加工业	8	2	135504	1496137
食品制造业	13		308849	894146
酒、饮料和精制茶制造业	7	1	127034	679767
烟草制品业				
纺织业	27	1	301237	1002445
纺织服装、服饰业	121	17	912839	3122672
皮革、毛皮、羽毛及其制品和制鞋业	131	25	843881	2260239
木材加工和木、竹、藤、棕、草制品业	3		24876	85841
家具制造业	80	8	428768	1665138
造纸和纸制品业	50	1	1078690	4485566
印刷和记录媒介复制业	47	3	355125	1067763
文教、工美、体育和娱乐用品制造业	140	21	875105	2931921
石油加工、炼焦和核燃料加工业				
化学原料和化学制品制造业	20	2	143494	474441
医药制造业	4		59499	192951
化学纤维制造业	3		9392	44100
橡胶和塑料制品业	169	27	1134915	3926942
非金属矿物制品业	30	7	344273	1074992
黑色金属冶炼和压延加工业	4		46442	127040
有色金属冶炼和压延加工业	5	1	14296	59378
金属制品业	85	8	961458	2458593
通用设备制造业	57	5	800237	4539382
专用设备制造业	73	5	664003	2187603
汽车制造业	19	1	361061	1221764
铁路、船舶、航空航天和其他运输设备制造业	14	2	109078	386694
电气机械和器材制造业	235	20	1858591	7320640
计算机、通信和其他电子设备制造业	498	66	9209982	67919824
仪器仪表制造业	42	9	411945	1096653
其他制造业	11	2	50298	171917
废弃资源综合利用业				
金属制品、机械和设备修理业				
电力、热力生产和供应业	5		1441302	5743040
燃气生产和供应业	1		67155	272339
水的生产和供应业	2		52409	125979

4-20 续表

(2016年)

项目	亏损企业亏损总额(万元)	利润总额(万元)	人均利润(元)
总计	352371	4084645	20648
按轻重工业分			
轻工业	170419	1452099	15573
重工业	181952	2632546	25173
按企业规模分			
大型企业	151166	2732290	29395
中型企业	201205	1352355	12895
按工业行业分（大类）			
煤炭开采和洗选业			
石油和天然气开采业			
黑色金属矿采选业			
有色金属矿采选业			
非金属矿采选业			
开采辅助活动			
其他采矿业			
农副食品加工业	13868	13137	39333
食品制造业		79450	51574
酒、饮料和精制茶制造业	42635	15112	24406
烟草制品业			
纺织业	2158	56267	18489
纺织服装、服饰业	8389	178361	15295
皮革、毛皮、羽毛及其制品和制鞋业	37479	443	30
木材加工和木、竹、藤、棕、草制品业		5883	27973
家具制造业	10552	54615	10071
造纸和纸制品业	57	320790	81730
印刷和记录媒介复制业	3276	64024	16728
文教、工美、体育和娱乐用品制造业	18988	60212	4139
石油加工、炼焦和核燃料加工业			
化学原料和化学制品制造业	506	35733	38968
医药制造业		40270	162906
化学纤维制造业		1046	8962
橡胶和塑料制品业	26636	133814	10161
非金属矿物制品业	12838	69881	29035
黑色金属冶炼和压延加工业		6743	15147
有色金属冶炼和压延加工业	1434	-97	-467
金属制品业	12159	139232	15289
通用设备制造业	7488	167634	23975
专用设备制造业	1617	146963	23925
汽车制造业	1461	123138	67499
铁路、船舶、航空航天和其他运输设备制造业	1704	23726	29407
电气机械和器材制造业	7486	390527	19536
计算机、通信和其他电子设备制造业	123290	1582114	23270
仪器仪表制造业	16024	46356	10348
其他制造业	2329	2291	3663
废弃资源综合利用业			
金属制品、机械和设备修理业			
电力、热力生产和供应业		269562	119344
燃气生产和供应业		51664	1106293
水的生产和供应业		5755	33341

4-21 大中型工业企业主要经济效益指标（2016年）

Main Indicators on Economic Benefit of Large and Medium-sized Industrial Enterprises (2016)

项 目	工业增加值率 (%)	总资产贡献率 (%)	资产负债率 (%)	流动资产周转率 (次/年)	成本费用利润率 (%)	全员劳动生产率 (元/人)	产品销售率 (%)
总 计	19.7	8.5	59.9	2.2	3.5	116931	97.7
按轻重工业分							
轻工业	26.1	8.4	51.0	1.7	4.7	93059	96.9
重工业	17.2	8.5	64.5	2.4	3.1	138216	98.0
按企业规模分							
大型企业	17.2	9.1	63.0	2.4	3.3	151517	97.8
中型企业	25.6	7.4	54.4	1.7	4.0	86277	97.5
按工业行业分（大类）							
煤炭开采和洗选业							
石油和天然气开采业							
黑色金属矿采选业							
有色金属矿采选业							
非金属矿采选业							
开采辅助活动							
其他采矿业							
农副食品加工业	10.4	3.2	73.3	3.3	0.8	405699	107.6
食品制造业	32.7	17.0	50.8	1.5	9.9	200486	93.2
酒、饮料和精制茶制造业	18.0	16.3	76.8	2.8	2.3	205158	97.3
烟草制品业							
纺织业	29.0	5.6	30.4	1.2	5.8	98984	97.5
纺织服装、服饰业	24.3	9.2	50.4	1.2	6.1	78277	87.7
皮革、毛皮、羽毛及其制品和制鞋业	35.9	2.1	61.2	1.8	0.02	57227	97.8
木材加工和木、竹、藤、棕、草制品业	28.7	22.3	64.3	2.4	7.4	118288	99.0
家具制造业	25.6	8.3	51.0	2.0	3.4	79062	98.6
造纸和纸制品业	23.7	10.9	43.5	2.0	7.6	274825	98.7
印刷和记录媒介复制业	33.0	7.2	43.0	1.3	6.3	92785	99.5
文教、工美、体育和娱乐用品制造业	30.0	5.2	56.6	1.9	2.1	60153	98.8
石油加工、炼焦和核燃料加工业							
化学原料和化学制品制造业	29.7	15.5	46.6	1.9	8.2	156482	98.6
医药制造业	29.5	8.8	36.3	0.9	23.9	240691	95.5
化学纤维制造业	19.2	5.3	50.6	2.2	2.4	80479	90.4
橡胶和塑料制品业	27.5	6.7	51.4	1.8	3.5	86180	94.8
非金属矿物制品业	31.5	7.2	49.7	1.3	6.9	143042	99.0
黑色金属冶炼和压延加工业	36.0	14.4	71.0	2.2	5.5	104316	101.9
有色金属冶炼和压延加工业	20.4	4.4	73.0	1.9	-0.2	69031	100.7
金属制品业	37.4	8.3	46.2	1.6	5.9	105575	94.7
通用设备制造业	17.3	7.3	63.9	2.1	3.8	114450	98.6
专用设备制造业	29.4	10.6	49.6	1.6	7.1	108098	97.0
汽车制造业	29.6	17.2	41.6	2.0	11.2	197917	100.0
铁路、船舶、航空航天和其他运输设备制造业	28.4	5.3	71.9	0.8	6.6	135198	100.7
电气机械和器材制造业	24.3	7.6	49.1	1.5	5.6	92977	96.4
计算机、通信和其他电子设备制造业	14.2	8.0	73.1	2.5	2.3	135461	98.1
仪器仪表制造业	36.6	6.3	35.9	2.1	4.4	91956	98.6
其他制造业	27.2	2.2	52.2	1.8	1.4	80425	92.9
废弃资源综合利用业							
金属制品、机械和设备修理业							
电力、热力生产和供应业	25.1	12.1	46.7	7.8	4.9	638111	99.6
燃气生产和供应业	24.5	24.3	51.6	4.5	22.6	1438006	100.0
水的生产和供应业	40.3	5.8	78.3	1.2	4.7	303643	96.8

4-22 主要年份规模以上工业企业经济效益指标

Main Indicators on Economic Benefit of Industrial Enterprises above Designated Size in Main Years

项　　目	单位	1985年	1990年	1995年	2000年	2005年	2010年	2015年	2016年
产品销售率	%	85.6	94.7	98.7	99.8	99.5	99.9	97.9	97.7
成本费用利润率	%	6.5	1.5	5.0	5.4	3.3	4.8	3.3	3.4
产值利税率	%	6.9	6.4	9.8	9.2	4.6	6.1	5.1	5.6
资金利税率	%	9.0	6.3	6.9	7.5	5.5	7.8	7.8	8.5
销售利税率	%	8.2	6.7	9.1	9.2	4.7	6.1	5.2	5.6
每百元固定资产原值实现的产值	元	174.85	133.63	108.70	125.49	212.40	240.60	292.63	312.52
每百元固定资产原值实现的利税	元	14.24	8.48	10.65	11.54	9.90	14.60	14.88	17.59
每百元固定资产原值实现的利润	元	4.36	1.76	5.52	6.90	6.70	11.00	9.36	10.69
每百元流动资产实现的产值	元	210.15	247.80	169.43	178.59	216.30	204.30	205.91	197.34
每百元流动资产实现的利税	元	17.12	15.73	16.59	16.42	10.00	12.40	10.47	11.11
每百元流动资产实现的利润	元	4.89	3.29	8.60	9.83	6.80	9.30	6.58	6.75
亏损企业亏损面	%	7.2	11.1	25.9	31.3	30.1	16.2	15.0	13.7
全部流动资产周转天数	天	173.69	155.62	201.07	189.04	169.80	179.40	175.88	177.24
全员劳动生产率	元/人	2906	6439	13778	36101	53340	60854	102756	118291

注：由于1993年财务会计制度改革，本表中有关财务指标1993年起数据与往年不可比；全员劳动生产率1993年起按增加值计算，以前年份按净产值计算；1993年以前的流动资产按定额资金计算，下同。

4-23 主要年份规模以上国有经济工业企业经济效益指标

Main Indicators on Economic Benefit of State-owned and State-holding Industrial Enterprises above Designated Size in Main Years

项　　目	单位	1985年	1990年	1995年	2000年	2005年	2010年	2015年	2016年
产品销售率	%	89.6	102.0	100.8	98.3	100.0	99.8	99.7	98.6
成本费用利润率	%	8.0	-0.8	15.5	7.0	5.8	3.2	5.4	5.6
产值利税率	%	13.2	9.2	40.6	69.4	11.3	7.3	10.0	10.1
资金利税率	%	20.4	8.3	14.9	21.6	10.6	6.7	12.2	11.2
销售利税率	%	14.8	9.0	20.6	19.2	11.3	7.3	9.6	9.6
每百元固定资产原值实现的产值	元	142.93	85.48	61.08	63.42	105.00	79.00	70.94	70.66
每百元固定资产原值实现的利税	元	21.11	7.82	24.82	43.98	11.80	5.70	7.07	7.16
每百元固定资产原值实现的利润	元	9.55	-0.63	10.81	14.46	5.60	2.40	3.79	3.96
每百元流动资产实现的产值	元	445.06	397.84	96.27	73.38	443.40	794.50	417.58	321.50
每百元流动资产实现的利税	元	65.73	36.41	39.12	50.89	50.00	57.70	41.60	32.58
每百元流动资产实现的利润	元	27.46	-2.44	17.03	16.73	23.80	24.60	22.33	18.01
亏损企业亏损面	%	9.9	16.7	20.9		20.0		25.8	14.3
全部流动资产周转天数	天	80.86	88.69	299.83	137.70	83.00	46.10	82.33	105.41
全员劳动生产率	元/人	3641	11253	73910	456736	2320312	405232	533494	461074

4-24 主要年份规模以上集体经济工业企业经济效益指标

Main Indicators on Economic Benefit of Collective-owned Industrial Enterprises above Designated Size in Main Years

项 目	单位	1985年	1990年	1995年	2000年	2005年	2010年	2015年	2016年
产品销售率	%	85.1	92.2	98.0	97.0	100.5	97.4	99.0	98.9
成本费用利润率	%	5.9	3.3	5.2	2.7	3.3	9.7	-1.4	6.8
产值利税率	%	9.3	6.9	9.0	5.1	5.8	10.4	0.3	8.5
资金利税率	%	15.1	9.7	6.0	2.9	3.2	9.7	0.3	4.4
销售利税率	%	11.0	7.5	8.7	5.2	5.8	10.7	0.4	8.4
每百元固定资产原值实现的产值	元	236.65	159.39	127.97	99.30	98.10	131.10	71.76	52.33
每百元固定资产原值实现的利税	元	22.07	10.98	11.46	5.01	5.70	13.60	0.25	4.43
每百元固定资产原值实现的利润	元	10.77	4.54	6.43	2.44	3.00	11.50	-0.85	3.40
每百元流动资产实现的产值	元	509.04	225.69	179.47	113.76	157.70	214.90	145.21	89.70
每百元流动资产实现的利税	元	47.47	15.55	16.07	5.74	9.10	22.40	0.50	7.60
每百元流动资产实现的利润	元	23.16	6.44	9.02	2.79	4.80	18.80	-1.72	5.82
亏损企业亏损面	%	6.6	8.8	12.8	18.6	25.9	22.5	41.9	22.2
全部流动资产周转天数	天	84.25	175.32	197.36	340.07	241.70	175.10	293.10	396.23
全员劳动生产率	元/人	2664	5437	5820	16344	28414	31412	80545	76840

4-25 主要年份大中型工业企业经济效益指标

Main Indicators on Economic Benefit of Large and Medium-sized Industrial Enterprises in Main Years

项 目	单位	1985年	1990年	1995年	2000年	2005年	2010年	2015年	2016年
产品销售率	%	104.3	103.5	99.7	98.6	99.5	100.6	98.0	97.7
成本费用利润率	%	14.3	2.2	12.9	12.0	3.8	5.1	3.4	3.5
产值利税率	%	16.1	8.7	19.9	21.4	4.7	6.4	5.1	5.7
资金利税率	%	14.8	6.5	14.0	15.3	6.1	8.4	8.1	9.0
销售利税率	%	15.5	8.4	19.8	21.7	4.7	6.4	5.2	5.6
每百元固定资产原值实现的产值	元	106.02	87.07	112.80	98.43	229.80	221.60	286.90	319.06
每百元固定资产原值实现的利税	元	17.10	7.57	22.40	21.06	10.70	14.20	14.59	18.14
每百元固定资产原值实现的利润	元	11.50	1.69	13.09	12.98	8.40	10.90	9.34	11.10
每百元流动资产实现的产值	元	758.81	329.30	174.27	183.41	227.40	220.60	221.16	209.19
每百元流动资产实现的利税	元	122.37	28.61	34.60	39.24	10.60	14.20	11.24	11.89
每百元流动资产实现的利润	元	82.34	6.39	20.22	24.18	8.30	10.90	7.20	7.28
亏损企业亏损面	%		17.2	22.2	12.8	20.1	12.2	14.8	12.3
全部流动资产周转天数	天	46.12	107.14	209.45	210.16	160.80	164.80	163.80	167.05
全员劳动生产率	元/人	6202	16492	81787	280810	72657	66101	98655	116931

4-26 主要年份规模以上港澳台商投资工业企业经济效益指标

Main Indicators on Economic Benefit of Industrial Enterprises above Designated Size with Hong Kong, Macao and Taiwan Funds in Main Years

项　　目	单位	1995年	2000年	2005年	2010年	2015年	2016年
产品销售率	%	99.6	100.8	99.4	99.7	97.6	98.4
成本费用利润率	%	2.1	4.6	3.2	5.4	3.5	4.0
产值利税率	%	4.9	6.6	4.0	6.3	4.8	5.5
资金利税率	%	3.8	5.4	4.6	7.6	6.5	7.4
销售利税率	%	4.9	6.5	4.1	6.3	5.0	5.7
每百元固定资产原值实现的产值	元	114.79	114.54	198.10	216.60	221.70	220.08
每百元固定资产原值实现的利税	元	5.61	7.54	8.00	13.60	10.68	12.10
每百元固定资产原值实现的利润	元	2.58	5.07	6.00	11.10	7.22	8.27
每百元流动资产实现的产值	元	165.18	182.24	192.30	189.10	187.80	183.60
每百元流动资产实现的利税	元	8.08	12.00	7.80	11.80	9.05	10.10
每百元流动资产实现的利润	元	3.71	8.09	5.80	9.70	6.12	6.90
亏损企业亏损面	%	46.4	36.1	35.1	20.2	19.9	15.9
全部流动资产周转天数	天	199.12	199.88	191.10	194.10	196.26	200.28
全员劳动生产率	元/人	17478	28933	41933	54793	86953	97233

4-27 主要年份规模以上外商投资工业企业经济效益指标

Main Indicators on Economic Benefit of Foreign-funded Industrial Enterprises above Designated Size in Main Years

项　　目	单位	1995年	2000年	2005年	2010年	2015年	2016年
产品销售率	%	91.0	99.2	99.4	100.1	97.6	98.2
成本费用利润率	%	-2.6	4.7	2.8	4.4	3.1	4.0
产值利税率	%	-0.6	5.7	3.2	5.3	4.2	5.2
资金利税率	%	-0.5	7.4	4.1	7.5	7.0	8.3
销售利税率	%	-0.6	5.7	3.2	5.3	4.3	5.2
每百元固定资产原值实现的产值	元	155.45	231.22	285.20	286.90	310.33	295.22
每百元固定资产原值实现的利税	元	-0.87	13.08	9.20	15.30	12.93	15.34
每百元固定资产原值实现的利润	元	-1.90	10.26	7.60	12.10	9.23	11.35
每百元流动资产实现的产值	元	94.26	250.96	223.60	211.10	224.39	210.81
每百元流动资产实现的利税	元	-1.53	14.20	7.20	11.20	9.35	10.95
每百元流动资产实现的利润	元	5.53	11.14	5.90	8.90	6.67	8.10
亏损企业亏损面	%	38.2	31.3	34.5	18.8	20.2	18.3
全部流动资产周转天数	天	174.06	148.44	164.40	173.00	163.11	169.38
全员劳动生产率	元/人	3646	50318	70722	66212	95545	109193

4-28 主要年份规模以上工业产品产量

Output of Main Industrial Products of Industrial Enterprises above Designated Size in Main Years

产品名称	单位	1985年	1990年	1995年	2000年	2005年	2010年	2015年	2016年
精制食用植物油	吨	5571	4431	6824	5180	181869	1135677	1004136	972212
饮料酒	千升	4034	2441	1720			493644	347668	356882
软饮料	吨		44061	71566	158599	861853	3142076	544380	520099
棉　纱	吨		321	9902	3048	49383	11252	2525	1488
布	万米		82	31045	28139	65669	15794	6729	4287
服　装	万件	108	1835	112177	85635	70054	140556	145609	137783
#衬　衫	万件			2518	3624	2210	6372	8742	6653
西服套装	万件			205	1761	555	204	146	143
轻　革	万平方米		5	1076	378	1391	744	267	193
皮革鞋靴	万双	17	457	27184	23474	31942	43062	16797	14457
人造板	立方米		7100	40666		167088	266113	272481	213298
家　具	万件	815	8657	77501	151374	7974	7390	5386	3749
机制纸及纸板	万吨	3	11	34	62	408	933	1399	1508
中成药	吨		216	6268	2354	1759	2478	2581	2812
塑料制品	吨	3089	17335	624476	571900	1265865	3998208	1200458	1179573
#塑料薄膜	吨		1928	59128	71394	83954	134737	119648	120976
水　泥	万吨	41	140	283	435	305	249	336	209
砖	万块	159305	296962	252783		2903		1456	
卫生陶瓷制品	万件	561	480	2414	1860	5745	2426	132	465
耐火材料制品	吨	7600	9928	9144			62512		
钢　材	吨	4678	1730	19690	14550	1087242	191656	173394	200070
铝　材	吨		881	3536	4080	61510	69933	119678	148274
输送机械	吨		8622	3736		33200		2880	1001
电动手提式工具	万台		1.89	471	357	6	1520	2550	2690
滚动轴承	万套	36	373	691	594	1333	4232	39427	20930
民用钢质船舶	载重吨	1916	841	3620	2894		18186	122913	63024

注：2000年以前家具的计量单位为“万元”。

4-28 续表

产品名称	单位	1985年	1990年	1995年	2000年	2005年	2010年	2015年	2016年
交流电动机	万千瓦	23	19	43	87		193	188	187
变压器	千伏安				6730	816409	2980343	2324960	3147563
电力电缆	千米		15091	20694	61996	78266	383829	2676097	3415175
原电池及原电池组	万只	12354	7607	63237	69401	214507	417215	354876	405795
家用吸尘器	万台	0.13	7.35	483	67	464	428	85	61
家用电风扇	万台		106	474	436	964	2081	833	960
房间空气调节器	台	31		26480	39582	4941			
自行车	辆			95439	185608	885211	1014533	877566	511812
家用电冰箱	台			35336		19360			
白炽灯泡	万只			5778	8560	45164	13198	6409	7627
灯具及照明装置	万件		87	42407	25135	14017	22819	26393	24308
电话单机	万部		17	877	1074	3651	4809	3326	3159
移动通信手持机（手机）	万部				619	639	1995	23643	35909
电子计算机整机	万台				27	180	44	108	126
电子元件	亿只	0.14	2.05	72	104	4642	9185	11385	12319
显示器	万台						157	195	305
打印机	万台						57	97	60
硬盘存储器	万台						30	208	229
半导体分立器件	亿只			248.48	3.23	220.32	404.44	517.49	520.06
彩色电视机	万台		1.04	81	134	135	536	345	301
组合音响	万台			1136	1572	2446	3637	2559	2238
照相机	万台		3	374	122	1355	210	26	58
表	万只		15	8514	954	1370	2168	1934	1707
钟	万只			1986	984	1193	3776	569	341
发电量	亿千瓦时	0.29	93	139	269	344	356	315.19	338.48
自来水生产量	万吨			21070	102083	94962	179639	165647	158720

4-29 规模以上五大支柱产业及四个特色产业主要经济指标（2016年）

Main Indicators of Five Pillar Industries & Four Characteristic Industries above Designated Size (2016)

项　目	企业单位数（个）	#亏损企业	工业增加值（万元）	主营业务收入（万元）
总　计	4458	618	23352321	126411438
按轻重工业分				
轻工业	5006	691	25143453	132408222
重工业	5321	731	27890428	142899498
按企业规模分				
大型企业	4493	625	25887941	135205142
中型企业	4745	656	25023014	131900846
小型企业	5501	745	25242117	133978260
微型企业	4504	632	23585450	127046346
按工业行业分（大类）				
五大支柱产业	3560	506	20424966	115364574
电子信息制造业	1064	175	9887848	71608357
电气机械及设备制造业	1368	167	5569515	22430991
纺织服装鞋帽制造业	815	125	2765293	8842653
食品饮料加工制造业	111	20	843762	6418662
造纸及纸制品业	202	19	1358548	6063912
四个特色产业	898	112	2927354	11046863
玩具及文体用品制造业	271	44	1086306	3690209
家具制造业	298	29	702653	2802221
化工制品制造业	209	24	627023	3007195
包装印刷业	120	15	511372	1547238

4-29　续表

(2016年)

项　目	亏损企业亏损总额（万元）	利润总额（万元）	人均利润（元）
总　计	487579	3905336	18739
按轻重工业分			
轻工业	515375	4189308	18563
重工业	577504	4743357	20302
按企业规模分			
大型企业	503230	4337017	19687
中型企业	527323	4199699	18622
小型企业	528702	4192328	18901
微型企业	508783	4014294	19252
按工业行业分（大类）			
五大支柱产业	437874	3469475	19759
电子信息制造业	189855	1612564	21113
电气机械及设备制造业	79951	1121941	21243
纺织服装鞋帽制造业	66748	247956	6721
食品饮料加工制造业	97348	140863	39521
造纸及纸制品业	3973	346151	58268
四个特色产业	49705	435862	13282
玩具及文体用品制造业	24031	68217	4079
家具制造业	13957	69506	8312
化工制品制造业	5682	200990	73623
包装印刷业	6035	97148	19432

4-30 规模以上电子信息、电气机械及仪器仪表制造业主要指标(2012-2016年)

Main Indicators of Electronic Information, Machinery and Instrument Manufacturing above Designated Size (2012-2016)

指　　标	单位	2012年	2013年	2014年	2015年	2016年
企业单位数	个	1373	1539	1066	1728	1804
#亏损企业单位数	个	239	224	161	287	270
工业增加值	亿元	775.11	976.71	782.88	1039.00	1282.42
主营业务收入	亿元	4264.03	4944.96	4924.69	6236.17	8294.22
成本费用总额	亿元	4180.21	4865.67	4884.52	6173.07	8221.13
#营业成本及销售费用	亿元	3973.63	4627.66	4645.96	5659.08	7789.76
管理费用	亿元	198.47	230.54	237.00	341.81	424.30
财务费用	亿元	8.12	7.47	1.56	-2.91	7.07
利润总额	亿元	102.10	115.02	129.04	174.91	213.46
应交增值税	亿元	67.43	91.75	58.01	65.44	126.21
亏损企业亏损总额	亿元	17.88	26.70	25.11	22.86	23.41
企业资产总额	亿元	2645.73	3089.40	2789.34	3801.31	4784.38
#流动资产	亿元	1823.10	2225.10	2022.16	2916.84	3795.03
#应收帐款余额	亿元	729.51	904.43	798.44	1219.75	1397.45
产成品存货	亿元	161.77	155.21	142.76	777.49	251.02
企业负债总额	亿元	1557.62	1945.82	1779.39	2439.83	3237.44
企业资产负债率	%	58.9	63.0	63.8	64.2	67.7
成本费用利润率	%	2.4	2.4	2.6	2.8	2.6

注：本表统计范围为规模以上计算机、通信和其他电子设备制造业、电气机械和器材制造业、仪器仪表制造业。

4-31 规模以上先进制造业企业主要经济指标（2016年）

Main Indicators of Advanced Manufacturing Enterprises above Designated Size (2016)

项目	企业单位数（个）	#亏损企业	工业增加值（万元）	主营业务收入（万元）
总计	2588	333	15052007	91308197
按企业规模分				
大型企业	152	16	8376858	63764020
中型企业	666	79	3859984	14851749
小型企业	1689	204	2732070	12196037
微型企业	82	34	83094	496391
按工业行业分				
装备制造业	2280	301	14216737	87351318
金属制品业	338	37	1135123	3317680
通用设备制造业	232	25	659385	3546415
专用设备制造业	266	28	933302	3112553
汽车制造业	58	4	468539	1598233
铁路、船舶、航空航天和其他运输设备制造业	7	2	68173	201015
电气机械和器材制造业	367	42	1387018	5953828
计算机、通信和其他电子设备制造业	950	154	9369358	68940525
仪器仪表制造业	61	9	193831	675607
船舶、航空航天器修理	1		2009	5462
钢铁冶炼及加工	20	4	55288	357782
炼铁				
炼钢				
钢压延加工	19	4	55288	357782
铁合金冶炼				
石油及化学	289	28	779982	3599098
石油和天然气开采业				
石油加工、炼焦及核燃料加工业	4		24157	61079
化学原料和化学制品制造业	205	24	602866	2946117
橡胶制品业	80	4	152959	591902

4-31 续表 1

(2016年)

项目	亏损企业亏损总额(万元)	利润总额(万元)	人均利润(元)	工业增加值率(%)	产品销售率(%)
总计	264167	2663744	22428	17.0	97.9
按企业规模分					
大型企业	78904	1540568	28092	13.9	98.1
中型企业	77812	667585	16372	25.2	97.1
小型企业	73254	477061	20688	22.1	97.7
微型企业	34198	-21470	-225289	16.8	104.2
按工业行业分					
装备制造业	254679	2429527	21281	16.8	97.9
金属制品业	17226	95597	9418	33.0	95.2
通用设备制造业	9873	166575	27458	18.5	99.4
专用设备制造业	15011	189026	23078	29.2	97.2
汽车制造业	2494	146948	59203	28.7	97.6
铁路、船舶、航空航天和其他运输设备制造业	597	19751	70439	33.5	98.3
电气机械和器材制造业	13355	269261	18509	22.2	95.7
计算机、通信和其他电子设备制造业	180029	1519583	21489	14.3	98.2
仪器仪表制造业	16093	22761	13242	28.0	99.4
船舶、航空航天器修理		26	1806	31.7	95.2
钢铁冶炼及加工	1020	7978	37579	15.2	98.6
炼铁					
炼钢					
钢压延加工	1020	7978	37579	15.2	98.6
铁合金冶炼					
石油及化学	8469	226240	51476	21.1	98.1
石油和天然气开采业					
石油加工、炼焦及核燃料加工业		2537	104403	38.3	102.0
化学原料和化学制品制造业	5682	198453	73346	19.8	97.4
橡胶制品业	2787	25249	15164	26.0	101.0

4−31 续表 2

(2016年)

项　　目	总资产贡献率(%)	资　产负债率(%)	流动资产周转率(次/年)	成本费用利润率(%)	全员劳动生产率(元/人)
总　计	8.0	66.0	2.1	3.0	126731
按企业规模分					
大型企业	8.3	73.7	2.5	2.4	152753
中型企业	8.0	52.9	1.7	4.7	94662
小型企业	7.5	58.4	1.5	4.1	118477
微型企业	-3.1	71.8	1.4	-4.2	871921
按工业行业分					
装备制造业	7.8	66.9	2.2	2.8	124529
金属制品业	5.6	54.0	1.6	2.9	111831
通用设备制造业	8.6	62.4	1.8	4.8	108693
专用设备制造业	9.5	52.2	1.4	6.4	113944
汽车制造业	14.5	49.4	1.7	10.1	188767
铁路、船舶、航空航天和其他运输设备制造业	6.0	78.9	0.5	11.1	243127
电气机械和器材制造业	7.4	53.8	1.5	4.7	95346
计算机、通信和其他电子设备制造业	7.7	72.7	2.4	2.2	132498
仪器仪表制造业	6.1	38.9	1.7	3.5	112764
船舶、航空航天器修理	3.2	88.7	1.8	0.4	139548
钢铁冶炼及加工	5.4	54.0	1.8	2.3	260423
炼铁					
炼钢					
钢压延加工	5.4	54.0	1.8	2.3	260423
铁合金冶炼					
石油及化学	10.9	52.4	1.5	6.7	177466
石油和天然气开采业					
石油加工、炼焦及核燃料加工业	8.7	58.3	1.0	4.2	994132
化学原料和化学制品制造业	11.4	50.6	1.6	7.2	222813
橡胶制品业	8.5	61.0	1.5	4.5	91861

4-32 规模以上高技术制造业企业主要经济指标（2016年）

Main Indicators of High-tech Manufacturing Enterprises above Designated Size (2016)

项　目	企业单位数(个)	#亏损企业	工业增加值(万元)	主营业务收入(万元)
总　计	1246	204	11031963	76111936
按企业规模分				
大型企业	124	13	7616038	60991052
中型企业	443	62	2537230	10712392
小型企业	629	102	835811	4069479
微型企业	50	27	42885	339013
按工业行业分				
信息化学品制造业	2	1	15677	79217
医药制造业	12	2	78729	238915
航空航天器制造业	2		29321	75593
电子及通信设备制造业	993	166	9479326	67931528
电子工业专用设备制造	33	4	86251	289928
光纤、光缆制造	3		14838	76949
锂离子电池制造	42	7	363165	1126407
通信设备制造	64	12	3703590	40982997
广播电视设备制造	30	4	115583	457752
雷达及配套设备制造	2	1	5662	34647
视听设备制造	114	21	518490	2667832
电子器件制造	144	31	873160	6493569
电子元件制造	429	65	3320540	13856695
其他电子设备制造	132	21	478047	1944752
电子计算机及办公设备制造业	164	25	1195789	6985847
计算机整机制造业	6	1	23642	97795
计算机零部件制造业	88	10	621719	3537374
计算机外围设备制造业	42	5	158179	1014237
其他计算机制造业	13	4	69234	520707
办公设备制造业	15	5	323014	1815734
医疗设备及仪器仪表制造业	73	10	233121	800836
医疗仪器设备及器械制造业	12	1	39290	125230
仪器仪表制造业	61	9	193831	675607

4-32 续表 1

(2016年)

项目	亏损企业亏损总额(万元)	利润总额(万元)	人均利润(元)	工业增加值率(%)	产品销售率(%)
总计	215930	1878417	21981	15.1	98.1
按企业规模分					
大型企业	77185	1415385	29741	13.3	98.4
中型企业	61482	406640	14510	22.6	96.1
小型企业	47143	81429	8311	20.7	98.4
微型企业	30120	-25036	-576866	12.3	99.1
按工业行业分					
信息化学品制造业	34	9248	140976	17.9	92.6
医药制造业	282	41372	121718	32.2	96.4
航空航天器制造业		19297	273716	38.7	99.8
电子及通信设备制造业	182859	1630548	23548	14.7	98.0
电子工业专用设备制造	1091	16991	24950	28.8	98.4
光纤、光缆制造		4914	37059	16.7	82.9
锂离子电池制造	3922	96993	34659	32.1	97.9
通信设备制造	46640	523631	32636	10.1	98.2
广播电视设备制造	5349	12152	8938	25.6	98.1
雷达及配套设备制造	1672	-803	-11932	14.6	89.8
视听设备制造	9826	92981	16419	18.3	96.2
电子器件制造	53616	205762	27993	13.4	99.1
电子元件制造	51168	560314	18297	23.6	98.5
其他电子设备制造	9575	117613	26003	23.4	91.0
电子计算机及办公设备制造业	15612	152152	11267	16.0	98.6
计算机整机制造业	75	1202	3436	24.3	100.4
计算机零部件制造业	3695	70355	9343	15.8	98.7
计算机外围设备制造业	4738	20380	10589	15.2	99.1
其他计算机制造业	3501	8978	9552	13.2	99.3
办公设备制造业	3603	51238	18563	17.2	97.9
医疗设备及仪器仪表制造业	17144	25800	11564	28.3	98.7
医疗仪器设备及器械制造业	1050	3038	5931	29.9	94.7
仪器仪表制造业	16093	22761	13242	28.0	99.4

4-32 续表 2

(2016年)

项　　目	总资产贡献率(%)	资产负债率(%)	流动资产周转率(次/年)	成本费用利润率(%)	全员劳动生产率(元/人)
总　计	7.7	70.2	2.3	2.5	129096
按企业规模分					
大型企业	8.4	75.5	2.6	2.3	160034
中型企业	6.9	55.4	1.7	3.9	90536
小型企业	5.6	62.3	1.6	2.0	85310
微型企业	-4.8	66.9	1.3	-6.9	988122
按工业行业分					
信息化学品制造业	18.3	63.0	1.5	13.3	238976
医药制造业	8.4	41.0	0.9	19.4	231624
航空航天器制造业	57.5	65.3	2.7	34.6	415904
电子及通信设备制造业	8.0	72.2	2.3	2.4	136898
电子工业专用设备制造	7.0	56.3	0.9	6.2	126654
光纤、光缆制造	14.5	67.5	1.8	6.9	111902
锂离子电池制造	8.5	48.5	1.0	9.3	129771
通信设备制造	8.0	92.7	2.7	1.3	230829
广播电视设备制造	7.2	64.6	1.6	2.7	85013
雷达及配套设备制造	0.5	23.8	1.2	-2.2	84127
视听设备制造	9.0	65.5	1.9	3.6	91558
电子器件制造	7.5	53.8	2.4	3.3	118791
电子元件制造	7.5	51.6	2.0	4.2	108430
其他电子设备制造	10.7	60.2	1.8	6.4	105690
电子计算机及办公设备制造业	5.1	62.0	2.3	2.2	88547
计算机整机制造业	1.5	53.2	1.8	1.2	67588
计算机零部件制造业	4.0	62.2	2.2	2.0	82566
计算机外围设备制造业	10.2	59.7	2.8	2.1	82188
其他计算机制造业	4.8	53.3	2.6	1.7	73661
办公设备制造业	5.5	65.7	2.2	2.9	117025
医疗设备及仪器仪表制造业	6.1	39.6	1.7	3.3	104487
医疗仪器设备及器械制造业	5.9	44.8	2.0	2.5	76709
仪器仪表制造业	6.1	38.9	1.7	3.5	112764

4-33 规模以上IT制造业企业主要经济指标（2016年）

Main Indicators of IT Manufacturing Enterprises above Designated Size (2016)

项目	企业单位数（个）	#亏损企业	工业增加值（万元）	主营业务收入（万元）
总计	1316	214	11070147	74487893
按企业规模分				
大型企业	124	13	7469874	58824446
中型企业	490	69	2674965	10989394
小型企业	648	103	882911	4344345
微型企业	54	29	42398	329709
按工业行业分（小类）				
训练健身器材制造	2		4507	21933
玩具制造	138	19	615245	1583201
信息化学品制造	2	1	15677	79217
照相机及器材制造	8	2	40452	189679
复印和胶印设备制造	10	2	170576	1012010
计算器及货币专用设备制造	5	3	152438	803725
医疗诊断、监护及治疗设备制造	2		3296	11788
微电机及其他电机制造	25	1	222467	778410
电线、电缆制造	133	13	399349	1967097
光纤、光缆制造	3		14838	76949
锂离子电池制造	42	7	363165	1126407
镍氢电池制造	2	1	6672	24538
其他电池制造	16	5	59522	252605
计算机整机制造	6	1	23642	97795
其他计算机制造	13	4	69234	520707
通信系统设备制造	17	2	857452	4031043
通信终端设备制造	47	10	2846138	36951954
电视机制造	6	1	48041	403778
音响设备制造	87	16	320100	1508436
影视录放设备制造	21	4	150350	755619
电子真空器件制造	1		3154	15709
集成电路制造	13	4	130413	870306
光电子器件及其他电子器件制造	128	27	692760	5391605
电子元件及组件制造	374	57	2994799	12835719
印制电路板制造	55	8	325741	1020977
其他电子设备制造	132	21	478047	1944752
电子测量仪器制造	4		10713	47724
其他未列明制造业	24	5	51361	164213

4-33 续表 1

(2016年)

项目	亏损企业亏损总额(万元)	利润总额(万元)	人均利润(元)	工业增加值率(%)	产品销售率(%)
总计	196261	1831131	20405	15.6	97.9
按企业规模分					
大型企业	77185	1387528	29517	13.6	98.3
中型企业	49778	387757	11975	23.4	96.1
小型企业	40535	79788	7743	20.3	97.9
微型企业	28764	-23942	-522747	12.3	98.7
按工业行业分(小类)					
训练健身器材制造		738	16503	19.9	96.8
玩具制造	8465	29164	2763	39.7	99.4
信息化学品制造	34	9248	140968	17.9	92.6
照相机及器材制造	827	5911	12214	21.2	99.7
复印和胶印设备制造	963	46630	38360	16.4	99.4
计算器及货币专用设备制造	2641	4608	2983	18.3	96.1
医疗诊断、监护及治疗设备制造		452	9264	28.7	102.8
微电机及其他电机制造	560	54540	29397	26.5	92.8
电线、电缆制造	3219	56988	12215	19.5	96.0
光纤、光缆制造		4914	37062	16.7	82.9
锂离子电池制造	3922	96993	34659	32.1	97.9
镍氢电池制造	250	931	10315	17.6	95.1
其他电池制造	740	6202	14102	21.2	95.5
计算机整机制造	75	1202	3437	24.3	100.4
其他计算机制造	3501	8978	9552	13.2	99.4
通信系统设备制造	1123	68527	12332	21.4	100.5
通信终端设备制造	45517	455104	43392	8.7	97.9
电视机制造	2626	19269	44327	11.9	92.9
音响设备制造	6610	28372	6667	19.3	96.4
影视录放设备制造	590	45340	46622	19.7	97.6
电子真空器件制造		717	23505	25.3	100.0
集成电路制造	7960	36027	40782	14.7	97.6
光电子器件及其他电子器件制造	45656	166257	27543	12.8	99.3
电子元件及组件制造	46917	520573	18672	23.0	98.5
印制电路板制造	4251	39741	14481	30.9	98.6
其他电子设备制造	9575	117613	26003	23.4	91.0
电子测量仪器制造		2048	18804	22.3	99.2
其他未列明制造业	242	4044	6795	32.1	96.8

4-33 续表 2

(2016年)

项目	总资产贡献率(%)	资产负债率(%)	流动资产周转率(次/年)	成本费用利润率(%)	全员劳动生产率(元/人)
总计	7.7	70.5	2.3	2.5	123360
按企业规模分					
大型企业	8.6	75.9	2.6	2.4	158905
中型企业	6.6	56.3	1.7	3.6	82610
小型企业	4.9	63.0	1.6	1.9	85687
微型企业	-4.3	65.0	1.3	-6.8	925720
按工业行业分（小类）					
训练健身器材制造	7.0	66.7	1.6	3.5	100818
玩具制造	4.4	59.9	1.9	1.9	58289
信息化学品制造	18.3	63.0	1.5	13.3	238976
照相机及器材制造	5.6	50.0	1.8	3.2	83577
复印和胶印设备制造	11.8	55.8	2.9	4.9	140322
计算器及货币专用设备制造	1.4	72.0	1.6	0.6	98691
医疗诊断、监护及治疗设备制造	4.0	16.0	1.1	4.0	67543
微电机及其他电机制造	11.2	39.5	1.8	7.5	119909
电线、电缆制造	5.5	55.8	1.4	3.0	85598
光纤、光缆制造	14.5	67.5	1.8	6.9	111902
锂离子电池制造	8.5	48.5	1.0	9.3	129771
镍氢电池制造	1.9	48.8	1.0	3.8	73886
其他电池制造	3.8	53.5	1.7	2.5	135338
计算机整机制造	1.5	53.2	1.8	1.2	67588
其他计算机制造	4.8	53.4	2.6	1.8	73661
通信系统设备制造	15.7	78.1	6.7	1.7	154312
通信终端设备制造	7.4	93.8	2.6	1.2	271368
电视机制造	5.8	80.9	0.9	4.7	110514
音响设备制造	6.4	55.8	2.3	1.9	75215
影视录放设备制造	19.5	69.6	2.3	6.4	154601
电子真空器件制造	17.0	74.8	2.5	4.8	103414
集成电路制造	7.5	51.1	2.1	4.3	147626
光电子器件及其他电子器件制造	7.9	56.1	2.5	3.2	114766
电子元件及组件制造	7.8	52.0	2.0	4.2	107420
印制电路板制造	5.4	48.3	1.7	4.0	118693
其他电子设备制造	10.7	60.2	1.8	6.4	105690
电子测量仪器制造	15.8	49.8	3.5	4.5	98377
其他未列明制造业	4.0	44.8	2.0	2.5	86306

主要统计指标解释

Explanatory Notes on Main Statistical Indicators

工业 指从事自然资源的开采，对采掘品和农产品进行加工和再加工的物质生产部门。具体包括：对自然资源的开采，如采矿、晒盐、森林采伐等（但不包括禽兽捕猎和水产捕捞）；对农副产品的加工、再加工，如粮油加工、食品加工、轧花、缫丝、纺织、制革等；对采掘品的加工、再加工，如炼铁、炼钢、化工生产、石油加工、机器制造、木材加工等，以及电力、自来水、煤气的生产和供应等；对工业品的修理、翻新，如机器制造设备的修理、交通运输工具（包括小卧车）的修理等。

轻工业 是指主要提供生活消费品和制作手工工具的工业。按其所使用的原料不同，可分为两大类：以农产品为原料的轻工业，是指直接或以农产品为基本原料的轻工业，主要包括食品制造、饮料制造、烟草加工、纺织、缝纫、皮革和毛皮制作、造纸以及印刷等工业；以非农产品为原料的轻工业，是以工业品为原料的轻工业，主要包括文教体育用品、化学药品制造、合成纤维制造、日用化学制品、日用玻璃制品、日用金属制品、手工工具制造、医疗器械制造、文化和办公用机械制造等工业。

重工业 是指为国民经济各部门提供物质技术基础的主要生产资料的工业。按其生产性质和产品用途，可以分为下列三类：采掘（伐）工业，是对自然资源的开采，包括石油开采、煤炭开采、金属矿开采等工业；原材料工业，指向国民经济各部门提供基本材料、动力和燃料的工业，包括金属冶炼及加工、炼焦及焦炭化学、化学原料、水泥、人造板以及电力、石油和煤炭加工等工业；加工工业，是指对工业原材料进行再加工制造的工业，包括装备国民经济各部门的机械设备制造工业、金属结构、水泥制造等工业，以及为农业提供的生产资料如化肥、农药等工业。

资产总额 是指企业拥有或控制的能以货币计量的经济资源，包括各种财产、债权和其他权利。资产按其流动性（即资产的变现能力和支付能力）划分为：流动资产、长期投资、固定资产、无形资产、递延资产和其他资产，即为企业资产负债表中的资产总计项。

流动资产 是企业资产的重要组成部分，通常是指一年内或超过一年的一个营业周期内可以变现或耗用的资产。其特点是在企业的生产经营或者业务活动中不断地在生产循环中周转，不断改变其形态。其价值一次性消耗、转移或者实现。包括：货币资金、短期投资、应收票据、应收账款、预付账款、其他应收款、存货、待摊费用、待处理流动资产损失、一年内到期的本期债券投资及其他流动资产。

固定资产原价 是指企业在建造、购置、安装、改建、扩建、技术改造某项固定资产时实际支出的全部货币总额。它一般包括买价、包装费、运杂费和安装费等。

固定资产合计 包括固定资产净值、固定资产清理、在建工程、待处理固定资产净损失所占用的资金合计。

固定资产净值 是指固定资产原价减去历年已提折旧额后的净额。

负债 是指企业所承担的能以货币计量，将以资产或劳务偿付的债务。其偿还形式可以用货币，也可以用资产或提供劳务的方式进行。包括流动负债、长期负债和递延税款贷项等，即为企业资产负债表的负债合计项。

实收资本 是指企业实际收到的投资人投入的资本。包括有国家资本、集体资本、法人资本、个人资本、外商资本、港澳台资本等。

主营业务收入 是企业在销售商品、提供劳务及让渡资产使用权等日常活动中所产生的收入。

主营业务税金及附加 是指企业日常活动应负担的税金及附加，包括营业税、消费税、城市维护建设税、资源税、土地增值税和教育费附加等。

主营业务成本 是指企业因销售商品、提供劳务或让渡资产使用权等日常活动而发生的实际成本。

营业利润 是企业生产经营活动所取得的利润，包括主营业务利润和其他业务利润。

利润总额 是指企业在一定时期内生产经营活动的最终的财务成果，是企业的收入减去有关成本与费用后的差额，收入大于相关的成本费用，企业就盈利，反之则亏损。包括营业利润、补贴收入、投资净收益、营业外收支净额、以前年度损失调整。

应交增值税 是指企业按税法规定，从事货物销售或提供加工、修理修配劳务等增加货物价值的活动本期应交纳的税金，即企业在报告期应交的增值税额。计算公式为：

应交增值税 = 销项税额-(进项税额-进项税额转出)-出口抵减内销产品应纳税额-减免税款+出口退税

从业人员平均人数 从业人员指企业工作并取得劳动报酬的全部人员数。包括在岗职工、再就业的离退休人员、民办教师及在企业工作的外方人员和港澳台方人员、兼职人员、借用的外单位人员和第二职业者。不包括离开本单位但仍保留劳动关系的职工。而从业人员平均人数指报告期内每天平均拥有的从业人员人数。其计算公式为：

月平均人数=报告月内每天实有人数之和÷报告月日历日数

季平均人数=季内各月平均人数之和÷3

年平均人数=全年各月平均人数之和÷12

资产利税率 是在一定时期内已实现的利润、税金总额与同期的资产总额之比。计算公式：

$$资产利税率（\%）= \frac{报告期累计实现利税总额}{资产总额} \times 100\%$$

资产利税率反映每单位（通常是每万元）资产所提供的利税金额。它是考察和评价部门或企业资金运用的经济效益，分析资金投入效果的主要分析指标。

产值利税率 是报告期已实现的利润、税金总额（包括利润总额、产品销售税金及附加和应交增值税）占同期全部工业总产值的百分比，计算公式为：

$$产值利税率（\%）= \frac{利税总额}{工业总产值（现价）} \times 100\%$$

工业经济效益综合指数 是现行综合评价工业经济效益总体水平及工业经济运行质量的指数，它是以若干项代表性经济效益指标，分别除以各项指标的标准值，再乘以各自的权数，加总后除以总权数求得。其计算公式为：

$$工业经济效益综合指数= \Sigma（\frac{某项经济效益指标报告期数值}{该项指标标准值} \times 权数）\div 总权数$$

上式总权数为 100。

工业产品销售率 是反映工业产品已实现销售的程度，是分析工业产销衔接情况、研究工业产品满足社会需求的指标。计算公式是：

$$产品销售率（\%）= \frac{现价工业销售产值}{现价工业总产值} \times 100\%$$

总资产贡献率 是指企业一定时期内全部资产获利能力，是企业经营业绩和管理水平的集中体现，是评价和考核企业盈利能力的核心指标。计算公式为：

$$总资产贡献率（\%）=\frac{利润总额+税金总额+利息支出}{平均资产总额}\times 100\%\times\frac{12}{累计月数}$$

注：税金总额为主营业务税金及附加与应交增值税之和，平均资产总额为期初、期末资产总计的算术平均值。

资本保值增值率 是反映企业净资产变动状况的一个重要指标，是企业发展能力的集中体现。是指期末所有者权益总额与期初所有者权益总额的比率。计算公式为：

$$资本保值增值率（\%）=\frac{期末所有者权益}{期初所有者权益}\times 100\%$$

所有者权益等于资产总计减负债总计。

资产负债率 是指反映企业经营风险的大小，反映企业利用债权人提供的资金从事经营活动的能力。计算公式为：

$$资产负债率（\%）=\frac{负债总额}{资产总额}\times 100\%$$

资产及负债均为报告期期末数。

流动资产周转率 是指一定时期内流动资产完成的周转次数，反映投入工业企业流动资金的周转速度，一般以一年内周转多少次表示。计算公式为：

$$流动资产周转率（次）=\frac{产品销售收入}{流动资产平均余额}\times\frac{12}{累计月数}$$

成本费用利润率 是指工业企业投入的生产成本及费用的经济效益，同时也反映企业降低成本所取得的经济效益。计算公式为：

$$成本费用利润率（\%）=\frac{利润总额}{成本费用总额}\times 100\%$$

注：成本费用总额为产品销售成本、销售费用、管理费用、财务费用之和。

全员劳动生产率 是指反映企业的生产效率和劳动投入的经济效益。一般用平均每人一年创造的工业增加值表示。计算公式为：

$$全员劳动生产率（元/人）=\frac{工业增加值}{全部职工平均人数}\times\frac{12}{累计月数}$$

五、固定资产投资与建筑业

Investment in Fixed Assets and Construction

5-1 主要年份固定资产投资与建筑业主要指标

Main Indicators of Investment in Fixed Assets and Construction in Main Years

项　　目	单　位	1990年	1995年	2000年	2005年	2010年	2015年	2016年
固定资产投资总额	万元	75052	631355	1028914	5972443	11149822	14465180	15574580
#国有单位	万元	50658	106935	197658	686333	1479886	1782379	1206638
私营个体经济	万元				1027969	2077250	3304853	4172283
港澳台投资经济	万元		10281	130501	1246450	1326063	1343480	1851731
外商投资经济	万元		230409	92699	507322	938943	1336845	1079654
新增固定资产	万元				1732967	5778616	7269377	7425999
固定资产交付使用率	%				29.0	51.8	50.3	47.7
房屋竣工面积	万平方米				696.99	686.22	499.49	320.55
房屋面积竣工率	%				22.5	20.7	9.4	5.6
固定资产计划总投资	万元				13905355	45000174	68582894	77048003
固定资产投资建设周期	年				2.32	4.04	4.74	4.95
固定资产投资资金来源	万元	50100	480875	1047861	6717711	18550102	26149934	30918002
#国家预算内资金	万元	3600	10858	10490	536	130717	553110	322080
国内贷款	万元	2900	27439	122561	651723	1882278	2087480	2479501
利用外资	万元	17000	194486	207444	940432	1400920	698707	624388
自筹资金	万元	25400	163090	587176	3901138	8390847	8998227	8819572
房地产开发投资	万元		85163	112498	1444277	2989853	5752145	6427591
房地产开发当年房屋施工面积	万平方米		160.74	315.45	1160.17	2060.54	3921.20	4408.65
房地产开发当年房屋竣工面积	万平方米		76.78	103.20	132.88	296.59	325.43	232.68
#住宅	万平方米		68.36	77.97	115.23	256.09	266.01	169.62
商品房销售面积	万平方米		25.42	63.21	321.85	511.25	1040.65	1024.25
#住宅	万平方米		20.49	51.02	297.19	469.90	948.50	887.01
建筑企业（单位）个数	个	8	8	99	361	431	540	542
建筑企业平均人数	人	6803	22200	64300	79965	57473	81440	100723
建筑企业总产值	万元	12678	94941	404493	843540	1220569	2245873	2672168
劳动生产率（按总产值计算）	元/人	18636	42766	60849	108136	218076	275770	265299
建筑业房屋施工面积	万平方米	66.30	278.72	1218.00	1234.98	733.44	1072.42	914.05
建筑业房屋竣工面积	万平方米	29.95	94.99	53.76	707.77	311.94	453.13	349.06

注：从2011年起，固定资产投资统计起点由计划投资50万元提高到计划投资500万元，下同。

5-2 历年固定资产投资

Total Investment in Fixed Assets over Years

单位：万元

年份	固定资产投资总额	#民营	#外资	#港澳台	#房地产开发
1978	2319				
1979	1641				
1980	2395				
1981	3756				
1982	18102				
1983	18370				
1984	30050				
1985	70600				
1986	115173				
1987	141856				
1988	165459				
1989	50135				
1990	75052				
1991	137464				
1992	188824				
1993	327630		62600		52110
1994	1407621		1038599		78392
1995	631355		240690		85163
1996	676185		259705		86258
1997	658941		69055		86662
1998	769953		91719	35868	95451
1999	883201		188036	116708	104411
2000	1028914		146887	96112	112498
2001	1254945		224812	181822	148544
2002	1915741		466569	213458	268350
2003	3193889		888664	619193	551184
2004	4548691		1094045	716611	1144195
2005	5972443		1753772	1246450	1444277
2006	7054511	2410417	2297486	1584104	1642398
2007	8412074	2841860	2356983	1136955	2094187
2008	9443426	3240949	2710398	1469186	2714197
2009	10940753	4279669	2038232	1114631	2776623
2010	11149822	4847208	2265006	1326063	2989853
2011	10793144	4438880	2228117	1460388	3733062
2012	11803493	6662441	2942143	1891724	3773210
2013	13839352	8835235	2566790	1460423	4976593
2014	14271099	9496756	2234743	1174881	5880630
2015	14465180	9475855	2680325	1343480	5752145
2016	15574580	10610512	2931385	1851731	6427591

5-3 按登记类型和行业分的固定资产投资（2016年）

Total Investment in Fixed Assets by Registration Status and Sector (2016)

单位：万元

项　目	全市合计	#房地产
合　计	15574580	6427591
按登记注册类型分		
内资	12643195	5804301
国有	682349	
集体	751381	256575
股份合作	1800	
国有联营	25673	
集体联营	248	
国有与集体联营	167469	
其他联营		
国有独资公司	498616	7807
其他有限责任公司	5703838	3186560
股份有限公司	282893	24456
私营	4121258	2274706
其他	356645	54197
个体经营：个体户	50425	
个人合伙	600	
港澳台商投资	1851731	425994
#合资经营	230866	38125
合作经营	190158	176203
独资	1224856	190201
股份有限公司		
外商投资	1079654	197296
#合资经营	199449	110304
合作经营	2727	1450
独资	862098	85542
股份有限公司		
按国民经济行业分		
第一产业	11665	
第二产业	5660622	
制造业	5037401	
电力、热力、燃气及水的生产和供应业	617045	
建筑业	10000	
第三产业	9902293	6427591
交通运输、仓储和邮政业	1333819	
信息传输、软件和信息技术服务业	172826	
批发和零售业	178852	
住宿和餐饮业	28047	
金融业	55934	
房地产业	7092286	6427591
租赁和商务服务业	21262	
科学研究和技术服务业	173136	
水利、环境和公共设施管理业	453295	
居民服务、修理和其他服务业	5100	
教育	251368	
卫生和社会工作	65507	
文化、体育和娱乐业	37400	
公共管理、社会保障和社会组织	27957	

5-4 固定资产投资主要指标（2016年）

Main Indicators of Total Investment in Fixed Assets (2016)

单位：万元

项目	计划总投资	本年完成投资	建筑工程	安装工程	设备工器具购置	其他费用
合计	36117388	9146989	4532237	473706	3446851	694195
按登记注册类型分						
内资	31311838	6838894	3955676	337214	1910998	635006
国有	6617077	682349	551384	43173	26737	61055
集体	1099600	494806	401162	62822	19878	10944
股份合作	10000	1800			1447	353
国有联营	27000	25673			25673	
集体联营	21275	248	248			
国有与集体联营	1120700	167469	126619			40850
其他联营						
国有独资公司	1639249	490809	219866	11058	185309	74576
其他有限责任公司	12389317	2517278	1285284	112302	845165	274527
股份有限公司	1686061	258437	106889	54255	83194	14099
私营个体	5811096	1897577	1018846	42418	717099	119214
其他	890463	302448	245378	11186	6496	39388
港澳台商投资	3341028	1425737	355959	94187	946791	28800
外商投资	1464522	882358	220602	42305	589062	30389
按国民经济行业分						
第一产业	18295	11665	10116	286	950	313
第二产业	14445344	5660622	2058813	232521	3103904	265384
制造业	12697928	5037401	1845482	185560	2824079	182280
电力、热力、燃气及水的生产和供应业	1734967	617045	211786	45021	277556	82682
建筑业	20000	10000	3698	2000	3200	1102
第三产业	21653749	3474702	2463308	240899	341997	428498
交通运输、仓储和邮政业	13095011	1333819	930341	15430	161566	226482
信息传输、软件和信息技术服务业	300357	172826	32510	43108	95717	1491
批发和零售业	847175	178852	90760	10538	33599	43955
住宿和餐饮业	116764	28047	22108	4783	909	247
金融业	385905	55934	39788	16033	105	8
房地产业	2631089	664695	523252	53763	6762	80918
租赁和商务服务业	299480	21262	14710	5435		1117
科学研究和技术服务业	1174441	173136	114613	25529	14241	18753
水利、环境和公共设施管理业	1501428	453295	398448	37414	6509	10924
居民服务、修理和其他服务业	5100	5100		4000	1100	
教育	886368	251368	214080	16225	2325	18738
卫生和社会工作	240429	65507	44532	2533	15253	3189
文化、体育和娱乐业	91532	37400	12541	2265	2980	19614
公共管理、社会保障和社会组织	69439	27957	23262	2313		2382
按建设性质分						
新建	28670226	5208148	3717907	272604	619241	598396
扩建	2169113	511284	346883	32298	76136	55967
改建和技术改造	2854056	1456431	423158	164214	835370	33689
单纯建造生活设施	59545	22991	13096	990	2762	6143
迁建	233011	33002	25592	3600	3810	
恢复	33205	5601	5601			
单纯购置	2098232	1909532			1909532	

注：本表不含房地产开发投资。

5-4 续表 1

(2016年)

单位：万元

项目	本年新增固定资产	本年施工房屋面积(万平方米)	本年竣工房屋面积(万平方米)	本年资金来源合计	#上年末结余资金
合计	5875926	1291.71	87.87	9717582	908973
按登记注册类型分					
内资	4242865	1117.38	81.20	7071556	630446
国有	131062	69.01	0.63	757986	138541
集体	508178	155.27	9.04	508882	22181
股份合作				1800	
国有联营				25673	
集体联营				250	
国有与集体联营				135000	69339
其他联营					
国有独资公司	264161	17.95		494141	44054
其他有限责任公司	1172637	302.07	17.84	2627729	295521
股份有限公司	814073	28.90	0.99	281497	10006
私营个体	1188112	493.85	48.45	1928931	43182
其他	164642	50.32	4.25	309667	7622
港澳台商投资	1039079	115.98	3.19	1792030	203772
外商投资	593982	58.35	3.49	853996	74755
按国民经济行业分					
第一产业	6064	1.22		11665	
第二产业	3951789	790.67	63.93	6112583	432764
制造业	3574014	789.44	63.93	5467495	380318
电力、热力、燃气及水的生产和供应业	384026	0.43		638911	52446
建筑业		2.16		10001	
第三产业	1918073	499.83	23.94	3593334	476209
交通运输、仓储和邮政业	294281	85.64		1296111	319483
信息传输、软件和信息技术服务业	44572	1.08		189572	28945
批发和零售业	75857	38.96	1.06	211598	17808
住宿和餐饮业	12179	3.41	0.63	29314	608
金融业	1491	20.93		69002	1000
房地产业	1015954	214.16	17.37	622572	34339
租赁和商务服务业	3420	9.59		20705	62
科学研究和技术服务业	19908	11.41		258305	4859
水利、环境和公共设施管理业	302214	23.06	1.28	488660	33625
居民服务、修理和其他服务业	5100			5100	
教育	85848	53.61	1.85	256988	12115
卫生和社会工作	22756	17.90		65970	
文化、体育和娱乐业	11377	16.39	0.43	39695	18956
公共管理、社会保障和社会组织	15185	2.33	1.33	34238	4409
按建设性质分					
新建	2785881	1143.81	76.65	5698907	675009
扩建	241437	95.09	6.80	545297	68194
改建和技术改造	1042558	52.81	4.43	1410862	66462
单纯建造生活设施	28000			14628	3
迁建	27928			32122	
恢复	560			5233	
单纯购置	1749562			2010533	99305

5-4 续表 2

(2016年)

单位：万元

项目	本年资金来源					
	#本年资金来源小计	国家预算内资金	国内贷款	利用外资	自筹资金	其他资金来源
合计	8808609	322080	768025	623529	6619053	475922
按登记注册类型分						
内资	6441110	322080	723325	8060	5040934	346711
国有	619445	253580	37361		274519	53985
集体	486701	15961			338261	132479
股份合作	1800				1499	301
国有联营	25673				25673	
集体联营	250				250	
国有与集体联营	65661				65661	
其他联营						
国有独资公司	450087	29550	334569		85968	
其他有限责任公司	2332208	21056	234502	848	1998536	77266
股份有限公司	271491		24401	4800	240742	1548
私营个体	1885749	1770	84542	2412	1752985	44040
其他	302045	163	7950		256840	37092
港澳台商投资	1588258		26986	412278	1112904	36090
外商投资	779241		17714	203191	465215	93121
按国民经济行业分						
第一产业	11665				11665	
第二产业	5679819	14448	513841	563866	4398142	189522
制造业	5087177		176913	563346	4178661	168257
电力、热力、燃气及水的生产和供应业	586465	14448	336928	520	213304	21265
建筑业	10001				10001	
第三产业	3117125	307632	254184	59663	2209246	286400
交通运输、仓储和邮政业	976628	124229	195060	51350	554001	51988
信息传输、软件和信息技术服务业	160627		9000	2326	147393	1908
批发和零售业	193790		3600	5987	174003	10200
住宿和餐饮业	28706	498	874		24672	2662
金融业	68002				67971	31
房地产业	588233	11299	9200		537120	30614
租赁和商务服务业	20643	391	8500		11752	
科学研究和技术服务业	253446	60607	17950		169473	5416
水利、环境和公共设施管理业	455035	80934			253817	120284
居民服务、修理和其他服务业	5100				5100	
教育	244873	15218	10000		162854	56801
卫生和社会工作	65970	5650			56760	3560
文化、体育和娱乐业	20739	1211			18730	798
公共管理、社会保障和社会组织	29829	7595			20096	2138
按建设性质分						
新建	5023898	274195	706142	89887	3654963	298711
扩建	477103	11609		22441	387620	55433
改建和技术改造	1344400	35373	46532	84848	1116731	60916
单纯建造生活设施	14625	70		1187	3859	9509
迁建	32122		1525		30597	
恢复	5233	833				4400
单纯购置	1911228		13826	425166	1425283	46953

5-5 固定资产投资分类情况（2016年）

Basic Statistics on Total Investment in Fixed Assets by Type (2016)

单位：万元

项目	计划总投资	自开始建设累计完成投资	本年完成投资	#住宅	本年新增固定资产
固定资产投资总额	36117388	22545079	9146989	74907	5875926
#基础设施	15366604	9460652	2197811	94	804603
#基础产业	16046243	9706494	2357342	94	930191
#城市建设	3578158	2649212	655440	94	332192
#原材料	924399	380818	220268		160991
#能源	1535199	884007	521980		355859
#工业合计	14432895	9046565	5654446	3568	3958040
#工业九大产业	9565898	6019939	3692136	750	2552752
#电子信息业	4646288	2962904	1841187		1217857
电气机械及专用设备	1786406	1336541	922679	750	755751
石油及化学	615612	178172	111670		111316
纺织及服装	402909	264996	145542		133477
食品饮料	898298	576738	243306		80803
建筑材料	242994	141040	78481		53221
森工造纸	372315	265684	178225		134471
医药	188067	106436	48004		24574
汽车	413009	187428	123042		41282

注：本表不含房地产开发投资。

5-6 房地产开发主要指标

Main Indicators of Real Estate Development

项目	单位	2005年	2010年	2015年	2016年
本年土地购置面积	万平方米	45	136	122	89
本年完成投资额	万元	1444277	2989853	5752145	6427591
#住宅	万元	1197154	2504525	4016931	4391349
资金来源	万元	1632570	6533564	10836961	14121627
#国内贷款	万元	114755	1271530	1112220	1711476
利用外资	万元	2075	75182	2960	859
自筹资金	万元	867824	2025670	2405896	2200519
房屋施工面积	万平方米	1160	2061	3921	4409
#住宅	万平方米	890	1687	2831	3158
房屋竣工面积	万平方米	133	297	325	233
#住宅	万平方米	115	256	266	170
商品房屋销售额	万元	1193991	3737742	10191063	14181733
#住宅	万元	1091095	3341485	9145019	12223119
商品房屋销售面积	万平方米	322	511	1041	1024
#住宅	万平方米	297	470	949	887

5-7　房地产开发企业主要经济指标（2016年）

Main Indicators of Real Estate Enterprises (2016)

单位：万元

项　　目	资产总计	负债总计	主营业务收入	主营业务税金及附加	利润总额
合　　计	37875537	31601872	10075958	1036887	1488572
按登记注册类型分					
＃内源型经济	34224500	29102783	9169385	957210	1296052
＃国有经济					
集体经济	941813	826773	134378	17105	13375
私营个体经济	10235479	9110536	2743379	259259	365307
外源型经济	3651036	2499090	906572	79676	192520
＃港澳台商投资	2058040	1245844	616103	49777	142450
外商投资	1592996	1253246	290469	29899	50070
民营经济	34003137	28722919	9268364	973797	1377863
按控股情况分					
国有控股	747354	675789	161513	12762	12367
集体控股	1678350	1491129	395128	51276	60139
私人控股	19558808	17097658	5743468	540989	738007
港澳台控股	1446848	808987	516576	42410	100421
外商控股	1678198	1394178	129505	7918	-2079
其他控股	12765979	10134131	3129768	381532	579717
按资质等级分					
一级	3719063	2323550	387122	128398	18306
二级	4732361	4133626	604473	57171	133769
三级	3874701	2915961	821680	76272	173548
四级	6200196	4629307	2719868	229455	402650
暂定	17717831	16170474	5170944	519389	724397
其他	1631385	1428955	371871	26204	35902

5-8 房地产开发投资情况（2015-2016年）

Investment in Real Estate Development (2015-2016)

项 目	2015年		2016年	
	房地产开发投资（万元）	#住宅	房地产开发投资（万元）	#住宅
合 计	5752145	4016931	6427591	4391349
内资	5274226	3697717	5804301	3928623
国有				
集体	205846	149852	256575	191275
国有独资公司	15510	15401	7807	7807
其他有限责任公司	3504643	2527434	3186560	2089119
私营独资	17523	12266	68509	23950
私营有限责任公司	1464235	935441	2180328	1541755
私营股份有限公司	7522	7522	25869	21047
其他（内资企业）	20971	14982	54197	30009
港澳台商投资	211499	156143	425994	333000
外商投资	266420	163071	197296	129726

5-9 房地产开发企业、房屋建筑面积及价值（2015-2016年）

Floor Space and Value of Buildings in Real Estate Development (2015-2016)

项 目	2015年			2016年		
	房屋建筑面积（平方米）		竣工房屋价值（万元）	房屋建筑面积（平方米）		竣工房屋价值（万元）
	施工面积	竣工面积		施工面积	竣工面积	
合 计	39212029	3254272	1494203	44086547	2326810	1186996
内资	36032870	3025551	1390378	39663515	2182160	1057774
国有						
集体	1620424	109139	32242	1618892	245530	85067
国有独资公司	221312	31084	215	104976		
其他有限责任公司	22130404	2184773	1122084	22664278	1040476	608004
私营独资	71448			296248	78197	15500
私营有限责任公司	11372308	642471	224220	14230740	817957	349203
私营股份有限公司	85034			220173		
其他（内资企业）	263701			287819		
港澳台商投资	1977539	126141	49780	3262456	57431	70475
外商投资	1201620	102580	54045	1160576	87219	58747

5-10 商品房屋销售情况（2016年）

Sale of Commercialized Buildings (2016)

项　目	商品房屋销售面积（平方米）	#住宅	商品房屋销售额（万元）	#住宅
合　计	10242482	8870113	14181733	12223119
内资	9534027	8265811	13103596	11360140
国有				
集体	715928	703945	742793	726366
国有独资公司	18617	12865	19347	13659
其他有限责任公司	5096295	4361621	7417085	6345513
私营独资	91857	89533	126834	122717
私营有限责任公司	3429505	2919021	4562371	3922275
私营股份有限公司	49369	49165	60071	59645
其他内资企业	68208	65413	101814	96684
港澳台商投资	607580	522005	931965	750842
外商投资	100875	82297	146172	112137

5-11 劳务分包建筑业企业主要指标（2015-2016年）

Main Indicators of Labour Subcontract Construction Enterprises (2015-2016)

指　标	单　位	2015年	2016年
企业单位数	个	63	63
年平均人数	人	13821	29857
固定资产原价	万元	8787	18954
建筑业总产值	万元	123405	220353
资产合计	万元	90209	120331
主营业务收入	万元	123208	228557
利润总额	万元	1854	5892

5-12 总承包和专业承包建筑业企业主要指标（2015-2016年）

Main Indicators of Construction Enterprises Qualified for General Contracts and Specialized Contracts (2015-2016)

指　　标	单　位	2015年	2016年
企业单位数	个	477	479
年平均人数	人	67619	70866
固定资产原价	万元	337445	338775
固定资产净值	万元	168270	192570
自有施工机械设备年末总台数	台	9005	11029
自有施工机械设备年末净值	万元	51407	60102
自有施工机械设备年末总功率	万千瓦	42	52
建筑业总产值	万元	2122468	2451815
建筑工程产值	万元	1820341	2094076
安装工程产值	万元	237391	296677
其他产值	万元	64735	61062
建筑业竣工产值	万元	1349919	1411221
房屋建筑施工面积	万平方米	1072	914
房屋建筑竣工面积	万平方米	453	349
资产合计	万元	4474986	4795166
主营业务收入	万元	2183415	2774754
利润总额	万元	94852	80806

主要统计指标解释

Explanatory Notes on Main Statistical Indicators

固定资产投资额 是以货币形式表现的在一定时期内建造和购置固定资产的工作量以及与此有关的费用的总称。按构成可分为建筑工程、安装工程、设备工器具购置和其他费用。

房屋建筑施工面积 指报告期内施工的全部房屋建筑面积。包括本期新开工的面积和上期开工跨入本期继续施工的房屋面积，以及上期已停建在本期复工的房屋面积。本期竣工和本期施工后又停缓建的房屋，其建筑面积仍计入本期施工房屋面积中。

房屋建筑竣工面积 指在报告期内房屋建筑按照设计要求已全部完工，达到住人和使用条件，经验收鉴定合格(或达到竣工验收标准)，可正式移交使用的各栋房屋建筑面积的总和。

房屋建筑面积竣工率 指一定时期内房屋竣工面积占同期房屋施工面积的比率。它是从房屋建筑施工速度的角度反映投资效果和建筑业经济效益的指标。

固定资产交付使用率 指一定时期新增固定资产与同期完成投资额的比率。它反映各个时期固定资产动用速度、衡量建设过程中投资效果的一个综合性指标。

六、运输邮电

Transport, Postal and Telecommunication Services

6-1　主要年份运输邮电主要指标

Main Indicators of Transport, Postal and Telecommunication Services in Main Years

项　　目	单　位	1985年	1990年	1995年	2000年	2005年	2010年	2015年	2016年
公路通车里程	公里	1240	1325	2327	2519	2871	4751	5165	5266
#高速公路	公里				89	154	217	335	388
一级公路	公里		6	679	782	1315	2394	2601	2649
内河通航里程	公里	532	598	598	798	664	643	643	643
公路桥梁	座	211	267	338	538	826	1211	1422	1432
民用汽车	辆	7897	19394	88311	153684	406577	920766	1844948	2246220
#载客	辆	1878	7225	25366	69658	268918	772701	1694322	2082986
载货	辆	5980	12087	52242	80405	129298	143005	145659	158212
摩托车	辆	11786	47881	255591	482636	775838	423766	32698	772
机动船	艘	2883	5885	5292	806	467	286	422	424
机动船净载重	吨位	80324	186056	259329	152661	148737	557846	1767170	1852267
邮电局(所)	处	52	53	273	594	702	555	797	787
邮路长度	公里	790	459	685	3550	6835	4667	5168	9032
局用交换机容量	万门	1.14	6.98	52.29	103.13	286.25	365.02	358.00	358.00
移动电话交换机总容量	万户			4.8	154.2	1059.1	1657.0	2033.0	2424.0
本地电话用户	万户	0.77	4.90	31.57	78.12	384.52	332.42	298.23	272.63
移动电话用户(含充值卡)	万户		0.05	4.77	123.68	1016.41	1607.60	1756.75	1575.08
互联网用户	万户			0.05	13.78	52.90	153.92	201.74	185.27
邮政业务收入(含快递)	万元						63178	992490	1395519
电信业务收入	万元						1490174	1497315	1555812
客运量	万人	2072	5758	10237	30697	33551	77446	4961	4874
#公路	万人	1940	5728	10210	30680	33510	77415	4928	4847
旅客周转量	万人公里	95237	322236	446230	1001906	1185290	1290692	771316	773194
#公路	万人公里	90950	320690	444293	1000492	1182000	1288675	769168	771437
货运量	万吨	2913	2701	4266	5431	6400	9312	15385	15594
#公路	万吨	1922	1571	2377	3440	4586	7640	10469	10325
货物周转量	万吨公里	171591	184700	264605	404678	424829	1090340	5048509	4552331
#公路	万吨公里	113038	72162	128026	246046	272500	510801	716902	716734
港口货物吞吐量	万吨	276	233	201	746	2280	5657	13149	14584

注：1．2006年起公路通车里程含专用公路和村道，下同。
2．2010年起，邮政业务相关指标不包括速递物流及邮政储蓄银行独立运营部分；2015年起采用邮管局数据，含快递业务，下同。
3．2014年起，客运量和旅客周转量不含城市客运量，数据与往年不可比，下同。

6-2 历年运输线路长度与公路密度

Length of Transportation Routes and Road Density over Years

年 份	公路通车里程(公里)	等级公路	#一级	等外公路	高级、次高级路面通车里程(公里)	内河通航里程(公里)	公路密度(公里/百平方公里)
1978	1259	287		972		530	51.08
1979	1225	355		870		603	49.70
1980	1225	355		870		603	49.70
1981	1225	845		380		415	49.70
1982	1225	845		380		115	49.70
1983	1225	872		353		132	49.70
1984	1240	896		344		132	50.30
1985	1240	490		750		132	50.30
1986	1248	977		271		274	50.63
1987	1261	991		270		598	51.16
1988	1302	1068	6	234		598	52.82
1989	1325	1091	6	234		598	53.75
1990	1325	1102	6	223	750	598	53.75
1991	1759	1226	6	533	1137	598	71.36
1992	2055	1431	151	624	1442	599	83.37
1993	2260	1673	315	587	1675	598	91.68
1994	2292	1868	599	424	1773	598	92.98
1995	2327	1930	679	397	1650	598	94.40
1996	2330	2087	689	243	1653	598	94.50
1997	2330	2087	690	243	1563	598	94.50
1998	2429	1897	714	480	1958	598	98.52
1999	2467	1935	717	480	2048	798	100.06
2000	2519	2339	782	91	2253	798	102.15
2001	2570	2393	845	78	2321	798	104.26
2002	2641	2464	908	78	2406	798	107.14
2003	2688	2508	967	75	2472	716	109.05
2004	2759	2609	1148	37	2637	798	111.93
2005	2871	2686	1315	31	2774	664	116.47
2006	3891	3619	1585	117	3823	664	157.85
2007	3924	3650	1591	116	3860	535	159.19
2008	4001	3884	1639	117	3864	643	162.31
2009	4713	4598	2389	115	4643	643	191.21
2010	4751	4637	2394	114	4681	643	192.74
2011	4828	4716	2420	112	4759	643	196.24
2012	4969	4861	2484	108	4800	643	201.98
2013	5002	4896	2507	106	4937	643	202.94
2014	5145	5058	2580	87	5093	643	208.72
2015	5165	5078	2601	86	5165	643	209.53
2016	5266	5180	2649	86	5225	643	214.08

注：公路密度数据来源于交通运输局，下同。

6-3 主要年份运输线路长度

Length of Transport Routes in Main Years

项目	单位	1980年	1990年	1995年	2000年	2005年	2010年	2015年	2016年
公路通车里程合计	公里	1225	1325	2327	2519	2871	4751	5165	5266
#按等级分									
等级公路	公里	355	1102	1930	2339	2686	4637	5078	5180
高速公路	公里				89	154	217	335	388
一级	公里		6	679	782	1315	2394	2601	2649
二级	公里		65	361	684	703	1317	1366	1363
三级	公里		60	135	310	297	178	256	259
四级	公里	355	971	755	563	371	532	520	522
等外公路	公里	870	223	397	91	31	114	86	86
#按路面分									
有路面里程	公里		800	1808	2508	2858	4689	5165	5225
#高级、次高级	公里		750	1650	2253	2774	4681	5165	5225
无路面里程	公里		524	519	11	13	62	41	41
桥梁合计	座		267	338	538	826	1211	1422	1432
	延米				39956	112385	162767	242319	245370
公路密度	公里/百平方公里	49.70	53.75	94.40	102.15	116.47	192.74	209.53	214.08
#等级公路密度	公里/百平方公里	14.40	44.71	78.30	94.89	108.97	188.12	206.00	210.57
内河通航里程	公里	603	598	598	798	664	643	643	643

6-4 主要年份运输工具拥有量

Possession of Main Means of Transport in Main Years

项目	单位	1985年	1990年	1995年	2000年	2005年	2010年	2015年	2016年
民用车辆拥有量									
汽车	辆	7897	19394	88311	153684	406577	920766	1844948	2246220
载客汽车	辆	1878	7225	25366	69658	268918	772701	1694322	2082986
	客位	23462	66361	302844	560155	2420591	5101240	9742352	11728222
载货汽车	辆	5980	12087	55000	81623	129298	143005	145659	158212
	吨位	20428	38010	133757	332621	243390	253879	305135	347079
其他汽车	辆	39	82	7945	2403	8361	5060	4967	5022
摩托车	辆	11786	47881	255591	482636	775838	423766	32698	772
挂车	辆				8	2222	2983	3757	4155
民用运输船舶拥有量									
机动船	艘	2883	5885	5292	806	467	286	422	424
	净载重吨位	80323	186056	259329	152661	148737	557846	1767170	1852267
	客位	2056	776	1881	1054	604	902	550	550
#货船	艘	2866	5875	5259	796	465	283	420	422
	净载重吨位	80285	186038	259314	152661	148431	557236	1766865	1851962
客船	艘			26	10	2	3	2	2
	客位			1295	1054	604	902	550	550
期末机动车驾驶员	人	44186	118229	351947	563564	798086	1287738	2254668	2565483
#汽车驾驶员	人	10661	28768	94778	173865	428912	1110932	2202712	2524781

注：2002年起民用汽车拥有量按新的口径分类，部分指标数值与往年不可比。

6–5 历年客货运输量

Passenger and Freight Traffic over Years

年 份	客运量（万人）	公 路	水 运	旅客周转量（万人公里）	公 路	水 运
1978	403	224	179	9425	5097	4328
1979	467	272	195	11162	6354	4808
1980	572	362	210	13584	8285	5299
1981	578	349	229	13845	7943	5902
1982	639	405	234	16026	9683	6343
1983	1281	1071	210	54075	47939	6136
1984	1287	1130	157	62107	56890	5217
1985	2072	1940	132	95237	90950	4287
1986	2304	2224	80	127458	124322	3136
1987	3359	3283	76	159117	156578	2539
1988	3223	3176	47	173335	171575	1760
1989	5288	5254	34	240999	239193	1806
1990	5758	5728	30	322236	320690	1546
1991	6749	6719	30	373284	371720	1564
1992	9267	9247	20	503973	502607	1366
1993	10907	10897	10	577800	576116	1684
1994	11234	11229	5	595134	594100	1034
1995	10237	10210	27	446230	444293	1937
1996	10749	10723	26	477466	476072	1394
1997	11300	11273	27	511592	509614	1978
1998	17485	17463	22	577452	575541	1911
1999	25404	25385	19	804278	802590	1688
2000	30697	30680	17	1001906	1000492	1414
2001	31220	31203	17	1031579	1030192	1387
2002	32100	32081	19	1091821	1090155	1666
2003	32588	32566	22	1126964	1125098	1866
2004	33240	33200	40	1166262	1163010	3352
2005	33551	33510	41	1185290	1182000	3290
2006	35182	35143	39	1213809	1210944	2865
2007	37182	37136	46	1264982	1261777	3205
2008	122468	122431	37	2248521	2246128	2393
2009	73324	73291	33	1053469	1051324	2145
2010	77446	77415	31	1290692	1288675	2017
2011	80337	80306	31	1458811	1456782	2029
2012	79739	79707	32	1568758	1566652	2106
2013	78113	78082	31	1559856	1557823	2033
2014	5555	5524	31	854598	852594	2004
2015	4961	4928	33	771316	769168	2148
2016	4874	4847	27	773194	771437	1757

6-5 续表 1

年 份	货运量(万吨)	公 路	#个体及联户	水 运	#个体及联户
1978	394	73		321	
1979	399	68		331	
1980	349	51		298	
1981	317	37		280	
1982	319	35		284	
1983	2366	1519	1515	847	535
1984	2738	1728	1710	1018	718
1985	3110	1922	1906	1188	814
1986	3296	2208	2190	1088	725
1987	2618	1304	1288	1314	928
1988	2685	1374	1358	1311	912
1989	3233	1516	1501	1717	1375
1990	2701	1571	1557	1130	837
1991	2456	1300	1286	1156	282
1992	2895	1703	1688	1192	902
1993	3256	1976	1960	1280	1011
1994	3646	2233	2222	1413	1147
1995	4266	2377	2368	1889	1599
1996	4451	2645	2636	1806	1556
1997	4644	2748	2740	1896	1622
1998	4776	2808	2808	1968	1678
1999	5016	3039	3039	1977	1653
2000	5431	3440	3440	1991	1660
2001	5527	3539	3539	1988	1659
2002	5857	4015	4015	1842	1504
2003	5877	4046	4046	1831	1496
2004	6054	4250	4250	1804	721
2005	6400	4586	4586	1814	1484
2006	5481	4930	4930	551	
2007	5676	5115	1194	561	75
2008	9273	8010	1273	1263	86
2009	8733	6944	1973	1789	159
2010	9312	7640	2080	1672	158
2011	10165	8210	2155	1955	133
2012	11191	8421	2310	2770	84
2013	12863	9162	2897	3701	80
2014	15375	10915	4033	4460	81
2015	15385	10469	4523	4916	100
2016	15594	10325	4493	5269	90

6-5 续表 2

年份	货物周转量(万吨公里)	公路	#个体及联户	水运	#个体及联户	港口货物吞吐量(万吨)
1978	15148	924		14224		293
1979	15390	636		14654		297
1980	16353	1479		14874		295
1981	15606	304		15302		272
1982	17185	252		16933		253
1983	108634	70723	70572	37911	20317	319
1984	140113	91774	91702	48339	29179	268
1985	171591	113038	113002	58553	31784	276
1986	126898	71392	71358	55506	27916	268
1987	174942	101285	101253	73657	41049	296
1988	169112	69014	68986	100098	82351	320
1989	186626	70942	70921	115684	82351	297
1990	184700	72162	72141	112538	83094	233
1991	194101	82555	82534	111546	82075	267
1992	232752	116698	116673	116054	85084	292
1993	248230	134918	134890	113312	87574	313
1994	273053	151108	148152	121945	93235	370
1995	264605	128026	127928	136579	105099	201
1996	267193	121625	121603	145568	118169	289
1997	278649	126336	126244	152313	122428	338
1998	285889	130378	130378	155511	123343	516
1999	300410	143465	143465	156945	119120	654
2000	404678	246046	246046	158632	119855	746
2001	406247	250121	250121	156126	118112	883
2002	420684	265908	265908	154776	115444	1611
2003	422822	268998	268998	153824	114812	2352
2004	423669	272220	272220	151449	48377	2600
2005	424829	272500	272500	152329	113249	2280
2006	336783	278566	278566	58217		1951
2007	356677	297223	50803	59454	6414	2017
2008	1747489	462797	38398	1284692	5598	3208
2009	1016490	452880	126052	563610	8787	3530
2010	1090340	510801	131929	579539	9399	5657
2011	1874802	531304	138976	1343498	9606	6848
2012	2967132	543633	147604	2423499	5941	9228
2013	4322745	683889	216590	3638856	5296	11187
2014	4480052	755240	389342	3724812	4103	12900
2015	5048509	716902	307772	4331607	5629	13149
2016	4552331	716734	311885	3835597	4909	14584

6-6 历年主要运输工具年末拥有量

Possession of Main Means of Transport at Year-end over Years

年 份	民用汽车(辆)	#客车	货车	摩托车(辆)	机动船(艘)	万人拥有公共汽(电)车数量(标台)
1978	623	78	506	134	2169	
1979	1115	178	1089	156	2034	
1980	2009	516	1457	170	1948	
1981	3039	751	2031	517	2107	
1982	3419	791	2724	1168	2285	
1983	4473	854	3580	1636	2313	
1984	6059	1243	4822	7060	2563	
1985	7897	1878	5980	11786	2883	
1986	8632	2245	6334	18006	4368	
1987	9983	2954	6973	21308	4884	
1988	13581	3456	8690	26995	4911	
1989	16340	4214	10434	36820	4901	
1990	19394	7225	12087	47881	5885	
1991	20734	5206	15423	65770	4405	
1992	32625	5753	25048	106013	4351	
1993	48145	8710	35421	153014	4379	
1994	61572	11550	43925	200543	4562	
1995	88311	25366	55000	255591	5292	
1996	90793	29430	54870	249492	5313	
1997	103425	40101	62507	287076	5064	
1998	113435	47769	64434	382010	456	
1999	127007	55715	69470	399324	690	
2000	153684	69658	82841	482636	806	
2001	183638	89677	91304	560310	536	
2002	220134	116783	102253	642034	483	
2003	255603	155206	97047	692562	392	
2004	319725	210531	105050	687651	417	
2005	406577	268918	129298	775838	467	
2006	489306	351265	131704	697175	440	
2007	608933	466999	134825	567002	393	
2008	701600	557359	136295	521118	326	
2009	795554	653273	137334	470818	293	
2010	920766	772701	143005	423766	286	
2011	1061373	906454	149635	352553	312	
2012	1207044	1047922	153655	276401	333	
2013	1389103	1225695	158298	154568	351	17.47
2014	1559588	1405878	148612	88339	386	18.36
2015	1844948	1694322	145659	32698	422	16.88
2016	2246220	2082986	158212	772	424	19.73

6-7 主要年份邮电通信业务基本情况

Basic Statistics on Postal and Telecommunication Services in Main Years

项　　目	单位	1978年	1990年	1995年	2000年	2005年	2010年	2015年	2016年
邮电通信网									
邮电局、所	处	50	53	273	594	702	555	797	787
邮路长度	公里	513	459	685	3550	6835	4667	5168	9032
农村投递线路长度	公里	1985	1812	2057	8865	19722	13261	21549	22390
邮电通信工具									
邮政汽车	辆		7	10	35	192	131	190	222
移动电话交换机总容量	万户			4.8	154.2	1059.1	1657.0	2033.0	2424.0
移动电话用户(含充值卡)	万户				123.68	1016.41	1607.60	1756.75	1575.08
移动电话用户(不含充值卡)	万户		0.05	4.77	80.97	176.83	174.04	752.06	787.43
局用交换机容量	万门		6.98	52.29	103.13	286.25	365.02	358.00	358.00
本地电话用户	万户	0.20	4.90	31.57	78.12	384.52	332.42	298.23	272.63
市内电话用户	万户	0.04	1.50	9.78	19.69	68.30	85.76	65.12	58.00
农村电话用户	万户	0.16	3.40	21.80	58.43	316.22	246.66	233.10	214.61
数字数据用户(DDN)	端口				2741	2170	1098	375	375
互联网用户	万户			0.05	13.78	52.90	153.92	201.74	185.27
邮电业务量									
邮电业务收入(含快递)	亿元					132.82	155.34	248.98	295.13
#电信业务	亿元						149.02	149.73	155.58
#移动通信业务	亿元						105.78	108.99	113.81
邮政业务收入(含快递)	亿元							99.25	139.55
邮政函件业务量	万件		3372	10407	8124	9429.79	4507.00	6718.32	9201.45
快递业务量	万件							75122	106896
快递业务收入	万元							854642	1226029

6-8 历年邮电通信业务主要指标

Main Indicators of Postal and Telecommunication Services over Years

年 份	邮 电 局、所 (处)	局用交换机容量 (万门)	本地电话用户 (万户)	移动电话用户 (万户)	邮电业务收入 (亿元)
1978	50		0.20		
1979	50		0.21		
1980	50		0.31		
1981	50		0.34		
1982	51		0.35		
1983	51		0.39		
1984	52		0.48		
1985	52		0.77		
1986	53		0.88		
1987	45		1.63		
1988	48		2.52		
1989	50		4.30	0.02	
1990	53	6.98	4.90	0.05	
1991	60	9.82	7.50	0.11	
1992	91	11.07	9.70	0.30	
1993	161	21.24	14.98	0.72	
1994	216	36.37	23.19	2.41	
1995	273	52.29	31.57	4.77	
1996	310	52.79	36.91	8.24	
1997	339	57.76	42.65	15.29	
1998	397	73.09	50.13	26.17	
1999	458	84.79	60.87	51.01	
2000	594	103.13	78.12	123.68	
2001	689	155.29	98.96	295.76	
2002	696	176.94	127.93	412.39	90.56
2003	846	220.28	206.11	660.86	105.12
2004	854	265.66	281.35	856.09	120.78
2005	702	286.25	384.52	1016.41	132.82
2006	560	299.19	461.31	1216.34	146.69
2007	567	329.50	469.17	1408.23	161.90
2008	547	340.71	439.41	1454.29	172.38
2009	546	347.15	378.40	1409.29	156.31
2010	555	365.02	332.42	1607.60	155.34
2011	626	357.00	319.55	1677.77	164.86
2012	595	364.00	330.79	1797.75	169.96
2013	611	295.26	314.48	1850.39	175.78
2014	715	363.83	327.22	1763.09	169.46
2015	797	358.00	298.23	1756.75	248.98
2016	787	358.00	272.63	1575.08	295.13

注：本地电话2015年起取消小灵通用户。

6-9 邮电通信企业财务指标（2015-2016年）

Main Financial Indicators of Postal and Telecommunication Enterprises（2015-2016）

单位：万元

指　　标	2015年	2016年
年初存货	8655	6219
期末资产负债		
流动资产合计	91465	89304
#应收账款	60331	55994
存货	6288	3213
固定资产原价	3679753	3757697
本年折旧	278161	2416676
资产总计	1759348	1788246
负债合计	1331405	1521902
所有者权益合计	427943	266344
损益及分配		
营业收入	1752735	1837553
#主营业务收入	1737064	1825206
营业成本	854953	898760
#主营业务成本	807430	886443
营业税金及附加	8468	5947
#主营业务税金及附加	3147	3309
销售费用	203223	185393
管理费用	49090	54570
#税金	2726	1438
财务费用	1842	-33
#利息收入	295	240
利息支出	2866	137
投资收益(损失以“-”号记)		
营业利润	620321	625739
营业外收入	11042	6919
营业外支出	10806	12275
利润总额	619632	620383
应交所得税	107839	107549
人工成本及增值税		
应付职工薪酬(本年贷方累计发生额)	123646	146393
应交增值税	106678	96782
从事服务业活动的从业人员平均人数(人)	9611	8297

主要统计指标解释

Explanatory Notes on Main Statistical Indicators

公路通车里程　指在一定时点上实际达到交通部规定的公路技术等级标准，并经公路主管部门正式验收交付使用的公路里程数。包括大、中城市的郊区公路以及公路通过城镇（指县城、集镇）街道的里程数。但不包括大、中城市街道，厂矿、林区内部生产用道、农业生产用道，以及新建公路尚未进行验收交付使用的路段里程。公路按工程技术等级分为高速、一、二、三、四级公路；按公路是否铺设路面分为有路面和无路面公路；按公路通车情况分为晴雨通车里程和晴通雨阻里程。

民用汽车拥有量　指报告期末，在公安交通管理部门按照《机动车注册登记工作规范》，已注册登记领有民用车辆牌照的全部汽车数量。汽车拥有量统计的主要分类：根据汽车结构分为载客汽车、载货汽车及其他汽车；根据汽车所有者不同分为个人（私人）汽车、单位汽车；根据汽车的使用性质分为营运汽车、非营运汽车；根据汽车大小规格不同，载客汽车分为大型、中型、小型和微型，载货汽车分为重型、中型、轻型和微型。

机动船　又称自航船，指装有各种发动机推进装置，以机械动力行驶的船舶。

货（客）运量　在一定时期内，各运输部门实际运送的货物（旅客）数量。货运按吨计算，客运按人计算。货物不论运输距离长短，货物类型，均按实际重量统计；旅客不论行程远近或票价多少，均按一人一次作为客运量统计。半价票，小孩票也按一人统计。货（客）运量反映运输业为国民经济和人民生活服务的数量，也是制定和检查运输生产计划，研究运输发展规模和速度的重要指标。

货物（旅客）周转量　指在一定时期内，由各种运输工具运输业运送的货物（旅客）数量与其相应运输距离的乘积，通常以吨公里和人公里为计算单位。计算货物周转量通常按发出站与到达站之间的最短距离，也就是计费距离计算。它是反映运输业生产总成果的重要指标，也是编制和检查运输生产计划，计算运输效率，劳动生产率以及核算运输单位成本的主要基础资料。

港口货物吞吐量　是指经由水运运进、运出港区范围，并经过装卸的货物数量。货物吞吐量分别按国内进口（装卸）、出口（装船），外贸进口、出口统计。货物吞吐量按货物实际重量吨统计，以货物交接清单或货单上记载的重量吨为准。如无实际重量吨，可根据船舶装载情况来推算。在本港区内的水运转口分别按进口和出口各计算一次吞吐量。货物吞吐量是衡量港口生产规模的一个主要数量指标。

邮电业务收入　是指邮电营运企业从事邮政、电信、移动及其他邮电业务所取得的营业收入。

局用交换机容量　指安装在本地电信运营商内用于接读本地固定电话的电话交换机容量，有倍增设备按倍增后的数量计数。包括现用和备用的人工或自动交换全部容量。

本地电话用户　是指接入本地电信运营商固定电话网上的电话用户。包括：住宅电话、单位用户、公用电话用户等。按电话用户位置又分城市电话用户和乡村电话用户。按通信手段又分为固定电话用户和无线电话用户。

移动电话用户　是指在移动通信部门办理登记手续，通过移动电话交换机进入移动电话网，占用移动电话号码的电话用户。包括签约用户和智能网预付费用户。一个移动电话号码统计为一户。

移动电话交换机容量　是指移动电话交换机根据一定话务模型和交换机处理能力计算出来的最大同时服务用户的数量。

邮政局所　指经邮政部门审批许可，有固定的地址，领有上级发给的邮政日戳或邮政戳记，对外营业直接为用户办理邮政业务（至少办理出售邮票和收寄给据函件）的服务机构。邮政局所按经营方式分为自办局所和代办局所；按设置地点分为城市局所和农村局所。

七、国内贸易

Domestic Trade

7-1 历年社会消费品零售总额

Total Retail Sales of Consumer Goods over Years

年份	社会消费品零售总额		按城乡分	
	绝对值（万元）	增速（%）	城镇(万元)	乡村(万元)
1978	21269			
1979	24956	17.3		
1980	31595	26.6		
1981	40201	27.2		
1982	48126	19.7		
1983	52255	8.6		
1984	73930	41.5		
1985	93640	26.7		
1986	122420	30.7		
1987	150511	23.0		
1988	246518	63.8		
1989	270354	9.7		
1990	319738	18.3		
1991	364972	14.2		
1992	443464	21.5		
1993	636882	43.6		
1994	851556	33.7		
1995	1130081	32.7		
1996	1255311	11.1		
1997	1460396	16.3		
1998	1751551	19.9		
1999	2023008	15.5		
2000	2351634	16.2		
2001	2757143	17.2		
2002	3212436	16.5		
2003	3697814	15.1		
2004	4264704	15.3		
2005	5062917	18.7		
2006	5993201	18.4		
2007	7224491	20.5		
2008	8811519	22.0		
2009	10290420	16.7		
2010	12233380	18.9	11290960	942420
2011	14412451	17.8	13418775	993676
2012	16004124	11.0	14932002	1072122
2013	17866589	11.6	16684394	1182195
2014	19422889	8.7	18083947	1338942
2015	21846996	10.9	20116701	1730296
2016	24707782	13.1	22049314	2658468

注：本表1979—2003年数据根据东莞市第一次全国经济普查结果重新核定，2005—2008年数据根据东莞市第二次全国经济普查结果重新核定，2009—2013年数据根据东莞市第三次全国经济普查结果重新核定。

7-2 历年批发零售贸易企业与个体户数

Wholesale and Retail Trades Enterprises and Self-employed Individuals over Years

单位：个

年　份	单位数合计	国有经济	集体经济	其他经济	#私营个体经济
1979	2459	406	1918	135	135
1980	2613	395	1679	539	537
1981	4603	371	1954	2278	2274
1982	3323	373	1838	1112	1107
1983	8723	401	1539	6783	6783
1984	18917	431	6720	11766	11766
1985	16885	670	4543	11672	11671
1986	18547	823	3063	14661	14660
1987	23468	739	4102	18627	18626
1988	26247	665	4405	21177	21176
1989	28453	695	4196	23562	23561
1990	27931	709	3512	23710	23709
1991	29474	678	3934	24862	24862
1992	34465	803	4193	29469	29469
1993	43511	886	7640	34985	34985
1994	49706	633	11396	37677	37677
1995	56339	745	14492	41102	41101
1996	60078	670	15183	44225	44224
1997	48910	811	8477	39622	39546
1998	52543	1064	4046	47433	46615
1999	55925	1056	3843	51026	50172
2000	57474	1024	3581	5289	51914
2001	68909	866	2960	65083	63760
2002	89246	748	2424	86078	84614
2003	113531	530	2068	110933	109236
2004	149067	539	1941	146587	144304
2005	192525	393	1451	190681	188082
2006	236124	283	1090	234751	231930
2007	284109	268	930	282911	279524
2008	301996	288	833	300875	296613
2009	300088	256	744	299088	294753
2010	300668	239	654	299775	295166
2011	288904	223	629	288052	283209
2012	305784	227	594	304963	299666
2013	313612	197	555	312860	307352
2014	339933	183	513	339237	333920
2015	378148	198	482	377468	371503
2016	437800	199	457	437144	430547

7-3 历年限额以上批发和零售企业商品购进、销售、库存总额

Total Purchases, Sales and Inventory of Enterprises above Designated Size in wholesale and Retail Trades over Years

单位：万元

年 份	商品购进 总 额	商品销售 总 额	批发总额	零售总额	年末库存 总 额
1978	82347	74936	50207	24729	7576
1979	91074	82878	55528	27350	8378
1980	109147	99324	66547	32777	10041
1981	131797	119936	80357	39579	12125
1982	156730	142615	95552	47063	14418
1983	160485	146042	97848	48194	14764
1984	214364	195072	130698	64374	19721
1985	254458	231557	155143	76414	23410
1986	630988	283945	190243	93702	28706
1987	380242	346021	231834	114187	34982
1988	714661	650342	435729	214613	65749
1989	729163	663539	444570	218969	67083
1990	766549	697560	467365	230195	70523
1991	796488	672666	433991	238675	74092
1992	881697	743990	473014	270976	64939
1993	1141163	1063567	725979	337588	92249
1994	1323263	1296363	912457	383906	177377
1995	1584470	1556882	1044334	512548	143404
1996	1694496	1737121	1117111	620010	166267
1997	1857884	1922001	1212399	709602	175715
1998	779319	863214	696921	166293	91640
1999	1064070	1106048	875799	230249	73620
2000	1232026	1354640	1072929	281711	58304
2001	1312924	1405409	1080688	324721	67415
2002	1588853	1682579	1188961	493618	102657
2003	1712564	1805840	1138496	667344	107996
2004		5406921	3479209	1927712	251427
2005	4798504	5683548	3882222	1801326	322445
2006	5324450	6487742	4215562	227179	335108
2007	6706290	8102415	4875668	3226748	485401
2008	8349926	10772768	6604662	4168106	790691
2009	8689984	10167222	6137228	4029994	839175
2010	12846503	14271362	9046899	5224463	1002940
2011	15777469	18129917	11738336	6391581	1401733
2012	20036523	22307974	15515426	6792549	1699355
2013	26698507	29369393	21570487	7798906	3189454
2014	25329332	29033764	20733048	8300715	2551678
2015	27857102	32191772	21844876	10346896	4769611
2016	35341899	39108916	27811404	11297512	2113452

注：本表2004年采用经济普查数据，由于普查报表制度没有设“商品购进”指标，故数据空缺。

7-4 限额以上批发和零售业商品购进、销售、库存总额（2016年）

Total Purchases, Sales and Inventory of Enterprises above Designated Size in Wholesale and Retail Trades (2016)

单位：万元

项目	法人企业(个)	从业人数(人)	商品购进总额	商品销售总额			年末库存总额
					批发额	零售额	
总计	1423	93726	35341899	39108916	27811404	11297512	2113452
批发企业	884	40114	25300513	27464658	26985504	479154	1260653
按登记注册类型分							
内资企业	802	34638	23772267	25704013	25251724	452289	1122838
港、澳、台商投资企业	54	4806	846672	1025435	1012787	12648	107481
外商投资企业	28	670	681575	735210	720993	14217	30334
按国民经济行业分							
农、林、牧产品批发业	7	283	749143	731024	730994	30	29556
食品、饮料及烟草制品批发业	61	6421	2573168	2964690	2946601	18089	150656
纺织、服装及家庭用品批发业	129	6899	3127974	3256982	3233433	23549	127595
文化、体育用品及器材批发业	33	2672	447115	494181	485778	8403	88305
医药及医疗器材批发业	33	3234	761610	833461	806719	26743	116374
矿产品、建材及化工产品批发业	375	10369	7931543	8581178	8327169	254009	450709
机械设备、五金交电及电子产品批发业	146	6832	6909108	7578644	7435078	143566	175609
贸易经纪与代理	48	1169	1745240	1913695	1913562	133	13101
其他批发业	52	2235	1055613	1110804	1106170	4634	108748
零售企业	539	53612	10041386	11644258	825900	10818358	852799
按登记注册类型分							
内资企业	501	45109	8865847	10305584	801212	9504372	776186
港、澳、台商投资企业	20	3095	524879	572356	6319	566037	39380
外商投资企业	18	5408	650659	766318	18369	747949	37234
按国民经济行业分							
综合零售业	60	12975	810835	932994	2440	930555	76963
食品、饮料及烟草制品专门零售业	12	491	39271	51090	1993	49097	7438
纺织、服装及日用品专门零售业	16	810	43686	50601	503	50098	18317
文化、体育用品及器材专门零售业	4	488	39854	42985	2220	40765	9715
医药及医疗器材专门零售业	35	4753	207246	248891	15128	233763	35251
汽车、摩托车、燃料及零配件专门零售业	330	24852	6805938	8151196	340975	7810221	521300
家用电器及电子产品专门零售业	35	5866	809361	816135	436780	379355	170012
五金、家具及室内装修材料专门零售业	10	578	48423	50387	1411	48976	6026
货摊、无店铺及其他零售业	37	2799	1236773	1299979	24450	1275528	7779

7-5 限额以上批发和零售企业财务状况（2016年）

Main Financial Indicators of Enterprises above Designated Size in Wholesale and Retail Trade (2016)

单位：万元

项目	法人企业数（个）	年末资产负债				
		流动资产合计	#存货	固定资产原价	累计折旧	#本年折旧
总计	1423	14009321	1902284	1545190	620759	85957
批发企业	884	8989866	1102858	883976	331009	44144
按登记注册类型分						
内资企业	802	8062856	972039	836084	311544	41259
港、澳、台商投资企业	54	602979	103123	34103	10676	1890
外商投资企业	28	324032	27696	13789	8790	995
按国民经济行业分						
农、林、牧产品批发业	7	86810	22218	721	259	111
食品、饮料及烟草制品批发业	61	855489	88575	61462	22146	3075
纺织、服装及家庭用品批发业	129	1023325	115556	31413	17708	2059
文化、体育用品及器材批发业	33	318124	95748	10857	5063	861
医药及医疗器材批发业	33	456178	111701	30116	9707	2566
矿产品、建材及化工产品批发业	375	3192367	408133	619918	223066	28873
机械设备、五金交电及电子产品批发业	146	2101181	153154	84061	38248	4612
贸易经纪与代理	48	612621	12493	8997	5409	635
其他批发业	52	343772	95279	36429	9403	1352
零售企业	539	5019454	799426	661214	289749	41813
按登记注册类型分						
内资企业	501	4689836	727059	514325	221788	33503
港、澳、台商投资企业	20	174365	36971	69033	29561	3941
外商投资企业	18	155253	35396	77856	38400	4369
按国民经济行业分						
综合零售业	60	259466	67475	146831	79744	9231
食品、饮料及烟草制品专门零售业	12	16114	6490	6047	3302	312
纺织、服装及日用品专门零售业	16	34611	20930	14477	4004	722
文化、体育用品及器材专门零售业	4	22989	10504	421	274	33
医药及医疗器材专门零售业	35	95668	35731	14069	5997	630
汽车、摩托车、燃料及零配件专门零售业	330	3930050	476295	350835	158057	24014
家用电器及电子产品专门零售业	35	445381	165980	36275	11652	2018
五金、家具及室内装修材料专门零售业	10	22360	6647	4781	3537	199
货摊、无店铺及其他零售业	37	192814	9374	87480	23184	4653

7-5 续表 1

（2016年）

单位：万元

项目	年末资产负债				损益及分配	
	资产总计	负债合计	所有者权益合计	#实收资本	营业收入合计	#主营业务收入
总计	16433768	12528451	3905317	1624396	36578703	36291909
批发企业	10606579	8596969	2009610	1111582	25651237	25574823
按登记注册类型分						
内资企业	9555904	7897262	1658642	913016	24066562	23992795
港、澳、台商投资企业	718433	420238	298194	152906	902992	900376
外商投资企业	332243	279469	52774	45660	681683	681652
按国民经济行业分						
农、林、牧产品批发业	124279	88261	36018	35125	656981	656976
食品、饮料及烟草制品批发业	1253379	878197	375182	104380	2650523	2601236
纺织、服装及家庭用品批发业	1110293	929241	181052	122067	3058121	3050201
文化、体育用品及器材批发业	348214	278630	69584	62198	448758	448494
医药及医疗器材批发业	482364	408320	74044	38583	745744	745301
矿产品、建材及化工产品批发业	3991561	3081906	909655	542152	7707908	7696561
机械设备、五金交电及电子产品批发业	2286406	2045594	240812	135237	7458160	7452934
贸易经纪与代理	629305	575918	53387	34621	1895055	1894163
其他批发业	380779	310902	69876	37219	1029986	1028958
零售企业	5827189	3931482	1895707	512814	10927466	10717086
按登记注册类型分						
内资企业	5378022	3644061	1733961	403385	9673730	9496494
港、澳、台商投资企业	229696	137063	92633	40736	571132	557273
外商投资企业	219471	150358	69113	68692	682604	663319
按国民经济行业分						
综合零售业	412323	361969	50354	58433	892486	837224
食品、饮料及烟草制品专门零售业	22253	7649	14604	7949	49460	48617
纺织、服装及日用品专门零售业	51795	50714	1081	6412	48371	45734
文化、体育用品及器材专门零售业	28467	19272	9195	6782	43085	42772
医药及医疗器材专门零售业	108435	88860	19575	6825	222053	221729
汽车、摩托车、燃料及零配件专门零售业	4411371	2777725	1633646	310963	7692551	7564528
家用电器及电子产品专门零售业	494279	419370	74909	38304	800238	783396
五金、家具及室内装修材料专门零售业	25841	29702	-3861	11024	45406	45135
货摊、无店铺及其他零售业	272425	176222	96204	66123	1133814	1127950

7-5 续表 2

(2016年)

单位：万元

项目	损益及分配					
	主营业务成本	主营业务税金及附加	其他业务利润	销售费用	管理费用	#税金
总计	33729004	159814	197985	1266809	685332	14107
批发企业	23897247	139669	92673	732735	491364	7796
按登记注册类型分						
内资企业	22464102	137321	90901	652190	454347	6817
港、澳、台商投资企业	778215	1719	777	68474	26179	613
外商投资企业	654930	629	996	12072	10838	367
按国民经济行业分						
农、林、牧产品批发业	651444	48	0.3	2767	1301	283
食品、饮料及烟草制品批发业	2237200	119328	127	94648	55858	1319
纺织、服装及家庭用品批发业	2929334	5786	6299	55139	44551	933
文化、体育用品及器材批发业	416435	488	65	20125	7619	85
医药及医疗器材批发业	684908	1049	935	16631	21152	570
矿产品、建材及化工产品批发业	7269615	5672	2882	208907	73250	2539
机械设备、五金交电及电子产品批发业	6873052	5956	78738	290540	259299	1139
贸易经纪与代理	1864529	278	1495	14733	13797	613
其他批发业	970730	1064	2132	29246	14538	315
零售企业	9831757	20145	105312	534074	193968	6311
按登记注册类型分						
内资企业	8769591	16807	87648	449636	164827	5040
港、澳、台商投资企业	488042	1592	10854	35063	13997	440
外商投资企业	574124	1746	6809	49375	15144	832
按国民经济行业分						
综合零售业	704921	3697	26507	154095	18691	637
食品、饮料及烟草制品专门零售业	39752	194	385	3477	1478	50
纺织、服装及日用品专门零售业	31587	171	-51	11733	4647	175
文化、体育用品及器材专门零售业	36196	108	146	4467	1026	1.2
医药及医疗器材专门零售业	181365	543	294	22637	13196	168
汽车、摩托车、燃料及零配件专门零售业	7037282	11768	59090	229918	117555	4301
家用电器及电子产品专门零售业	734209	1241	15812	45389	15039	47
五金、家具及室内装修材料专门零售业	35098	172	1208	9029	441	110
货摊、无店铺及其他零售业	1031349	2252	1922	53329	21895	824

7-5 续表 3

(2016年)

单位：万元

项目	损益及分配				应付职工薪酬	应交增值税
	财务费用	营业利润	利润总额	应交所得税		
总　计	156102	532752	546637	116517	516898	361879
批发企业	97541	295462	300890	71579	244444	228138
按登记注册类型分						
内资企业	90651	263207	270689	64649	205189	208238
港、澳、台商投资企业	6131	30121	30741	5318	31841	16076
外商投资企业	759	2134	-539	1612	7414	3824
按国民经济行业分						
农、林、牧产品批发业	206	1138	1239	69	2985	371
食品、饮料及烟草制品批发业	10342	138225	142071	33071	49719	54522
纺织、服装及家庭用品批发业	3175	17530	18977	8347	37764	38099
文化、体育用品及器材批发业	3298	3835	2146	996	13089	3277
医药及医疗器材批发业	8992	13287	14764	3833	16447	9433
矿产品、建材及化工产品批发业	61801	79152	78651	15806	62598	48237
机械设备、五金交电及电子产品批发业	6851	29181	28435	5766	42334	58856
贸易经纪与代理	-548	3088	4759	1144	6102	5108
其他批发业	3423	10026	9847	2547	13405	10234
零售企业	58561	237290	245747	44939	272454	133741
按登记注册类型分						
内资企业	52800	170492	177934	31264	224759	108798
港、澳、台商投资企业	3435	32188	32965	7478	19822	11804
外商投资企业	2326	34610	34848	6198	27873	13139
按国民经济行业分						
综合零售业	2947	5343	8620	3603	52929	13698
食品、饮料及烟草制品专门零售业	134	4125	4108	1075	2777	1213
纺织、服装及日用品专门零售业	1776	-1908	-1761	101	4213	1804
文化、体育用品及器材专门零售业	67	1026	1623	408	2021	648
医药及医疗器材专门零售业	1372	2901	3123	1028	19742	5103
汽车、摩托车、燃料及零配件专门零售业	47397	201160	205097	32160	145976	88866
家用电器及电子产品专门零售业	3700	901	1160	516	24408	5659
五金、家具及室内装修材料专门零售业	396	289	317	270	4088	1254
货摊、无店铺及其他零售业	773	23454	23460	5778	16301	15496

7-6 限额以上批发和零售业商品销售情况（2016年）

Total Sales of Commodities above Designated Size in Wholesale and Retail Trades (2016)

单位：万元

项　　目	商品销售总额	批发额	零售额
粮油、食品类	2062579	1651988	410590
#粮油类	1127922	1010694	117228
肉禽蛋类	49913	1142	48770
水产品类	21171	40	21131
蔬菜类	56739	22497	34242
干鲜果品类	91327	22975	68352
饮料类	343078	265280	77798
烟酒类	1180797	1128234	52563
服装鞋帽、针纺织品类	2131495	1810513	320982
#服装类	1218946	1022121	196825
鞋帽类	219477	167497	51981
针、纺织品类	693071	620895	72176
化妆品类	69954	10495	59458
金银珠宝类	104056	75476	28580
日用品类	551195	412945	138251
#儿童玩具类	67577	57324	10253
五金、电料类	544332	524243	20089
体育、娱乐用品类	23095	10317	12777
#照相器材类	32.9		33
书报杂志类	38369	18857	19512
电子出版物及音像制品类	1602	513	1089
家用电器和音像器材类	1181918	557942	623976
中西药品类	1008873	759679	249194
#西药	445480	283752	161728
中草药及中成药	417335	355367	61968
文化办公用品类	888864	130969	757895
#计算机及其配套产品	721096	9776	711320
家具类	1125080	1120515	4565
通讯器材类	3939103	3709565	229538
煤炭及制品类	1001057	1000149	908
木材及制品类	147659	147659	
石油及制品类	5467014	3608088	1858926
化工材料及制品类	2489457	2489457	
#化肥类	11070	11070	
金属材料类	755618	755618	
建筑及装潢材料类	212938	156128	56810
机电产品及设备类	971489	945090	26399
#农机类	214	214	
汽车类	6374648	403061	5971587
种子饲料类	2479	2479	
棉麻类	60	60	
其它	2754443	2626694	127750

注：分类别情况采用月度数据。

7-7 限额以上住宿业和餐饮业经营情况（2016年）

Business of Hotels and Catering Services above Designated Size (2016)

项目	法人企业（个）	从业人数（人）	营业额（万元）	客房收入	餐费收入	商品销售收入	其它收入
总计	318	45950	718201	153944	485047	28560	50651
住宿业	162	27141	371668	150443	171557	2132	47536
按登记注册类型分							
内资企业	149	24090	331574	135814	150922	1722	43116
港、澳、台商投资企业	9	1881	26526	10093	13175	409	2850
外商投资企业	4	1170	13568	4537	7460	1	1570
按国民经济行业分							
旅游饭店	134	25655	351930	138098	166389	2023	45419
一般旅馆	22	1281	16796	9764	5004	42	1987
其它住宿服务业	6	205	2943	2582	163	67	130
餐饮业	156	18809	346533	3501	313490	26428	3115
按登记注册类型分							
内资企业	136	13795	236988	3501	206200	25361	1926
港、澳、台商投资企业	10	998	25397		23151	1066	1179
外商投资企业	10	4016	84149		84139		10
按国民经济行业分							
正餐服务业	120	9648	151016	3501	137603	6838	3074
快餐服务业	11	5224	102113		102113		
饮料及冷饮服务业	1	415	1813		137	1675	
其他餐饮服务业	24	3522	91593		73637	17914	42

7-8 限额以上住宿和餐饮企业财务状况（2016年）

Main Financial Indicators of Enterprises above Designated Size in Hotels and Catering Services (2016)

单位：万元

项目	法人企业数（个）	年末资产负债				
		流动资产合计	存货	固定资产原价	累计折旧	本年折旧
总计	318	646096	35422	1065990	584212	42986
住宿业	162	486914	24523	973754	534515	37527
按登记注册类型分						
内资企业	149	396623	22729	792578	406432	33361
港、澳、台商投资企业	9	83609	1315	138383	107230	2546
外商投资企业	4	6682	479	42793	20854	1620
按国民经济行业分						
旅游饭店	134	474817	23505	945361	520683	36743
一般旅馆	22	11799	949	26995	13112	706
其它住宿服务业	6	299	69	1398	720	77
餐饮业	156	159181	10899	92236	49696	5460
按登记注册类型分						
内资企业	136	118058	7179	43601	24238	2848
港、澳、台商投资企业	10	26581	410	25350	11371	1073
外商投资企业	10	14542	3309	23285	14088	1539
按国民经济行业分						
正餐服务业	120	63327	5087	60180	30608	2936
快餐服务业	11	62654	3217	28445	17491	1868
饮料及冷饮服务业	1	520	496	417	134	5
其他餐饮服务业	24	32681	2099	3194	1464	651

7-8 续表 1

(2016年)

单位：万元

项目	年末资产负债				损益及分配	
	资产总计	负债合计	所有者权益合计	#实收资本	营业收入	#主营业务收入
总计	1468253	1558740	-90487	301946	710477	700213
住宿业	1197022	1453402	-256379	223674	366555	358490
按登记注册类型分						
内资企业	1038651	1180969	-142319	153445	327021	319061
港、澳、台商投资企业	125572	242294	-116722	48682	25967	25967
外商投资企业	32799	30138	2661	21547	13568	13463
按国民经济行业分						
旅游饭店	1167433	1433676	-266243	212539	347354	339321
一般旅馆	26958	16220	10738	10835	16745	16712
其它住宿服务业	2632	3505	-874	300	2457	2457
餐饮业	271231	105339	165892	78271	343922	341723
按登记注册类型分						
内资企业	185682	77186	108496	49616	235201	234805
港、澳、台商投资企业	45684	33359	12325	12460	24675	24529
外商投资企业	39865	-5206	45071	16196	84046	82389
按国民经济行业分						
正餐服务业	107069	67526	39542	40692	148856	148382
快餐服务业	121724	17000	104724	25147	101988	100340
饮料及冷饮服务业	803	201	602	240	1813	1813
其他餐饮服务业	41635	20612	21024	12193	91265	91189

7-8 续表 2

(2016年)

单位：万元

项　　目	损益及分配					
	主营业务成本	主营业务税金及附加	其他业务利润	销售费用	管理费用	#税　金
总　　计	319268	17169	27331	228018	142701	2137
住宿业	119838	10751	11885	137804	108203	1506
按登记注册类型分						
内资企业	107742	9614	7242	120753	92723	1367
港、澳、台商投资企业	7319	500	4538	10322	11686	103
外商投资企业	4778	637	105	6729	3795	36
按国民经济行业分						
旅游饭店	109519	10192	11657	133407	104622	1389
一般旅馆	9133	491	228	3565	3202	115
其它住宿服务业	1186	69		831	380	2
餐饮业	199430	6418	15446	90215	34498	631
按登记注册类型分						
内资企业	153624	4404	13779	45111	27024	351
港、澳、台商投资企业	10026	492	10	10432	2408	53
外商投资企业	35780	1522	1657	34673	5066	227
按国民经济行业分						
正餐服务业	80914	3522	567	42857	18525	363
快餐服务业	43825	1882	14705	41857	8225	251
饮料及冷饮服务业	1262			473	32	
其他餐饮服务业	73428	1014	175	5028	7716	17

7-8 续表 3

(2016年)

单位：万元

项目	损益及分配				应付职工薪酬	应交增值税
	财务费用	营业利润	利润总额	应交所得税		
总计	25617	-24954	-20763	3538	175142	13417
住宿业	25556	-36501	-31343	667	105146	8483
按登记注册类型分						
内资企业	21893	-26349	-24678	667	92279	7364
港、澳、台商投资企业	3554	-7673	-7651		8519	670
外商投资企业	109	-2479	986		4348	449
按国民经济行业分						
旅游饭店	25262	-36404	-31272	576	99674	8074
一般旅馆	281	-22	28	88	4764	361
其它住宿服务业	14	-75	-99	4	708	48
餐饮业	61	11547	10579	2871	69996	4935
按登记注册类型分						
内资企业	500	4296	3477	1309	50068	4066
港、澳、台商投资企业	-112	1301	1126	199	4890	449
外商投资企业	-328	5950	5976	1362	15039	420
按国民经济行业分						
正餐服务业	334	2379	1440	608	34198	2579
快餐服务业	-348	5130	5239	1360	18268	774
饮料及冷饮服务业	1	45	45	11	793	
其他餐饮服务业	73	3992	3856	892	16736	1582

7–9 历年住宿餐饮企业与个体户数

Enterprises and Self-employed Individuals in Hotels and Catering Services over Years

单位：个

年 份	单位数合 计	国有经济	集体经济	其他经济	#私营个体经济
1979	147	22	115	10	10
1980	182	23	121	38	38
1981	622	24	283	315	315
1982	308	24	102	182	182
1983	2069	31	98	1940	1940
1984	4012	31	445	3536	3536
1985	2982	36	389	2557	2557
1986	3268	38	270	2960	2956
1987	2281	35	308	1938	1934
1988	2265	31	296	1938	1934
1989	2850	32	276	2542	2538
1990	3387	30	439	2918	2914
1991	3438	44	225	3169	3165
1992	4456	25	320	4111	4106
1993	7119	12	1851	5256	5232
1994	7819	12	1748	6059	6051
1995	8918	26	1802	7090	7082
1996	9708	9	1900	7799	7789
1997	9968	28	606	9334	9210
1998	11069	102	368	10599	10532
1999	11904	80	337	11487	11392
2000	8335	78	361	7896	7831
2001	9776	67	343	9366	9318
2002	15128	74	265	14789	14740
2003	17615	64	229	17322	17276
2004	19802	39	424	19339	19224
2005	25972	28	315	25629	25522
2006	27108	16	247	26845	26747
2007	38435	11	219	38205	38094
2008	40154	9	177	39968	39687
2009	38220	5	130	38085	37795
2010	36156	4	113	36039	35728
2011	29280	4	91	29185	28825
2012	29381	4	81	29296	28874
2013	31780	2	70	31708	31205
2014	36172	2	55	36115	35559
2015	41690	3	53	41634	41021
2016	54831	1	49	54781	54115

7-10　专业市场分类基本情况（2015-2016年）

Basic Statistics on Specialized Market Classification (2015-2016)

单位：个

项　目	2015年			2016年		
	合　计	城　市	农　村	合　计	城　市	农　村
合　计	203	83	114	227	101	126
消费品市场	153	72	81	176	84	92
消费品综合市场	86	33	53	92	37	55
农副产品市场	11	5	6	11	7	4
农副产品综合市场	11	5	6	10	7	3
农副产品专业市场				1		1
工业品消费市场	42	24	18	49	25	24
工业消费品综合市场	14	10	4	14	9	5
工业消费品专业市场	28	14	14	35	16	19
其他消费品市场	14	10	4	24	15	9
生产资料市场	48	16	32	51	17	34
生产资料综合市场	13	1	12	13	1	12
工业生产资料市场	18	7	11	28	10	18
机动车交易市场	6	2	4	7	3	4
钢材交易市场	2	1	1	2	1	1
煤炭交易市场						
木材交易市场	5	1	4	4		4
其他工业生产资料市场	16	6	10	15	6	9
其他生产资料市场	11	6	5	10	6	4

注：本表数据来源于市工商局，不包括集贸市场数。

7-11 历年城乡集市贸易

Statistics on Urban and Rural Trade Fairs over Years

单位：个

年 份	集贸市场		
	总 数	城 市	农 村
1978	35		35
1979	35		35
1980	35		35
1981	38		38
1982	40		40
1983	41		41
1984	43		43
1985	48		48
1986	57	7	50
1987	63	10	53
1988	66	12	54
1989	69	11	58
1990	73	10	63
1991	75	10	65
1992	53	7	46
1993	155	13	142
1994	162	12	150
1995	189	17	172
1996	219	20	199
1997	241	23	218
1998	252	25	227
1999	286	36	250
2000	308	29	279
2001	375	31	344
2002	495	28	467
2003	576	34	542
2004	610	35	575
2005	665	36	629
2006	812	39	773
2007	845	36	809
2008	871	228	643
2009	883	225	658
2010	792	194	598
2011	812	181	631
2012	816	186	630
2013	815	185	630
2014	779	146	633
2015	816	392	424
2016	390	78	312

注：1.2008年以前的城市集贸市场数只包括莞城的集贸市场，2008年起包括莞城、东城、南城和万江四大街道办的市场数。
2.2016年起，按统计标准要求，剔除了部分不符合要求的集贸市场数据。

主要统计指标解释

Explanatory Notes on Main Statistical Indicators

社会消费品零售总额 指企业（单位、个体户）通过交易直接售给个人、社会集团非生产、非经营用的实物商品金额，以及提供餐饮服务所取得的收入金额。个人包括城乡居民和入境人员，社会集团包括机关、社会团体、部队、学校、企事业单位、居委会或村委会等。

商品购进总额 指从本企业以外的单位和个人购进（包括从国外直接进口）作为转卖或加工后转卖的商品金额（含增值税）。本指标反映批发和零售业从国内外市场上购进商品的总价。

商品销售总额 指对本单位以外的单位和个人出售的商品金额（包括售给本单位消费用的商品，含增值税），本指标反映批发和零售业在国内市场上销售商品以及出口商品的总量。

期末库存 对于批发和零售业法人企业和个体经营户，是指取得所有权的全部商品金额（含增值税）；对于批发和零售业产业活动单位，是指期末实际在库且归属法人具有所有权的全部商品金额（含增值税）。这个指标反映批发和零售业的商品库存情况，以及对市场商品供应的保证程度。

批发额 指售给国民经济各行业企业（单位）用于生产、经营用的商品金额。

零售额 指售给城乡居民用于生活消费和社会集团用于公共消费的商品金额。

住宿和餐饮业零售额 指住宿和餐饮业单位因为提供就餐服务或销售商品取得的全部收入，包括餐费收入和商品销售收入（含增值税）。

流动资产合计 资产满足以下条件之一应归为流动资产：（1）预计在一个正常营业周期中变现、出售或耗用，主要包括存货、应收帐款等；（2）主要为交易目的而持有；（3）预计在资产负债表日起一年内（含一年）变现；（4）自资产负债日起一年内，交换其他资产或清偿负债的能力不受限制的现金或现金等价物。包括货币资金、应收票据、应收账款、存货等项目。根据会计“资产负债表”中“流动资产合计”项目的期末余额数填报。

固定资产合计 指企业为生产商品、提供劳务、出租或经营管理而持有的，使用寿命超过一个会计年度的有形资产。包括使用期限超过一年的房屋、建筑物、机器、机械、运输工具以及其他与生产、经营有关的设备、器具、工具等。固定资产合计是时点指标，表示固定资产经过扣减折旧、减值准备等后的期末余额。根据会计“资产负债表”中“固定资产”项目的期末余额数填报。

所有者权益合计 指企业资产扣除负债后由所有者享有的剩余权益。公司的所有者权益又称股东权益。包括实收资本、资本公积、盈余公积、未分配利润等。根据会计“资产负债表”中“所有者权益合计”项目的期末余额数填报。

营业税金及附加 指企业因从事生产经营活动按税法规定缴纳的应从经营收入中抵扣的税金和附加，包括营业税、消费税、城市维护建设税、教育费附加等。根据会计“利润表”中“营业税金及附加”项目的本期金额数填报。

利润总额 指企业在一定会计期间的经营成果，是生产经营过程中各种收入扣除各种耗费后的盈余，反映企业在报告期内实现的亏盈总额。根据会计“利润表”中“利润总额”项目的本期金额数填报。执行2006 年《企业会计准则》的企业，利润总额为营业利润加上营业外收入，减去营业外支出后的金额；未执行 2006 年《企业会计准则》的企业，利润总额为营业利润加上投资收益、补贴收入、营业外收入，再减去营业外支出后的金额。

应交增值税 指企业按税法规定，从事货物销售或提供加工、修理修配劳务等增加货物价值的活动本期应交纳的税金。指企业在报告期应交增值税额。

计算公式一 本年应交增值税＝销项税额－（进项税额－进项税额转出）－出口抵减内销产品应纳税额－减免税款＋出口退税

计算公式二 应交增值税 = 销项税额－（进项税额－进项税额转出－免、抵、退应退税额） + 简易计税办法计算的应纳税额 + 按简易计税办法计算的纳税检查应补缴税额 － 应纳税额减征额

批发零售贸易、餐饮业统计限额标准

行业类别	统计指标名称	限额标准
批发业	年主营业务收入	2000万元
零售业	年主营业务收入	500万元
住宿业、餐饮业	年主营业务收入	200万元

说明：

1. 外贸企业包括在批发业中，其年销售额以外币计量的，应折合成人民币，按批发业标准执行。

2. 本限额标准对象为批发和零售业、住宿和餐饮业法人企业和个体经营户、非批发和零售业、住宿和餐饮业法人单位附营的批发和零售业、住宿和餐饮业产业活动单位。

八、价格指数

Price Indices

8-1 历年物价总指数（以上年价格为100）

General Price Indices over Years (Preceding Year=100)

年 份	商品零售价格总指数	#食品	#家用电器及音像器材	居民消费价格总指数	#食品	# 服 务价格指数	工业生产者出厂价格指数
1978	100.4	101.6					
1979	102.6	107.1					
1980	110.9	114.5					
1981	109.3	110.3					
1982	101.2	100.8					
1983	99.6	99.5					
1984	98.6	97.5		99.3	97.5	102.0	
1985	106.9	108.7		106.5	108.7	103.3	
1986	104.4	105.0		104.2	105.0	102.3	
1987	112.2	113.6		112.0	113.6	109.6	
1988	132.8	133.9		136.0	133.9	168.0	
1989	122.4	125.7		122.0	127.5	118.8	
1990	94.9	92.8		96.6	92.8	111.0	
1991	101.4	101.1		102.4	101.1	109.8	
1992	107.7	109.0		109.2	109.0	117.9	
1993	119.5	123.7		121.8	123.7	134.6	
1994	118.4	125.9	99.6	123.5	126.4	141.2	
1995	109.7	119.5	95.6	113.9	119.1	128.9	
1996	104.7	108.1	94.5	106.8	107.8	115.0	
1997	99.7	100.0	92.7	101.5	99.4	113.1	
1998	98.7	99.9	93.3	99.9	99.5	108.4	
1999	95.9	95.6	94.9	97.9	95.7	109.5	
2000	100.1	100.3	97.2	101.5	100.4	112.8	
2001	97.8	99.1	97.0	96.6	98.9	101.1	
2002	99.1	100.9	98.0	98.1	99.0	98.7	
2003	101.7	103.6	99.0	100.7	103.5	97.8	
2004	103.2	108.6	98.7	103.0	108.6	99.7	
2005	103.0	106.5	101.1	102.4	106.5	100.4	100.4
2006	102.8	100.1	100.5	101.2	100.1	101.6	100.7
2007	104.2	108.3	98.2	103.1	108.0	100.2	101.4
2008	107.9	115.6	100.4	105.5	115.1	100.1	101.7
2009	95.3	97.9	95.6	96.9	98.1	96.3	96.8
2010	103.2	104.8	95.6	102.8	104.6	102.6	102.6
2011	104.7	111.1	99.3	104.9	111.1	103.0	102.9
2012	102.4	106.4	95.2	102.9	106.1	101.1	99.8
2013	100.6	103.2	96.9	101.9	103.1	102.1	98.9
2014	101.2	106.1	95.9	102.3	106.0	101.4	99.0
2015	99.4	104.0	98.6	101.4	103.8	101.9	98.2
2016	100.9	106.0	99.7	102.7	106.1	102.1	99.9

8-2 居民消费价格分类指数（2016年，以上年价格为100）

Consumer Price Indices by Category (2016, Preceding Year=100)

项　　目	指 数	项　　目	指 数
居民消费价格总指数	102.7	水电燃料	100.0
非食品烟酒价格指数	101.1	自有住房	100.4
服务价格指数	102.1	生活用品及服务	102.0
扣除鲜菜鲜果总指数	102.5	家具及室内装饰品	105.6
消费品价格指数	103.1	家用器具	98.7
食品烟酒	106.3	家用纺织品	102.2
食品	106.1	家庭日用杂品	101.5
粮食	104.2	个人护理用品	101.9
薯类	109.2	家庭服务	104.2
豆类	104.8	交通和通信	98.6
食用油	98.7	交通	97.8
菜	111.8	交通费	100.7
畜肉类	109.7	通信	100.1
禽肉类	102.2	邮递服务	100.8
水产品	109.2	教育文化和娱乐	101.3
蛋类	94.2	教育	102.3
奶类	99.1	教育用品	101.6
干鲜瓜果类	102.4	教育服务	102.4
茶及饮料	99.4	文化娱乐	99.9
烟酒	101.9	旅游	98.8
在外餐饮	108.1	医疗保健	107.5
衣着	101.2	药品及医疗器具	104.5
服装	101.4	中药	103.3
服装材料	103.6	西药	111.1
其他衣着及配件	97.5	医疗服务	109.5
衣着加工服务费	104.9	其他用品和服务	100.5
居住	100.8	其他用品类	100.1
租赁房房租	103.3	其他服务类	100.9
住房保养维修及管理	101.8	旅馆住宿	104.6
住房装潢材料	100.2		

8-3 居民消费价格分月指数（2016年，以上年同月价格为100）

Consumer Price Indices by Month (2016, Same Month of Preceding Year=100)

项　　目	1 月	2 月	3 月	4 月	5 月	6 月
居民消费价格总指数	102.1	103.1	102.7	103.4	102.7	102.7
非食品烟酒价格指数	100.4	100.7	100.2	100.2	100.4	101.2
服务价格指数	101.4	101.8	101.0	101.0	101.2	102.5
扣除鲜菜鲜果总指数	101.6	101.6	101.6	102.4	102.7	103.0
消费品价格指数	102.4	103.9	103.7	104.7	103.6	102.7
食品烟酒	105.8	108.4	108.2	110.4	107.9	105.9
#食品	106.1	111.2	110.4	111.7	107.9	105.5
粮食	103.4	105.2	101.7	104.7	106.6	107.4
菜	127.5	160.3	145.4	137.9	104.2	91.8
畜肉类	108.1	109.8	113.1	117.3	119.1	115.3
水产品	105.6	105.5	108.6	111.2	112.0	108.7
衣着	102.7	102.5	102.7	102.6	101.5	100.8
#服装	102.0	101.6	102.1	101.8	101.6	101.3
居住	100.2	100.4	100.0	100.3	101.0	101.1
#租赁房房租	102.2	103.2	103.1	103.2	103.2	102.9
#水电燃料	98.2	98.2	98.2	99.0	100.4	100.7
#自有住房	100.7	101.0	100.2	100.3	100.5	100.6
生活用品及服务	102.5	103.1	103.2	102.9	103.1	103.1
#家具及室内装饰品	100.9	101.8	104.6	105.6	105.6	105.8
#家用器具	101.4	100.5	100.9	101.1	101.4	99.5
交通和通信	98.8	100.6	97.3	97.2	97.1	97.8
#交通	98.7	101.1	95.9	95.7	95.4	96.1
#通信	98.9	99.6	99.7	100.0	100.2	100.9
教育文化和娱乐	101.4	100.5	100.8	100.6	100.7	100.2
#教育	100.1	101.1	100.8	100.5	100.5	100.5
#文化娱乐	103.0	99.8	100.8	100.8	101.0	99.9
旅游	105.8	98.6	100.5	100.2	101.4	99.9
医疗保健	100.4	100.7	101.5	101.6	102.1	111.8
#药品及医疗器具	101.0	101.7	103.7	103.8	105.0	105.5
#医疗服务	100.0	100.0	100.0	100.0	100.0	116.2
其他用品和服务	97.1	95.9	99.1	98.7	99.1	99.4
#其他用品类	93.2	94.9	98.1	97.0	97.7	98.3
#其他服务类	100.3	96.6	99.9	100.1	100.2	100.3
旅馆住宿	99.8	98.3	98.9	102.8	103.2	104.7

8-3 续表

项　　目	7 月	8 月	9 月	10 月	11 月	12 月
居民消费价格总指数	102.5	102.5	103.0	102.6	102.9	102.5
非食品烟酒价格指数	101.2	101.5	102.0	101.6	101.8	101.8
服务价格指数	102.2	102.3	102.9	102.6	103.0	102.7
扣除鲜菜鲜果总指数	102.7	102.6	103.1	102.8	102.7	102.7
消费品价格指数	102.7	102.5	103.1	102.6	102.8	102.4
食品烟酒	105.3	104.5	105.3	104.7	105.1	104.1
#食品	104.5	103.0	103.7	102.5	104.1	103.2
粮食	106.7	105.1	103.5	102.6	101.0	102.6
菜	94.8	93.7	97.6	94.1	107.0	96.9
畜肉类	110.7	104.1	104.8	104.3	105.0	106.9
水产品	106.7	109.7	111.5	110.3	110.4	110.4
衣着	100.6	100.6	100.5	100.1	99.9	99.6
#服装	101.1	101.2	101.2	101.1	100.8	100.6
居住	101.0	101.2	101.1	101.1	101.1	101.3
#租赁房房租	102.0	103.8	103.9	103.7	104.3	103.8
#水电燃料	100.7	100.8	100.9	100.9	100.9	101.5
#自有住房	100.5	100.4	100.3	100.3	100.3	100.2
生活用品及服务	102.2	102.3	102.0	100.8	99.7	99.5
#家具及室内装饰品	106.8	106.3	107.2	108.1	107.7	107.2
#家用器具	98.1	97.6	97.9	96.6	95.1	94.9
交通和通信	97.6	98.7	100.0	99.1	99.5	100.0
#交通	95.8	97.8	99.5	98.5	99.4	100.4
#通信	101.0	100.3	100.9	100.2	99.7	99.3
教育文化和娱乐	100.6	100.3	101.9	102.4	103.2	102.7
#教育	100.4	100.5	105.9	105.9	105.8	105.9
#文化娱乐	100.8	100.1	96.9	97.9	99.7	98.6
旅游	100.1	97.8	91.3	95.0	99.3	96.4
医疗保健	111.9	112.0	112.1	111.7	111.8	111.8
#药品及医疗器具	105.9	106.1	106.2	105.3	105.2	105.0
#医疗服务	116.2	116.2	116.2	116.2	116.5	116.5
其他用品和服务	102.5	103.3	103.2	102.2	103.6	102.8
#其他用品类	105.0	105.6	103.8	101.6	104.4	102.9
#其他服务类	100.5	101.6	102.7	102.6	103.0	102.7
旅馆住宿	106.8	106.9	107.9	107.3	112.2	106.9

8-4 居民消费价格分月指数（2016年，以上月价格为100）

Consumer Price Indices by Month (2016, Preceding Month=100)

项　　目	1 月	2 月	3 月	4 月	5 月	6 月
居民消费价格总指数	100.5	102.5	98.9	100.3	99.5	100.5
非食品烟酒价格指数	100.3	100.5	99.3	100.0	100.2	100.9
服务价格指数	100.4	100.9	98.4	100.0	100.2	101.7
扣除鲜菜鲜果总指数	100.2	101.1	99.3	100.7	100.3	100.7
消费品价格指数	100.5	103.3	99.2	100.5	99.1	99.9
食品烟酒	100.9	106.6	98.1	101.0	98.0	99.7
#食品	101.5	109.9	97.0	99.6	96.8	99.6
粮食	99.1	102.2	97.8	101.6	100.8	99.4
菜	107.9	140.5	91.4	89.8	77.8	95.2
畜肉类	100.6	106.5	97.9	103.3	101.1	99.8
水产品	102.2	107.4	97.8	100.7	101.9	100.0
衣着	100.3	99.7	101.4	99.8	100.4	99.8
#服装	100.2	99.6	101.6	99.5	100.8	100.0
居住	99.7	100.0	100.1	100.4	100.1	100.1
#租赁房房租	99.5	100.2	101.5	100.2	100.4	100.4
#水电燃料	100.0	100.0	100.0	100.8	99.5	100.0
#自有住房	99.5	100.0	100.0	100.2	100.3	100.2
生活用品及服务	99.9	101.1	100.0	100.0	99.6	99.9
#家具及室内装饰品	99.7	101.1	102.4	100.7	100.2	100.1
#家用器具	99.6	99.7	100.5	99.8	100.0	98.7
交通和通信	100.4	101.6	96.9	99.7	100.4	100.5
#交通	100.6	102.3	95.6	99.5	100.6	100.9
#通信	100.0	100.3	99.2	100.0	100.1	99.8
教育文化和娱乐	101.4	100.0	98.5	100.0	100.1	100.5
#教育	100.0	101.0	100.0	99.7	100.0	100.0
#文化娱乐	103.3	98.7	96.6	100.2	100.2	101.2
旅游	106.4	97.2	91.5	101.0	100.8	104.3
医疗保健	100.2	100.3	100.6	100.1	100.6	109.6
#药品及医疗器具	100.4	100.6	101.5	100.2	101.0	100.7
#医疗服务	100.0	100.0	100.0	100.0	100.3	116.2
其他用品和服务	100.2	101.7	99.9	99.8	100.3	100.0
#其他用品类	100.3	101.9	101.6	99.4	100.7	99.8
#其他服务类	100.1	101.5	98.6	100.1	100.1	100.1
旅馆住宿	101.4	99.0	101.5	101.9	100.7	101.3

8-4 续表

项　　目	7 月	8 月	9 月	10 月	11 月	12 月
居民消费价格总指数	100.1	100.0	100.6	99.6	100.2	99.8
非食品烟酒价格指数	100.4	99.7	100.5	99.9	100.1	99.9
服务价格指数	100.6	99.8	100.7	100.0	100.2	99.9
扣除鲜菜鲜果总指数	100.1	99.9	100.5	99.9	100.1	100.0
消费品价格指数	99.8	100.1	100.6	99.4	100.3	99.7
食品烟酒	99.5	100.6	100.8	99.1	100.4	99.5
#食品	99.2	100.6	101.1	98.4	100.7	99.2
粮食	99.6	100.1	99.8	99.7	100.4	102.3
菜	100.4	104.3	104.1	95.8	109.3	92.1
畜肉类	99.0	98.8	101.1	98.8	99.9	100.3
水产品	98.1	101.8	101.3	99.2	98.1	101.7
衣着	99.5	99.1	100.5	99.4	100.5	99.3
#服装	99.5	99.2	100.8	99.3	100.7	99.4
居住	100.1	100.2	100.0	100.0	100.3	100.1
#租赁房房租	100.4	100.8	100.5	100.0	100.6	99.3
#水电燃料	100.0	100.0	100.0	100.0	100.5	100.6
#自有住房	100.1	100.0	100.0	100.0	100.1	99.9
生活用品及服务	99.7	100.0	100.3	100.0	99.5	99.5
#家具及室内装饰品	100.3	100.0	101.2	101.4	100.4	99.6
#家用器具	99.0	99.4	100.1	99.1	99.3	99.7
交通和通信	100.1	99.4	100.5	100.3	100.2	100.3
#交通	100.0	99.1	100.8	100.4	100.4	100.4
#通信	100.2	99.7	100.1	100.0	100.0	100.0
教育文化和娱乐	102.0	98.9	102.1	99.8	100.0	99.6
#教育	99.9	100.0	105.2	100.0	99.9	100.0
#文化娱乐	104.8	97.4	98.1	99.6	100.0	99.0
旅游	109.5	94.5	95.7	100.0	99.5	97.4
医疗保健	100.3	100.0	100.0	100.0	99.9	100.0
#药品及医疗器具	100.8	100.0	100.0	100.0	99.9	100.0
#医疗服务	100.0	100.0	100.0	100.0	100.0	100.0
其他用品和服务	101.4	100.9	99.8	99.0	100.5	99.3
#其他用品类	103.1	100.7	98.3	97.8	101.0	98.5
#其他服务类	100.1	101.0	101.0	100.0	100.2	100.0
旅馆住宿	100.4	99.6	100.3	99.5	102.0	99.2

8-5 居民消费价格分月指数（2016年，以上年同期价格为100）

Consumer Price Indices by Month (2016, Cumulative Month(s) of Preceding Year=100)

项目	1月	2月	3月	4月	5月	6月
居民消费价格总指数	102.1	102.6	102.6	102.8	102.8	102.8
非食品烟酒价格指数	100.4	100.5	100.4	100.4	100.4	100.5
服务价格指数	101.4	101.6	101.4	101.3	101.3	101.5
扣除鲜菜鲜果总指数	101.6	101.6	101.6	101.8	102.0	102.2
消费品价格指数	102.4	103.2	103.3	103.7	103.7	103.5
食品烟酒	105.8	107.1	107.5	108.2	108.1	107.8
#食品	106.1	108.7	109.3	109.9	109.5	108.8
粮食	103.4	104.3	103.4	103.8	104.3	104.8
菜	127.5	144.8	145.0	143.3	135.3	127.5
畜肉类	108.1	109.0	110.4	112.1	113.5	113.8
水产品	105.6	105.6	106.6	107.7	108.6	108.6
衣着	102.7	102.6	102.6	102.6	102.4	102.1
#服装	102.0	101.8	101.9	101.9	101.8	101.7
居住	100.2	100.3	100.2	100.2	100.4	100.5
#租赁房房租	102.2	102.7	102.8	102.9	103.0	103.0
#水电燃料	98.2	98.2	98.2	98.4	98.8	99.1
#自有住房	100.7	100.8	100.6	100.5	100.5	100.5
生活用品及服务	102.5	102.8	102.9	102.9	103.0	103.0
#家具及室内装饰品	100.9	101.4	102.4	103.2	103.7	104.1
#家用器具	101.4	100.9	100.9	101.0	101.1	100.8
交通和通信	98.8	99.7	98.9	98.5	98.2	98.1
#交通	98.7	99.9	98.6	97.9	97.4	97.2
#通信	98.9	99.2	99.4	99.5	99.7	99.9
教育文化和娱乐	101.4	100.9	100.9	100.8	100.8	100.7
#教育	100.1	100.6	100.6	100.6	100.6	100.6
#文化娱乐	103.0	101.4	101.2	101.1	101.1	100.9
旅游	105.8	102.1	101.6	101.3	101.3	101.1
医疗保健	100.4	100.6	100.9	101.1	101.3	103.0
#药品及医疗器具	101.0	101.4	102.1	102.6	103.0	103.5
#医疗服务	100.0	100.0	100.0	100.0	100.0	102.7
其他用品和服务	97.1	96.5	97.3	97.7	98.0	98.2
#其他用品类	93.2	94.0	95.4	95.8	96.2	96.5
#其他服务类	100.3	98.4	98.9	99.2	99.4	99.6
旅馆住宿	99.8	99.1	99.0	99.9	100.6	101.3

8-5 续表

项　　目	7 月	8 月	9 月	10 月	11 月	12 月
居民消费价格总指数	102.7	102.7	102.7	102.7	102.7	102.7
非食品烟酒价格指数	100.6	100.7	100.8	100.9	101.0	101.1
服务价格指数	101.6	101.7	101.8	101.9	102.0	102.1
扣除鲜菜鲜果总指数	102.2	102.3	102.4	102.4	102.4	102.5
消费品价格指数	103.4	103.3	103.3	103.2	103.2	103.1
食品烟酒	107.4	107.0	106.8	106.6	106.5	106.3
#食品	108.2	107.5	107.1	106.6	106.4	106.1
粮食	105.1	105.1	104.9	104.7	104.3	104.2
菜	122.6	118.7	116.2	113.8	113.2	111.8
畜肉类	113.3	112.1	111.2	110.5	109.9	109.7
水产品	108.3	108.5	108.8	109.0	109.1	109.2
衣着	101.9	101.7	101.6	101.4	101.3	101.2
#服装	101.7	101.6	101.6	101.5	101.4	101.4
居住	100.6	100.6	100.7	100.7	100.8	100.8
#租赁房房租	102.8	102.9	103.1	103.1	103.2	103.3
#水电燃料	99.3	99.5	99.7	99.8	99.9	100.0
#自有住房	100.5	100.5	100.5	100.5	100.4	100.4
生活用品及服务	102.9	102.8	102.7	102.5	102.2	102.0
#家具及室内装饰品	104.4	104.7	104.9	105.3	105.5	105.6
#家用器具	100.4	100.1	99.8	99.5	99.1	98.7
交通和通信	98.0	98.1	98.3	98.4	98.5	98.6
#交通	96.9	97.0	97.3	97.4	97.6	97.8
#通信	100.0	100.1	100.2	100.2	100.1	100.1
教育文化和娱乐	100.7	100.6	100.8	100.9	101.2	101.3
#教育	100.5	100.5	101.1	101.6	102.0	102.3
#文化娱乐	100.9	100.8	100.3	100.1	100.1	99.9
旅游	100.9	100.5	99.4	98.9	99.0	98.8
医疗保健	104.3	105.3	106.0	106.6	107.1	107.5
#药品及医疗器具	103.8	104.1	104.3	104.4	104.5	104.5
#医疗服务	104.6	106.1	107.2	108.1	108.9	109.5
其他用品和服务	98.8	99.4	99.8	100.0	100.3	100.5
#其他用品类	97.7	98.6	99.2	99.4	99.9	100.1
#其他服务类	99.7	99.9	100.2	100.5	100.7	100.9
旅馆住宿	102.0	102.6	103.2	103.6	104.4	104.6

8-6 商品零售价格分类指数（2016年，以上年价格为100）

Retail Price Indices by Category (2016, Preceding Year=100)

项　　目	指　数	项　　目	指　数
商品零售价格总指数	100.9	专业音像器材	97.2
食品	106.0	文化办公用品	101.1
粮食	104.0	日用品	100.5
薯类	109.2	日用百货	102.8
豆类	104.8	厨具餐具茶具	100.4
食用油	98.7	清洗用品	100.1
菜	111.7	其他日用品	97.8
畜肉类	109.4	体育娱乐用品	100.8
禽肉类	102.2	体育用品	101.8
水产品	109.2	娱乐用品	100.3
蛋类	94.3	交通、通信用品	96.2
奶类	99.2	交通运输机械	95.5
干鲜瓜果类	102.6	通信器材	98.4
糖果糕点类	107.0	家具	106.1
调味品	102.5	化妆品	101.6
其他食品类	102.3	金银饰品	105.6
在外餐饮	106.4	中西药品及医疗保健用品类	105.4
饮料、烟酒	101.1	医疗卫生器具	99.9
茶及饮料	99.5	中药	103.2
烟草	102.4	西药	110.8
酒类	101.0	保健器具及用品	100.7
服装、鞋帽	101.0	书报杂志及电子出版物类	99.7
服装	101.5	教材及参考书	101.6
鞋帽袜	100.0	书报杂志	100.0
其他衣着配件	96.3	计算机办公软件	96.1
纺织品	103.5	燃料	96.4
服装材料	103.6	煤炭及制品	101.2
床上用品	103.4	石油及制品	96.3
家用电器及音像器材	99.7	建筑材料及五金电料类	100.3
家庭设备	98.5	建筑装璜材料	100.1
文娱用耐用消费品	102.4	五金水暖	100.6

8-7 工业生产者出厂价格指数（2015—2016年，以上年价格为100）
Producer Price Index (PPI) for Manufactured Goods (2015-2016, Preceding Year=100)

项　　目	2015年	2016年
工业生产者出厂价格指数	98.2	99.9
#轻工业	99.2	101.1
重工业	97.7	99.3
#农副食品加工业	89.7	102.6
食品制造业	103.3	101.7
酒、饮料和精制茶制造业	100.6	99.5
纺织业	99.2	99.8
纺织服装、服饰业	101.1	101.3
皮革、皮毛、羽毛及其制品和制鞋业	102.7	101.4
木材加工和木、竹、藤、棕、草制品业	99.9	100.1
家具制造业	101.2	102.1
造纸和纸制品业	99.7	100.3
印刷和记录媒介复制业	100.8	100.8
文教、美工、体育和娱乐用品制造业	98.7	103.6
石油加工、炼焦和核燃料加工业	73.5	90.8
化学原料和化学制品制造业	94.3	96.6
医药制造业	101.2	101.3
化学纤维制造业	95.0	96.4
橡胶和塑料制品业	97.6	98.9
非金属矿物制品业	95.4	97.9
黑色金属冶炼和压延加工业	86.6	99.3
有色金属冶炼和压延加工业	93.6	98.9
金属制品业	97.5	99.2
通用设备制造业	98.7	101.3
专用设备制造业	99.9	98.1
汽车制造业	98.9	98.2
铁路、船舶、航空航天和其他运输设备制造业	99.7	100.3
电气机械和器材制造业	98.3	99.4
计算机、通信和其他电子设备制造业	98.4	99.7
仪器仪表制造业	98.2	100.4
其他制造业	102.0	103.1
废弃资源综合利用业	93.2	92.9
金属制品、机械和设备修理业	92.4	
电力、热力的生产和供应业	98.5	98.5
燃气生产和供应业	76.0	87.2
水的生产和供应业	100.4	102.9

主要统计指标解释

Explanatory Notes on Main Statistical Indicators

居民消费价格指数 是度量消费商品及服务项目价格水平随着时间而变动的相对数，反映居民家庭购买的消费品及服务价格水平的变动情况。它是宏观经济分析、决策、调控和价格总水平监测以及国民经济核算的重要指标。其按年度计算的变动率通常被用来作为反映通货膨胀(或紧缩)程度的指标。

商品零售价格指数 是度量市场商品零售价格水平变动趋势和变动程度的相对数，反映商品在流通过程中最后一个环节的价格即工业、商业、餐饮业和其他零售企业向城乡居民、机关团体出售生活消费品和办公用品价格水平的变动趋势。它可以为国家宏观调控和国民经济核算提供参考依据，并在此基础上派生其他价格指数。

工业生产者出厂价格总指数 是反映各工业部门主要工业产品出厂价格变动趋势和程度的相对数。编制该价格指数，用以观察和分析在生产环节中工业品价格变动对企业经济效益及宏观经济运行的影响，并为工业增长速度的科学计算提供重要的依据。

九、对外经济贸易与旅游

Foreign Trade and Tourism

9-1 主要年份对外经济与旅游业主要指标

Main Indicators of Foreign Trade and Economic Cooperation and Tourism in Main Years

指　　标	单 位	1985年	1995年	2000年	2005年	2010年	2015年	2016年
进出口总额	万美元(万元)		1539112	3204526	7437150	12133773	16767331	114159947
出口总额	万美元(万元)	17545	779867	1715927	4092905	6959751	10371861	65568458
进口总额	万美元(万元)		759245	1488599	3344245	5174022	6395470	48591489
新签利用外资协议（合同）数	宗	625	3077	1276	992	875	440	446
"三来一补"项目	宗	514	2094	871	219	6		
"三资"项目	宗	111	983	405	773	869	440	446
利用外资增资项目宗数	宗				1138	1059	552	488
合同规定外商投资额	万美元	6815	330920	183633	475238	307282	509080	479046
"三来一补"项目	万美元	1870	97428	69302	166363	47542	3226	5873
"三资"项目	万美元	4945	233492	114331	308875	259740	505854	473173
合同规定外商增资项目	万美元				187422	180723	429045	375001
实际利用外资	万美元	2894	105665	164712	375139	316287	546838	398385
"三来一补"项目	万美元	1511	38418	55975	93023	43116	14856	5768
"三资"项目	万美元	1383	67247	108737	282116	273171	531982	392617
本年止累计"三来一补"企业投产宗数	宗	1592	8447	9917	8997	5688	1112	978
年末"三来一补"企业从业人员	万人	9.82	59.44	72.89	126.49	81.00	23.70	10.60
本年止累计"三资"企业投产数	宗	51	2629	3908	6657	8338	10016	10240
年末"三资"企业从业人员	万人	0.64	25.01	87.17	145.50	163.53	203.50	207.47
当年来料加工企业转为三资或民营企业	家					1250	68	58
合同规定外商投资额（新口径）	万美元				298029	259740	505854	473173
实际利用外资（新口径）	万美元				146796	273171	531982	392617
全年接待旅游人数	万人次		89	291	1156	2251	3199	3792
#国际及港澳台旅游者	万人次		27	106	169	327	373	400
#外国人	万人次		6	15	70	109	105	111
国内旅客	万人次		62	185	987	1924	2826	3392
国际旅游收入	万美元		5679	7617	28189	67592	157743	153117
星级以上宾馆酒店客房数	间		7568	18024	18258	16631	12127	10354
宾馆酒店客房开房率	%		68.80	61.88	58.90	58.12	54.00	57.38

注：1. 对外经济部分除有注明新口径的以外均为旧口径，旧口径包括"三资"和"三来一补"，新口径不含"三来一补"且以验资作为统计标准，后同。
2. 2002年起，旅游业指标采用旅游局口径，与往年数不可比。
3. 2016年起，进出口相关数据采用人民币口径，后同。

9-2 进出口贸易（2015-2016年）

Total Imports and Exports（2015-2016）

单位：亿元

项　　目	2015年	2016年
进出口总额	10399.92	11415.99
出口总额	6428.91	6556.85
按贸易方式分		
#一般贸易	2345.95	2360.95
加工贸易	3861.95	3794.46
来料加工	654.43	559.69
进料加工	3207.53	3234.77
保税物流	219.49	262.40
其他	1.25	139.03
按经济类型分		
#国有企业	149.02	143.13
三资企业	3955.09	3907.19
集体企业	8.96	4.07
民营企业	2310.79	2486.96
其他企业	4.79	5.78
进口总额	3971.19	4859.15
按贸易方式分		
#一般贸易	869.28	991.21
加工贸易	2340.64	2255.11
来料加工	445.54	326.98
进料加工	1895.10	1928.12
保税物流	742.42	1585.85
其他	25.87	26.98
按经济类型分		
#国有企业	80.64	70.64
三资企业	2429.22	2246.34
集体企业	4.91	1.51
民营企业	1455.95	2526.85
其他企业	0.34	5.66
贸易顺差	2457.72	1697.70

9−3 历年进出口总额

Total Value of Imports and Exports over Years

单位：万美元（万元）

年份	进出口总额	出口总额	#一般贸易	来料加工装配	进料加工	进口总额	#一般贸易	来料加工装配	进料加工
1978		3938							
1979		5382							
1980		7737							
1981		9173							
1982		10879							
1983		11890							
1984		12966							
1985		17545							
1986		23280							
1987		26755							
1988		31781							
1989		34868							
1990	108229	56828				51401			
1991	317463	165159				152304			
1992	509007	260272				248735			
1993	675647	321137				354510			
1994	882997	429416				453581			
1995	1539112	779867	23180	434646	320186	759245	5394	353138	259397
1996	1784222	918683	16377	496833	405066	865539	8956	383988	309710
1997	2129885	1136768	18020	582863	535708	993117	7598	445237	420014
1998	2327324	1306055	15409	652853	636822	1021269	10406	462194	463450
1999	2846291	1515391	16347	759638	738191	1330900	51726	584224	582721
2000	3204526	1715927	20937	834347	858409	1488599	72475	645562	616319
2001	3445457	1898924	25945	940908	931766	1546533	68392	684323	656910
2002	4424706	2373646	34848	1171688	1167047	2051060	83522	922916	886699
2003	5210623	2800227	48988	1257934	1492723	2410396	144235	962367	1127404
2004	6451775	3519237	85056	1503757	1929967	2932538	222262	1090197	1402413
2005	7437150	4092905	175502	1611676	2304325	3344245	236133	1216566	1625629
2006	8422107	4737640	265784	1661399	2806910	3684467	259709	1265725	1879233
2007	10687290	6023212	357941	2235125	3398212	4664078	371073	1702595	2196521
2008	11329947	6553738	487193	2428365	3585619	4776209	455447	1712939	2206139
2009	9415458	5516861	571682	1823160	3055047	3898597	456075	1297315	1820882
2010	12133773	6959751	954098	1955379	3946227	5174022	755349	1424118	2457194
2011	13522382	7832871	1341146	1693479	4654300	5689511	988370	1174341	2881689
2012	14441587	8506606	1692301	1216525	5398579	5934981	1096531	901512	3322199
2013	15307167	9086371	2007791	1070242	5758315	6220796	1237293	806988	3573281
2014	16253046	9706918	2687709	1102722	5472315	6546128	1614999	775951	3333100
2015	16767331	10371861	3796284	1054049	5167717	6395470	1400324	718358	3055447
2016	114159947	65568458	23609477	5596949	32347693	48591489	9912140	3269824	19281239

注：1.出口总额1990年以前为外经贸口径，1990年起为海关口径。
2.2016年起，进出口相关数据采用人民币口径。

9-4 分国别（地区）进出口总值（2015-2016年）

Total Value of Imports and Exports by Countries（Regions）(2015-2016)

单位：亿元

国别（地区）	实际出口		进口到货	
	2015年	2016年	2015年	2016年
亚洲	3348.48	3548.91	3521.85	4348.48
东南亚联盟	569.12	583.16	640.89	798.93
非洲	112.88	81.80	16.03	23.26
欧洲	1049.30	1102.57	168.41	176.20
欧盟	998.77	1043.37	153.50	166.32
拉丁美洲	212.42	200.78	75.34	96.85
北美洲	1620.31	1532.11	172.56	188.12
大洋洲	85.25	80.96	16.86	18.06
美国	1537.15	1460.91	146.99	160.38
香港	1614.93	1713.57	18.16	17.92
日本	442.90	486.56	470.24	494.31
荷兰	175.88	194.85	8.71	9.84
德国	205.04	190.62	41.36	49.26
英国	188.92	175.98	21.03	19.05
韩国	293.74	316.87	594.87	881.89
台湾	106.15	98.12	631.40	802.62
法国	76.71	80.44	10.98	10.19
加拿大	83.16	71.20	25.56	27.74
澳大利亚	74.71	70.72	14.15	14.69
新加坡	106.70	72.09	78.81	118.18
马来西亚	89.81	108.18	150.85	155.28

9-5 主要商品类别出口总值（2015-2016年）

Total Export Value by Category of Main Commodities（2015-2016）

单位：亿元

商品名称	2015年	2016年
机电产品（包括本目录已具体列名的机电产品）	4384.83	4659.17
高新技术产品	2198.02	2586.40
电话机	402.00	657.53
文化产品	481.52	558.19
自动数据处理设备及其部件	448.80	410.87
服装及衣着附件	429.56	354.77
家具及其零件	318.30	291.31
静止式变流器	191.89	195.99
玩具	154.30	175.73
自动数据处理设备的零件	196.24	172.53
鞋类	199.36	164.79
贵金属或包贵金属的首饰	76.01	164.45
灯具、照明装置及零件	176.82	150.48
通断保护电路装置及零件	137.49	144.22
箱包及类似容器	162.08	141.18
电线和电缆	139.76	137.55
塑料制品	138.92	127.55
纺织纱线、织物及制品	113.18	102.46
电视、收音机及无线电讯设备的零附件	76.88	97.23
打印机（包括多功能一体机）	106.83	71.76
眼镜及其零件	57.97	66.93
印刷电路	58.74	58.25

9-6 主要商品进口数量与金额（海关口径，2015-2016年）

Main Import Commodities in Volume and Value（Custom Statistics）(2015-2016)

金额单位：万元

商品名称	数量单位	2015年		2016年	
		数量	金额	数量	金额
谷物及谷物粉	万吨	25.14	58098	22.13	57987
食用植物油	万吨	37.36	143386	21.44	92742
食糖	万吨	16.85	32786	17.63	39979
天然橡胶（包括胶乳）	万吨	3.22	26541	2.90	22821
合成橡胶（包括胶乳）	万吨	5.38	86054	5.04	76369
原木	万立方	19147.12	37381	40996.43	64541
锯材	万立方	27640.23	115639	32582.53	120388
羊毛（包括羊毛条）	吨	838.14	4655	957.90	5332
纺织用合成纤维	万吨	0.76	11739	0.69	11555
#聚酯纤维	万吨	0.57	6431	0.54	6181
人造纤维短纤	吨	440.63	804	403.98	771
成品油	万吨	4.17	21245	4.28	23074
合成有机染料	吨	1668.64	10398	1339.51	8975
初级形状的塑料	万吨	160.87	1960930	152.75	1886530
#初级形状的聚乙烯	万吨	13.77	124280	12.23	109648
初级形状的聚丙烯	万吨	22.88	209159	20.98	190696
初级形状的苯乙烯聚合物	万吨	44.22	501271	41.07	454227
初级形状的聚氯乙烯	万吨	15.15	97274	13.82	91812
初级形状的聚酯	万吨	17.26	334460	17.30	334558
牛皮革及马皮革	万吨	6.26	366467	4.49	275660
纸及纸板（未切成形的）	万吨	23.44	135944	19.72	119026
毛纱线	万吨	0.52	37090	0.38	28639
合成纤维纱线	万吨	3.63	105954	3.49	104281
棉机织物	万米	7743.86	99359	5230.16	75026
涂覆浸渍塑料的织物	万吨	1.72	74620	1.40	66926
针织或钩编织物	万米	13006	131741	11195.23	121048
钢材	万吨	68.83	492381	65.29	458195
#钢铁板材	万吨	56.71	351951	53.10	331206
未锻轧铜及铜材	万吨	16.02	692513	15.32	644201
#铜材	万吨	11.56	527646	10.88	499648
未锻轧铝及铝材	万吨	2.89	91085	2.10	67277
#铝材	万吨	2.32	82387	1.71	59198

9-6 续表

金额单位：万元

商品名称	数量单位	2015年		2016年	
		数量	金额	数量	金额
钢铁或铝制结构体及其部件	吨	1402.76	1567	1249.07	849
蒸汽锅炉及过热水锅炉	台	6	223	3	93
液泵及液体提升机	万台	190.43	10484	144.68	9410
冷冻机和制冷设备	金额		839		203
机械提升搬运装卸设备及零件	金额		31704		25871
制造纸及纸制品用机械及零件	金额		10681		10103
印刷、装订机械及零件	金额		438150		298494
纺织机械及零件	金额		20796		35554
#针织机及缝编机	台	389	10507	525	25037
纱线织物等后整理机器	台	131	3823	202	4991
工业用缝纫机	台	833	1918	323	1413
金属加工机床	台	3240	140831	2338	94245
橡胶或塑料加工机械及零件	金额		54787		47386
型模及金属铸造用型箱	金额		48725		60179
自动数据处理设备及其部件	万台	4798.19	752054	5819.06	916836
自动数据处理设备的零件	吨	9794.64	1114671	8596.48	830410
电动机及发电机	万台	27173.86	146114	19993.00	116449
发电机组及旋转式变流机	台	146	7749	74	6360
电视、收音机及无线电讯设备	吨	3786.26	587903	3328.87	415047
通断保护电路装置及零件	金额		1146589		1258740
二极管及类似半导体器件	亿个	883.41	1382210	630.44	1429339
电线和电缆	吨	26256.25	325785	21702.33	262616
计量检测分析自控仪器及器具	金额		358447		460080
塑料制品	吨	18127.20	113843	17895.79	123667

9-7 主要商品出口数量与金额（海关口径，2015-2016年）

Main Export Commodities in Volume and Value（Custom Statistics）(2015-2016)

金额单位：万元

商品名称	数量单位	2015年		2016年	
		数 量	金 额	数 量	金 额
活猪（种猪除外）	万头	14.82	182	14.20	223
水海产品	万吨	0.18	4469	0.17	5482
蔬菜	万吨	1.06	3942	0.92	3764
食用植物油（包括棕榈油）	吨	1411.27	1230	259.17	531
成品油	万吨		5	42.04	114936
医药品	吨	891.55	6593	1017	9732
美容化妆品及护肤品	吨	3972.48	16528	3828	23393
洗衣粉	吨	19440.20	9524	17693.43	9193
初级形状的聚氯乙烯	万吨	0.83	7797	1.20	9885
家用或装饰用木制品	万吨	1.01	37974	0.84	30398
纸及纸板（未切成形的）	万吨	13.81	90983	22.74	92250
纺织纱线、织物及制品	金额		1132123		1025873
#棉纱线	吨	12542.50	42599	7811.24	26547
亚麻及苎麻机织物	万米	5.84	103	4.58	103
棉机织物	万米	1158.99	25447	1262.05	24140
玻璃制品	吨	22412.58	86457	16382.94	48626
家用陶瓷	万吨	5.91	231874	2.84	87697
钢材	万吨	5.92	70670	2.32	29113
未锻轧铜及铜材	吨	33573.87	142415	33459.30	130609
未锻轧铝及铝材	万吨	0.76	23947	0.69	20470
手用或机用工具	万吨	2.51	202503	2.56	231095
电扇	万台	11058.58	261105	10532.83	261545
纺织机械及零件	金额		22832		21183
金属加工机床	万台	2.96	35574	1.64	41510
电子计算器	亿台	0.14	25107	0.10	16934
电动机及发电机	亿台	5.12	417247	5.14	426824

9-7 续表

金额单位：万元

商品名称	数量单位	2015年		2016年	
		数量	金额	数量	金额
静止式变流器	亿个	4.89	1919297	4.70	1960235
原电池	亿个	15.93	94999	16.25	109169
蓄电池	万个	594.13	33955	391.66	21418
电话机	万台	10259.68	4019960	12454.83	6577658
扬声器	亿个	1.33	473808	1.33	563878
收音设备（包括收录音组合机）	万台	3259.86	443907	3258.03	425428
电视机	万台	168.30	309072	178.05	400571
#彩色电视机	万台	168.30	309072	178.05	400571
电视、收音机及无线电讯零附件	万吨	4.48	768767	3.62	974471
电容器	万吨	1.00	679546	0.92	445571
通断及保护电路装置及零件	金额		1375350		1447350
二极管及类似半导体器件	亿个	981.59	493458	691.64	445988
电线和电缆	万吨	18.90	1397501	18.48	1376699
照相机	万架	784.98	204419	552.97	142908
医疗仪器及器械	金额		170094		180117
手表	万只	5383.41	127126	4549.32	107211
#电动手表	万只	5350.72	124666	4525.97	104788
家具及其零件	金额		3183163		2914422
灯具、照明装置及零件	金额		1768579		1515785
箱包及类似容器	万吨	17.86	1621211	16.88	1412598
服装及衣着附件	金额		4296585		3548516
#织物制服装	金额		3779359		3090101
裘皮服装	吨	84.03	6137	78.17	8235
帽类	万个	8070.41	136698	5450.92	120433
鞋	亿双	1.60	1866378	1.30	1516238
塑料制品	万吨	58.87	1392189	55.87	1276752
玩具	金额		1544128		1759532
贵金属或包贵金属的首饰	千克	17017.40	760108	15851.64	1644502

9-8 历年新签利用外资协议（合同）宗数

Number of Signed Agreements or Contracts of Utilization of Foreign Capital over Years

单位：宗

年 份	新签协议（合同）数	"三来一补"企业	"三资"企业
1979	184	184	
1980	415	415	
1981	555	553	2
1982	470	468	2
1983	454	447	7
1984	551	508	43
1985	625	514	111
1986	618	559	59
1987	824	729	95
1988	2048	1839	209
1989	939	779	160
1990	1267	1075	192
1991	1636	1268	368
1992	2232	1374	858
1993	3118	1773	1345
1994	2678	1521	1157
1995	3077	2094	983
1996	1678	1343	335
1997	1685	1492	193
1998	1383	1051	332
1999	1362	1135	227
2000	1276	871	405
2001	1395	705	690
2002	1391	524	867
2003	1524	392	1132
2004	1423	391	1032
2005	992	219	773
2006	786	177	609
2007	790	82	708
2008	588	35	553
2009	601	22	579
2010	875	6	869
2011	1325	1	1324
2012	690		690
2013	506		506
2014	465		465
2015	440		440
2016	446		446

9-9 历年新签利用外资协议（合同）规定外商投资额

Amount of Signed Agreements or Contracts of Utilization of Foreign Capital over Years

单位：万美元

年　份	协议（合同）规定外商投资额	"三来一补"企业	"三资"企业
1979	476	476	
1980	1055	1055	
1981	806	784	22
1982	787	771	16
1983	1616	841	775
1984	3217	1013	2204
1985	6815	1870	4945
1986	3398	1593	1805
1987	18513	14082	4431
1988	62173	42507	19666
1989	23365	9268	14097
1990	30180	12346	17834
1991	64483	19348	45135
1992	208825	29720	179105
1993	355515	54823	300692
1994	349703	47700	302003
1995	330920	97428	233492
1996	208861	62811	146050
1997	121351	62114	59237
1998	163677	58709	104968
1999	147247	69756	77491
2000	183633	69302	114331
2001	209779	56833	152946
2002	248914	47285	201629
2003	325633	59538	266095
2004	413216	124089	289127
2005	475238	166363	308875
2006	552758	197836	354922
2007	625088	176903	448185
2008	393701	134952	258749
2009	203040	41420	161620
2010	307282	47542	259740
2011	370189	19353	350836
2012	415522	34491	381031
2013	415614	11504	404110
2014	443973	12514	431459
2015	509080	3226	505854
2016	479046	5873	473173

9-10 历年实际利用外资

Foreign Capital Actually Utilized over Years

单位：万美元

年 份	累计实际利用外资	当年实际利用外资		
			"三来一补"企业	"三资"企业
1979	173	173	173	
1980	1107	934	934	
1981	1642	535	528	7
1982	2357	715	668	47
1983	3258	901	871	30
1984	5175	1917	1233	684
1985	8069	2894	1511	1383
1986	11111	3042	1553	1489
1987	22370	11259	9185	2074
1988	46496	24126	17717	6409
1989	71445	24949	16559	8390
1990	95764	24319	14309	10010
1991	121918	26154	11478	14676
1992	168510	46592	13716	32876
1993	261938	93428	14181	79247
1994	366750	104812	26938	77874
1995	472415	105665	38418	67247
1996	579979	107564	38061	69503
1997	701406	121427	33467	87960
1998	835219	133813	40780	93033
1999	980951	145732	48620	97112
2000	1145663	164712	55975	108737
2001	1327225	181562	66841	114721
2002	1542073	214848	68980	145868
2003	1798409	256336	80936	175400
2004	2101839	303430	89555	213875
2005	2476978	375139	93023	146796
2006	2910751	433773	98543	180789
2007	3415146	504395	94365	211759
2008	3737716	322570	77902	244668
2009	4031873	294157	34758	259399
2010	4348160	316287	43116	273171
2011	4353694	321821	16769	305052
2012	4725598	371904	34966	336938
2013	5128533	402935	9160	393775
2014	5590667	462134	9215	452919
2015	6137505	546838	14856	531982
2016	6535890	398385	5768	392617

9-11 主要年份“三资”企业利用外资

Utilization of Foreign Capital of Enterprises with Foreign Investment in Main Years

项　　目	计量单位	1990年	1995年	2000年	2005年	2010年	2015年	2016年
全部“三资”企业利用外资情况								
当年新签协议宗数	宗	192	983	405	773	869	440	446
本年止累计执行宗数	宗	591	2807	4012	6657	8338	10016	10240
#已投产	宗	454	2629	3908	5870	7469	9561	9746
项目（协议）终止宗数	宗	24	48	338	193	471	270	260
实际利用外资总额	万美元	18642	75853	115801	290553	277547	531982	392617
引进设备价值	万美元	6619	50267	80215	118401	63822	15852	11508
出口总值	万美元	13439	178351	835600	2353253	4426236	6371274	5918937
期末职工人数	万人	3.81	25.01	87.17	145.50	163.53	203.50	207.47
中外合作企业利用外资情况								
当年新签协议宗数	宗	72	195	19	2			
本年止累计执行宗数	宗	237	730	705	337	184	107	104
#已投产	宗	177	682	700	299	184	107	104
项目（协议）终止宗数	宗	15	12	130	25	23	10	6
实际利用外资总额	万美元	5072	15159	10045	13529	1345	4264	2049
引进设备价值	万美元	2411	9320	5033	4060	651		
出口总值	万美元	2423	35718	92100	116157	117188	46676	39566
期末职工人数	万人	1.02	5.82	13.57	10.38	3.50	1.49	2.11

注：本表2000年起出口总值是海关口径。

9-11 续表

项目	计量单位	1990年	1995年	2000年	2005年	2010年	2015年	2016年
中外合资企业利用外资情况								
当年新签协议宗数	宗	93	378	29	31	18	43	52
本年止累计执行宗数	宗	338	1590	1690	712	507	502	553
#已投产	宗	251	1498	1650	668	489	459	525
项目（协议）终止宗数	宗	9	31	159	53	99	9	5
实际利用外资总额	万美元	13070	39659	23966	25672	36342	40981	5512
引进设备价值	万美元	3920	25557	14365	4060	28850	2886	312
出口总值	万美元	10934	90357	248800	289344	348622	299587	276141
期末职工人数	万人	2.69	13.51	24.68	17.95	11.60	9.57	11.20
外商独资企业利用外资情况								
当年新签协议宗数	宗	27	410	357	740	851	397	394
本年止累计执行宗数	宗	16	487	1614	5607	7641	9388	9583
#已投产	宗	8	449	1555	4903	6790	8991	9313
项目（协议）终止宗数	宗		5	49	115	349	251	249
实际利用外资总额	万美元	500	21035	79113	252194	239860	482771	243182
引进设备价值	万美元	288	15390	58140	91288	34321	12966	11196
出口总值	万美元	82	52276	494700	1947751	3960425	6025010	5603230
期末职工人数	万人	0.10	5.67	48.92	117.17	148.43	192.44	194.16

9-12 主要年份分方式、分国别（地区）实际利用外资

Foreign Capital Actually Utilized by Type and Countries（Regions）in Main Years

单位：万美元

项　　目	1990年	1995年	2000年	2005年	2010年	2014年	2015年	2016年
按引进方式分								
总　计	10167	68438	164712	375139	316287	462134	546841	398385
外商直接投资	10010	67247	108737	282116	273171	452919	531985	392617
合资经营企业	5871	31314	18865	18195	32135	42022	40981	36796
合作经营企业	3645	14983	8305	12669	1176	277	4264	2049
外资（独资）经营企业	494	20950	78890	251252	239634	410372	482771	347321
外商投资股份公司			2677		226	248	3969	6451
外商其他投资	157	1191	55975	93023	43116	9215	14856	5768
国际租赁								
补偿贸易								
加工装配	157	1191	55975	93023	43116	9215	14856	5768
按国家和地区分								
总　计	10167	67247	164712	375139	316287	462134	546841	392617
香　港	10167	58333	88950	185214	182600	236826	373441	271386
澳　门		13		44	442	482	389	798
台　湾		3016	23722	130682	82674	110805	100227	1323
日　本		391	7476	25253	12861	36228	19413	735
泰　国		96	33	20		14	2	38
新加坡		822	3511	3994	6094	32609	9070	4908
德　国		3	1884	487	1488	2994	250	
法　国			89	20	688	2669	881	43
瑞　士			546		127	2607		410
加拿大		46	15	99	568	37	4226	8
美　国		3230	2391	8122	3309	12971	8685	2085
澳大利亚		56	14	48	61	112	215	81
韩　国			2362	6958	5955	7155	4970	3042
利比亚			153					
英　国		79		12	277	507	572	25
其　他		1162	33566	14186	19143	16118	24500	107735

注：1995年分国别地区的外商投资额是外商直接投资额。

9-13　外商直接投资分行业情况（2015-2016年）

Foreign Direct Investment by Sector（2015-2016）

单位：万美元

行　业	2015年			2016年		
	项　目 个数（个）	合同外 资金额	实际投 资金额	项　目 个数（个）	合同外 资金额	实际投 资金额
总　计	440	505854	531982	446	473173	392617
农、林、牧、渔业	2	311	38	1	19858	
采矿业			4	1	6518	776
制造业	221	226696	342799	186	187114	169644
#纺织业	5	11760	17168	5	11948	9200
化学原料及化学制品制造业	4	848	5946	7	584	1898
医药制造业		52	1100	2	164	53
通用设备制造业	10	7111	21147	10	2472	5017
专用设备制造业	19	14477	24671	15	15785	14762
通信设备、计算机及其他电子设备制造业	39	51600	66062	32	27960	26625
电力、燃气及水的生产和供应业	2	10591	7005		46146	48105
建筑业		26	133	4	24048	6869
交通运输、仓储和邮政业	6	16506	14747	8	12763	6904
信息传输、计算机服务和软件业	2	94	37	10	220	29
批发和零售业	162	56754	30649	169	27463	23529
住宿和餐饮业	5	53	980	5	5200	16
金融业			605			
房地产业	1	-4029	15222	9	16971	10018
#房地产开发经营	1	-4029	15222	9	16971	10018
租赁和商务服务业	26	196684	117502	25	125601	124282
科学研究、技术服务和地质勘查业	11	3692	2198	24	2291	2417
居民服务和其他服务业	1	28	69	2	126	25
卫生、社会保障和社会福利业						
公共管理和社会组织						

9-14　主要年份宾馆酒店接待能力和接待人数

Capacity and Tourists Received by Hotels in Main Years

项　目	单 位	1990年	1995年	2000年	2005年	2010年	2015年	2016年
三星级以上宾馆（酒店）	家	3	16	30	63	82	54	36
三星级	家	3	16	23	27	35	18	8
四星级	家			6	22	25	17	12
五星级	家			1	14	22	19	16
客房（已评1星以上）	间	3793	7568	18024	18258	16631	12127	10354
床位（已评1星以上）	张	8531	15136	30895	25014	24841	16444	14324
开房率	%	60.2	68.8	61.9	58.9	58.1	54.0	57.4
全年接待人数	万人次	125	89	291	1156	2251	3199.09	3791.98
国际及港澳台旅游者	万人次	27	27	106	169	327	373.40	399.54
#外国人	万人次	1	6	15	70	109	105.02	110.62
港澳台同胞	万人次	26	21	89	99	219	268.38	288.92
国内旅客	万人次	98	62	185	987	1924	2825.69	3392.43
外出旅游人数	万人次					154	142.88	148.04
国内旅游人数	万人次					139	124.64	131.31
出国（境）游人数	万人次					15	18.24	16.72

9-15 历年旅游业情况

Basic Statistics on Tourism over Years

年份	三星级以上宾馆（酒店）（家）	客房（已评1星以上）（间）	床位（已评1星以上）（张）	开房率（%）	全年接待人数（万人次）	国际及港澳台旅游者	外国人	港澳台同胞	国内游客	国际旅游外汇收入（万美元）
1986					80	11		10	69	554
1987					107	19	1	18	87	453
1988		6435	7641	65.8	125	20		19	105	710
1989		3324	7376	64.8	115	18		18	97	504
1990		3793	8531	60.2	125	27	1	26	98	1025
1991		4004	8701	64.9	155	37	1	36	118	2443
1992		4042	8770	72.6	172	47	2	46	125	2473
1993		4258	8517	75.1	169	52	2	50	117	2888
1994		3542	7443	77.6	119	44	4	40	75	3464
1995	16	7568	15136	68.8	89	27	6	21	62	5679
1996	16	13409	26818	50.3	175	36	6	29	139	6464
1997	19	10420	19142	50.6	171	59	5	54	112	6778
1998	20	17428	31987	53.3	216	75	11	63	141	6601
1999	20	17931	25482	63.5	253	97	17	77	156	7055
2000	30	18024	30895	61.9	291	106	15	89	185	7617
2001	48	20572	32789	62.0	327	110	22	88	217	8200
2002	53	9427	14652	69.0	930	108	22	86	822	11847
2003	52	8170	12599	65.0	1086	80	24	56	1006	13825
2004	60	10530	14934	61.2	1131	149	66	83	982	23437
2005	63	18258	25014	58.9	1156	169	70	99	987	28189
2006	71	18258	25014	60.1	1363	193	81	112	1170	33180
2007	74	19023	26132	63.4	1725	248	102	146	1477	42702
2008	77	19510	26864	58.9	1872	268	103	165	1604	45614
2009	80	16332	24389	58.0	2037	286	104	182	1751	51756
2010	82	16631	24841	58.1	2251	327	109	219	1924	67592
2011	77	17899	24348	60.0	2615	357	121	236	2258	90975
2012	75	17254	23612	59.9	2744	415	135	280	2329	126924
2013	75	18611	24437	56.9	2826	418	138	280	2408	144981
2014	58	12855	16921	51.2	2791	356	122	234	2435	157493
2015	54	12127	16444	54.0	3199	373	105	268	2826	157743
2016	36	10354	14324	57.4	3792	400	111	289	3392	153117

注：国际旅游外汇收入1995年以前单位为万元（外汇券），1995年起为万美元。

主要统计指标解释

Explanatory Notes on Main Statistical Indicators

海关进出口总额 指实际进出我国国境的货物（包括贸易和非贸易）的价值总和。主要包括对外贸易实际进出口货物，来料加工装配、补偿贸易、进料加工进出口货物，国家间及国际组织无偿援助物资和赠送品，华侨、港澳台同胞和外籍华人捐赠品，租赁期满归承租人所有的租赁货物，边境地方贸易及边境地区小额贸易进出口货物（边民互市贸易除外），中外合资、合作经营企业、外商独资经营企业进出口货物和公用物品，到、离岸价格在规定限额以上的进出口货样和广告品（无商业价值、无使用价值和免费提供出口的除外），从保税仓库提取在中国境内销售的进出口货物，以及其他进出口货物。海关进出口总额反映一个国家在对外经济贸易方面实际进出口货物的总规模。

贸易出口 指由外贸进出口公司、工农贸易进出口公司和地方性的进出口公司由国家统一安排的出口、代理出口和自营、联营出口，其中包括进料加工出口，以及各进出口公司在国内以外汇结算方式售给友谊商店、华侨商店、出国人员服务公司和中外合资、合作经营和外资企业等的出口商品。

"三来一补"出口 指来料加工装配出口按工缴费计算，中小型补偿贸易按金额计算。

"三资"企业出口 指三资企业自己出口的本企业产品。不包括委托外贸进出口公司出口的商品。

利用外资 指我国各级政府、部门、企业和其他经济组织通过对外借款、吸收外商直接投资以及向境外发行债券、股票等方式筹措的境外资金。

外资的形式可以是现汇、实物、工业产权或专有技术等有形资本和无形资本。

我国自有外汇如国家外汇、中国银行等金融机构用自有资金发放的外汇贷款等，华侨、港澳同胞的捐赠，联合国或其他国际组织的无偿赠送资金、无偿援建的项目均不属于外资范围。

利用外资的方式有：对外借款，外国（或港澳地区）企业和经济组织或个人在我国境内开办独资企业，与我国境内的企业或组织共同开办合资企业合作经营（企业）项目或合作开发资源，以及补偿贸易、国际租赁等。

外商直接投资 指外国企业和经济组织或个人（包括华侨、港澳同胞以及我在境外注册的企业）按我国有关政策、法规，在我国境内开办外商独资企业，与我国境内的企业或经济组织共同举办中外合资企业、合作经营企业或合作开发资源的投资以及外商从企业得到收益的再投资。

新口径合同利用外资 根据2003年修订的《利用外资统计制度》，明确指出合同外资的统计指外商直接投资（三资企业）企业设立时，根据合同（章程）规定，外方投资者应缴付的注册资本。

国际旅游（外汇）收入 指国内各部门为来我国旅游的外国人、华侨、港澳和台湾同胞提供商品和劳务而得到的外汇收入。包括供应商品、饮食和提供住宿、交通、邮电、文化娱乐、导游等各项服务所得的全部外汇收入。

十、财政、金融与保险

Finance, Banking and Insurance

10-1 主要年份财政收支主要指标

Main Indicators of Government Revenue and Expenditure in Main Years

单位：万元

项　　目	1978年	1980年	1985年	1990年	2000年	2005年
财政收入						
来源于东莞的财政收入	6604	6710	11118	35719	1035561	3319079
中央财政收入					617151	1935069
#关税和海关代征税					273972	483327
省级财政收入					113681	344330
一般公共预算收入	6604	6710	11118	35719	304730	1039680
工商税收						
工商税收总额					867584	2923001
国税（不含关税）					607216	1849818
地税					260368	1073183
财政支出						
一般公共预算支出	1792	2015	4999	22779	336102	1170427
#基本建设支出					27426	276646
企业挖潜改造支出		88	15	37	1584	9107
科技三项费用支出		7		140	9963	31572
农林水气部门事业费支出		304	1154	3261	40097	62181
工交部门事业费支出		2	7	180	192	20499
城市维护费支出		31	219	1350	41267	162370
科教文卫体事业费支出		1051	2139	7357	86737	210620
#科学事业费				404	936	3956
教育事业费		760	1504	3786	68194	171055
卫生事业费		185	262	743	12083	11469
体育事业费		18	50	827	1517	2860
抚恤和社会福利救济支出		75	132	368	2888	8335
行政管理费支出		293	320	1324	29817	102296
公检法司支出			92	740	46446	166055

注：1. 1995年及以前年份，来源于东莞的财政收入不含关税。
2. 从2007年起财政收支按新的分类项目，在10-1续表中反映。

10-1 续表

单位：万元

指　　标	2010年	2015年	2016年
来源于东莞的财政收入	7851003	11554989	15691913
财政总收入	6542697	12792586	14110668
#中央	2940745	5818477	5886391
省级	823548	1794427	2776735
一般公共预算收入	2778404	5179682	5447543
#增值税	626301	1421654	1659498
营业税	458712	538241	330255
企业所得税	247986	396494	467438
个人所得税	110441	144828	197378
房产税	92706	184115	134380
契税	186994	354276	481239
罚没收入	78400	88266	69064
一般公共预算支出	2898306	5812410	5992899
#一般公共服务	269505	470871	636650
公共安全	388243	635334	815375
教育	653090	1309337	1429470
科学技术	79830	308338	279373
社会保障和就业	264017	529597	352863
农林水事务	229613	312956	283313
交通运输	90609	542551	244051
税收总额	6887249	14130921	17049638
#国税	4394366	9552458	12296585
地税	2492883	4578463	4753053

注：1．2009及以前年份，国税不含海关代征税。
　　2．2010年及以前年份，地税不含契税和耕地占用税。
　　3．2011年起，来源于东莞的财政收入含政府性基金和出口退税。

10-2 历年财政收入

Government Revenue over Years

单位：万元

年份	来源于东莞的财政收入	财政总收入	中央财政收入	省级财政收入	一般公共预算收入	各项税收	工商税收	专项收入	其他收入
1978	6604				6604	6595	5826		9
1979	6634				6634	6625	5725		9
1980	6710				6710	6699	5785		11
1981	6823				6823	6805	5942		18
1982	8103				8103	8068	7184		35
1983	8578				8578	8501	7599		77
1984	8469				8469	8385	7442		84
1985	11118				11118	10998	9708		120
1986	16053				16053	15865	14574	45	143
1987	20221				20221	19989	18551	50	182
1988	27076				27076	26837	25309	76	163
1989	31888				31888	30997	29331	116	775
1990	35719				35719	33544	31911	686	1489
1991	44374				44374	41659	39302	913	1802
1992	56204				56204	52620	48272	1351	2233
1993	93828				93828	88920	83462	1947	2961
1994	130531				76940	70451	60889	2697	3792
1995	180051				115618	106388	95463	4070	5160
1996	283506				96541	85648	74323	4470	6423
1997	335044				114069	96980	85245	4794	12295
1998	472422				151012	123816	106700	5693	21503
1999	717847				182577	159873	134852	8759	13945
2000	1035561				304730	265565	248159	14709	24456
2001	1259961				450163	402668	381660	18356	29139
2002	1678848				552933	489780	467998	26438	36715
2003	2064052				674461	575342	536390	30710	68409
2004	2591086				826389	707954	655571	35273	83162
2005	3319079				1039680	879653	797038	36423	123604
2006	4065412	3358095	1638195	430455	1289445	1077152	990029	49285	163008
2007	5395362	4574778	2151906	558404	1864468	1652620	1291335	55863	155985
2008	6010642	5234746	2476902	665596	2092248	1682270	1555499	60590	349388
2009	6278114	5402140	2392927	697658	2311555	1822650	1618514	60007	428899
2010	7851003	6542697	2940745	823548	2778404	2217675	1950773	72153	488576
2011	8385226	7665371	3422151	1112580	3130639	2433937	2171228	133951	562751
2012	8456419	8624762	3777465	1284053	3563245	2792883	2514813	159582	610780
2013	9747062	9963650	4432671	1438081	4092897	3318201	2938124	221062	553634
2014	10662149	11226068	5148379	1525570	4552119	3651289	3364746	233430	667400
2015	11554989	12792586	5818477	1794427	5179682	3995152	3564401	412612	771918
2016	15691913	14110668	5886391	2776735	5447543	4311691	3786326	420802	715050

注：1．1995年及以前年份，来源于东莞的财政收入不含关税。
　　2．2011年起，来源于东莞的财政收入含政府性基金和出口退税。

10-3　历年财政支出

Government Expenditure over Years

单位：万元

年 份	一般公共预算支出	#基本建设支出	科技三项费用	农林水气等部门事业费	城市维护费	科教文卫体育事业费	教育事业费	行政管理费
1978	1792							
1979	1908		20	451	74	852	618	202
1980	2015		7	304	31	1051	760	293
1981	2139		4	341	36	1182	818	246
1982	2612		1	359	141	1346	912	336
1983	2804		1	413	28	1672	1004	287
1984	3013			264	48	1868	1309	340
1985	4999			1154	219	2139	1504	320
1986	9916			2541	1431	2887	1793	330
1987	12512			3479	1624	4759	1871	510
1988	17475		100	4094	1614	6950	3339	888
1989	21623		103	3509	2286	7958	3733	1159
1990	22779		140	3261	1350	7357	3786	1324
1991	27499		30	4938	866	7956	4720	1484
1992	38162		50	5637	567	17505	7682	2348
1993	72910	5400	1289	8882	5737	25716	14427	4002
1994	88984	14575	1496	12835	5254	20725	13552	6158
1995	124173	13736	441	15798	9947	31021	23110	8433
1996	124059	17285	1332	14962	5199	28927	21237	10384
1997	148510	16923	1479	15349	6258	36614	23262	11691
1998	179064	26144	1164	19255	7264	36710	25578	11082
1999	212641	40681	1429	26648	12994	40863	30631	12979
2000	336102	27426	9963	40097	41267	86737	68194	29817
2001	478646	119692	4113	28957	43706	105990	85544	28961
2002	649606	165283	28013	37348	64483	143225	120195	43678
2003	765190	201077	30062	41164	44240	193138	163390	50022
2004	941554	179039	27110	53855	164770	162573	139337	84798
2005	1170427	276646	31572	62181	162370	210620	171055	102296
2006	1478955	242829	87397	64911	205426	291467	244113	119034

注：从2007年起财政支出按新的分类项目，在10-1续表中反映。

10-4 税务登记情况及税种征收情况（2015-2016年）

Taxes (2015-2016)

指　　标	国税		地税	
	2015年	2016年	2015年	2016年
税务登记情况（户）	436896	545448	510362	599349
#国有企业	320	403	264	410
集体企业	1746	3296	5836	5780
私营企业	83559	117079	83772	116459
港澳台投资企业	7699	7798	9730	8599
外商投资企业	5228	5475	4540	4828
个体经营	230515	274336	270381	306835
工商税收总额（万元）	9552458	12296585	4578463	4753053
#国有企业	14073	29855	38920	29129
集体企业	19472	39902	181511	140603
私营企业	1354900	1850349	604404	844884
港澳台投资企业	1850052	1893012	657985	675034
外商投资企业	1525066	1489155	464714	496505
个体经营	564496	586401	472369	564061
#增值税	7728411	10273070		23792
消费税	105142	129298		
营业税			1456346	905558
企业所得税	1278713	1447046	756776	926138
个人所得税	5	5	724133	986884
房产税			184115	134380
印花税			106870	121790
城镇土地使用税			137741	81669
土地增值税			298635	515104
车船税			83661	92532
车辆购置税	438124	443156		
#第一产业	194	809	982	1515
第二产业	5585502	6002223	1574873	1533297
#采矿业	1498	1057	1269	2951
制造业	5316066	5612772	1148366	1210511
农副食品加工业	17936	17818	8075	10438
食品制造业	78403	96119	44607	30668
酒、饮料和精制茶制造业	33872	29977	21704	20131
纺织业	183094	146942	18463	15667
纺织服装、服饰业	269483	267495	39167	35304
皮革、毛皮、羽毛及其制品和制鞋业	231028	209803	34860	27431
木材加工和木、竹、藤、棕、草制品业	20233	24223	3677	3271
家具制造业	145330	147072	22838	18306
造纸和纸制品业	166497	202783	38856	51326

10-4 续表

单位：万元

指　　标	国税		地税	
	2015年	2016年	2015年	2016年
印刷和记录媒介复制业	93548	98745	19157	18643
文教、工美、体育和娱乐用品制造业	167118	175956	25784	28760
石油加工、炼焦和核燃料加工业	19005	15295	1214	1361
化学原料和化学制品制造业	110276	112544	23356	22682
医药制造业	40863	28930	9557	8610
化学纤维制造业	7140	9732	683	630
橡胶和塑料制品业	400149	469807	74863	70113
非金属矿物制品业	82478	94639	14184	13510
黑色金属冶炼和压延加工业	2341	2333	1592	1867
有色金属冶炼和压延加工业	7477	8167	2855	2831
金属制品业	382127	482521	64406	73106
通用设备制造业	251558	225920	22999	23652
专用设备制造业	184473	222665	32424	41246
汽车制造业	69035	79754	9523	10094
铁路、船舶、航空航天和其他运输设备制造业	18591	13683	6423	7722
电气机械和器材制造业	466192	458035	93741	96543
计算机、通信和其他电子设备制造业	1685701	1748311	412320	459968
仪器仪表制造业	70561	82655	12684	12630
其他制造业	111557	140848	88354	103660
电力、燃气及水的生产和供应业	259971	250222	49743	45968
建筑业	7967	138172	375495	273867
房屋和土木工程建筑业	1529	40872	70367	31919
建筑安装业	2671	62065	168407	162973
建筑装饰和其他建筑业	3767	35235	136721	78975
第三产业	3966762	6293553	3002608	3218241
#交通运输、仓储及邮政业	68943	76004	56639	42214
信息传输、软件和信息技术服务业	77911	47517	28283	146117
批发和零售业	742333	997480	193803	213167
住宿和餐饮业	2185	19436	75210	39618
金融业	240792	360456	575352	427032
房地产业	127121	410213	1088580	1396651
租赁和商务服务业	71017	133187	264972	217141
科学研究和技术服务业	47340	67734	34482	34443
居民服务、修理和其他服务业	33047	109136	159003	137349
教育	5728	5918	8308	10797
卫生和社会工作	2606	5840	9501	11030
文化、体育和娱乐业	2432	4482	16642	10883
公共管理、社会保障和社会组织	406069	274304	467571	510615
其他行业	2139238	3776246	24262	21184

10-5 历年金融机构各项存贷款余额

Deposits and Loans in All Financial institutions over Years

单位：万元

年 份	各项本外币存款余额	#住户存款	各项本外币贷款余额	各项人民币存款余额	#住户存款	各项人民币贷款余额
1978	10496	5410	19607	10496	5410	19607
1979	14875	7185	21302	14875	7185	21302
1980	26093	11718	30797	26093	11718	30797
1981	38003	20339	40243	38003	20339	40243
1982	45120	27650	45525	45120	27650	45525
1983	60547	38597	57618	60547	38597	57618
1984	110265	61823	121891	110265	61823	121891
1985	134867	91941	142437	134867	91941	142437
1986	195948	131352	206813	195948	131352	206813
1987	284819	189654	312431	284819	189654	312431
1988	380511	249134	415818	380511	249134	415818
1989	468203	325670	493737	468203	325670	493737
1990	680696	455140	630355	680696	455140	630355
1991	1029899	679935	852849	949713	614737	783957
1992	1577735	895260	1185126	1473354	815404	1059794
1993	1946346	1186421	1512129	1795701	1071713	1338033
1994	2737104	1700582	1990311	2497834	1515445	1709945
1995	4114645	2526179	2828201	3836761	2329685	2548512
1996	5201272	3392956	3404854	4896463	3180215	3128076
1997	7083202	4507195	4076237	6711687	4258238	3826560
1998	9166048	5724445	4641324	8640053	5337482	4427394
1999	11169344	6740770	5426244	10408377	6163430	5243735
2000	13277901	7537819	6421906	12286706	6720704	6308405
2001	15659074	8868348	7656842	14586491	7991768	7501801
2002	19024082	10930292	9517967	17901799	10016909	9334054
2003	22377551	13173589	12472347	21267775	12310616	12067237
2004	25769443	15142762	14502244	24628693	14316777	14052461
2005	30367695	17966871	15404787	29334026	17282760	15005217
2006	34643620	20739887	17752094	33656508	20133979	17305554
2007	38433605	21640637	22179330	37518345	21207413	21547660
2008	44602450	26775123	24328833	43545340	26380433	23803585
2009	50949212	29455910	30170741	49866108	29045704	29037984
2010	60778667	34258874	34419920	59433885	33868535	33298244
2011	67566598	37503559	38609164	66093904	37109919	37160847
2012	76912423	42469653	44468248	74304570	42042032	41956074
2013	88749114	45175855	49894985	86307325	44764310	47742282
2014	93232801	46482691	55623579	90699213	46067942	53316348
2015	99687961	46306942	59808985	97362437	45913850	58160376
2016	115450990	49435649	65456575	111984273	48829068	64024779

注：2015年起，“城乡居民储蓄存款余额”改名为“住户存款”，口径有变，数据与往年不可比。

10-6 保险行业主要指标（2010-2016年）

Main Indicators of Insurance (2010-2016)

指　标	单位	2010年	2011年	2012年	2013年	2014年	2015年	2016年
保险公司	家	37	38	46	52	52	54	56
保险业从业人员	人	27281	28064	33449	40867	43886	57664	71226
保费收入	万元	1597166	1636513	1776566	2071338	2580654	3053737	4726882
寿险类	万元	1129950	1085528	1166113	1355224	1731887	2062920	3650822
#传统寿险	万元	72494	72212	79299	110599	465876	717225	1351292
分红险	万元	867738	813006	966343	1072335	1026853	945344	1015713
万能险	万元	110035	18650	17032	16823	18354	16280	307938
投连险	万元	18953	805	724	680	768	827	883
意外险	万元	18718	23730	27899	37653	54475	79625	104923
健康险	万元	42012	57507	74816	117135	165561	303619	870073
财险类	万元	467216	550985	610453	716114	848797	990817	1076060
#机动车险	万元	400405	460241	515282	612210	722660	852862	945118
企财险	万元	32123	34107	32135	35318	35246	32487	31770
家财险	万元	1832	1806	1476	1761	1482	1634	2379
货运险	万元	4576	6917	7164	5695	6218	3622	3648
责任险	万元	9772	10516	12930	16584	19837	22055	27050
短健险	万元	4289	7222	6924	7268	7382	8362	7998
短意险	万元	11073	10271	11959	13650	14914	17525	20409
农业险	万元	55	35	61	130	25	27	47

主要统计指标解释

Explanatory Notes on Main Statistical Indicators

一般公共预算收入 指国家财政参与社会产品分配所取得的收入，是实现国家职能的财力保证，主要包括：

（1）各项税收：包括国内增值税、国内消费税、进口货物增值税和消费税、出口货物退增值税和消费税、营业税、企业所得税、个人所得税、资源税、城市维护建设税、房产税、印花税、城镇土地使用税、土地增值税、车船税、船舶吨税、车辆购置税、关税、耕地占用税、契税、烟叶税等。

（2）非税收入：包括专项收入、行政事业性收费、罚没收入和其他收入。

一般公共预算支出 指国家财政将筹集起来的资金进行分配使用，以满足经济建设和各项事业的需要。主要包括：一般公共服务、外交、国防、公共安全、教育、科学技术、文化体育与传媒、社会保障和就业、医疗卫生、环境保护、城乡社区事务、农林水事务、交通运输、资源勘探电力信息等事务、商业服务等事务。

信贷资金 指金融机构以信用方式积聚和分配的货币资金。金融机构信贷资金的来源有各项存款、金对国际金融机构负债、流通中现金、银行自有资金及当年结益等；信贷资金的运用有各项贷款、黄金占款、外汇占款、财政借款及在国际金融机构中的资产等。

存款 指机构或个人在保留资金或者货币所有权的条件下，以不可流通的存款凭证为依据，暂时让渡或者接受资金使用权所形成的债权或者债务。存款对象或性质的不同可划分为单位存款、个人存款、财政性存款等项目。

贷款 指机构或个人在保留资金或者货币所有权的条件下，以不可流通的贷款凭证或类似凭证为依据，暂时让渡或者接受资金使用权所形成的债权或者债务。贷款分单位贷款、个人贷款、融资租赁等项目。

住户存款 个人客户在其他存款性公司开立账户并存入资金或者货币，由其他存款性公司出具存款凭证，个人客户凭存款凭证可以支取本金或利息的存款。

保费 指投保人为取得保险人在约定范围内所承担赔偿责任而支付给保险人的费用。

十一、人民生活

People's Living Conditions

11-1 主要年份人民生活主要指标

Basic Statistics on People's Living Conditions in Main Years

指　　标	单位	1985年	1990年	1995年	2000年	2005年	2010年	2015年	2016年
全市职工年平均工资	元				7765	10639	16108	41864	46242
城镇在岗职工年平均工资	元	1456	3552	9682	14051	28253	46576	53221	57649
国有单位	元	1400	3600	9390	16371	37919	57275	91982	109565
城镇集体单位	元	1501	3507	7507	10475	15958	27391	63105	72895
其他各种单位	元	1571	3525	7891	14218	20882	37803	50487	54026
城镇常住居民人均可支配收入	元	791	2508	9588	14142	22882	35690	39793	43096
城镇常住居民人均消费性支出	元	689	2038	9220	12529	21768	25733	29001	30688
食品烟酒	元	493	1295	3644	4048	6035	8732	9625	9966
衣着	元	28	95	604	487	1285	1706	1637	1836
居住	元	58	184	1084	1218	1242	2089	4870	5407
生活用品及服务	元	48	153	694	623	1165	1771	1643	1688
医疗保健	元	14	42	258	431	811	1294	1315	1344
交通通信	元	4	25	1562	3309	7482	5925	5820	6146
教育文化娱乐	元	21	113	991	1517	3205	3443	3168	3383
其他用品和服务	元	23	131	383	896	543	773	924	917
农村常住居民人均可支配收入	元	803	1542	4769	8484	13076	20486	24225	26526
农村常住居民人均消费性支出	元						11842	19889	21539
居民人均可支配收入	元							38651	41902
居民人均消费性支出	元							28256	29906

注：1．2012年起城镇在岗职工含劳务派遣人员；2013年起，将原属于乡镇企业且符合城镇非私营单位条件的“四上”企业纳入城镇单位从业人员及工资统计的范围，下同。

2．全市职工年平均工资调查范围为东莞市辖区内除农户以外各类经济实体。

3．按照国家统计局的统一部署，自2012年12月起正式启动城乡住户调查一体化改革工作。2014年起正式对外发布全体居民人均可支配收入和消费性支出指标。　新口径指标将城市居民人均可支配收入改为城镇常住居民人均可支配收入，农民人均纯收入改为农村常住居民人均可支配收入，与往年数不可比，下同。

11-2 历年城镇在岗职工工资总额与平均工资

Total and Average Wage of Employed Persons in Urban Areas over Years

年 份	工资总额(万元)	国有单位	城镇集体单位	其他单位	平均工资(元)	国有单位	城镇集体单位	其他单位
1978	4485	2911	1574		474	630	325	
1979	5869	3611	2258		650	708	574	
1980	7255	4210	3045		750	867	632	
1981	9416	5000	4416		887	979	801	
1982	11839	6440	5399		1095	1089	1102	
1983	12808	6834	5974		1197	1138	1273	
1984	14963	7002	7961		1383	1333	1431	
1985	17260	7619	9238	403	1456	1400	1501	1571
1986	20980	10336	10026	618	2616	1698	1525	1940
1987	27610	12300	14159	1151	2067	2028	2094	2166
1988	35007	17931	14854	2222	2757	2942	2588	2574
1989	42947	20340	20808	1799	3320	3355	3295	3236
1990	46780	22321	21012	3447	3552	3600	3507	3525
1991	54002	24456	23268	6278	3777	3841	3674	3933
1992	68360	30469	28886	9005	4531	4610	4404	4696
1993	107088	47088	40171	19829	6228	7007	5583	6044
1994	131160	61869	49323	19968	8360	9390	7507	7891
1995	171543	75157	51398	44988	9682	10802	8007	10367
1996	178968	83372	52581	43015	10382	11623	8658	10775
1997	175156	87890	47185	40081	10691	12160	8774	10610
1998	187636	98109	50302	39225	11422	13123	9362	10959
1999	204550	109437	52217	42896	12557	14601	9966	12062
2000	229404	125711	53903	49790	14051	16371	10475	14218
2001	261645	152564	52645	56436	16183	19869	11001	15238
2002	291778	165611	58907	67260	17804	22228	11640	17348
2003	362935	230464	55866	76605	22598	29773	12940	19140
2004	432893	282512	62898	87483	25326	35163	13954	19223
2005	518216	349572	70872	97772	28253	37919	15958	20882
2006	608670	413718	74637	120315	31135	41457	17174	23032
2007	707007	487826	74408	144773	35284	46197	18807	26218
2008	809893	570134	82432	157327	39516	51441	20833	28838
2009	944243	639161	76001	229081	42585	56129	22077	31195
2010	1029873	678673	96664	254537	46576	57275	27391	37803
2011	1229001	826777	104824	297400	50398	61504	30549	39591
2012	1434133	960274	126456	347404	57007	66857	35977	47726
2013	10499782	1138596	218818	9142369	42870	75846	38409	40776
2014	11319163	1189178	226508	9903477	47600	78384	47024	45469
2015	12308012	1288341	255177	10764494	53221	91982	63105	50487
2016	13160504	1511235	235480	11413789	57649	109565	72895	54026

11-3 城镇在岗职工工资总额及平均工资(2016年，按经济类型、行业分)

Total and Average Wage of Fully Employed Persons in Urban Areas (2016, by Status of Registration and Sector)

项目	工资总额(万元)	国有单位	城镇集体单位	其他单位	平均工资(元)	国有单位	城镇集体单位	其他单位
总计	13160504	1511235	235480	11413789	57649	109565	72895	54026
按企业、事业和机关分								
企业	11820596	229395	209486	11381714	55011	155123	73452	54058
事业	738118	733837	1712	2569	105112	105273	81519	84500
机关	548003	548003			102557	102557		
按国民经济行业分								
农、林、牧、渔业	3218	2964		254	126208	135963		68730
工业	9759614	3137	42928	9713550	52658	49946	40517	52729
建筑业	208554	789	21637	186128	52982	62126	64243	51892
交通运输、仓储和邮政业	191644	49816	389	141439	69238	121533	41860	60220
信息传输、软件和信息技术服务业	123778	1212		122567	116202	113224		116232
批发和零售业	316474	2187	6149	308137	54056	166969	43032	54072
住宿和餐饮业	101912		1996	99916	38441		38901	38432
金融业	399810	170022	98110	131678	167117	168991	165084	166261
房地产业	206797	213	4652	201932	80058	142000	65701	80425
租赁和商务服务业	238910	7753	32302	198855	56364	103791	48575	56832
科学研究、技术服务业	116436	13201	5050	98185	89573	130061	167222	84048
水利、环境和公共设施管理业	14648	2938	598	11112	35692	62782	45626	31703
居民服务、修理和其他服务业	44213	805	26	43382	34252	64424	51000	33951
教育	358691	298078	142	60471	95429	107980	49034	60756
卫生和社会工作	470693	384174	20742	65777	103825	105929	84455	99481
文化、体育和娱乐业	44727	13560	760	30407	67158	85934	92695	60813
公共管理、社会保障和社会组织	560386	560386			102374	102374		
国际组织								

11-4 主要年份各种分组的城镇在岗职工平均工资

Average Wage of Employed Persons in Urban Areas by Item in Main Years

单位：元

项　　目	1985年	1990年	1995年	2000年	2005年	2010年	2015年	2016年
职工平均工资	1456	3552	9682	14051	28253	46576	53221	57649
按经济类型分								
国有单位	1400	3600	10802	16371	37919	57275	91982	109565
城镇集体单位	1501	3507	8007	10475	15958	27391	63105	72895
其他单位	1571	3525	10367	14218	20882	37803	50487	54026
按国民经济行业分								
农、林、牧、渔业	1312	3639	12412	14000	37046	61606	99510	126208
工　业	1450	3481	8945	12316	18371	30418	48893	52658
建筑业	2052	3813	9125	9820	18385	31020	47757	52982
交通运输、仓储和邮政业					31989	40809	61710	69238
信息传输、软件和信息技术服务业					71801	110207	124608	116202
批发和零售业					28565	38986	50656	54056
住宿和餐饮业					18257	21955	34957	38441
金融业	1500	3303	13254	20560	40655	94569	176578	167117
房地产业	1779	4414	11184	17993	34805	53939	74262	80058
租赁和商务服务业					29824	47505	52828	56364
科学研究、技术服务业					37423	51017	84770	89573
水利、环境和公共设施管理业					34573	51426	44510	35692
居民服务、修理和其他服务业					44853	56776	32474	34252
教育					27255	37734	89780	95429
卫生和社会工作					37991	52867	86091	103825
文化、体育和娱乐业					37710	58317	58686	67158
公共管理、社会保障和社会组织	1519	3666	12347	15424	37888	56817	79271	102374
国际组织								

11-5 各种经济类型分行业城镇在岗职工工资总额、平均工资(2015-2016年)

Total and Average Wage of Employed Persons in Urban Areas by Status of Registration and Sector (2015-2016)

项　　目	国有经济		城镇集体经济		其他经济类型	
	2015年	2016年	2015年	2016年	2015年	2016年
职工工资总额(万元)	1288341	1511235	255177	235480	10764494	11413789
农、林、牧、渔业	2273	2964			205	254
工业	2982	3137	61897	42928	9186446	9713550
建筑业	351	789	26673	21637	156932	186128
交通运输、仓储和邮政业	51594	49816	2209	389	116738	141439
信息传输、软件和信息技术服务业	1552	1212			99779	122567
批发和零售业	1755	2187	5444	6149	279874	308137
住宿和餐饮业			2615	1996	97268	99916
金融业	164513	170022	89274	98110	222074	131678
房地产业	148	213	4025	4652	167209	201932
租赁和商务服务业	5092	7753	32974	32302	164847	198855
科学研究、技术服务业	10636	13201	9059	5050	94142	98185
水利、环境和公共设施管理业	4184	2938	496	598	7729	11112
居民服务、修理和其他服务业	679	805	26	26	38281	43382
教育	272649	298078		142	47095	60471
卫生和社会工作	312955	384174	19764	20742	57041	65777
文化、体育和娱乐业	10532	13560	722	760	28300	30407
公共管理、社会保障和社会组织	446446	560386				
国际组织						
职工平均工资(元)	91982	109565	63105	72895	50487	54026
农、林、牧、渔业	108751	135963			51225	68730
工业	49693	49946	41188	40517	48954	52729
建筑业	92474	62126	53366	64243	46869	51892
交通运输、仓储和邮政业	102899	121533	48118	41860	52673	60220
信息传输、软件和信息技术服务业	66051	113224			126351	116232
批发和零售业	134000	166969	40994	43032	50691	54072
住宿和餐饮业			38224	38901	34877	38432
金融业	157745	168991	149688	165084	210377	166261
房地产业	86765	142000	55290	65701	74871	80425
租赁和商务服务业	117875	103791	46429	48575	53390	56832
科学研究、技术服务业	105311	130061	60679	167222	86163	84048
水利、环境和公共设施管理业	61080	62782	43912	45626	38840	31703
居民服务、修理和其他服务业	57050	64424	51000	51000	32221	33951
教育	101902	107980		49034	53166	60756
卫生和社会工作	85734	105929	81065	84455	90084	99481
文化、体育和娱乐业	67170	85934	74454	92695	55763	60813
公共管理、社会保障和社会组织	79271	102374				
国际组织						

11-6 国有企、事业和机关单位城镇在岗职工工资总额及平均工资(2016年)

Total and Average Wage of Employed Persons in Urban State-owned Enterprises, Institutions and Government Agencies (2016)

项目	单位从业人员劳动报酬(万元)	在岗职工工资总额	其他从业人员工资总额	在岗职工平均工资(元)
总计	1541982	1511235	30747	109565
按企事业机关分				
企业	252325	229395	22930	155123
#地方	178135	177781	354	151535
事业	736427	733837	2590	105273
#地方	734230	731640	2590	105242
机关	553230	548003	5228	102557
#地方	553230	548003	5228	102557
按行业分				
农、林、牧、渔业	3054	2964	90	135963
工业	3257	3137	120	49946
建筑业	789	789		62126
交通运输、仓储和邮政业	49816	49816		121533
信息传输、软件和信息技术服务业	1212	1212		113224
批发和零售业	2194	2187	7	166969
住宿和餐饮业				
金融业	192793	170022	22772	168991
房地产业	213	213		142000
租赁和商务服务业	7774	7753	21	103791
科学研究、技术服务业	13305	13201	104	130061
水利、环境和公共设施管理业	2981	2938	43	62782
居民服务、修理和其他服务业	805	805		64424
教育	298100	298078	22	107980
卫生和社会工作	386541	384174	2367	105929
文化、体育和娱乐业	13576	13560	16	85934
公共管理、社会保障和社会组织	565573	560386	5187	102374
国际组织				

11-7 工业、建筑业城镇在岗职工工资总额和平均工资（2015-2016年）

Total and Average Wage of Employed Persons in Urban Industrial and Construction Units (2015-2016)

项　　目	2015年		2016年	
	工资总额（万元）	平均工资（元）	工资总额（万元）	平均工资（元）
工业总计	9251324	48893	9759614	52658
按经济类型分				
国有单位	2982	49693	3137	49946
城镇集体单位	61897	41188	42928	40517
其他各种单位	9186446	48954	9713550	52729
按工业行业分(大类)				
农副食品加工业	31324	62925	32997	67148
食品制造业	56263	42300	66350	42625
酒、饮料和精制茶制造业	47011	70208	42342	75543
烟草制品业				
纺织业	139027	44200	129542	48841
纺织服装、服饰业	415517	42719	389908	44623
皮革、毛皮、羽毛及其制品和制鞋业	781207	43149	643183	46070
木材加工和木、竹、藤、棕、草制品业	6260	40386	8255	46557
家具制造业	248285	44526	256318	47845
造纸和纸制品业	197335	49584	215920	56042
印刷和记录媒介复制业	181634	48112	199780	50083
文教、工美、体育和娱乐用品制造业	576490	39999	605768	43462
石油加工、炼焦和核燃料加工业	1691	72871	1808	75333
化学原料和化学制品制造业	104460	67990	122503	75188
医药制造业	20214	75062	22078	77986
化学纤维制造业	6588	43835	7210	51245
橡胶和塑料制品业	651459	44511	733317	50664
非金属矿物制品业	83408	49380	110048	54977
黑色金属冶炼和压延加工业	27368	56863	16290	57460
有色金属冶炼和压延加工业	28233	45589	29463	47066
金属制品业	493738	51881	554246	54567
通用设备制造业	382903	54252	435433	59434
专用设备制造业	289189	53928	377878	57049
汽车制造业	119434	62738	132916	69386
铁路、船舶、航空航天和其他设备制造业	50096	60067	45495	64587
电气机械和器材制造业	873440	46560	935596	49484
计算机、通信和其他电子设备制造业	3056929	52672	3260633	55934
仪器仪表制造业	249163	51544	255951	53890
其他制造业	60146	49951	52012	50853
废弃资源综合利用业	366	71686	211	47932
电力、热力生产和供应业	37041	98961	39743	109877
燃气生产和供应业	7870	84260	8306	95356
水的生产和供应业	26938	59584	27369	62990
建筑业总计	183955	47757	208554	52982
国有单位	351	92474	789	62126
城镇集体单位	26673	53366	21637	64243
其他单位	156932	46869	186128	51892

11-8 历年城乡居民收入

Income of Households over Years

单位：元

年 份	全体居民人均可支配收入	城镇常住居民人均可支配收入	农村常住居民人均可支配收入
1978			149
1979			188
1980			272
1981			463
1982			567
1983			618
1984			691
1985		791	803
1986		1033	951
1987		1247	1142
1988		1778	1325
1989		2282	1424
1990		2508	1542
1991		3068	1673
1992		4026	2290
1993		5970	2903
1994		8270	3769
1995		9588	4769
1996		10824	5554
1997		11032	6132
1998		11506	6830
1999		12954	7704
2000		14142	8484
2001		16938	9383
2002		16949	10178
2003		18471	11033
2004		20526	11941
2005		22882	13076
2006		25320	14313
2007		27025	15747
2008		30275	16904
2009		33045	18098
2010		35690	20486
2011		39513	22842
2012		42944	24944
2013		46594	27214
2014	35712	36764	22327
2015	38651	39793	24225
2016	41902	43096	26526

注：本表城镇居民人均可支配收入1997年以前是生活费收入口径，1997年起是可支配收入口径，2014年起为新口径，下同。

11-9 历年城镇常住居民人均可支配收入

Income of Urban Households over Years

单位：元

年 份	可支配收入	工资性收入	经营净收入	财产净收入	转移净收入
1985	791	603			
1986	1033	974			
1987	1247	989			
1988	1778	1097			
1989	2282	1185			
1990	2508	1459	46	30	417
1991	3062	2160	226	55	534
1992	4026	2560	411	175	709
1993	5969	3684	749	889	319
1994	8270	5758	840	553	994
1995	9588	6260	1210	659	1329
1996	10824	8428	1127	455	1273
1997	11032	8024	625	349	1544
1998	11506	8334	884	319	1207
1999	12954	7910	1799	357	1541
2000	14142	8702	2740	895	720
2001	16938	11037	2643	895	1879
2002	16949	13050	1662	1076	1923
2003	18471	15282	1598	1210	1388
2004	20526	17153	1634	1553	1535
2005	22882	18524	2709	1894	1536
2006	25320	18318	4389	2504	1946
2007	27025	18930	3359	4849	2101
2008	30275	20872	4521	3527	3047
2009	33045	23723	4724	4209	3094
2010	35690	26799	4171	4771	3220
2011	39513	27272	4075	7481	4374
2012	42944	30518	3940	9099	3484
2013	46594	33051	4003	10136	3941
2014	36764	28256	3993	6711	-2196
2015	39793	29750	3973	7397	-1326
2016	43096	31826	4576	7505	-810

11-10 历年城镇常住居民人均消费性支出

Living Expenditure of Urban Resident over Years

单位：元

年 份	年人均消费性支出	食品烟酒	衣 着	居 住	生活用品及服务	医疗保健	交通通信	教育文化娱乐	其他用品和服务	恩格尔系数(%)
1985	689	493	28	58	48	14	4	21	23	71.6
1986	883	588	43	66	84	15	6	46	35	66.6
1987	1174	709	64	79	128	55	9	106	24	60.4
1988	1583	977	64	136	171	22	12	124	77	61.7
1989	1980	1235	101	156	196	55	24	115	98	62.4
1990	2038	1295	95	184	153	42	25	113	131	63.5
1991	2481	1476	188	254	122	47	47	211	136	59.5
1992	3901	1834	259	369	263	94	587	331	164	47.0
1993	5533	2615	373	333	583	133	855	389	252	47.3
1994	7270	3172	420	761	925	192	850	714	236	43.6
1995	9220	3644	604	1084	694	258	1562	991	383	39.5
1996	8585	3682	706	674	660	225	990	847	802	42.9
1997	8309	3681	594	880	435	415	916	939	449	44.3
1998	8644	3785	457	659	612	455	1025	1074	577	43.8
1999	11348	3712	400	898	601	371	3398	1043	923	32.7
2000	12529	4048	487	1218	623	431	3309	1517	896	32.3
2001	14669	4572	648	1173	746	513	4258	1429	1330	31.2
2002	15157	4818	748	1060	611	529	4303	2660	428	31.8
2003	15446	4804	921	2966	1093	693	2062	2512	395	31.1
2004	18426	5041	1134	2517	925	811	4973	2673	352	27.4
2005	21768	6035	1285	1242	1165	811	7482	3205	543	27.7
2006	18995	6321	1238	2341	1229	809	3531	3001	525	33.3
2007	21545	6966	1213	1903	1342	860	5208	3515	538	32.3
2008	23208	7778	1349	2585	1539	1332	4462	3464	699	33.5
2009	24270	7972	1492	2232	1616	1400	5456	3326	776	32.8
2010	25733	8732	1706	2089	1771	1294	5925	3443	773	33.9
2011	27495	9513	1806	2128	1902	1251	6035	3886	974	34.6
2012	31369	11103	2121	2852	2173	1521	6108	4348	1143	35.4
2013	33251	11704	2280	3034	2328	1619	6408	4666	1212	35.2
2014	27071	9022	1653	4550	1932	1280	4712	3200	723	33.3
2015	29001	9625	1637	4870	1643	1315	5820	3168	924	33.2
2016	30688	9966	1836	5407	1688	1344	6146	3383	917	32.5

11−11 历年农村常住居民人均收入

Per Capita Actual Income of Rural Households over Years

单位：元

年 份	可支配收入	工资性收入	经营净收入	财产净收入	转移净收入
2006	17676	8522	4195	4171	789
2007	19945	9446	4388	5191	920
2008	20622	9876	4326	5531	889
2009	22077	10442	4517	6210	908
2010	22537	11201	3629	6402	1305
2011	26460	13254	4150	7232	1822
2012	27008	14045	3829	7013	2121
2013	29399	15147	4171	7368	2713
2014	22327	21030	2286	1846	-2836
2015	24225	21405	2241	2181	-1602
2016	26526	23113	2250	2207	-1043

11−12 历年农村常住居民人均消费性支出

Per Capita Consumption Expenditure of Rural Households over Years

单位：元

年 份	年人均消费性支出	食品烟酒	衣 着	居 住	生活用品及服务	医疗保健	交通通信	教育文化娱乐服务	其他用品和服务
2006	9370	3380	448	1458	474	510	1543	932	625
2007	10771	3805	602	2001	581	494	1953	1029	306
2008	10887	3823	691	1500	622	545	1799	1198	709
2009	10598	3711	633	1485	471	565	1764	1223	746
2010	11842	4447	627	1877	480	569	2120	1082	640
2011	14055	5313	655	2345	574	665	2698	1225	580
2012	16103	5980	751	2817	771	765	2828	1533	659
2013	17003	6291	812	2744	752	748	3103	1769	784
2014	18505	7154	1131	3191	817	471	3811	1684	245
2015	19889	7493	1197	2861	975	881	3861	2316	304
2016	21539	8102	1263	3150	1079	904	4153	2567	323

11-13 居民人均收入和支出（2015-2016年）

Income and Expenditure of Households (2015-2016)

单位：元

项目	2015年			2016年		
	常住居民	城镇常住居民	农村常住居民	常住居民	城镇常住居民	农村常住居民
人均可支配收入	38651	39793	24225	41902	43096	26526
工资性收入	29370	29750	21405	31466	31826	23113
经营净收入	3851	3973	2241	4316	4576	2250
财产净收入	6949	7397	2181	7053	7505	2207
转移净收入	-1520	-1326	-1602	-933	-810	-1043
人均消费支出	28256	29001	19889	29906	30688	21539
食品烟酒	9463	9625	7493	9837	9966	8102
衣着	1601	1637	1197	1705	1836	1263
居住	4689	4870	2861	5205	5407	3150
生活用品及服务	1583	1643	975	1634	1688	1079
交通通信	5642	5820	3861	5960	6146	4153
教育文化娱乐	3134	3168	2316	3347	3383	2567
医疗保健	1281	1315	881	1316	1344	904
其他用品和服务	862	924	304	902	917	323

主要统计指标解释

Explanatory Notes on Main Statistical Indicators

可支配收入 指调查户在调查期内获得的、可用于最终消费支出和储蓄的总和，即调查户可以用来自由支配的收入。可支配收入既包括现金，也包括实物收入。按照收入的来源，可支配收入包含四项，分别为：工资性收入、经营净收入、财产净收入和转移净收入。计算公式为：

可支配收入 = 工资性收入 + 经营净收入 + 财产净收入 + 转移净收入

其中：经营净收入 = 经营收入 − 经营费用 − 生产性固定资产折旧 − 生产税

财产净收入 = 财产性收入 − 财产性支出

转移净收入 = 转移性收入 − 转移性支出

工资性收入 指就业人员通过各种途径得到的全部劳动报酬和各种福利，包括受雇于单位或个人、从事各种自由职业、兼职和零星劳动得到的全部劳动报酬和福利。

经营净收入 指住户或住户成员从事生产经营活动所获得的净收入，是全部经营收入中扣除经营费用、生产性固定资产折旧和生产税之后得到的净收入。

财产净收入 指住户或住户成员将其所拥有的金融资产、住房等非金融资产和自然资源交由其他机构单位、住户或个人支配而获得的回报并扣除相关的费用之后得到的净收入。财产净收入包括利息净收入、红利收入、储蓄性保险净收益、转让承包土地经营权租金净收入、出租房屋净收入、出租其他资产净收入和自有住房折算净租金等。

转移净收入 计算公式为：转移净收入 = 转移性收入 − 转移性支出

转移性收入 指国家、单位、社会团体对住户的各种经常性转移支付和住户之间的经常性收入转移。包括政府、非行政事业单位、社会团体对居民转移的养老金或退休金、社会救济和补助、惠农补贴、政策性生活补贴、救灾款、经常性捐赠和赔偿以及报销医疗费等；住户之间的赡养收入、经常性捐赠和赔偿以及在外（含国外）工作的本住户非常住成员寄回带回的收入等。

转移性支出 指调查户对国家、单位、住户或个人的经常性或义务性转移支付。包括缴纳的税款、各项社会保障支出、赡养支出、经常性捐赠和赔偿支出、外来从业人员寄给家人的支出以及其他经常转移支出等。

消费支出 指住户用于满足家庭日常生活消费需要的全部支出，包括用于消费品的支出和用于服务性消费的支出。根据用途不同，消费支出可划分为食品烟酒、衣着、居住、生活用品及服务、交通通信、教育文化娱乐、医疗保健、其他用品及服务八大类。根据来源不同，消费支出可划分为现金消费支出、实物消费支出（含自产自用、来自单位、来自政府和其他社会组织）。

职工工资总额 指各单位在一定时期内直接支付给本单位全部职工的劳动报酬总额。工资总额的计算原则应以直接支付给职工的全部劳动报酬为根据。各单位支付给职工的劳动报酬以及其他根据有关规定支付的工资，不论是计入成本的还是不计入成本的，不论是按国家规定列入计征奖金税项目的，还是未列入计征奖金税项目的，不论是以货币形式支付的还是以实物形式支付的，均包括在工资总额内。

职工平均工资 指企业、事业、机关单位的职工在一定时期内平均每人所得的货币工资额。它表明一定时期职工工资收入的高低程度，是反映职工工资水平的主要指标。计算公式为：职工平均工资=报告期实际支付全部职工工资总额/报告期全部职工平均人数。

十二、社会事业

Social Undertakings

12-1 主要年份社会事业主要指标

Main Indicators of Social Undertakings in Main Years

项　　目	单位	1985年	1990年	1995年	2000年	2005年	2010年	2015年	2016年
公有企事业单位科学技术人员数	人	9166	11629	16856		42593	40025	42624	43225
专利申请量	件		34	325	1653	6694	21654	38094	56653
专利授权量	件		30	262	1399	3114	20397	26820	28559
各类技术合同签订项目数	项		5	46	110	50	90	177	178
各类技术合同签订项目金额	万元		12	1804	3469	4058	18366	9853	17370
在校学生数									
普通高等学校	人			1628	3241	16645	38293	114626	112603
成人高等学校	人	403	531	1254	3642	12665	21703	43894	22301
中等职业技术学校	人	3363	8919	18737	23144	29487	47531	69734	74700
普通中学	人	46596	61188	92481	112418	191044	258276	287582	295753
小学	人	134421	162664	195063	272793	480923	552377	719263	738686
小学学龄儿童入学率	%	99.8	99.9	100.0	100.0	100.0	100.0	100.0	100.0
小学毕业生升学率	%	79.5	95.4	99.2	99.8	99.9	100.0	100.0	100.0
初中毕业生升学率	%	38.5	43.6	85.4	90.3	94.1	97.9	98.5	98.4
普通高中毕业生升学率	%	26.5	31.2	64.9	70.5	96.5	95.1	98.0	98.9
电影放映单位	个	60	114	218	192	70	46	79	96
艺术表演团体	个	1	7	2	1		4	20	20
文化馆（群众艺术馆）	个	1	1	1	1	1	1	1	1
公共图书馆	个	3	5	15	18	473	505	641	605
博物馆	个	2	2	2	3	16	30	48	49
档案馆	个	1	1	1	1	1	1	1	1
《东莞日报》发行量	万份		177	987	1578	2751	4563	4356	5691
广播电台	座		1	1	1	1	1	1	1
电视台	座	1	1	1	1	1	1	1	1
镇街文化广电服务中心	个						28	28	33
卫生事业机构病床床位数	张	2323	3866	5798	7081	11972	19980	27457	28138
卫生技术人员数	人	3305	3902	5290	6915	16608	37487	45226	47668
#执业（助理）医师	人	1201	1721	2299	3309	6901	13214	15889	16680
举办全民健身活动	次							367	417
参加全民健身活动人数	万人次							20.12	41.80
律师人数	人	6	12	85	130	625	1366	2035	2282
公证人员数	人	6	10	19	20	48	96	120	115
人民调解委员会调解人员数	人	3603	3664	3664	3644	4556	17438	14683	14350
优抚收养单位收养人数	人次		19	11	7	8	8	7	7
一般工业固体废物综合利用率	%	37.5	17.9	18.2	63.8	86.5	95.0	88.7	83.7
城市环境空气质量达标天数	天						357	307	319

注：1. 2010年起，公有企事业单位科学技术人员数只统计在编在岗人员数，与往年数不可比。
2. 中等职业技术学校包含市技工学校，不含一般成人中专。
3. 2004年起，卫生方面包含诊所、卫生所、医务室及村卫生室的数据，与往年数不可比。

12-2 科技活动基本情况（2016年）

Basic Statistics on Scientific and Technological Activities (2016)

项　目	单位	2016年	项　目	单位	2016年
科技企业			专利授权数	件	218
企业数			科技园区和基地		
#国家高新技术企业	个	2028	国家级高新区	个	1
省创新型试点企业	个	58	省级高新区	个	
省创新型企业	个	29	专业镇	个	34
省创新百强企业	个	10	#工业总产值	亿元	13612
重点培育上市后备科技企业	个	76	全镇科技投入	亿元	113
科技合作			国家高新技术企业数	个	1695
国际合作项目立项数	项	2	火炬计划特色产业基地	个	6
#国家立项数	项		#工业总产值	亿元	1835
省级立项数	项	2	国家高新技术企业数	个	253
国际科技合作示范基地	个	1	科技企业孵化器/加速器	个	59
#国家级基地	个	1	#建筑场地面积	万平方米	140.89
省级基地	个		在孵企业数	个	1800
产学研项目立项数	项	17	毕业企业数	个	207
资助金额	万元	2069	工程中心		
科技特派员入驻数	人		国家级工程中心	个	1
省部产学研示范基地	个		省级工程中心	个	163
省部产学研创新联盟	个		#工程中心职工总数	人	19122
科技机构			经费收入	万元	497958
机构数	个	40	研究开发课题（项目）	项	1508
职工总数	人	3244	专利授权数	项	2674
#单位在职从事科技活动人员	人	2536	研究与发展（R&D）人员	人	13208
#大学本科及以上学历	人	2219	研究与发展经费	万元	451087
科技活动收入	万元	68198.3	市级工程中心	个	110
#政府拨款	万元	58620.8	#工程中心职工总数	人	12278
科技经费内部支出	万元	54374.6	经费收入	万元	357549
课题数	项	322	研究开发课题（项目）	项	909
课题经费支出额	万元	31560	专利授权数	项	1984
科技论文数	篇	293	研究与发展（R&D）人员	人	8392
专利申请受理	件	485	研究与发展经费	万元	319119

12-3 规模以上工业企业R&D活动及相关情况（2010-2016年）

The Main Indicators on R&D of Industrial Enterprises above Designated Size (2010-2016)

指 标	单位	2010年	2011年	2012年	2013年	2014年	2015年	2016年
R&D企业情况								
有研发机构的企业数	家	314	351	321	372	563	950	2004
有R&D活动的企业数	家	436	428	607	709	855	1145	1709
企业办研发机构情况								
机构数	个	376	468	417	476	716	1126	2264
机构人员合计	人	26376	29772	27060	29943	40012	54234	98662
机构经费支出	万元	330015	395075	440568	558771	746857	1016937	1966566
R&D项目情况								
全部R&D项目数	项	1955	2448	3083	3973	4307	4484	5812
R&D活动人员情况								
R&D人员合计	人	36064	39400	51386	53258	58752	59469	64963
#研究人员	人	6095	5513	6807	9109	8707	13851	14562
R&D人员折合全时当量合计	人年	26634	31743	44335	43635	49457	47449	48209
#研究人员	人年	4542	4421	5999	7727	7432	11240	11133
R&D经费支出合计	万元	495099	612516	748347	983720	1150506	1267890	1434038
其中：①经常费支出	万元	420877	493831	676645	855711	1041473	1142706	1295452
②资产性支出	万元	74222	118686	71702	128009	109034	125183	138586
其中：①基础研究支出								
②应用研究支出	万元	9740	7790	348	183	3754	4302	1086
③试验发展支出	万元	485360	604726	747999	983537	1146753	1263587	1432952
其中：①政府资金	万元	20388	23729	16789	16012	11334	15031	18231
②企业资金	万元	455496	576732	720243	938785	1114200	1232605	1365448
③境外资金	万元	10021	3045	5626	22682	14807	7670	26395
④其他资金	万元	9194	9010	5690	6241	10165	12583	23965
委托外单位开展研发的经费支出合	万元	11050	13888	28331	49266	143368	278714	601287
#对境内研究机构支出	万元	6467	10703	4437	14379	120399	236268	522990
对境内高等学校支出	万元	2622	2577	2980	2142	1626	1692	1760
对境内企业支出						8166	9354	26272
对境外支出	万元	982	225	1245	7380	13177	31401	50265
科技活动产出及相关情况								
自主知识产权情况								
专利申请数	件	4654	5746	8038	10946	9586	9209	15068
#发明专利	件	1301	1177	2574	4256	3819	2772	4427
有效发明专利数	件	1926	3320	2064	3217	5363	6084	10236
#境外授权	件	112	237	119	210	283	287	596
专利所有权转让及许可数	件	161	537	136	112	119	184	183
专利所有权转让及许可收入	万元	8640	15859	10584	2908	3733	2917	11498
新产品开发、生产及销售情况								
新产品开发项目数	项	2276	2534	3094	6376	5978	6414	9929
新产品开发经费支出	万元	589036	776818	765927	1232410	1497801	1638609	2203250
新产品产值	万元	5501675	6945494	8643848	11744374	22172598	24746366	45756078
新产品销售收入	万元	5391190	6373687	8385864	11951808	21901522	24215567	46427486
#出口	万元	1988713	3109605	3466739	3786174	8113170	7917504	16506231
其他情况								
发表科技论文	篇	205	340	309	209	190	174	218
拥有注册商标数量	件	2287	3047	3194	3580	4327	5421	7603
#境外注册	件	310	326	309	482	752	612	690
形成国家或行业标准	项	171	50	201	172	139	83	154

12-4 规模以上服务业企业R&D活动及相关情况（2016年）

The Main Indicators on R&D of Service Enterprises above Designated Size (2016)

指　　标	单位	2016年
R&D企业情况		
有研发机构的企业数	家	18
有R&D活动的企业数	家	14
企业办研发机构情况		
机构数	个	21
机构人员合计	人	2854
机构经费支出	万元	50387
R&D项目情况		
全部R&D项目数	项	129
R&D活动人员情况		
R&D人员合计	人	4194
#研究人员	人	1724
R&D人员折合全时当量合计	人年	3352
#研究人员	人年	1374
R&D经费支出合计	万元	134449
其中：①经常费支出	万元	128011
②资产性支出	万元	6438
其中：①基础研究支出		
②应用研究支出	万元	716
③试验发展支出	万元	133733
其中：①政府资金	万元	56
②企业资金	万元	134393
③境外资金	万元	
④其他资金	万元	
委托外单位开展研发的经费支出合计	万元	1974
#对境内研究机构支出	万元	
对境内高等学校支出	万元	
对境内企业支出	万元	21
对境外支出	万元	1953
科技活动产出及相关情况		
专利申请数	件	4974
#发明专利	件	4619
有效发明专利数	件	901

12-5 主要年份公有企事业单位科学技术人员

Scientific and Technical Personnel in Public Enterprises and Institutions in Main Years

单位：人

项　　目	1990年	1995年	2005年	2010年	2015年	2016年
公有企事业单位科技人员数	11629	16856	42593	40025	42624	43225
#工程技术人员	1084	1718	1839	1438	1795	1948
农业技术人员	432	230	290	172	205	210
卫生技术人员	1430	1988	16188	11171	10360	10411
科学研究人员	21	52	77	16	58	85
教学人员	7524	11553	21717	24010	25937	25951
经济人员	278	329	636	1184	1971	1990
会计人员	581	484	1299	1454	1561	1737
统计人员	170	77	82	91	94	91

注：2010年起，公有企事业单位科学技术人员数只统计在编在岗人员数，与往年数不可比，下同。

12-6 主要年份三种专利申请量与授权量

Three Kinds of Patents Application Accepted and Granted in Main Years

单位：件

项　　目	1990年	1995年	2000年	2005年	2010年	2015年	2016年
申请量	34	325	1653	6694	21654	38094	56653
发　明	1	5	35	245	3143	11166	17024
实用新型	5	70	386	1971	7677	17567	28096
外观设计	28	250	1232	4478	10834	9361	11533
授权量	30	262	1399	3114	20397	26820	28559
发　明	1	8	4	24	442	2795	3682
实用新型	4	41	344	1116	7529	14074	16454
外观设计	25	213	1051	1974	12426	9951	8423

12-7 主要年份各类技术合同签订情况

Basic Statistics on Technical Contracts Signed by Type in Main Years

项　　目	1990年	1995年	2000年	2005年	2010年	2015年	2016年
技术合同项目数（项）	5	46	110	50	90	177	178
#技术开发合同	3		1	41	79	156	159
技术咨询合同				2		1	
技术转让合同	2	44	78	1	2	2	6
技术服务合同		2	31	6	9	18	13
技术合同金额（万元）	12	1804	3469	4058	18366	9853	17370
#技术开发合同			1000	1888	6878	7677	11804
技术咨询合同				80		10	
技术转让合同	12	1656	2007	2000	11046	750	5198
技术服务合同		148	1362	90	442	1416	368
技术合同实现金额（万元）	7	1623	2398	2522	17891	9571	15002
#技术开发合同			700	1427	6402	7505	9437
技术咨询合同				35		10	
技术转让合同	7	1535	1260	1000	11046	750	5198
技术服务合同		88	438	60	442	1306	367

12-8 主要年份高新科技发展情况

Basic Statistics on High-tech Development in Main Years

项　　目	单 位	1995年	2000年	2005年	2010年	2015年	2016年
高新技术企业							
企业数	个	11	66	247	334	986	2028
总产值	亿元	30.55	274.41	925.07	1240.59	2719.73	4073.20
总收入	亿元	26.76	266.49	927.72	1249.50	2989.10	4438.20
出口总额	亿美元	0.54	7.34	71.59	99.08	774.69	1221.90
从业人员数	人	6400	36304	171812	246134	320119	510073
#科技活动人员	人	832	8663	34448	72833	64010	94424
高新技术产品							
企业数	家			543	924	1155	1551
产品	个	27	177	947	1430	2079	3148
总产值	亿元	31.43	186.00	1062.40	2353.70	4920.90	6898.62
销售收入	亿元			1033.64	2316.74	4828.91	6818.07
#出口销售收入	亿元			651.99	1510.87	2076.73	2372.93
实现利税	亿元			66.06	116.82	246.07	296.02

注：1．高新技术企业情况2009年以前为省级高新技术企业情况，2009年起为国家级高新技术企业情况。
2．高新技术产品情况从2010年起，统计口径为规模以上工业企业。

12-9 主要年份科学技术成果项数

Achievements for Scientific and Technological Research in Main Years

单位：项

项　目	1985年	1990年	1995年	2000年	2005年	2010年	2015年	2016年
获省级科技进步奖		1	4	6	3	8	5	4
市级科技进步奖	68	31	22	47	75	87	63	63
农业方面	30	8	3	13	9	7	6	4
一等奖	1	4		2	1	2	1	1
二等奖	3	3		5	3	2	1	
三等奖	18	1	3	6	5	3	4	3
工业方面	32	18	14	24	42	57	37	37
特等奖				1	2			
一等奖	1	3		5	7	13	6	6
二等奖	8	11	5	8	19	21	13	14
三等奖	10	4	9	10	14	23	18	18
医药卫生方面	6	5	5	10	25	23	20	21
特等奖								
一等奖			1			5	1	1
二等奖		1		2	4	6	6	6
三等奖	2	4	4	8	19	12	13	14
市长奖						5	3	3
技术成果类						1		
荣誉类						4	3	3

12-10 科技创新平台情况（2011-2016年）

Basic Statistics on Technology Innovation Platform (2011-2016)

单位：个

项　目	2011年	2012年	2013年	2014年	2015年	2016年
科技创新平台						
#公共科技创新平台（新型研发机构）	11	13	16	17	27	24
专业镇创新服务平台	12	12	12	12	15	3
企业创新平台						
#企业工程技术研究开发中心	124	124	161	186	219	289
#国家级	2	1	1	1	1	1
省级	42	45	76	92	126	166
市级	80	78	84	93	92	122
实验室					76	90
#国家级					1	1
省级	9	11	11	11	12	12
市级	31	31	35	37	42	77
#重点实验室	31	31	35	37	42	51

12-11 历年公有企事业单位科学技术人员数

Scientific and Technical Personnel in Public Enterprises and Institutions over Years

单位：人

年份	科学技术人员	#工程技术人员	农业技术人员	卫生技术人员	科学研究人员	教学人员	经济人员	会计人员	统计人员
1980	6619	370	190	1076	19	4282		564	99
1981	7473	463	217	1166	23	4978		501	109
1982	7547	468	243	1241	28	4954		509	101
1983	8453	525	315	1699		5257		109	109
1984	9033	615	307	1791		5534		261	201
1985	9166	663	318	2319	6	5129		491	214
1986	9490	768	358	2398	5	5222		501	203
1987	10945	797	378	2426	6	6495		583	222
1988	12495	1014	359	3093	24	7064	72	590	197
1989	11306	960	388	1393	19	7394	281	632	181
1990	11629	1084	432	1430	21	7524	278	581	170
1991	15004	2170	405	3347	13	7843	308	558	153
1992	16809	2522	375	3690	18	8659	313	613	153
1993	18491	2871	264	4074	112	9511	290	916	141
1994	20198	3490	272	4513	57	9949	300	657	112
1995	23104	3944	255	4878	66	11613	329	750	171
1996	24693	4037	263	5356	51	12287	360	740	143
1997	26103	4258	294	5504	48	13371	418	882	280
1998	26582	4321	310	4862	48	14316	376	894	171
1999	28789	4620	288	5246	48	15604	416	946	152
2000									
2001	24677	795	121	5493	31	17309	252	273	40
2002	34168	5261	246	6538	28	18756	555	1319	184
2003	33070	996	159	11145	44	19614	314	741	57
2004	39398	1752	276	14541	141	20905	561	613	74
2005	42593	1839	290	16188	77	21717	636	1299	82
2006	46371	1913	462	18401	70	22434	763	1512	93
2007	49032	2037	492	19528	71	23364	892	1832	92
2008	51729	2375	343	20955	50	24063	1048	1827	100
2009	55097	2302	284	21679	43	26741	1129	1940	122
2010	40025	1438	172	11171	16	24010	1184	1454	91
2011	41370	1427	216	11117	21	25084	1393	1426	90
2012	41336	1426	217	10762	24	25412	1261	1556	79
2013	41812	1378	208	10613	17	25707	1678	1514	169
2014	42141	1552	205	10290	19	25807	1954	1628	87
2015	42624	1795	205	10360	58	25937	1971	1561	94
2016	43225	1948	210	10411	85	25951	1990	1737	91

12-12 历年三种专利与技术合同签订情况

Basic Statistics on Three Kinds of Patents and Technical Contracts Signed by Type over Years

年 份	三种专利申请量(件)	#发明	三种专利授权量(件)	#发明	技术合同签订项目数(项)	技术合同签订金额(万元)	技术合同实现金额(万元)
1990	34	1	30	1	5	12	7
1991	70	3	50	1	4	10	10
1992	102	5	78	2	3	23	10
1993	100	3	90	1	2	24	2
1994	104	4	100	2	14	2537	1756
1995	325	5	262	8	46	1804	1623
1996	333	3	312	4	133	4839	3756
1997	725	1	321		78	2036	800
1998	890	15	709	9	62	3048	2398
1999	1221	15	819	16	20	1124	1077
2000	1653	35	1399	4	110	3469	2398
2001	2914	71	1753	5	89	1335	953
2002	3100	90	2680	10	91	766	730
2003	3865	93	2858	14	58	700	680
2004	4325	185	3167	26	69	4278	2726
2005	6694	245	3114	24	50	4058	2522
2006	9879	553	4872	28	25	13644	13402
2007	13842	876	6752	44	53	8510	8138
2008	14406	1188	8093	115	54	12838	3694
2009	19106	1593	12918	254	60	6996	6264
2010	21654	3143	20397	442	70	15760	15572
2011	24455	4214	19353	758	163	31966	29923
2012	29199	5568	20900	1381	152	14516	13577
2013	29013	6454	22595	1495	175	25960	24610
2014	28432	6912	20340	1624	177	11241	10298
2015	38094	11166	26820	2795	177	9853	9571
2016	56653	17024	28559	3682	178	17370	15002

12-13 历年科学技术成果项数

Scientific and Technological Achievements over Years

单位：项

年 份	获国家级科技进步奖	获省级科技进步奖	获市级科技进步奖					
				特等奖	一等奖	二等奖	三等奖	四等奖
1979			25			5	4	16
1980			27			2	11	14
1981			35		2	4	11	18
1982			62		1	3	21	37
1983			38		2	6	11	19
1984			35			11	11	13
1985			68		2	11	30	25
1986			86		5	14	27	40
1987			59		2	19	25	13
1988		1	37		6	10	16	5
1989		1	32		4	6	22	
1990		1	31		7	15	9	
1991		4	35	1	3	18	13	
1992		3	19		4	7	8	
1993			18	1	3	8	6	
1994		6	23		4	9	10	
1995		4	22		1	5	16	
1996		3	32		7	6	19	
1997		4	32		7	6	19	
1998		6	38	1	2	11	24	
1999		9	39		6	11	22	
2000		6	47	1	7	15	24	
2001		4	51		4	23	24	
2002		3	47		7	15	25	
2003		4	50		7	14	29	
2004		6	60	1	6	19	34	
2005		3	75	2	10	25	38	
2006		2	70	1	8	24	37	
2007		7	83	1	18	26	38	
2008		7	83		19	28	36	
2009		19	85		22	24	39	
2010		8	87		20	29	38	
2011		13	77		21	30	26	
2012		9	93		22	33	38	
2013		9	93		26	33	34	
2014		8	75		12	27	36	
2015		5	63		8	20	35	
2016		4	63		8	20	35	

12-14 主要年份各类学校情况

Basic Statistics on Schools by Type in Main Years

项　　目	单位	1985年	1990年	1995年	2000年	2005年	2010年	2015年	2016年
普通高等专业学校									
学校数	所			1	1	4	5	8	9
毕业生数	人			395	985	1439	8105	23927	22974
招生数	人			576	1440	7273	12660	33319	31362
在校学生数	人			1628	3241	16645	38293	114626	112603
教职工数	人			262	293	1761	3192	7451	6440
#专任教师	人			119	161	1081	2174	6569	4651
中等职业技术学校									
学校数	所	3	17	20	23	21	26	25	26
毕业生数	人	234	2210	4641	9554	9062	14028	17119	20593
招生数	人	1508	3866	8697	8759	10971	18477	26074	29139
在校学生数	人	3363	8919	18737	23144	29487	47531	69734	74700
教职员工数	人	217	619	1134	1608	2230	2996	3783	4126
#专任教师	人	150	434	859	1221	1621	2341	2973	3257
普通中学									
学校数	所	106	64	69	77	134	190	218	231
毕业生数	人	12317	18688	24165	30261	48935	73810	84541	85524
#高中生	人	2055	2527	3231	7120	12233	20816	25322	25673
招生数	人	16978	20441	33086	41488	70843	93196	103313	110681
#高中生	个	2915	3389	6099	9048	19540	24668	26720	27153
在校学生数	人	46596	61188	92481	112418	191044	258276	287582	295753
#高中生	人	6304	8572	13653	24677	52283	70398	78905	79851
教职员工数	人	3266	4001	5900	6012	12177	16946	23537	25527
#专任教师	个	2420	2963	4381	5027	9640	14572	17701	18885
小　学									
学校数	所	583	570	595	552	414	330	327	328
毕业生数	人	17901	18262	27257	33684	61173	77429	89575	98789
招生数	人	20264	26158	36702	53786	84784	108900	140200	138179
在校学生数	人	134421	162664	195063	272793	480923	552377	719263	738686
教职员工数	人	7009	7797	9560	9131	21964	28298	33427	35959
#专任教师	人	6017	6785	8060	7946	17478	23733	30281	32302

注：中等职业技术学校包含市技工学校，不含一般成人中专，下同。

12-14 续表

项目	单位	1985年	1990年	1995年	2000年	2005年	2010年	2015年	2016年
成人高等专业教育									
当年招生人数	人				1697	6387	6086	14435	9074
在校学生数	人	403	531	1254	3642	12665	21703	43894	22301
小学适龄儿童入学									
小学适龄儿童总数	人	103460	133011	177791	247555	423058	511439	697780	717224
小学已入学儿童数	人	103282	132934	177787	247539	423058	511439	697780	717224
小学学龄儿童入学率	%	99.8	99.9	100.0	100.0	100.0	100.0	100.0	100.0
小学毕业生升学									
小学毕业生人数	人	17901	18262	27257	33684	61173	77429	89575	98789
已升学人数	人	14235	17413	27166	33627	61095	77429	89575	98606
小学毕业生升学率	%	79.5	95.4	99.2	99.8	99.9	100.0	100.0	100.0
初中毕业生升学									
初中毕业生人数	人	10262	16161	20933	23141	36702	52994	59219	59851
已升学人数	人	3955	7134	17876	20896	34536	51881	58333	58587
初中毕业生升学率	%	38.5	43.6	85.4	90.3	94.1	97.9	98.5	98.4
普通高中毕业生升学									
高考录取人数	人	543	759	2095	5017	12461	20099	27426	24094
#高考升本科人数	人	274	250	697	1678	5161	11033	12592	15234
普通高中毕业生升学率	%	26.5	31.2	64.9	70.5	96.5	95.1	98.0	98.9
幼儿园									
幼儿园数	所	83	86	258	452	511	727	949	1016
在园幼儿数	人	31382	47040	84263	111763	111330	208373	314449	331710
幼教职工数	人	984	1387	1427	7517	12567	22122	39492	43000
#专任教师	人	841	1160	1160	4618	7002	13947	20561	22089
特殊教育									
学校数	所						1	2	2
毕业生数	人						89	35	78
招生数	人						55	111	90
在校学生数	人						501	739	747
教职员工数	人						55	185	211
#专任教师	人						41	134	159
国家各大（学）专院校在我市招生人数	人				11680	35831	40795	46049	46541
全市教育经费投入总额	亿元				15.5	50.2	94.4	188.6	226.7

12-15 历年各类学校在校学生数

Number of Students Enrollment by Type of School over Years

单位：人

年份	普通高等学校	中等职业技术学校	#技工学校	普通中学	#高中	小学	幼儿园	特殊教育
1949		151		1960	318	52781		
1952		543		3394	296	70359		
1957		561		6652	848	88001		
1962		380		9736	1513	119998		
1965		358		10469	1397	160931		
1970				60150	9873	118128		
1975		689		49569	10847	168236		
1978		595		76025	12092	161114	18228	
1979		450		62292	7010	158008	12774	
1980		386		54829	6909	154871	7630	
1981		450		43514	5755	150857	8103	
1982		661		41683	4654	144754	14650	
1983		967		42777	4798	135440	15436	
1984		1070		46488	5766	134567	23702	
1985		3363		46596	6304	134421	31382	
1986		3891	60	49445	7880	140700	38195	
1987		5847	117	54435	8367	144287	42569	
1988		7120	229	59268	8201	150097	42845	
1989		7878	293	61955	7687	155852	44110	
1990		8919	582	61188	8572	162664	47040	
1991		10938	915	60146	8725	170064	51051	
1992		13161	1277	65171	9711	175203	57537	
1993	1079	14176	1516	75305	10297	180114	65310	
1994	1451	16084	2025	85827	11409	186244	72552	
1995	1628	18737	2404	92481	13653	195063	84263	
1996	1771	22614	2567	95150	16887	205957	85709	
1997	2025	24821	2598	98005	20609	221838	100059	
1998	2171	25588	2291	101202	22490	235787	103585	
1999	2241	25073	2001	105518	23084	248759	109773	
2000	3241	23144	1746	112418	24677	272793	111763	
2001	3802	23638	2039	122115	28232	295384	112963	
2002	5144	25363	2152	135256	32398	342804	108898	
2003	6884	27664	2564	149656	38143	386890	104832	
2004	9104	28487	2559	171336	45050	448296	112538	
2005	16645	29487	2618	191044	52283	480923	111330	
2006	22005	35403	2905	214638	57662	496828	118683	
2007	25178	40429	3063	234578	61151	520684	130932	
2008	28656	45419	3238	248442	63962	528644	156362	
2009	33992	46538	3268	249464	66750	511160	176249	
2010	38293	47531	2955	258276	70398	552377	208373	501
2011	45081	48159	2915	263076	73644	578279	227656	384
2012	52381	50092	2833	267918	75851	608118	255657	421
2013	60877	61011	13101	278289	77045	659138	277777	380
2014	69866	64412	14192	284648	78053	687269	290548	449
2015	114626	69734	16300	287582	78905	719263	314449	739
2016	112603	74700	17457	295753	79851	738686	331710	747

注：2013年起中等职业技术学校含东莞市技师学院、东莞市实验技工学校、东莞市联合技工学校数据。

12-16 历年各类学校当年招收学生数

Number of New Students Enrollment by Type of School over Years

单位：人

年 份	普通高等学校	中等职业技术学校	#技工学校	普通中学	#高中	小 学	特殊教育
1949		102					
1952		285		1666	190		
1957		80		2516	259		
1962		45		3716	566		
1965		134		3656	476		
1970				45069	7919		
1975		188		28329	5930		
1978		250		29788	3436	30152	
1979		200		25364	3900	28315	
1980		186		24083	3906	26857	
1981		266		16808	2594	26461	
1982		162		17492	2317	23970	
1983		573		18111	2344	19604	
1984		1964		16609	2477	17644	
1985		1508		16978	2915	20264	
1986		1977	60	17944	2781	25867	
1987		2883	64	21720	2665	28926	
1988		2832	112	23280	2925	29437	
1989		2966	124	21877	2686	27539	
1990		3866	343	20441	3389	26158	
1991		5008	445	21430	3266	27539	
1992		5696	487	26161	3751	28804	
1993	567	5835	633	29948	3944	31841	
1994	569	7064	952	32229	4440	34495	
1995	576	8697	996	33086	6099	36702	
1996	711	10119	978	33576	7385	39689	
1997	750	9718	798	35140	8273	42066	
1998	750	9664	852	36423	8118	43802	
1999	802	9060	665	38400	8199	47715	
2000	1440	8759	527	41488	9048	53786	
2001	1597	8850	1116	44729	10727	56521	
2002	2190	9417	1153	49881	11852	65066	
2003	3104	9809	874	55564	15147	71476	
2004	3804	10618	1044	63085	17467	80525	
2005	7273	10971	1100	70843	19540	84784	
2006	8032	13357	1250	79985	20866	89663	
2007	8519	16491	1297	85816	21146	92860	
2008	10218	17475	1163	89808	22313	94641	
2009	12863	15767	1598	88325	23631	92281	
2010	12660	18477	2052	93196	24668	108900	55
2011	16837	17812	1180	95155	25647	114763	78
2012	20507	18269	1306	96348	25758	123290	55
2013	20816	24687	7069	100170	26039	127237	57
2014	22830	24524	5110	102112	26741	125039	92
2015	33319	26074	6060	103313	26720	140200	111
2016	31362	29139	7442	110681	27153	138179	90

12–17 历年各类学校当年毕业生数

Number of Graduates by Type of School over Years

单位：人

年 份	普通高等学校	中等职业技术学校	#技工学校	普通中学	#高中	小 学	特殊教育
1949				414	83		
1952		48		588	44	14349	
1957		87		1365	203	59056	
1962		209		2680	468	28418	
1965		44		2363	393	32508	
1970				15081	1954	26187	
1975		374		20842	4937	25009	
1978		244		43035	8533	30480	
1979		244		33554	8004	28925	
1980		250		19578	3096	27294	
1981		191		13308	3046	27215	
1982				10483	3004	27348	
1983		260		10752	1940	26723	
1984		230		10969	1404	17870	
1985		234		12317	2055	17901	
1986		660		13527	1271	17533	
1987		819		13895	2296	23183	
1988		1323		15322	2966	23054	
1989		1960	60	15310	2716	20315	
1990		2210	57	18688	2527	18262	
1991		2634	112	19820	2559	19186	
1992		2126	123	19323	2643	23308	
1993	30	2915	390	18363	3020	26893	
1994	197	5035	445	20360	2787	28500	
1995	395	4641	541	24165	3231	27257	
1996	560	5813	753	27675	3483	27156	
1997	484	6745	691	28729	3834	27992	
1998	556	8316	918	29839	5448	29794	
1999	714	9044	796	30109	6585	31426	
2000	985	9554	634	31291	7120	33684	
2001	1019	7748	684	32409	7553	37077	
2002	753	7171	542	34204	8277	40611	
2003	1350	7217	509	39031	8784	45599	
2004	1506	8630	917	43471	10676	51831	
2005	1439	9062	777	48935	12233	61173	
2006	2269	9422	677	55856	15486	70474	
2007	5096	10061	754	60436	17354	74681	
2008	6486	10728	821	66594	19315	78037	
2009	7292	11927	962	71811	20550	78027	
2010	8105	14028	956	73810	20816	77429	89
2011	9463	14774	831	76816	22095	80463	64
2012	12625	14099	993	79449	23398	87733	64
2013	11630	16660	2426	78364	24341	84641	66
2014	12990	17521	2834	82718	25180	86693	48
2015	23927	17119	2985	84541	25322	89575	35
2016	22974	20593	5278	85524	25673	98789	78

12-18 历年各级各类学校专任教师数

Number of Full-time Teachers by Level and Type of School over Years

单位：人

年 份	普通高等学校	中等职业技术学校	#技工学校	普通中学	#高中	小 学	幼儿园	特殊教育
1978		34		3641	638	5641		
1979		31		3367	369	6136		
1980		29		2996	370	6022		
1981		32		2343	344	6433		
1982		38		2210	284	6186		
1983		61		2361	296	5830		
1984		63		2352	309	5971		
1985		150		2420	354	6017	841	
1986		168	5	2463	407	6515	720	
1987		208	7	2709	490	6878	941	
1988		306	9	3007	540	7112	967	
1989		422	11	2949	462	6743	980	
1990		434	12	2963	488	6785	1160	
1991		513	15	3019	500	6831	1470	
1992		600	17	3198	479	7164	1569	
1993	99	737	16	3583	610	7314	1773	
1994	113	767	26	4001	710	7610	1920	
1995	119	859	34	4381	733	8060	1160	
1996	119	924	40	4310	886	7410	2175	
1997	123	1151	89	4404	991	7518	2753	
1998	125	1338	93	4632	1065	7912	3247	
1999	133	1205	92	4699	1149	7198	3715	
2000	161	1221	84	5027	1310	7946	4618	
2001	231	1286	121	5348	1411	8693	4701	
2002	290	1445	125	6373	1769	10880	5351	
2003	312	1548	124	7069	1976	12490	5505	
2004	560	1531	134	8437	2367	15512	6218	
2005	1081	1621	150	9640	2817	17478	7002	
2006	1357	1801	122	10953	3215	18717	7919	
2007	1569	1965	156	12272	3678	20511	9279	
2008	1691	2218	161	12995	3976	21203	11072	
2009	1890	2321	160	13598	4178	21130	12419	
2010	2174	2341	171	14572	4541	23733	13947	41
2011	2435	2403	167	15262	4851	24787	15232	43
2012	2729	2448	180	15858	5026	25379	16689	48
2013	2952	2677	458	16422	5114	26681	17640	47
2014	3148	2861	628	17148	5291	28679	18748	54
2015	6569	2973	647	17701	5387	30281	20561	134
2016	4651	3257	700	18885	5671	32302	22089	159

12-19 历年各类学校入(升)学率与高考入围人数

Number of Passing College Entrance Examination and Proportion of Students Entering Schools over Years

年 份	学龄儿童入学率(%)	小学毕业生升学率(%)	初中毕业生升学率(%)	高中毕业生升学率(%)	高考入围人数(人)
1978	98.36	85.80	14.30	8.14	846
1979	98.70	76.00	16.00	6.71	566
1980	98.85	73.40	25.40	7.15	222
1981	98.72	50.56	27.40	8.64	239
1982	99.06	54.40	34.40	8.04	252
1983	99.75	57.60	37.40	12.34	245
1984	99.65	70.80	29.86	43.32	619
1985	99.83	79.52	38.54	26.50	534
1986	99.90	84.71	33.89	43.69	595
1987	99.94	83.60	40.10	27.09	644
1988	99.93	89.88	42.00	30.63	925
1989	99.92	96.18	43.30	32.92	977
1990	99.94	95.35	43.60	31.20	759
1991	99.92	96.18	45.20	26.22	861
1992	99.94	97.58	56.00	35.59	994
1993	99.95	97.79	68.50	39.23	1102
1994	99.96	98.94	79.02	62.75	1823
1995	99.99	99.16	85.40	64.90	2095
1996	99.98	96.45	86.70	66.80	2160
1997	99.99	99.90	87.35	60.00	2212
1998	99.99	99.86	88.25	47.69	2348
1999	99.99	99.87	89.80	53.15	3501
2000	99.99	99.83	90.30	70.50	5017
2001	100.00	99.77	90.50	74.82	5651
2002	100.00	99.80	91.10	83.00	6873
2003	100.00	99.80	92.10	93.60	9167
2004	100.00	99.90	93.30	96.70	10756
2005	100.00	99.90	94.10	96.50	11196
2006	100.00	100.00	94.80	82.90	11359
2007	100.00	100.00	95.20	89.10	13275
2008	100.00	100.00	96.60	91.00	15047
2009	100.00	100.00	97.00	87.50	17487
2010	100.00	100.00	97.90	95.10	18845
2011	100.00	100.00	98.00	94.50	19588
2012	100.00	100.00	97.80	95.90	22127
2013	100.00	100.00	98.40	95.40	22840
2014	100.00	100.00	98.40	98.37	23900
2015	100.00	100.00	98.50	97.97	26519
2016	100.00	100.00	98.40	98.90	24094

12−20 历年文化艺术、文物事业机构数

Number of Institutions in Culture and Cultural Relics over Years

年份	电影放映单位(个)	#影剧院	艺术表演团体(个)	群众艺术馆(个)	文化站(广电文化中心)(个)	公共图书馆(个)	公共图书馆藏书量(万册)	博物馆(个)	档案馆(座)
1978	167	5	1	1	33	1	11	2	1
1979	157	5	1	1	33	1	15	2	1
1980	65	5	1	1	33	1	16	2	1
1981	75	6	1	1	33	1	17	2	1
1982	53	6	1	1	33	1	19	2	1
1983	49	6	1	1	33	1	19	2	1
1984	65	6	1	1	33	1	24	2	1
1985	60	7	1	1	33	3	30	2	1
1986	61	9	2	1	33	3	30	2	1
1987	70	13	4	1	33	8	30	2	1
1988	78	15	5	1	33	3	30	2	1
1989	102	26	6	1	33	3	30	2	1
1990	114	26	7	1	33	5	30	2	1
1991	126	36	5	1	33	6	31	2	1
1992	150	50	2	1	33	8	37	2	1
1993	163	53	2	1	33	11	47	2	1
1994	193	63	2	1	33	14	58	2	1
1995	218	97	2	1	33	15	68	2	1
1996	225	111	4	1	33	16	73	2	1
1997	229	130	4	1	33	26	84	2	1
1998	233	147	4	1	32	26	106	3	1
1999	210	87	4	1	32	20	133	3	1
2000	192	87	1	1	32	18	97	3	1
2001	145	84	1	1	32	21	99	3	1
2002	162	81	2	1	32	24	109	3	2
2003	107	55	2	1	32	346	289	3	2
2004	88	78		1	32	397	631	6	2
2005	70	31		1	32	473	660	16	2
2006	51	34		1	33	1222	771	21	2
2007	51	34		1	33	1271	896	23	2
2008	40	34	1	1	33	387	515	23	1
2009	40	62	4	1	33	504	599	31	1
2010	46	62	4	1	33	505	701	30	1
2011	52	62	5	1	33	622	771	31	1
2012	59	11	6	1	33	649	1020	31	1
2013	66	11	10	1	33	641	1061	31	1
2014	60	11	16	1	33	641	996	33	1
2015	79	9	20	1	33	641	1015	48	1
2016	96	7	20	1	33	605	1014	49	1

12-21 主要年份广播电视事业发展情况

Basic Statistics on Radio and Television Industry in Main Years

项　　目	单位	1985年	1990年	1995年	2000年	2005年	2010年	2015年	2016年
广播电台	个		1	1	1	1	1	1	1
电视台	个	1	1	1	1	1	1	1	1
镇街文化广电服务中心	个						28	28	28

12-22 主要年份火灾事故发生情况

Statistics on Fire Accidents in Main Years

项　　目	单位	2010年	2014年	2015年	2016年
发生起数	起	1900	2575	1675	1670
受伤人数	人	8	10	3	10
死亡人数	人	15	14	12	14
损失折款	万元	4017	6068	5609	6364
平均每起事故损失	万元	2.00	2.40	3.35	3.81

注：本表数据来源于市公安局。

12-23 主要年份交通事故发生情况

Basic Statistics on Traffic Accidents in Main Years

项　　目	单位	1995年	2000年	2005年	2010年	2015年	2016年
发生起数	起	2015	7386	7124	4874	3595	3648
受伤人数	人	2061	8217	8642	5355	3934	3927
死亡人数	人	692	903	921	528	483	486
损失折款	万元	685	1759	934	682	551	814
平均每起事故损失	元	3400	2382	1312	1400	1533	2231

注：本表数据来源于市公安局和海事局，含道路和水上交通事故。

12-24 各类卫生事业机构及床位、人员数（2016年）

Number of Health Care Institutions, Beds and Employed Personnel by Type of Institution (2016)

项　　目	机构数（个）	实有床位数（张）	卫生工作人员（人）	#卫生技术人员	#执业（助理）医师
总　　计	2344	28138	57167	47668	16680
医疗机构	2304	28138	56406	47097	16557
县及县以上及其他医院	89	27450	41513	34084	11203
#综合医院	60	24088	37062	30706	10151
中医医院	7	1438	1851	1563	526
专科医院	22	1924	2600	1815	526
社区卫生服务中心（站）	399		6154	4965	1937
村（社区）卫生站	35		88	76	36
门诊部（含18所分院个数）	476		3754	3465	1604
诊所、卫生所、医务室	1303		3343	3276	1421
妇幼保健院	1	568	1286	1001	292
专科疾病防治院	1	120	268	230	64
急救中心（站）					
采供血机构	1		130	106	9
疾病预防控制中心（防疫站）	1		220	170	94
卫生监督所	34		309	228	
健康教育所	1				
其他卫生机构	2		73	46	20

12-25 主要年份卫生事业机构各类人员数

Number of Personnel in Health Institutions in Main Years

单位：人

项　　目	1980年	1985年	1990年	1995年	2000年	2005年	2010年	2015年	2016年
卫生工作人员	3599	3945	4503	6149	9289	22127	46102	54950	57167
#卫生技术人员	2960	3305	3902	5290	8065	18757	37487	45226	47668
执业（助理）医师	1167	1201	1721	2299	3309	8130	13214	15889	16680
注册护士	584	643	1164	1751	2673	6303	14689	19782	21268
药剂人员	236	572	546	602	706	1281	2284	2694	2828
检验人员	120	147	152	216	367	781	1412	1633	1739
其　他	1040	766	316	395	350	2262	5888	5228	5153
其他技术人员	8		13	96	174	786	1217	1361	1526
管理人员	299	282	243	432	597	1080	2418	2307	2178
工勤人员	332	358	345	331	453	1504	4980	6056	5795

注：2004年起，卫生方面包含诊所、卫生所、医务室及村卫生室的数据，与往年数不可比。

12-26 医疗机构服务情况（2016年）

Services in Medical Institutions (2016)

指标名称	诊疗人数（人次）	#门、急诊	入院人数（人）	病死率（%）
总　　计	64816196	64617805	919429	0.42
医院	35506761	35414951	883033	0.43
#公立医院	29579128	29509991	659121	0.46
#卫生部门办	29004022	28935367	648003	0.45
其他部门办	575106	574624	11118	0.62
民营医院	5927633	5904960	223912	0.36
基层医疗机构	27586535	27480042		
社区卫生服务中心（站）	17064476	16970867		
村卫生室	256744	253333		
门诊部	2845822	2843056		
诊所、卫生所、医务室	7419493	7412786		
#诊所	1420412	1419518		
卫生所、医务室	5999081	5993268		
专业公共卫生服务机构	1722900	1722812	36396	0.04
专科疾病防治院	250788	250788	2129	0.10
妇幼保健院	1472112	1472024	34267	0.04

12-27 历年卫生事业机构、床位、人员数

Number of Health Care Institutions, Beds and Personnel over Years

年 份	机构数(个)	实有床位数(张)	卫生工作人员(人)	#卫生技术人员	#执业(助理)医师
1978	82	2257	3242	2636	768
1979	81	2271	3466	2863	971
1980	83	2207	3599	2960	1167
1981	83	2210	3724	3091	1102
1982	83	2292	3886	3253	1097
1983	83	2098	3985	3335	1088
1984	83	2231	4005	3351	1132
1985	87	2323	3945	3305	1201
1986	88	3054	4084	3454	1179
1987	88	3393	4475	3490	1304
1988	87	3640	4582	3829	1537
1989	87	3677	4522	3874	1620
1990	85	3866	4503	3902	1721
1991	85	4085	4578	3946	1755
1992	83	4517	4705	4127	1832
1993	99	4940	5247	4524	2023
1994	98	5365	5689	4930	2221
1995	99	5798	6149	5290	2299
1996	99	5288	6712	5766	2449
1997	151	5505	7286	6283	2605
1998	171	5892	8306	7139	2955
1999	176	6241	8697	7575	3080
2000	174	7081	9289	8065	3309
2001	173	7474	9323	8064	3429
2002	178	8641	10692	9011	3523
2003	172	9820	11584	9807	3758
2004	944	10797	15058	13053	4870
2005	874	11972	22127	18757	8130
2006	1210	13293	27128	22904	8629
2007	1649	15227	34151	28758	10446
2008	2106	16778	40449	33113	11869
2009	2106	18080	43561	35766	12884
2010	2229	19980	46102	37487	13214
2011	2249	22814	48142	39582	13644
2012	2222	24617	49353	40597	14043
2013	2254	25736	52325	42132	14864
2014	2194	26704	53013	43091	15081
2015	2237	27457	54950	45226	15889
2016	2344	28138	57167	47668	16680

注：2004年起本表包含诊所、卫生所、医务室及村卫生室的数据，与往年数不可比。

12-28 历年体育运动情况

Basic Statistics on Sports over Years

年份	破（超）世界纪录（次）	破（超）亚洲纪录（次）	破（超）全国纪录（次）	在国际比赛中获得金牌总数（枚）	在全国比赛中获得金牌总数（枚）	在省级比赛中获得金牌总数（枚）	市级运动会参赛运动员人数（人）	为国家省输送运动员（人）
1978			9	1	7	26	2500	11
1979	2		2	1	7		2250	18
1980			12		2		2400	14
1981			11	4	19		2500	13
1982			14	4	30	15	2650	9
1983	1		7	5	6		2420	7
1984			1	16	5		2500	33
1985		2	1	5	2		1960	7
1986		7	4	7	4	52	2420	16
1987	1	1	8	35	9		2130	19
1988	3	1	4	14	25		2540	15
1989			27	5	43	92	6430	18
1990	13	5		4	6		2370	25
1991	2	1	8	12	14		4800	16
1992	2	3	21	10	6		15000	30
1993	2	8	5	12	9		10350	16
1994	34	2	24	6	23	157	2720	14
1995	10	1		5	37		1500	14
1996				3	16		7800	13
1997	10	9		1	6	36	6000	74
1998	2	4	28	4	28	87	1560	74
1999				4	33		6000	6
2000			3	4	91		4000	6
2001				13	22	48	8000	5
2002				2	35	58		11
2003		7		2	31	82		6
2004	3	4	4	49	34			18
2005				2	13	46	8564	44
2006				20	21	32	16000	
2007				3	25	46	2740	9
2008				3	16	49	630	17
2009		1	3	8	20	94	1550	17
2010				4	6	40	9895	16
2011				8	27	116	3300	25
2012					10	127	3400	16
2013					5	55	3600	10
2014					8	113	3998	31
2015					48	135	2010	18
2016				5	96	212	2325	31

12-29　主要年份体育比赛成绩

Basic Statistics on Sports Achievements in Main Years

项　　目	单位	1980年	1985年	1990年	1995年	2000年	2005年	2010年	2015年	2016年
破世界纪录	次			13	10					
获得国际赛冠军	个		5	4	5	4		4		
破亚洲纪录	次		2	5	1					
破全国纪录	次	12	1			3				
获国际比赛奖牌										
金牌	枚		5	4	5	4	2	4		
银牌	枚			4	3	2	1	2		
铜牌	枚						2			
获全国比赛金牌	枚	2	2	6	37	91	13	6	48	96

注：“获得国际赛冠军”及“获国际比赛奖牌”含地区赛。

12-30　主要年份群众体育活动情况

Basic Statistics on Activities of Mass Sports in Main Years

项　　目	单位	1980年	1985年	1990年	1995年	2000年	2005年	2010年	2015年	2016年
举办市级运动会	次	5	4	9	4	2	4	16	8	13
市级运动会参赛	人	2400	1960	2370	1500	4000	8564	9895	2010	2560
举办全民健身活动	次								367	417
参加全民健身活动人数	万人次								20.12	41.80
为国家和省输送运动员人数	人	14	7	25	14	6	47	16	18	31

12−31 主要年份治安案件情况

Basic Statistics on Public Security Cases in Main Years

项　目	单位	2005年	2010年	2015年	2016年
治安案件受理数	起	13760	44979	128576	117779
扰乱公共秩序	起	2816	198	336	475
妨害公共安全	起	243	630	395	637
侵犯人身、财产权利	起	6044	24551	102807	94609
#盗窃	起	2599	10513	57235	54513
妨害社会管理秩序	起	4296	19600	25038	22058
#吸毒	起	2697	4455	15165	13612
卖淫、嫖娼	起	153	663	527	741
赌博或为赌博提供条件	起	942	10464	5495	1969
治安案件查处数	起	12490	37818	58375	57176
扰乱公共秩序	起	2797	186	256	411
妨害公共安全	起	237	583	293	606
侵犯人身、财产权利	起	4865	17687	32943	34377
#盗窃	起	2007	5476	16391	18821
妨害社会管理秩序	起	4246	19362	24883	21782
#吸毒	起	2665	4317	15127	13608
卖淫、嫖娼	起	147	659	524	734
赌博或为赌博提供条件	起	938	10408	5478	1945
查处违法人员数	人	20692	42815	49312	51116
扰乱公共秩序	人	4486	363	609	641
妨害公共安全	人	218	618	293	585
侵犯人身、财产权利	人	6769	14145	7984	6846
#盗窃	人	2676	3802	2579	2272
妨害社会管理秩序	人	8201	27689	40426	43044
#吸毒	人	3922	4885	17049	17861
卖淫、嫖娼	人	415	1506	1209	1763
赌博或为赌博提供条件	人	3179	17191	18265	17670

注：本表数据来源于市公安局。

12-32 主要年份刑事案件情况

Basic Statistics on Criminal Cases in Main Years

单位：起

项　目	2005年	2010年	2015年	2016年
刑事案件立案数	44641	36965	94541	83440
危害公共安全	264	586	1170	1293
破坏市场经济秩序	451	577	2359	1531
侵犯公民人身权利	3748	3587	2715	2315
#杀人	87	69	21	40
伤害	3071	2882	2057	1701
强奸	266	336	333	311
侵犯财产	39657	31251	85100	75769
#抢劫	9144	5045	5290	3813
抢夺	3736	3250	10705	8947
入室盗窃	4150	8779	15834	13598
盗窃机动车	16050	3526	1707	1304
诈骗	897	3203	14450	13936
妨害社会管理秩序	571	963	3194	2530
#毒品犯罪	215	587	1863	1848
刑事案件破案数	13682	16271	19495	20675
危害公共安全	161	550	693	1014
破坏市场经济秩序	439	388	1032	739
侵犯公民人身权利	2037	1933	1198	1077
#杀人	73	61	23	34
伤害	1586	1449	887	783
强奸	171	224	164	146
侵犯财产	10598	12534	13887	15730
#抢劫	3582	2531	1274	965
抢夺	1525	1700	2066	2114
入室盗窃	1081	4182	2707	2682
盗窃机动车	1880	631	246	237
诈骗	202	536	260	1267
妨害社会管理秩序	490	866	2684	2114
#毒品犯罪	210	569	1664	1703

注：本表数据来源于市公安局。

12-33 主要年份道路交通违法情况

Basic Statistics on Traffic Offense in Main Years

项 目	单位	2005年	2010年	2015年	2016年
处理违法起数	万起	61.04	282.48	174.98	193.08
#机动车	万起		280.44	174.21	192.15
非机动车	起		10084	7667	9243
行人和乘车人	起		10281	14	23
教育人次	人次		261411	36134	
#机动车	人次		253789	36134	
非机动车	人次		3479		
行人和乘车人	人次		4143		
罚款总额	万元	9991.70	44359.52	32453.86	35709.53
#机动车	万元		44355.07	32411.54	35655.34
非机动车	万元		2.80	42.31	54.17
行人和乘车人	元		16500	100	23

注：本表数据来源于市公安局。

12-34 主要年份律师、公证、基层司法及普法教育

Basic Statistics on Lawyers, Notarization, Grassroots Judicial Work and Law Education in Main Years

项 目	单位	1990年	1995年	2000年	2005年	2010年	2015年	2016年
律师工作								
律师事务所	个	2	8	22	46	115	163	188
律师	人	12	85	221	625	1366	2035	2282
担任常年法律顾问	家	102	364	416	1426	2752	3245	4695
民事诉讼代理	件	145	343	1203	6543	12041	16122	19746
非诉讼法律事务	件	110	1162	2079	13391	19967	22678	26476
刑事辩护及代理	件	295	235	438	2496	2776	3566	3847
经济案件诉讼代理	件	107	348	1100	1801	1133	1641	1523
#涉外及港澳台	件	165	11	27	160	299	63	154
公证工作								
公证处	个	1	1	1	1	3	3	3
公证人员	人	10	19	20	48	96	120	115
办结公证总数	件	5347	11377	28910	60685	48296	81253	104845
#国内民事公证	件	113	2795	19607	19627	35104	66946	89703
国内经济公证	件	236	898	1776	34015	3536	3027	2562
涉外公证（含港澳台）	件	4998	7684	4809	4607	9656	14307	11037
基层司法工作								
法律服务所	个	24	29	32	32	32	32	32
法律服务工作者	人					58	80	72
担任法律顾问	家	62	482	695	1208	724	316	274
民事诉讼代理	件	26	568	1221	1790	1090	426	338
非诉讼代理	件	129	1045	3016	3837	1549	440	362
调解工作								
人民调解委员会	个	904	813	750	814	1552	1554	1483
调解人员	人	3664	3466	3644	4556	17438	14683	14350
调解民间纠纷	件	2005	2632	2642	15210	15239	13471	12880
参加普法教育人数	万人	79.9	170	79	571	288	651	319

12－35 历年计划生育情况

Basic Statistics on Family Planning over Years

年 份	已婚育龄妇女人数（人）	女性初婚人数（人）			落实各种节育措施	
			#23周岁及以上	不足20周岁	育龄夫妇（对）	节育率（%）
1978	130438	10974			103414	79.28
1979	134483	11914			104612	77.79
1980	136742	9270			101190	74.00
1981	141079	13714			112956	80.07
1982	142324	8729			115302	81.01
1983	149928	12664			129035	86.06
1984	156444	9579			138785	88.71
1985	159985	11208			142974	89.37
1986	168611	13983	11899		150545	89.30
1987	176868	13492	11252		158857	89.80
1988	183022	12419	10072		164889	90.10
1989	196042	13691	10228	15	172799	88.20
1990	202505	13264	9670	29	177425	87.60
1991	211544	13790	10834	12	184254	87.10
1992	224624	15295	10375	13	190151	84.70
1993	235150	13932	9793	6	200673	85.30
1994	243456	13213	9833	9	208234	85.50
1995	252627	13921	10430	26	215339	85.20
1996	258873	13556	10114	20	221805	85.70
1997	263646	12968	9623	9	226674	85.98
1998	267982	12366	9260	7	233007	86.95
1999	280455	12114	8999	4	249368	88.92
2000	285244	11122	7050	14	249741	87.55
2001	295395	10903	6755	14	260077	88.04
2002	303134	11635	7082	8	268243	88.49
2003	306157	12441	7767	5	266832	87.16
2004	312941	13957	9318	2	273387	87.36
2005	317062	13251	9057	5	275685	86.95
2006	323479	12460	9117	3	279246	86.33
2007	331556	13621	10333	1	293733	85.29
2008	343051	14485	11053	1	291049	84.84
2009	352115	14450	11157	5	297559	84.51
2010	367607	14265	11019	4	309054	84.07
2011	380570	14899	11820	1	320135	84.12
2012	384854	14875	12049	12	320907	83.38
2013	391864	13549	10952	5	327002	83.45
2014	399044	14871	12118	6	333848	83.66
2015	401786	12933	10667	6	338726	84.31
2016	418882	14465	12078	13	339885	81.14

12−35 续表

年份	领取独生子女证		人口出生率（‰）	政策生育率（%）	多孩率（%）
	累计（人）	领证率（%）			
1978			18.73		
1979			24.13		
1980			24.41		
1981			21.86		
1982			19.07		
1983			16.74		
1984			15.54		
1985	1954	1.22	15.37	88.94	4.27
1986	2029	1.20	16.44	92.45	2.93
1987	2257	1.28	16.11	93.16	1.97
1988	2408	1.32	16.75	93.58	2.14
1989	2116	1.10	17.06	92.35	2.54
1990	2288	1.13	17.07	89.08	3.71
1991	2514	1.19	17.91	89.55	3.65
1992	2335	1.04	19.31	86.08	4.44
1993	2905	1.24	18.38	87.29	4.50
1994	3245	1.33	17.88	86.50	4.71
1995	3389	1.34	17.76	85.09	4.33
1996	4028	1.63	17.05	83.83	4.87
1997	4514	1.71	16.50	83.98	4.68
1998	4971	1.85	15.31	90.01	2.92
1999	21228	7.57	14.55	89.31	2.92
2000	30921	10.84	12.11	90.17	1.77
2001	41636	14.10	11.16	91.75	1.57
2002	49188	16.23	10.35	91.80	1.31
2003	51814	16.92	10.34	92.45	1.24
2004	55425	17.71	10.86	93.48	1.14
2005	60426	19.06	10.62	94.32	0.80
2006	69507	21.49	10.14	94.69	0.71
2007	73766	22.25	10.39	95.48	0.63
2008	77919	22.71	10.77	96.28	0.54
2009	80738	22.93	10.67	96.75	0.75
2010	81736	22.23	10.90	96.97	0.99
2011	83312	21.89	10.92	98.65	0.90
2012	81341	21.14	13.32	84.23	3.42
2013	81215	20.73	11.79	83.52	3.65
2014	80769	20.24	11.20	89.21	2.57
2015	77688	19.34	11.34	92.47	1.20
2016	69298	16.54	13.92	97.06	1.88

注：领证率是期末已领取独生子女证人数除以全市已婚育龄妇女人数。

12-36 主要年份优抚和社会救济、福利事业

Basic Statistics on Special Care, Social Relief and Welfare in Main Years

项　　目	单位	1990年	1995年	2000年	2005年	2010年	2013年	2014年	2015年	2016年
优抚事业										
优抚收养性事业单位数	个	1	1	1	1	1	1	1	1	1
优抚收养性单位收养人数	人次	19	11	7	8	8	6	7	7	7
优抚事业费用	万元	340	213	412	2400	4555	331	345	327	424
社会救济										
社会救济人数	人次	4433	7273	19914	23886	36516	24020	21032	19000	12552
年末社会散居孤幼人数	人	2026	2444	1596	875	11	239	119	109	97
#定期救济对象	人	142	569	29	18	11	239	119	109	97
社会救济福利事业费	万元		190	993	6955	21199	18113	22444	24991	20552
自然灾害生活救助费	万元	4.6	70	50	744	139	584	467	536	687
社会福利										
社会福利事业单位数	个	1	1	3	36	38	34	37	37	37
#民政部门办	个	1	1	3	4	3	3	3	3	3
社会福利事业单位收养人数	人	363	351	406	2240	2609	2389	2724	2737	2810
#民政部门办	人	363	351	406	893	1715	1158	1121	1252	1122
安排“四残”人员就业人数	人	199	239	393	351	321	314	685	395	
社会福利事业单位费用支出	万元					9770	19130	22404	24991	18112
敬老院情况										
全市敬老院个数	个			32	31	35	31	34	34	34
年末敬老院供养人数	人			833	1347	894	1231	1603	1485	1688
“五保户”情况										
年末列入“五保户”户数	户			1545	1575	1254	907	847	833	824
年末列入“五保户”人数	人			1587	1575	1263	913	854	833	824
全年“五保户”费用支出	万元			2198	1594	1536	1882	2123	1484	1371
城乡基层社会保障										
建立社会保障网络镇街数	个	33	24	32	32	32	32	32	32	32

注：“五保户”人数及费用支出含敬老院供养人数及费用支出。

12-37 主要年份婚姻登记情况

Basic Statistics on Marriage Registration in Main Years

项　　目	单位	1985年	1990年	1995年	2000年	2005年	2010年	2015年	2016年
准予登记结婚	对	11870	13668	14170	10535	14293	11415	18101	17555
#涉外、华侨、港澳台同胞	对	638	709	510	213	113	79	169	159
准予登记离婚	对				448	1319	1856	3672	3987
#涉外、华侨、港澳台同胞	对						9	45	55

12-38 主要年份环境保护基本情况

Basic Statistics on Environmental Protection in Main Years

项　　目	单 位	1985年	1990年	1995年	2000年	2005年	2010年	2015年	2016年
废水									
废水排放总量	万吨	3100	5259	9681	40703	69049	87953	114086	125185
#工业废水	万吨	2686	4124	5511	11753	21355	29742	20429	17245
污水厂集中处理率	%						71.5	95.0	96.2
废气									
工业废气排放量	亿立方米	34	307	556	1318	1695	2340	3219	3643
一般工业固体废物									
一般工业固体废物产生量	万吨	16	112	108	149	284	313	486	457
一般工业固体废物处置量	万吨	8	2	1	5	12	15	55	47
一般工业固体废物处置率	%	48.2	1.8	0.9	66.9	99.8	4.8	11.3	10.3
一般工业固体废物综合利用率	%	37.5	17.9	18.2	63.8	86.5	95.0	88.7	89.7
城市环境质量及污染控制									
空气质量指数	范围值				21-87	24-123	14-108	20-201	22-203
交通干线噪声平均值	db				68.4	67.9	67.7	68.8	65.0
汽车尾气排放达标率	%				81.2	88.1	81.0	86.0	88.0
全市生活垃圾无害化处理率	%						37.3	74.9	100.0

12-39 主要年份社会保险事业情况

Basic Statistics on Social Insurance in Main Years

项目	单位	1995年	2000年	2005年	2010年	2015年	2016年
参加各种社会保险人数	万人次	149.33	338.33	804.71	2726.37	2659.94	2558.79
#失业保险	万人次	6.49	17.84	177.78	279.90	412.14	409.11
养老保险	万人次	8.46	82.95	182.49	421.84	670.60	651.66
医疗保险	万人次	7.60	88.21	189.40	592.27	601.92	574.47
工伤保险	万人次	126.78	136.53	235.10	469.08	464.46	445.07
社会保险基金总收入	万元	18155	127964	491540	1544112	4309420	4763827
#失业保险	万元	60	2732	28954	27008	186278	117224
养老保险	万元	7697	85245	343429	976257	3340876	3668720
医疗保险	万元	2057	23488	82138	333342	643199	783623
工伤保险	万元	8341	15891	35073	62806	132895	119483
社会保险基金总支出	万元	10520	40454	217413	547470	1684737	1955338
#失业保险	万元	16	440	6676	9681	58297	85722
养老保险	万元	7450	24130	135958	194055	781414	1074526
医疗保险	万元	1436	3694	51021	299975	555937	624366
工伤保险	万元	1618	11703	22220	41910	120276	119060

注：1. 1997年起养老保险因口径调整，与以前年份不可比。
2. 参加各种社会保险总人数包含生育保险人数。

12-40 主要年份最低生活保障情况

Basic Statistics on Minimum Income Relief in Main Years

项目	单位	2005年	2010年	2015年	2016年
居民最低生活保障线	元/人月	320	440	610	610
村民最低生活保障线	元/人月	300	440	610	610
居民最低生活保障户数	户	1911	1599	2707	1938
居民最低生活保障人数	人	4885	3643	5466	3569
居民最低生活保障金支出	万元	790	673	6098	2510
村民最低生活保障户数	户	6705	12214	5566	4090
村民最低生活保障人数	人	17426	30785	11961	8343
村民最低生活保障金支出	万元	2318	5922	3228	5317

12-41 主要年份市政建设情况

Basic Statistics on Municipal Construction in Main Years

项目	单位	1995年	2000年	2005年	2010年	2015年	2016年
水厂日供水能力	万立方米	66	187	480	700	746	747
年末供水管道总长度	公里	1580	2106	3680	16268	20100	20841
全年供水量	万立方米	18802	70046	155100	165607	155441	156401
#生活用水量	万立方米	7361	21433	51100	28560	42685	44543
建成区绿地面积	万平方米	800	1396	10298	33092	38801.81	41402.29
#公园绿地面积	万平方米				9075	11535.60	14455.69
建成区绿化覆盖面积	万平方米	1885	1364	9436	35571	41667.00	45620.01
建成区土地面积	平方公里	82.00	147.68	657.17	798.48	928.87	956.54
公园数	个		273	931	1004	1223	1509
公园面积	公顷		1423	2887	11130	14493.14	20692.80

注：公园数和公园面积不含森林公园数及其面积。

12-42 主要年份液化石油气及天然气供应情况

Basic Statistics on Supply of Liquefied Petroleum Gas and Natural Gas in Main Years

项目	单位	1995年	2000年	2005年	2010年	2015年	2016年
年末液化石油气用户数	户	63419	110172	144797	956018	885176	917933
#居民用户数	户	62246	106910	144035	870921	853945	873251
全年液化石油气供气量	吨	25935	58287	161930	344762	289410	230000
#家庭用量	吨	18948	22104	24354	188108	234500	197640
年末天然气用户数	户			5027	147047	594731	813000
#居民用户数	户			5000	116239	586339	807000
全年天然气供气量	万立方米			350	23414	73866	105000
#家庭用量	万立方米			45	1600	16400	13578
年末汽车天然气加气站	个				10	15	38
天然气汽车加气全年供应量	万立方米				5324	3836	13000

注：本表2000—2006年为市喜威液化石油气有限公司与市中液石油气有限公司的业务量，2007年起调整为市城市管理局统计口径。

12-43 历年环境保护基本情况

Basic Statistics on Environmental Protection over Years

年份	降水PH均值	酸雨PH均值	酸雨频率(%)	酸雨占总降水量(%)	交通干线噪声平均值(db)	工业废水排放量(万吨)
1982						1842
1983						2068
1984	6.53					2127
1985						2686
1986					76.8	2416
1987	6.64	5.38		38.4	78.9	3501
1988	4.85	4.72	63.6	75.1	77.6	3029
1989	5.44	5.21	31.0	31.8	74.1	3976
1990	6.15	5.30	29.5	43.3	75.9	4124
1991	5.24	4.78	35.4	30.4	72.2	5506
1992	5.10	4.71	36.8	35.9	76.0	5849
1993	4.93	4.41	22.5	29.1	75.8	6500
1994	5.33	4.81	23.2	25.5	72.6	7057
1995	5.89	5.49	9.2	13.7	70.3	5511
1996	5.83	5.40	14.7	10.9	70.4	6033
1997	4.94	4.84	56.6	76.4	70.6	8930
1998	4.79	4.70	60.3	80.4	70.3	7989
1999	4.97	4.68	40.0	50.5	69.1	11719
2000	4.90	4.67	50.7	56.6	68.7	11753
2001	5.06	4.74	31.6	43.9	68.2	11694
2002	5.47	5.09	29.3	28.8	68.0	25587
2003	4.55	4.44	60.5	77.2	67.9	23389
2004	4.47	4.41	69.6	85.7	68.0	22501
2005	4.07	4.00	65.7	86.2	67.9	21355
2006	3.57-6.57	4.70	50.0	42.4	68.0	24134
2007	5.21	4.36-7.59	54.2	59.2	67.9	91260
2008	4.83	4.65	60.1	63.6	63.6	33359
2009	5.03	4.88	51.8	67.3	63.8	29960
2010	5.11	4.97	52.2	65.3	67.7	29742
2011	5.02	4.59	47.6	31.9	67.8	29091
2012	5.26	4.98	33.7	47.2	67.9	26909
2013	5.23	4.93	30.8	46.7	68.3	23463
2014	5.46	5.16	38.2	40.2	68.5	28292
2015	5.91	5.35	8.2	7.8	68.8	20429
2016	5.88	5.45	12.6	14.6	65.0	17245

注：2007年起，工业废水排放量统计口径变更，与往年不可比。

主要统计指标解释

Explanatory Notes on Main Statistical Indicators

工程技术人员 指在国民经济各行业从事工程技术工作的自然科学技术专业人员，包括：高级工程师、工程师、助理工程师、技术员和未评定职称的技术人员。

农业技术人员 指在国民经济各行业从事农业技术工作的自然科学技术专业人员，包括：高级农艺师、农艺师、助理农艺师、技术员和未评定职称的技术人员。

科学研究人员 指在国民经济各行业从事科学技术活动的科学技术专业人员，包括：正副研究员、助理研究员、研究实习员、技术员和未评定职称的技术人员。

专利申请量 指企业当年向国家知识产权局提出专利申请并被受理项数。

专利授权量 指企业当年获国家知识产权局授予专利权的项数。

发明 专利法及其实施细则所称的发明是指对有关产品、方法或其改进所提出的新的技术方案。

实用新型 专利法及其实施细则所称的实用新型是指对产品的形状、构造或者其结合所提出的适于实用的新的技术方案。

外观设计 专利法及其实施细则所称的外观设计是指对产品的形状、图案、色彩或者其结合所作出的富有美感并适于工业上应用的新设计。

科技活动经费使用总额(内部支出) 指报告期内调查单位用于科技活动的实际支出。包括劳务费、科研业务费、科研管理费、非基建投资购建的固定资产、科研、基建支出以及其他用于科技活动的支出。但不包括生产性活动支出、归还贷款支出及转拨外单位支出。

毕业生数 毕业生数是指上学年内，具有学籍的学生学完教学计划规定的全部课程，考试及格，实际毕业的学生数。不包括结业生和肄业生。

招生数 招生数是指新学年开始时，按规定实际招收入学的新生数，不包括重读生和复学生（高等教育包括春秋两季招收的学生）。

在校学生数 是指具有学籍的注册学生总数。

学龄儿童入学率 指调查范围内已入小学学习的学龄儿童占校内外学龄儿童总数（包括弱智儿童在内，但不包括盲聋哑儿童）的比重。

电影放映单位 指具有放映机器设备、固定或不固定的放映场所与专职或兼职的放映技术人员，经有关部门登记批准，经常为一定的观众对象放映电影的机构。包括经批准对外开放进行营业，并与电影发行放映管理机构分帐的专用放映单位和军委系统租片单位。

公共图书馆藏书量 是指本馆已编目的古籍、图书、期刊和报纸的合订本、小册子、手稿，以及缩徽制品、录像带、录音带、光盘等视听文献资料数量之和。

医疗机构 是指根据《医疗机构管理条例》的规定，经登记取得《医疗机构执业许可证》的机构。包括医院、社区卫生服务中心（站）、卫生院、门诊所、诊疗所、医务室、村卫生室、妇幼保健院（所、站）、专科疾病防治院（所、站）、急救中心、临床检验中心。

医院 指设有固定床位能收容病人住院并能为病人提供医疗、护理服务的医疗机构。包括县及县以上医院、农村乡卫生院、其他医院三部分。按所属性质分为卫生部门、工业及其他部门、集体经济单位三类。其中县及县以上医院按业务性质分为综合医院和专科医院。

实有床位 是指报告期末固定实有床位数，包括正规床、简易床、监护床、正在消毒和修理床位、因扩建或修理而停用的床位，不包括产科新生儿床、待产室待产床、库存床、观察床、临时加床和病人家属陪伴床。

诊疗人数 是指所有诊疗工作的总人数。包括病人来院就诊的门诊、急诊人次和出诊、下地段、赴家庭病床、到工厂、农村、工地、会议、集体活动等外出诊疗的人次数，以及外出进行的单项健康检查及健康咨询指导人次数。并包括本院职工的诊疗的人次数及局部的单项健康检查人数。

卫生技术人员 指卫生事业机构支付工资的全部固定职工和合同制职工中现任职务为卫生技术工作的专业人员。包括中医师、西医师、中西医结合高级医师、护师、中药师、西药师、检验师、其他技师、中医士、西医士、护士、助产士、中药剂士、西药剂士、检验士、其他技士、其他中医、护理员、中药剂员、西药剂员、检验员，其他初级卫生技术人员。

病死率 是指年内住院病人中死亡人数占出院人数的比例。

刑事案件立案 是指实施违反我国刑事法律的行为，构成犯罪的案件。根据《关于公安机关办理刑事案件程序规定》第一百六十二条，公安机关受理案件后，经过审查，认为有犯罪事实需要追究刑事责任，且属于自己管辖的，由接受单位制作《刑事案件立案报告书》，经县级以上公安机关负责人批准，予以立案。

刑事案件破案 根据《关于公安机关办理刑事案件程序规定》第一百六十六条的规定，刑事案件破案应当具备下列条件：（一）犯罪事实已有证据证明；（二）有证据证明犯罪事实是犯罪嫌疑人实施的；（三）犯罪嫌疑人或者主要犯罪嫌疑人已经归案。

治安案件查处 是指触犯了《中华人民共和国治安管理处罚条例》规定，给社会或个人造成一定危害，公安机关依照相关法律、法规和规定，应当给予处罚的行为事件。

律师 指受聘参加法律顾问处工作，担任法律顾问、刑（民）事代理人、刑事辩护人，办理非诉讼事件、解答法律询问，代写法律事务文书等主要从事律师业务的专职法律工作者和兼职律师。

公证人员 指在国家公证机关依法办理公证事务的司法人员。包括公证员、助理公证员和在公证处工作的其他人员。

调解人员 在人民调解委员会担负调解民间一般民事纠纷和轻微违法行为所引起的纠纷的工作人员。包括调解委员会的委员和调解小组的调解员。

社会保险基金收入 是指根据国家规定，由纳入基本社会保险范围的单位，按照国家规定的缴费基数和缴费比例缴纳的社会统筹基金，以及通过其他方式取得的形成基金来源的收入，包括：单位缴纳的社会统筹基金收入、财政补贴收入、利息收入、其他收入。

社会保险基金支出 是指按照国家政策规定的开支范围和开支标准从社会统筹基金中支付给参加基本社会保险人员个人的费用，以及由于保险关系转移、上下级之间调剂资金等原因而发生的支出。

社会福利事业单位 指集中收养社会孤老、残、幼的机构。包括由民政部门管理的社会福利院、儿童福利院、精神病人福利院和城镇集体办的福利院，以及农村集体举办的敬老院。

社会福利事业单位收养人数包括民政部门管理的和城镇及农村集体举办的社会福利事业单位中收养的老人、少年儿童、缺乏生活自理能力的残疾人员和精神病人。

废水排放总量 包括工业废水和生活污水。工业废水指工业企业在生产、科研过程中向企业外部排放的所有排放口的废水量总和。生活污水指居民或职工在饮用、洗涤、烹饪、清洁卫生等过程中排放的污水量。

十三、能　源

Energy

13-1 主要节能情况

Main Condition of Energy Conservation

单位：±%

年　份	单位生产总值能耗上升率或下降率	单位生产总值电耗上升率或下降率	单位工业增加值能耗上升率或下降率
2006	-4.86	-5.69	-10.66
2007	-5.36	-7.64	-10.07
2008	-5.11	-12.49	-10.94
2009	-4.48	-8.42	-0.26
2010	-2.02	2.84	-10.92
2011	-4.61	-3.40	-6.12
2012	-4.46	-2.85	-11.42
2013	-5.35	-6.17	-8.45
2014	-5.88	-1.50	-9.74
2015	-7.90	-6.54	-10.88
2016	-4.65	-2.62	-3.93

13-2 规模以上工业企业能源加工转换情况（2016年）

Energy Convertion of Industrial Enterprises Above Designated Size (2016)

能源名称	计量单位	工业生产消费量	#加工转换投入合计	火力发电	供热	加工煤制品	能源加工转换产出	回收利用
原煤	吨	15876475	15313605	11009600	3966838	337168		
煤制品	吨	386921	354301	162482	191820		403904	
天然气（气态）	万立方米	123844	113731	109199	4531			
柴油	吨	7371	4303	4303				
润滑油	吨	87						
热力	百万千焦	56505468					69183946	
电力	万千瓦时	930821					3379145	
城市生活垃圾（用于燃料）	吨	2290075	2290075	2290075				
余热余压	百万千焦	107669	107669	107669				107669
能源合计	吨标准煤	16148477	12610619	9717299	2667766	225554	6736363	3672

13-3 全市规模以上工业企业能源购进、消费及库存量（2016年）

Energy Purchases, Consumptton and Stock of Industrial Enterprises of Whole Municipality Above Designated Size (2016)

能源品种	单　位	购进量	消费量	#工业生产	年末库存量
原煤	吨	16681510	16943679	16939387	644536
煤制品	吨	73694	460039	459662	946
焦炭	吨	5636	5360	5360	431
天然气（气态）	万立方米	160637	160541	159366	61
液化天然气（液态）	吨	5119	5106	4640	
汽油	吨	18062	18136	3116	39
煤油	吨	56	56	16	1
柴油	吨	68780	69993	47326	3400
燃料油	吨	41758	43311	42729	12539
液化石油气	吨	9868	10030	8793	271
润滑油	吨	496	498	494	14
溶剂油	吨	49	49	49	2
热力	百万千焦	10439791	64866893	64714902	
电力	万千瓦时	2457571	3338467	3177335	
城市生活垃圾（用于燃料）	吨	2311537	2290075	2290075	47765
生物燃料	吨标准煤	68424	67982	66893	999
余热余压	百万千焦		107669	107669	
其他燃料	吨标准煤	1484	2535	2156	

13−4 全市规模以上工业企业分行业能源消费量（2016年）

Total Energy Consumption of Industrial Enterprises Above Designated Size by Sector (2016)

行　　业	原煤（吨）	煤制品（吨）	焦炭（吨）	天然气（气态）（万立方米）	液化天然气（液态）（吨）	汽油（吨）
总　计	16943679	460039	5360	160541	5106	18136
采矿业						8
煤炭开采和洗选业						
石油和天然气开采业						
黑色金属矿采选业						
有色金属矿采选业						
非金属矿采选业						8
开采辅助活动						
其他采矿业						
制造业	8194232	460039	5360	47314	5047	17815
农副食品加工业	132111	52618		433	3	117
食品制造业	393			1589		237
酒、饮料和精制茶制造业				1183	135	15
烟草制品业						
纺织业	445575			1061	549	1019
纺织服装、服饰业	16	2520		242	13	828
皮革、毛皮、羽毛及其制品和制鞋业	152			273	43	1330
木材加工和木、竹、藤、棕、草制品业	1335					325
家具制造业	400			699	279	555
造纸和纸制品业	7474367	354301		822	2	703
印刷和记录媒介复制业	6664	487		265	52	644
文教、工美、体育和娱乐用品制造业	2990			361		430
石油加工、炼焦和核燃料加工业				162		
化学原料和化学制品制造业	32379		1632	1296		743
医药制造业				311		77
化学纤维制造业				213		30
橡胶和塑料制品业	42603	456		976	25	1204
非金属矿物制品业	54080	49657		28408		132
黑色金属冶炼和压延加工业			2810	67	3179	79
有色金属冶炼和压延加工业				1118		264
金属制品业			917	1957	41	921
通用设备制造业				431	1	1219
专用设备制造业				584	28	1074
汽车制造业				916	2	268
铁路、船舶、航空航天和其他运输设备制造业				121	378	30
电气机械和器材制造业	1067			1241	231	1491
计算机、通信和其他电子设备制造业	100			2424	85	3631
仪器仪表制造业				161		297
其他制造业						154
废弃资源综合利用业						
金属制品、机械和设备修理业						
电力、热力、燃气及水生产和供应业	8749447			113228	59	314
电力、热力生产和供应业	8749447			113197	59	109
燃气生产和供应业				31		8
水的生产和供应业						197

13-4 续表 1

(2016年)

行业	煤油(吨)	柴油(吨)	燃料油(吨)	液化石油气(吨)	润滑油(吨)	溶剂油(吨)
总计	56	69993	43311	10030	498	49
采矿业						
煤炭开采和洗选业						
石油和天然气开采业						
黑色金属矿采选业						
有色金属矿采选业						
非金属矿采选业						
开采辅助活动						
其他采矿业						
制造业	56	65769	43311	10015	407	49
农副食品加工业		1617	120	11		
食品制造业		1924		164		
酒、饮料和精制茶制造业		1144				
烟草制品业						
纺织业		2635	249	6		
纺织服装、服饰业	1	2716	272	292		
皮革、毛皮、羽毛及其制品和制鞋业		2768	98	487	4	41
木材加工和木、竹、藤、棕、草制品业		531				
家具制造业		674	12	502		6
造纸和纸制品业	31	11169	557	483		
印刷和记录媒介复制业		1861		11		
文教、工美、体育和娱乐用品制造业		2003	131	99	1	
石油加工、炼焦和核燃料加工业						
化学原料和化学制品制造业		3055	2082	57		
医药制造业		51				
化学纤维制造业		199				
橡胶和塑料制品业	4	4279	102	270		
非金属矿物制品业		4220	39003	421		
黑色金属冶炼和压延加工业		85				
有色金属冶炼和压延加工业		2017	110	29		
金属制品业		3198		867	138	
通用设备制造业	17	1622	25	1266	203	
专用设备制造业		2550	73	37	23	
汽车制造业	2	601		1	2	
铁路、船舶、航空航天和其他运输设备制造业		2711		32		
电气机械和器材制造业		2936	182	3389	5	
计算机、通信和其他电子设备制造业	1	8519	295	1582	28	2
仪器仪表制造业		469		11		
其他制造业		212			2	
废弃资源综合利用业						
金属制品、机械和设备修理业						
电力、热力、燃气及水生产和供应业		4224		15	91	
电力、热力生产和供应业		3321		15	91	
燃气生产和供应业						
水的生产和供应业		904				

13-4 续表 2

(2016年)

行业	热力(百万千焦)	电力(万千瓦时)	城市生活垃圾(用于燃料)(吨)	生物燃料(吨标准煤)	余热余压(百万千焦)	其他燃料(吨标准煤)
总计	64866893	3338467	2290075	67982	107669	2535
采矿业		301				
煤炭开采和洗选业						
石油和天然气开采业						
黑色金属矿采选业						
有色金属矿采选业						
非金属矿采选业		301				
开采辅助活动						
其他采矿业						
制造业	64866893	3099129		67982	107669	2535
农副食品加工业	2918879	46715		4490		
食品制造业	425981	23744		4876		
酒、饮料和精制茶制造业	291318	14610		314		
烟草制品业						
纺织业	5764790	74061		5080		
纺织服装、服饰业	90776	51896		10151		
皮革、毛皮、羽毛及其制品和制鞋业	290268	85424		896		
木材加工和木、竹、藤、棕、草制品业		6100		3384		
家具制造业		58751		3169		
造纸和纸制品业	53947389	785320		12205		
印刷和记录媒介复制业	4575	49929		818		
文教、工美、体育和娱乐用品制造业		99108		80		
石油加工、炼焦和核燃料加工业		220				
化学原料和化学制品制造业	250040	51837		872		
医药制造业		3233		2238		
化学纤维制造业		8480		4275		
橡胶和塑料制品业	818236	283897		10821		514
非金属矿物制品业		122259		2778	107669	
黑色金属冶炼和压延加工业		14279				
有色金属冶炼和压延加工业		18811				
金属制品业	7239	141337		62		62
通用设备制造业		71035				
专用设备制造业		78145				
汽车制造业		31602				
铁路、船舶、航空航天和其他运输设备制造业	56892	10589				
电气机械和器材制造业	464	224409		655		1484
计算机、通信和其他电子设备制造业	45	695161		819		475
仪器仪表制造业		38626				
其他制造业		8761				
废弃资源综合利用业		96				
金属制品、机械和设备修理业		692				
电力、热力、燃气及水生产和供应业		239037	2290075			
电力、热力生产和供应业		198547	2290075			
燃气生产和供应业		1175				
水的生产和供应业		39315				

13-5 主要年份全社会用电量

Total Consumption of Electricity in Main Years

单位：万千瓦时

项　　目	2005年	2010年	2015年	2016年
全社会用电量总计	4198289	5619996	6668438	7020063
#各行业用电量合计	3855742	5036303	5822942	6114137
第一产业	9761	10279	14115	16046
第二产业	3397588	4317267	4877762	5100277
第三产业	448393	708757	931065	997814
城乡居民生活用电量合计	342547	583693	845497	905927
各行业用电分类				
农、林、牧、渔业	9761	10279	14115	16046
工　业	3374306	4262339	4833053	5060048
#轻工业	1357858	1821542	1990103	2076914
重工业	2016448	2440797	2842950	2983134
#采矿业	8112	8044	531	603
制造业	3044575	3953169	4493951	4739265
电力、燃气及水的生产和供应业	321619	301126	338572	320180
电力、热力的生产和供应业	240737	183361	229753	216778
#电厂生产全部耗用电量	41656	51096	55866	64138
线路损失电量	190736	132265	163744	127989
燃气生产和供应业	654	1778	382	450
水的生产和供应业	80228	115987	108436	102952
建筑业	23282	54928	44709	40228
交通运输、仓储和邮政业	14425	26524	51705	66732
交通运输业	8614	16173	30546	42253
仓储业	2084	5774	16094	19121
邮政业	3727	4577	5065	5358
信息传输、计算机服务和软件业	15277	35085	61673	64937
商业住宿和餐饮业	282238	376037	511790	533834
批发和零售业	148555	194549	335417	353663
住宿和餐饮业	130153	181488	176372	180171
金融、房地产、商务及居民服务业	65223	117690	95148	104831
金融业	16158	14156	8311	9411
房地产业	21976	23489	14002	15330
租赁和商务服务、居民服务和其他服务	27089	80045	72835	80090
公共事业及管理组织	71230	153421	210750	227480
科学研究、技术服务和地质勘查业	4550	2950	4724	7567
#地质勘查业	248	45	215	217
水利、环境和公共设施管理业	26633	56514	70396	75455
#水利管理业	12157	5208	4823	5027
教育、文化、体育和娱乐业	13596	29655	51512	56975
#教育	4793	8615	42007	47300
卫生、社会保障和社会福利业	12151	8964	36193	38417
公共管理和社会组织、国际组织	14300	55338	47926	49066

13-6 规模以上工业综合能源消费量（2015-2016年）

Overall Energy Consumpiton of Industrial Enterprises above Designated Size (2015-2016)

单位：万吨标准煤

指　　标	2015年	2016年
合　计	1329.38	1388.87
采矿业		0.04
煤炭开采和洗选业		
石油和天然气开采业		
黑色金属矿采选业		
有色金属矿采选业		
非金属矿采选业		0.04
开采辅助活动		
其他采矿业		
制造业	855.90	890.44
农副食品加工业	26.01	27.83
食品制造业	6.42	6.95
酒、饮料和精制茶制造业	4.81	4.41
烟草制品业		
纺织业	52.41	44.76
纺织服装、服饰业	8.41	7.83
皮革、毛皮、羽毛及其制品和制鞋业	13.29	11.10
木材加工和木、竹、藤、棕、草制品业	1.53	1.19
家具制造业	7.58	7.96
造纸和纸制品业	452.32	473.78
印刷和记录媒介复制业	6.26	6.68
文教、工美、体育和娱乐用品制造业	12.45	12.10
石油加工、炼焦和核燃料加工业	0.28	0.24
化学原料和化学制品制造业	12.55	11.78
医药制造业	0.99	0.99
化学纤维制造业	1.27	1.69
橡胶和塑料制品业	38.84	41.37
非金属矿物制品业	49.22	61.29
黑色金属冶炼和压延加工业	2.19	2.54
有色金属冶炼和压延加工业	3.73	3.83
金属制品业	17.72	18.94
通用设备制造业	9.12	8.93
专用设备制造业	7.95	9.82
汽车制造业	4.97	4.88
铁路、船舶、航空航天和其他运输设备制造业	2.37	1.87
电气机械和器材制造业	26.41	28.40
计算机、通信和其他电子设备制造业	80.69	83.96
仪器仪表制造业	4.74	4.22
其他制造业	1.35	1.05
废弃资源综合利用业	0.005	0.01
金属制品、机械和设备修理业	0.005	0.08
电力、热力、燃气及水生产和供应业	473.48	498.39
电力、热力生产和供应业	468.43	493.34
燃气生产和供应业	0.16	0.14
水的生产和供应业	4.88	4.92

主要统计指标解释

Explanatory Notes on Main Statistical Indicators

能源购进量 指能源使用企业（单位）在报告期购进、用于本企业（单位）消费的各种能源数量。本指标解释不涉及能源贸易企业的能源购进量。

工业企业能源消费量 指工业企业在工业生产活动和非工业生产活动中消费的能源，包括工业生产活动中作为燃料、动力、原料、辅助材料使用的能源，生产工艺中使用的能源，用于能源加工转换的能源；非工业生产活动中使用的能源。

工业生产能源消费量 指工业企业为进行工业生产活动所消费的能源。主要包括：

（1）用于本企业产品生产、工业性作业的能源，包括用作原料、材料、燃料、动力的能源；作为能源加工转换企业，还包括用作加工转换的能源。

（2）产品生产过程中作为辅助材料使用的能源。

（3）生产工艺过程使用的能源。

（4）新技术研究、新产品试制、科学试验使用的能源。

（5）为了工业生产活动而在进行的各种修理过程中使用的能源。

（6）生产区内的劳动保护用能等。

能源库存量 指能源使用企业（单位）在报告期的某时间点所拥有的、用于企业（单位）消费的各种能源的库存量。本指标解释不涉及能源生产企业的能源产成品库存和能源贸易企业的能源商品库存。

综合能源消费量 指企业（单位）在报告期内工业生产实际消费的各种能源（扣除能源加工转换和能源回收利用等重复因素）的总和。计算综合能源消费量时，需要将各种能源品种的消费量换算成按照标准计量单位（如：吨标准煤）计量的消费量。

能源加工转换投入 能源加工转换，指为了特定的用途，将一种能源（一般为一次能源），经过一定的工艺，加工或转换成另外一种能源（二次能源）。

火力发电的加工转换投入 指火力发电企业为发电而投入发电锅炉燃烧室的燃料数量。通常燃料主要有：煤炭、燃料油、天然气、焦炉煤气、高炉煤气、转炉煤气、生物质燃料、可燃废弃物和可燃垃圾等。

供热的加工转换投入 指热力生产企业为生产热力而投入供热锅炉燃烧室的燃料数量，以及热电联产机组按照热电产出比例分摊的用于供热的燃料投入量。

加工煤制品的加工转换投入 指煤制品生产企业，在不改变煤炭基本属性的情况下，为生产型煤（煤球、煤饼、蜂窝煤）、煤粉、水煤浆等煤制品而使用的原煤或其他煤炭产品的数量。

能源加工转换产出量 指一次能源经过加工转换产出的二次能源产品（包括不作能源使用的其他副产品和联产品）的数量，比如火力发电产出的电力，热电联产同时产出的电力、蒸汽、热水，原煤洗选产出的洗精煤、洗中煤、洗煤泥等，炼焦产出的焦炭、焦炉煤气和其他焦化产品（煤焦油、粗苯等），炼油和煤制油产出的汽油、煤油、柴油、燃料油、液化石油气、炼厂干气 、石脑油、润滑油、石蜡、溶剂油、石油焦、石油沥青等，制气（指煤气生产）产出的发生炉煤气、焦炭和其他焦化产品（煤焦油、粗苯等）。

十四、镇街主要指标

Main Indicators of Towns

14-1 镇街生产总值

Gross Domestic Product by Town

单位：万元

镇街	(1991年)				(1992年)			
	地区生产总值	第一产业	第二产业	第三产业	地区生产总值	第一产业	第二产业	第三产业
莞城	22046	174	16612	5260	28881	108	22263	6510
石龙	25154	907	17669	6578	29467	1026	21163	7278
虎门	44900	10059	16412	18429	56539	10336	24781	21422
东城	23500	7179	13793	2528	32770	7362	21392	4016
万江	18518	3874	11653	2991	27997	3968	18928	5102
南城	13339	2219	8181	2939	18147	1973	12681	3493
中堂	14889	3300	9065	2524	19902	4360	10669	4873
望牛墩	11950	2794	7394	1762	13789	2854	8683	2252
麻涌	24449	10489	11478	2482	26907	9797	14294	2816
石碣	12556	2686	7660	2210	16967	2888	11140	2939
高埗	11546	3352	5163	3031	14295	4017	6503	3775
道滘	15659	4540	9542	1577	19009	4805	12003	2201
洪梅	6492	3879	1872	741	6906	2441	3435	1030
沙田	12616	6467	4552	1597	16779	6511	7850	2417
厚街	31303	5679	22403	3221	38272	6064	28528	3680
长安	24850	7961	13185	3704	36298	8980	21883	5435
寮步	23700	9030	8979	5691	30083	9256	12627	8200
大岭山	10557	5918	3123	1516	16175	6342	4928	4905
大朗	19481	11277	4870	3334	24694	10104	9836	4754
黄江	20403	2765	15888	1750	28355	3244	22864	2247
樟木头	10515	10515	2107	6426	13972	2212	8536	3224
清溪	8673	2076	4428	2169	12742	2405	6936	3401
塘厦	17826	6128	9049	2649	30454	6300	19988	4166
凤岗	8676	2698	5550	428	12119	3257	8146	716
谢岗	9472	2019	5197	2256	7178	2339	4236	603
常平	38008	13134	14511	10363	45046	11625	20103	13317
桥头	14030	4083	8114	1833	22099	5429	10336	6334
横沥	11125	2499	6349	2277	15673	2710	9342	3621
东坑	16245	3544	11393	1308	22332	3368	17294	1670
企石	16155	3731	9575	2849	21159	4699	13097	3363
石排	16123	2350	10727	3046	18091	2704	11839	3548
茶山	13328	3385	7146	2797	16377	4160	8782	3435

注：各镇街合计不等于全市数，下同。

14-1 续表 1

单位：万元

镇街	(1993年) 地区生产总值	第一产业	第二产业	第三产业	(1994年) 地区生产总值	第一产业	第二产业	第三产业
莞城	41307		32838	8469	55021		43120	11901
石龙	34182	582	21188	12412	48891	216	32738	15937
虎门	74808	11281	37710	25816	103070	14350	51597	37123
东城	37567	4379	25901	7287	44963	5223	30065	9675
万江	39317	4818	26939	7561	45953	5499	31186	9268
南城	23341	2767	16312	4262	46416	2811	38511	5094
中堂	31352	7282	16982	7089	34819	6271	19472	9076
望牛墩	15717	2642	10196	2879	18449	2796	11974	3679
麻涌	34553	9305	22223	3025	42676	9160	27917	5599
石碣	23877	2542	16311	5024	34401	2816	24582	7003
高埗	17843	4751	8347	4745	22368	5495	10877	5996
道滘	24306	5086	15471	3749	37062	5698	27835	14072
洪梅	8069	2265	4292	1512	9020	2406	4756	1858
沙田	24446	6574	14434	3438	31950	6196	20646	5107
厚街	57912	6707	44408	6796	101289	7615	77637	16037
长安	49862	9995	31962	7905	68914	11024	46939	10951
寮步	46311	9423	21926	14962	63089	12428	30205	20456
大岭山	22611	6717	7660	8234	27722	6725	11258	9739
大朗	32720	10237	15152	7331	46550	13958	21052	11540
黄江	37008	3021	30171	3816	47096	3254	39031	4811
樟木头	18265	1361	13994	2910	23438	1680	18008	3750
清溪	19533	3299	12076	4158	30510	4230	20391	5889
塘厦	41635	4353	31001	6281	80870	6396	65620	8854
凤岗	16961	3282	12778	901	24520	4166	19054	1300
谢岗	12063	2367	8997	699	16093	3365	11143	1585
常平	67921	12564	34518	20839	100294	13561	62109	24624
桥头	27654	5023	15085	7546	40632	6225	22445	11962
横沥	23825	23825	2604	13815	33565	3922	17444	12198
东坑	33565	4073	25007	4485	36161	4245	26665	5251
企石	28573	5167	17684	5722	34915	6545	21854	6516
石排	25462	2992	17949	4521	31920	3699	21172	7049
茶山	21196	4908	12096	4192	30233	6017	18221	5995

14-1 续表 2

单位：万元

镇街	(1995年) 地区生产总值	第一产业	第二产业	第三产业	(1996年) 地区生产总值	第一产业	第二产业	第三产业
莞城	69318		52710	16608	72335		50523	21812
石龙	70501	318	46550	23633	72190	303	36303	35584
虎门	130282	18388	68784	43110	158257	25193	85444	47620
东城	85114	6208	57257	21649	100581	6744	66136	27701
万江	55648	6705	37884	11059	63649	8488	40934	14227
南城	83707	2938	63407	17362	103785	3667	79347	20771
中堂	41537	6593	23358	11585	50533	7418	28908	14206
望牛墩	21961	3197	14061	4703	25963	3440	16512	6011
麻涌	47340	11783	28584	6973	49764	15494	26884	7386
石碣	46831	3332	33206	10293	66081	3495	45532	17054
高埗	28324	6213	14403	7708	36274	6945	19348	9981
道滘	47605	5698	27835	14072	55596	6031	35931	13634
洪梅	15209	2667	6923	5619	16733	2908	7657	6168
沙田	42922	7741	29376	5806	49023	10655	32354	6015
厚街	118353	9670	90642	18041	140036	10906	83151	45979
长安	93323	12505	65233	15585	131672	12882	97066	21724
寮步	75398	14727	32311	28360	85876	15651	37022	33203
大岭山	39228	8485	17265	13478	49383	9773	21083	18527
大朗	66807	17319	25844	23644	78506	16982	29641	31883
黄江	61098	3708	46392	10998	63391	3929	46558	12904
樟木头	31914	2662	24710	4543	41323	3443	32232	5647
清溪	52550	5721	35627	11202	82953	6083	55419	21451
塘厦	112158	6909	90588	14661	139903	9900	112916	17087
凤岗	37051	4767	30135	2149	48015	5521	39670	2824
谢岗	18872	4356	12655	1861	25536	5213	18242	2081
常平	135315	18444	87856	29015	146594	19303	86033	41258
桥头	54012	7206	30626	16180	64694	8418	38393	17883
横沥	44663	4484	23559	16620	54922	4717	29045	21161
东坑	34654	5179	19727	9748	50965	5274	32218	13473
企石	44588	7760	28861	7967	54066	8947	35535	9584
石排	34349	4898	20547	8904	37946	5718	21459	10769
茶山	41484	6017	18221	5995	51339	7159	24892	9433

14-1 续表 3

单位：万元

镇街	(1997年) 地区生产总值	第一产业	第二产业	第三产业	(1998年) 地区生产总值	第一产业	第二产业	第三产业
莞城	80298		49962	30336	110076		49677	60399
石龙	95560	293	48361	46906	133953	116	77910	55927
虎门	246823	25799	130963	90061	362826	29535	176729	156562
东城	125730	5850	78959	40921	161819	5246	105142	51431
万江	69516	8749	42333	18434	82239	9424	50075	22922
南城	130392	3490	103126	23776	160524	3933	128850	27741
中堂	61741	7610	35991	18140	76980	7727	45359	23894
望牛墩	30854	3780	19390	7684	36531	3941	22769	9821
麻涌	52217	15965	29345	6907	62531	16443	35485	10603
石碣	85990	3782	54674	27534	109255	3852	70872	34531
高埗	46630	7586	26579	12465	60242	8235	36383	15624
道滘	69424	6383	47525	15516	80887	6756	54039	20092
洪梅	20052	4501	7602	7949	23134	4607	9569	8958
沙田	54881	11342	36602	6936	71203	16829	42167	12207
厚街	184205	11448	96880	75877	247177	12150	146229	88798
长安	180377	13111	134235	33031	245676	13562	183031	49083
寮步	103656	17341	45112	41203	129731	18768	60452	50511
大岭山	65246	10538	31884	22824	83268	9134	45040	29094
大朗	95301	19093	38996	37212	122409	15008	53085	54316
黄江	67618	4139	47073	16406	83585	4244	58492	20849
樟木头	55682	4725	43020	7936	71299	5333	51615	14351
清溪	120961	7519	84276	29166	160483	7802	115314	37367
塘厦	178757	11467	140870	26420	230580	12121	177569	40890
凤岗	63066	5925	51486	5655	79286	6187	65440	7659
谢岗	29488	6379	20521	2588	34881	6958	24888	3035
常平	185390	20195	98068	67127	231059	19811	131252	79995
桥头	79685	8523	51919	19243	96661	9712	61140	25809
横沥	67894	6411	34892	26591	81263	5364	45427	30472
东坑	63718	4810	44682	14226	78576	5726	54359	18491
企石	62625	9562	42240	10823	72065	9827	47551	14687
石排	43477	6463	23530	13484	53842	6606	28932	18304
茶山	63955	9321	39524	15110	77319	9878	47785	19656

14-1 续表 4

单位：万元

镇街	(1999年) 地区生产总值	第一产业	第二产业	第三产业	(2000年) 地区生产总值	第一产业	第二产业	第三产业
莞城	131005		58104	72901	184225		67030	117195
石龙	157715	349	86171	71195	184256	189	98240	85827
虎门	442633	31013	213607	198014	532946	30479	263928	238539
东城	207432	4126	125159	78147	262854	4233	153667	104954
万江	97379	9435	59636	28308	138724	11604	85526	41594
南城	198820	2756	149678	46386	233013	3119	171413	58481
中堂	94412	7001	57217	30194	123213	7032	76571	39610
望牛墩	43303	4012	26738	12553	51516	4072	31399	16045
麻涌	75449	12466	44768	18215	90816	12213	45965	32638
石碣	137148	3866	88152	45130	175180	4021	111038	60121
高埗	78709	8792	50131	19786	102516	9155	67888	25473
道滘	93751	7151	61687	24913	109999	7569	67841	34589
洪梅	26118	4162	11872	10084	29921	4383	14095	11443
沙田	86339	12167	53505	20667	109128	12714	71503	24911
厚街	300721	12412	171495	116814	405317	12705	221947	170665
长安	332335	13820	240690	77825	419347	14256	299650	105441
寮步	161782	19944	82582	59256	202379	20732	110577	71070
大岭山	108469	9238	67662	31569	138789	9742	89991	39056
大朗	156427	16699	69193	70535	201504	17826	94065	89613
黄江	97621	4410	67206	26005	123331	5243	83748	34340
樟木头	94385	4225	64138	26021	147697	4639	71921	71138
清溪	206524	8790	151219	46515	303131	9984	231303	61844
塘厦	288110	12783	217897	57430	363971	13486	272234	78251
凤岗	100753	6267	61392	33094	128298	6336	79138	42824
谢岗	42142	3610	29017	9515	50174	3975	35779	10420
常平	302805	15703	166347	120755	395318	16116	218229	160974
桥头	111892	9062	69595	33235	130380	9093	82261	39026
横沥	97209	6178	55276	35756	116749	8593	62314	45842
东坑	101287	5363	65010	30913	118430	6241	76250	35940
企石	85313	10000	51789	23524	99467	11339	58897	29231
石排	69030	6772	37874	24384	87817	6913	48532	32372
茶山	90250	9514	55468	25268	105432	10712	64726	29994

14-1 续表 5

单位：万元

镇街	(2001年) 地区生产总值	第一产业	第二产业	第三产业	(2002年) 地区生产总值	第一产业	第二产业	第三产业
莞城	222233		80203	142030	312742		76890	235852
石龙	215738	150	115691	99897	248664	144	135163	113357
虎门	618557	30469	304781	283307	717425	26838	350636	339951
东城	342044	3785	188628	149631	466960	2110	232502	232348
万江	175693	13015	90857	71821	213919	11026	106945	95948
南城	286473	2929	211622	71922	350029	2711	262431	84887
中堂	153366	7155	95677	50533	194263	5908	122819	65536
望牛墩	60921	3540	36872	20509	73104	3591	43299	26214
麻涌	127061	12298	74806	39957	173557	1002	120426	43079
石碣	243163	4139	150613	88411	340162	4141	209830	126191
高埗	133362	9477	90730	33155	173004	9701	120415	42888
道滘	128327	8011	76692	43624	153201	8479	87039	57683
洪梅	34245	4587	16543	13115	41756	4793	21676	15287
沙田	142060	13641	92266	36153	182363	13912	119778	48673
厚街	483117	13088	253149	216880	583689	13976	297707	272006
长安	529219	14496	371263	143460	679022	14622	469032	195368
寮步	252526	21246	143824	87456	314871	20276	182688	111907
大岭山	194021	10089	133489	50443	251078	5741	178811	66526
大朗	264929	17764	128283	118882	341930	15525	181234	145171
黄江	154595	5176	98438	50981	199781	5288	122001	72492
樟木头	176062	4460	84195	87407	210845	5545	101237	104063
清溪	393471	10517	302613	80341	501941	11106	382584	108251
塘厦	457175	13796	335872	107507	573947	13603	425078	135266
凤岗	162854	6400	97540	58914	205006	2035	126903	76068
谢岗	58323	4115	41585	12623	71092	5665	40790	24637
常平	493419	16451	272983	203985	557039	16077	310537	230425
桥头	151979	8366	98054	45559	179442	7245	118564	53633
横沥	140251	9252	74148	56851	168932	9380	90576	68976
东坑	132805	6013	84256	42535	149147	5438	92587	51122
企石	115314	12403	63421	39490	127616	9088	68807	49721
石排	107585	6925	61859	38801	131394	6967	75798	48629
茶山	123931	9801	75341	38789	153215	9801	91916	51498

14-1 续表 6

单位：万元

镇街	(2003年) 地区生产总值	第一产业	第二产业	第三产业	(2004年) 地区生产总值	第一产业	第二产业	第三产业
莞城	415993		80802	335191	552370		94035	458335
石龙	287713	116	167126	120471	317521	51	186652	130820
虎门	905165	27106	462105	415954	1139827	27168	598000	514659
东城	652408	1657	314094	336657	897727	900	411172	485655
万江	269593	9622	129625	130346	329849	5617	156431	167801
南城	452911	2743	314752	135416	741609	1869	349496	390244
中堂	256251	7013	162945	86292	338808	5956	206693	126159
望牛墩	87872	3520	50846	33506	106086	3550	59709	42827
麻涌	234612	8769	177540	48303	292911	8664	226131	58116
石碣	463023	4253	290495	168275	590604	3649	381862	205093
高埗	224078	9891	157949	56238	282716	9943	202317	70456
道滘	178954	8975	100566	69413	217400	9499	119688	88213
洪梅	53960	5113	29668	19179	76686	4770	41140	30776
沙田	236769	13944	155438	67387	310921	13975	202383	94563
厚街	721188	12275	374482	334431	878666	12341	454284	412041
长安	887947	14863	603308	269776	1162826	15040	759582	388204
寮步	394322	13167	234806	146349	498253	5327	303435	189491
大岭山	322872	4937	226565	91370	447412	4571	313857	128984
大朗	443891	10640	240983	192268	574604	6986	325826	241792
黄江	258682	4567	152903	101212	331432	3294	187369	140769
樟木头	250877	4863	119145	126869	291893	4350	139729	147814
清溪	645553	11218	495035	139300	848426	9610	660589	178227
塘厦	710030	13565	526730	169735	882099	13700	653816	214583
凤岗	284608	2048	170574	111986	373309	2015	220434	150860
谢岗	91482	4266	51312	35904	119007	4328	69024	45655
常平	657385	12627	377679	267079	796109	10792	468642	316674
桥头	213712	5419	134937	73356	264849	4495	144282	116072
横沥	205872	9602	117554	78716	253887	9075	153884	90928
东坑	181394	8423	113270	59701	230057	7943	145998	76116
企石	142717	5216	72284	65217	167279	3848	80461	82970
石排	157729	7144	92020	58565	190127	7259	109953	72915
茶山	195098	8607	118895	67596	268473	7413	161070	99990

14-1 续表 7

单位：万元

镇街	(2005年) 地区生产总值	第一产业	第二产业	第三产业	(2006年) 地区生产总值	第一产业	第二产业	第三产业
莞城	617849		153367	464482	712319		230144	482174
石龙	349301	141	194749	154411	384329	35	213392	170902
虎门	1283052	22937	668632	591483	1492628	11446	763086	718096
东城	1049758	480	473888	575389	1264850	427	571728	692694
万江	375471	4209	164099	207164	440346	4711	187932	247702
南城	1016644	1900	440431	574313	1229016	1995	508223	718798
中堂	424212	6122	276399	141691	507968	6428	332766	168774
望牛墩	126751	3511	73191	50049	156949	3480	87638	65831
麻涌	387211	8588	310275	68348	494018	7106	398466	88445
石碣	728816	3782	491498	233535	868731	3091	588622	277018
高埗	366593	10020	254017	102556	456695	6552	320225	129918
道滘	255589	8753	143285	103551	301036	9568	174820	116648
洪梅	102660	3939	61138	37583	123863	4082	77274	42507
沙田	364800	13695	240822	110283	442784	12585	293854	136345
厚街	1033929	11722	531019	491188	1199117	6929	609223	582965
长安	1339428	9492	917732	412204	1539236	7505	1042139	489592
寮步	598969	7765	364261	226943	739610	1136	451671	286803
大岭山	547734	4102	370108	173524	675091	2329	431260	241502
大朗	707369	14112	411161	282096	850356	1491	499588	349277
黄江	364377	3065	220654	140658	441152	741	276062	164349
樟木头	330537	3463	157434	169640	393688	600	185556	207532
清溪	984943	9036	761281	214626	1097986	8012	828219	261755
塘厦	1057175	13661	771724	271790	1186644	12312	830537	343794
凤岗	517427	1762	320177	195488	623929	1750	373375	248804
谢岗	148917	4467	91026	53424	192841	4795	118714	69332
常平	951464	10062	556932	384470	1119659	6338	644544	468777
桥头	287240	4495	168473	114271	388604	1387	210763	176454
横沥	304870	8593	195659	100619	373304	7274	242406	123624
东坑	261238	11543	165441	84254	295233	5703	194653	94877
企石	200581	3129	102183	95269	244027	2266	129255	112506
石排	234709	7268	128132	99308	294009	7283	154259	132467
茶山	305183	6652	190620	107911	384988	3215	245078	136695

14-1 续表 8

单位：万元

镇街	(2007年) 地区生产总值	第一产业	第二产业	第三产业	(2008年) 地区生产总值	第一产业	第二产业	第三产业
莞城	897597		298250	599347	1015311		294311	721000
石龙	427216	10	235821	191385	475742	7	239943	235792
虎门	1846638	10373	936639	899626	2153489	11940	1093014	1048535
东城	1559123	377	699730	859017	1816793	339	773623	1042831
万江	520636	3405	221314	295917	604659	3702	262498	338459
南城	1425257	2015	583496	839747	1632407	1285	618209	1012913
中堂	588085	6553	379181	202351	659949	6760	419455	233734
望牛墩	193635	3462	105983	84190	236495	3359	127759	105377
麻涌	651344	5985	537412	107947	834681	7564	693959	133158
石碣	994532	3096	670790	320646	1082524	2795	694349	385380
高埗	568276	6530	384637	177109	690604	6526	442377	241701
道滘	362268	8202	211240	142826	439328	7218	240510	191600
洪梅	163384	4281	110958	48145	206785	4381	147969	54435
沙田	515106	12403	327706	174997	588063	12863	337140	238060
厚街	1420026	7270	719643	693113	1616483	7971	797404	811108
长安	1770272	7746	1152474	610052	2029075	4979	1158887	865209
寮步	886584	1118	531815	353650	1038493	2141	584767	451585
大岭山	822554	2241	502679	317634	960138	2248	554712	403178
大朗	1025864	2098	592111	431655	1100875	877	688340	411658
黄江	556305	740	347972	207593	721414	724	438204	282486
樟木头	461719	505	228647	232567	507743	311	253050	254382
清溪	1266762	6207	924401	336153	1417816	5170	966538	446108
塘厦	1365736	11206	903107	451422	1602945	10447	980030	612468
凤岗	747757	1752	409163	336843	901696	1725	472782	427189
谢岗	239771	5178	143093	91500	273944	9273	160217	104454
常平	1311744	6665	747353	557726	1495652	6058	796227	693366
桥头	467790	1326	242928	223536	536868	2692	254438	279737
横沥	443014	4350	275399	163265	522130	6972	300380	214778
东坑	320991	4532	204804	111654	372361	4017	231268	137076
企石	291765	2868	150052	138844	320630	2314	159252	159064
石排	360806	7308	187787	165711	417073	7313	216033	193727
茶山	476010	3131	293991	178888	593265	4327	353036	235902
松山湖					618635		297419	321216

14-1 续表 9

单位：万元

镇街	(2009年) 地区生产总值	第一产业	第二产业	第三产业	(2010年) 地区生产总值	第一产业	第二产业	第三产业
莞城	1039596		304342	735255	1120356		302272	818084
石龙	504196	7	251309	252880	563812	18	304608	259186
虎门	2424929	12828	1214281	1197820	2712345	16705	1300263	1395378
东城	1972630	500	746158	1225972	2308515	656	963402	1344456
万江	608904	3390	242069	363446	681580	3222	271521	406837
南城	1838797	1284	700382	1137130	1996248	1269	503015	1491965
中堂	667852	7100	403004	257748	680472	7310	409239	263924
望牛墩	287776	3472	164372	119932	304774	3658	169114	132002
麻涌	936352	7862	783010	145479	1097963	8234	904031	185698
石碣	1086458	2648	641252	442558	1119051	3295	741995	373761
高埗	606138	5999	383433	216706	691277	5892	444102	241283
道滘	451406	8351	239202	203854	524691	8861	301184	214645
洪梅	259432	4740	193219	61473	341015	4887	262817	73311
沙田	611189	13163	359306	238720	671307	13446	415810	242050
厚街	1678345	8479	898569	771297	1900402	9339	1049787	841276
长安	2191401	4875	1290474	896052	2476284	5739	1522056	948489
寮步	1113184	1661	635046	476478	1331469	1897	785661	543911
大岭山	978589	2294	513473	462823	1065349	2490	541915	520944
大朗	1169527	1280	684678	483568	1380864	1436	828791	550638
黄江	759627	770	426511	332346	850323	852	478420	371051
樟木头	525108	370	253945	270793	550792	387	238952	311453
清溪	1355016	5502	890772	458742	1432701	6065	944468	482168
塘厦	1737670	11238	1072265	654167	1854479	11288	1148809	694383
凤岗	1019431	1233	520978	497220	1130971	1248	560451	569272
谢岗	295849	9452	170525	115872	364081	8230	226867	128984
常平	1527726	6940	797473	723314	1647385	7562	785535	854288
桥头	533939	3291	258057	272591	591569	4943	291724	294902
横沥	544391	6058	334338	203994	593004	3689	338669	250646
东坑	407774	1903	257886	147986	495426	1420	325976	168030
企石	317899	2160	178008	137731	330285	1973	196062	132250
石排	443189	7210	248863	187116	521559	6950	314768	199840
茶山	610347	4214	359288	246846	624169	2729	343837	277602
松山湖	807836		384075	423761	994690		473193	521497

14-1 续表 10

单位：万元

镇街	(2011年) 地区生产总值	第一产业	第二产业	第三产业	(2012年) 地区生产总值	第一产业	第二产业	第三产业
莞城	1222655		345656	876999	1312960		336032	976928
石龙	629604	20	335392	294192	674289	28	351445	322817
虎门	3083685	16073	1354138	1713474	3449740	16086	1528888	1904766
东城	2549277	869	994680	1553728	2759681	1210	957773	1800698
万江	771560	2832	302715	466013	806233	2684	297329	506219
南城	2324783	1316	568939	1754528	2602379	1230	565615	2035535
中堂	759504	8362	452733	298409	759839	8500	438227	313112
望牛墩	362001	4049	203523	154429	372158	4493	193674	173991
麻涌	1225141	9587	949921	265633	1274486	10132	936615	327739
石碣	1120241	3031	737704	379506	1126839	3139	727501	396199
高埗	796174	5677	505676	284821	835235	5775	516211	313249
道滘	597487	10424	336278	250785	632178	11771	344767	275640
洪梅	367244	5430	271593	90221	368660	5029	267867	95764
沙田	722343	16062	420766	285516	770194	18396	369414	382384
厚街	2183188	10109	1238029	935050	2672266	10596	1612391	1049279
长安	2700394	5630	1623068	1071697	2997437	5850	1888651	1102936
寮步	1474860	1431	860989	612441	1585830	8556	906576	670698
大岭山	1230485	2592	604612	623281	1340909	2738	678908	659263
大朗	1519385	1701	889042	628642	1647461	2111	942467	702883
黄江	953803	936	511631	441236	1092088	1103	592122	498864
樟木头	626259	417	264935	360907	654566	328	272232	382006
清溪	1519387	6889	954224	558274	1554412	7990	941313	605109
塘厦	2136115	11593	1250805	873717	2296084	13283	1262674	1020128
凤岗	1338390	1414	655037	681939	1443889	1634	671346	770909
谢岗	429711	10748	273012	145951	482047	14028	315477	152542
常平	1863138	8627	884541	969971	2066421	9493	923396	1133532
桥头	636208	3917	319231	313060	754630	3897	412213	338520
横沥	654815	4617	367161	283037	713002	4492	394598	313912
东坑	624978	1621	425730	197628	704773	1549	473215	230010
企石	373472	2380	215989	155103	405816	2780	230741	172295
石排	550833	6716	311739	232378	554266	6839	309790	237638
茶山	696375	3086	355755	337534	737038	3438	396459	337141
松山湖	1322103		625162	696941	1507742		719184	788558

14-1 续表 11

单位：万元

镇街	(2013年) 地区生产总值	第一产业	第二产业	第三产业	(2014年) 地区生产总值	第一产业	第二产业	第三产业
莞城街道	1339920		317520	1022401	1419815		316944	1102870
石龙镇	768510	40	411491	356979	828879	42	444840	383998
虎门镇	3824840	16924	1634600	2173316	4132811	17675	1745903	2369233
东城街道	3303629	1679	1229249	2072701	3456419	1753	1268004	2186663
万江街道	939750	2724	350319	586707	986999	2845	359822	624332
南城街道	3012235	1269	650744	2360222	3239733	1243	623104	2615386
中堂镇	793906	9280	435852	348775	833920	9688	460049	364183
望牛墩镇	486471	4921	251694	229856	520110	5139	262892	252078
麻涌镇	1470511	11042	1000864	458605	1535610	11510	1046529	477571
石碣镇	1152872	3046	754524	395302	1245249	3184	814839	427226
高埗镇	1023272	5958	649450	367864	1102860	6220	698804	397836
道滘镇	701067	13120	381843	306105	747656	13676	397045	336935
洪梅镇	432280	5536	313316	113428	501312	5782	353550	141980
沙田镇（虎门港）	889532	20113	393891	475528	977426	20998	425057	531371
厚街镇	2848938	11491	1553664	1283783	3029896	11978	1555886	1462032
长安镇	3404500	6274	2226636	1171590	3636575	6540	2378672	1251363
寮步镇	1872441	7996	1080016	784429	2006549	8335	1140825	857389
大岭山镇	1521845	2899	831833	687112	1633407	3026	883138	747243
大朗镇	1851180	2338	1009803	839039	2007114	2502	1075277	929335
黄江镇	1215390	1263	649602	564525	1256520	1317	661385	593819
樟木头镇	754398	344	320684	433370	795822	358	359653	435810
清溪镇	1806184	8817	1088267	709101	1923374	9221	1148214	765939
塘厦镇	2612946	13965	1577367	1021614	2788544	14754	1680339	1093451
凤岗镇	1749523	1734	849065	898724	1945158	1808	1007922	935428
谢岗镇	536402	12346	358653	165403	622337	12894	428006	181437
常平镇	2450935	10491	1136304	1304139	2599815	10935	1186883	1401996
桥头镇	907965	3873	497587	406505	1036247	4037	602304	429906
横沥镇	840177	4630	470940	364606	920083	4834	511149	404100
东坑镇	825806	1490	550685	273632	903038	1556	596840	304642
企石镇	467766	3258	263467	201041	496360	3396	279580	213384
石排镇	641382	7042	359996	274345	687253	7355	390947	288952
茶山镇	849677	3585	460233	385858	911046	3737	495466	411843
松山湖	1705264		816223	889041	2109233		1094934	1014299

14-1 续表 12

单位：万元

镇街	(2015年)				(2016年)			
	地区生产总值	第一产业	第二产业	第三产业	地区生产总值	第一产业	第二产业	第三产业
莞城街道	1469204		312012	1157192	1596846		318961	1277885
石龙镇	866308	42	451583	414683	914812	46	446278	468488
虎门镇	4471700	17799	1696749	2757152	4976610	19276	1716255	3241079
东城街道	3728664	1765	1317384	2409514	4131408	1912	1409087	2720410
万江街道	1047196	2865	368943	675387	1144808	3103	394803	746902
南城街道	3525763	1252	571781	2952730	3920288	1258	530606	3388424
中堂镇	846736	9756	444721	392259	899291	10565	458413	430313
望牛墩镇	550965	5175	266361	279429	580416	5605	257012	317799
麻涌镇	1673252	11855	1101360	560036	1859559	12839	1041693	805027
石碣镇	1331428	3232	849448	478748	1459867	3394	917183	539290
高埗镇	1177880	6264	748243	423374	1263080	6783	760909	495388
道滘镇	773870	13772	382549	377549	900844	13813	427741	459289
洪梅镇	509711	5822	355860	148030	536652	6305	362318	168029
沙田镇（虎门港）	1068619	21145	450820	596654	1180318	22900	453467	703951
厚街镇	3219431	12062	1507369	1700000	3589044	13063	1565044	2010937
长安镇	4005148	6586	2551639	1446924	4630793	7132	2823825	1799836
寮步镇	2104805	8393	1129050	967361	2305636	9091	1178537	1118008
大岭山镇	1758093	3047	899316	855729	1940908	3300	946048	991560
大朗镇	2201519	2534	1127473	1071512	2421432	2745	1215171	1203516
黄江镇	1339779	1325	680780	657674	1455853	1435	715803	738615
樟木头镇	851972	361	384459	467152	943524	391	428839	514294
清溪镇	2080511	9285	1204527	866700	2294645	10056	1318757	965832
塘厦镇	3029267	14858	1848880	1165529	3341244	16091	1936561	1388593
凤岗镇	2128717	1820	1084089	1042808	2416729	1971	1238958	1175800
谢岗镇	675484	12984	474917	187583	731978	14062	522617	195299
常平镇	2801648	11012	1276021	1514615	3052627	11926	1280844	1759857
桥头镇	1102103	4065	620647	477391	1246345	4402	713321	528622
横沥镇	1007554	4868	551780	450907	1120967	5272	610220	505475
东坑镇	1004595	1567	687782	315246	1102297	1697	760121	340478
企石镇	539762	3420	306508	229834	596920	3704	332534	260683
石排镇	731026	7406	417557	306063	831670	8021	476079	347570
茶山镇	975074	4040	512132	458902	1070327	4396	559262	506669
松山湖	2592604		1969666	622938	3039613		2336516	703097

14-2 镇街第三产业增加值（2016年）

Value-added of the Tertiary Industry by Town (2016)

单位：万元

镇　街	第三产业增加值	#交通运输及仓储业	批发和零售业	住宿和餐饮业	金融业	房地产业
莞城街道	1277885	106268	262644	27513	240511	152243
石 龙 镇	468488	24377	134098	25398	54936	69802
虎 门 镇	3241079	276241	722141	163279	297168	688062
东城街道	2720410	179372	470919	133861	483081	345765
万江街道	746902	55620	159218	58269	96169	120526
南城街道	3388424	59516	536883	68981	675676	421664
中 堂 镇	430313	9313	121993	31701	38781	55393
望牛墩镇	317799	38941	67778	18408	31802	46714
麻 涌 镇	805027	144555	410348	17057	43993	75469
石 碣 镇	539290	12878	185272	38792	46106	68143
高 埗 镇	495388	29354	108349	41365	37115	122794
道 滘 镇	459289	19635	128797	27073	44900	133179
洪 梅 镇	168029	23474	58072	6715	12887	18054
沙田镇（虎门港）	703951	220690	143181	26023	28094	108803
厚 街 镇	2010937	47559	552750	153965	182967	615191
长 安 镇	1799836	34265	687610	101617	175160	198461
寮 步 镇	1118008	114948	465035	55907	81318	130065
大岭山镇	991560	31723	290042	59485	83531	200308
大 朗 镇	1203516	55318	384047	60162	123547	208520
黄 江 镇	738615	18598	302677	54583	84407	125035
樟木头镇	514294	33028	120101	37266	57704	110901
清 溪 镇	965832	33696	408283	69537	74863	127310
塘 厦 镇	1388593	41656	426033	117584	162747	253336
凤 岗 镇	1175800	34839	252606	66766	138764	277343
谢 岗 镇	195299	10923	48068	17532	25497	32349
常 平 镇	1759857	56091	491158	118547	141519	290843
桥 头 镇	528622	4828	203576	36607	53145	62998
横 沥 镇	505475	21674	170363	47053	60323	79256
东 坑 镇	340478	17220	106360	17303	27605	67559
企 石 镇	260683	16589	57529	11449	29095	61815
石 排 镇	347570	16253	96534	29300	46939	60657
茶 山 镇	506669	26844	139945	37673	62075	70229
松 山 湖	703097	10503	148359	10961	96594	166085

14−3 镇街户籍户数与人口数（2016年）

Population of Household by Town (2016)

单位：人

镇　街	户数(户)	城镇户	乡村户	人口数	按性别分 男	按性别分 女	按城镇、乡村分 城镇人口	按城镇、乡村分 乡村人口
全　市	582644	518832	63812	2009352	1014678	994674	1781973	227379
莞城街道	41807	41807		182173	91960	90213	182173	
石龙镇	22073	22073		72779	36143	36636	72779	
虎门镇	36014	31206	4808	135689	68625	67064	115855	19834
东城街道	29462	29462		104706	53087	51619	104706	
万江街道	27806	27806		87425	44337	43088	87425	
南城街道	28469	28469		94869	48293	46576	94869	
中堂镇	23012	21985	1027	79379	40312	39067	75980	3399
望牛墩镇	12538	11079	1459	48361	24065	24296	42246	6115
麻涌镇	22295	12318	9977	77098	38541	38557	39733	37365
石碣镇	15795	15795		47716	24261	23455	47716	
高埗镇	11867	9263	2604	40286	20297	19989	31554	8732
道滘镇	17378	12895	4483	58783	29478	29305	42569	16214
洪梅镇	7310	4348	2962	23838	11965	11873	13464	10374
沙田镇（虎门港）	13317	6711	6606	44652	22350	22302	21891	22761
厚街镇	30196	28017	2179	104031	52137	51894	95674	8357
长安镇	14976	14976		52579	26867	25712	52579	
寮步镇	24448	22239	2209	80124	40354	39770	73514	6610
大岭山镇	14112	12127	1985	49720	25018	24702	42766	6954
大朗镇	20364	18965	1399	77104	39691	37413	71757	5347
黄江镇	9287	5037	4250	29528	14782	14746	15332	14196
樟木头镇	9001	9001		31452	15849	15603	31452	
清溪镇	12571	10117	2454	38888	19342	19546	31309	7579
塘厦镇	19212	18071	1141	55357	27604	27753	52001	3356
凤岗镇	8110	8110		28811	13981	14830	28811	
谢岗镇	5337	3314	2023	21753	10832	10921	13015	8738
常平镇	26769	26579	190	81860	42077	39783	81227	633
桥头镇	12008	9073	2935	38194	19271	18923	28193	10001
横沥镇	12094	10470	1624	39964	20486	19478	34012	5952
东坑镇	10790	9059	1731	31110	16079	15031	25597	5513
企石镇	13932	10714	3218	44843	22984	21859	34002	10841
石排镇	13566	13566		45217	22848	22369	45217	
茶山镇	14146	11598	2548	46870	23408	23462	38362	8508
松山湖	2582	2582		14193	7354	6839	14193	

14-4 镇街户籍人口自然变动情况（2016年）

Population Household by Town (2016)

镇　街	出　生		死　亡		自然增长	
	人　数（人）	出生率（‰）	人　数（人）	死亡率（‰）	人　数（人）	自然增长率（‰）
全　市	27613	13.92	10475	5.28	17138	8.64
莞城街道	2140	11.82	852	4.70	1288	7.11
石 龙 镇	717	9.71	459	6.22	258	3.50
虎 门 镇	1741	12.77	839	6.15	902	6.62
东城街道	1542	15.13	446	4.38	1096	10.75
万江街道	1155	13.41	465	5.40	690	8.01
南城街道	1801	20.02	274	3.05	1527	16.97
中 堂 镇	1157	14.70	462	5.87	695	8.83
望牛墩镇	540	11.19	250	5.18	290	6.01
麻 涌 镇	1089	14.28	426	5.59	663	8.69
石 碣 镇	652	13.80	213	4.51	439	9.29
高 埗 镇	579	14.35	208	5.16	371	9.20
道 滘 镇	646	10.81	327	5.47	319	5.34
洪 梅 镇	336	14.19	131	5.53	205	8.66
沙田镇（虎门港）	605	13.74	248	5.63	357	8.11
厚 街 镇	1205	11.86	579	5.70	626	6.16
长 安 镇	930	18.30	249	4.90	681	13.40
寮 步 镇	1165	14.90	427	5.46	738	9.44
大岭山镇	907	18.55	237	4.85	670	13.70
大 朗 镇	1266	16.70	441	5.82	825	10.88
黄 江 镇	392	13.52	134	4.62	258	8.90
樟木头镇	415	13.22	134	4.27	281	8.95
清 溪 镇	538	14.03	220	5.74	318	8.29
塘 厦 镇	839	15.54	216	4.00	623	11.54
凤 岗 镇	416	14.40	162	5.61	254	8.79
谢 岗 镇	338	15.79	124	5.79	214	10.00
常 平 镇	950	11.82	458	5.70	492	6.12
桥 头 镇	508	13.33	231	6.06	277	7.27
横 沥 镇	583	14.91	245	6.27	338	8.65
东 坑 镇	348	11.25	215	6.95	133	4.30
企 石 镇	596	13.16	269	5.94	327	7.22
石 排 镇	594	13.23	245	5.46	349	7.77
茶 山 镇	573	12.35	286	6.16	287	6.18
松 山 湖	350	28.08	3	0.24	347	27.84

14-5 镇街人口迁移变动情况（2016年）

Population Migration by Town (2016)

单位：人

镇　街	迁移总计	省　内	省　外	迁入总计	省内迁入	省外迁入	迁出总计	迁往省内	迁往省外
全　市	50368	19188	31180	43738	16126	27612	6630	3062	3568
莞城街道	2690	1250	1440	2182	978	1204	508	272	236
石龙镇	1189	640	549	894	501	393	295	139	156
虎门镇	2111	998	1113	1794	838	956	317	160	157
东城街道	4114	1566	2548	3614	1383	2231	500	183	317
万江街道	2732	976	1756	2552	903	1649	180	73	107
南城街道	6961	2388	4573	6252	1969	4283	709	419	290
中堂镇	498	279	219	422	235	187	76	44	32
望牛墩镇	172	88	84	132	59	73	40	29	11
麻涌镇	712	287	425	584	236	348	128	51	77
石碣镇	842	321	521	678	257	421	164	64	100
高埗镇	311	111	200	276	94	182	35	17	18
道滘镇	500	186	314	448	160	288	52	26	26
洪梅镇	187	73	114	157	65	92	30	8	22
沙田镇（虎门港）	656	265	391	607	247	360	49	18	31
厚街镇	1402	513	889	1264	458	806	138	55	83
长安镇	3362	1149	2213	3024	944	2080	338	205	133
寮步镇	3044	1146	1898	2737	963	1774	307	183	124
大岭山镇	1003	370	633	927	344	583	76	26	50
大朗镇	1381	529	852	1278	502	776	103	27	76
黄江镇	1157	455	702	1078	406	672	79	49	30
樟木头镇	1325	468	857	1169	400	769	156	68	88
清溪镇	1175	428	747	979	391	588	196	37	159
塘厦镇	3140	1129	2011	2888	1014	1874	252	115	137
凤岗镇	1486	605	881	1292	530	762	194	75	119
谢岗镇	231	128	103	188	116	72	43	12	31
常平镇	2588	904	1684	2319	817	1502	269	87	182
桥头镇	445	213	232	345	172	173	100	41	59
横沥镇	697	221	476	583	189	394	114	32	82
东坑镇	314	87	227	228	75	153	86	12	74
企石镇	386	117	269	231	97	134	155	20	135
石排镇	399	155	244	247	128	119	152	27	125
茶山镇	477	179	298	318	150	168	159	29	130
松山湖	2681	964	1717	2051	505	1546	630	459	171

注：本表按户籍人口统计。

14-6 镇街土地面积和人口密度（2016年）

Land Area and Population Density by Town (2016)

镇　街	土地面积（平方公里）	人口密度（人/平方公里）	
		户籍人口	常住人口
莞城街道	11.2	16265	14857
石 龙 镇	13.8	5274	10290
虎 门 镇	166.5	815	3819
东城街道	105.1	996	4578
万江街道	48.5	1803	5062
南城街道	56.6	1676	5461
中 堂 镇	59.9	1325	2327
望牛墩镇	31.6	1530	2703
麻 涌 镇	87.2	884	1367
石 碣 镇	36.2	1318	6633
高 埗 镇	34.6	1164	6199
道 滘 镇	54.3	1083	2604
洪 梅 镇	33.2	718	1750
沙田镇（虎门港）	117.7	379	1518
厚 街 镇	125.7	828	3462
长 安 镇	89.5	588	7376
寮 步 镇	72.5	1105	5639
大岭山镇	95.5	521	2907
大 朗 镇	97.5	791	3207
黄 江 镇	92.9	318	2448
樟木头镇	118.8	265	1109
清 溪 镇	140.1	278	2206
塘 厦 镇	128.2	432	3808
凤 岗 镇	82.4	350	3854
谢 岗 镇	91.0	239	1073
常 平 镇	103.3	792	3734
桥 头 镇	56.0	682	2943
横 沥 镇	44.7	894	4562
东 坑 镇	23.7	1313	5646
企 石 镇	58.2	770	2088
石 排 镇	48.7	928	3222
茶 山 镇	45.4	1032	3485
松 山 湖	89.6	158	1278

注：土地面积数据来源于市国土局，不包括海域面积。

14-7 镇街常住人口（2015-2016年）

Permanent Population by Town (2015-2016)

单位：万人

镇　街	2015年	2016年	镇　街	2015年	2016年
莞城街道	16.65	16.64	寮 步 镇	40.80	40.88
石 龙 镇	14.21	14.20	大岭山镇	27.56	27.76
虎 门 镇	63.83	63.58	大 朗 镇	31.11	31.27
东城街道	48.14	48.11	黄 江 镇	22.80	22.74
万江街道	24.39	24.55	樟木头镇	13.16	13.18
南城街道	30.24	30.91	清 溪 镇	31.00	30.91
中 堂 镇	13.92	13.94	塘 厦 镇	48.48	48.82
望牛墩镇	8.56	8.54	凤 岗 镇	31.85	31.76
麻 涌 镇	11.88	11.92	谢 岗 镇	9.81	9.76
石 碣 镇	24.10	24.01	常 平 镇	38.59	38.57
高 埗 镇	21.51	21.45	桥 头 镇	16.52	16.48
道 滘 镇	14.16	14.14	横 沥 镇	20.45	20.39
洪 梅 镇	5.81	5.81	东 坑 镇	13.45	13.38
沙田镇（虎门港）	17.93	17.87	企 石 镇	12.15	12.15
厚 街 镇	43.75	43.52	石 排 镇	15.74	15.69
长 安 镇	66.06	65.94	茶 山 镇	15.72	15.82
松 山 湖	11.08	11.45			

14-8 镇街外来暂住人口数（2015-2016年）

Migrant Population by Town (2015-2016)

单位：人

镇　街	2015年			2016年		
	外来暂住人口	男	女	外来暂住人口	男	女
全　市	4008120	2047374	1960746	4283923	2274363	2009560
莞城街道	39811	21694	18117	50936	26969	23967
石 龙 镇	53202	24088	29114	54300	24636	29664
虎 门 镇	366917	179575	187342	354968	181136	173832
东城街道	156567	84888	71679	156312	83258	73054
万江街道	66252	34423	31829	68951	36792	32159
南城街道	141029	75305	65724	140981	75107	65874
中 堂 镇	42850	20646	22204	42235	24458	17777
望牛墩镇	29351	14345	15006	30146	15462	14684
麻 涌 镇	34986	21410	13576	37586	23401	14185
石 碣 镇	101192	47684	53508	97546	45291	52255
高 埗 镇	73663	41818	31845	86675	45283	41392
道 滘 镇	34503	15519	18984	35051	17514	17537
洪 梅 镇	22982	12560	10422	23547	12934	10613
沙田镇（虎门港）	67592	36694	30898	61084	34416	26668
厚 街 镇	298178	141905	156273	240479	143316	97163
长 安 镇	392013	207523	184490	393260	209753	183507
寮 步 镇	192062	105474	86588	206112	120105	86007
大岭山镇	107509	60280	47229	200994	118753	82241
大 朗 镇	131929	62337	69592	201248	94266	106982
黄 江 镇	158136	90700	67436	144085	78505	65580
樟木头镇	89099	36388	52711	90825	49303	41522
清 溪 镇	152148	59042	93106	158515	66671	91844
塘 厦 镇	288823	150997	137826	417889	219069	198820
凤 岗 镇	185262	97398	87864	179193	96521	82672
谢 岗 镇	52343	27268	25075	46516	24202	22314
常 平 镇	180399	90734	89665	178036	89859	88177
桥 头 镇	68923	35615	33308	70943	36478	34465
横 沥 镇	98029	59186	38843	97362	56123	41239
东 坑 镇	55802	25110	30692	56103	28514	27589
企 石 镇	35167	19052	16115	43717	24665	19052
石 排 镇	88520	42588	45932	91816	44552	47264
茶 山 镇	72542	38218	34324	72871	36274	36597
松 山 湖	130339	66910	63429	146762	86748	60014

14-9 镇街计划生育情况（2016年）

Basic Statistics on Family Planning by Town (2016)

镇　　街	已婚育龄妇女人数（人）	女性初婚人数（人）	#23周岁及以上	落实各种节育措施育龄夫妇（对）	节育率（%）	领取独生子女证累　计（人）	领证率（%）	政　策生育率（%）	多孩率（%）
全　　市	418882	14465	12078	339885	81.14	69298	16.54	97.06	1.88
莞城街道	34768	980	896	28429	81.77	7404	21.30	97.62	1.26
石 龙 镇	13690	503	450	10880	79.47	3011	21.99	97.91	2.51
虎 门 镇	27611	1027	849	20898	75.69	3472	12.57	96.73	3.10
东城街道	23930	581	513	18451	77.10	3597	15.03	97.99	2.01
万江街道	18704	614	536	15807	84.51	3723	19.90	96.80	1.21
南城街道	25262	750	693	19635	77.73	3281	12.99	95.95	2.22
中 堂 镇	14609	633	530	11627	79.59	2548	17.44	97.58	0.86
望牛墩镇	8946	418	360	7375	82.44	1361	15.21	96.67	1.85
麻 涌 镇	15186	699	626	12286	80.90	3313	21.82	97.34	1.84
石 碣 镇	9781	325	250	8599	87.92	1896	19.38	98.93	1.23
高 埗 镇	7679	344	287	6683	87.03	1405	18.30	98.10	2.07
道 滘 镇	10519	417	348	8419	80.04	1850	17.59	97.68	2.48
洪 梅 镇	4651	201	166	3913	84.13	803	17.27	98.81	1.49
沙田镇（虎门港）	9384	322	251	7525	80.19	1913	20.39	97.02	1.82
厚 街 镇	20145	630	512	16696	82.88	3020	14.99	95.77	1.83
长 安 镇	12523	467	397	10773	86.03	1277	10.20	97.74	2.04
寮 步 镇	17176	631	506	13438	78.24	2292	13.34	95.79	2.32
大岭山镇	11109	516	402	9392	84.54	1600	14.40	97.91	2.32
大 朗 镇	15719	556	427	13055	83.05	2988	19.01	95.58	1.34
黄 江 镇	6834	217	160	5947	87.02	1363	19.94	95.92	2.04
樟木头镇	7495	243	188	5705	76.12	678	9.05	98.07	3.61
清 溪 镇	8716	277	228	6612	75.86	1207	13.85	97.58	1.67
塘 厦 镇	12769	420	361	9582	75.04	1988	15.57	96.19	1.79
凤 岗 镇	7036	225	181	5830	82.86	557	7.92	93.99	1.68
谢 岗 镇	4707	129	104	4037	85.77	628	13.34	95.56	1.48
常 平 镇	16766	506	410	13410	79.98	3311	19.75	98.32	1.79
桥 头 镇	7987	260	214	6865	85.95	1485	18.59	97.44	0.98
横 沥 镇	8115	221	156	6943	85.56	1232	15.18	98.28	1.54
东 坑 镇	5645	240	184	4729	83.77	1075	19.04	96.84	0.86
企 石 镇	9131	315	252	7837	85.83	1337	14.64	96.14	2.35
石 排 镇	9197	356	287	7578	82.40	1682	18.29	97.64	1.52
茶 山 镇	9114	345	259	7588	83.26	1181	12.96	97.91	2.79
松 山 湖	3978	97	95	3341	83.99	820	20.61	96.29	1.43

14-10 镇街农林牧渔业总产值（2016年）

Gross Output Value of Agriculture by Town (2016)

单位：万元

镇　街	农林牧渔业总产值	农业	林业	牧业	渔业
石龙镇	170		84		86
虎门镇	28201	9948	170	9025	9057
东城街道	2997	2348	113	26	510
万江街道	10701	9931	96	7	667
南城街道	1021	937	77	6	
中堂镇	29664	26324	84	1287	1969
望牛墩镇	4661	3912	57	24	669
麻涌镇	15496	13216	120		2159
石碣镇	5585	4973	54		558
高埗镇	10882	10080	46		756
道滘镇	16573	11702	67	64	4740
洪梅镇	5841	2006	27	16	3793
沙田镇（虎门港）	30382	13568	50	1846	14918
厚街镇	24304	20741	163	359	3040
长安镇	6703	1310	99	59	5235
寮步镇	50549	49651	87		811
大岭山镇	6184	5124	67	821	172
大朗镇	3123	2211	87	230	595
黄江镇	5139	1490	266	2938	446
樟木头镇	566	373	86	108	
清溪镇	20995	19170	264	1310	251
塘厦镇	20536	16823	185	2623	905
凤岗镇	2503	2050	325	2	126
谢岗镇	24851	17757	68	1486	5540
常平镇	19652	15078	271	3351	952
桥头镇	7364	5474	43	51	1796
横沥镇	13570	3421	46	6375	3728
东坑镇	2759	2574	3	70	111
企石镇	6535	3933	51	1773	778
石排镇	9515	5128	52	305	4030
茶山镇	5694	2705	55	794	2140

注：2015年起，林业总产值统计口径有变，数据与往年不可比。

14－11　镇街主要农产品生产及产品产量（2016年）

Production and Output of Main Agricultural Products by Town (2016)

镇　街	粮食播种面积（亩）	粮　食总产量（吨）	稻谷播种面积（亩）	稻　谷产　量（吨）	蔬菜（含菜用瓜）播种面积（亩）	蔬菜（含菜用瓜）产量（吨）	水　果总面积（亩）	水　果总产量（吨）
石 龙 镇								
虎 门 镇	1801	588	607	230	17585	19111	6425	1584
东城街道	1312	551	1312	551	3120	4475	1798	966
万江街道	776	259	506	185	15090	22817	169	169
南城街道	545	162	38	15	440	369	1790	163
中 堂 镇	2307	724	674	245	18064	26256	4757	7564
望牛墩镇	1741	446	208	79	1913	2765	3543	6716
麻 涌 镇	3043	992	2348	785	5932	6084	16646	19470
石 碣 镇	671	203	5	2	10454	12652	143	99
高 埗 镇	1900	609	390	156	14806	21942	140	227
道 滘 镇	3342	1067	999	390	12070	29652	1106	2504
洪 梅 镇	3058	967	1308	471	660	792	1626	2104
沙田镇（虎门港）	3201	1008	706	263	22468	25870	1757	1948
厚 街 镇	1602	468			43573	49147	30784	3596
长 安 镇	350	99			1560	1623	4832	905
寮 步 镇	757	212			1923	2194	2850	477
大岭山镇	761	187			9191	11518	9865	510
大 朗 镇	716	175			4249	4115	17852	646
黄 江 镇	730	215			2207	2889	14260	184
樟木头镇	460	97			405	581	5120	120
清 溪 镇	900	258			12151	13105	14634	386
塘 厦 镇	953	255			36765	43748	11827	1354
凤 岗 镇	680	185			3507	3560	9073	579
谢 岗 镇	2661	788	96	34	19660	27830	14430	1484
常 平 镇	1540	423			16529	25054	8128	222
桥 头 镇	1096	302	6	2	7752	11101	2148	431
横 沥 镇	720	213			6670	6389	3180	1037
东 坑 镇	729	170			1972	2005	2010	1224
企 石 镇	1291	372	47	22	7025	9618	3487	844
石 排 镇	1061	307			9520	11439	1092	1297
茶 山 镇	960	275			5810	5596	3398	600

14-11 续表 1

(2016年)

镇 街	香(大)蕉面积(亩)	香(大)蕉产量(吨)	荔枝面积(亩)	荔枝产量(吨)	林业用地面积(亩)	当年种植面积(亩)	生猪年末存栏量(头)	生猪出栏量(头)
石龙镇					109			
虎门镇	220	232	4622	408	29355		10000	38780
东城街道	280	405	316	71	10081	238		
万江街道	122	125	16	4				
南城街道			1050	80	11706			
中堂镇	4005	6596	42	8				5699
望牛墩镇	3200	6226	8	1				
麻涌镇	14537	17288						
石碣镇			50	15				
高埗镇								
道滘镇	966	2415						
洪梅镇	1526	2081	40	4				
沙田镇(虎门港)	1437	1833	50	7	484			
厚街镇	1295	1628	25042	1050	50861		160	1752
长安镇			4700	875	18204	180		283
寮步镇	20	59	2200	155	11500			
大岭山镇			9000	180	49280	57	1494	3769
大朗镇	30	22	15987	500	27257			
黄江镇			13140	60	72361	500	24702	14200
樟木头镇			4470	90	52806	500		
清溪镇			11934	65	67731	500	2193	5243
塘厦镇			10537	450	33644	12	3296	4600
凤岗镇			6528	433	39084			
谢岗镇	610	834	13000	154	58448			
常平镇	86	55	6875	122	22527	1000		
桥头镇	420	138	680	18	6085			
横沥镇	280	655	2780	347	4594		20100	31238
东坑镇	170	640	1128	33	3128			
企石镇	1200	695	1741	118	9726			8060
石排镇	526	958	115	14	1168		518	1315
茶山镇	155	238	2930	230	6900			

注：林业用地面积、当年种植面积指标采用林业局数据。

14–11 续表 2

(2016年)

镇　　街	三鸟年末存栏量(只)	三鸟出栏量(只)	畜牧总肉量(吨)	#猪肉	禽蛋产量(吨)	淡水养殖面积(亩)	水产品产量(吨)	#淡水产量
石龙镇						101	93	93
虎门镇	107100	614770	3426	2686	1	10920	7303	3744
东城街道	8800	8090	10			1320	626	626
万江街道	950	1971	3			1605	1605	1605
南城街道		1947	2					
中堂镇	500	39262	488	413		3525	2018	2018
望牛墩镇	3850	7860	9			1567	1036	1036
麻涌镇						2820	1591	1591
石碣镇						930	594	594
高埗镇						1710	810	810
道滘镇		21080	26			6435	4368	4368
洪梅镇	4486	4787	6			5512	2811	2811
沙田镇（虎门港）	58320	481660	680		14	16287	10762	6619
厚街镇	5000	8332	137	127		5430	1891	1891
长安镇	10870	6244	29	21			115	
寮步镇						1605	803	803
大岭山镇	30000	30000	310	254		765	179	179
大朗镇	16011	45278	62		23	1429	756	756
黄江镇	9500	14100	1110	1066		4635	502	502
樟木头镇	4080	31956	38					
清溪镇	13529	15201	411	392				
塘厦镇	243959	518234	968	345		2700	977	977
凤岗镇		590	1			195	146	146
谢岗镇	101560	471390	700			11385	6239	6239
常平镇	98000	1008300	1081		224	4110	930	930
桥头镇	3000	10986	13		12	3705	2237	2237
横沥镇	34500	53970	2431	2364	9	2289	1442	1442
东坑镇	10971	20880	25			330	110	110
企石镇		51800	659	561		1472	915	915
石排镇	6000	5118	103	97	29	7000	3177	3177
茶山镇	13500	79000	209			2175	2587	2587

14-12 镇街农业主要物质消耗（2016年）

Main Material Consumption of Agriculture by Town (2016)

镇　街	农　村 用 电 量 (万千瓦时)	化肥施用 实 物 量 (吨)	农　药 使用量 (吨)
石 龙 镇	1909		
虎 门 镇	486107	1431	54
东城街道	64089	108	1
万江街道	86200	743	31
南城街道	37848	47	2
中 堂 镇	153021	1599	39
望牛墩镇	87493	384	10
麻 涌 镇	13803	1225	22
石 碣 镇	184316	554	19
高 埗 镇	129250	274	3
道 滘 镇	110376	926	49
洪 梅 镇	1509	510	15
沙田镇（虎门港）	61461	1372	75
厚 街 镇	337265	1640	79
长 安 镇	643749	330	3
寮 步 镇	31627	301	7
大岭山镇	27728	822	16
大 朗 镇	328174	776	35
黄 江 镇	12509	178	24
樟木头镇	101602	196	14
清 溪 镇	294165	1419	70
塘 厦 镇	463871	2802	31
凤 岗 镇	299634	436	8
谢 岗 镇	5210	1557	35
常 平 镇	301172	640	16
桥 头 镇	136530	708	7
横 沥 镇	131796	395	5
东 坑 镇	61308	205	5
企 石 镇	100224	635	1
石 排 镇	17365	620	28
茶 山 镇	165523	665	7

14-13 镇街农村集体（经联社、经济社两级合计）经济收益分配（2016年）

Income Distribution of Rural Economy by Town（2016）

单位：万元

镇　街	经营总收入	经营总费用	经营纯收入
全　市	1903450	673615	1229835
莞城街道	20102	5047	15055
石 龙 镇	20304	8797	11507
虎 门 镇	187164	63771	123394
东城街道	117397	42560	74837
万江街道	54902	20984	33918
南城街道	79018	24363	54655
中 堂 镇	77626	17742	59884
望牛墩镇	11217	3571	7646
麻 涌 镇	23429	7684	15746
石 碣 镇	73122	28551	44571
高 埗 镇	26338	8719	17619
道 滘 镇	26866	9299	17567
洪 梅 镇	6460	2654	3806
沙田镇（虎门港）	30897	11555	19342
厚 街 镇	131030	57547	73483
长 安 镇	184656	54368	130289
寮 步 镇	99586	41641	57944
大岭山镇	50145	13854	36291
大 朗 镇	89556	38066	51490
黄 江 镇	28282	8450	19832
樟木头镇	25215	13893	11323
清 溪 镇	63036	23011	40025
塘 厦 镇	87846	23321	64524
凤 岗 镇	88993	22683	66310
谢 岗 镇	18272	3467	14804
常 平 镇	81135	31447	49688
桥 头 镇	37311	14412	22898
横 沥 镇	30694	14731	15963
东 坑 镇	28213	10593	17620
企 石 镇	20861	9848	11013
石 排 镇	37218	16020	21197
茶 山 镇	46561	20965	25596

14-14 镇街规模以上工业企业主要经济指标（2016年）

Main Indicators of Industrial Enterprises above Designated Size by Town (2016)

单位：万元

镇 街	企业单位数（个）	亏损企业	工业销售产值	工业增加值
莞城街道	32	6	1094398	292584
石 龙 镇	51	9	2079320	440245
虎 门 镇	352	33	4950039	1476607
东城街道	271	31	3876315	1183104
万江街道	95	14	972517	262814
南城街道	55	9	1188911	351073
中 堂 镇	131	18	2420944	513963
望牛墩镇	94	10	996758	239185
麻 涌 镇	99	22	5456645	1067368
石 碣 镇	152	16	4526212	894577
高 埗 镇	149	28	2662750	813492
道 滘 镇	130	13	1531200	358870
洪 梅 镇	50	9	1883357	397041
沙田镇（虎门港）	126	12	1833283	411547
厚 街 镇	329	50	8101555	1483517
长 安 镇	304	52	20215262	3055689
寮 步 镇	297	46	4666809	1148631
大岭山镇	223	30	4714368	887711
大 朗 镇	352	38	3830979	934039
黄 江 镇	156	23	3189453	676979
樟木头镇	96	13	1354826	367035
清 溪 镇	306	46	5453355	1232620
塘 厦 镇	351	53	6334699	1595495
凤 岗 镇	257	31	3859518	1076377
谢 岗 镇	109	18	1107545	281671
常 平 镇	262	35	3933008	903662
桥 头 镇	198	21	3595206	674264
横 沥 镇	161	17	1898215	485801
东 坑 镇	125	17	3168760	774834
企 石 镇	134	16	1231306	313860
石 排 镇	142	14	1328272	373629
茶 山 镇	176	30	1997820	527735
松 山 湖	99	24	22116152	2605686

14-14 续表 1

(2016年)

单位：万元

镇　　街	资产总额	#流动资产	固定资产净值	负债总额
莞城街道	1026088	524755	333758	560832
石 龙 镇	1619186	1221827	161690	827893
虎 门 镇	4866690	3506259	943157	2577036
东城街道	3583745	2282967	1038317	1995740
万江街道	862910	656081	163790	565921
南城街道	1406669	929663	315163	563660
中 堂 镇	2106607	1202117	632597	1367275
望牛墩镇	826908	549288	199427	473800
麻 涌 镇	5749637	2980272	2019935	3005341
石 碣 镇	2796824	2134776	508474	1694684
高 埗 镇	2000257	1404449	462965	1231110
道 滘 镇	1609288	1106870	240412	661867
洪 梅 镇	2152520	1375221	664821	940543
沙田镇（虎门港）	1275867	792411	367461	651832
厚 街 镇	4405818	3469085	624861	2315353
长 安 镇	10590173	8394404	1371104	7893005
寮 步 镇	3504053	2571986	640241	1994768
大岭山镇	3947481	3163986	530892	2791148
大 朗 镇	3401828	2663015	482410	2256413
黄 江 镇	2211091	1516167	569556	1247717
樟木头镇	1032820	728585	224280	615410
清 溪 镇	4558377	3408197	885290	2526097
塘 厦 镇	4662429	3500413	841964	2481454
凤 岗 镇	3654483	2380243	1077696	1926239
谢 岗 镇	857801	604481	171297	556767
常 平 镇	3181282	2387883	591721	1510450
桥 头 镇	2388944	1844905	381995	1594252
横 沥 镇	1854818	1154460	400544	1092847
东 坑 镇	1892871	1282274	440764	1181917
企 石 镇	992597	806366	150735	639068
石 排 镇	1015629	660871	219026	578674
茶 山 镇	1496800	1090342	305495	795165
松 山 湖	14047668	11262044	1305427	10976141

14－14 续表 2

（2016年）

单位：万元

镇　街	主营业务收入	主营业务税金及附加	利润总额	本年应交增值税	全部从业人员平均人数（人）
莞城街道	1104092	5524	84180	29288	13418
石龙镇	2091048	8461	132391	27015	29409
虎门镇	5001503	22774	295788	102715	155349
东城街道	3914218	31308	282330	111282	98445
万江街道	978051	5982	31719	20598	29908
南城街道	1189239	7068	94594	30832	24229
中堂镇	2504395	11770	80666	107844	29608
望牛墩镇	1000589	3658	52077	25667	18662
麻涌镇	6371060	13618	276460	109550	37702
石碣镇	4484185	15027	144917	56424	88609
高埗镇	2699611	10092	78848	22596	85150
道滘镇	1546375	6658	76429	34416	27635
洪梅镇	1857065	2603	114785	34093	20053
沙田镇（虎门港）	1814297	5506	56359	25734	32479
厚街镇	8184149	22532	313935	80581	161602
长安镇	23708196	25382	221256	643986	250579
寮步镇	4682181	14976	121650	57030	111143
大岭山镇	4665972	13989	118763	77415	86300
大朗镇	3715314	15350	138434	75430	89570
黄江镇	2889167	12335	79428	50157	75517
樟木头镇	1365720	5404	93992	21716	31755
清溪镇	5336300	17680	140550	46393	142200
塘厦镇	6227746	24898	212962	77906	179628
凤岗镇	3714234	13248	138124	92141	113485
谢岗镇	1053053	4264	29724	20563	28449
常平镇	3769416	13827	127851	44697	105160
桥头镇	3747786	9324	92348	31214	63723
横沥镇	1896218	7239	93954	13011	55116
东坑镇	3177832	10243	83173	46442	76773
企石镇	1230175	5747	28263	29761	33751
石排镇	1406732	6267	30520	31762	53718
茶山镇	1938685	8017	52924	35340	47711
松山湖	23666807	65218	725876	250050	90450

14-15 镇街规模以上工业企业主要经济效益指标（2016年）

Main Indicators on Economic Benefit of Industrial Enterprises above Designated Size by Town (2016)

镇　街	工业增加值率 (%)	总资产贡献率 (%)	资产负债率 (%)	流动资产周转率 (次/年)	成本费用利润率 (%)	全员劳动生产率 (元/人)	产品销售率 (%)
莞城街道	26.7	12.8	54.7	2.1	8.2	218053	100.0
石龙镇	20.6	10.4	51.1	1.7	6.7	149697	97.5
虎门镇	27.2	8.8	53.0	1.5	6.1	95051	91.1
东城街道	29.6	12.4	55.7	1.7	7.7	120179	96.8
万江街道	25.7	7.7	65.6	1.5	3.4	87874	95.2
南城街道	27.4	9.5	40.1	1.3	8.6	144898	92.8
中堂镇	20.9	11.2	64.9	2.1	3.3	173589	98.5
望牛墩镇	24.0	10.5	57.3	1.8	5.5	128167	100.2
麻涌镇	19.9	7.5	52.3	2.2	4.3	283107	101.6
石碣镇	19.5	7.9	60.6	2.1	3.3	100958	98.7
高埗镇	30.1	6.0	61.5	1.9	3.0	95536	98.7
道滘镇	23.4	8.0	41.1	1.4	5.2	129861	99.7
洪梅镇	19.0	6.9	43.7	1.4	6.5	197996	90.0
沙田镇（虎门港）	21.5	7.7	51.1	2.3	3.2	126712	95.6
厚街镇	18.2	9.8	52.6	2.4	4.0	91801	99.5
长安镇	14.6	8.5	74.5	2.9	0.9	121945	96.8
寮步镇	24.9	5.9	56.9	1.8	2.7	103347	101.1
大岭山镇	18.6	6.5	70.7	1.5	2.6	102863	99.0
大朗镇	23.3	7.2	66.3	1.4	3.9	104280	95.6
黄江镇	20.6	6.6	56.4	1.9	2.8	89646	97.2
樟木头镇	27.0	12.5	59.6	1.9	7.4	115584	99.7
清溪镇	21.9	4.8	55.4	1.6	2.7	86682	97.0
塘厦镇	24.2	6.6	53.2	1.8	3.5	88822	96.1
凤岗镇	26.3	7.2	52.7	1.6	3.8	94847	94.3
谢岗镇	23.4	6.7	64.9	1.7	2.9	99009	91.9
常平镇	22.6	6.1	47.5	1.6	3.5	85932	98.2
桥头镇	18.9	5.5	66.7	2.0	2.5	105812	101.0
横沥镇	24.9	6.6	58.9	1.7	5.2	88141	97.3
东坑镇	24.8	7.6	62.4	2.5	2.7	100925	101.4
企石镇	24.6	7.3	64.4	1.5	2.3	92993	96.6
石排镇	27.5	7.3	57.0	2.1	2.2	69554	97.8
茶山镇	25.2	7.0	53.1	1.8	2.8	110611	95.2
松山湖	11.6	7.2	78.1	2.2	3.0	288080	98.5

14-16 镇街规模以上工业企业R&D人员情况（2016年）

R&D Personnel of Industrial Enterprises above Designated Size by Town (2016)

镇街	有R&D活动的工业企业数（个）	R&D人员合计（人）	#参加项目人员	#女性	#研究人员	#全时人员	非全时人员
全市	1709	64963	61620	12971	14562	51161	13802
莞城街道	14	555	493	93	195	454	101
石龙镇	29	1541	1515	427	258	1268	273
虎门镇	86	2635	2242	440	634	1889	746
东城街道	98	3694	3604	747	769	2671	1023
万江街道	42	1584	1534	236	280	1270	314
南城街道	22	656	626	115	121	439	217
中堂镇	38	888	833	137	162	591	297
望牛墩镇	26	618	588	117	142	509	109
麻涌镇	43	1781	1708	255	448	1338	443
石碣镇	45	4084	3841	917	1001	3334	750
高埗镇	46	962	956	244	191	854	108
道滘镇	23	529	527	80	147	423	106
洪梅镇	19	1149	1141	226	167	850	299
沙田镇（虎门港）	45	1151	1119	250	177	854	297
厚街镇	47	2059	2052	463	449	1715	344
长安镇	97	4232	4093	825	611	3298	934
寮步镇	103	4319	4050	1035	1083	3625	694
大岭山镇	60	1627	1581	241	355	1344	283
大朗镇	98	2678	2562	508	486	2098	580
黄江镇	58	1737	1683	302	279	1374	363
樟木头镇	21	629	579	134	132	465	164
清溪镇	82	3241	2842	773	766	2730	511
塘厦镇	93	4963	4637	1098	1222	3904	1059
凤岗镇	56	2291	2153	482	399	1771	520
谢岗镇	41	991	920	195	144	842	149
常平镇	59	1702	1611	339	286	1387	315
桥头镇	32	873	832	172	158	635	238
横沥镇	55	1227	1190	168	201	1009	218
东坑镇	33	1056	958	224	254	755	301
企石镇	46	1463	1428	236	341	1053	410
石排镇	37	1033	975	251	172	800	233
茶山镇	37	940	896	181	172	698	242
松山湖	78	6075	5851	1060	2360	4914	1161

14-17 镇街规模以上工业企业R&D人员全时当量情况（2016年）

R&D Personnel Full-time-equivalent of Industrial Enterprises above Designated Size by Town (2016)

镇 街	有R&D活动的工业企业数（个）	R&D人员全时当量（人年）	#研究人员	#应用研究人员	#试验发展人员
全 市	1709	48209	11133	22	48187
莞城街道	14	406	142		406
石龙镇	29	1097	196	3	1095
虎门镇	86	1990	487		1990
东城街道	98	2698	578	4	2695
万江街道	42	1068	197		1068
南城街道	22	430	88		430
中堂镇	38	495	90		495
望牛墩镇	26	522	114		522
麻涌镇	43	1343	358		1343
石碣镇	45	3417	834		3417
高埗镇	46	802	164		802
道滘镇	23	416	119		416
洪梅镇	19	621	88	10	611
沙田镇（虎门港）	45	908	134		908
厚街镇	47	1622	361		1622
长安镇	97	3074	477		3074
寮步镇	103	3167	777	6	3161
大岭山镇	60	1179	268		1179
大朗镇	98	1975	364		1975
黄江镇	58	1298	205		1298
樟木头镇	21	464	104		464
清溪镇	82	2278	534		2278
塘厦镇	93	4027	1012		4027
凤岗镇	56	1481	278		1481
谢岗镇	41	746	106		746
常平镇	59	1203	199		1203
桥头镇	32	634	112		634
横沥镇	55	900	142		900
东坑镇	33	765	179		765
企石镇	46	1011	249		1011
石排镇	37	765	121		765
茶山镇	37	584	101		584
松山湖	78	4822	1955		4822

14−18 镇街规模以上工业企业R&D经费情况（2016年）

The R&D Funds of Industrial Enterprises above Designated Size by Town (2016)

镇　街	R&D经费支出合计（万元）	按活动类型分组			按资金来源分组			
		基础研究支出	应用研究支出	试验发展支出	政府资金	企业资金	境外资金	其他资金
全　市	1434038		1086	1432952	18231	1365448	26395	23965
莞城街道	15221			15221		11984		3236
石龙镇	33290		207	33083	666	29149		3475
虎门镇	63243			63243	257	60746	1999	242
东城街道	74465		122	74343	1627	71832		1006
万江街道	17601			17601	338	17026		237
南城街道	20411			20411	480	19901		29
中堂镇	19156			19156	685	17999		472
望牛墩镇	11214			11214		10949		265
麻涌镇	60225			60225	248	59945		33
石碣镇	65653			65653		65511	126	17
高埗镇	18181			18181	130	18051		
道滘镇	13186			13186	256	12930		
洪梅镇	19712		715	18997	80	19632		
沙田镇（虎门港）	20883			20883	136	20291		456
厚街镇	43965			43965	171	21060	22107	628
长安镇	62181			62181	1584	60352		245
寮步镇	67801		42	67759	1648	65371		782
大岭山镇	31412			31412	472	30707		233
大朗镇	44518			44518	1493	42563		462
黄江镇	31590			31590	235	28498	136	2722
樟木头镇	8157			8157	37	7989		132
清溪镇	47121			47121	1191	42106		3825
塘厦镇	80363			80363	116	79296	101	851
凤岗镇	33712			33712	652	31644		1416
谢岗镇	16646			16646	7	15339	850	450
常平镇	34763			34763	170	32552	1076	964
桥头镇	21676			21676		21439		238
横沥镇	18933			18933	928	17955		50
东坑镇	20181			20181	51	20130		
企石镇	16432			16432	4	16178		250
石排镇	14102			14102	65	13858		179
茶山镇	17367			17367	240	17127		
松山湖	370677			370677	4264	365341		1072

14-18 续表

(2016年)

镇　街	按使用项目分		委托外单位开展研发的经费支出合计(万元)	对境内研究机构支出	对境内高等院校支出	对境内企业支出	对境外支出
	经常性支出	资产性支出					
全　市	1295452	138586	601288	522990	1760	26272	50265
莞城街道	13644	1576	240	140	100		
石龙镇	25988	7302	7861	67	20	7653	120
虎门镇	60233	3010	112	27	80	4	
东城街道	65317	9149	117	1	5	111	
万江街道	16022	1579	83	36	38	6	2
南城街道	14832	5579					
中堂镇	15929	3227	8	2		6	
望牛墩镇	10217	997					
麻涌镇	55453	4772	399	138	6	254	
石碣镇	62120	3533	154	22	88	43	
高埗镇	16826	1356	22	17	5		
道滘镇	12118	1068	87		59	28	
洪梅镇	17900	1812	244	150		94	
沙田镇（虎门港）	18848	2034	23	0.1	14	9	
厚街镇	41939	2026	2	2		0.1	
长安镇	57480	4701	510		499	11	
寮步镇	62891	4910	378	14	23	341	
大岭山镇	24799	6613	79	13	1	65	
大朗镇	39447	5071	316	2	16	298	
黄江镇	27530	4060	4			4	
樟木头镇	7318	839	7		7		
清溪镇	41526	5595	213	50	81	82	
塘厦镇	76377	3987	343	103	178	12	49
凤岗镇	32536	1176	72		24	48	
谢岗镇	15192	1454	45	45			
常平镇	31536	3226	90	32	59		
桥头镇	20173	1503	22	18	4		
横沥镇	17278	1656	76	35	19	22	
东坑镇	18433	1748	23	0.1	23		
企石镇	15019	1413	1			1	
石排镇	11831	2271	9			9	
茶山镇	14769	2598	260		24	236	
松山湖	333929	36747	589492	522076	386	16936	50093

14-19 镇街规模以上工业企业全部R&D项目情况（2016年）

Basic Statistics on R&D Projects of Industrial Enterprises above Designated Size by Town (2016)

镇　街	项目数（个）	项目人员折合全时当量（人年）	全部项目经费内部支出（万元）
全　市	5812	45237	1361758
莞城街道	64	350	14216
石 龙 镇	132	1077	32135
虎 门 镇	217	1682	59727
东城街道	384	2599	69896
万江街道	140	1020	16946
南城街道	79	398	18940
中 堂 镇	118	455	19024
望牛墩镇	98	496	10829
麻 涌 镇	150	1268	59087
石 碣 镇	192	3165	64237
高 埗 镇	138	787	17775
道 滘 镇	110	401	12234
洪 梅 镇	101	608	18750
沙田镇（虎门港）	148	880	19788
厚 街 镇	156	1584	42932
长 安 镇	324	2919	60787
寮 步 镇	412	2950	65660
大岭山镇	181	1130	29467
大 朗 镇	280	1855	42471
黄 江 镇	188	1242	30399
樟木头镇	53	418	7674
清 溪 镇	252	2048	44340
塘 厦 镇	327	3699	78896
凤 岗 镇	194	1364	33138
谢 岗 镇	132	680	15580
常 平 镇	161	1121	32514
桥 头 镇	107	605	21147
横 沥 镇	162	873	18494
东 坑 镇	93	684	19543
企 石 镇	126	967	15577
石 排 镇	97	712	13534
茶 山 镇	126	557	17051
松 山 湖	370	4643	338974

14-20 镇街规模以上工业企业办科技机构情况（2016年）

Basic Statistics on Scientific and Technological Institutions of Industrial Enterprises above Designated Size by Town (2016)

镇街	有研发机构的工业企业数（个）	机构数（个）	机构人员合计（人）	#博士毕业	#硕士毕业	机构经费支出（万元）
全市	2004	2264	98662	619	3889	1966566
莞城街道	12	13	570	2	17	10800
石龙镇	32	32	1800	7	38	39781
虎门镇	121	127	5273	19	92	103165
东城街道	101	107	4461	26	209	83463
万江街道	48	54	2071	16	40	24096
南城街道	22	26	684	2	28	16418
中堂镇	43	45	771	5	29	22600
望牛墩镇	30	32	1112	4	17	18576
麻涌镇	50	58	3250	14	90	97088
石碣镇	48	58	4976	9	61	57884
高埗镇	60	60	2166	11	41	37335
道滘镇	33	33	900	8	47	18207
洪梅镇	21	25	1615	7	17	31018
沙田镇（虎门港）	51	52	1702	13	41	31877
厚街镇	64	73	2419	5	72	51754
长安镇	86	91	4659	31	140	72180
寮步镇	122	126	5448	37	103	82441
大岭山镇	58	58	2738	19	73	63437
大朗镇	108	118	3662	27	91	67381
黄江镇	69	77	3002	20	65	47650
樟木头镇	32	44	943	3	15	17692
清溪镇	100	125	6992	32	94	88668
塘厦镇	120	143	9007	36	268	125592
凤岗镇	73	86	4243	8	99	62453
谢岗镇	42	44	1088	7	24	21588
常平镇	77	82	3060	16	48	56159
桥头镇	44	46	1846	9	26	37690
横沥镇	76	78	2444	11	52	35968
东坑镇	48	58	2393	18	304	49598
企石镇	58	65	1591	11	26	22124
石排镇	56	62	1957	11	36	29862
茶山镇	43	47	1398	4	24	23096
松山湖	56	119	8421	171	1562	418926

14-21 镇街规模以上工业企业高新技术产品情况（2016年）

Basic Statistics on High-tech Products of Industrial Enterprises above Designated Size by Town (2016)

镇街	生产高新技术产品企业数（家）	高新产品个数（个）	高新产品产值（万元）	高新产品销售收入（万元）	#高新产品出口销售收入	高新产品实现利税（万元）
全 市	1551	3148	68986201	68180721	23729337	2960230
莞城街道	9	15	639203	639878	49443	96026
石 龙 镇	19	26	1698787	1653261	1230479	93788
虎 门 镇	80	165	1756803	1674644	590270	62587
东城街道	76	200	726935	704815	165266	50060
万江街道	33	66	260220	256921	83209	15654
南城街道	18	37	210690	205105	52674	32612
中 堂 镇	23	46	307228	307454	39875	31754
望牛墩镇	40	66	304828	308642	81964	19620
麻 涌 镇	24	77	1834137	1810629	244762	179068
石 碣 镇	42	85	2200141	2060193	1458766	74379
高 埗 镇	38	57	721482	725454	266504	41822
道 滘 镇	32	68	500447	504686	50959	26391
洪 梅 镇	14	34	655535	659152	214390	87996
沙田镇（虎门港）	33	73	734246	698117	170726	39607
厚 街 镇	39	75	3404883	3390913	3133248	214423
长 安 镇	87	195	14856276	14697219	1227442	118585
寮 步 镇	106	157	2731027	2767512	2139458	81705
大岭山镇	65	135	2792287	2757881	1059912	138020
大 朗 镇	59	112	1021684	981899	270795	58816
黄 江 镇	50	104	1012997	964527	647444	63598
樟木头镇	14	37	137714	138364	78466	9441
清 溪 镇	86	190	1967721	1939577	1061882	50016
塘 厦 镇	106	195	2066793	1996698	1091469	128232
凤 岗 镇	51	115	738340	727015	229280	56545
谢 岗 镇	22	33	309057	265878	92996	22584
常 平 镇	110	182	1585765	1462178	1109044	62269
桥 头 镇	34	83	1794039	1783554	1584397	31559
横 沥 镇	50	101	699527	672521	267950	37333
东 坑 镇	27	69	601557	601605	278023	27634
企 石 镇	26	50	233346	229257	90017	11306
石 排 镇	19	50	287490	272449	24923	49801
茶 山 镇	48	97	827719	774648	326411	45511
松 山 湖	71	153	19367297	19548074	4316895	901488

14-22 镇街固定资产投资总额（2016年）

Total Investment in Fixed Assets by Town (2016)

单位：万元

镇街	固定资产投资	#第二产业	#工业	第三产业	#房地产开发投资	#民营
莞城街道	238416	75117	75117	163299	124956	144518
石龙镇	209909	57107	57107	152802	137903	94596
虎门镇	1208987	289343	289343	919644	755022	929750
东城街道	643268	202728	192728	440540	237086	437226
万江街道	282049	72477	72477	209572	186350	197941
南城街道	595479	91345	91345	504134	485477	478641
中堂镇	161264	26346	26346	131881	78614	142256
望牛墩镇	137572	56942	56942	80630	17675	128189
麻涌镇	667773	281191	281191	384018	235216	391375
石碣镇	262695	118232	118232	144463	131801	183256
高埗镇	157979	80426	80426	77553	73581	92475
道滘镇	218613	60649	60649	152384	140574	213070
洪梅镇	160483	50675	50675	109808		50609
沙田镇（虎门港）	514244	57693	57693	456551	250769	330697
厚街镇	562544	152304	152304	410240	310520	335455
长安镇	655261	450534	450534	204727	78333	380859
寮步镇	552002	97153	97153	454849	435053	474028
大岭山镇	361391	145256	145256	216135	203297	276956
大朗镇	559672	188311	188311	371361	206497	457295
黄江镇	387249	117792	117792	269457	260187	215701
樟木头镇	253152	97819	97819	155333	143022	219759
清溪镇	625103	295321	295321	328832	265621	502801
塘厦镇	729394	170759	170759	558635	507163	595105
凤岗镇	779867	160184	160184	619683	495651	635609
谢岗镇	182563	145333	145333	37230		126154
常平镇	558906	179573	179573	379333	240115	504847
桥头镇	292925	196107	196107	96818	94549	194070
横沥镇	195884	90541	90541	105343	99485	139036
东坑镇	241325	205905	205905	35420	32518	115496
企石镇	179291	109034	109034	70257	16567	163791
石排镇	253059	171398	171398	80447	19505	217167
茶山镇	334686	119317	119317	215369	53209	222614
松山湖	1184702	729896	729896	454806	146947	1019170

14-23 镇街邮电局、所通信能力及服务网点（2015-2016年）

Communication Capacity and Service Establishments of Telecommunication Offices by Town (2015-2016)

镇　街	邮电局（所、综合营业厅）(处)		服务网点（含报刊亭）(处)		固定电话用户 (户)	
	2016年	2015年	2016年	2015年	2016年	2015年
全　市	787	797	9455	7728	2447838	2610440
市　区	80	82	1263	1484	468838	528307
石龙镇	13	16	70	95	78375	79177
虎门镇	52	58	845	528	185796	196498
中堂镇	22	16	123	139	43850	47114
望牛墩镇	14	13	92	82	21499	23149
麻涌镇	9	11	99	33	28354	30133
石碣镇	19	17	299	286	64237	66531
高埗镇	20	16	120	113	37937	40563
道滘镇	9	13	85	108	40623	42224
洪梅镇	8	8	44	77	15612	14866
沙田镇（虎门港）	16	17	142	126	38628	42852
厚街镇	41	41	734	190	145188	151242
长安镇	55	55	901	602	169168	178857
寮步镇	24	24	484	352	100524	102122
大岭山镇	29	31	140	231	68847	72802
大朗镇	29	31	364	305	113204	121153
黄江镇	25	28	263	234	59060	63395
樟木头镇	20	23	309	165	62930	65369
清溪镇	25	28	495	399	72047	73927
塘厦镇	46	46	473	422	114098	121641
凤岗镇	36	34	327	255	74653	77961
谢岗镇	12	10	107	96	28637	30837
常平镇	43	47	458	385	131306	141549
桥头镇	26	24	271	222	50527	50368
横沥镇	25	25	250	182	45551	51718
东坑镇	19	15	217	150	31387	32520
企石镇	14	17	134	84	38465	40942
石排镇	19	17	175	186	52217	52413
茶山镇	32	30	163	188	48450	51688
松山湖	5	7	8	9	17829	18524

注：市区指莞城、南城、东城、万江四个街道。

14-24 镇街商贸情况（2016年）

Statistics on Commerce by Town (2016)

单位：万元

镇　街	社会消费品零售总额	限额以上批发和零售业销售额	限额以上住宿和餐饮业营业额
莞城街道	1160089	2578104	28048
石 龙 镇	411915	172731	13613
虎 门 镇	2091339	1159687	87046
东城街道	1387678	2932296	97251
万江街道	591275	705347	28484
南城街道	2061833	5516532	103898
中 堂 镇	317682	466922	13982
望牛墩镇	110489	165876	1767
麻 涌 镇	1258534	3025223	4060
石 碣 镇	418563	285365	16556
高 埗 镇	268880	264494	10902
道 滘 镇	196673	310108	5850
洪 梅 镇	65888	68682	3566
沙田镇（虎门港）	297515	3188500	10504
厚 街 镇	1671340	1299133	88448
长 安 镇	1342400	3825917	49946
寮 步 镇	2724688	3159152	39640
大岭山镇	660821	356316	12806
大 朗 镇	884183	987509	29428
黄 江 镇	416062	333059	6013
樟木头镇	629563	1022133	18491
清 溪 镇	525373	240229	13890
塘 厦 镇	1004046	479877	47376
凤 岗 镇	529156	335715	17169
谢 岗 镇	137561	118263	1967
常 平 镇	1301944	859032	37884
桥 头 镇	295365	101789	14674
横 沥 镇	283148	210339	6844
东 坑 镇	193659	122254	4836
企 石 镇	177404	65513	3991
石 排 镇	266135	138910	5813
茶 山 镇	345011	260418	8381
松 山 湖	55773	628829	29568

14–25 镇街注册工商企业及个体户数（2016年）

Registered Industrial & Commercial Enterprises and Self-employed Individuals by Town (2016)

单位：户

镇　街	总户数	#内资企业	外商投资企业	三来一补	私营企业	个体户
全　市	840367	18854	12614	1386	296005	510754
莞城街道	21486	749	238	4	8314	12146
石 龙 镇	13327	268	115	5	2290	10641
虎 门 镇	75398	1202	739	50	23575	49800
东城街道	57780	1659	717	39	22468	32819
万江街道	27554	508	206	8	11027	15799
南城街道	50821	2185	659	12	29437	18414
中 堂 镇	14860	300	109	15	3504	10921
望牛墩镇	4665	149	104	4	1273	3130
麻 涌 镇	8506	346	86	6	1730	6316
石 碣 镇	21133	324	252	29	6131	14388
高 埗 镇	12604	214	158	6	3557	8661
道 滘 镇	10044	233	176	8	3304	6316
洪 梅 镇	3359	109	89	1	790	2364
沙田镇（虎门港）	12127	438	249	6	3538	7880
厚 街 镇	43226	787	637	35	13759	27956
长 安 镇	73711	1165	1174	200	32501	38587
寮 步 镇	41151	766	467	14	14278	25610
大岭山镇	28926	527	364	23	10576	17418
大 朗 镇	42377	585	472	60	11443	29804
黄 江 镇	19883	430	370	38	7260	11763
樟木头镇	19737	390	247	20	7314	11747
清 溪 镇	22881	397	610	101	7576	14185
塘 厦 镇	44098	777	963	175	17805	24362
凤 岗 镇	26123	589	608	157	8675	16088
谢 岗 镇	8037	170	232	35	2071	5514
常 平 镇	39064	865	716	120	13734	23558
桥 头 镇	15252	310	337	42	4130	10428
横 沥 镇	18762	390	405	52	5523	12367
东 坑 镇	10536	268	182	15	3443	6623
企 石 镇	11878	270	198	29	2910	8467
石 排 镇	18185	309	243	40	4507	13080
茶 山 镇	18328	349	270	37	4681	12987
松 山 湖	4548	826	222		2881	615

注：本表数据来源于市工商局。

14-26 镇街集市贸易市场数及私营个体户注册资金额（2015-2016年）

Fair Trades and Registered Capital of Private Enterprises & Self-employed Individuals by Town (2015-2016)

镇街	集市贸易市场数（个）		个体工商户注册资金额（万元）		私营企业注册资金额（万元）	
	2016年	2015年	2016年	2015年	2016年	2015年
全　市	390	816	1471722	1255162	66699226	41544668
莞城街道	9	21	30460	26641	6040719	5235530
石龙镇	6	16	24565	21339	387582	230791
虎门镇	37	76	137424	115875	4027429	2430795
东城街道	25	58	81219	69681	6954210	4204008
万江街道	23	35	40896	35955	2323855	1432103
南城街道	21	31	57082	46390	11368623	7562325
中堂镇	9	21	33768	31782	558919	310564
望牛墩镇	4	6	10407	9069	294149	200262
麻涌镇	8	14	18791	14781	417750	201288
石碣镇	13	25	41516	35875	676470	319382
高埗镇	11	21	26159	23093	767545	396032
道滘镇	3	13	18219	16260	1071834	434896
洪梅镇	3	4	6608	5900	236820	106511
沙田镇（虎门港）	10	19	21731	18511	715777	1658528
厚街镇	16	58	78189	66878	2418365	1658528
长安镇	19	38	100209	83550	4320794	2780892
寮步镇	8	41	66651	54954	2732243	1646701
大岭山镇	10	19	48402	42673	1580776	946812
大朗镇	12	32	109955	85362	1902992	1212678
黄江镇	7	23	35360	29829	1307820	531225
樟木头镇	12	26	32711	29263	1219251	584227
清溪镇	14	21	43748	36341	1086708	596503
塘厦镇	22	30	59598	49656	2916403	1827543
凤岗镇	12	16	47355	41066	943578	584630
谢岗镇	8	8	22182	19199	156597	42810
常平镇	21	42	81372	71890	2838205	1517957
桥头镇	6	17	31176	27937	639953	385712
横沥镇	7	18	38207	33340	789648	416931
东坑镇	3	14	19989	17483	531349	130969
企石镇	9	9	30177	25778	446434	241580
石排镇	9	18	38280	34046	470821	245800
茶山镇	11	24	34468	30716	627309	369114
松山湖	2	2	4847	4047	3928300	1101041

注：本表数据来源于市工商局；2016年起，按统计标准剔除部分不符合要求的集贸市场数据。

14−27 镇街来料加工装配签约宗数、出口值及引进设备价值（2016年）

Contracts of Processing and Assembling of Import Materials, Export Value and Value of Equipments Imported by Town (2016)

镇　　街	累计投产宗数（宗）	出口值（万元）	引进设备价值（万元）
莞城街道	8	706	
石 龙 镇	4	1724	
虎 门 镇	57	4625	
东城街道	33	34964	2167
万江街道	7	3627	10
南城街道	12	2706	
中 堂 镇	9	1026	0.2
望牛墩镇	2		
麻 涌 镇	2		
石 碣 镇	28	5477	
高 埗 镇	2		
道 滘 镇	5	4256	8
洪 梅 镇	1		
沙田镇（虎门港）	1		
厚 街 镇	22	24493	
长 安 镇	162	1299718	3363
寮 步 镇	32	943	
大岭山镇	17	102162	77
大 朗 镇	34	5662	
黄 江 镇	32	519315	165
樟木头镇	30	6648	
清 溪 镇	73	97591	16
塘 厦 镇	126	117803	37
凤 岗 镇	70	27297	12
谢 岗 镇	22	22668	
常 平 镇	56	3413	
桥 头 镇	23	8547	17
横 沥 镇	35	16581	
东 坑 镇	7	4977	
企 石 镇	20	8957	
石 排 镇	28	7464	
茶 山 镇	18	38502	
松 山 湖			

14-28 镇街“三资”企业签约、实际利用外资及出口值(新口径)(2016年)

Contracts, Foreign Capital Actually Utilized and Export Value of Enterprises with Foreign Investment by Town (2016)

镇　　街	签约宗数(宗)	投产企业宗数(宗)	协议（合同）规定外商投资总额(万美元)	外商实际投资总额(万美元)	出口值(万元)
莞城街道	5	101	6572	1536	1122484
石 龙 镇	3	76	91	356	1211855
虎 门 镇	17	598	490	4003	2010193
东城街道	15	472	16904	16898	3308459
万江街道	8	154	837	4147	329001
南城街道	50	330	4296	3813	2828889
中 堂 镇	5	93	4154	3284	206397
望牛墩镇	2	95	1924	1898	184340
麻 涌 镇	2	66	35098	29565	680413
石 碣 镇	8	245	1640	2536	2411113
高 埗 镇	2	123	583	762	1005627
道 滘 镇	3	159	816	1257	440039
洪 梅 镇	4	77	15324	13069	206990
沙田镇（虎门港）	14	230	14869	8746	2258926
厚 街 镇	20	461	1133	9782	6076224
长 安 镇	31	882	21167	7355	6613558
寮 步 镇	13	421	8579	5963	3554696
大岭山镇	15	310	6586	7295	1764518
大 朗 镇	12	419	4612	4508	1327893
黄 江 镇	8	316	6595	7450	2324384
樟木头镇	6	196	21422	1602	629828
清 溪 镇	19	545	13822	6653	3116319
塘 厦 镇	23	878	5366	5644	3083275
凤 岗 镇	18	510	29843	28356	1681351
谢 岗 镇	8	222	29468	8663	461443
常 平 镇	25	607	19530	5966	3848389
桥 头 镇	11	308	3408	9620	2589679
横 沥 镇	7	353	8086	12582	1004238
东 坑 镇	5	159	1538	884	1509513
企 石 镇	13	180	4408	1822	467696
石 排 镇	6	223	2894	6397	667242
茶 山 镇	11	211	8488	9006	734686
松 山 湖	52	220	132436	126062	5943824

14-29 镇街进出口总额（2015-2016年，海关口径）

Total Value of Exports and Imports by Town (2015-2016, Custom Statistics)

镇街	2015年			2016年		
	进出口总额（万美元）	进口	出口	进出口总额（万元）	进口	出口
莞城街道	214872	61981	152891	1431237	308753	1122484
石龙镇	288835	87496	201339	1704353	492499	1211855
虎门镇	454158	145468	308690	3169586	1159393	2010193
东城街道	638142	94072	544069	3964887	656428	3308459
万江街道	59544	13839	45705	435280	106279	329001
南城街道	794996	178797	616200	3568304	739415	2828889
中堂镇	85260	53157	32103	519855	313458	206397
望牛墩镇	48785	10828	37957	248637	64298	184340
麻涌镇	372293	231238	141055	1746454	1066042	680413
石碣镇	666705	235218	431487	3865641	1454527	2411113
高埗镇	233698	72489	161208	1472736	467109	1005627
道滘镇	136142	29645	106498	734419	294380	440039
洪梅镇	130185	98831	31354	1035299	828308	206990
沙田镇（虎门港）	529705	227702	302003	4484264	2225338	2258926
厚街镇	1410837	491081	919757	9437140	3360916	6076224
长安镇	1899616	991451	908165	18885160	12271602	6613558
寮步镇	1123860	439591	684269	5837277	2282581	3554696
大岭山镇	392732	163006	229726	3104268	1339751	1764518
大朗镇	365487	90399	275088	1907081	579188	1327893
黄江镇	635006	224282	410724	3661912	1337527	2324384
樟木头镇	155537	42747	112790	916291	286464	629828
清溪镇	818726	301075	517650	4599070	1482751	3116319
塘厦镇	701581	209912	491669	4523047	1439772	3083275
凤岗镇	492912	159881	333031	2324413	643062	1681351
谢岗镇	91894	22583	69311	594187	132744	461443
常平镇	906825	333978	572847	6206922	2358533	3848389
桥头镇	603175	251766	351409	4461596	1871917	2589679
横沥镇	220009	60792	159217	1375967	371729	1004238
东坑镇	384626	165017	219609	2468231	958718	1509513
企石镇	85546	15927	69619	591042	123346	467696
石排镇	127951	25360	102591	822205	154963	667242
茶山镇	163617	54781	108836	1084123	349436	734686
松山湖	1335065	759039	576025	12937446	7036529	5943824

注：2016年起，进出口相关数据采用人民币口径。

14-30 镇街实际利用外资（2015-2016年）

Foreign Capital Actually Utilized by Town (2015-2016)

单位：万美元

镇　街	2015年	2016年	镇　街	2015年	2016年
莞城街道	5375	1536	寮 步 镇	20984	5963
石 龙 镇	9534	356	大岭山镇	12047	7295
虎 门 镇	15203	4003	大 朗 镇	15919	4508
东城街道	18778	16898	黄 江 镇	14150	7450
万江街道	6994	4147	樟木头镇	2168	1602
南城街道	5408	3813	清 溪 镇	9351	6653
中 堂 镇	2594	3284	塘 厦 镇	27293	5644
望牛墩镇	1416	1898	凤 岗 镇	52401	28356
麻 涌 镇	36541	29565	谢 岗 镇	6687	8663
石 碣 镇	7056	2536	常 平 镇	24390	5966
高 埗 镇	4920	762	桥 头 镇	11113	9620
道 滘 镇	3922	1257	横 沥 镇	8241	12582
洪 梅 镇	9568	13069	东 坑 镇	6985	884
沙田镇（虎门港）	13524	8746	企 石 镇	2805	1822
厚 街 镇	9821	9782	石 排 镇	8128	6397
长 安 镇	33391	7355	茶 山 镇	11234	9006
松 山 湖	91303	126062			

14-31 镇街税收总额（2015-2016年）

Taxes by Town (2015-2016)

单位：万元

镇 街	2015年			2016年		
	税收总额	国税	地税	税收总额	国税	地税
莞城街道	434934	198230	236705	400843	200228	200615
石 龙 镇	181436	108606	72829	184582	116868	67713
虎 门 镇	725688	445182	280506	785126	449185	335941
东城街道	1197398	734639	462758	1134742	722364	412378
万江街道	187880	107025	80855	208940	139890	69050
南城街道	1175734	524740	650994	1349929	797722	552207
中 堂 镇	134672	98337	36335	148222	109116	39106
望牛墩镇	75866	61017	14850	82671	64625	18046
麻 涌 镇	227824	133643	94181	299038	180033	119004
石 碣 镇	287019	207428	79592	309985	211778	98207
高 埗 镇	170671	125428	45243	156924	108062	48863
道 滘 镇	147142	100374	46767	174659	112101	62558
洪 梅 镇	73605	47877	25729	75455	55029	20426
沙田镇（虎门港）	231715	138636	93080	257731	147517	110215
厚 街 镇	500215	285142	215072	552257	325583	226674
长 安 镇	846000	588117	257883	1029707	773091	256616
寮 步 镇	509956	349278	160678	622613	450227	172386
大岭山镇	300150	204821	95329	371087	235724	135364
大 朗 镇	322309	222754	99555	374632	255520	119112
黄 江 镇	259121	149885	109236	330912	179017	151895
樟木头镇	165746	78691	87055	203200	102813	100387
清 溪 镇	376191	257456	118735	434989	291748	143241
塘 厦 镇	684172	408533	275639	751692	487426	264267
凤 岗 镇	450738	217800	232938	503460	289618	213842
谢 岗 镇	93566	72434	21132	90164	68319	21845
常 平 镇	336870	226209	110661	386499	262277	124222
桥 头 镇	157603	112483	45120	202639	140713	61925
横 沥 镇	186433	135825	50608	217110	159303	57808
东 坑 镇	137698	80849	56849	149505	105314	44191
企 石 镇	94681	64997	29684	100450	73220	27230
石 排 镇	117543	82955	34588	135322	99225	36098
茶 山 镇	166034	121142	44892	192761	140781	51980
松 山 湖	811185	498799	312386	1008810	619166	389644

14-32 镇街财政收支情况（2016年）

Government Revenue and Expenditure by Town (2016)

单位：万元

镇 街	地方财政总收入	地方财政总支出	地方财政总财力
莞城街道	130522	90368	157837
石 龙 镇	52399	80755	83680
虎 门 镇	184808	263636	271856
东城街道	302082	306229	480839
万江街道	206852	265958	404256
南城街道	176993	182261	305258
中 堂 镇	41110	84328	95829
望牛墩镇	59861	59941	60144
麻 涌 镇	128233	169892	170381
石 碣 镇	76496	195341	194433
高 埗 镇	37887	126092	131431
道 滘 镇	44831	137290	149070
洪 梅 镇	32798	105841	107871
沙田镇（虎门港）	143554	284658	284912
厚 街 镇	148824	241779	267223
长 安 镇	237303	365716	417108
寮 步 镇	127681	204301	208696
大岭山镇	466406	392893	523313
大 朗 镇	362937	288634	453717
黄 江 镇	529165	295015	605798
樟木头镇	57232	121209	163119
清 溪 镇	170683	301310	351040
塘 厦 镇	182218	461681	482887
凤 岗 镇	162241	309591	359042
谢 岗 镇	60995	60461	64503
常 平 镇	145998	186569	216286
桥 头 镇	61692	154592	166272
横 沥 镇	174383	130523	181094
东 坑 镇	49025	129348	134833
企 石 镇	58187	60200	61674
石 排 镇	233438	216280	353822
茶 山 镇	269662	253209	334988
松 山 湖	249022	209852	881252

注：为进一步规范镇街财政收支数据，2016年起，分镇街财政数据按市财政局指导的统计方式填报，数据与往年不可比。

14-33 镇街各项人民币存贷款余额（2015-2016年）

Balance of Deposits and Loans by Town (2015-2016)

单位：万元

镇　街	年末各项存款余额		年末各项贷款余额	
	2015年	2016年	2015年	2016年
莞城街道	11975172	11982852	4809971	5776053
石 龙 镇	1776219	1867726	947010	1001517
虎 门 镇	6659704	6765009	3673642	4478489
东城街道	8556327	11047407	6129743	7333482
万江街道	1916652	2100728	1319638	1379358
南城街道	18320329	24203519	14581266	13900019
中 堂 镇	1115982	1168817	754814	741041
望牛墩镇	550870	565558	247376	324669
麻 涌 镇	886852	954376	496144	735591
石 碣 镇	1819987	1884379	655696	568348
高 埗 镇	942294	1016738	426261	472410
道 滘 镇	914041	972666	455334	556095
洪 梅 镇	347221	379505	322645	308503
沙田镇（虎门港）	1051132	1192861	682154	738439
厚 街 镇	4476935	4690976	3733141	4049311
长 安 镇	7128138	8221377	2540230	2545792
寮 步 镇	2250409	2541486	1336148	1659390
大岭山镇	1670383	1979080	784468	1079293
大 朗 镇	2848842	3367976	1942048	2029773
黄 江 镇	1598970	2100636	778940	919027
樟木头镇	1421091	1478876	947498	947457
清 溪 镇	1831268	1930896	730998	723408
塘 厦 镇	3323396	3722984	2555389	3120169
凤 岗 镇	2452013	2712779	1980088	2457202
谢 岗 镇	684559	715000	353311	228436
常 平 镇	3198580	3679344	1537966	1900958
桥 头 镇	1101797	1216839	569869	737598
横 沥 镇	1143788	1297397	537849	668547
东 坑 镇	726107	781346	417903	425937
企 石 镇	789277	828796	382454	347410
石 排 镇	1127273	1274603	433782	535506
茶 山 镇	1211073	1389880	379686	443764
松 山 湖	1545758	1951861	716912	891787

注：本表数据来源于市人民银行。

14-34 镇街普通中学情况（2016年）

Basic Statistics on Regular Secondary Schools by Town (2016)

镇　街	学校数（所）	毕业生数（人）	#普通高中	招生数（人）	#普通高中	在校学生数（人）	#普通高中	教职工数（人）	#专任教师
全　市	231	85524	25673	110681	27153	295753	79851	25527	18885
莞城街道									
石龙镇	4	1362		1405		4141		317	281
虎门镇	13	4008	433	4504	369	12642	1152	1543	855
东城街道	16	3636	441	5605	1012	13970	2253	1329	882
万江街道	6	1931		2212		5825		485	385
南城街道	9	3359	656	3731	399	10434	1796	1030	711
中堂镇	7	2014	210	2522	244	6981	667	592	419
望牛墩镇	4	1221		1248		3449		300	243
麻涌镇	2	764		794		2064		243	218
石碣镇	10	1762		2512		6319		539	418
高埗镇	6	885		1284		3182		362	218
道滘镇	4	1803	468	1888	405	5391	1233	481	352
洪梅镇	1	160		276		839		69	56
沙田镇（虎门港）	4	1719	608	2262	575	5895	1671	599	381
厚街镇	11	2408		3345		8709		818	525
长安镇	6	2033		3271		7907		520	435
寮步镇	7	2576		3369		8931		646	538
大岭山镇	8	1885	297	2428	277	6458	781	624	430
大朗镇	7	3033	524	4211	477	10731	1481	813	574
黄江镇	3	1001		1309		3333		275	198
樟木头镇	3	1060		1257		3424		265	227
清溪镇	8	1672		2719		6682		587	402
塘厦镇	5	2785	482	3898	390	10433	1462	894	580
凤岗镇	10	2344	294	3380	278	8775	894	682	469
谢岗镇	3	686		868		2426		180	146
常平镇	11	2693		3336		8893		745	536
桥头镇	5	1634	426	2438	475	6666	1571	748	443
横沥镇	5	1101		1598		4200		362	231
东坑镇	6	1102		1775		4519		471	249
企石镇	3	965		1218		3321		259	202
石排镇	5	940		1351		3648		370	246
茶山镇	8	2361	733	4131	1274	10947	3773	1150	653
松山湖	3	574	295	1344	493	3108	1258	507	259
市直属	28	28047	19806	33192	20485	91510	59859	6722	6123

14-35 镇街小学情况（2016年）

Basic Statistics on Primary Schools by Town (2016)

镇 街	学校数（所）	毕业生数（人）	招生数（人）	在校学生数（人）	教职工数（人）	#专任教师
全 市	328	98789	138179	738686	35959	32302
莞城街道	9	2153	2339	13514	823	785
石 龙 镇	6	1597	2209	11906	627	567
虎 门 镇	24	5720	8530	45091	2303	2009
东城街道	15	5800	8924	44215	2124	1928
万江街道	16	3709	4829	26421	1176	1101
南城街道	10	3842	5336	28916	1568	1483
中 堂 镇	9	2367	3221	17068	790	765
望牛墩镇	4	938	1263	6434	366	345
麻 涌 镇	8	921	1611	7450	432	399
石 碣 镇	6	3263	3802	22019	954	931
高 埗 镇	6	1898	2235	12233	640	534
道 滘 镇	7	1659	2094	11325	572	547
洪 梅 镇	3	256	397	2135	125	108
沙田镇（虎门港）	4	1652	2631	13775	623	581
厚 街 镇	15	4744	7174	37238	1768	1599
长 安 镇	23	5973	9566	48811	2222	1965
寮 步 镇	16	4405	6054	32168	1504	1344
大岭山镇	10	2979	4108	21158	1117	954
大 朗 镇	18	4947	6594	36549	1651	1361
黄 江 镇	9	2225	3161	17069	807	661
樟木头镇	7	2132	2853	15349	721	640
清 溪 镇	8	3221	4511	24105	1178	1046
塘 厦 镇	13	4685	6706	35594	1806	1527
凤 岗 镇	16	4429	6414	33888	1619	1481
谢 岗 镇	3	1055	1368	7743	361	344
常 平 镇	18	5098	6470	36250	1604	1512
桥 头 镇	8	2333	2925	15953	800	747
横 沥 镇	7	2344	4003	19831	946	809
东 坑 镇	5	2085	2897	15875	676	638
企 石 镇	8	1590	2050	11398	559	502
石 排 镇	8	2105	2801	15908	771	674
茶 山 镇	5	2836	3777	20481	962	951
松 山 湖	2	758	1373	6640	389	365
市 直 属	2	3070	3953	24176	1375	1099

14-36 镇街卫生事业机构、床位及人员数（2016年）

Number of Health Care Institutions, Beds and Personnel by Town (2016)

镇街	机构数（个）	#医院	病床床位（张）	卫生工作人员（人）	#卫生技术人员	#执业（助理）医师	注册护士	药剂人员	检验人员
全市	2344	89	28138	57167	47668	16680	21268	2828	1739
莞城街道	52	4	386	1231	989	350	438	68	29
石龙镇	22	3	1811	2703	2323	787	1073	156	83
虎门镇	192	10	2162	4540	3831	1401	1714	244	150
东城街道	187	11	3670	7370	5982	1937	2592	321	232
万江街道	70	3	2994	5522	4651	1577	2304	213	127
南城街道	115	6	1265	3953	3205	1196	1395	140	166
中堂镇	66	2	971	990	861	253	439	49	31
望牛墩镇	37	1	150	745	620	246	235	55	16
麻涌镇	43	2	480	706	566	191	234	38	27
石碣镇	59	1	270	1105	919	343	383	86	27
高埗镇	58	2	327	725	597	227	244	47	24
道滘镇	58	1	200	606	541	186	210	47	26
洪梅镇	25	1	188	416	338	103	128	38	17
沙田镇（虎门港）	51	2	217	746	610	235	251	26	17
厚街镇	109	3	1055	2561	2193	781	997	138	76
长安镇	126	6	1655	2313	1920	733	922	90	72
寮步镇	109	3	1039	1884	1521	501	713	72	55
大岭山镇	94	2	450	1124	989	395	426	54	31
大朗镇	102	2	890	1838	1548	553	686	81	54
黄江镇	57	2	646	1247	1059	393	447	63	37
樟木头镇	32	2	521	1215	985	308	433	55	30
清溪镇	82	3	703	1381	1141	409	465	68	45
塘厦镇	83	4	1029	2112	1774	643	775	110	78
凤岗镇	75	3	1001	1754	1427	492	662	97	63
谢岗镇	30	1	180	495	443	169	200	18	13
常平镇	99	3	1500	2070	1729	621	769	104	64
桥头镇	53	1	500	1095	958	319	452	62	30
横沥镇	68	1	420	1235	987	349	436	60	22
东坑镇	43	1	350	669	581	190	240	28	20
企石镇	42	1	448	975	842	254	338	72	24
石排镇	46	1	360	856	718	237	325	64	22
茶山镇	47	1	300	892	753	273	322	61	29
松山湖	12			93	67	28	20	3	2

14-37 镇街优抚和社会救济基本情况（2016年）

Basic Statistics on Special Care and Social Relief by Town (2016)

镇　街	敬老院 个　数 (个)	敬 老 院 供养人数 (人)	最低生活 保障户数 (户)	最低生活 保障人数 (人)	最低生活 保障费支出 (万元)
全　　市	34	1688	6028	11912	7826.48
莞城街道	1	23	211	369	264.93
石 龙 镇	1	17	169	326	250.81
虎 门 镇	1	41	155	307	233.76
东城街道	1	16	12	19	16.44
万江街道	1	41	285	562	374.98
南城街道		4	27	49	33.62
中 堂 镇	1	29	417	840	518.37
望牛墩镇	1	63	357	795	569.39
麻 涌 镇	1	20	933	1580	962.85
石 碣 镇	1	23	37	78	53.23
高 埗 镇	1	15	267	633	350.15
道 滘 镇	1	44	380	753	535.02
洪 梅 镇	1	26	216	382	197.07
沙田镇（虎门港）	1	25	213	396	194.35
厚 街 镇	1	41	273	511	328.41
长 安 镇	1	25	4	4	3.00
寮 步 镇	1	41	136	272	163.76
大岭山镇	1	24	241	401	280.65
大 朗 镇	1	27	158	395	272.49
黄 江 镇	1	35	69	127	94.01
樟木头镇	1	27	54	102	54.34
清 溪 镇	1	41	128	257	180.71
塘 厦 镇	1	21	71	138	81.95
凤 岗 镇	1	7	13	25	16.25
谢 岗 镇	1	12	102	270	169.54
常 平 镇	1	17	107	196	148.54
桥 头 镇	1	41	57	105	73.91
横 沥 镇	1	7	132	276	200.98
东 坑 镇	1	18	105	179	135.32
企 石 镇	1	22	151	362	234.62
石 排 镇	1	14	379	820	579.49
茶 山 镇	1	17	169	383	253.56

14-38 镇街专利申请与授权数（2016年）

Basic Statistics on Patents Application Accepted and Granted by Town (2016)

单位：件

镇 街	专利申请数	#发明	实用新型	外观设计	专利授权数	#发明	实用新型	外观设计
全 市	56653	17024	28096	11533	28559	3682	16454	8423
莞城街道	484	64	273	147	310	27	167	116
石 龙 镇	341	51	222	68	147	31	68	48
虎 门 镇	2394	376	1397	621	1370	163	763	444
东城街道	3460	1000	1735	725	1819	266	1009	544
万江街道	1581	288	1064	229	880	74	662	144
南城街道	1951	369	1197	385	1068	130	703	235
中 堂 镇	552	120	372	60	183	21	117	45
望牛墩镇	410	72	239	99	246	30	130	86
麻 涌 镇	305	84	194	27	140	27	93	20
石 碣 镇	1211	154	665	392	764	68	434	262
高 埗 镇	632	101	314	217	276	30	133	113
道 滘 镇	750	151	457	142	496	53	274	169
洪 梅 镇	218	31	130	57	154	27	87	40
沙田镇（虎门港）	770	172	470	128	355	38	230	87
厚 街 镇	2339	174	825	1340	1655	65	536	1054
长 安 镇	10533	6562	3307	664	2992	683	1871	438
寮 步 镇	2269	311	1393	565	1296	103	728	465
大岭山镇	1955	219	805	931	1272	66	522	684
大 朗 镇	1315	219	883	213	815	83	580	152
黄 江 镇	1369	178	752	439	814	56	491	267
樟木头镇	1047	133	603	311	614	45	369	200
清 溪 镇	1543	199	1092	252	975	69	695	211
塘 厦 镇	3054	453	2080	521	1886	137	1404	345
凤 岗 镇	1556	143	930	483	870	39	494	337
谢 岗 镇	432	53	299	80	271	14	194	63
常 平 镇	2068	267	1231	570	1118	87	671	360
桥 头 镇	806	95	476	235	535	31	284	220
横 沥 镇	1229	146	807	276	652	72	422	158
东 坑 镇	548	91	312	145	351	18	246	87
企 石 镇	703	91	395	217	428	30	230	168
石 排 镇	965	100	578	287	584	42	343	199
茶 山 镇	1099	295	553	251	636	77	315	244
松 山 湖	6714	4248	2029	437	2571	977	1182	412
其 它	50	14	17	19	16	3	7	6

14-39 镇街总用电量和总售水量（2015-2016年）

Gross Comsumption of Electicity and Water by Town (2015-2016)

镇 街	总用电量（万千瓦时）		总售水量（万吨）	
	2015年	2016年	2015年	2016年
莞城街道	49491	57059	1753	1758
石龙镇	74883	75415	1781	1736
虎门镇	429929	450114	8590	8563
东城街道	298794	312936	10072	9874
万江街道	134025	139628	4075	3968
南城街道	110319	113908	5001	4907
中堂镇	338315	356489	2118	2246
望牛墩镇	76521	87493	1232	1203
麻涌镇	148577	150367	2432	2416
石碣镇	175002	184316	3919	3668
高埗镇	131310	129251	2585	2619
道滘镇	109741	112574	2356	2318
洪梅镇	52984	47845	1109	967
沙田镇（虎门港）	141916	150241	2020	3225
厚街镇	329932	337265	7888	7331
长安镇	627436	643749	10251	10117
寮步镇	260887	272827	5796	5948
大岭山镇	201966	220251	2878	3211
大朗镇	297644	331822	6677	6615
黄江镇	180251	190201	3188	3498
樟木头镇	99980	101602	2375	2283
清溪镇	275305	294165	5123	5203
塘厦镇	412363	463871	7782	7860
凤岗镇	282089	299634	4751	4962
谢岗镇	91537	95837	1665	1721
常平镇	292555	301173	6587	6843
桥头镇	164412	177266	3064	2969
横沥镇	151797	161287	3599	3730
东坑镇	103064	109637	2148	2101
企石镇	92307	102031	2175	2275
石排镇	146507	167620	2116	2089
茶山镇	153025	165523	3636	3553
松山湖	97378	117492	2009	2261

注：总售水量数据来源于市水务局。

十五、村（居）委会主要指标

Main Indicators of Villagers' (Neighborhood) Committees

15 村（居）委会主要指标（2016年）

Main Indicators of Villagers' (Neighborhood) Committees (2016)

村（居）委会	土地面积（平方公里）	户籍人口（人）	外来暂住人口（人）	全部企业及个体户数（个）	#工业企业	资产总额（万元）	负债总额（万元）	资产负债率（%）	村组两级经营纯收入（万元）
莞　城									
东正社区	1.7	21938	2980	1062	13	642	4	0.6	
市桥社区	0.9	32688	1144	1172		553	31	5.6	
北隅社区	1.1	28287	9386	1586	3	919	101	11.0	
西隅社区	0.6	11958	213	203	2	948	171	18.0	
罗沙社区	1.8	20100	5902	1987	3	445	146	32.8	
博厦社区	1.0	9820	1082	230	3	218	15	6.9	
兴塘社区	2.6	15240	11752	3900	2	227	68	30.0	
创业社区	1.5	24023	9983	2719	13	394	29	7.4	
罗沙联合社						25857	2083	8.1	10638
博厦联合社						6821	539	7.9	1614
细村联合社						19336	1537	8.0	2803
石　龙									
中山东社区	0.5	21524	11368	776	11	1021	261	25.6	
中山西社区	0.5	21178	2540	728	23	1097	174	15.9	
兴龙社区		20585	7884	2733	9	3609	1006	27.9	
忠 维 村	0.8	1033	2317	275	16	7248	844	11.7	752
林 屋 村	0.7	670	1967	521	5	3805	1044	27.4	627
新 维 村	0.6	557	1210	834	63	16851	1549	9.2	1840
蒲 溪 村	0.7	634	360	4		4749	1854	39.0	664
西 湖 村	3.5	2958	9486	2390	132	83432	7407	8.9	5979
王屋洲村	3.2	1648	6912	608	38	13440	956	7.1	1105
黄家山村	2.5	1992	6107	568	55	33944	13567	40.0	540
虎　门									
东方社区	0.8	9099	2350	505	2	994	424	42.7	22
则徐社区	1.2	15768	8600	1562	48	1403	464	33.1	54
虎门寨社区	2.0	7965	9150	6300	22	26136	2138	8.2	7409
树田社区	4.0	1560	8216	830	540	11679	3827	32.8	1486
怀德社区	13.8	6596	27316	1459	224	60336	7452	12.4	9776
居岐社区	1.6	1356	13450	448	55	17894	2947	16.5	2642
村头社区	1.3	829	6800	228	68	12041	1804	15.0	1792
陈村社区	1.3	803	4429	60	36	6873	1161	16.9	530
黄村社区	0.9	598	4900	86	31	3304	484	14.6	536
大宁社区	5.4	2955	25600	700	330	182731	5873	3.2	15252
北栅社区	5.9	4843	38800	2098	339	36775	4788	13.0	7978
龙眼社区	3.0	3005	43600	1540	580	112891	10505	9.3	7731
赤岗社区	7.5	4390	55000	547	120	41045	3249	7.9	3423
博涌社区	5.9	7586	25500	2380	264	169123	81917	48.4	10262
新联社区	4.0	1235	6300	608	80	14167	3233	22.8	1702

注：村（居）委会主要指标为镇、村自报数据。

15 续表 1

(2016年)

村（居）委会	土地面积（平方公里）	户籍人口（人）	外来暂住人口（人）	全部企业及个体户数（个）	#工业企业	资产总额（万元）	负债总额（万元）	资产负债率（%）	村组两级经营纯收入（万元）
白沙社区	7.8	7419	8400	1237	178	47135	11705	24.8	3824
镇口社区	1.8	3229	10982	1518	179	23749	1891	8.0	3342
金洲社区	4.8	4201	18000	1400	75	88888	21728	24.4	5697
小捷滘社区	2.0	966	4100	550	150	15408	3191	20.7	1544
南栅社区	8.2	5647	37500	1664	364	102337	18783	18.4	13285
东风社区	2.8	1844	5602	431	53	18548	7134	38.5	1411
寮岗社区	1.3	1168	7000	190	25	8947	1628	18.2	1116
路东社区	5.6	3414	23000	860	212	67888	7233	10.7	10417
沙角社区	11.2	5953	22647	1402	476	47663	13952	29.3	7371
九门寨社区	2.6	1524	5300	291	41	14510	4698	32.4	1079
南面社区	7.3	2932	3230	290	7	21709	2087	9.6	1585
北面社区	5.5	2718	3673	80	56	13099	4551	34.7	1251
武山沙社区	2.9	2427	3533	184	61	7480	3069	41.0	1175
新湾社区	1.0	10059	3800	201	23	8622	1731	20.1	852
民泰社区									
东　　城									
岗贝社区	1.7	16187	13190	4246		1974	278	14.1	62
花园新村社区	0.8	1585	1152	784		2236	412	18.4	
东泰社区	1.4	18188	14037	1540		4183	234	5.6	
温塘社区	11.6	10037	33100	715	649	27206	1398	5.1	14840
桑园社区	4.0	3867	25300	435	125	11350	1405	12.4	4855
周屋社区	2.8	2434	7213	360	61	6587	414	6.3	2095
余屋社区	2.0	1707	3320	287	63	6379	258	4.0	1756
鳌峙塘社区	2.0	1076	2322	145	80	4516	1354	30.0	677
峡口社区	1.6	1244	5130	237	96	7741	1374	17.7	1695
柏洲边社区	1.0	1135	4035	220	61	7116	461	6.5	2107
上桥社区	1.0	1419	3605	260	42	3344	179	5.4	1580
下桥社区	2.0	2587	7440	869	47	9084	1324	14.6	4730
樟村社区	3.0	3340	3990	530	42	44309	8982	20.3	3866
梨川社区	1.0	1694	3566	269	62	7054	1163	16.5	2781
堑头社区	1.5	3216	3800	295	35	9617	406	4.2	3768
主山社区	6.6	6415	11000	1150	303	36186	553	1.5	10831
石井社区	6.7	2154	2980	145	60	11225	2994	26.7	3497
同沙社区	4.6	2515	5900	100	128	15616	805	5.2	3065
光明社区	1.9	1470	2340	250	20	10035	930	9.3	1385
牛山社区	11.0	4321	13825	843	87	15835	1789	11.3	3989
立新社区	2.5	3405	5823	573	38	6519	3360	51.5	4338
火炼树社区	1.2	1429	13622	475	18	7194	2369	32.9	2920
星城社区	2.7	12398	25150	635		187	27	14.5	
万　　江									
万江墟社区	1.0	6859	1261	240	31	3494	1997	57.2	297
万江社区	2.6	4319	2769	80	74	15451	2531	16.4	2696
石美社区	2.5	4283	2971	238	96	12921	1291	10.0	3187
莫屋社区	1.0	1527	1670	165	96	5378	953	17.7	1242

15 续表 2

(2016年)

村（居）委会	土地面积（平方公里）	户籍人口（人）	外来暂住人口（人）	全部企业及个体户数（个）	#工业企业	资产总额（万元）	负债总额（万元）	资产负债率（%）	村组两级经营纯收入（万元）
拔蛟窝社区	1.3	2277	2151	269	79	19300	929	4.8	1012
黄粘洲社区	0.3	815	907	43	24	3581	817	22.8	207
蚬涌社区	2.0	2138	1979	244	115	4348	1195	27.5	1630
谷涌社区	2.0	3257	1520	173	26	22013	1450	6.6	2472
小享社区	3.8	5202	2208	220	136	19673	910	4.6	1984
滘联社区	2.1	3572	1127	138	40	8825	7269	82.4	343
金泰社区	1.0	2227	1592	130	33	5292	1254	23.7	1238
曲海社区	1.2	1620	361	34	2	16128	328	2.0	1163
牌楼基社区	1.6	1670	1250	285	45	19462	775	4.0	972
大莲塘社区	0.8	1043	267	78	41	8974	606	6.8	697
水蛇涌社区	1.5	2409	1497	140	45	14759	1354	9.2	73
共联社区	1.3	2129	7915	164	69	6557	532	8.1	1589
新谷涌社区	1.4	2271	1379	91	45	11713	1355	11.6	1093
坝头社区	1.4	1620	2591	19	14	12785	3306	25.9	1570
胜利社区	0.9	1003	7713	31	28	3145	296	9.4	947
官桥滘社区	1.9	1792	1780	161	58	11127	1105	9.9	1167
简沙洲社区	1.6	1770	3717	144	125	3231	4711	145.8	1081
新和社区	3.7	2860	7975	236	135	12933	1102	8.5	2459
上甲社区	1.4	2509	1278	99	79	9405	3065	32.6	230
严屋社区	1.0	1158	1879	39	34	4926	1068	21.7	426
大汾社区	2.6	3503	1467	280	75	16858	1136	6.7	1730
新村社区	5.8	8460	2295	436	184	15874	3448	21.7	1619
流涌尾社区	2.5	2457	1162	108	56	5177	1341	25.9	1091
新城社区		12675	4270	2300	32	508	394	77.6	53
南　　城									
鸿福社区		20620	41340	2408	10				
元美社区	0.4	2745	3026	562	2	10678	2086	19.5	810
胜和社区	4.0	6847	19352	3423	1	36025	1559	4.3	14696
亨美社区	0.5	2038	4400	270	22	32146	4238	13.2	2628
三元里社区	0.2	1188	885	70	7	32428	4246	13.1	3403
篁村社区	1.0	3127	6168	728	13	30262	2929	9.7	2331
新基社区	2.0	2933	5238	1526	15	100190	1610	1.6	4672
周溪社区	5.0	4140	7826	412	15	47460	2232	4.7	4906
袁屋边社区	2.1	2126	7763	673	12	132572	484	0.4	5885
白马社区	4.0	3455	8150	2475	39	38434	2312	6.0	3476
石鼓社区	2.0	1861	4768	256	25	37633	2852	7.6	3245
蛤地社区	8.0	2918	3900	89	20	25537	3365	13.2	2521
西平社区	3.9	3239	8235	632	11	40293	13296	33.0	3186
水濂社区	6.0	2174	1987	110	28	20279	9574	47.2	1881
雅园社区	1.8	1282	2163	267	81	27667	1048	3.8	1015
新城社区	2.2	3550	2310	2408					
宏远社区	1.2	14097	22000	1505	1				
宏图社区		10869	52700	734					

15　续表 3

(2016年)

村（居）委会	土地面积（平方公里）	户籍人口（人）	外来暂住人口（人）	全部企业及个体户数（个）	#工业企业	资产总额（万元）	负债总额（万元）	资产负债率（%）	村组两级经营纯收入（万元）
中　　堂									
中心社区	0.7	9859	8132	2469	42	1970	1827	92.7	
斗朗社区	2.5	2748	873	488	50	7732	1995	25.8	1192
红锋社区	0.1	811	49	27	3	1564	869	55.6	144
东泊社区	2.9	3907	4123	924	288	16047	3805	23.7	1080
江南社区	2.1	2625	4180	1675	646	14232	496	3.5	1236
潢 涌 村	9.3	10102	2208	1178	175	406355	12021	3.0	43323
三 涌 村	4.0	3961	1825	645	129	9147	4052	44.3	1456
湛 翠 村	1.8	2469	905	262	88	8620	5321	61.7	303
袁家涌村	4.0	5834	2094	695	196	9314	1544	16.6	1121
吴家涌村	3.4	2849	2250	529	129	8100	1718	21.2	805
凤 冲 村	1.3	1698	685	119	50	3307	1781	53.9	76
鹤 田 村	2.2	2330	1243	497	161	3498	1828	52.3	525
中 堂 村	1.1	2070	1925	256	57	5322	1622	30.5	841
一 村 村	0.7	1917	2280	603	30	8611	1063	12.3	1334
东 向 村	2.4	3410	1360	512	138	4110	722	17.6	938
蕉 利 村	4.6	5178	5287	717	263	5896	1165	19.8	1485
槎 滘 村	9.4	10745	1595	820	202	40236	10727	26.7	2779
下 芦 村	1.3	1268	403	86	52	3785	1359	35.9	318
马 沥 村	1.9	2078	486	86	34	11451	1229	10.7	591
四 乡 村	4.2	3399	332	126	19	3828	1291	33.7	340
望 牛 墩									
望牛墩社区		4709	542						
李 屋 村	0.6	682	608	61	26	6516	1539	23.6	233
望 东 村	1.4	2153	746	193	16	3452	1309	37.9	393
扶 涌 村	0.6	960	3127	49	9	3092	1117	36.1	223
赤 滘 村	1.9	3176	2855	48	38	15212	2747	18.1	1063
五 涌 村	1.4	1573	814	48	48	3690	1106	30.0	189
下 漕 村	3.5	4542	3211	88	39	7194	3523	49.0	573
上 合 村	1.9	3148	3732	62	35	4985	1950	39.1	577
聚龙江村	0.7	1033	2857	146	28	7418	1054	14.2	388
望 联 村	2.8	5305	1638	446	18	6556	1519	23.2	622
洲 湾 村	1.6	1978	650	31	10	4318	2153	49.9	166
洲 涡 村	1.9	2709	546	42	22	5911	2138	36.2	296
寮 厦 村	1.4	1470	501	36	22	5243	1939	37.0	424
官桥涌村	0.7	1007	763	12	10	3623	384	10.6	365
芙蓉沙村	0.8	1068	548	24	17	3756	1283	34.2	408
杜 屋 村	1.8	2512	436	66	30	8187	1851	22.6	342
横 沥 村	1.8	2337	1450	40	8	5213	2166	41.5	191
福 安 村	0.6	1133	317	36	6	4107	902	22.0	257
官 洲 村	1.0	1078	823	30	14	3479	1576	45.3	264
石 排 村	0.4	665	850	14	7	2342	1016	43.4	185
朱平沙村	2.7	3518	2216	60	17	14971	4080	27.3	271
锦 涡 村	2.2	1605	916	35	5	7323	1453	19.8	216

15 续表 4

(2016年)

村（居）委会	土地面积（平方公里）	户籍人口（人）	外来暂住人口（人）	全部企业及个体户数（个）	#工业企业	资产总额（万元）	负债总额（万元）	资产负债率（%）	村组两级经营纯收入（万元）
麻　　涌									
麻涌社区		7214							
麻二社区	6.8	3718	2345	156	22	15029	5150	34.3	803
麻 一 村	4.0	4306	2310	409	39	15632	5653	36.2	515
麻 三 村	3.7	3972	4500	1857	179	15493	1513	9.8	661
麻 四 村	4.5	5060	710	313	30	18851	2395	12.7	684
大 步 村	10.7	7631	2776	1250	67	32368	2010	6.2	1675
东 太 村	4.8	4679	4007	575	27	12701	2974	23.4	793
新 基 村	4.4	5916	3874	531	59	16772	1148	6.8	1357
川 槎 村	3.0	4135	1623	357	55	698	553	79.2	983
鸥 涌 村	2.8	4043	4471	379	21	767	474	61.8	1300
黎 滘 村	1.3	1402	743	89	22	3428	819	23.9	561
华 阳 村	5.5	5559	550	329	20	18990	3987	21.0	977
南 洲 村	3.3	2959	2448	258	21	10034	899	9.0	326
大 盛 村	6.9	3153	10322	998	50	27345	2571	9.4	2158
漳 澎 村	25.7	13351	2448	640	74	61229	29629	48.4	2952
石　　碣									
城中社区		9202	5325	2671	139	7169	6993	97.5	122
唐 洪 村	1.0	1831	2827	678	44	14245	4124	29.0	1392
水 南 村	2.8	3722	5101	1642	151	18775	4044	21.5	5337
石 碣 村	4.6	5515	10239	1706	210	14545	2961	20.4	7672
刘 屋 村	4.9	4758	4727	771	127	9491	2768	29.2	3370
横 滘 村	1.6	2076	6198	1050	111	13431	4857	36.2	3095
鹤田厦村	2.5	2006	4230	338	36	10758	2749	25.6	1588
四 甲 村	4.0	4843	7738	839	132	17030	2101	12.3	5850
沙 腰 村	4.0	3724	4430	513	86	17464	1718	9.8	2354
梁 家 村	2.0	2553	2272	153	61	16843	1268	7.5	981
桔 洲 村	1.2	1532	9521	442	76	42170	1516	3.6	3636
单 屋 村	2.3	1339	2335	201	93	17743	3319	18.7	1016
涌 口 村	1.6	1848	4200	471	125	16500	5160	31.3	1156
西 南 村	2.6	2042	6300	1045	93	55360	4347	7.9	5833
黄泗围村	1.2	725	1835	480	58	12708	764	6.0	1289
高　　埗									
新创社区		2552	2520						
冼 沙 村	7.2	7928	19513	407	175	12682	10961	86.4	3207
卢 溪 村	1.6	1785	3591	225	55	4772	668	14.0	512
宝 莲 村	0.9	1074	798	51	15	2050	572	27.9	93
塘 厦 村	2.7	2016	2808	124	19	2713	691	25.5	1061
草 墩 村	0.8	843	1350	24	21	3711	912	24.6	467
护安围村	1.5	1187	1250	98	45	6317	945	15.0	558

15 续表 5

(2016年)

村（居）委会	土地面积(平方公里)	户籍人口(人)	外来暂住人口(人)	全部企业及个体户数(个)	#工业企业	资产总额(万元)	负债总额(万元)	资产负债率(%)	村组两级经营纯收入(万元)
保安围村	2.8	2523	2635	126	44	19569	16633	85.0	-17
三联村	1.1	1394	862	30	5	4491	2408	53.6	411
横滘头村	0.9	1133	510	30	8	4451	484	10.9	509
低涌村	2.4	2985	6560	360	25	5883	1932	32.8	1746
朱磡村	1.0	1586	753	40	20	1808	360	19.9	251
欧邓村	0.7	959	6012	31	9	3108	1657	53.3	261
芦村村	1.4	1785	1561	58	22	3671	601	16.4	234
高埗村	3.3	3509	21039	1209	50	5841	1953	33.4	3434
凌屋村	1.4	1312	2333	60	8	4720	1886	40.0	423
上江城村	2.5	2382	6829	83	20	9837	4282	43.5	1178
下江城村	1.5	1618	3890	120	24	6197	2671	43.1	2035
新联村	0.9	1783	950	142	6	1487	889	59.8	1253
道滘									
兴隆社区		12409	726				408	78.3	
南城村	5.8	4455	2205	577	70	14492	1095	7.6	2444
闸口村	4.5	2900	3733	467	18	10605	1392	13.1	1333
北永村	4.8	3861	2220	380	110	8989	2987	33.2	1470
永庆村	2.3	1721	1675	180	104	8206	690	8.4	1020
厚德村	3.4	2577	3076	235	41	12421	989	8.0	521
蔡白村	6.5	4973	2423	352	62	22305	5858	26.3	952
南丫村	6.1	4355	7890	466	146	9158	2153	23.5	2689
九曲村	4.0	3225	1597	165	55	10290	3009	29.2	848
大罗沙村	3.8	3083	2410	85	35	8713	866	9.9	693
小河村	4.8	5956	2316	209	76	7045	1795	25.5	1746
昌平村	3.0	3661	1686	166	45	4734	1556	32.9	1308
大岭丫村	3.5	3818	2773	365	131	14062	3820	27.2	1981
大鱼沙村	1.8	1789	1047	210	31	6153	557	9.1	561
洪梅									
洪梅社区	1.4	1237	5178	451	3				
洪屋涡村	14.1	7284	5380	354	21	23760	4058	17.1	1042
新庄村	1.7	926	1623	67	9	4370	1267	29.0	294
梅沙村	4.7	4293	1486	125	13	10081	2639	26.2	396
金鳌沙村	1.7	1385	665	42	12	5472	1473	26.9	514
乌沙村	3.9	2358	1195	45	23	11227	1432	12.8	311
尧均村	1.0	640	2053	75	19	3293	1140	34.6	178
夏汇村	0.9	788	211	11	6	2899	1121	38.7	280
氹涌村	2.1	2106	1690	106	11	8024	2193	27.3	271
黎洲角村	1.6	2890	6512	385	10	15482	1897	12.3	520
沙田									
横流社区	0.4	3949	2754	1608	120	6164	537	8.7	500
滨港社区		1813							

15 续表 6

(2016年)

村（居）委会	土地面积（平方公里）	户籍人口（人）	外来暂住人口（人）	全部企业及个体户数（个）	#工业企业	资产总额（万元）	负债总额（万元）	资产负债率（%）	村组两级经营纯收入（万元）
中围村	2.9	1887		30	2	20606	3153	15.3	1323
和安村	2.7	3397		23	2	14447	3549	24.6	912
大流村	2.2	2192		45	5	15766	6607	41.9	1242
泥洲村	5.1	4125		33	1	18576	8340	44.9	1127
杨公洲村	3.2	2038	4153	921	315	10203	3070	30.1	1439
阇西村	2.5	2357	3945	1134	143	32286	7482	23.2	1965
民田村	3.0	2762	7235	1145	293	14956	3652	24.4	1263
大泥村	2.5	1958	12214	1374	629	10849	1477	13.6	767
福禄沙村	3.4	2060	2865	361	85	8535	1816	21.3	1194
西大坦村	2.5	2247		69	6	9693	3357	34.6	540
穗丰年村	4.2	2918	3675	539	197	23827	5235	22.0	1839
齐沙村	2.3	2134	8645	747	214	14287	2450	17.2	1746
稔洲村	3.3	2578	21423	1665	593	22104	12791	57.9	1254
义沙村	3.5	1977	11234	470	171	10508	1780	16.9	830
西太隆村	3.7	2108	3888	937	414	7691	2872	37.3	986
先锋村	0.3	2113	321	79	17	7840	2301	29.4	415
厚街									
竹溪社区		12618		150		4614	244	5.3	32
厚街社区	5.7	9347	20395	5941	1045	39761	12282	30.9	3636
珊美社区	2.0	2594	13812	4506	242	9679	1150	11.9	2291
寮厦社区	3.4	2669	10230	4506	379	30370	2612	8.6	4632
河田社区	10.1	6476	22425	3727	625	53454	9616	18.0	5476
汀山社区	4.3	2023	14200	1144	588	37496	1754	4.7	1538
环冈社区	5.0	2163	4611	722	189	18486	6193	33.5	1023
三屯社区	3.5	2812	15630	2021	447	91698	7659	8.4	7197
宝屯社区	3.1	2680	5680	2184	650	19223	8871	46.1	3403
陈屋社区	2.5	1570	8563	1528	298	32924	2035	6.2	3418
赤岭社区	6.2	3830	26552	2006	604	66502	24788	37.3	5708
桥头社区	11.7	8335	12015	2705	659	41404	7076	17.1	5207
南五社区	1.2	1659	4032	907	253	16526	3839	23.2	1088
溪头社区	4.5	8335	12015	2705	659	41404	7076	17.1	5207
沙塘社区	1.4	2095	4300	337	131	15883	2644	16.6	1661
宝塘社区	1.7	1636	6310	584	233	22670	2399	10.6	2013
下汴社区	6.0	1789	6760	887	303	21411	1383	6.5	1847
白濠社区	5.5	5563	22530	2156	840	49525	5170	10.4	5508
新塘社区	4.4	5855	15925	2375	446	53566	26308	49.1	5576
双岗社区	4.5	7075	6542	1700	535	23901	5632	23.6	2794
涌口社区	3.7	5653	10159	1594	390	55140	4710	8.5	3632
大迳社区	13.2	3737	3296	313	105	12412	3396	27.4	748
新围社区	17.6	4620		416	163	12434	2236	18.0	566
湖景社区		3189							
长安									
长盛社区	0.8	15468	22193	5068	6	12974	3238	25.0	

15　续表 7

(2016年)

村（居）委会	土地面积(平方公里)	户籍人口(人)	外来暂住人口(人)	全部企业及个体户数(个)	#工业企业	资产总额(万元)	负债总额(万元)	资产负债率(%)	村组两级经营纯收入(万元)
涌头社区	3.8	1823	32145	892	190	29831	11285	37.8	5930
霄边社区	7.4	3601	53438	3142	62	143996	5290	3.7	9492
咸西社区	3.9	1379	27887	1050	150	86665	25144	29.0	3395
锦厦社区	8.1	4535	50756	3897	282	155651	38569	24.8	23148
新安社区	10.4	3637	50177	3122	346	54271	7448	13.7	9985
乌沙社区	11.7	4123	80507	5439	727	72776	11812	16.2	29822
新民社区	2.4	995	28244	1160	180	41573	22019	53.0	4659
沙头社区	14.2	6596	84669	1143	266	113980	16201	14.2	13329
上沙社区	7.4	3037	52691	2567	332	66731	6264	9.4	10225
厦岗社区	8.9	3369	46390	2122	529	57111	3229	5.7	5878
厦边社区	5.0	2616	34889	2480	531	25431	4320	17.0	6563
上角社区	3.2	1410	42840	1135	206	55815	12530	22.4	7862
寮　步									
寮步社区	1.7	8723	4600	2813	20	6631	1136	17.1	475
塘边社区	0.7	1737	2979	299	34	4504	5724	127.1	2174
岭厦社区	0.9	1053	3972	209	73	18653	723	3.9	2254
新旧围社区	1.4	1034	1140	281	198	8362	691	8.3	823
横坑社区	5.9	5141	23236	139	139	119064	10905	9.2	8943
牛杨社区	1.2	1629	9230	286	92	31477	15549	49.4	2165
泉塘社区	2.3	1616	6250	69	30	7922	2014	25.4	1179
坑口社区	1.6	1264	6032	802	45	9500	1267	13.3	1022
缪边社区	1.6	1263	2972	194	39	17932	7163	39.9	1281
良平社区		11130	98000						
西溪村	4.5	4834	8300	850	433	19162	7842	40.9	2153
凫山村	4.0	6392	9510	778	123	12903	2564	19.9	6513
石步村	2.3	4747	7500	473	124	20454	2373	11.6	2769
良边村	2.7	3290	4555	400	200	6083	930	15.3	2553
富竹山村	3.5	2089	5683	354	21	13953	1756	12.6	2338
塘唇村	3.4	2428	5036	508	56	21980	1310	6.0	3389
向西村	2.9	2676	4220	475	81	12146	5589	46.0	867
下岭贝村	1.8	1648	5112	226	38	14933	1748	11.7	3007
霞边村	1.3	945	1525	114	22	10466	910	8.7	1694
竹园村	1.5	938	1580	143	40	7501	2845	37.9	401
上屯村	4.5	3500	3995	495	51	20996	4062	19.3	2664
石龙坑村	1.9	3768	5120	508	236	9948	645	6.5	2596
浮竹山村	3.4	1648	2780	161	33	14682	1694	11.5	1474
上底村	2.0	1534	1250	112	22	5800	3005	51.8	622
刘屋巷村	1.6	611	3140	66	33	4720	1035	21.9	476
药勒村	2.4	1193	2070	189	54	24084	1767	7.3	2431
陈家埔村	1.6	991	800	215	28	11153	3262	29.2	748

15 续表 8

(2016年)

村（居）委会	土地面积(平方公里)	户籍人口(人)	外来暂住人口(人)	全部企业及个体户数(个)	#工业企业	资产总额(万元)	负债总额(万元)	资产负债率(%)	村组两级经营纯收入(万元)
小坑村	1.5	823	1500	59	18	11416	1108	9.7	656
长坑村	1.5	1015	730	32	21	9952	780	7.8	928
井巷村	1.1	958	1130	56	49	8385	1744	20.8	859
大岭山									
大岭山社区	10.0	6881	8466	1910	17	693	182	26.3	344
农场社区	1.0	791	3820	454	15	10478	335	3.2	2392
马蹄岗村	0.8	2315	6000	254	121	6884	1839	26.7	1462
大塘朗村	3.0	1704	3300	80	47	6612	506	7.7	708
新塘村	2.0	2376	10003	286	86	24120	2279	9.4	3090
元岭村	0.3	1034	2219	120	3	16055	966	6.0	623
金桔村	4.3	3918	8560	533	60	25188	2828	11.2	2018
鸡翅岭村	4.5	1394	2030	198	19	6553	1806	27.6	1156
大沙村	3.0	2008	4327	285	268	10018	1679	16.8	1859
旧飞鹅村	3.1	500	1500	20	13	5415	151	2.8	419
连平村	7.2	3191	13801	289	88	7465	670	9.0	3265
梅林村	1.5	588	5980	142	72	3267	434	13.3	1152
下高田村	0.5	499	838	63	38	3339	713	21.4	262
大环村	2.0	658	2500	85	35	5281	1272	24.1	415
太公岭村	2.2	1819	8000	230	60	4827	348	7.2	1368
百花洞村	4.8	1387	7010	281	62	12345	3205	26.0	894
大片美村	2.6	1055	9000	232	22	5509	510	9.3	1126
矮岭冚村	5.5	3960	20000	1185	196	15169	5896	38.9	4136
大岭村	7.0	2514	8300	126	80	7583	1301	17.2	992
水朗村	4.5	1546	3120	60	36	43907	3573	8.1	1738
大塘村	8.5	3513	20000	480	252	13488	2124	15.7	1732
杨屋村	12.0	5250	15200	930	420	13005	1008	7.8	4424
颜屋村	3.0	816	9600	480	108	6349	810	12.8	607
大朗									
大朗社区	0.3	6751	3721	1123	195	3574	509	14.2	325
竹山社区	1.3	1688	4363	507	274	14429	1174	8.1	612
巷头社区	3.5	4687	22387	6969	2286	121008	23864	19.7	6643
巷尾社区	1.6	2065	9839	2003	540	51824	14758	28.5	4411
求富路社区	1.4	1560	9725	1091	274	46389	1434	3.1	2410
长塘社区	2.7	5168	16548	2770	654	129228	19191	14.9	5621
大井头社区	4.1	6044	11848	4067	834	103138	31703	30.7	6091
圣堂社区	0.9	1711	3928	2398	222	30481	2484	8.1	1860
黄草朗社区	1.5	2526	7295	1377	693	18638	8760	47.0	526
佛新社区	0.6	950	942	424	216	16948	1522	9.0	2710
屏山社区	2.3	554	619	146	91	6083	785	12.9	231
长富社区	1.5	3805	1005	657	68				
高英村	1.7	1868	6468	630	323	16287	3761	23.1	1070

15 续表 9

(2016年)

村（居）委会	土地面积（平方公里）	户籍人口（人）	外来暂住人口（人）	全部企业及个体户数（个）	#工业企业	资产总额（万元）	负债总额（万元）	资产负债率（%）	村组两级经营纯收入（万元）
蔡边村	6.1	4454	7828	2491	1071	47460	5597	11.8	1756
水口村	3.3	3112	10426	1401	602	28630	4758	16.6	1769
洋乌村	2.1	1771	4451	850	468	17501	2489	14.2	1547
洋坑塘村	1.1	1154	8744	817	402	12879	3194	24.8	872
松柏朗村	2.5	4500	7430	1213	457	21618	11196	51.8	842
黎贝岭村	1.9	2338	5421	1286	448	18613	1617	8.7	2344
佛子凹村	1.1	2591	1622	632	187	12507	1953	15.6	1100
松木山村	2.7	2798	11393	1335	666	24911	4909	19.7	1792
犀牛陂村	8.0	3577	12870	2146	1091	18773	1525	8.1	2747
水平村	7.9	1995	7173	982	381	24892	3697	14.9	1548
宝陂村	0.5	769	183	114	54	13452	5237	38.9	656
石厦村	8.0	3154	7938	1337	650	18743	1607	8.6	1207
杨涌村	1.5	1451	5881	772	276	7944	843	10.6	486
沙步村	3.1	2401	5304	1405	652	860	661	76.9	862
新马莲村	6.6	1662	5896	987	463	4114	2042	49.6	1010
黄江									
新市社区	1.6	8722	10542	620		1579	423	26.8	
三新社区	16.0	3151	11612	660	83	22667	1641	7.2	2258
田美社区	15.9	4943	35742	1493	391	35332	3006	8.5	5636
北岸社区	5.9	1693	13008	255	66	12951	1392	10.7	1950
长龙社区	18.0	2687	8100	285	71	11390	1792	15.7	1467
梅塘社区	25.6	5348	33557	1283	294	49093	6176	12.6	4518
宝山社区	4.9	3028	20740	671	145	40736	3617	8.9	3978
樟木头									
圩镇社区	4.3	11872	9372	2208	121	22386	9999	44.7	600
樟罗社区	6.8	3731	15532	2983	77	33005	7406	22.4	2823
百果洞社区	2.4	1016	5200	1160	32	13070	3842	29.4	371
樟洋社区	13.5	2540	26473	1912	51	21517	5715	26.6	1552
石新社区	7.3	2521	8960	2137	232	43504	21356	49.1	3801
柏地社区	6.6	1483	10500	1634	27	15675	6911	44.1	496
官仓社区	3.0	1176	2500	260	35	7225	2349	32.5	488
裕丰社区	10.0	2186	9368	613	87	9515	3736	39.3	532
金河社区	14.0	1822	9010	794	185	9995	2943	29.5	637
樟新社区									
清溪									
清溪社区	7.0	9163	14021	3051	20	5880	3324	56.5	1580
罗马村	7.0	1947	7200	350	53	4575	2728	59.6	1745
长山头村	4.3	1201	5000	79	32	13813	3180	23.0	1709
荔横村	3.4	1576	8576	484	58	6832	5296	77.5	3022
浮岗村	3.0	1990	6200	532	50	13890	4518	32.5	2180
松岗村	3.9	1284	3050	232	46	2100	906	43.1	1070
上元村	4.3	973	3500	225	29	4818	2663	55.3	1212

15 续表 10

(2016年)

村（居）委会	土地面积（平方公里）	户籍人口（人）	外来暂住人口（人）	全部企业及个体户数（个）	#工业企业	资产总额（万元）	负债总额（万元）	资产负债率（%）	村组两级经营纯收入（万元）
重河村	8.4	2786	6800	350	40	9315	1238	13.3	4420
清厦村	2.3	1636	8347	700	48	5927	3132	52.8	1597
铁松村	5.6	2635	8886	220	92	11719	3567	30.4	2436
铁场村	7.4	824	284	23	6	7317	4002	54.7	746
九乡村	7.5	1731	3000	200	62	8569	5890	68.7	1615
大埔村	1.8	752	2400	79	8	3037	1293	42.6	468
大利村	9.6	2722	11250	895	65	14715	3323	22.6	4190
渔樑围村	2.5	1186	19000	360	78	11826	3051	25.8	2653
三星村	2.5	1110	3268	131	23	2517	1274	50.6	1091
厦垊村	1.7	925	5750	335	35	8992	7393	82.2	492
土桥村	1.2	624	5800	249	40	8956	4746	53.0	1652
谢坑村	3.2	813	4615	95	50	7514	1696	22.6	1107
三中村	9.0	1833	57213	672	135	17061	7297	42.8	3430
青皇村	6.5	1177	3900	65	36	3000	497	16.6	1610
塘厦									
塘厦社区	0.9	3701	46300	2080	315	4959	813	16.4	1237
三局社区		2800							
林村社区	21.0	6059	41102	1923	280	104789	10288	9.8	15989
莲湖社区	9.0	2354	24000	710	138	18902	3468	18.4	3773
石潭埔社区	6.8	1727	10000	145	68	43212	1854	4.3	3183
横塘社区	4.0	1208	9676	270	104	14645	2124	14.5	1955
莆心湖社区	6.1	2248	11000	229	76	39732	2282	5.7	5359
诸佛岭社区	2.4	1216	10200	322	60	32657	4516	13.8	3860
振兴围社区	2.4	1046	16500	235	48	18940	893	4.7	1895
四村社区	4.0	1205	11900	993	39	22428	3200	14.3	2842
蛟乙塘社区	4.9	1516	9850	322	102	30409	3243	10.7	2784
大坪社区	13.0	1506	12896	155	94	80560	29836	37.0	2347
田心社区	4.5	967	9550	104	92	18094	1868	10.3	2287
龙背岭社区	8.2	1068	10000	316	80	11988	1645	13.7	1160
石鼓社区	6.4	2763	16000	300	160	42943	2346	5.5	4763
平山社区	4.8	850	13000	160	170	24827	2509	10.1	2197
桥陇社区	2.8	1134	12361	169	73	12922	1559	12.1	1613
凤凰岗社区	3.5	1430	10483	389	81	19204	1963	10.2	2434
沙湖社区	4.0	635	7713	120	102	14953	808	5.4	1714
石马社区	2.7	534	10000	200	70	6895	1154	16.7	655
清湖头社区	4.1	1552	19556	210	160	24487	1674	6.8	4526
塘新社区		17761							
凤岗									
凤岗社区	1.1	9053	3867	741	14				1036
雁田村	21.8	3930	68198	3044	320	329322	49538	15.0	25831
官井头村	10.4	2044	12186	1442	169	148628	9656	6.5	7120
油甘埔村	6.9	2097	20327	419	402	40409	6004	14.9	7431

15 续表 11

(2016年)

村（居）委会	土地面积（平方公里）	户籍人口（人）	外来暂住人口（人）	全部企业及个体户数（个）	#工业企业	资产总额（万元）	负债总额（万元）	资产负债率（%）	村组两级经营纯收入（万元）
凤德岭村	3.4	1300	5375	460	130	17472	4247	24.3	3501
塘沥村	6.7	1983	12711	312	84	13034	4445	34.1	4853
黄洞村	11.7	2268	14574	312	112	14601	2919	20.0	2878
竹塘村	5.7	1308	16083	505	109	8261	2570	31.1	3833
竹尾田村	1.5	757	5714	205	40	8508	557	6.5	1135
三联村	3.4	1525	4613	1450	34	5885	411	7.0	3589
五联村	5.6	1380	9147	482	216	17752	5630	31.7	2741
天堂围村	4.2	1166	6398	421	80	23431	2189	9.3	2364
谢岗									
泰园社区	0.8	3208	6312	1340	102	1446	1558	107.7	88
黎村村	12.8	4057	4250	168	76	25450	4779	18.8	3669
南面村	31.6	1611	1000	60	20	6423	1561	24.3	664
窖山村	1.0	545	1850	108	35	3440	695	20.2	301
大龙村	5.9	1093	2155	70	49	3320	1259	37.9	649
大厚村	6.3	1116	5080	187	58	20890	974	4.7	2226
谢山村	3.9	672	3200	302	32	15525	347	2.2	1108
谢岗村	10.4	3165	2597	158	81	20483	1275	6.2	2673
赵林村	7.1	1802	5641	141	79	18285	1734	9.5	1641
曹乐村	7.1	2380	9158	491	141	7387	660	8.9	1201
五星村	1.8	1411	3195	121	23	3259	1165	35.7	399
稔子园村	2.4	690	2078	80	50	22504	3675	16.3	1046
常平									
常平社区	0.7	21689	21671	1378		985	449	45.6	
新民社区									
下墟村	0.4	878	2007	158	38	26064	5303	20.3	2959
岗梓村	2.7	2633	3500	106	72	8256	3342	40.5	1292
桥梓村	2.0	2517	3880	333	161	19022	1901	10.0	2000
塘角村	1.1	995	3655	185	105	9404	1393	14.8	962
苏坑村	4.0	3815	6850	980	280	6621	1068	16.1	2249
袁山贝村	5.0	3749	7000	443	290	21547	5692	26.4	2400
金美村	3.0	2651	19038	310	140	46108	7036	15.3	4963
还珠沥村	5.5	2899	11205	550	150	12159	4783	39.3	1991
朗贝村	3.3	2119	6800	280	75	8870	1759	19.8	2487
板石村	3.1	2097	11200	672	56	3847	761	19.8	2438
桥沥村	9.8	3698	6710	510	293	12073	1248	10.3	3356
卢屋村	3.0	858	4343	165	165	3163	1686	53.3	886
土塘村	8.7	2960	31126	1586	168	21916	2114	9.6	1903
麦元村	2.4	1117	3900	696	25	11339	1429	12.6	1091
九江水村	9.0	1507	6500	226	65	24168	1293	5.4	1355
朗洲村	4.1	630	500	112	29	5225	755	14.4	315
陈屋贝村	2.2	1130	2970	150	35	11979	546	4.6	878

15 续表 12

(2016年)

村（居）委会	土地面积（平方公里）	户籍人口（人）	外来暂住人口（人）	全部企业及个体户数（个）	#工业企业	资产总额（万元）	负债总额（万元）	资产负债率（%）	村组两级经营纯收入（万元）
司马村	8.1	2879	10982	620	84	22822	4438	19.4	2594
霞坑村	1.6	754	4500	220	23	8645	503	5.8	503
漱旧村	2.0	1140	3650	130	28	7791	971	12.5	1490
漱新村	2.4	1298	6300	403	93	11192	4082	36.5	1137
黄泥塘村	1.0	900	2000	94	45	3355	1662	49.5	122
元江元村	2.1	1540	8300	212	90	7503	1094	14.6	920
横江厦村	5.0	2859	1600	236	85	11945	5083	42.6	889
田尾村	2.1	1587	2300	132	27	4701	2315	49.2	337
白花沥村	1.1	711	350	18	15	3192	882	27.6	100
沙湖口村	1.3	1040	2980	95	20	3806	2097	55.1	279
白石岗村	5.0	3866	4334	98	91	6065	3960	65.3	1493
松柏塘村	3.8	2446	5347	84	34	7878	3724	47.3	676
上坑村	1.3	962	2100	104	27	8592	1447	16.8	786
木棆村	3.5	2303	1003	541	42	35091	4120	11.7	5005
桥头									
莲城社区	14.6	10414	62454						
桥头社区	1.0	1428	3962	297	31	27711	1588	5.7	3059
迳联社区	1.5	1857	3643	120	51	22545	3198	14.2	1779
田新社区	2.2	2292	4086	298	180	21180	5242	24.7	1695
岭头社区	1.3	1209	3586	413	64	14888	358	2.4	1329
大洲社区	4.6	3387	3200	182	76	16072	2319	14.4	1684
东江村	4.8	2529	2870	193	42	7880	3491	44.3	665
山和村	2.5	1017	6850	113	28	7282	1741	23.9	541
屋厦村	2.0	733	2230	85	35	5201	448	8.6	675
岗头村	0.6	509	2580	48	28	3728	864	23.2	325
李屋村	2.3	1671	4201	72	38	15034	3347	22.3	765
邓屋村	2.7	1993	9860	56	36	22087	1595	7.2	2250
朗厦村	4.1	1693	4520	79	70	20108	2551	12.7	1815
邵岗头村	1.3	912	1474	50	35	5584	2041	36.6	713
石水口村	7.8	4724	7300	430	152	31983	3138	9.8	2895
禾坑村	1.5	1034	1920	85	35	6956	452	6.5	690
田头角村	1.2	792	1870	97	53	6973	643	9.2	940
横沥									
恒泉社区	0.2	7705	1713	2322	21	1828	820	44.9	275
石涌村	3.7	1892	6033	1919	110	15541	1896	12.2	1475
隔坑村	2.2	2852	5300	1288	68	15127	4796	31.7	2717
半仙山村	2.2	1797	2800	1180	35	18661	5700	30.5	846
横沥村	4.6	3103	3200	1756	46	14616	7669	52.5	1693
田头村	4.1	2647	7348	1423	54	13751	335	2.4	1932
田坑村	4.8	3006	4876	2256	72	7521	2770	36.8	1895
村头村	3.5	2434	6371	914	95	13716	3538	25.8	634
长巷村	2.1	1752	899	187	12	6071	1497	24.7	241

15 续表 13

(2016年)

村（居）委会	土地面积（平方公里）	户籍人口（人）	外来暂住人口（人）	全部企业及个体户数（个）	#工业企业	资产总额（万元）	负债总额（万元）	资产负债率（%）	村组两级经营纯收入（万元）
田饶步村	2.8	1904	1658	532	70	14868	6629	44.6	56
六甲村	1.4	1140	3265	320	66	7504	2887	38.5	369
村尾村	2.7	1583	3954	991	42	13920	4474	32.1	339
水边村	4.0	2999	4057	579	45	8767	2854	32.6	611
新四村	2.9	2170	7039	738	118	1606	925	57.6	1514
山厦村	2.3	1107	2021	957	64	13408	829	6.2	672
月塘村	0.5	1156	1560	239	35	11828	1130	9.6	464
张坑村	1.0	643	2591	153	25	7160	1467	20.5	506
东坑									
草塘社区	0.1	2953	285	270	51				
骏达社区	0.1	452	13569	95	18				
东坑村	2.0	3131	11000	1739	331	27855	5807	20.8	4126
黄麻岭村	0.8	1125	1800	364	69	8835	3502	39.6	315
长安塘村	1.3	1891	2810	504	96	15004	5528	36.8	1260
寮边头村	0.8	1609	2805	458	87	7400	2120	28.6	820
塔岗村	2.1	1787	4752	467	89	15100	1922	12.7	863
坑美村	2.2	2021	3892	477	91	11853	1633	13.8	868
新门楼村	2.1	1720	6870	578	110	13795	4545	32.9	767
井美村	1.9	2500	5000	1048	199	20227	2521	12.5	1726
初坑村	2.8	2572	17500	1183	226	3018	606	20.1	2757
凤大村	0.3	758	1308	192	36	6851	2221	32.4	368
丁屋村	1.1	1105	2600	232	44	5230	1624	31.1	682
彭屋村	2.1	1952	3248	421	81	6695	908	13.6	1349
黄屋村	2.0	2042	5000	1595	305	14083	2683	19.1	1185
角社村	2.4	3492	5788	789	152	27779	1842	6.6	1278
企石									
宝石社区	0.9	5732	3195	700	70	156	56	36.0	22
铁岗村	5.7	2634	4296	128	40	12412	4279	34.5	667
深巷村	4.1	2406	2415	200	70	6695	2005	29.9	653
湖美村	1.0	808	173	26	20	5130	2303	44.9	207
博厦村	6.9	3739	915	85	34	10006	1129	11.3	290
上洞村	5.1	2864	1126	56	17	7185	1407	19.6	234
清湖村	4.4	2129	2362	42	32	7592	2760	36.4	626
江边村	4.9	3107	1520	65	21	6785	1593	23.5	250
旧围村	3.8	2039	3502	52	38	5816	1254	21.6	339
东平村	1.6	758	2133	215	51	4738	3478	73.4	364
上截村	0.9	1232	2040	97	65	5863	4425	75.5	306
下截村	1.2	1528	1961	38	20	6745	2109	31.3	748
东山村	6.0	4493	4896	739	126	33304	7282	21.9	3093
铁炉坑村	3.4	3353	3351	122	40	11757	531	4.5	501
企石村	1.5	1558	656	41	19	6746	2193	32.5	272
杨屋村	0.8	686	718	50	15	4862	2794	57.5	108
莫屋村	1.0	1322	1300	80	30	6180	2430	39.3	264

15 续表 14

(2016年)

村（居）委会	土地面积(平方公里)	户籍人口(人)	外来暂住人口(人)	全部企业及个体户数(个)	#工业企业	资产总额(万元)	负债总额(万元)	资产负债率(%)	村组两级经营纯收入(万元)
霞朗村	1.0	964	1736	301	32	13110	2055	15.7	1662
新南村	2.8	2198	2300	341	52	9670	2708	28.0	809
南坑村	1.4	1293	2000	76	42	9819	2330	23.7	269
石　排									
太和社区		3298				2063	471	22.8	142
石排村	2.4	3754	10180	751	34	3643	692	19.0	1928
下沙村	2.2	2643	4500	506	144	5041	1279	25.4	2456
庙边王村	2.0	2499	7620	672	236	5627	1676	29.8	1880
福隆村	3.7	6121	10012	1147	275	17009	7228	42.5	1813
沙角村	3.4	2649	4500	153	39	4032	836	20.7	599
黄家壆村	2.4	1980	2450	152	30	8964	1436	16.0	506
赤坎村	3.2	1452	4879	150	85	9295	2578	27.7	585
向西村	2.0	1229	6460	478	63	6503	706	10.9	861
水贝村	3.5	3384	4325	357	69	6498	1091	16.8	1536
田寮村	3.3	2017	1432	120	45	5958	1244	20.9	853
横山村	3.8	2110	6017	173	46	2760	845	30.6	1405
谷吓村	2.0	1961	4098	212	115	7197	2216	30.8	1505
埔心村	2.2	1677	10963	680	140	11313	584	5.2	2450
塘尾村	0.9	1100	2431	233	59	10342	1730	16.7	436
李家坊村	0.9	960	2800	191	57	5959	1082	18.2	509
田边村	4.2	2176	3299	185	72	4474	1273	28.5	1074
中坑村	3.2	5570	3170	228	35	15112	1529	10.1	738
燕窝村	3.6	1800	4200	389	108	8836	1182	13.4	1342
茶　山									
茶山圩社区	0.3	6704	2460	642	16				
茶溪社区		1299							
上元村	5.1	3244	3080	695	90	10763	843	7.8	1473
茶山村	2.3	1793	4100	610	50	11720	3242	27.7	1504
下朗村	1.8	1461	2045	242	34	24874	9055	36.4	1643
横江村	4.3	3271	4300	420	212	16229	1967	12.1	1480
卢边村	3.6	2877	3800	377	121	11705	2756	23.5	850
寒溪水村	1.3	1008	2110	108	47	3556	1024	28.8	693
增埗村	6.3	7535	10525	655	360	9626	3941	40.9	5080
南社村	4.1	3690	8016	476	228	32760	2709	8.3	1808
塘角村	2.8	3114	6141	386	145	15421	721	4.7	4014
京山村	4.2	2579	6035	362	55	16715	3853	23.1	2860
博头村	0.9	696	1250	40	33	4752	577	12.1	340
冲美村	0.7	807	1300	95	39	8083	471	5.8	684
粟边村	2.2	2089	2700	231	82	8190	709	8.7	934
刘黄村	1.5	1013	3603	171	62	6777	1968	29.0	627
孙屋村	0.8	721	1220	46	25	2542	953	37.5	152
超朗村	3.3	2969	10186	192	74	39417	13834	35.1	1454

十六、历年国民经济和社会发展主要指标

Main Indicators of National Economy and Social Development over Years

16 历年国民经济和社会发展主要指标

Main Indicators of National Economy and Social Development over Years

年 份	户籍人口(万人)	常住人口(万人)	外来暂住人口(万人)	户籍人口自然增长率(‰)	外来暂住从业人员(万人)	城镇在岗职工人数(万人)	城镇在岗职工平均工资(元)
1949	68.24						
1952	71.68						
1957	77.48					3.90	400
1962	79.64					2.93	552
1965	86.46			29.60		3.17	524
1970	98.56			20.60		3.29	534
1975	107.94			14.51		3.80	577
1978	111.23			13.81		8.20	474
1979	112.04			19.00		9.68	650
1980	112.70			19.31		9.86	750
1981	114.46			16.57		10.66	887
1982	116.19			14.14		11.41	1095
1983	117.59			11.53		11.59	1197
1984	118.95			10.60		11.76	1383
1985	120.85			10.83		12.30	1456
1986	123.01		15.62	11.56	10.41	13.27	2616
1987	124.86		25.29	11.67	18.03	13.67	2067
1988	126.76		36.89	12.09	29.25	12.71	2757
1989	128.76		47.19	12.39	40.53	13.10	3320
1990	131.85	175.62	65.59	12.31	57.20	13.16	3552
1991	133.65	200.01	80.58	13.34	70.20	14.59	3777
1992	136.06	227.78	114.48	14.50	107.10	15.47	4531
1993	138.92	259.41	121.70	13.41	112.68	17.66	6228
1994	141.40	295.43	139.09	13.37	124.18	16.09	8360
1995	143.65	336.45	142.18	12.75	126.54	17.87	9682
1996	145.25	383.17	143.32	11.97	127.66	17.50	10382
1997	147.12	436.38	144.68	12.09	130.73	16.50	10691
1998	148.77	496.97	199.11	10.86	183.19	16.40	11422
1999	150.82	565.98	244.81	10.22	216.15	16.39	12557
2000	152.61	644.84	254.72	7.52	244.84	16.41	14051
2001	153.89	654.43	457.82	7.01	449.68	16.42	16183
2002	156.19	654.84	433.65	5.91	426.01	16.42	17804
2003	158.96	655.25	440.45	5.65	432.73	16.60	22598
2004	161.97	655.66	486.95	5.96	473.39	17.54	25326
2005	165.65	656.07	584.98	6.02	553.42	18.86	28253
2006	168.31	685.66	586.76	5.86	566.98	19.99	31135
2007	171.26	717.02	557.80	5.98	538.95	20.56	35284
2008	174.87	750.60	552.50	6.23	530.30	20.72	39516
2009	178.73	786.08	429.96	6.31	413.46	22.60	42585
2010	181.77	822.48	411.47	6.23	391.23	22.63	46576
2011	184.77	825.48	413.62	6.13	394.71	24.61	50398
2012	187.02	829.23	416.74	8.10	397.94	25.02	57007
2013	188.93	831.66	434.68	7.18	412.80	239.82	42870
2014	191.39	834.31	415.86	5.83	389.33	234.25	47600
2015	195.01	825.41	400.81	6.41	376.54	226.78	53221
2016	200.94	826.14	428.39	8.64	395.39	226.94	57649

注：2012年起城镇在岗职工含劳务派遣人员；2013年起，将原属于乡镇企业且符合城镇非私营单位条件的“四上”企业纳入城镇单位从业人员及工资统计的范围。

16 续表 1

年　份	地区生产总值(亿元)	第一产业	第二产业	第三产业	#工　业	#建筑业	人均地区生产总值(元)
1978	6.11	2.72	2.68	0.71			553
1979	6.62	2.65	2.92	1.05			593
1980	7.22	2.63	3.33	1.26			643
1981	9.11	3.28	4.30	1.54			802
1982	11.43	3.73	5.81	1.89			991
1983	13.03	3.98	6.90	2.15			1115
1984	15.96	4.57	7.81	3.59			1350
1985	22.60	6.15	11.66	4.80			1885
1986	30.02	8.14	13.57	8.30	10.54	3.03	2462
1987	39.29	9.82	17.72	11.74	14.24	3.49	3170
1988	55.46	11.89	28.28	15.29	25.05	3.23	4408
1989	60.92	12.66	27.97	20.29	27.22	0.75	4768
1990	80.44	13.28	40.53	26.63	39.18	1.34	6173
1991	95.91	13.45	50.32	32.13	48.34	1.98	5095
1992	110.89	14.41	59.27	37.21	56.63	2.64	5038
1993	157.05	14.40	87.31	55.34	82.89	4.42	5850
1994	217.03	17.48	119.49	80.06	110.77	8.72	6357
1995	296.29	21.43	166.97	107.89	154.19	12.78	7421
1996	361.75	24.86	199.48	137.40	187.85	11.63	8444
1997	448.60	25.64	243.28	179.68	230.79	12.50	9747
1998	558.00	25.94	305.68	226.37	290.69	14.99	11265
1999	667.24	25.79	367.05	274.40	349.53	17.52	12494
2000	820.25	25.91	450.71	343.64	430.45	20.25	13679
2001	991.89	26.10	540.51	425.28	517.03	23.48	15268
2002	1186.94	24.88	648.81	513.25	621.86	26.96	18131
2003	1452.52	22.82	798.20	631.51	757.18	41.01	22174
2004	1806.03	22.71	1016.04	767.28	968.01	48.03	27554
2005	2183.20	20.55	1227.86	934.78	1173.23	54.63	33287
2006	2627.98	12.01	1506.60	1109.37	1441.69	64.91	39173
2007	3160.05	11.90	1754.66	1393.49	1681.83	72.83	45057
2008	3703.60	14.83	1901.61	1787.17	1819.22	82.38	50471
2009	3785.83	14.79	1836.01	1935.03	1754.46	81.55	49273
2010	4278.21	16.57	2191.78	2069.86	2109.42	82.37	53913
2011	4771.93	17.88	2417.54	2336.52	2339.75	77.79	57913
2012	5039.21	18.76	2444.61	2575.85	2366.49	78.12	60907
2013	5517.47	19.55	2622.67	2875.25	2542.60	86.69	66440
2014	5881.32	20.35	2794.42	3066.55	2709.00	91.35	70605
2015	6275.07	21.03	2922.05	3332.00	2840.35	88.81	75616
2016	6827.69	24.20	3173.24	3630.25	3089.26	91.37	82682

注：1．本表按当年价格计算。
　　2．人均生产总值1990年及以前年份按年平均户籍人口计算，1991年起按年平均常住人口计算。

16 续表 2

（上年＝100）

年　份	地区生产总值指数	第一产业	第二产业	第三产业	#工　业	#建筑业	人均地区生产总值指　数
1979	99.5	86.5	107.0	146.4			98.6
1980	102.7	90.3	117.3	113.9			102.0
1981	116.6	115.0	122.1	110.8			115.4
1982	116.9	105.3	131.0	117.6			115.1
1983	110.4	104.8	115.7	111.3			108.9
1984	114.2	109.0	107.0	140.9			112.9
1985	132.3	118.9	144.5	132.7			130.5
1986	126.1	111.9	110.3	174.7			124.0
1987	122.5	111.6	127.7	126.0	125.8	147.0	120.5
1988	115.7	90.6	143.7	103.0	151.4	77.9	114.0
1989	107.1	99.8	106.2	113.7	106.4	103.7	105.5
1990	123.2	104.4	127.6	128.0	130.6	76.4	120.8
1991	117.5	103.1	121.5	118.6	121.8	113.2	108.8
1992	108.3	100.0	112.6	105.1	113.7	78.0	92.6
1993	127.9	79.4	139.2	129.0	138.5	168.1	104.8
1994	122.5	107.2	124.7	122.3	124.3	138.5	96.3
1995	127.4	110.5	135.1	116.8	135.3	128.3	108.9
1996	117.5	109.4	115.5	123.5	116.2	91.2	109.5
1997	119.6	104.5	119.8	121.8	120.1	106.1	111.3
1998	121.8	100.9	122.1	124.5	122.2	115.1	113.1
1999	119.7	102.3	120.6	120.3	120.7	115.2	111.0
2000	119.7	99.8	120.7	120.0	120.9	110.5	106.6
2001	119.9	103.0	121.6	118.9	122.0	113.0	110.7
2002	120.5	97.6	122.6	119.1	123.0	114.1	119.6
2003	120.5	90.2	122.3	119.7	121.4	143.5	120.4
2004	121.0	90.0	125.6	115.8	126.5	106.8	120.9
2005	119.5	102.3	120.0	119.3	120.2	113.5	119.4
2006	119.2	58.9	121.9	117.1	122.0	118.7	116.6
2007	118.3	89.9	114.8	123.3	115.0	108.7	113.1
2008	114.0	110.6	106.1	124.0	106.4	100.9	109.0
2009	105.3	102.3	100.3	110.8	100.1	104.7	100.6
2010	110.3	101.6	117.1	103.7	118.0	97.1	105.4
2011	108.0	100.5	107.4	108.7	108.1	87.8	105.4
2012	106.1	100.0	106.1	106.2	106.4	98.5	105.7
2013	109.8	100.1	111.9	107.7	112.1	104.5	109.4
2014	107.8	102.8	109.1	106.3	109.3	103.3	107.4
2015	108.0	101.9	106.1	110.2	106.3	98.9	108.4
2016	108.1	105.6	108.7	107.6	108.9	102.1	108.6

注：本表按可比价格计算。

年 份	固定资产投资总额（亿元）	一般公共预算收入（亿元）	一般公共预算支出（亿元）	居民消费价格指数（上年=100）	商品零售价格指数（上年=100）	农林牧渔业总 产 值（亿元）	农林牧渔业总产值指数（1978年=100）
1949						0.54	
1952		0.28	0.02			0.66	
1957		0.32	0.04			0.78	
1962		0.31	0.07			0.76	
1965		0.47	0.07			1.28	
1970		0.48	0.08			1.47	
1975		0.65	0.11			2.53	
1978	0.23	0.66	0.18		100.4	4.24	100.0
1979	0.16	0.66	0.19		102.6	4.15	96.5
1980	0.24	0.67	0.20		110.9	4.19	98.0
1981	0.38	0.68	0.21		109.3	5.04	102.1
1982	1.81	0.81	0.26		101.2	5.59	117.6
1983	1.84	0.86	0.28		99.6	5.64	117.4
1984	3.01	0.85	0.30	99.3	98.6	7.02	126.7
1985	7.06	1.11	0.50	106.5	106.9	9.12	138.9
1986	11.52	1.61	0.99	104.2	104.4	12.30	174.6
1987	14.19	2.02	1.25	112.0	112.2	14.84	186.4
1988	16.55	2.71	1.75	136.0	132.8	20.37	182.1
1989	5.01	3.19	2.16	122.0	122.4	22.11	181.9
1990	7.51	3.57	2.28	96.6	94.9	23.64	195.3
1991	13.75	4.44	2.75	102.4	101.4	24.26	199.5
1992	18.88	5.62	3.82	109.2	107.7	27.13	211.3
1993	32.76	9.38	7.29	121.8	119.5	28.45	175.5
1994	140.76	7.69	8.90	123.5	118.4	34.75	188.4
1995	63.14	11.56	12.42	113.9	109.7	42.69	207.8
1996	67.62	9.65	12.41	106.8	104.7	49.72	216.3
1997	65.89	11.41	14.85	101.5	99.7	51.44	225.0
1998	77.00	15.10	17.91	99.9	98.7	53.60	227.3
1999	88.32	18.26	21.26	97.9	95.9	53.74	242.8
2000	102.89	30.47	33.61	101.5	100.1	54.64	243.3
2001	125.49	45.02	47.86	96.6	97.8	55.93	246.3
2002	191.57	55.29	64.96	98.1	99.1	53.67	263.2
2003	319.39	67.45	76.52	100.7	101.7	49.02	209.7
2004	454.87	82.64	94.16	103.0	103.2	44.19	213.5
2005	597.24	103.97	117.04	102.4	103.0	42.05	222.2
2006	705.45	128.94	147.90	101.2	102.8	21.26	121.0
2007	841.21	186.45	193.10	103.1	104.2	19.98	105.6
2008	944.34	209.22	218.26	105.5	107.9	25.53	118.3
2009	1094.08	231.16	232.62	96.9	95.3	25.31	122.2
2010	1114.98	277.84	289.83	102.8	103.2	28.31	126.2
2011	1079.31	313.06	351.92	104.9	104.7	30.66	126.1
2012	1180.35	356.32	385.58	102.9	102.4	32.01	126.9
2013	1383.94	409.29	444.66	101.9	100.6	33.15	125.1
2014	1427.11	455.21	457.68	102.3	101.2	33.94	126.4
2015	1446.52	517.97	581.24	101.4	99.4	34.35	126.1
2016	1557.46	544.75	599.29	102.7	100.9	38.44	130.0

注：农林牧渔总产值1952—1970年按1957年不变价计算，1975年按1970年不变价计算，1978年起按当年价计算。

16 续表 4

年 份	农作物总播种面积（千公顷）	#粮食	粮食产量（万吨）	油料产量（万吨）	水果产量（万吨）	肉类产量（万吨）	水产品产量（万吨）
1949	141.26	127.26	21.07	0.15			0.32
1952	167.61	149.68	26.95	0.35			0.34
1957	188.98	165.53	28.80	0.33			0.42
1962	155.97	138.18	33.12	0.38			0.63
1965	158.97	121.64	43.71	0.72	4.54		0.99
1970	174.60	127.25	45.08	0.96	6.95		1.62
1975	202.00	137.03	50.72	1.11	3.68		2.19
1978	190.63	138.15	53.23	1.42	2.65	2.69	3.09
1979	172.36	129.16	53.53	1.91	2.33	2.92	2.23
1980	162.41	117.12	52.94	2.90	2.37	2.77	2.55
1981	151.17	107.13	44.75	3.55	4.69	2.80	2.49
1982	146.96	106.68	54.33	2.99	5.82	3.30	2.77
1983	146.21	109.02	56.12	1.97	7.72	3.57	3.03
1984	144.35	105.12	55.82	2.31	10.59	3.33	3.25
1985	130.01	93.05	48.87	2.10	18.94	3.33	3.26
1986	119.41	83.81	45.52	2.01	30.77	4.33	4.65
1987	119.73	83.40	46.28	1.70	36.31	4.61	6.57
1988	119.53	82.42	46.09	1.51	26.37	5.61	6.81
1989	122.27	85.61	48.76	1.37	22.14	5.86	6.23
1990	123.25	85.74	49.43	1.34	28.24	6.22	6.85
1991	119.42	81.77	47.37	1.15	34.32	6.88	6.90
1992	104.10	64.26	36.81	0.93	34.48	6.80	7.32
1993	71.20	36.74	20.21	0.56	27.13	7.66	6.50
1994	67.30	35.75	20.24	0.37	26.49	8.54	6.74
1995	71.89	39.90	22.74	0.37	24.32	9.76	7.48
1996	72.23	41.89	24.32	0.31	20.63	11.61	8.11
1997	72.17	41.61	24.69	0.29	16.50	12.90	9.19
1998	73.46	41.63	24.72	0.26	11.41	15.35	9.69
1999	72.59	41.77	24.73	0.22	13.63	15.99	9.40
2000	65.73	35.18	20.41	0.20	12.94	17.90	9.51
2001	56.95	22.56	12.84	0.16	15.01	19.84	8.96
2002	42.28	9.88	5.37	0.09	18.93	18.88	8.24
2003	33.97	5.65	3.05	0.04	14.64	15.46	7.58
2004	30.82	5.41	3.04	0.02	17.54	14.62	7.15
2005	27.38	4.14	2.00	0.01	15.13	17.17	6.74
2006	22.26	2.29	1.00	0.01	13.96	3.49	4.71
2007	21.37	2.15	0.99	0.01	13.16	2.03	4.73
2008	23.48	2.72	1.19	0.01	10.15	2.41	7.23
2009	24.72	2.77	1.19	0.01	9.15	2.55	7.33
2010	24.62	2.79	1.25	0.01	7.55	2.88	7.63
2011	24.46	2.76	1.29	0.01	7.39	2.60	7.82
2012	24.83	2.75	1.25	0.03	6.49	2.67	7.70
2013	24.52	2.74	1.24	0.02	6.11	2.28	7.45
2014	24.41	2.75	1.24	0.02	6.25	2.01	7.27
2015	24.97	2.81	1.27	0.02	6.30	1.52	6.89
2016	25.10	2.78	1.26	0.02	5.94	1.29	5.66

16 续表 5

年 份	工业企业单位数（个）	工 业增加值（亿元）	工业增加值指数（上年=100）	规模以上工业增加值（亿元）	总 供电 量（亿千瓦时）	全社会用电量（亿千瓦时）	建筑业总产值（亿元）	建筑业增加值（亿元）
1949	1							
1952	23							
1957	262							
1962	280				0.08			
1965	260				0.36			
1970	220				0.71			
1975	324				1.24			
1978	1290				1.64			
1979	1250				1.93			
1980	1293				2.17			
1981	1479				2.22			
1982	1862				2.69			
1983	1964				3.15			
1984	2329				3.26			
1985	4187				3.82			
1986	5949	10.54		4.28	3.93			3.03
1987	8106	14.24	125.8	5.67	6.43			3.49
1988	8408	25.05	151.4	7.93	9.48			3.23
1989	8757	27.22	106.4	9.36	12.09		1.03	0.75
1990	9892	39.18	130.6	13.44	18.01	18.01	1.27	1.34
1991	10094	48.34	121.8	17.63	24.05	24.05	2.19	1.98
1992	11639	56.63	113.7	25.66	32.00	32.00	3.19	2.64
1993	12449	82.89	138.5	35.05	43.62	43.62	5.39	4.42
1994	14086	110.77	124.3	56.61	58.58	58.58	7.99	8.72
1995	15215	154.19	135.3	64.99	68.00	68.00	9.49	12.78
1996	15326	187.85	116.2	84.14	80.03	80.03	9.66	11.63
1997	16857	230.79	120.1	103.90	94.93	94.83	28.73	12.50
1998	16406	290.69	122.2	168.71	109.48	109.48	35.92	14.99
1999	16877	349.53	120.7	232.15	132.78	134.37	40.73	17.52
2000	16975	430.45	120.9	259.44	178.03	179.66	40.45	20.25
2001	18094	517.03	122.0	290.67	207.72	209.17	50.13	23.48
2002	21313	621.86	123.0	466.61	258.55	259.86	65.84	26.96
2003	21935	757.18	121.4	595.48	321.65	323.53	76.48	41.01
2004	22156	968.01	126.5	800.45	372.84	375.85	77.01	48.03
2005	21868	1173.23	120.2	1062.42	415.66	419.83	84.35	58.61
2006	22447	1441.69	122.0	1318.58	464.45	472.01	94.58	64.91
2007	22587	1681.83	115.0	1430.60	507.89	515.40	112.87	72.83
2008	25656	1819.22	106.4	1689.90	507.35	514.16	108.81	82.38
2009	31160	1754.46	100.1	1453.37	488.85	495.58	99.40	81.55
2010	38273	2109.42	118.0	1708.31	556.89	562.00	122.06	82.37
2011	46413	2339.75	108.6	1642.45	579.35	586.07	130.85	77.79
2012	57808	2366.49	106.4	1978.13	600.58	604.28	157.58	78.12
2013	67332	2542.60	112.1	2425.62	617.20	622.51	188.13	86.69
2014	80567	2709.00	109.3	2490.84	655.72	660.99	204.21	91.35
2015	97944	2840.35	106.3	2611.96	661.26	666.84	224.59	88.81
2016	121762	3089.26	108.9	2968.16	695.59	702.01	267.22	91.37

16 续表 6

年 份	公路通车里程（公里）	民用汽车拥有量（万辆）	旅客周转量（万人公里）	货物周转量（万吨公里）	邮电业务收入（万元）	本地电话用户（万户）	移动电话用户（万户）
1949	204	0.002					
1952	219	0.002	1350	139			
1957	373	0.005	2100	195			
1962	598	0.007	4120	293			
1965	882	0.010	4725	457			
1970	1134	0.012	2800	900			
1975	1173	0.025	3890	694			
1978	1259	0.06	9425	15148	686	0.20	
1979	1225	0.11	11162	15290	790	0.21	
1980	1225	0.20	13584	16353	927	0.31	
1981	1225	0.30	13845	15606	962	0.34	
1982	1225	0.34	16026	17185	940	0.35	
1983	1225	0.45	54075	108634	1018	0.39	
1984	1240	0.61	62107	140113	1263	0.48	
1985	1240	0.79	95237	171591	1560	0.77	
1986	1248	0.86	127458	126898	2015	0.88	
1987	1261	1.00	159117	174942	3410	1.63	
1988	1302	1.36	173335	169112	5728	2.52	
1989	1325	1.63	240999	186626	9620	4.30	0.02
1990	1325	1.94	322236	184700	17555	4.90	0.05
1991	1759	2.07	373284	194101	27733	7.50	0.11
1992	2055	3.26	503973	232752	42155	9.70	0.30
1993	2260	4.81	577800	248230	65699	14.98	0.72
1994	2292	6.16	595134	273053	102238	23.19	2.41
1995	2327	8.83	446230	264605	152761	31.57	4.77
1996	2330	9.08	477466	267193	207573	36.91	8.24
1997	2330	10.34	511592	278649	284278	42.65	15.29
1998	2377	11.34	577452	285889	376708	50.13	26.17
1999	2467	12.70	804278	300410	515916	60.87	51.01
2000	2518	15.37	1001906	404678	724593	78.12	123.68
2001	2570	18.36	1031579	406247	1225474	98.96	295.76
2002	2641	22.01	1091821	420684	1816802	127.93	412.39
2003	2688	25.56	1126964	422822	1051220	206.11	660.86
2004	2759	31.97	1166262	423669	1207778	281.35	856.09
2005	2871	40.66	1185290	424829	1328172	384.52	1016.41
2006	3891	48.93	1213809	336783	1466871	461.31	1216.34
2007	3924	60.89	1264982	356677	1619048	469.17	1408.23
2008	4001	70.16	2248521	1747489	1723829	439.41	1454.29
2009	4713	79.56	1053469	1016490	1563077	378.40	1409.29
2010	4751	92.08	1290692	1090340	1553352	332.42	1607.60
2011	4828	106.14	1458811	1874802	1648579	319.55	1677.77
2012	4969	120.70	1568758	2967132	1699619	330.79	1797.75
2013	5002	138.91	1559856	4322745	1758017	314.48	1850.39
2014	5145	155.96	854598	4480052	1694637	327.22	1763.09
2015	5165	184.49	771316	5048509	2489805	298.23	1756.75
2016	5266	224.62	773194	4552331	2951331	272.63	1575.08

注：1．公路通车里程2006年起含专用公路和村道。
2．邮电业务收入2003年以前为邮电业务总量，按1990年不变价计算，2003年起为邮电业务收入。
3．2014年客运量和旅客周转量不含城市客运量，数据与往年不可比。

年 份	社会消费品零售总额（亿元）	进出口总额 亿美元（亿元）	出口总额	进口总额	协议(合同)规定外商投资额（亿美元）	实际利用外资（亿美元）	#外商直接投资
1957			0.02				
1962			0.04				
1965			0.08				
1970			0.10				
1975			0.25				
1978	2.13		0.39				
1979	2.50		0.54		0.05	0.02	
1980	3.16		0.77		0.11	0.09	
1981	4.02		0.92		0.08	0.05	0.001
1982	4.81		1.09		0.08	0.07	0.005
1983	5.23		1.19		0.16	0.09	0.003
1984	7.39		1.30		0.32	0.19	0.07
1985	9.36		1.75		0.68	0.29	0.14
1986	12.24		2.33		0.34	0.30	0.15
1987	15.05		2.68		1.85	1.13	0.21
1988	24.65		3.18		6.22	2.41	0.64
1989	27.04		3.49		2.34	2.49	0.84
1990	31.97	10.82	5.68	5.14	3.02	2.43	1.00
1991	36.50	31.75	16.52	15.23	6.45	2.62	1.47
1992	44.35	50.90	26.03	24.87	20.88	4.66	3.29
1993	63.69	67.56	32.11	35.45	35.55	9.34	7.92
1994	85.16	88.30	42.94	45.36	34.97	10.48	7.79
1995	113.01	153.91	77.99	75.92	33.09	10.57	6.72
1996	125.53	178.42	91.87	86.55	20.89	10.76	6.95
1997	146.04	212.99	113.68	99.31	12.14	12.14	8.80
1998	175.16	232.73	130.61	102.13	16.37	13.38	9.30
1999	202.30	284.63	151.54	133.09	14.72	14.57	9.71
2000	235.16	320.45	171.59	148.86	18.36	16.47	10.87
2001	275.71	344.55	189.89	154.65	20.98	18.16	11.47
2002	321.24	442.47	237.36	205.11	24.89	21.48	14.59
2003	369.78	521.06	280.02	241.04	32.56	25.63	17.54
2004	426.47	645.18	351.92	293.25	41.32	30.34	21.39
2005	506.29	743.72	409.29	334.42	47.52	37.51	14.68
2006	599.32	842.21	473.76	368.45	55.28	43.38	18.08
2007	722.45	1068.73	602.32	466.41	62.51	50.44	21.18
2008	881.15	1132.99	655.37	477.62	39.37	32.26	24.47
2009	1029.04	941.55	551.69	389.86	20.30	29.42	25.94
2010	1223.34	1213.38	695.98	517.40	30.73	31.63	27.32
2011	1441.25	1352.24	783.29	568.95	37.02	32.18	30.51
2012	1600.41	1444.16	850.66	593.50	41.55	37.19	33.69
2013	1786.66	1530.72	908.64	622.08	41.56	40.29	39.38
2014	1942.29	1625.30	970.69	654.61	44.39	46.21	45.29
2015	2184.70	1676.73	1037.19	639.55	50.91	54.68	53.20
2016	2470.78	11415.99	6556.85	4859.15	47.90	39.84	39.26

注：1.出口总额1990年起为海关口径，1990年以前为外经贸口径。
2.外商直接投资2004年起为新口径，是以验资作为统计标准，与往年数不可比。
3.2016年起，进出口相关数据采用人民币口径。

16 续表 8

年 份	国际及港澳台旅游者（万人次）	旅游总收入（亿元）	国际旅游外汇收入（万美元）	接待国内游客人次（万人次）	各项人民币存款余额（亿元）	#住户存款	各项人民币贷款余额（亿元）
1952						0.003	0.004
1957						0.02	0.26
1962					0.08	0.04	0.75
1965					0.16	0.09	0.81
1970					0.39	0.16	0.87
1975					0.96	0.41	1.39
1978					1.05	0.54	1.96
1979					1.49	0.72	2.13
1980					2.61	1.17	3.08
1981					3.80	2.03	4.02
1982					4.51	2.77	4.55
1983					6.05	3.86	5.76
1984					11.03	6.18	12.19
1985					13.49	9.19	14.24
1986	11		554	69	19.59	13.14	20.68
1987	19		453	87	28.48	18.97	31.24
1988	20		710	105	38.05	24.91	41.58
1989	18		504	97	46.82	32.57	49.37
1990	27		1025	98	68.07	45.51	63.04
1991	37		2443	118	94.97	61.47	78.40
1992	47		2473	125	147.34	81.54	105.98
1993	52		2888	117	179.83	107.17	134.31
1994	44		3464	75	249.78	151.54	173.44
1995	27		5679	62	383.68	232.97	254.85
1996	36		6464	139	489.65	318.02	312.81
1997	59		6778	112	671.17	425.82	382.66
1998	75		6601	141	864.01	533.75	442.74
1999	97		7055	156	1040.84	616.34	524.37
2000	106		7617	185	1228.67	672.07	630.84
2001	110	39.80	8200	217	1458.65	799.18	750.18
2002	108	72.51	11847	822	1790.18	1001.69	933.41
2003	80	79.92	13825	1006	2126.78	1231.06	1206.72
2004	149	85.70	23437	982	2462.87	1431.68	1405.25
2005	169	90.72	28189	987	2933.40	1728.28	1500.52
2006	193	96.01	33180	1170	3365.65	2013.40	1730.56
2007	248	118.88	42702	1477	3751.83	2120.74	2154.77
2008	268	128.69	45614	1604	4354.53	2638.04	2380.36
2009	286	151.49	51756	1751	4986.61	2904.57	2903.80
2010	327	191.32	67592	1924	5943.39	3386.85	3329.82
2011	357	249.37	90975	2258	6609.39	3710.99	3716.08
2012	415	306.35	126924	2329	7430.46	4204.20	4195.61
2013	418	346.43	144981	2408	8630.73	4476.43	4774.23
2014	356	374.60	157493	2435	9069.92	4606.79	5331.63
2015	373	395.18	157743	2826	9736.24	4591.38	5816.04
2016	400	445.40	153117	3392	11198.43	4882.91	6402.48

注：2015年起，“城乡居民储蓄存款余额”更名为“住户存款”，口径有变，数据与往年不可比。

16 续表 9

年 份	在校学生数（万人）			小学学龄儿童入学率（%）	高考入围人数（人）
	普通高等学校	普通中学	小学		
1949		0.20	5.28		
1952		0.34	7.04		
1957		0.67	8.80		
1962		0.97	12.00		
1965		1.05	16.09		
1970		6.02	11.81		
1975		4.96	16.82		
1978		7.60	16.11	98.36	846
1979		6.23	15.80	98.70	566
1980		5.48	15.49	98.85	222
1981		4.35	15.09	98.72	239
1982		4.17	14.48	99.06	252
1983		4.28	13.54	99.75	245
1984		4.65	13.46	99.65	619
1985		4.66	13.44	99.83	534
1986		4.94	14.07	99.90	595
1987		5.44	14.43	99.94	644
1988		5.93	15.01	99.93	925
1989		6.20	15.59	99.92	977
1990		6.12	16.27	99.94	759
1991		6.01	17.01	99.92	861
1992		6.52	17.52	99.94	994
1993	0.11	7.53	18.01	99.95	1102
1994	0.15	8.58	18.62	99.96	1823
1995	0.16	9.25	19.51	99.99	2095
1996	0.18	9.52	20.60	99.98	2160
1997	0.20	9.80	22.18	99.99	2212
1998	0.22	10.12	23.58	99.99	2348
1999	0.22	10.55	24.88	99.99	3501
2000	0.32	11.24	27.28	99.99	5017
2001	0.38	12.21	29.54	100.00	5651
2002	0.51	13.53	34.28	100.00	6873
2003	0.69	14.97	38.69	100.00	9167
2004	0.91	17.13	44.83	100.00	10756
2005	1.66	19.10	48.09	100.00	11196
2006	2.20	21.46	49.68	100.00	11359
2007	2.52	23.46	52.07	100.00	13275
2008	2.87	24.84	52.86	100.00	15047
2009	3.40	24.95	51.12	100.00	17487
2010	3.83	25.83	55.24	100.00	18845
2011	4.51	26.31	57.83	100.00	19588
2012	5.24	26.79	60.81	100.00	22127
2013	6.09	27.83	65.91	100.00	22840
2014	6.99	28.46	68.73	100.00	23900
2015	11.46	28.76	71.93	100.00	26519
2016	11.26	29.58	73.87	100.00	24094

16 续表 10

年 份	医疗机构病床床位数（张）	卫生机构技术人员数（万人）	#执 业（助理）医 师	每万人口拥有 床位数（张）	执业(助理)医师（人）	年末参加基本养老保险人数（万人次）	年末参加基本医疗保险人数（万人次）
1949	219	0.02		3.21			
1952	179	0.01		2.50			
1957	403	0.03		5.20			
1962	1376	0.13		17.28			
1965	1308	0.16		15.13			
1970	1476	0.17		14.98			
1975	1970	0.23		18.25			
1978	2257	0.26	0.08	20.29	6.90		
1979	2271	0.29	0.10	20.27	8.67		
1980	2207	0.30	0.12	19.58	10.35		
1981	2210	0.31	0.11	19.31	9.63		
1982	2292	0.33	0.11	19.73	9.44		
1983	2098	0.33	0.11	17.84	9.25		
1984	2231	0.34	0.11	18.76	9.52		
1985	2323	0.33	0.12	19.22	9.94		
1986	3054	0.35	0.12	24.83	9.58		
1987	3393	0.35	0.13	27.17	10.44		
1988	3640	0.38	0.15	28.72	12.13		
1989	3677	0.39	0.16	28.56	12.58		
1990	3866	0.39	0.17	22.01	9.80		
1991	4085	0.39	0.18	20.42	8.77		
1992	4517	0.41	0.18	19.83	8.04		
1993	4940	0.45	0.20	19.04	7.80		
1994	5365	0.49	0.22	18.16	7.52	7.55	7.77
1995	5798	0.53	0.23	17.23	6.83	8.46	7.60
1996	5288	0.58	0.24	13.80	6.39	9.16	7.65
1997	5505	0.63	0.26	12.62	5.97	7.53	8.29
1998	5892	0.71	0.30	11.86	5.95	7.84	9.05
1999	6241	0.76	0.31	11.03	5.44	8.35	9.95
2000	7081	0.81	0.33	10.98	5.13	82.95	88.21
2001	7474	0.81	0.34	11.42	5.24	83.01	84.99
2002	8641	0.90	0.35	13.20	5.38	103.19	105.19
2003	9820	0.98	0.38	14.99	5.74	104.13	105.90
2004	10797	1.31	0.49	16.47	7.43	104.44	105.95
2005	11972	1.88	0.69	18.25	10.52	182.49	189.40
2006	13293	2.29	0.86	22.21	12.58	204.08	212.16
2007	15227	2.88	1.04	21.24	14.57	227.98	236.32
2008	16778	3.31	1.19	22.35	15.81	262.63	513.25
2009	18080	3.58	1.29	23.00	16.39	315.81	536.57
2010	19980	3.75	1.32	24.29	16.07	421.84	592.27
2011	22814	3.96	1.36	27.64	16.53	481.05	602.41
2012	24617	4.06	1.40	29.69	16.93	513.29	616.86
2013	25736	4.21	1.49	30.95	17.87	521.91	618.09
2014	26704	4.31	1.51	32.01	18.08	632.03	615.69
2015	27457	4.52	1.59	33.26	19.25	670.60	601.92
2016	28138	4.77	1.67	34.06	20.19	651.66	574.57

注：每万人口拥有床位数、执业(助理)医师数按常住人口计算。

16 续表 11

年　份	专　利 申请量 （件）	专　利 授权量 （件）	城镇居 民最低 生活保 障人数 （人）	城镇常住 居民人均 可支配 收　入 （元）	农村常住 居民人均 可支配 收　入 （元）
1978					149
1979					188
1980					272
1981					463
1982					567
1983					618
1984					691
1985				791	803
1986				1033	951
1987				1247	1142
1988				1778	1325
1989				2282	1424
1990	34	30		2508	1542
1991	70	50		3068	1673
1992	102	78		4026	2290
1993	100	90		5970	2903
1994	104	100		8270	3769
1995	325	262		9588	4769
1996	333	312		10824	5554
1997	725	321		11032	6132
1998	890	709		11506	6830
1999	1221	819		12954	7704
2000	1653	1399	1825	14142	8484
2001	2914	1753	2003	16938	9383
2002	3100	2680	2711	16949	10178
2003	3865	2858	2876	18471	11033
2004	4325	3167	4968	20526	11941
2005	6694	3114	4885	22882	13076
2006	9879	4872	6091	25320	14313
2007	13842	6752	3129	27025	15747
2008	14406	8093	3653	30275	16904
2009	19106	12918	3770	33045	18098
2010	21654	20397	3643	35690	20486
2011	24455	19352	9415	39513	22842
2012	29199	20900	6598	42944	24944
2013	29013	22595	6584	46594	27214
2014	28432	20340	6560	36764	22327
2015	38094	26820	5466	39793	24225
2016	56653	28559	3569	43096	26526

注：按照国家统计局的统一部署，2014年起，把原来的城市居民人均可支配收入和农民人均纯收入分别改为城镇常住居民人均可支配收入和农村常住居民人均可支配收入。

十七、东莞与全国、全省、三角洲城市及港澳台主要指标比较

Comparison of Main Indicators between Dongguan and China, Guangdong Province, the Cities of the Pearl River Delta Hong Kong Macao Taiwan

17-1 主要年份全国国民经济与社会发展指标

Main Indicators on National Economy and Social Development of China

指 标	单 位	1980年	1990年	2000年	2005年	2010年	2015年	2016年
人口与劳动力								
年末总人口	万人	98705	114333	126743	130756	134091	137462	138271
年末就业人员人数	万人	42361	64749	72085	74647	76105	77451	77603
#城镇就业人员	万人	10525	17041	23151	28389	34687	40410	41428
经济总量								
国内生产总值	亿元	4588	18873	100280	187319	413030	689052	744127
第一产业增加值	亿元	1360	5017	14717	21807	39363	60862	63671
第二产业增加值	亿元	2205	7744	45665	88084	191630	282040	296236
第三产业增加值	亿元	1023	6111	39898	77428	182038	346150	384221
人均国内生产总值	元	468	1663	7942	14368	30876	50251	53980
农业								
主要农产品产量								
粮食	万吨	32056	44624	46218	48402	54678	62144	61625
水果	万吨	679	1874	6225	16120	21401	27375	28351
肉类	万吨		2857	6014	6939	7926	8625	8538
水产品	万吨	450	1237	3706	4420	5373	6700	6901
工业								
工业增加值	亿元	2015	6905	40260	77961	165126	236506	247860
主要工业产品产量								
机制纸及纸板	万吨	535	1372	2487	5404	9833	11743	12105
彩电	万台	3	1033	3936	8283	11830	14476	15770
发电量	亿千瓦时	3006	6212	13556	25003	42072	58146	61425
钢材	万吨	2716	5153	13146	37771	80277	112350	113801
运输邮电								
货运量	亿吨	31.08	97.06	135.87	186.21	324.18	417.59	438.68
货物周转量	亿吨公里	11629	26208	44321	80258	141837	178356	186629
客运量	亿人	34.18	77.27	147.86	184.70	326.95	194.33	190.02
旅客周转量	亿人公里	2281	5628	12261	17467	27894	30059	31258
邮电业务总量	亿元	39	156	4793	12029	31979	28425	43346
年末固定电话用户	万户	214	685	14483	35045	29434	23100	20662
年末移动电话用户	万户		2	8453	39341	85900	127140	132193

注：1.城镇就业人员1998年起为城镇在岗职工人数。
2.2014年起，客运量和旅客周转量不含城市客运量，数据与往年不可比。
3.实施研发支出核算方法改革后，对各年度GDP数据进行了系统修订。

17−1 续表

指　　标	单　位	1980年	1990年	2000年	2005年	2010年	2015年	2016年
固定资产投资								
固定资产投资总额	亿元	911	4517	32918	88774	278122	562000	596501
#房地产开发	亿元		253	4984	15909	48259	95979	102581
商业								
社会消费品零售总额	亿元	2140	8300	39106	68353	156998	300931	332316
物价总指数								
商品零售价格指数	上年=100	106.0	102.1	98.5	100.8	103.1	100.1	100.7
居民消费价格指数	上年=100	107.5	103.1	100.4	101.8	103.3	101.4	102.0
外贸外经								
海关进出口总额	亿美元/亿元	381	1154	4743	14219	29740	39530	243386
进口总额	亿美元/亿元	200	533	2251	6599	13962	16796	104932
出口总额	亿美元/亿元	181	621	2492	7620	15778	22735	138455
实际利用外资	亿美元		35	407	603	1057	1263	1260
财政、金融								
一般公共预算收入	亿元	1160	2937	13395	31649	83102	152269	159552
一般公共预算支出	亿元	1229	3084	15887	33930	89874	175878	187841
各项人民币存款余额	亿元	1690	13943	123804	287170	718238	1357022	1505864
#住户存款余额	亿元	400	7120	64332	141051	303302	546078	597751
各项人民币贷款余额	亿元	2478	17511	99371	194690	479196	939540	1066040
人民生活								
在岗职工平均工资	元	762	2140	9371	18364	37147	63241	67569
城镇居民人均可支配收入	元	478	1510	6280	10493	19109	31195	33616
农村居民人均可支配收入	元	191	686	2253	3255	5919	11422	12363
教育								
在校学生数								
普通高等学校	万人	114	206	556	1562	2232	2625	2696
普通中学	万人	5508	4586	7369	8581	7703	6686	6696
小学	万人	14627	12241	13013	10864	9941	9692	9913
卫生								
医院床位数	万张	120	187	217	245	338.7	533.1	568.9
卫生技术人员	万人	280	390	449	456	587.6	800.8	845.4
#执业（助理）医师	万人	115	176	208	204	241.3	303.9	319.1

注：1.实际利用外资不含对外借款，2005年起为实际使用外商直接投资口径。
　　2.2016年起，进出口相关数据采用人民币。

17-2 主要年份广东省国民经济与社会发展指标

Main Indicators on National Economy and Social Development of Guangdong Province

指　　标	单　位	1980年	1990年	2000年	2005年	2010年	2015年	2016年
人口与劳动力								
年末常住人口	万人		6347	8650	9194	10441	10849	10999
年末就业人员人数	万人	2368	3118	3989	5023	5870	6219.31	6279.22
#城镇就业人员	万人	564	785	759	904	1119	1948.04	1957.57
经济总量								
地区生产总值	亿元	250	1559	10741	22557	46036	72812.55	79512.05
第一产业增加值	亿元	83	385	986	1428	2287	3345.54	3694.37
第二产业增加值	亿元	103	616	5000	11357	22822	32613.54	34001.31
第三产业增加值	亿元	64	559	4755	9773	20928	36853.47	41816.37
人均地区生产总值	元	481	2484	12736	24647	44758	67503	72787
农业								
主要农产品产量								
粮食	万吨	1682	1896	1822	1395	1317	1358.13	1360.22
水果	万吨	29	329	644	832	1129	1519.89	1580.96
肉类	万吨	63	202	324	384	441	424.25	415.49
水产品	万吨	63	208	593	695	729	857.23	873.79
工业								
工业增加值	亿元	90	523	4463	10490	21270	30259.49	31539.56
主要工业产品产量								
机制纸及纸板	万吨	31	104	260	691	1435	2078.29	2127.52
彩电	万台	1	262	1532	4090	4495	7003.58	8116.89
发电量	亿千瓦时	109	344	1293	2163	3101	3900.21	4081.97
成品钢材	万吨	45	134	406	1366	2919	3271.01	4113.34
运输邮电								
货运量	万吨	14201	85809	119216	133992	205034	376434	377645
货物周转量	亿吨公里	1413	2599	3065	3917	5934	15130.59	22032.27
客运量	万人	21444	78046	164791	161357	467049	207345	144262
旅客周转量	亿人公里	114	453	1219	2043	3342	4335.79	3842.58
邮电业务总量	亿元	2	26	602	2122	4833	4397.09	6892.41
年末固定电话用户	万户		113	1415	3443	3169	2807.11	2609.71
年末移动电话用户	万户		1	1357	6407	9710	15009.75	14348.96

注：1.2010年年末人口数为第六次全国人口普查数据。
　　2.2014年客运量和旅客周转量不含城市客运量，数据与往年不可比。

17-2 续表

指　　标	单　位	1980年	1990年	2000年	2005年	2010年	2015年	2016年
固定资产投资								
固定资产投资总额	亿元	38	381	3234	7164	16113	30031.20	33008.86
#房地产开发	亿元		33	859	1592	3660	8538.47	10307.80
商业								
社会消费品零售总额	亿元	118	667	4380	7916	17458	31517.56	34739.00
物价总指数								
商品零售价格指数	上年=100	108.5	95.6	99.9	101.8	103.3	99.6	100.8
居民消费价格指数	上年=100		97.5	101.4	102.3	103.1	101.5	102.3
外贸外经								
海关进出口总额	亿美元/亿元	26	419	1701	4280	7849	10227.96	63099.68
进口总额	亿美元/亿元	4	197	782	1898	3317	3793.28	23579.14
出口总额	亿美元/亿元	22	222	919	2382	4532	6434.68	39520.54
实际利用外资	亿美元	2	20	146	152	210	270.25	234.07
财政、金融								
地方一般公共预算收入	亿元	38	131	911	1807	4517	9366.78	10390.35
地方一般公共预算支出	亿元	27	151	1070	2289	5422	12827.80	13446.09
各项人民币存款余额	亿元		1577	16920	35959	79958	153551.79	171024.47
#住户存款余额	亿元	30	752	8667	19051	36319	54238.30	58618.89
各项人民币贷款余额	亿元		1704	11787	20966	47192	89289.27	103649.79
人民生活								
在岗职工平均工资	元	789	2929	13823	23959	40358	66296	72848
全省常住居民人均可支配收入	元						27858.86	30295.80
城镇常住居民人均可支配收入	元	473	2303	9762	14770	23898	34757.16	37684.25
农村常住居民人均可支配收入	元	274	1043	3654	4690	7890	13360.44	14512.15
教育								
在校学生数								
#普通高等学校	万人	4	10	30	87	143	185.64	189.29
中等职业教育学校	万人	6	45	66	71	155	117.21	106.57
普通中学	万人	252	234	461	612	709	560.72	545.22
小学	万人	749	747	930	1067	849	868.88	905.22
卫生								
医院及卫生院床位数	万张	8	11	16	19	28	40.07	42.84
卫生技术人员	万人	14	19	26	30	46	62.00	66.75
#执业（助理）医师	万人	6	8	11	12	18	22.94	24.41

注：2016年起，进出口相关数据采用人民币口径，后同。

17–3 主要经济指标东莞占全国、全省的比重（2016年）

Proportion of Main Indicators of Dongguan to China and Guangdong Province (2016)

指　　标	单 位	绝 对 值			东莞占全国的比重(%)	东莞占全省的比重(%)
		全 国	全 省	东 莞		
人口						
年末常住人口	万 人	138271	10999	826.14	0.60	7.51
经济总量						
地区生产总值	亿 元	744127	79512.05	6827.69	0.92	8.59
第一产业增加值	亿 元	63671	3694.37	24.20	0.04	0.66
第二产业增加值	亿 元	296236	34001.31	3173.24	1.07	9.33
第三产业增加值	亿 元	384221	41816.37	3630.25	0.94	8.68
工业						
工业增加值	亿 元	247860	31539.56	3089.26	1.25	9.79
主要工业产品产量						
机制纸及纸板	万 吨	12105	2127.52	1507.86	12.46	70.87
彩电	万 台	15770	8116.89	300.70	1.91	3.70
发电量	亿千瓦时	61425	4081.97	338.48	0.55	8.29
农业						
主要农产品产量						
粮食	万 吨	61625	1360.22	1.26	0.002	0.09
水果	万 吨	28351	1580.96	5.94	0.02	0.38
肉类	万 吨	8538	415.49	1.29	0.02	0.31
水产品	万 吨	6901	873.79	5.66	0.08	0.65
固定资产投资额						
固定资产投资总额	亿 元	596501	33008.86	1577.46	0.26	4.78
运输邮电						
货物周转量	亿吨公里	186629	22032.27	455.23	0.24	2.07
旅客周转量	亿人公里	31258	3842.58	77.32	0.25	2.01
年末固定电话用户	万 户	20662	2609.71	272.63	1.32	10.45
年末移动电话用户	万 户	132193	14348.96	1575.08	1.19	10.98
财政、金融						
一般公共预算收入	亿 元	159552	10390.35	544.75	0.34	5.24
一般公共预算支出	亿 元	187841	13446.09	599.29	0.32	4.46
各项人民币存款余额	亿 元	1505864	171024.47	11198.43	0.74	6.55
#住户存款余额	亿 元	597751	58618.89	4882.91	0.82	8.33
各项人民币贷款余额	亿 元	1066040	103649.79	6402.48	0.60	6.18
外经外贸						
进出口总额	亿 元	243386	63099.68	11415.99	4.69	18.09
进口总额	亿 元	104932	23579.14	4859.15	4.63	20.61
出口总额	亿 元	138455	39520.54	6556.85	4.74	16.59
实际利用外资	亿美元	1260	234.07	39.26	3.12	16.77
商业、物价						
社会消费品零售总额	亿 元	332316	34739.00	2470.78	0.74	7.11
商品零售价格指数	上年=100	100.7	100.8	100.9		
居民消费价格指数	上年=100	102.0	102.3	102.7		
人民生活						
城镇在岗职工年平均工资	元	67569	72848	57649	85.32	79.14
城镇常住居民人均可支配收入	元	33616	37684.25	43096	128.20	114.36
农村常住居民人均可支配收入	元	12363	14512.15	26526	214.56	182.78

17-4 主要经济指标东莞占全国、全省的比重（2015年）

Proportion of Main Indicators of Dongguan to China and Guangdong Province (2015)

指标	单位	绝对值			东莞占全国的比重(%)	东莞占全省的比重(%)
		全国	全省	东莞		
人口						
年末常住人口	万人	137462	10849	825.41	0.60	7.61
经济总量						
地区生产总值	亿元	689052	72812.55	6275.07	0.91	8.62
第一产业增加值	亿元	60862	3345.54	21.03	0.03	0.63
第二产业增加值	亿元	282040	32613.54	2922.05	1.04	8.96
第三产业增加值	亿元	346150	36853.47	3332.00	0.96	9.04
工业						
工业增加值	亿元	236506	30259.49	2840.35	1.20	9.39
主要工业产品产量						
机制纸及纸板	万吨	11743	2078.29	1399.23	11.92	67.33
彩电	万台	14476	7003.58	344.94	2.38	4.93
发电量	亿千瓦时	58146	3900.21	315.19	0.54	8.08
农业						
主要农产品产量						
粮食	万吨	62144	1358.13	1.27	0.002	0.09
水果	万吨	27375	1519.89	6.30	0.02	0.41
肉类	万吨	8625	424.25	1.52	0.02	0.36
水产品	万吨	6700	857.23	6.89	0.10	0.80
固定资产投资额						
固定资产投资总额	亿元	562000	30031.20	1446.52	0.26	4.82
运输邮电						
货物周转量	亿吨公里	178356	15130.59	504.85	0.28	3.34
旅客周转量	亿人公里	30059	4335.79	77.13	0.26	1.78
年末固定电话用户	万户	23100	2807.11	298.23	1.29	10.62
年末移动电话用户	万户	127140	15009.75	1756.75	1.38	11.70
财政、金融						
一般公共预算收入	亿元	152269	9366.78	517.97	0.34	5.53
一般公共预算支出	亿元	175878	12827.80	581.24	0.33	4.53
各项人民币存款余额	亿元	1357022	153551.79	9736.24	0.72	6.34
#住户存款余额	亿元	546078	54238.30	4591.38	0.84	8.47
各项人民币贷款余额	亿元	939540	89289.27	5816.04	0.62	6.51
外经外贸						
进出口总额	亿美元	39530	10227.96	1676.73	4.24	16.39
进口总额	亿美元	16796	3793.28	639.55	3.81	16.86
出口总额	亿美元	22735	6434.68	1037.19	4.56	16.12
实际利用外资	亿美元	1263	270.25	53.20	4.21	19.69
商业、物价						
社会消费品零售总额	亿元	300931	31517.56	2184.70	0.73	6.93
商品零售价格指数	上年=100	100.1	99.6	99.4		
居民消费价格指数	上年=100	101.4	101.5	101.4		
人民生活						
城镇在岗职工年平均工资	元	63241	66296	53221	84.16	80.28
城镇常住居民人均可支配收入	元	31195	34757	39793	127.56	114.49
农村常住居民人均可支配收入	元	11422	13360	24225	212.09	181.32

17-5 主要经济指标人均水平东莞与全国、全省的比较（2016年）

Comparison of Per Capita Level of Main Economic Indicators between Dongguan and China, Guangdong Province (2016)

指标	单位	人均水平			东莞相当于全国(%)	东莞相当于全省(%)
		全国	全省	东莞		
地区生产总值	元	53980	72787	82682	153.2	113.6
一般公共预算收入	元	11573	9511	6597	57.0	69.4
出口总额	元	10043	36178	79402	790.6	219.5
各项人民币存款余额	元	108907	155491	135551	124.5	87.2
住户存款余额	元	43230	53295	59105	136.7	110.9
固定资产投资总额	元	43267	30217	19103	44.2	63.2
社会消费品零售总额	元	24104	31801	29921	124.1	94.1
实际利用外资	美元	91	214	475	520.2	221.9
城镇在岗职工年平均工资	元	67569	72848	57649	85.3	79.1
城镇常住居民人均可支配收入	元	33616	37684	43096	128.2	114.4
农村常住居民人均可支配收入	元	12363	14512	26526	214.6	182.8
粮食产量	公斤	447	125	2	0.3	1.2
水产品产量	公斤	50	80	7	13.7	8.6
水果产量	公斤	206	145	7	3.5	5.0
工业发电量	千瓦时	4455	3737	4099	92.0	109.7
医院卫生院床位数	张/千人	4.11	3.90	3.41	82.8	87.4
卫生技术人员数	人/千人	6.11	6.07	5.77	94.4	95.1

注：本表人均指标时点数按常住人口计算，时期数按年平均常住人口计算。

17-6 主要经济指标人均水平东莞与全国、全省的比较（2015年）

Comparison of Per Capita Level of Main Economic Indicators between Dongguan and China, Guangdong Province (2015)

指标	单位	人均水平			东莞相当于全国(%)	东莞相当于全省(%)
		全国	全省	东莞		
地区生产总值	元	50251	67503	75616	150.5	112.0
一般公共预算收入	元	11105	8684	6242	56.2	71.9
出口总额	美元	1658	5965	12498	753.8	209.5
各项人民币存款余额	元	98720	141535	117956	119.5	83.3
住户存款余额	元	39726	49994	55625	140.0	111.3
固定资产投资总额	元	40985	27841	17431	42.5	62.6
社会消费品零售总额	元	21946	29219	26326	120.0	90.1
实际利用外资	美元	92	251	641	696.2	255.9
城镇在岗职工年平均工资	元	63241	66296	53221	84.2	80.3
城镇常住居民人均可支配收入	元	31195	34757	39793	127.6	114.5
农村常住居民人均可支配收入	元	11422	13360	24225	212.1	181.3
粮食产量	公斤	453	126	2	0.3	1.2
水产品产量	公斤	49	79	8	17.0	10.4
水果产量	公斤	200	141	8	3.8	5.4
工业发电量	千瓦时	4240	3616	3798	89.6	105.0
医院卫生院床位数	张/千人	3.88	3.69	3.33	85.8	90.1
卫生技术人员数	人/千人	5.83	5.71	5.48	94.1	95.9

注：本表人均指标时点数按年末常住人口计算，时期数按年平均常住人口计算。

17-7 珠江三角洲国民经济和社会发展主要指标（2016年）

指　　标	单 位	广州市	深圳市	珠海市
综合				
土地面积	平方公里	7249	1997	1732
年末常住人口	万人	1404.35	1190.84	167.53
年末户籍人口	万人	870.49	400.47	114.78
地区生产总值	亿元	19547.44	19492.60	2226.37
第一产业增加值	亿元	239.28	7.17	43.53
第二产业增加值	亿元	5751.59	7780.45	1079.89
第三产业增加值	亿元	13556.57	11704.97	1102.96
人均生产总值（按常住人口计算）	元	141933	167411	134548
农村经济				
农林牧渔业总产值	亿元	436.65	16.73	84.13
粮食产量	万吨	43.65	0.01	4.28
水果产量	万吨	49.48	1.23	6.64
水产品产量	万吨	47.70	3.99	29.93
工业				
规模以上工业企业数	个	4660	6627	1048
规模以上工业增加值	亿元	4387.90	7108.87	1022.86
规模以上工业企业主营业务收入	亿元	17599.01	26764.55	4213.59
规模以上工业企业利润总额	亿元	1225.15	1769.91	420.58
规模以上工业产品销售率	%	97.87	97.49	92.33
固定资产投资				
固定资产投资总额	亿元	5703.59	4078.16	1389.75
#房地产开发投资额	亿元	2540.85	1756.52	641.03
商品房屋销售面积	万平方米	1949.10	736.19	653.15
商品房屋销售额	亿元	3193.33	3323.64	1215.60
交通、邮电				
民用汽车拥有量	万辆	230.04	317.88	47.37
年末固定电话用户数	万户	462.48	514.52	74.08
年末移动电话用户数	万户	2782.68	2846.35	337.27
全年总用电量	亿千瓦时	823.57	842.09	152.90

Main Indicators of National Economy and Social Development of the Pearl River Delta Economic Zone (2016)

佛山市	惠州市	肇庆市	江门市	东莞市	中山市
3798	11347	14891	9505	2460	1784
746.27	477.50	408.46	454.40	826.14	323.00
400.18	364.31	444.17	393.93	200.94	161.25
8630.00	3412.17	2084.02	2418.78	6827.69	3202.78
145.31	171.66	317.07	188.97	24.20	68.26
5146.02	1837.53	999.43	1150.77	3173.24	1677.26
3338.68	1402.98	767.52	1079.05	3630.25	1457.26
115891	71605	51178	53374	82682	99471
293.05	277.51	479.80	345.61	38.44	116.08
9.83	59.99	116.05	95.83	1.26	7.69
4.96	77.37	155.62	28.40	5.94	18.26
63.12	17.15	44.37	78.66	5.66	33.79
5671	2140	1100	1998	5869	3089
4671.23	1763.69	921.14	1065.80	2968.16	1319.96
20199.21	7398.15	3864.90	3980.91	14889.63	6221.56
1589.80	483.72	225.23	238.18	502.73	332.69
97.19	96.81	97.74	94.23	97.67	95.21
3512.04	2039.71	1373.74	1517.77	1557.46	1149.01
1229.97	747.63	145.20	353.62	642.76	543.59
2221.51	1771.91	499.96	679.78	1024.25	1158.23
2117.23	1415.00	239.33	410.23	1418.17	844.81
202.01	87.62	41.05	61.05	224.62	83.16
235.59	106.48	62.97	120.95	272.63	105.80
1196.47	537.13	306.47	461.59	1575.08	598.79
620.82	323.41	159.31	248.50	702.01	259.33

17-7 续表

(2016年)

指标	单位	广州市	深圳市	珠海市
金融、贸易、财政				
年末金融机构本外币存款余额	亿元	47530.20	64407.81	6124.26
#住户存款	亿元	14430.11	10755.66	1457.49
年末金融机构本外币贷款余额	亿元	29669.82	40526.90	4098.08
社会消费品零售总额	亿元	8706.49	5512.76	1016.13
地方一般公共预算收入	亿元	1393.64	3136.49	292.37
地方一般公共预算支出	亿元	1943.75	4211.04	417.16
对外经济				
进出口总额	亿美元	1293.09	3984.36	417.32
进口总额	亿美元	511.32	1610.97	144.02
出口总额	亿美元	781.77	2373.39	273.29
合同利用外资金额	亿美元	99.01	521.93	90.56
实际利用外商直接投资	亿美元	57.01	67.32	22.95
人民生活、物价				
在岗职工年平均工资	元	89096	89757	74931
全体常住居民人均可支配收入	元	46667	48695	40154
全体常住居民人均消费支出	元	35388	36481	30479
城镇常住居民人均可支配收入	元	50941	48695	42537
城镇常住居民人均消费支出	元	38398	36481	32151
农村常住居民人均可支配收入	元	21449		22889
农村常住居民人均消费性支出	元	17595		18373
居民消费价格总指数（以上年为100）	%	102.7	102.4	101.9
教育、R&D、卫生				
学校数				
中等职业技术学校	所	83	15	9
普通中学	所	514	352	73
小学	所	953	337	118
在校学生数				
中等职业技术学校	人	216974	39665	21597
普通中学	人	505685	396455	86928
小学	人	968531	910974	155269
规上工业企业R&D活动人员	人	80509	202684	16737
规上工业企业R&D经费内部支出	万元	2317659	7600311	490503
卫生事业机构	个	3806	3957	721
#医院	个	243	134	41
医院床位数	张	79037	34936	7864
执业（助理）医师	人	46791	30757	5806

佛山市	惠州市	肇庆市	江门市	东莞市	中山市
13281.61	4974.48	2041.58	4030.37	11545.10	5031.00
6736.22	1961.99	1272.68	2454.80	4943.56	2309.44
8717.81	3460.97	1293.43	2469.83	6545.66	3367.09
3017.76	1227.88	731.98	1159.06	2470.78	1205.84
604.50	361.30	91.70	204.17	544.75	295.04
695.85	509.08	248.16	293.21	599.29	367.57
621.84	461.44	69.37	190.89	1723.14	338.48
152.04	162.67	22.58	40.59	732.79	71.88
469.80	298.78	46.80	150.31	990.35	266.61
22.28	21.34	13.51	10.77	47.32	10.63
14.72	11.43	3.70	4.76	39.26	4.74
67187	64766	59591	61366	57649	64790
41941	28061	20580	24427	41902	40012
30562	20461	13928	17282	29906	26637
43120	33213	25907	29557	43096	41613
31303	23779	17883	20459	30688	27631
24159	17603	15115	15226	26526	27529
16736	13726	9976	11584	21539	19276
102.3	101.9	101.7	102.2	102.7	101.9
36	24	18	21	26	11
198	252	179	188	231	102
408	456	222	316	328	206
71963	55446	58290	43523	74700	23139
313354	275031	235651	208611	295753	148682
512455	530498	356373	313894	738686	285941
74427	34929	12100	17120	64963	38970
1948807	676932	214433	402769	1434048	747859
1469	2668	3096	1590	2344	727
105	70	54	41	89	53
32187	15737	12172	15487	27450	13656
16534	11283	7151	9298	16680	7425

17-8 长江三角洲国民经济和社会发展主要指标（2016年）

指　　标	单 位	上海市	南京市	苏州市	无锡市	常州市	镇江市
综合							
行政区域土地面积	平方公里	6341	6587	8488	4627	4372	3847
年末常住人口	万人	2419.70	827.00	1062.57	652.90	470.80	318.13
年末户籍人口	万人	1439.50	662.79	678.20	486.20	374.90	271.98
地区生产总值	亿元	27466.15	10503.02	15475.09	9210.02	5773.86	3833.84
第一产业增加值	亿元	109.47	252.51	221.81	135.19	152.67	137.78
第二产业增加值	亿元	7994.34	4117.20	7277.46	4346.78	2682.29	1870.40
第三产业增加值	亿元	19362.34	6133.31	7975.82	4728.05	2938.90	1825.66
人均地区生产总值	元	113615	127264	145556	141258	122721	120603
工业							
规模以上工业增加值	亿元	7452.58	3050.55	6365.29	3075.49	2827.16	2064.56
规模以上工业企业主营业务收入	亿元	34292.43	12421.68	30135.00	14643.13	12441.40	8852.71
规模以上工业企业利润总额	亿元	2898.52	941.81	1761.11	977.92	730.65	585.40
工业用电量	亿千瓦时	798.18	310.81	1116.30	493.73	334.78	173.78
固定资产投资							
固定资产投资总额	亿元	6755.88	5533.56	5648.49	4795.25	3605.08	2873.43
#工业投资额	亿元	979.56	1761.65	1982.29	2045.54	1918.48	1475.13
#房地产开发投资额	亿元	3709.03	1845.60	2163.24	1033.62	446.70	448.64
交通、邮电							
民用汽车拥有量	万辆	322.94	221.68	313.30	158.50	109.80	43.68
年末固定电话用户数	万户	731.62	250.28	252.00	155.15	123.40	75.79
年末移动电话用户数	万户	3156.14	1107.20	1690.60	864.62	526.20	305.89
金融、贸易、财政							
年末金融机构本外币存款余额	亿元	110510.96	28355.89	27727.55	14612.00	8850.03	4835.19
#住户存款	亿元	25112.99	6095.08	8068.20	4957.02	3415.31	1899.19
年末金融机构本外币贷款余额	亿元	59982.25	22268.94	22752.22	10517.75	6081.37	3472.35
社会消费品零售总额	亿元	10946.57	5088.20	4936.79	3119.56	2202.83	1236.78
地方一般公共预算收入	亿元	6406.13	1142.60	1730.04	875.00	480.29	293.01
地方一般公共预算支出	亿元	6918.94	1173.79	1617.20	867.66	505.50	360.10
对外经济							
进出口总额	亿美元	4338.05	502.12	2737.58	698.05	275.81	103.16
进口总额	亿美元	2503.38	206.20	1098.17	268.95	67.30	33.65
出口总额	亿美元	1834.67	295.92	1639.41	429.10	208.51	69.51
实际利用外商直接投资	亿美元	185.14	34.79	60.03	34.13	25.00	13.51
人民生活、物价							
城镇常住居民人均可支配收入	元	57692	49997	54341	48628	46058	41794
农村常住居民人均可支配收入	元	25520	21156	27691	26158	23780	20922
居民消费价格总指数（以上年为100）	%	103.2	102.7	102.3	102.2	102.5	102.2

注：1.杭州、南通民用汽车拥有量为机动车拥有量；台州、嘉兴为汽车保有量；苏州为汽车拥有量；无锡为全社会拥有车辆

Main Indicators on National Economy and Social Development of the Yangtze River Delta Economic Zone (2016)

南通市	扬州市	泰州市	杭州市	宁波市	嘉兴市	湖州市	绍兴市	舟山市	台州市
8001	6591	5787	16596	9816	3915	5820	8279	1440	9411
730.20	449.14	464.58	918.80	787.50	461.40	297.50	498.8	115.80	608.00
766.70	461.67	508.21	736.00	591.00	352.12	264.84	444.53	97.33	600.17
6768.20	4449.38	4101.78	11050.49	8541.11	3760.12	2243.06	4710.19	1228.51	3842.81
366.08	251.49	240.00	304.84	304.62	143.85	127.75	209.86	130.00	254.93
3170.30	2197.63	1933.89	3977.39	4239.64	1911.57	1058.14	2319.17	489.34	1645.14
3231.82	2000.26	1927.89	6768.26	3996.85	1704.70	1057.17	2181.16	609.17	1942.74
92702	99150	88330	121394	108804	81751	75715	94620	106364	64172
3330.36	2298.10	2766.85	2983.91	2799.12	1543.70	828.29	1678.63	403.34	894.64
14683.60	9603.10	12190.18	1236.54	13205.19	7303.77	4217.38	9237.68	1375.99	3758.09
1109.95	603.00	936.76	927.94	993.84	495.72	282.81	575.49	27.28	244.71
265.65	156.60	176.20	401.55	476.74	368.50	165.73	291.98	23.47	183.43
4811.95	3288.70	3164.12	5842.42	4961.39	2790.16	1592.18	2882.48	1311.14	2272.63
2406.36	1714.40	1957.87	883.95	1469.95	1225.39	678.03	1300.84	360.83	876.02
584.14	410.20	250.71	2606.41	1270.33	478.40	274.22	641.19	171.89	424.21
177.72		61.93	234.15	237.99	105.27	64.20	129.98	17.31	132.78
179.70	614.01	100.46	265.70	238.00	110.46	81.90	127.48	32.82	106.81
819.00	506.88	461.10	1734.41	1209.83	608.41	456.20	559.34	162.10	770.84
11330.57	5448.23	5406.35	33386.04	16989.30	6848.41	3552.42	7433.53	1915.84	7068.62
5597.93	2585.52	2487.93	8493.27	5788.07	3275.82	1756.02	3431.62	725.97	3728.59
6896.58	3526.36	3720.85	26169.00	16622.90	5286.90	2757.57	6151.84	1521.82	5826.03
2632.87	1358.80	1118.34	5176.20	3667.63	1638.49	1068.86	1783.34	457.40	2013.14
590.18	345.30	327.60	1402.38	1114.50	387.93	211.18	390.30	120.32	343.28
750.10	484.25	450.88	1404.31	1289.26	442.19	288.62	456.10	250.54	514.40
308.59	96.25	103.81	679.92	948.69	313.48	102.22	276.05	105.51	198.69
78.48	23.66	37.07	177.33	287.82	78.41	12.06	20.41	42.88	21.36
230.11	72.59	66.74	502.59	660.87	235.07	90.16	255.64	62.63	177.33
23.87	12.04	13.44	72.09	45.13	26.92	10.01	8.00	2.10	3.37
39247	35659	36828	52185	51560	48926	45794	50305	48423	47162
18741	18058	17861	27908	28572	28997	26508	27744	28308	23164
102.3	102.4	102.1	102.6	102.1	101.8	101.6	101.9	101.8	101.7

2. 数据为初步统计数，来自统计公报、网站等，最终数据以各地2017年统计年鉴为准。

17-9 中国香港特别行政区主要社会经济指标

Main Statistical Indicators of Hong Kong Special Administrative Region

指　　标	单　位	1990年	2000年	2010年	2015年	2016年
人口及生命统计						
年中人口	万人	570.4	666.5	702.4	729.1	733.7
粗出生率	‰	12.0	8.1	12.6	8.2	8.3
粗死亡率	‰	5.2	5.1	6.0	6.3	6.4
劳动、就业						
劳动人口	万人	274.8	337.4	363.1	390.3	392.0
劳动人口参与率	%	63.2	61.4	59.6	61.1	61.1
失业率	%	1.3	4.9	4.3	3.3	3.4
本地生产总值						
按2014年环比物量计算 ①						
本地生产总值年增长率	%	3.8	7.7	6.8	2.4	1.9
本地生产总值	亿港元	9112	13426	20011	23136	23586
人均本地生产总值	港元	159737	201441	284885	317305	321487
按当年价格计算						
本地生产总值年增长率	%	11.7	4.0	7.1	6.1	3.8
本地生产总值	亿港元	5993	13375	17763	23984	24891
人均本地生产总值	港元	105050	200675	252887	328941	339273
政府收支、货币、金融						
政府收入总额 ②	亿港元	895	2251	3765	4500	5595
政府支出总额 ②	亿港元	856	2329	3014	4356	4667
货币供应量M_3	亿港元	12880	36928	71563	116550	125512
居民消费物价指数						
(2014年10月至2015年9月=100)						
综合消费物价指数		46.6	78.4	81.8	100.6	103.0
本地居民总收入（按当年价格计算）						
本地居民总收入	亿港元		13482	18139	24428	25732
人均本地居民总收入	港元		202287	258240	335027	350738
工业生产						
工业生产指数 ③（2008年=100）				95.0	93.2	92.7
工业电力消费量	万亿焦耳	24934	17769	11080	11436	11252
工业煤气消费量	万亿焦耳	583	982	917	1649	1477

17-9 续表

指标	单位	1990年	2000年	2010年	2015年	2016年
房屋及物业						
已登记物业买卖合约涉及的价值	亿港元		2225	6895	5487	5329
住宅	亿港元		1684	5607	4165	4280
非住宅	亿港元		541	1288	1321	1048
楼宇售价指数						
私人住宅单位	1999年=100	44.8	89.6	150.9	296.8	286.1
私人写字楼（甲级、乙级及丙级）	1999年=100	99.1	89.9	230.4	448.9	426.2
楼宇租金指数						
私人住宅单位	1999年=100	76.7	98.1	119.7	172.8	168.2
私人写字楼（甲级、乙级及丙级）	1999年=100	137.7	98.5	147.6	226.7	232.3
运输、通讯						
进出香港的货物						
总卸下	万吨	6076	13035	17282	16877	16441
总装上	万吨	2997	8692	12882	11491	11673
集装箱吞吐量 ④	万标准集装箱单位	510	1810	2370	2007	1981
电话服务	万条操作线路	245	395	426	421	420
对外商品贸易						
港产品出口	亿港元	2259	1810	695	469	429
转口	亿港元	4140	13917	29615	35584	35454
进口	亿港元	6425	16580	33648	40464	40084
旅　游						
访港旅客 ⑤	万人次	658	1306	3603	5931	5665
酒店入住率	%	79	83	87	86	87
教　育						
小学学生人数	人	526720	493979	331112	337558	349008
中学学生人数	人	453423	466710	452581	354135	339437
大学教育学生人数	人	57824	78295	166018	189484	187544

注：本表数据由香港特别行政区政府统计处提供，国家统计局整理编辑。1996年及以前年份数据均指原香港地区。
①以环比物量计算的本地生产总值及其组成部分的参照年为2014年。
②财政年度数字。指当年4月1日至第二年3月31日。
③自2005年统计年度开始，所有工业生产指数均按《香港标准行业分类2.0版》编制。
④1998年起，采用一系列新的集装箱吞吐量数字，与1998年以前的数字不可比。
⑤1996年及以后的数字包括澳门访港的非澳门居民旅客人数。

17-10 中国澳门特别行政区主要社会经济指标

Main Statistical Indicators of Macao Special Administrative Region

指　　标	单　位	1990年	2000年	2010年	2015年	2016年
人口及生命统计						
年中人口	万人	33.5	43.1	53.7	64.3	65.3
出生率	‰	20.5	8.9	9.5	11.0	11.0
死亡率	‰	4.4	3.1	3.3	3.1	3.4
劳动力						
劳动人口	万人	16.9	20.9	32.4	40.4	39.7
劳动力参与率	%	66.6	64.3	72.0	73.7	72.3
失业率	%	3.2	6.8	2.8	1.8	1.9
就业不足率	%	2.3	3.0	1.7	0.4	0.5
本地生产总值 ①						
以2014年环比物量计算						
本地生产总值实际增长率（支出法）	%	8.0	5.7	25.3	-21.5	-2.1
本地生产总值	亿澳门元	797.2	1037.7	3027.4	3468.6	3394.5
人均本地生产总值	万澳门元	23.8	24.1	56.4	54.1	52.6
按当年价格计算						
本地生产总值名义增长率（支出法）	%	19.8	4.0	31.3	-18.0	-1.2
本地生产总值	亿澳门元	258.3	539.4	2250.5	3626.4	3582.0
人均本地生产总值	万澳门元	7.7	12.5	41.9	56.5	55.5
政府收支、货币、金融						
政府总收入 ①	亿澳门元	60.2	153.4	884.9	1161.1	1024.1
政府总开支 ①	亿澳门元	55.1	150.2	383.9	807.5	807.3
货币供应（广义货币供应量M_2）	亿澳门元	307.4	849.2	2430.5	4728.3	5324.5
消费价格指数						
(2013年10月至2014年9月=100)						
综合消费价格指数			64.82	80.50	105.72	108.23
工业生产						
工业电力消耗量	亿千瓦小时		1.5	1.5	1.7	1.8
建　筑						
建成的私人楼宇单位数目	个	11574	3146	4527	4364	498
建成的私人楼宇总建筑面积	万平方米	105.7	37.0	127.2	257.8	19.2
新动工的私人楼宇单位数目	个		1167	870	5405	5122
新动工的私人楼宇总建筑面积	万平方米		20.3	18.4	198.4	86.8

17-10 续表

指　　标	单　位	1990年	2000年	2010年	2015年	2016年
楼宇单位买卖数目	个	8463	10211	29617	9771	14108
不动产买卖契约数目	宗	8559	12484	12707	8771	13262
不动产按揭贷款数目	宗	6610	7367	15127	16570	18529
房屋（期末值）						
公共房屋 ②	个	4871	9084	8174	11507	12219
运输、通讯						
进出澳门货运车辆数目 ③	万辆	26.4	45.4	35.8	38.5	36.3
领牌车辆 ④	万辆	5.1	11.4	19.7	24.9	25.0
电话线	万条	9.6	17.7	16.8	14.7	13.9
对外商品贸易						
出口	亿澳门元	136.4	203.8	69.6	106.9	100.5
本地产品出口	亿澳门元		170.8	23.9	18.2	19.6
转口	亿澳门元		33.0	45.7	88.7	80.8
进口	亿澳门元	123.4	181.0	441.2	846.6	713.5
旅　游						
访澳旅客 ⑤	万人次	594.2	916.2	2496.5	3071.5	3095.0
酒店入住率	%	69	58	80	82	83
教　育 ⑥						
幼儿教育学生	人	20814	14978	10804	16789	17757
小学生	人	34972	45474	23785	26436	28438
中学生	人	17601	38156	37224	28745	27473
高等教育学生	人	7425	8358	25539	31970	32750

注：本表数据由澳门特别行政区政府统计暨普查局提供，国家统计局整理编辑。1998年及以前数据均指原澳门地区。
①数字在日后得到更多资料时会作出修订。
②不包括已出售者。
③自2000年开始包括进出关闸及路(氹)城边检站的数字。而自2007年开始亦包括进出跨境工业区边检站的数字。
④自2007年开始不包括单车。
⑤自2008年开始访澳旅客不包括外地雇员及学生等。
⑥不包括特殊教育学生。第n年的学生人数是指n/n+1学年年底学生人数。2007/2008学年起不包括回归教育学生人数；2010/2011学年起为注册学生人数。

17-11 中国台湾省主要社会经济指标

Main Statistical Indicators of Taiwan Province

指　　标	单　位	1995年	2000年	2010年	2015年	2016年
人口						
户籍登记人口数 ①	万人	2136	2228	2316	2349	2354
人口自然增加率	‰	9.90	8.08	0.91	2.12	1.53
人口密度	人/平方公里	590	616	640	649	650
劳动、就业						
劳动力人口	万人	921	978	1107	1164	1173
劳动参与率	%	58.7	57.7	58.1	58.7	58.8
失业率	%	1.8	3.0	5.2	3.8	3.9
国民经济核算						
本地居民生产总值	新台币亿元	71291	101716	145489	173179	177166
本地生产总值	新台币亿元	70179	100320	141192	167590	171113
人均本地居民生产总值	新台币元	336042	459729	628706	738097	753565
物价年涨跌率						
批发	%		1.82	5.46	-8.84	-2.99
消费者	%		1.26	0.96	-0.31	1.40
工　业						
工业生产指数（2011年＝100）				95.8	104.9	106.5
制造业				95.5	105.3	107.4
运输、旅游						
铁路客运人数	亿人次	1.6	4.6	7.8	10.6	10.9
公路客运人数	亿人次	12.0	11.0	11.1	12.2	12.2
港埠货物装卸量	万收费吨	42017	56695	65540	72139	73356
出岛旅客	万人次	519	733	942	1318	1459
来台湾旅客	万人次	233	262	557	1044	1069
对外贸易						
出口	亿美元	1117	1520	2780	2853	2803
进口	亿美元	1036	1407	2563	2372	2306
财政、金融及景气						
赋税实征净额 ②	新台币亿元	12323	19298	16222	21349	22241
货币供应量M_2 ①	新台币亿元	128054	188978	309544	398840	413018
存款 ①	新台币亿元	131309	193087	310063	393558	407174
放款与投资 ①	新台币亿元	121003	166220	228037	294064	305475

注：1.①为年底数。②为年度资料。
　　2.本表数据来源于台湾行政院主计总处。

第三部分 基本单位情况

Part Three Basic Units

1-1 按行业分的法人单位、产业活动单位数（2016年）

Number of Corporate Units and Industrial Establishments by Sector (2016)

项　　目	法　人单位数（个）	单产业法人单位	多产业法人单位	产业活动单位数（个）	#多产业法人单位的产业活动单位
合　　计	154402	151712	2685	170250	18538
农、林、牧、渔业	286	279	7	297	18
农业	125	122	3	128	6
林业	22	21	1	22	1
畜牧业	13	12	1	13	1
渔业	53	52	1	54	2
农、林、牧、渔服务业	73	72	1	80	8
采 矿 业	13	13		14	1
煤炭开采和洗选业					
石油和天然气开采业					
黑色金属矿采选业					
有色金属矿采选业					
非金属矿采选业	12	12		13	1
开采辅助活动	1	1		1	
其他采矿业					
制 造 业	71007	70582	423	71546	964
农副食品加工业	346	338	8	350	12
食品制造业	563	554	9	576	22
酒、饮料和精制茶制造业	135	128	7	140	12
烟草制品业					
纺织业	1952	1939	13	1964	25
纺织服装、服饰业	4506	4475	31	4522	47
皮革、毛皮、羽毛及其制品和制鞋业	3665	3651	14	3682	31
木材加工和木、竹、藤、棕、草制品业	678	676	2	687	11
家具制造业	2141	2118	23	2157	39
造纸和纸制品业	3227	3223	4	3236	13
印刷和记录媒介复制业	2272	2265	7	2277	12
文教、工美、体育和娱乐用品制造业	3185	3165	20	3195	30
石油加工、炼焦和核燃料加工业	87	85	2	94	9
化学原料和化学制品制造业	1950	1931	19	1962	31
医药制造业	70	66	4	79	13
化学纤维制造业	99	99		101	2
橡胶和塑料制品业	8249	8225	24	8280	55
非金属矿物制品业	1361	1353	8	1378	25
黑色金属冶炼和压延加工业	214	213	1	217	4
有色金属冶炼和压延加工业	480	479	1	487	8

1-1 续表 1

(2016年)

项 目	法 人 单位数 (个)	单 产 业 法人单位	多 产 业 法人单位	产业活动 单 位 数 (个)	#多产业法人单位的产业活动单 位
金属制品业	8384	8359	25	8415	56
通用设备制造业	4569	4523	45	4606	83
专用设备制造业	5896	5859	37	5934	75
汽车制造业	320	317	3	323	6
铁路、船舶、航空航天和其他运输设备制造业	177	176	1	181	5
电气机械和器材制造业	5808	5766	42	5849	83
计算机、通信和其他电子设备制造业	7987	7936	51	8049	113
仪器仪表制造业	1182	1171	11	1191	20
其他制造业	1218	1210	7	1217	7
废弃资源综合利用业	66	63	3	165	102
金属制品、机械和设备修理业	220	219	1	232	13
电力、燃气及水的生产和供应业	253	248	5	335	87
电力、热力生产和供应业	58	57	1	69	12
燃气生产和供应业	39	37	2	78	41
水的生产和供应业	156	154	2	188	34
建筑业	5289	5188	100	5983	795
房屋建筑业	564	534	30	821	287
土木工程建筑业	415	407	8	582	175
建筑安装业	1022	997	24	1111	114
建筑装饰和其他建筑业	3288	3250	38	3469	219
批发和零售业	36798	36366	432	42400	6034
批发业	21057	20897	160	22183	1286
零售业	15741	15469	272	20217	4748
交通运输、仓储和邮政业	3002	2892	110	4080	1188
铁路运输业	16	16		24	8
道路运输业	1048	1023	25	1187	164
水上运输业	82	79	3	89	10
航空运输业	10	9	1	19	10
管道运输业				1	1
装卸搬运和运输代理业	1381	1332	49	1707	375
仓储业	210	206	4	220	14
邮政业	255	227	28	833	606
住宿和餐饮业	2225	2064	160	2997	933
住宿业	874	784	90	969	185
餐饮业	1351	1280	70	2028	748
信息传输、软件和信息技术服务业	2124	2080	44	2578	498
电信、广播电视和卫星传输服务	71	61	10	390	329
互联网和相关服务	451	445	6	501	56
软件和信息技术服务业	1602	1574	28	1687	113
金融业	406	355	51	2093	1738
货币金融服务	132	111	21	1408	1297

1-1 续表 2

(2016年)

项目	法人单位数(个)	单产业法人单位	多产业法人单位	产业活动单位数(个)	#多产业法人单位的产业活动单位
资本市场服务	135	131	4	196	65
保险业	89	63	26	425	362
其他金融业	50	50		64	14
房地产业	4522	4293	229	5234	941
房地产业	4522	4293	229	5234	941
租赁与商务服务业	15184	14869	315	16671	1802
租赁业	338	335	3	365	30
商务服务业	14846	14534	312	16306	1772
科学研究、技术服务业	2135	2080	55	2350	270
研究和试验发展	320	313	7	323	10
专业技术服务业	1388	1346	42	1592	246
科技推广和应用服务业	427	421	6	435	14
水利、环境和公共设施管理业	527	514	13	589	75
水利管理业	59	57	2	68	11
生态保护和环境治理业	104	104		119	15
公共设施管理业	364	353	11	402	49
居民服务、修理和其他服务业	2636	2585	51	2887	302
居民服务业	1003	986	17	1166	180
机动车、电子产品和日用产品修理业	824	807	17	875	68
其他服务业	809	792	17	846	54
教育	2331	2284	47	3013	729
教育	2331	2284	47	3013	729
卫生和社会工作	1013	948	65	1595	647
卫生	903	838	65	1482	644
社会工作	110	110		113	3
文化、体育和娱乐业	2118	2095	22	2272	177
新闻和出版业	21	20	1	20	
广播、电视、电影和影视录音制作业	118	113	5	155	42
文化艺术业	295	293	2	300	7
体育	145	144	1	153	9
娱乐业	1539	1525	13	1644	119
公共管理、社会保障和社会组织	2533	1977	556	3316	1339
中国共产党机关	60	60		60	
国家机构	859	805	54	1425	620
人民政协、民主党派	15	15		15	
社会保障	18	18		30	12
群众团体、社会团体和其他成员组织	867	851	16	1008	157
基层群众自治组织	714	228	486	778	550
国际组织					
国际组织					

1-2 按注册类型分的法人单位、产业活动单位数（2016年）

Number of Corporate Units and Industrial Establishments by Registration Status (2016)

项目	法人单位数（个）	单产业法人单位	多产业法人单位	产业活动单位数（个）	#多产业法人单位的产业活动单位
合计	154402	151712	2685	170250	18538
内资	143071	140637	2429	157702	17065
国有	1769	1659	110	3497	1838
集体	2429	2330	99	3171	841
股份合作	602	593	9	741	148
国有联营	11	9	2	18	9
集体联营	79	77	2	100	23
国有与集体联营	12	11	1	31	20
其他联营	190	186	4	221	35
国有独资公司	87	74	13	93	19
其他有限责任公司	44482	43801	678	49080	5279
股份有限公司	2072	2002	70	3790	1788
私营独资	16458	16381	75	16991	610
私营合伙	4366	4336	30	4482	146
私营有限公司	57483	56805	678	60399	3594
私营股份有限公司	2001	1964	37	2121	157
其他	11030	10409	621	12967	2558
港澳台商投资	8132	7980	152	8651	671
与港澳台商合资经营	392	371	21	493	122
与港澳台商合作经营	219	216	3	248	32
港澳台商独资	7106	6982	124	7458	476
港澳台商投资股份有限公司	203	199	4	227	28
其他港、澳、台商投资	212	212		225	13
外商投资	3199	3095	104	3897	802
中外合资经营	271	252	19	456	204
中外合作经营	65	63	2	85	22
外资企业	2602	2524	78	3062	538
外商投资股份有限公司	125	123	2	143	20
其他外商投资	136	133	3	151	18

1-3 按地域分的法人单位、产业活动单位数（2016年）

Number of Corporate Units and Industrial Establishments by District (2016)

项目	法人单位数（个）	单产业法人单位	多产业法人单位	产业活动单位数（个）	#多产业法人单位的产业活动单位
全市	154402	151712	2685	170250	18538
莞城街道	6242	6024	218	7067	1043
石龙镇	1655	1604	51	2026	422
虎门镇	9254	9163	91	10176	1013
东城街道	9899	9626	272	11188	1562
万江街道	5035	4943	92	5476	533
南城街道	8931	8649	282	10213	1564
中堂镇	2937	2885	52	3281	396
望牛墩镇	1170	1141	29	1327	186
麻涌镇	1791	1752	39	2066	314
石碣镇	4519	4460	59	4861	401
高埗镇	2232	2184	48	2454	270
道滘镇	2577	2529	48	2786	257
洪梅镇	889	865	24	1024	159
沙田镇（虎门港）	3000	2953	47	3278	325
厚街镇	6628	6541	87	7412	871
长安镇	11371	11263	108	12387	1124
寮步镇	9674	9510	164	10433	923
大岭山镇	5028	4971	57	5437	466
大朗镇	9119	9014	105	9750	736
黄江镇	3796	3744	52	4195	451
樟木头镇	4660	4586	72	5169	583
清溪镇	4934	4870	64	5299	429
塘厦镇	9586	9489	97	10230	741
凤岗镇	5374	5311	62	5803	492
谢岗镇	1548	1523	25	1713	190
常平镇	7609	7461	148	8579	1118
桥头镇	2627	2593	33	2953	360
横沥镇	2946	2913	33	3224	311
东坑镇	1705	1664	41	1918	254
企石镇	1719	1674	45	1951	277
石排镇	2443	2401	42	2676	275
茶山镇	2585	2537	48	2870	333
松山湖	919	869	50	1028	159

1-4 星级酒店名单（2016年）

List of Star-ranking Hotels (2016)

酒店名称	星级	电话	地址
豪门大饭店	五星	85117888	虎门镇虎门大道
嘉华大酒店	五星	85928888	厚街镇家具大道1号
东莞富盈雅高美爵酒店	五星	85888888	厚街镇赤岭路段
东莞唐拉雅秀酒店	五星	22698888	东城区迎宾路8号
长安莲花山庄酒店	五星	85538388	长安镇莲花山
柏宁长安国际酒店	五星	85333333	长安镇德政路222号
东莞喜来登大酒店	五星	85988888	厚街镇S256省道莞太路段
塘厦三正半山酒店	五星	87299333	塘厦镇迎宾大道
汇华国际饭店	五星	83938888	常平镇常平大道2号
丰泰花园酒店	五星	85708888	虎门镇S358省道大板地路段
华尔登国际酒店	五星	81028888	桥头镇广场路3号
悦莱花园酒店	五星	81118888	寮步镇香市路8号
欧亚国际酒店	五星	82838888	常平镇常东路8号（嘉骏中心）
东莞虎门美思威尔顿酒店	五星	82888888	虎门镇虎门大道黄河商业城
厚街国际大酒店	五星	85088888	厚街镇东风路与S256省道交汇处
东莞观澜湖度假酒店	五星	87288888	塘厦镇大坪林坪路
东莞宾馆	四星	22222222	莞城区东正路11号
宏远酒店	四星	22418888	南城区宏远路1号
汇美酒店	四星	83918888	常平镇中元路9号

1-4 续表

(2016年)

酒店名称	星级	电话	地址
长安酒店	四星	85532388	长安镇中心S358省道旁
东莞汇源雅高美爵酒店	四星	85244888	虎门镇虎门大道
方中假日酒店	四星	86866666	茶山镇茶山大道西28号
常平半岛酒店	四星	83988888	常平镇北环路
华禧酒店	四星	85383888	长安镇S358省道上沙路段
嘉辉会酒店	四星	87563388	凤岗镇官井头嘉辉路
美怡登酒店	四星	83028888	常平镇中元路
天悦酒店	四星	81812222	石碣镇崇焕路18号
华庭花园酒店	四星	81633333	厚街镇广东现代国际展览中心南侧
石龙宾馆	三星	86613333	石龙镇绿化中路2号
广彩城酒店	三星	22402088	南城区莞太路
西湖大酒店	三星	22822888	南城区西平板岭
明苑大酒店	三星	85122918	虎门镇金龙大道南
宝石大酒店	三星	86662188	企石镇振华路1号
中明酒店	三星	88883368	中堂镇新兴路1号
宏信假日酒店	三星	87363888	清溪镇香芒西路
中青旅山水设计师酒店	三星	21988888	东城区东纵大道189号
冠城酒店	二星	82804888	常平镇中元街常平广场
海月酒店	二星	85926888	厚街镇涌口海月公园侧

1-5 高新技术企业名录（2016年）

List of High-tech Enterprises (2016)

企业名称	所在镇街	行业类别
东莞市捷联科技有限公司	莞城街道	互联网信息服务
东莞市政创软件科技有限公司	莞城街道	信息系统集成服务
东莞市乐琪光电科技有限公司	莞城街道	其他非金属加工专用设备制造
广东智通人才连锁股份有限公司	莞城街道	职业中介服务
广东慧讯计算机网络工程有限公司	莞城街道	信息系统集成服务
东莞市彩丽建筑维护技术有限公司	莞城街道	其他建筑安装业
广东玉兰集团股份有限公司	莞城街道	其他纸制品制造
东莞市茶搜搜网络科技有限公司	莞城街道	互联网信息服务
东莞市东信网络技术有限公司	莞城街道	信息技术咨询服务
东莞市科立电子设备有限公司	莞城街道	其他电子设备制造
东莞市新奥车用燃气发展有限公司	莞城街道	燃气生产和供应业
广东卓科电子科技有限公司	莞城街道	其他电子设备制造
东莞市邦邻信息科技有限公司	莞城街道	软件开发
东莞欧景乐厨卫有限公司	莞城街道	家用厨房电器具制造
东莞市博通科技服务有限公司	莞城街道	软件开发
东莞市车尚信息科技有限公司	莞城街道	软件开发
东莞市德华信息软件有限公司	莞城街道	软件开发
东莞市莞穗照明科技有限公司	莞城街道	电气安装
东莞市冠锋自动化科技有限公司	莞城街道	其他通用设备制造业
东莞市理工软件有限公司	莞城街道	计算机、软件及辅助设备零售
东莞市途安信息科技有限公司	莞城街道	其他未列明信息技术服务业
广东德鑫医疗科技有限公司	莞城街道	其他未列明专业技术服务业
广东快网科技有限公司	莞城街道	互联网信息服务
广东立升科技有限公司	莞城街道	软件开发
广东盈华信息科技有限公司	莞城街道	信息系统集成服务
广东远华电信科技有限公司	莞城街道	其他电信服务
东莞热道节能设备有限公司	莞城街道	泵及真空设备制造
东莞市安达发网络信息技术有限公司	莞城街道	软件开发
东莞市东烽网络科技有限公司	莞城街道	软件开发
广东宏达工贸集团有限公司	莞城街道	其他建筑安装业
东莞赋安实业有限公司	莞城街道	其他输配电及控制设备制造
东莞市臻智计算机科技有限公司	莞城街道	软件开发
广东绿巨人环境科技有限公司	莞城街道	节能技术推广服务
广东众生药业股份有限公司	石龙镇	中成药生产
东莞市广安电气检测中心有限公司	石龙镇	质检技术服务
广东华南药业集团有限公司	石龙镇	化学药品制剂制造
泰阳电子（东莞）有限公司	石龙镇	其他玻璃制品制造
东莞市光华实业有限公司	石龙镇	变压器、整流器和电感器制造
东莞市石龙富华电子有限公司	石龙镇	其他电子设备制造
日本电产三协电子（东莞）有限公司	石龙镇	电子元件及组件制造
东莞天意电子有限公司	石龙镇	其他电子设备制造
东莞市精航科技有限公司	石龙镇	其他金属工具制造
东莞市龙基电子有限公司	石龙镇	电子元件及组件制造
东莞市石龙联兴实业有限公司	石龙镇	其他纸制品制造
广东格林莱光电科技有限公司	石龙镇	电光源制造
东莞市德方斯电器科技有限公司	石龙镇	家用厨房电器具制造
东莞石龙津威饮料食品有限公司	石龙镇	含乳饮料和植物蛋白饮料制造
东莞市光烨节能科技有限公司	石龙镇	光伏设备及元器件制造
东莞市科纯电子有限公司	石龙镇	电子元件及组件制造
东莞市乐一电子有限公司	石龙镇	电子工业专用设备制造

1-5 续表 1

(2016年)

企业名称	所在镇街	行业类别
东莞市阳光信息科技有限公司	石龙镇	信息系统集成服务
东莞市振源机械设备有限公司	石龙镇	其他未列明电气机械及器材制造
广东开普云信息科技股份有限公司	石龙镇	软件开发
东莞泽龙线缆有限公司	石龙镇	电线、电缆制造
东莞长联电线电缆有限公司	虎门镇	电线、电缆制造
东莞市瑞辉机械制造有限公司	虎门镇	连续搬运设备制造
东莞市精铁机械有限公司	虎门镇	电工机械专用设备制造
广东力生智能有限公司	虎门镇	其他通用设备制造业
东莞康源电子有限公司	虎门镇	集成电路制造
广东励晶智能照明有限公司	虎门镇	照明灯具制造
东莞市热恒注塑科技有限公司	虎门镇	模具制造
东莞市连威电子有限公司	虎门镇	其他电子设备制造
东莞常禾电子有限公司	虎门镇	音响设备制造
东莞市科美斯制冷设备有限公司	虎门镇	制冷、空调设备制造
虎彩印艺股份有限公司	虎门镇	包装装潢及其他印刷
广东银禧科技股份有限公司	虎门镇	初级形态塑料及合成树脂制造
东莞市平波电子有限公司	虎门镇	电子元件及组件制造
兴科电子（东莞）有限公司	虎门镇	电子元件及组件制造
东莞令特电子有限公司	虎门镇	电子元件及组件制造
东莞市妙达电动工具制造有限公司	虎门镇	风动和电动工具制造
宝利根（东莞）电子科技有限公司	虎门镇	模具制造
东莞市晋诚机械有限公司	虎门镇	金属切削机床制造
东莞市康祥电子有限公司	虎门镇	电子元件及组件制造
东莞市科佳电路有限公司	虎门镇	印制电路板制造
东莞市怡合达自动化科技有限公司	虎门镇	其他通用设备制造业
广东福德电子有限公司	虎门镇	电力电子元器件制造
东莞市科达计算机系统工程有限公司	虎门镇	信息系统集成服务
东莞市联升电线电缆有限公司	虎门镇	电线、电缆制造
东莞中探探针有限公司	虎门镇	其他电子设备制造
东莞市鸿金顺机械制造有限公司	虎门镇	金属成形机床制造
东莞市睿绅生物技术有限公司	虎门镇	其他农业
东莞市广业电子有限公司	虎门镇	电力电子元器件制造
东莞市锐升电线电缆有限公司	虎门镇	电线、电缆制造
东莞市新杰电工机械有限公司	虎门镇	其他原动设备制造
东莞市誉晟电子科技有限公司	虎门镇	电子元件及组件制造
东莞星海丰电子有限公司	虎门镇	其他塑料制品制造
东莞恒涌电子制品有限公司	虎门镇	其他电子设备制造
东莞嘉盛照明科技有限公司	虎门镇	照明灯具制造
东莞市春藤实业有限公司	虎门镇	绳、索、缆制造
东莞市冠标电工机械有限公司	虎门镇	电工机械专用设备制造
东莞市嘉富汽车用品有限公司	虎门镇	电线、电缆制造
东莞市捷信纸品有限公司	虎门镇	其他纸制品制造
东莞市金铸机械设备有限公司	虎门镇	其他金属加工机械制造
东莞市精汇发电子有限公司	虎门镇	应用电视设备及其他广播电视设备制造
东莞市品胜水性涂料有限公司	虎门镇	专项化学用品制造
东莞市荣泉音响制造有限公司	虎门镇	音响设备制造
东莞市三苑宜友制衣有限公司	虎门镇	服饰制造
东莞市森动律电子有限公司	虎门镇	其他电子设备制造
东莞市士格电子机械有限公司	虎门镇	电容器及其配套设备制造
东莞市天翼通讯电子有限公司	虎门镇	其他电子设备制造

1-5　续表 2

(2016年)

企业名称	所在镇街	行业类别
东莞市婉晶电子科技有限公司	虎门镇	电子元件及组件制造
东莞鑫泰玻璃科技有限公司	虎门镇	其他玻璃制造
广东粤元机电科技有限公司	虎门镇	电动机制造
东莞东寰塑胶五金制品有限公司	虎门镇	日用塑料制品制造
东莞市比特硅橡胶模具有限公司	虎门镇	其他橡胶制品制造
东莞市恒锦印刷机械有限公司	虎门镇	印刷专用设备制造
东莞市衡正光学科技有限公司	虎门镇	其他塑料制品制造
东莞市汇海环保科技有限公司	虎门镇	环境保护专用设备制造
东莞市柯氏五金有限公司	虎门镇	其他有色金属压延加工
东莞市科冠机电有限公司	虎门镇	制冷、空调设备制造
东莞市蓝鹰环保科技有限公司	虎门镇	气体、液体分离及纯净设备制造
东莞市易辉自动化机械有限公司	虎门镇	其他通用设备制造业
东莞市银泰玻璃有限公司	虎门镇	其他玻璃制品制造
信义玻璃工程（东莞）有限公司	虎门镇	其他玻璃制品制造
兴科电子科技有限公司	虎门镇	通信终端设备制造
东莞昆嘉电子有限公司	虎门镇	电子元件及组件制造
东莞市贝斯特热流道科技有限公司	虎门镇	专用设备修理
东莞市翰胜金属制品有限公司	虎门镇	金属结构制造
东莞市庆丰电工机械有限公司	虎门镇	电工机械专用设备制造
东莞市瑞科五金塑胶制品有限公司	虎门镇	航空、航天相关设备制造
东莞市三信精密机械有限公司	虎门镇	电子工业专用设备制造
东莞市泰威电子有限公司	虎门镇	其他电子设备制造
东莞市益仁实业有限公司	虎门镇	电子工业专用设备制造
东莞奔迅汽车玻璃有限公司	虎门镇	其他玻璃制品制造
东莞市科越电子科技有限公司	虎门镇	商业、饮食、服务专用设备制造
广东杰思通讯股份有限公司	虎门镇	电子元件及组件制造
信义汽车玻璃（东莞）有限公司	虎门镇	其他玻璃制造
东莞市台工电子机械科技有限公司	东城街道	电子工业专用设备制造
东莞市骏宏电子科技有限公司	东城街道	其他电子设备制造
东莞市利瀚机械有限公司	东城街道	其他非金属加工专用设备制造
东莞市天勤仪器有限公司	东城街道	绘图、计算及测量仪器制造
东莞市菱锐机械有限公司	东城街道	其他通用设备制造业
东莞市普密斯精密仪器有限公司	东城街道	光学仪器制造
东莞市力星激光科技有限公司	东城街道	金属切削机床制造
东莞市嘉腾仪器仪表有限公司	东城街道	供应用仪表及其他通用仪器制造
东莞通华液晶有限公司	东城街道	光电子器件及其他电子器件制造
广东东日环保有限公司	东城街道	环境保护专用设备制造
广东宏远集团药业有限公司	东城街道	化学药品制剂制造
长园高能电气股份有限公司	东城街道	绝缘制品制造
东莞科威医疗器械有限公司	东城街道	假肢、人工器官及植（介）入器械制造
东莞市贝尔试验设备有限公司	东城街道	电工仪器仪表制造
东莞市伟煌试验设备有限公司	东城街道	试验机制造
东莞市冈田电子科技有限公司	东城街道	其他原动设备制造
东莞市百分百科技有限公司	东城街道	照明灯具制造
东莞市大能环保科技有限公司	东城街道	节能技术推广服务
东华机械有限公司	东城街道	塑料加工专用设备制造
东莞万德电子制品有限公司	东城街道	电子元件及组件制造
广东长天精密设备科技有限公司	东城街道	电子工业专用设备制造
东莞市嘉准电子科技有限公司	东城街道	电子元件及组件制造
东莞市新铂铼电子有限公司	东城街道	电子元件及组件制造

1-5 续表 3

(2016年)

企业名称	所在镇街	行业类别
东莞市星曜光电照明科技有限公司	东城街道	照明灯具制造
东莞科视自动化科技有限公司	东城街道	印刷专用设备制造
广东红旗家具有限公司	东城街道	木质家具制造
东莞美维电路有限公司	东城街道	印制电路板制造
东莞市奕东电子有限公司	东城街道	其他通用零部件制造
东莞市安拓普塑胶聚合物科技有限公司	东城街道	其他塑料制品制造
德科摩橡塑科技（东莞）有限公司	东城街道	橡胶加工专用设备制造
东莞市德瑞精密设备有限公司	东城街道	其他电子设备制造
广东合通建业科技股份有限公司	东城街道	电子元件及组件制造
东莞市金沃新材料科技有限公司	东城街道	其他橡胶制品制造
东莞市鸿铭机械有限公司	东城街道	其他原动设备制造
东莞市天唯智能科技有限公司	东城街道	信息系统集成服务
广东戈兰玛汽车系统有限公司	东城街道	汽车零部件及配件制造
岭南园林股份有限公司	东城街道	其他林业服务
东莞博力威电池有限公司	东城街道	锂离子电池制造
东莞市正新包装制品有限公司	东城街道	塑料薄膜制造
东莞丝丽雅电子科技有限公司	东城街道	电力电子元器件制造
广东立佳实业有限公司	东城街道	电工仪器仪表制造
广东守门神科技集团有限公司	东城街道	其他专用设备制造
东莞市大忠电子有限公司	东城街道	电子元件及组件制造
东莞市凯格精密机械有限公司	东城街道	其他电子设备制造
东莞市神州视觉科技有限公司	东城街道	光学仪器制造
东莞市佳晟实业有限公司	东城街道	其他非家用纺织制成品制造
东莞市康星运动用品有限公司	东城街道	其他体育用品制造
东莞市莱宝机电科技有限公司	东城街道	其他通用设备制造业
东莞市新宇机械有限公司	东城街道	其他通用设备制造业
东莞市鑫华仪器有限公司	东城街道	其他电子设备制造
东莞市银通机械科技有限公司	东城街道	其他非金属加工专用设备制造
广东安盾安检排爆装备有限公司	东城街道	实验分析仪器制造
广东莞银信息科技有限公司	东城街道	其他计算机制造
广东汇嵘节能服务有限公司	东城街道	节能技术推广服务
广东索博智能科技有限公司	东城街道	其他综合零售
广东拓扑中润科技发展有限公司	东城街道	涂料制造
伸铭电子（东莞）有限公司	东城街道	电子元件及组件制造
东莞市东穗电子科技有限公司	东城街道	其他建筑安装业
广东源兴光学仪器有限公司	东城街道	光学仪器制造
东莞京能新能源科技有限公司	东城街道	照明灯具制造
东莞锐视光电科技有限公司	东城街道	灯用电器附件及其他照明器具制造
东莞市艾思荔检测仪器有限公司	东城街道	试验机制造
东莞市宝华数控科技有限公司	东城街道	金属成形机床制造
东莞市鼎盛机械有限公司	东城街道	锂离子电池制造
东莞市福瑞德橡塑制品有限公司	东城街道	合成橡胶制造
东莞市嘉刚机电科技发展有限公司	东城街道	工业自动控制系统装置制造
东莞市嘉靖食品科技有限公司	东城街道	其他未列明食品制造
东莞市交通规划勘察设计院有限公司	东城街道	工程勘察设计
东莞市杰贡机械设备有限公司	东城街道	电子工业专用设备制造
东莞市精准通检测服务有限公司	东城街道	质检技术服务
东莞市矩正电子科技有限公司	东城街道	其他通用设备制造业
东莞市蓝天电脑软件咨询有限公司	东城街道	软件开发
东莞市乐辰日用品有限公司	东城街道	日用塑料制品制造

1-5 续表 4

(2016年)

企业名称	所在镇街	行业类别
东莞市利名自动化科技有限公司	东城街道	集成电路制造
东莞市鹏博盛实业有限公司	东城街道	其他通用零部件制造
东莞市庆声试验设备有限公司	东城街道	试验机制造
东莞市瑞为电器配件有限公司	东城街道	其他橡胶制品制造
东莞市叁益机械科技有限公司	东城街道	其他通用设备制造业
东莞市鑫圣五金机械有限公司	东城街道	其他通用设备制造业
东莞市星马焊锡有限公司	东城街道	锡冶炼
东莞市粤丰展示用品有限公司	东城街道	其他工艺美术品制造
东莞市兆丰精密仪器有限公司	东城街道	光学仪器制造
东莞市正品五金电子有限公司	东城街道	金属结构制造
东莞市卓益塑胶制品有限公司	东城街道	塑料板、管、型材制造
东莞优聚信息科技有限公司	东城街道	教育辅助服务
广东华思科金属科技有限公司	东城街道	金属门窗制造
广东莫莱卡焊接科技有限公司	东城街道	其他有色金属压延加工
广东台泉环保科技有限公司	东城街道	日用家电设备零售
东莞博登运动用品有限公司	东城街道	运动防护用具制造
东莞力嘉塑料制品有限公司	东城街道	其他塑料制品制造
东莞仕能机械设备有限公司	东城街道	其他通用设备制造业
东莞市爱酷防潮设备科技有限公司	东城街道	工业自动控制系统装置制造
东莞市澳星通信设备有限公司	东城街道	电子工业专用设备制造
东莞市创科自动化设备有限公司	东城街道	其他通用设备制造业
东莞市东莞通有限公司	东城街道	其他未列明信息技术服务业
东莞市房讯资讯股份有限公司	东城街道	房地产中介服务
东莞市高品计量技术服务有限公司	东城街道	质检技术服务
东莞市光博士激光科技股份有限公司	东城街道	纺织专用设备制造
东莞市环联自动化设备有限公司	东城街道	其他专用设备制造
东莞市环瑞环境测试设备有限公司	东城街道	试验机制造
东莞市吉洋自动化科技有限公司	东城街道	电子工业专用设备制造
东莞市嘉仪自动化设备科技有限公司	东城街道	电子工业专用设备制造
东莞市杰美电器有限公司	东城街道	家用厨房电器具制造
东莞市金振电子有限公司	东城街道	电子工业专用设备制造
东莞市良展有机硅科技有限公司	东城街道	其他合成材料制造
东莞市榴花艺术有限公司	东城街道	其他工艺美术品制造
东莞市普强高分子材料有限公司	东城街道	其他未列明制造业
东莞市铨智科通信设备有限公司	东城街道	通信系统设备制造
东莞市热线家具有限公司	东城街道	木质家具制造
东莞市台塑实业有限公司	东城街道	塑料加工专用设备制造
东莞市天一电机有限公司	东城街道	电动机制造
东莞市万德光电科技有限公司	东城街道	电子元件及组件制造
东莞市鑫泰网络科技有限公司	东城街道	信息系统集成服务
东莞市雅弘自动化设备有限公司	东城街道	其他通用设备制造业
东莞市雅捷通电脑科技有限公司	东城街道	软件开发
东莞新奥燃气有限公司	东城街道	其他未列明商务服务业
广东利鑫智能科技有限公司	东城街道	其他专用设备制造
广东粤辉环保工程有限公司	东城街道	环境保护专用设备制造
生益电子股份有限公司	东城街道	印制电路板制造
东莞东超新材料科技有限公司	东城街道	其他基础化学原料制造
东莞华晶粉末冶金有限公司	东城街道	锻件及粉末冶金制品制造
东莞金迪照明科技有限公司	东城街道	照明灯具制造
东莞市爱迪机电科技有限公司	东城街道	其他仪器仪表制造业

1-5 续表 5

(2016年)

企业名称	所在镇街	行业类别
东莞市德隆自动化科技有限公司	东城街道	其他通用设备制造业
东莞市东联铝业有限公司	东城街道	铝压延加工
东莞市国亨塑胶科技有限公司	东城街道	其他塑料制品制造
东莞市好又快照明电器制造有限公司	东城街道	照明灯具制造
东莞市鸿远机械设备制造有限公司	东城街道	其他通用设备制造业
东莞市松菱实业有限公司	东城街道	其他医疗设备及器械制造
东莞市湘江电子科技有限公司	东城街道	其他家用电力器具制造
东莞市亿茂滤材有限公司	东城街道	其他合成材料制造
东莞市中天自动化科技有限公司	东城街道	电子工业专用设备制造
东莞泰升音响科技有限公司	东城街道	其他电子设备制造
广东爱车小屋实业发展股份有限公司	东城街道	香料、香精制造
广东红运家具有限公司	东城街道	木质家具制造
广东龙香食品有限公司	东城街道	糕点、面包制造
广东胜特建筑科技开发有限公司	东城街道	其他未列明建筑业
广东天一照明科技有限公司	东城街道	照明灯具制造
经续检验技术（东莞）有限公司	东城街道	质检技术服务
广东建邦计算机软件股份有限公司	东城街道	软件开发
东莞市达瑞电子有限公司	东城街道	其他电子设备制造
东莞市太业电子股份有限公司	东城街道	锂离子电池制造
广东鸿宝科技有限公司	东城街道	电子工业专用设备制造
广东晖速通信技术股份有限公司	东城街道	通信系统设备制造
广东聚光电子科技有限公司	东城街道	其他计算机制造
广东科源智能科技股份有限公司	东城街道	软件开发
东莞市同涞节能设备有限公司	东城街道	生态与环境
广东利扬芯片测试股份有限公司	万江街道	光电子器件及其他电子器件制造
东莞铭丰包装股份有限公司	万江街道	包装装潢及其他印刷
东莞安默琳机械制造技术有限公司	万江街道	其他金属加工机械制造
东莞市多贺自动化科技有限公司	万江街道	通用设备修理
东莞市鸿企机械有限公司	万江街道	其他未列明电气机械及器材制造
广东至诚化学工业有限公司	万江街道	涂料制造
广东五星太阳能股份有限公司	万江街道	燃气、太阳能及类似能源家用器具制造
东莞市长盛刀锯有限公司	万江街道	切削工具制造
东莞市今联实业有限公司	万江街道	其他计算机制造
东莞市明天纳米科技有限公司	万江街道	涂料制造
东莞市爱克斯曼机械有限公司	万江街道	纺织专用设备制造
广东广视通科教设备有限公司	万江街道	木质家具制造
广东硕源科技股份有限公司	万江街道	锦纶纤维制造
东莞基业电气设备有限公司	万江街道	配电开关控制设备制造
东莞市康源节能科技有限公司	万江街道	燃气、太阳能及类似能源家用器具制造
广东西奥物联网科技股份有限公司	万江街道	计算机外围设备制造
东莞市莱硕光电科技有限公司	万江街道	照明灯具制造
东莞市爱嘉义齿有限公司	万江街道	卫生材料及医药用品制造
东莞市宏祥机械设备有限公司	万江街道	其他专用设备制造
东莞市领冠半导体照明有限公司	万江街道	电力电子元器件制造
东莞市诺丽电子科技有限公司	万江街道	软件开发
东莞市欧西曼机械设备有限公司	万江街道	其他通用设备制造业
东莞市晴远电子有限公司	万江街道	电力电子元器件制造
东莞市瑞达电瓶车科技有限公司	万江街道	电车制造
东莞市银华生物科技有限公司	万江街道	饲料加工
东莞市卓安精机自动化设备有限公司	万江街道	电子工业专用设备制造

1-5 续表 6

(2016年)

企业名称	所在镇街	行业类别
广东迪奥技术有限公司	万江街道	电气安装
广东中科集创电力科技有限公司	万江街道	其他未列明电气机械及器材制造
东莞市同亚电子科技有限公司	万江街道	其他电子设备制造
东莞和创食品有限公司	万江街道	饼干及其他焙烤食品制造
东莞华尔泰装饰材料有限公司	万江街道	其他建筑材料制造
东莞华懋精密机械科技有限公司	万江街道	其他金属加工机械制造
东莞市艾立克机械制造有限公司	万江街道	其他通用设备制造业
东莞市爱康电子科技有限公司	万江街道	电子工业专用设备制造
东莞市百思特塑胶有限公司	万江街道	其他塑料制品制造
东莞市合鼎电路有限公司	万江街道	印制电路板制造
东莞市宏文机械科技有限公司	万江街道	其他通用设备制造业
东莞市嘉汇环保科技有限公司	万江街道	石灰和石膏制造
东莞市贾氏机械制造有限公司	万江街道	其他通用设备制造业
东莞市简创电子科技有限公司	万江街道	电子元件及组件制造
东莞市锦顺自动化工程有限公司	万江街道	其他未列明电气机械及器材制造
东莞市龙行胜机械有限公司	万江街道	其他金属加工机械制造
东莞市绿保纸塑制品有限公司	万江街道	其他纸制品制造
东莞市瑞丰源工艺包装制品有限公司	万江街道	木制容器制造
东莞市三人行环境科技有限公司	万江街道	水污染治理
东莞市天利太阳能有限公司	万江街道	太阳能发电
东莞市威立雅水处理设备有限公司	万江街道	污水处理及其再生利用
东莞市玮创电子设备有限公司	万江街道	电子工业专用设备制造
东莞市祥搏机电设备有限公司	万江街道	食品、酒、饮料及茶生产专用设备制造
东莞市逸顺音响科技有限公司	万江街道	音响设备制造
东莞市裕隆机械制造有限公司	万江街道	其他通用设备制造业
东莞永冠电子科技有限公司	万江街道	其他电子设备制造
广东凯德伦集团有限公司	万江街道	其他专用设备制造
广东尚而特太阳能有限公司	万江街道	燃气、太阳能及类似能源家用器具制造
广东尚鑫新材料股份有限公司	万江街道	其他纸制品制造
广东振远信息科技有限公司	万江街道	计算机、软件及辅助设备批发
广东中冶地理信息股份有限公司	万江街道	测绘服务
东莞市邦泰印刷机械有限公司	万江街道	印刷专用设备制造
东莞市超业精密设备有限公司	万江街道	电子工业专用设备制造
东莞市高鑫检测设备有限公司	万江街道	实验分析仪器制造
东莞市广传信息科技有限公司	万江街道	信息系统集成服务
东莞市汇如涞电能科技有限公司	万江街道	其他通用设备制造业
东莞市品耀自动化设备有限公司	万江街道	其他物料搬运设备制造
东莞市赛力自动化设备科技股份有限公司	万江街道	其他专用设备制造
东莞市胜高通讯科技有限公司	万江街道	其他电子设备制造
东莞市思齐橡胶技术有限公司	万江街道	橡胶零件制造
东莞市沃锐电子有限公司	万江街道	电子工业专用设备制造
东莞市亚布力气动液压设备科技有限公司	万江街道	其他通用零部件制造
东莞市亿辰模具科技有限公司	万江街道	模具制造
东莞市银屏电子科技有限公司	万江街道	光电子器件及其他电子器件制造
东莞市圆美精密电子有限公司	万江街道	平板玻璃制造
东莞市中锂自动化设备有限公司	万江街道	其他通用设备制造业
东莞市忠信橡胶制品有限公司	万江街道	日用及医用橡胶制品制造
东莞智邦机械科技有限公司	万江街道	其他通用设备制造业
广东能标检测技术服务有限公司	万江街道	质检技术服务
广东顺联动漫科技有限公司	万江街道	玩具制造

1-5 续表 7

(2016年)

企业名称	所在镇街	行业类别
广东沃特环保科技有限公司	万江街道	环境保护专用设备制造
广东雅迪环保设备有限公司	万江街道	污水处理及其再生利用
东莞吉川机械科技股份有限公司	万江街道	喷枪及类似器具制造
东莞市精茂机电制品有限公司	万江街道	微电机及其他电机制造
东莞市久锋纸箱机械有限公司	万江街道	印刷专用设备制造
东莞市力显仪器科技有限公司	万江街道	试验机制造
东莞市普华精密机械有限公司	万江街道	其他通用设备制造业
东莞市瑞鹏机器人自动化有限公司	万江街道	电子工业专用设备制造
东莞市三优塑料机械制造有限公司	万江街道	电工机械专用设备制造
东莞市顺如电子科技有限公司	万江街道	电工机械专用设备制造
东莞市沃德精密机械有限公司	万江街道	其他通用设备制造业
东莞市众度机械设备有限公司	万江街道	其他机械设备及电子产品批发
东莞市卓蓝自动化设备有限公司	万江街道	其他仪器仪表制造业
东莞斯巴复新能源有限公司	万江街道	其他电池制造
广东宝士电气有限公司	万江街道	其他输配电及控制设备制造
广东明日新能源有限公司	万江街道	燃气、太阳能及类似能源家用器具制造
广东每通测控科技股份有限公司	万江街道	其他通用设备制造业
广东大榕树信息科技有限公司	南城街道	软件开发
东莞市银雁金融配套服务有限公司	南城街道	其他未列明信息技术服务业
广东沃杰森环保科技股份有限公司	南城街道	水资源专用机械制造
广东技安科技有限公司	南城街道	互联网接入及相关服务
东莞新科技术研究开发有限公司	南城街道	工程和技术研究和试验发展
广东凌康科技有限公司	南城街道	信息系统集成服务
东莞方天软件科技股份有限公司	南城街道	软件开发
东莞市杉杉电池材料有限公司	南城街道	其他未列明制造业
东莞市骏翼电子科技有限公司	南城街道	其他未列明信息技术服务业
东莞市中大科技网络有限公司	南城街道	互联网信息服务
广东开源环境科技有限公司	南城街道	水污染治理
广东力拓网络科技有限公司	南城街道	软件开发
东莞市崴泰电子有限公司	南城街道	其他电子设备制造
东莞市富默克化工有限公司	南城街道	其他基础化学原料制造
广东万维博通信息技术有限公司	南城街道	软件开发
广东天新软件科技有限公司	南城街道	软件开发
东莞市鑫利机电有限公司	南城街道	其他电子设备制造
东莞市爱玛数控科技有限公司	南城街道	其他金属工具制造
东莞市钜大电子有限公司	南城街道	锂离子电池制造
广东优信无限网络股份有限公司	南城街道	其他电信服务
东莞市信测科技有限公司	南城街道	其他未列明信息技术服务业
东莞市斯宇自动化设备有限公司	南城街道	锂离子电池制造
东莞市正太合赢自动化设备有限公司	南城街道	其他专用设备制造
广东上川智能装备股份有限公司	南城街道	其他仪器仪表制造业
广东盘古信息科技有限公司	南城街道	软件开发
东莞市开创精密机械有限公司	南城街道	其他金属加工机械制造
广东宏泰照明科技有限公司	南城街道	照明灯具制造
东莞市凯诺德软件科技有限公司	南城街道	信息系统集成服务
东莞市贝迪自动化科技有限公司	南城街道	其他电子设备制造
东莞安本先天下智能科技有限公司	南城街道	通信终端设备制造
东莞传动电喷科技有限公司	南城街道	汽车零部件及配件制造
东莞市博拓自动化设备有限公司	南城街道	电子工业专用设备制造
东莞市创丰科技发展有限公司	南城街道	其他电子产品零售

1–5 续表 8

(2016年)

企业名称	所在镇街	行业类别
东莞市北测标准技术服务有限公司	南城街道	质检技术服务
东莞市鸿茂物联网科技有限公司	南城街道	其他电子设备制造
东莞市嘉松电子科技有限公司	南城街道	互联网信息服务
东莞市立迪电子科技有限公司	南城街道	其他通用设备制造业
东莞市联鼎电子科技有限公司	南城街道	质检技术服务
东莞市诺尔检测科技有限公司	南城街道	质检技术服务
东莞市三瑞自动化科技有限公司	南城街道	软件开发
东莞市新雷神仿真控制有限公司	南城街道	其他未列明信息技术服务业
东莞市中谱光电设备有限公司	南城街道	其他通用设备制造业
东莞市中旺精密仪器有限公司	南城街道	光学仪器制造
广东安标检测科技有限公司	南城街道	质检技术服务
广东日正实业有限公司	南城街道	其他金属制日用品制造
广东三鼎实业有限公司	南城街道	其他建筑安装业
广东网安科技有限公司	南城街道	信息系统集成服务
东莞市金状元网络科技有限公司	南城街道	其他互联网服务
易通百通网络科技股份有限公司	南城街道	其他计算机制造
东莞海金杜门五金制品有限公司	南城街道	其他金属制日用品制造
东莞宏强电子有限公司	南城街道	电容器及其配套设备制造
东莞纳萨斯通信科技有限公司	南城街道	软件开发
东莞市保得生物工程有限公司	南城街道	有机肥料及微生物肥料制造
东莞市北斗航盛通讯科技有限公司	南城街道	其他未列明信息技术服务业
东莞市辰宇电气有限公司	南城街道	工业自动控制系统装置制造
东莞市顾德电脑软件有限公司	南城街道	软件开发
东莞市华高网络科技有限公司	南城街道	互联网信息服务
东莞市华科建筑科技有限公司	南城街道	房屋建筑业
东莞市集创计算机科技有限公司	南城街道	软件开发
东莞市凌速电子科技有限公司	南城街道	导航、气象及海洋专用仪器制造
东莞市凌宇工业设备技术有限公司	南城街道	气体压缩机械制造
东莞市视帝测量软件有限公司	南城街道	软件开发
东莞市娃哈哈饮用水有限公司	南城街道	瓶（罐）装饮用水制造
东莞市维度自动化设备有限公司	南城街道	工业自动控制系统装置制造
东莞市信瑞智能科技有限公司	南城街道	工业自动控制系统装置制造
东莞市雅之雷德机电科技有限公司	南城街道	泵及真空设备制造
东莞市易比信息技术有限公司	南城街道	软件开发
东莞市银讯网络支付有限公司	南城街道	其他未列明金融业
东莞市正太合信自动化设备有限公司	南城街道	其他通用设备制造业
东莞云泰信息科技有限公司	南城街道	信息系统集成服务
东莞智标鞋业科技有限公司	南城街道	其他制鞋业
广东安源鼎盛检测评价技术服务有限公司	南城街道	质检技术服务
广东布鲁斯工业设计有限公司	南城街道	专业化设计服务
广东车云网络信息科技股份有限公司	南城街道	其他互联网服务
广东金颢轩环境工程设备科技有限公司	南城街道	环境保护专用设备制造
广东开能环保能源有限公司	南城街道	其他电力生产
广东绿家绿生态环境农业科技有限公司	南城街道	其他农业服务
广东普洛测控科技有限公司	南城街道	其他仪器仪表制造业
广东越联仪器有限公司	南城街道	试验机制造
广东中健检测技术有限公司	南城街道	质检技术服务
广东筑奥生态环境股份有限公司	南城街道	其他未列明建筑业
东莞科曼利智控有限公司	南城街道	通信终端设备制造
东莞市艾特姆射频科技有限公司	南城街道	其他未列明信息技术服务业

1-5 续表 9

(2016年)

企业名称	所在镇街	行业类别
东莞市彼联机械科技有限公司	南城街道	其他通用零部件制造
东莞市富驰电子科技有限公司	南城街道	软件开发
东莞市海川博通信息科技有限公司	南城街道	其他仪器仪表制造业
东莞市海川数控技术有限公司	南城街道	工业自动控制系统装置制造
东莞市瀚恒环境技术工程有限公司	南城街道	环境保护专用设备制造
东莞市乐普电子技术有限公司	南城街道	集成电路制造
东莞市亮宇自动化科技有限公司	南城街道	电线、电缆制造
东莞市麦迪工业装备有限公司	南城街道	其他通用设备制造业
东莞市欧特自动化技术有限公司	南城街道	计算机、软件及辅助设备批发
东莞市台通电子科技有限公司	南城街道	工业自动控制系统装置制造
东莞市天霸电子科技有限公司	南城街道	互联网接入及相关服务
东莞市微科光电科技有限公司	南城街道	光学玻璃制造
东莞市鑫品自动化科技有限公司	南城街道	工业自动控制系统装置制造
东莞市亦强软件有限公司	南城街道	软件开发
东莞市永铠自动化科技有限公司	南城街道	其他机械和设备修理业
东莞市远程自动化科技有限公司	南城街道	工业自动控制系统装置制造
东莞市掌商信息科技有限公司	南城街道	互联网信息服务
东莞市中南环保科技有限公司	南城街道	环境保护专用设备制造
东莞拓蓝自动化科技有限公司	南城街道	工业自动控制系统装置制造
高铁检测仪器（东莞）有限公司	南城街道	试验机制造
广东德鸿档案科技有限公司	南城街道	软件开发
广东广量测绘信息技术有限公司	南城街道	工程和技术研究和试验发展
广东鸿太升软件科技有限公司	南城街道	软件开发
广东数夫家具软件有限公司	南城街道	软件开发
广东通莞科技股份有限公司	南城街道	其他未列明信息技术服务业
广东物网智能科技有限公司	南城街道	信息系统集成服务
广东云关通科技有限公司	南城街道	软件开发
广东兆天纺织科技有限公司	南城街道	针织或钩针编织物印染精加工
广东中金环保科技有限公司	南城街道	环境保护专用设备制造
全天自动化能源科技（东莞）有限公司	南城街道	电工机械专用设备制造
广东盛世商潮网络科技有限公司	南城街道	互联网信息服务
东莞华迈通信技术有限公司	南城街道	信息系统集成服务
东莞市奥时达信息技术有限公司	南城街道	汽车零部件及配件制造
东莞市东测检测技术有限公司	南城街道	环境保护监测
东莞市盟大塑化科技有限公司	南城街道	互联网信息服务
东莞市易得网络科技有限公司	南城街道	软件开发
东莞市禹瑞机电设备有限公司	南城街道	其他专用设备制造
东莞市智软计算机有限公司	南城街道	软件开发
东莞市智赢智能装备有限公司	南城街道	机械零部件加工
东莞文胜鼎电子科技有限公司	南城街道	其他电子设备制造
广东瑞恩科技有限公司	南城街道	信息系统集成服务
广东思域信息科技有限公司	南城街道	信息系统集成服务
东莞市佛尔盛机电科技有限公司	南城街道	泵及真空设备制造
广东创锐电子技术股份有限公司	南城街道	电子测量仪器制造
广东华恒智能科技有限公司	南城街道	其他专用设备制造
派生科技集团股份有限公司	南城街道	互联网信息服务
广东唯一网络科技有限公司	南城街道	互联网接入及相关服务
广东伟旺达科技股份有限公司	南城街道	电子元件及组件制造
广东智政信息科技有限公司	南城街道	软件开发
东莞爱屋氏日用品有限公司	中堂镇	其他日用化学产品制造

1-5　续表 10

(2016年)

企业名称	所在镇街	行业类别
东莞市希贝实业有限公司	中堂镇	日用及医用橡胶制品制造
广东广益科技实业有限公司	中堂镇	食品及饲料添加剂制造
东莞建泰生物科技有限公司	中堂镇	淀粉及淀粉制品制造
东莞理文造纸厂有限公司	中堂镇	机制纸及纸板制造
东莞兆舜有机硅科技股份有限公司	中堂镇	有机化学原料制造
东莞市东兴铝业有限公司	中堂镇	其他未列明金属制品制造
东莞市嘉达磁电制品有限公司	中堂镇	稀有稀土金属压延加工
东莞市新华业纤维科技有限公司	中堂镇	纤维板制造
东莞市满贯包装有限公司	中堂镇	金属包装容器制造
广东高德品杰光电科技有限公司	中堂镇	照明灯具制造
东莞美哲塑胶制品有限公司	中堂镇	地板制造
东莞市本铃车业科技有限公司	中堂镇	摩托车零部件及配件制造
东莞市建远机电有限公司	中堂镇	金属切割及焊接设备制造
东莞耀铨顺塑料有限公司	中堂镇	塑料鞋制造
东莞环裕自动化机械有限公司	中堂镇	其他通用设备制造业
东莞市恩科化工有限公司	中堂镇	化学试剂和助剂制造
东莞市君容信息技术有限公司	中堂镇	其他电子设备制造
东莞市明聚塑胶有限公司	中堂镇	其他塑料制品制造
东莞市西芹电器有限公司	中堂镇	家用厨房电器具制造
东莞市晓马精密机械有限公司	中堂镇	塑料加工专用设备制造
东莞市毅新庆江机械制造有限公司	中堂镇	起重机制造
广东粤辉科技股份有限公司	中堂镇	其他橡胶制品制造
万宝力不锈钢制品（东莞）有限公司	中堂镇	其他金属制日用品制造
东莞市华汇精密机械有限公司	中堂镇	金属密封件制造
广东鑫发精密金属科技有限公司	中堂镇	金属表面处理及热处理加工
永磁电子（东莞）有限公司	中堂镇	变压器、整流器和电感器制造
东莞市金澜电工材料有限公司	望牛墩镇	其他有色金属压延加工
东莞市科力钢铁线材有限公司	望牛墩镇	金属丝绳及其制品制造
东莞智源彩印有限公司	望牛墩镇	包装装潢及其他印刷
东莞市亚美精密机械配件有限公司	望牛墩镇	电子工业专用设备制造
广东金达照明科技股份有限公司	望牛墩镇	照明灯具制造
东莞市华清净水技术有限公司	望牛墩镇	其他专用化学产品制造
东莞市精诚电能设备有限公司	望牛墩镇	家用厨房电器具制造
广东南方宏明电子科技股份有限公司	望牛墩镇	电子元件及组件制造
东莞市五鑫精密机器设备制造有限公司	望牛墩镇	其他金属加工机械制造
广东比伦生活用纸有限公司	望牛墩镇	其他纸制品制造
东莞市贝司通橡胶科技有限公司	望牛墩镇	其他橡胶制品制造
东莞市天尚太阳能有限公司	望牛墩镇	燃气、太阳能及类似能源家用器具制造
东莞市养生源蜂业有限公司	望牛墩镇	保健食品制造
东莞市屹泰水晶工艺有限公司	望牛墩镇	日用玻璃制品制造
东莞市盈尔电器有限公司	望牛墩镇	包装专用设备制造
广东侨盛防伪材料有限公司	望牛墩镇	其他纸制品制造
东莞市奥思睿德世浦电子科技有限公司	望牛墩镇	集成电路及电子元器件
东莞市天球实业有限公司	麻涌镇	其他电池制造
东莞南玻光伏科技有限公司	麻涌镇	其他电池制造
广东康达尔农牧科技有限公司	麻涌镇	饲料加工
东莞南玻工程玻璃有限公司	麻涌镇	平板玻璃制造
东莞超盈纺织有限公司	麻涌镇	化纤织物染整精加工
东莞市贝特利新材料有限公司	麻涌镇	油墨及类似产品制造
东莞玖龙纸业有限公司	麻涌镇	机制纸及纸板制造

1-5 续表 11

(2016年)

企业名称	所在镇街	行业类别
东莞南玻太阳能玻璃有限公司	麻涌镇	平板玻璃制造
东莞市山力高分子材料科研有限公司	麻涌镇	密封用填料及类似品制造
东莞太平洋博高润滑油有限公司	麻涌镇	原油加工及石油制品制造
广东省东莞电机有限公司	麻涌镇	电动机制造
广东中远船务工程有限公司	麻涌镇	金属船舶制造
广东汇美淀粉科技有限公司	麻涌镇	淀粉及淀粉制品制造
东莞市导谷电子材料科技有限公司	麻涌镇	其他电子设备制造
丰益油脂科技（东莞）有限公司	麻涌镇	其他日用化学产品制造
广东裕华兴建筑机械制造有限公司	麻涌镇	其他未列明制造业
东莞市奥莱克电子有限公司	麻涌镇	音响设备制造
东莞市伟力合机器人有限公司	麻涌镇	机械零部件加工
广东华兰海电测科技股份有限公司	麻涌镇	其他专用仪器制造
东莞一翔液体肥料有限公司	麻涌镇	其他肥料制造
广东凯力船艇股份有限公司	麻涌镇	金属船舶制造
广东龙马化学有限公司	麻涌镇	防水建筑材料制造
广东信力材料科技有限公司	麻涌镇	合成橡胶制造
东莞市冠晔电子科技有限公司	石碣镇	其他电子设备制造
东莞市维尔霓斯照明科技有限公司	石碣镇	照明灯具制造
东莞泉声电子有限公司	石碣镇	电力电子元器件制造
东莞市志基电子有限公司	石碣镇	半导体分立器件制造
东莞市科磊实业有限公司	石碣镇	其他塑料制品制造
东莞天龙阿克达电子有限公司	石碣镇	其他塑料制品制造
东莞市五株电子科技有限公司	石碣镇	印制电路板制造
东莞市金源电池科技有限公司	石碣镇	锂离子电池制造
广东广发制药有限公司	石碣镇	中成药生产
东莞市盈聚电子有限公司	石碣镇	电子元件及组件制造
东莞市铭冠电子科技有限公司	石碣镇	计算机外围设备制造
东莞市威力固电路板设备有限公司	石碣镇	其他电子设备制造
东莞市卓茂仪器有限公司	石碣镇	电子工业专用设备制造
东莞精塑电子科技有限公司	石碣镇	塑料零件制造
东莞莫仕连接器有限公司	石碣镇	电线、电缆制造
东莞市澳中电子材料有限公司	石碣镇	其他合成材料制造
东莞市辉胜自动化设备有限公司	石碣镇	其他金属加工机械制造
东莞市杰创电子测控科技有限公司	石碣镇	工业自动控制系统装置制造
东莞市奇立电源有限公司	石碣镇	其他通用设备制造业
东莞市瑞吉实业有限公司	石碣镇	其他通用设备制造业
东莞市声强电子有限公司	石碣镇	电子元件及组件制造
东莞市轩音电子科技有限公司	石碣镇	电力电子元器件制造
东莞市怡沁电子有限公司	石碣镇	电子元件及组件制造
东翔电子（东莞）有限公司	石碣镇	电子元件及组件制造
广东炜田环保新材料股份有限公司	石碣镇	塑料包装箱及容器制造
东莞市倍加自动化设备有限公司	石碣镇	纺织专用设备制造
东莞市大研自动化设备有限公司	石碣镇	其他通用设备制造业
东莞市焦点自动化科技有限公司	石碣镇	电工机械专用设备制造
东莞市鹏起塑胶有限公司	石碣镇	塑料板、管、型材制造
东莞市硕诚电子有限公司	石碣镇	电子元件及组件制造
东莞市思普电子有限公司	石碣镇	其他专用仪器制造
东莞市新亮点自动化设备科技有限公司	石碣镇	其他通用设备制造业
东莞市众隆泵业科技有限公司	石碣镇	泵及真空设备制造
广东德奥电梯科技有限公司	石碣镇	电梯、自动扶梯及升降机制造

1–5　续表 12

(2016年)

企业名称	所在镇街	行业类别
东莞凯科电子科技有限公司	石碣镇	电线、电缆制造
东莞市鼎力自动化科技有限公司	石碣镇	工业自动控制系统装置制造
东莞市孚朗仕照明科技有限公司	石碣镇	照明灯具制造
东莞市金华电子有限公司	石碣镇	电子元件及组件制造
东莞市卡萨帝电子科技有限公司	石碣镇	金属结构制造
东莞市良友五金制品有限公司	石碣镇	锻件及粉末冶金制品制造
东莞市万将机电设备有限公司	石碣镇	电子工业专用设备制造
东莞市益诚自动化设备有限公司	石碣镇	其他未列明电气机械及器材制造
东莞市荣旭自动化科技有限公司	高埗镇	电子工业专用设备制造
东莞市宏达聚氨酯有限公司	高埗镇	初级形态塑料及合成树脂制造
东莞市沁鑫热能科技有限公司	高埗镇	金属制厨房用器具制造
东莞东美食品有限公司	高埗镇	淀粉及淀粉制品制造
东莞精锐电器五金有限公司	高埗镇	切削工具制造
东莞市唯美陶瓷工业园有限公司	高埗镇	建筑陶瓷制品制造
东莞市中领生物科技有限公司	高埗镇	生物药品制造
东莞锂威能源科技有限公司	高埗镇	锂离子电池制造
东莞海宝电子热传科技有限公司	高埗镇	其他未列明金属制品制造
东莞市宝帅鞋材有限公司	高埗镇	其他合成材料制造
东莞市金富亮塑胶科技有限公司	高埗镇	颜料制造
东莞市晶磁科技有限公司	高埗镇	电力电子元器件制造
东莞市钜铧机械有限公司	高埗镇	其他通用设备制造业
东莞市秋天塑胶材料有限公司	高埗镇	其他塑料制品制造
东莞市锐达涂料有限公司	高埗镇	油墨及类似产品制造
东莞市锡达焊锡制品有限公司	高埗镇	其他未列明金属制品制造
东莞市永固绝缘材料有限公司	高埗镇	其他合成材料制造
东莞市兆荣节能科技有限公司	高埗镇	其他未列明制造业
东莞市中航自动化设备有限公司	高埗镇	其他通用设备制造业
广东星宇耐力新材料股份有限公司	高埗镇	油墨及类似产品制造
东莞市东田厨具设备有限公司	高埗镇	金属制厨房用器具制造
东莞市海德机械有限公司	高埗镇	金属切割及焊接设备制造
东莞市普济药业有限公司	高埗镇	化学药品制剂制造
东莞市意高节能科技有限公司	高埗镇	其他电子设备制造
东莞市粤行自动化设备科技有限公司	高埗镇	其他通用设备制造业
东莞市博晨塑料科技有限公司	高埗镇	塑料薄膜制造
东莞市佳盟照明科技有限公司	高埗镇	电子工业专用设备制造
广东顺力智能物流装备股份有限公司	高埗镇	金属结构制造
东莞市金瑞五金股份有限公司	道滘镇	金属结构制造
广东亿鑫丰智能装备股份有限公司	道滘镇	电子工业专用设备制造
东莞市派乐玛新材料技术开发有限公司	道滘镇	密封用填料及类似品制造
广东瑞星新能源科技有限公司	道滘镇	制冷、空调设备制造
东莞市国祥空调设备有限公司	道滘镇	制冷、空调设备制造
东莞市广华化工有限公司	道滘镇	其他基础化学原料制造
东莞市雄林新材料科技股份有限公司	道滘镇	其他橡胶制品制造
东莞市恒宇仪器有限公司	道滘镇	试验机制造
银禧工程塑料（东莞）有限公司	道滘镇	初级形态塑料及合成树脂制造
东莞洲亮通讯科技有限公司	道滘镇	通信系统设备制造
东莞市勤善美瓦楞纸品工艺科技有限公司	道滘镇	机械零部件加工
东莞市精心自动化设备科技有限公司	道滘镇	其他专用设备制造
东莞市圣茵环境科技有限公司	道滘镇	固体废物治理
广东天环创新科技股份有限公司	道滘镇	密封用填料及类似品制造

1-5 续表 13

(2016年)

企业名称	所在镇街	行业类别
东莞市优越检测技术服务股份有限公司	道滘镇	质检技术服务
广东东鹏维他命饮料有限公司	道滘镇	茶饮料及其他饮料制造
东莞市德鑫光学仪器有限公司	道滘镇	光学仪器制造
东莞市富基自动化设备有限公司	道滘镇	汽车零部件及配件制造
东莞市恒科自动化设备有限公司	道滘镇	实验分析仪器制造
东莞市良强机械有限公司	道滘镇	其他制鞋业
东莞市世通仪器检测服务有限公司	道滘镇	质检技术服务
东莞市亚马电子有限公司	道滘镇	其他电子设备制造
东莞市银禧光电材料科技股份有限公司	道滘镇	塑料板、管、型材制造
广东绿深环境工程有限公司	道滘镇	气体、液体分离及纯净设备制造
东莞鸿祥机械有限公司	道滘镇	橡胶加工专用设备制造
东莞市海达仪器有限公司	道滘镇	环境监测专用仪器仪表制造
东莞市金辉电源科技有限公司	道滘镇	锂离子电池制造
东莞市锦诚机械有限公司	道滘镇	电工机械专用设备制造
东莞市盟昌精密设备有限公司	道滘镇	其他通用设备制造业
东莞市沃府工程塑料科技有限公司	道滘镇	塑料零件制造
东莞市银锐精密机械有限公司	道滘镇	玻璃、陶瓷和搪瓷制品生产专用设备制造
必图实业（东莞）有限公司	道滘镇	其他建筑材料制造
东莞精诚数控科技有限公司	道滘镇	金属切削机床制造
东莞市和乐电子有限公司	道滘镇	其他电子设备制造
东莞市索康自动化设备有限公司	道滘镇	工业自动控制系统装置制造
东莞市天成热敏电阻有限公司	道滘镇	电子元件及组件制造
东莞市天耀高分子材料科技有限公司	道滘镇	其他塑料制品制造
东莞市天熠皮业科技股份有限公司	道滘镇	皮革鞣制加工
广东莞绿环保工程有限公司	道滘镇	水污染治理
广东力顺源智能自动化有限公司	道滘镇	其他日用品生产专用设备制造
广东国立科技股份有限公司	道滘镇	其他合成材料制造
广东理文造纸有限公司	洪梅镇	机制纸及纸板制造
广东福利龙复合肥有限公司	洪梅镇	复混肥料制造
东莞市海新金属科技有限公司	洪梅镇	家用厨房电器具制造
广东大众农业科技股份有限公司	洪梅镇	复混肥料制造
东莞市绿通高尔夫观光车有限公司	洪梅镇	其他未列明金属制品制造
东莞市亚洲制药有限公司	洪梅镇	中成药生产
东莞辰达电器有限公司	洪梅镇	电子元件及组件制造
东莞市中纺化工有限公司	洪梅镇	化学试剂和助剂制造
东莞统领新型材料纳米科技有限公司	洪梅镇	涂料制造
台玻华南玻璃有限公司	洪梅镇	平板玻璃制造
东莞万钧电子科技有限公司	洪梅镇	印制电路板制造
广东汇星新材料科技股份有限公司	洪梅镇	化纤织物染整精加工
东莞市邦泽电子有限公司	沙田镇（虎门港）	其他文教办公用品制造
东莞井上建上汽车部件有限公司	沙田镇（虎门港）	汽车零部件及配件制造
东莞市虎门港网络系统有限公司	沙田镇（虎门港）	软件开发
东莞市南星电子有限公司	沙田镇（虎门港）	其他电子设备制造
广东华坤新能源股份有限公司	沙田镇（虎门港）	电线、电缆制造
东莞市众志检测仪器有限公司	沙田镇（虎门港）	其他专用仪器制造
东莞百宏实业有限公司	沙田镇（虎门港）	化纤织造加工
东莞得康医疗制品有限公司	沙田镇（虎门港）	医疗诊断、监护及治疗设备制造
东莞宏石功能材料科技有限公司	沙田镇（虎门港）	初级形态塑料及合成树脂制造
东莞市豪辉精密机械有限公司	沙田镇（虎门港）	金属成形机床制造
东莞市坚华机械有限公司	沙田镇（虎门港）	其他通用设备制造业

1-5 续表 14

(2016年)

企业名称	所在镇街	行业类别
东莞市尚兰科技有限公司	沙田镇（虎门港）	雕塑工艺品制造
富加宜连接器（东莞）有限公司	沙田镇（虎门港）	光电子器件及其他电子器件制造
东莞林发电子有限公司	沙田镇（虎门港）	其他通用设备制造业
东莞市票友机电科技有限公司	沙田镇（虎门港）	其他文化、办公用机械制造
东莞市无极净化用品科技有限公司	沙田镇（虎门港）	化纤织造加工
东莞市信太通讯设备有限公司	沙田镇（虎门港）	通信系统设备制造
东莞市远大机械有限公司	沙田镇（虎门港）	纺织专用设备制造
广东安普智信电气有限公司	沙田镇（虎门港）	其他输配电及控制设备制造
东莞庞思化工机械有限公司	沙田镇（虎门港）	其他专用设备制造
东莞市多普森机械科技有限公司	沙田镇（虎门港）	印刷专用设备制造
东莞市华青微波设备制造有限公司	沙田镇（虎门港）	其他通用设备制造业
东莞市科迪实业有限公司	沙田镇（虎门港）	纺织面料鞋制造
东莞市银建玻璃工程有限公司	沙田镇（虎门港）	其他玻璃制造
东莞市银特丰光学玻璃科技有限公司	沙田镇（虎门港）	光学玻璃制造
东莞市银通玻璃有限公司	沙田镇（虎门港）	其他玻璃制品制造
东莞泰升玻璃有限公司	沙田镇（虎门港）	其他玻璃制造
广东威立瑞科技有限公司	沙田镇（虎门港）	其他输配电及控制设备制造
广东粤运佳富实业有限公司	沙田镇（虎门港）	原油加工及石油制品制造
金富科技股份有限公司	沙田镇（虎门港）	日用塑料制品制造
东莞市名菱工业自动化科技有限公司	厚街镇	缝制机械制造
东莞市铝美铝型材有限公司	厚街镇	铝压延加工
东莞市松燊塑料科技有限公司	厚街镇	有机化学原料制造
东莞市辉煌龙腾机械有限公司	厚街镇	其他未列明制造业
东莞乔登节能科技有限公司	厚街镇	锂离子电池制造
东莞威信运动用品有限公司	厚街镇	其他医疗设备及器械制造
南兴装备股份有限公司	厚街镇	木材加工机械制造
东莞市巨冈机械工业有限公司	厚街镇	金属切削机床制造
东莞朗诚微电子设备有限公司	厚街镇	电子工业专用设备制造
东莞市长泰尔电子有限公司	厚街镇	光电子器件及其他电子器件制造
东莞栢能电子科技有限公司	厚街镇	计算机零部件制造
东莞市金银丰机械实业有限公司	厚街镇	皮革、毛皮及其制品加工专用设备制造
东莞市金河田实业有限公司	厚街镇	计算机外围设备制造
东莞大鼎机械有限公司	厚街镇	其他通用设备制造业
东莞康众实业有限公司	厚街镇	其他家具制造
东莞市绰士食品有限公司	厚街镇	其他未列明食品制造
东莞市光纪光电科技有限公司	厚街镇	电子工业专用设备制造
东莞市联峰电机有限公司	厚街镇	电动机制造
东莞骅国电子有限公司	厚街镇	电子元件及组件制造
东莞市倡原机械有限公司	厚街镇	包装专用设备制造
东莞市兴扬机械制造有限公司	厚街镇	其他通用设备制造业
广东东华光电科技有限公司	厚街镇	其他塑料制品制造
东莞润信弹性织物有限公司	厚街镇	化纤织物染整精加工
东莞市宾澄电子有限公司	厚街镇	电子元件及组件制造
东莞市德威精密机械有限公司	厚街镇	其他金属加工机械制造
东莞市富立信影像科技有限公司	厚街镇	专业化设计服务
东莞市航展精密机械科技有限公司	厚街镇	缝制机械制造
东莞市宏昱新材料有限公司	厚街镇	其他塑料制品制造
东莞市克莱飞科仪器有限公司	厚街镇	试验机制造
东莞市凌木实业有限公司	厚街镇	其他未列明电气机械及器材制造
东莞市隆庆机械五金有限公司	厚街镇	电工机械专用设备制造

1-5 续表 15

(2016年)

企业名称	所在镇街	行业类别
东莞市奇峰液压科技有限公司	厚街镇	液压和气压动力机械及元件制造
东莞市穗丰装饰材料有限公司	厚街镇	刨花板制造
东莞市翔宇汽车装备有限公司	厚街镇	汽车零部件及配件制造
东莞市鑫海环保材料有限公司	厚街镇	日用塑料制品制造
东莞市星达建材有限公司	厚街镇	其他橡胶制品制造
东莞市星士达电子有限公司	厚街镇	音响设备制造
东莞市迅拓自动化科技有限公司	厚街镇	液压和气压动力机械及元件制造
东莞市毅豪精密机械有限公司	厚街镇	金属切削机床制造
东莞市兆生家具实业有限公司	厚街镇	木质家具制造
东莞市正工机电设备科技有限公司	厚街镇	其他机械和设备修理业
东莞中钜资讯光电有限公司	厚街镇	电线、电缆制造
广东莱多实业有限公司	厚街镇	服饰制造
老凤祥东莞珠宝首饰有限公司	厚街镇	珠宝首饰及有关物品制造
东莞吉研达自动化设备科技有限公司	厚街镇	其他通用设备制造业
东莞市达硕科技有限公司	厚街镇	音响设备制造
东莞市景曜防静电科技股份有限公司	厚街镇	其他通用设备制造业
东莞市凯成无纺设备有限公司	厚街镇	非织造布制造
东莞市科园防静电设备有限公司	厚街镇	其他电子设备制造
东莞市凌亚电子有限公司	厚街镇	其他文化、办公用机械制造
东莞市意利自动化科技有限公司	厚街镇	其他日用品生产专用设备制造
东莞市友联奕诺生物科技有限公司	厚街镇	其他专用设备制造
东莞市诚锋机械有限公司	厚街镇	其他通用设备制造业
东莞市城市之窗家具有限公司	厚街镇	木质家具制造
东莞市点亮软件有限公司	厚街镇	软件开发
东莞市隆威实业有限公司	厚街镇	生物药品制造
东莞市明珊机械制造有限公司	厚街镇	其他通用设备制造业
东莞市慕思寝室用品有限公司	厚街镇	其他家具制造
广东鼎泰机器人科技有限公司	厚街镇	其他通用设备制造业
广东星美灿照明科技股份有限公司	厚街镇	家用电力器具专用配件制造
广东利拿实业有限公司	厚街镇	其他机械和设备修理业
飞尔特能源（东莞）有限公司	厚街镇	发电机及发电机组制造
东莞市翔龙能源科技有限公司	厚街镇	照明灯具制造
东莞市惠峰商业有限公司	长安镇	其他合成材料制造
东莞明泰彩色包装印刷有限公司	长安镇	包装装潢及其他印刷
东莞市正旭新能源设备科技有限公司	长安镇	燃气、太阳能及类似能源家用器具制造
东莞市珍世好电子科技有限公司	长安镇	电子工业专用设备制造
广东欧珀移动通信有限公司	长安镇	其他未列明信息技术服务业
东莞市铱伦实业有限公司	长安镇	供应用仪表及其他通用仪器制造
广东冠辉科技有限公司	长安镇	建筑、家具用金属配件制造
胜蓝科技股份有限公司	长安镇	计算机零部件制造
东莞鸿图精密压铸有限公司	长安镇	有色金属铸造
东莞市扬明精密塑胶五金电子有限公司	长安镇	电子元件及组件制造
东莞市广正模具塑胶有限公司	长安镇	其他塑料制品制造
东莞市盟拓光电科技有限公司	长安镇	其他电子设备制造
东莞市长信模具有限公司	长安镇	其他通用设备制造业
东莞市东阳光电容器有限公司	长安镇	电子元件及组件制造
先锐模具配件（东莞）有限公司	长安镇	汽车零部件及配件制造
东莞市思拓达光电科技有限公司	长安镇	照明器具生产专用设备制造
东莞市胜大光电科技有限公司	长安镇	光学玻璃制造
维沃移动通信有限公司	长安镇	专业化设计服务

1-5 续表 16

(2016年)

企业名称	所在镇街	行业类别
东莞市台科精密机械有限公司	长安镇	金属成形机床制造
广东万濠精密仪器股份有限公司	长安镇	其他仪器仪表制造业
东莞市蓝光塑胶模具有限公司	长安镇	日用塑料制品制造
东莞市其利模具有限公司	长安镇	模具制造
广东小天才科技有限公司	长安镇	工程和技术研究和试验发展
东莞市汇鼎实业有限公司	长安镇	模具制造
祥鑫科技股份有限公司	长安镇	汽车零部件及配件制造
东莞市奥源电子科技有限公司	长安镇	集成电路制造
东莞市星河精密压铸模具有限公司	长安镇	其他未列明金属制品制造
东莞市长原科技实业有限公司	长安镇	制药专用设备制造
东莞市维峰五金电子有限公司	长安镇	电子元件及组件制造
东莞捷荣技术股份有限公司	长安镇	金属结构制造
东莞市运通环保科技有限公司	长安镇	环境保护专用设备制造
必诺机械（东莞）有限公司	长安镇	金属切割及焊接设备制造
东莞市龙顺自动化科技有限公司	长安镇	电工机械专用设备制造
东莞市凯登能源科技有限公司	长安镇	光伏设备及元器件制造
广东雷洋智能科技股份有限公司	长安镇	音响设备制造
东莞汇乐环保股份有限公司	长安镇	其他专用设备制造
东莞市爱加照明科技有限公司	长安镇	照明灯具制造
环球石材（东莞）股份有限公司	长安镇	建筑用石加工
东莞劲胜精密组件股份有限公司	长安镇	塑料零件制造
东莞成谦音响科技有限公司	长安镇	其他电子设备制造
东莞联基电业有限公司	长安镇	电子元件及组件制造
东莞市海圣光电科技有限公司	长安镇	其他通用设备制造业
东莞市汇诚塑胶金属制品有限公司	长安镇	塑料零件制造
东莞市瑞云电子科技有限公司	长安镇	计算机整机制造
东莞市硕信电子科技有限公司	长安镇	质检技术服务
东莞市鑫信模具机械有限公司	长安镇	模具制造
东莞市泽润电子科技有限公司	长安镇	光伏设备及元器件制造
东莞市中光光电科技有限公司	长安镇	玻璃仪器制造
广东柳道热流道系统有限公司	长安镇	模具制造
东莞亲亲我实业有限公司	长安镇	日用及医用橡胶制品制造
东莞市长原喷雾技术有限公司	长安镇	其他未列明金属制品制造
东莞市竹菱铜业有限公司	长安镇	金属及金属矿批发
广东宏伟泰精工实业股份有限公司	长安镇	机械零部件加工
东莞创先新材料科技有限公司	长安镇	其他塑料制品制造
东莞沁峰机器人有限公司	长安镇	其他通用设备制造业
东莞市艾佛杜电子科技有限公司	长安镇	计算机外围设备制造
东莞市缔网通讯科技有限公司	长安镇	铜压延加工
东莞市高登电器有限公司	长安镇	电力电子元器件制造
东莞市光志光电有限公司	长安镇	电视机制造
东莞市硅翔绝缘材料有限公司	长安镇	其他金属制日用品制造
东莞市恒博装订设备有限公司	长安镇	其他文化、办公用机械制造
东莞市汇高工业机械有限公司	长安镇	金属切削机床制造
东莞市晋源祥塑胶五金电子有限公司	长安镇	其他橡胶制品制造
东莞市京工自动化设备有限公司	长安镇	气体、液体分离及纯净设备制造
东莞市均准视觉科技有限公司	长安镇	电工机械专用设备制造
东莞市骏怡线棒制造有限公司	长安镇	金属结构制造
东莞市力华机械设备有限公司	长安镇	电工机械专用设备制造
东莞市明镜光学有限公司	长安镇	光学仪器制造
东莞市欧联电子科技有限公司	长安镇	计算机外围设备制造

1–5 续表 17

(2016年)

企业名称	所在镇街	行业类别
东莞市鹏讯电子科技有限公司	长安镇	其他文教办公用品制造
东莞市启航精密数控设备有限公司	长安镇	其他金属加工机械制造
东莞市千岛机械制造有限公司	长安镇	其他未列明制造业
东莞市千洪电子有限公司	长安镇	电子工业专用设备制造
东莞市三基电子有限公司	长安镇	电子元件及组件制造
东莞市翔景模具制品有限公司	长安镇	模具制造
东莞市鑫亚低碳设备科技有限公司	长安镇	汽车零部件及配件制造
东莞市鑫钻电子科技有限公司	长安镇	电子元件及组件制造
东莞市野田自动化设备有限公司	长安镇	其他通用设备制造业
东莞市银泽实业有限公司	长安镇	其他通用设备制造业
东莞市友卉机械有限公司	长安镇	其他通用零部件制造
东莞市粤钢不锈钢制品有限公司	长安镇	钢压延加工
东莞市泽恒机械有限公司	长安镇	其他通用设备制造业
东莞市展宏自动化科技有限公司	长安镇	电子工业专用设备制造
东莞市长瑞精密设备制造有限公司	长安镇	其他通用设备制造业
东莞市智晖机械科技有限公司	长安镇	电子工业专用设备制造
东莞伟时科技有限公司	长安镇	其他电子设备制造
东莞长发光电科技有限公司	长安镇	电子元件及组件制造
东莞洲煌塑胶五金制品有限公司	长安镇	其他塑料制品制造
广东大伦新材料股份有限公司	长安镇	机制纸及纸板制造
广东刀父精工科技有限公司	长安镇	金属切割及焊接设备制造
广东龙泽精密组件有限公司	长安镇	其他通用设备制造业
广东永畅兴精密制造股份有限公司	长安镇	其他塑料制品制造
广东造裕智能装备机器人有限公司	长安镇	其他专用设备制造
昱宇光电（东莞）有限公司	长安镇	光电子器件及其他电子器件制造
东莞常安精密工业有限公司	长安镇	其他金属加工机械制造
东莞市本量电子科技有限公司	长安镇	电力电子元器件制造
东莞市彩贝机电设备科技有限公司	长安镇	其他金属加工机械制造
东莞市诚志电子有限公司	长安镇	印制电路板制造
东莞市崇康电子有限公司	长安镇	通信终端设备制造
东莞市鼎通精密五金有限公司	长安镇	电力电子元器件制造
东莞市锋铭实业有限公司	长安镇	其他通用设备制造业
东莞市富饶光电有限公司	长安镇	光学玻璃制造
东莞市国正精密电子科技有限公司	长安镇	光电子器件及其他电子器件制造
东莞市浩琛热流道科技有限公司	长安镇	模具制造
东莞市和明机械有限公司	长安镇	其他专用设备制造
东莞市恒升环保科技有限公司	长安镇	环境保护专用设备制造
东莞市鸿展机电设备有限公司	长安镇	其他通用设备制造业
东莞市康永电子科技有限公司	长安镇	音响设备制造
东莞市科发盛实业有限公司	长安镇	其他塑料制品制造
东莞市科华精密塑胶模具有限公司	长安镇	模具制造
东莞市朗迪格林特电器有限公司	长安镇	其他塑料制品制造
东莞市乐鑫塑胶制品有限公司	长安镇	其他塑料制品制造
东莞市镭邦光电科技有限公司	长安镇	金属切割及焊接设备制造
东莞市龙芯光电有限公司	长安镇	其他计算机制造
东莞市摩卡信息科技股份有限公司	长安镇	汽车零部件及配件制造
东莞市磐锐机电科技有限公司	长安镇	其他通用设备制造业
东莞市鹏辉电子有限公司	长安镇	电力电子元器件制造
东莞市品宇电子科技有限公司	长安镇	计算机外围设备制造
东莞市普禄达电子科技有限公司	长安镇	其他橡胶制品制造
东莞市睿奇五金制品有限公司	长安镇	电子元件及组件制造

1-5 续表 18

(2016年)

企业名称	所在镇街	行业类别
东莞市三姆森光电科技有限公司	长安镇	光学仪器制造
东莞市松柏模具有限公司	长安镇	其他通用设备制造业
东莞市速美达自动化有限公司	长安镇	其他通用设备制造业
东莞市天富励德实业有限公司	长安镇	其他塑料制品制造
东莞市拓久柘电子科技有限公司	长安镇	其他电子设备制造
东莞市银钢机械设备有限公司	长安镇	其他通用设备制造业
东莞市御明电器科技有限公司	长安镇	家用厨房电器具制造
东莞市真品五金散热科技有限公司	长安镇	计算机外围设备制造
东莞市志远数控设备制造有限公司	长安镇	其他通用设备制造业
东莞亦准自动化科技有限公司	长安镇	工业自动控制系统装置制造
东莞煜森精密端子有限公司	长安镇	其他未列明制造业
巨力精密设备制造（东莞）有限公司	长安镇	机械零部件加工
东莞东兴商标织绣有限公司	长安镇	化纤织造加工
东莞富兰地工具股份有限公司	长安镇	金属切割及焊接设备制造
东莞华清光学科技有限公司	长安镇	光学玻璃制造
东莞市光劲光电有限公司	长安镇	电子元件及组件制造
东莞市广奥自动化科技有限公司	长安镇	其他通用设备制造业
东莞市佳的自动化设备科技有限公司	长安镇	其他专用设备制造
东莞市津舜康五金制品有限公司	长安镇	模具制造
东莞市酷柏净化科技有限公司	长安镇	家用空气调节器制造
东莞市铭皓照明有限公司	长安镇	照明灯具制造
东莞市鑫海金属制品有限公司	长安镇	灯用电器附件及其他照明器具制造
东莞市银辰精密光电股份有限公司	长安镇	其他未列明制造业
东莞市泽源机械有限公司	长安镇	其他通用设备制造业
东莞毅比道自动化设备有限公司	长安镇	其他电子设备制造
东莞汇美模具制造有限公司	长安镇	其他未列明金属制品制造
东莞市奥普特自动化科技有限公司	长安镇	光电子器件及其他电子器件制造
东莞市长江超声波机有限公司	长安镇	其他通用设备制造业
广东中塑新材料有限公司	长安镇	初级形态塑料及合成树脂制造
东莞市宇瞳光学科技股份有限公司	长安镇	光学仪器制造
广东瑞谷光纤通信有限公司	长安镇	光电子器件及其他电子器件制造
东莞市盛雄激光设备有限公司	长安镇	其他通用设备制造业
东莞五方光电科技有限公司	长安镇	集成电路及电子元器件
东莞钜升塑胶电子制品有限公司	长安镇	其他塑料制品制造
捷荣模具工业（东莞）有限公司	长安镇	金属结构制造
东莞市虹瑞机械五金有限公司	长安镇	其他金属加工机械制造
东莞市信诺橡塑工业有限公司	长安镇	初级形态塑料及合成树脂制造
东莞市瑞必达科技股份有限公司	寮步镇	其他玻璃制品制造
东莞市新泽谷机械制造股份有限公司	寮步镇	电子工业专用设备制造
广东飞新达智能设备股份有限公司	寮步镇	其他通用设备制造业
东莞阿李自动化股份有限公司	寮步镇	其他机械和设备修理业
东莞市开源塑化科技有限公司	寮步镇	其他合成材料制造
金龙机电（东莞）有限公司	寮步镇	光电子器件及其他电子器件制造
东莞市开关厂有限公司	寮步镇	配电开关控制设备制造
东莞汇海光电科技实业有限公司	寮步镇	光电子器件及其他电子器件制造
广东宏磊达光电科技有限公司	寮步镇	灯用电器附件及其他照明器具制造
康达新能源设备股份有限公司	寮步镇	发电机及发电机组制造
东莞市盛丰机械有限公司	寮步镇	其他金属加工机械制造
广东美塑塑料科技有限公司	寮步镇	其他塑料制品制造
东莞市蓝冠环保节能科技有限公司	寮步镇	燃气、太阳能及类似能源家用器具制造
东莞市永强汽车制造有限公司	寮步镇	汽车整车制造

1-5 续表 19

(2016年)

企业名称	所在镇街	行业类别
东莞电力设计院	寮步镇	工程勘察设计
东莞市国一精密机械有限公司	寮步镇	其他金属工具制造
东莞市得力仕机械科技有限公司	寮步镇	其他金属加工机械制造
东莞日进电线有限公司	寮步镇	电线、电缆制造
东莞市安达自动化设备有限公司	寮步镇	其他通用设备制造业
东莞三联热缩材料有限公司	寮步镇	其他塑料制品制造
东莞市琅菱机械有限公司	寮步镇	其他专用设备制造
东莞市汇星厨具有限公司	寮步镇	其他家具制造
东莞市科锐机电设备有限公司	寮步镇	其他原动设备制造
东莞市美之尊电子科技有限公司	寮步镇	其他家用电力器具制造
东莞快灵通卡西尼电子科技有限公司	寮步镇	电子工业专用设备制造
东莞唯佳电子有限公司	寮步镇	电子元件及组件制造
东莞长联新材料科技股份有限公司	寮步镇	涂料制造
广东永强奥林宝国际消防汽车有限公司	寮步镇	改装汽车制造
东莞宇球电子股份有限公司	寮步镇	电子元件及组件制造
东莞市科隆威自动化设备有限公司	寮步镇	光伏设备及元器件制造
东莞市蓝威实业有限公司	寮步镇	金属制厨房用器具制造
东莞市威骏不织布有限公司	寮步镇	非织造布制造
广东鼎立汽车空调有限公司	寮步镇	家用空气调节器制造
广东国邦清洁设备有限公司	寮步镇	环境保护专用设备制造
广东香勳生物科技有限公司	寮步镇	食用菌种植
广东新志密封技术有限公司	寮步镇	其他橡胶制品制造
东莞市雅思电子有限公司	寮步镇	家用美容、保健电器具制造
东莞市毅豪电子科技有限公司	寮步镇	信息系统集成服务
东莞市创智涂装设备工程有限公司	寮步镇	其他专用设备制造
春迅电子（东莞）有限公司	寮步镇	照明灯具制造
东莞波顿香料有限公司	寮步镇	香料、香精制造
东莞博力威新能源有限公司	寮步镇	锂离子电池制造
东莞高伟光学电子有限公司	寮步镇	电力电子元器件制造
东莞汉莎产品技术咨询服务有限公司	寮步镇	其他未列明专业技术服务业
东莞森玛德数控设备有限公司	寮步镇	其他通用设备制造业
东莞市阿比亚能源科技有限公司	寮步镇	其他合成材料制造
东莞市百盛聚氨酯材料有限公司	寮步镇	合成纤维单（聚合）体制造
东莞市丞冠橡塑制品有限公司	寮步镇	泡沫塑料制造
东莞市鸿泰鑫机械设备有限公司	寮步镇	皮革、毛皮及其制品加工专用设备制造
东莞市金业电子科技有限公司	寮步镇	其他电子设备制造
东莞市科瓦兹照明科技有限公司	寮步镇	照明灯具制造
东莞市可享光电科技有限公司	寮步镇	光电子器件及其他电子器件制造
东莞市瑞年塑胶科技有限公司	寮步镇	其他塑料制品制造
东莞市润华铝业有限公司	寮步镇	铝压延加工
东莞市田津电子科技有限公司	寮步镇	电子工业专用设备制造
东莞市象能电气设备有限公司	寮步镇	其他通用设备制造业
东莞市智盈自动化设备有限公司	寮步镇	其他通用设备制造业
东莞市紫能电子科技有限公司	寮步镇	集成电路制造
东莞威霸清洁器材有限公司	寮步镇	其他未列明制造业
广东东安电力工程有限公司	寮步镇	提供施工设备服务
广东华鑫检测技术有限公司	寮步镇	质检技术服务
广东柯保迪集团有限公司	寮步镇	皮箱、包（袋）制造
广东日芝电梯有限公司	寮步镇	电梯、自动扶梯及升降机制造
科广电子（东莞）有限公司	寮步镇	电子元件及组件制造
东莞当纳利印刷有限公司	寮步镇	包装装潢及其他印刷

1-5 续表 20

(2016年)

企业名称	所在镇街	行业类别
东莞钱锋特殊胶粘制品有限公司	寮步镇	其他纸制品制造
东莞市富滤盛滤清器有限公司	寮步镇	汽车零部件及配件制造
东莞市宏恩塑胶制品有限公司	寮步镇	泡沫塑料制造
东莞市金隆机械设备有限公司	寮步镇	其他专用设备制造
东莞市精和电子科技有限公司	寮步镇	其他通用零部件制造
东莞市路鑫五金制品有限公司	寮步镇	其他通用零部件制造
东莞市锐天机电科技有限公司	寮步镇	其他输配电及控制设备制造
东莞市天明环保节能工程有限公司	寮步镇	环境保护专用设备制造
东莞市信远无纺布有限公司	寮步镇	其他未列明制造业
东莞市宇智精密科技有限公司	寮步镇	其他专用仪器制造
东莞市玉榕包装制品有限公司	寮步镇	塑料包装箱及容器制造
东莞市泽风净化设备有限公司	寮步镇	气体、液体分离及纯净设备制造
东莞首科电子科技有限公司	寮步镇	电子元件及组件制造
东莞永腾自动化设备有限公司	寮步镇	电工机械专用设备制造
广东澳洋顺昌金属材料有限公司	寮步镇	其他未列明金属制品制造
广东宾士动力科技有限公司	寮步镇	发电机及发电机组制造
广东合邦新型粉末涂料科技股份有限公司	寮步镇	涂料制造
广东欧得森电源科技有限公司	寮步镇	变压器、整流器和电感器制造
东莞高端精密电子股份有限公司	寮步镇	光电子器件及其他电子器件制造
东莞辉科机器人自动化股份有限公司	寮步镇	其他物料搬运设备制造
东莞金研精密研磨机械制造有限公司	寮步镇	其他通用设备制造业
东莞市贝禹电子科技有限公司	寮步镇	塑料加工专用设备制造
东莞市高臻机械设备有限公司	寮步镇	其他通用设备制造业
东莞市景瑜实业有限公司	寮步镇	建筑、家具用金属配件制造
东莞市勒姆精密电子有限公司	寮步镇	其他电子设备制造
东莞市利腾达机械有限公司	寮步镇	其他原动设备制造
东莞市雅联电子有限公司	寮步镇	计算机外围设备制造
广东富行洗涤剂科技有限公司	寮步镇	有机化学原料制造
广东明利环保机电实业有限公司	寮步镇	环境保护专用设备制造
东莞嘉丰机电设备有限公司	寮步镇	其他金属加工机械制造
东莞洁澳思精密科技股份有限公司	寮步镇	家用厨房电器具制造
东莞市凯金新能源科技有限公司	寮步镇	石墨及碳素制品制造
东莞市维斗科技股份有限公司	寮步镇	电子元件及组件制造
广东百味佳味业科技股份有限公司	寮步镇	其他调味品、发酵制品制造
广东佳景科技有限公司	寮步镇	油墨及类似产品制造
广东方振新材料精密组件有限公司	寮步镇	其他塑料制品制造
永发印务（东莞）有限公司	大岭山镇	包装装潢及其他印刷
东莞市祺龙电业有限公司	大岭山镇	其他塑料制品制造
东莞市西特新能源科技有限公司	大岭山镇	锂离子电池制造
东莞泰硕电子有限公司	大岭山镇	计算机零部件制造
东莞优邦材料科技股份有限公司	大岭山镇	密封用填料及类似品制造
东莞市汇成真空科技有限公司	大岭山镇	泵及真空设备制造
东莞市奥达铝业有限公司	大岭山镇	铝压延加工
东莞优诺电子焊接材料有限公司	大岭山镇	化学试剂和助剂制造
东莞市宝瑞电子有限公司	大岭山镇	电子元件及组件制造
东莞市智高化学原料有限公司	大岭山镇	其他专用化学产品制造
东莞亿东机器有限公司	大岭山镇	塑料加工专用设备制造
东莞光群雷射科技有限公司	大岭山镇	塑料薄膜制造
东莞华威铜箔科技有限公司	大岭山镇	铜冶炼
东莞崧崴电子科技有限公司	大岭山镇	其他家具制造
东莞锦弘精密机械有限公司	大岭山镇	其他通用设备制造业

1-5 续表 21

(2016年)

企业名称	所在镇街	行业类别
东莞大宝化工制品有限公司	大岭山镇	涂料制造
东莞市宇佳电子实业有限公司	大岭山镇	其他电子设备制造
东莞市龙健电子有限公司	大岭山镇	音响设备制造
广东佳居乐厨房科技有限公司	大岭山镇	木质家具制造
东莞金太阳研磨股份有限公司	大岭山镇	其他非金属矿物制品制造
广东拓斯达科技股份有限公司	大岭山镇	工业自动控制系统装置制造
东莞市新时代新能源科技有限公司	大岭山镇	家用制冷电器具制造
东莞市瑞德丰生物科技有限公司	大岭山镇	生物化学农药及微生物农药制造
东莞市富宝家居集团有限公司	大岭山镇	木质家具制造
东莞定远陶齿制品有限公司	大岭山镇	卫生材料及医药用品制造
东莞市斯博锐高分子建筑材料科技有限公司	大岭山镇	其他建筑材料制造
利泰五金制品（东莞）有限公司	大岭山镇	其他金属制日用品制造
东莞市德翔鑫机械有限公司	大岭山镇	铸造机械制造
东莞市迪奥数控设备有限公司	大岭山镇	电子工业专用设备制造
东莞市锋驰印刷机械有限公司	大岭山镇	印刷专用设备制造
东莞市汉亚工业自动化设备有限公司	大岭山镇	其他通用设备制造业
东莞市航星针织机械有限公司	大岭山镇	纺织专用设备制造
东莞市锦顺包装机械有限公司	大岭山镇	包装专用设备制造
东莞市京润节能科技有限公司	大岭山镇	粘土砖瓦及建筑砌块制造
东莞市朗晟硅材料有限公司	大岭山镇	橡胶板、管、带制造
东莞市纳隆机械设备有限公司	大岭山镇	其他通用设备制造业
东莞市瑞科制冷设备有限公司	大岭山镇	制冷、空调设备制造
东莞市三文光电技术有限公司	大岭山镇	电力电子元器件制造
东莞市太阳线缆设备有限公司	大岭山镇	电工机械专用设备制造
东莞市万鑫机电有限公司	大岭山镇	电动机制造
东莞市伟思化学科技有限公司	大岭山镇	其他专用化学产品制造
东莞市鑫佳机械有限公司	大岭山镇	铸造机械制造
东莞市粤丰废水处理有限公司	大岭山镇	水污染治理
东莞市长和兴印刷机械有限公司	大岭山镇	印刷专用设备制造
东莞市智恒卓越电子有限公司	大岭山镇	其他电子设备制造
广东大群数控机床有限公司	大岭山镇	工业自动控制系统装置制造
东莞侨亨精密设备有限公司	大岭山镇	电子工业专用设备制造
东莞市大洋化工科技有限公司	大岭山镇	其他日用化学产品制造
东莞市豪顺精密科技有限公司	大岭山镇	金属结构制造
东莞市捷科五金有限公司	大岭山镇	机械零部件加工
东莞市金材五金有限公司	大岭山镇	其他金属加工机械制造
东莞市金铭电子有限公司	大岭山镇	通信终端设备制造
东莞市金众电子股份有限公司	大岭山镇	电子元件及组件制造
东莞市晋益电子科技有限公司	大岭山镇	有色金属铸造
东莞市旭瑞光电科技有限公司	大岭山镇	光学玻璃制造
东莞市耀盛工业炉有限公司	大岭山镇	锅炉及辅助设备制造
东莞市亿富机械科技有限公司	大岭山镇	其他通用设备制造业
东莞市悠乐厨户外休闲用品有限公司	大岭山镇	金属制厨房用器具制造
广东福临门世家智能家居有限公司	大岭山镇	金属门窗制造
广东哈弗石油能源有限公司	大岭山镇	原油加工及石油制品制造
广东威士达智能设备科技有限公司	大岭山镇	电子工业专用设备制造
东莞市博钺电子有限公司	大岭山镇	电子元件及组件制造
东莞市畅利莱机器人科技有限公司	大岭山镇	其他通用设备制造业
东莞市海天磁业股份有限公司	大岭山镇	稀有稀土金属压延加工
东莞市华诺合金有限公司	大岭山镇	其他通用零部件制造
东莞市四辉表面处理科技有限公司	大岭山镇	其他专用化学产品制造

1-5 续表 22

(2016年)

企业名称	所在镇街	行业类别
广东虹瑞智能设备股份有限公司	大岭山镇	其他金属加工机械制造
广东汇兴精工智造股份有限公司	大岭山镇	电工机械专用设备制造
东莞市燿安塑胶机器有限公司	大朗镇	其他塑料制品制造
东莞市冲宝模具有限公司	大朗镇	其他未列明制造业
东莞市东升压铸模具有限公司	大朗镇	其他金属加工机械制造
东莞信易电热机械有限公司	大朗镇	塑料加工专用设备制造
东莞市迈科科技有限公司	大朗镇	镍氢电池制造
东莞市安德丰电池有限公司	大朗镇	锂离子电池制造
东莞富强鑫塑胶机械制造有限公司	大朗镇	铸造机械制造
东莞市盛雄激光设备有限公司	大朗镇	其他仪器仪表制造业
东莞金准电器有限公司	大朗镇	灯用电器附件及其他照明器具制造
东莞市迈科新能源有限公司	大朗镇	锂离子电池制造
东莞钜鼎照明有限公司	大朗镇	照明灯具制造
广东伯朗特智能装备股份有限公司	大朗镇	其他通用设备制造业
东莞市润华光电有限公司	大朗镇	其他电子设备制造
东莞市海拓伟电子科技有限公司	大朗镇	锂离子电池制造
东莞市升微机电设备科技有限公司	大朗镇	环境保护专用设备制造
东莞欧德雅装饰材料有限公司	大朗镇	塑料家具制造
东莞市中一合金科技有限公司	大朗镇	电子元件及组件制造
东莞市百维科技有限公司	大朗镇	锂离子电池制造
东莞市三基音响科技有限公司	大朗镇	音响设备制造
东莞艾尔发自动化机械有限公司	大朗镇	其他非金属加工专用设备制造
东莞九州电器有限公司	大朗镇	电子元件及组件制造
东莞市宏扬数控设备有限公司	大朗镇	其他金属加工机械制造
东莞市永晟电线科技股份有限公司	大朗镇	其他电子设备制造
东莞信宝电子产品检测有限公司	大朗镇	质检技术服务
东莞市俊知自动机械有限公司	大朗镇	其他通用设备制造业
东莞捷邦实业有限公司	大朗镇	电子元件及组件制造
东莞市安德鑫通讯器材有限公司	大朗镇	其他电子设备制造
东莞市方荣精机工业有限公司	大朗镇	其他通用设备制造业
东莞市福是多电器有限公司	大朗镇	家用厨房电器具制造
东莞市汉萨自动化设备科技有限公司	大朗镇	铸造机械制造
东莞市弘融数控科技有限公司	大朗镇	其他金属加工机械制造
东莞市金耐尔能源科技有限公司	大朗镇	石墨及碳素制品制造
东莞市精亿五金有限公司	大朗镇	其他未列明金属制品制造
东莞市隆盛智能装备股份有限公司	大朗镇	连续搬运设备制造
东莞市全讯五金制品有限公司	大朗镇	其他未列明金属制品制造
东莞市三诚嘉五金塑胶制品有限公司	大朗镇	塑料零件制造
东莞市新懿电子材料技术有限公司	大朗镇	其他电子设备制造
东莞市智科智能科技有限公司	大朗镇	家用清洁卫生电器具制造
广东新科炬机械制造有限公司	大朗镇	其他通用设备制造业
广东中聪机器人科技有限公司	大朗镇	其他金属加工机械制造
东莞科多电气有限公司	大朗镇	电子工业专用设备制造
东莞市宝人电器科技有限公司	大朗镇	家用空气调节器制造
东莞市宝拓来金属有限公司	大朗镇	有色金属合金制造
东莞市凯旋照明科技有限公司	大朗镇	照明灯具制造
东莞市瑞科自动化设备有限公司	大朗镇	工业自动控制系统装置制造
东莞市仕研电子通讯有限公司	大朗镇	通信终端设备制造
东莞市泰基山机械设备有限公司	大朗镇	其他金属加工机械制造
东莞市新威环保科技有限公司	大朗镇	涂料制造
东莞市紫科环保设备有限公司	大朗镇	环境保护专用设备制造

1-5　续表 23

(2016年)

企业名称	所在镇街	行业类别
东莞祥龙五金制品有限公司	大朗镇	金属结构制造
广东春夏新材料科技有限公司	大朗镇	非织造布制造
广东快手机器人科技有限公司	大朗镇	其他通用设备制造业
广东统一机器人智能股份有限公司	大朗镇	其他通用设备制造业
长园电子（东莞）有限公司	大朗镇	塑料板、管、型材制造
东莞创群石英晶体有限公司	大朗镇	电子元件及组件制造
东莞市德尔能新能源股份有限公司	大朗镇	其他电池制造
东莞市飞洋光电科技有限公司	大朗镇	光电子器件及其他电子器件制造
东莞市厚威包装有限公司	大朗镇	纸和纸板容器制造
东莞市开方实业有限公司	大朗镇	其他通用设备制造业
东莞市台冠起重机械设备有限公司	大朗镇	起重机制造
东莞市旭田包装机械有限公司	大朗镇	包装专用设备制造
东莞市云通通讯科技有限公司	大朗镇	通信终端设备制造
东莞添慧软件有限公司	大朗镇	软件开发
鸿纳(东莞)新材料科技有限公司	大朗镇	石墨及碳素制品制造
广东宝杰环保科技有限公司	大朗镇	其他专用设备制造
广东飞触科技股份有限公司	大朗镇	光电子器件及其他电子器件制造
广东龙昕科技有限公司	大朗镇	通信终端设备制造
中广核高新核材集团（东莞）祈富新材料有限公司	大朗镇	其他塑料制品制造
东莞市天晖电子材料科技有限公司	黄江镇	其他电子设备制造
广东兴锐电子科技股份有限公司	黄江镇	橡胶零件制造
丽清电子科技（东莞）有限公司	黄江镇	电子元件及组件制造
东莞盛世科技电子实业有限公司	黄江镇	电子元件及组件制造
东莞泰欣照明有限公司	黄江镇	照明灯具制造
东莞市宏德电子设备有限公司	黄江镇	电子工业专用设备制造
东莞市精诚厨具实业有限公司	黄江镇	金属制厨房用器具制造
东莞市兰光光学科技有限公司	黄江镇	光学玻璃制造
东莞市纳川盈海照明有限公司	黄江镇	灯用电器附件及其他照明器具制造
东莞爱旺电子科技有限公司	黄江镇	计算机外围设备制造
鹏驰五金制品有限公司	黄江镇	紧固件制造
广东欧科空调制冷有限公司	黄江镇	制冷、空调设备制造
广东保迪环保电镀设备有限公司	黄江镇	环境保护专用设备制造
东莞正扬电子机械有限公司	黄江镇	汽车零部件及配件制造
广东惠伦晶体科技股份有限公司	黄江镇	电子元件及组件制造
东莞新东方科技有限公司	黄江镇	合成橡胶制造
东莞市森佳机械有限公司	黄江镇	电工机械专用设备制造
东莞倍力扣金属制品有限公司	黄江镇	金属表面处理及热处理加工
东莞市恒荣机械设备有限公司	黄江镇	塑料包装箱及容器制造
东莞市纳利光学材料有限公司	黄江镇	其他塑料制品制造
东莞市胜邦通讯配件科技有限公司	黄江镇	锂离子电池制造
东莞市佰荣臻机械设备有限公司	黄江镇	其他通用设备制造业
东莞市红富照明科技有限公司	黄江镇	照明灯具制造
东莞市古川胶带有限公司	黄江镇	其他塑料制品制造
东莞市华纬涂装设备有限公司	黄江镇	其他金属加工机械制造
东莞市华粤焊锡制品有限公司	黄江镇	其他未列明金属制品制造
东莞市黄江大顺电子有限公司	黄江镇	电子元件及组件制造
东莞市君奥连接器有限公司	黄江镇	电子元件及组件制造
东莞市凯圣自行车有限公司	黄江镇	脚踏自行车及残疾人座车制造
东莞市蓝天创达化工有限公司	黄江镇	专项化学用品制造
东莞市龙拓鑫电子有限公司	黄江镇	其他电子设备制造
东莞市胜创光电科技有限公司	黄江镇	光纤、光缆制造

1-5 续表 24

(2016年)

企业名称	所在镇街	行业类别
东莞市通骏电子科技有限公司	黄江镇	电线、电缆制造
东莞市亚力电器有限公司	黄江镇	灯用电器附件及其他照明器具制造
东莞市亿杰五金制品有限公司	黄江镇	其他未列明金属制品制造
广东奔迪新材料科技有限公司	黄江镇	泡沫塑料制造
广东荣意家居股份有限公司	黄江镇	木质家具制造
广东新吉欣实业有限公司	黄江镇	其他未列明金属制品制造
东莞市栢科电源有限公司	黄江镇	电力电子元器件制造
东莞市昶通通讯科技有限公司	黄江镇	电子元件及组件制造
东莞市固达机械制造有限公司	黄江镇	其他通用设备制造业
东莞市基烁实业有限公司	黄江镇	其他合成材料制造
东莞市科盛实业有限公司	黄江镇	其他机械和设备修理业
东莞市普锐米勒机床有限公司	黄江镇	金属切削机床制造
东莞市索艾电子科技有限公司	黄江镇	计算机外围设备制造
东莞市信为兴电子有限公司	黄江镇	电子元件及组件制造
泓凯电子科技（东莞）有限公司	黄江镇	计算机外围设备制造
金科伟业（中国）有限公司	黄江镇	日用塑料制品制造
东莞礼国光电科技有限公司	黄江镇	照明灯具制造
东莞盛翔精密金属有限公司	黄江镇	其他电子设备制造
东莞市超讯电子有限公司	黄江镇	电子元件及组件制造
东莞市合明光电科技有限公司	黄江镇	照明灯具制造
东莞市中佑机械科技有限公司	黄江镇	金属切削机床制造
广东延春高新材料科技股份有限公司	黄江镇	玻璃纤维增强塑料制品制造
东莞联通达电路制板有限公司	黄江镇	印制电路板制造
东莞市童星玩具制品有限公司	樟木头镇	玩具制造
广东摩尔达电器科技有限公司	樟木头镇	其他家用电力器具制造
东莞市张力机电科技有限公司	樟木头镇	其他专用仪器制造
东莞市德诚塑化科技有限公司	樟木头镇	其他塑料制品制造
东莞积信制造有限公司	樟木头镇	家用厨房电器具制造
广东广海大实业有限公司	樟木头镇	其他橡胶制品制造
东莞市恒越实业有限公司	樟木头镇	其他农、林、牧、渔业机械制造
东莞市力能电子科技有限公司	樟木头镇	电子元件及组件制造
东莞铿利五金制品有限公司	樟木头镇	有色金属铸造
东莞市卡帝德塑化科技有限公司	樟木头镇	初级形态塑料及合成树脂制造
博世激光仪器（东莞）有限公司	樟木头镇	其他仪器仪表制造业
东莞艾宝纳米科技有限公司	樟木头镇	其他基础化学原料制造
东莞市冠力实业有限公司	樟木头镇	其他专用化学产品制造
东莞市合宜电子有限公司	樟木头镇	电线、电缆制造
东莞市莱竣电子有限公司	樟木头镇	印制电路板制造
东莞市小耳朵电子有限公司	樟木头镇	电子元件及组件制造
东莞市源凯塑胶有限公司	樟木头镇	塑料板、管、型材制造
东莞市众一新材料科技有限公司	樟木头镇	其他未列明制造业
广东合即得能源科技有限公司	樟木头镇	其他科技推广和应用服务业
广东康福星科技有限公司	樟木头镇	水资源专用机械制造
东莞市格尼斯电子有限公司	樟木头镇	绝缘制品制造
东莞市辉碟自动化科技有限公司	樟木头镇	其他未列明电气机械及器材制造
东莞市秦基减速电机有限公司	樟木头镇	微电机及其他电机制造
永林电子有限公司	樟木头镇	电子元件及组件制造
东莞市怡丰锁业有限公司	樟木头镇	其他金属加工机械制造
广东凯威检测技术股份有限公司	樟木头镇	质检技术服务
广东罗曼智能科技股份有限公司	樟木头镇	家用美容、保健电器具制造
东莞市启天自动化设备有限公司	樟木头镇	光伏设备及元器件制造

1-5 续表 25

(2016年)

企业名称	所在镇街	行业类别
广东天元实业集团股份有限公司	清溪镇	包装装潢及其他印刷
东莞市科隆电机有限公司	清溪镇	微电机及其他电机制造
东莞建玮电子制品有限公司	清溪镇	计算机外围设备制造
东莞龙杰电子有限公司	清溪镇	其他电子设备制造
健富塑胶五金制品（东莞）有限公司	清溪镇	通信系统设备制造
东莞永钜电子有限公司	清溪镇	计算机外围设备制造
东莞宜安科技股份有限公司	清溪镇	金属结构制造
广东光阵光电科技有限公司	清溪镇	电子元件及组件制造
实盈电子（东莞）有限公司	清溪镇	电子元件及组件制造
东莞市荣烨五金制品有限公司	清溪镇	计算机外围设备制造
东莞市金铮自动冲压设备有限公司	清溪镇	金属切削机床制造
东莞市联臣电子科技有限公司	清溪镇	电子元件及组件制造
东莞市垠星科技发展有限公司	清溪镇	原油加工及石油制品制造
广东普赛达密封粘胶有限公司	清溪镇	密封用填料及类似品制造
东莞市鸿德电池有限公司	清溪镇	其他电池制造
东莞市捷和光电有限公司	清溪镇	照明灯具制造
模德模具（东莞）有限公司	清溪镇	金属表面处理及热处理加工
东莞清溪华晖电器有限公司	清溪镇	家用厨房电器具制造
东莞泰星五金制品厂有限公司	清溪镇	金属结构制造
快意电梯股份有限公司	清溪镇	电梯、自动扶梯及升降机制造
东莞华明灯具有限公司	清溪镇	照明灯具制造
广东粤林电气科技股份有限公司	清溪镇	计算机外围设备制造
东莞市湘华五金科技有限公司	清溪镇	计算机零部件制造
东莞立德精密工业有限公司	清溪镇	电子元件及组件制造
广东德瑞新材料科技有限公司	清溪镇	其他金属制日用品制造
东莞市黄刀实业有限公司	清溪镇	计算机零部件制造
东莞市嘉龙海杰电子科技有限公司	清溪镇	电子元件及组件制造
东莞市三润田自动化设备有限公司	清溪镇	电子工业专用设备制造
东莞市特旺通信科技有限公司	清溪镇	光纤、光缆制造
东莞市伟创东洋自动化设备有限公司	清溪镇	金属结构制造
东莞硕仕儿童用品有限公司	清溪镇	其他家具制造
东莞华辉数控机床有限公司	清溪镇	金属切削机床制造
东莞市必德电子科技有限公司	清溪镇	变压器、整流器和电感器制造
东莞市丰华印铁制罐有限公司	清溪镇	包装装潢及其他印刷
东莞市美迈士机械科技有限公司	清溪镇	其他机械和设备修理业
东莞市丘彼特婴儿用品有限公司	清溪镇	其他日用杂品制造
东莞市泰有源电池科技有限公司	清溪镇	锂离子电池制造
东莞市鑫濠信精密工业有限公司	清溪镇	其他电子设备制造
东莞市兴开泰电子科技有限公司	清溪镇	光电子器件及其他电子器件制造
东莞市致格电池科技有限公司	清溪镇	锂离子电池制造
东莞市致一五金制品有限公司	清溪镇	模具制造
东莞伊洛斯制冷科技有限公司	清溪镇	制冷、空调设备制造
广东力人科技有限公司	清溪镇	电子元件及组件制造
锦美运动用品（东莞）有限公司	清溪镇	体育器材及配件制造
东莞町强机电有限公司	清溪镇	其他电子设备制造
东莞金旺儿童用品有限公司	清溪镇	其他塑料制品制造
东莞南科玻璃有限公司	清溪镇	其他玻璃制造
东莞市艾畅电子制品有限公司	清溪镇	其他电子设备制造
东莞市昶宏金属科技有限公司	清溪镇	其他金属工具制造
东莞市鸿德医用塑料制品有限公司	清溪镇	塑料薄膜制造
东莞市鸿愃实业有限公司	清溪镇	锂离子电池制造

1-5 续表 26

(2016年)

企业名称	所在镇街	行业类别
东莞市慧江平成机械有限公司	清溪镇	工业自动控制系统装置制造
东莞市佳丹润滑油有限公司	清溪镇	其他专用化学产品制造
东莞市久制电子有限公司	清溪镇	电子元件及组件制造
东莞市钜欣电子有限公司	清溪镇	电子元件及组件制造
东莞市开胜电子有限公司	清溪镇	电气设备批发
东莞市锐鼎五金制品有限公司	清溪镇	金属结构制造
东莞市特瑞斯电池科技有限公司	清溪镇	锂离子电池制造
东莞市惟实电子材料科技有限公司	清溪镇	其他塑料制品制造
东莞市亚琪五金塑胶科技有限公司	清溪镇	橡胶零件制造
东莞市颖锋光电材料有限公司	清溪镇	其他未列明制造业
东莞市正生瑞生物医学科技有限公司	清溪镇	其他医疗设备及器械制造
东莞市致腾塑胶制品有限公司	清溪镇	塑料薄膜制造
东莞讯滔电子有限公司	清溪镇	光电子器件及其他电子器件制造
东莞优品电子制造有限公司	清溪镇	其他电子设备制造
广东铭利达科技有限公司	清溪镇	机械零部件加工
广东裕利智能科技股份有限公司	清溪镇	玩具制造
东莞力朗电池科技有限公司	清溪镇	锂离子电池制造
东莞市华源光电科技有限公司	清溪镇	光伏设备及元器件制造
东莞英伍电子有限公司	清溪镇	其他电子设备制造
广东纳特康电子股份有限公司	清溪镇	电子元件及组件制造
东莞福泽尔电子科技有限公司	塘厦镇	影视录放设备制造
东莞市中汇瑞德电子股份有限公司	塘厦镇	电子元件及组件制造
东莞市锐祥智能卡科技有限公司	塘厦镇	工业自动控制系统装置制造
东莞星晖真空镀膜塑胶制品有限公司	塘厦镇	日用塑料制品制造
东莞永安科技有限公司	塘厦镇	其他未列明金属制品制造
东莞市现代精工实业有限公司	塘厦镇	其他塑料制品制造
东莞市三友联众电器有限公司	塘厦镇	电子元件及组件制造
东莞市千岛金属锡品有限公司	塘厦镇	锡冶炼
东莞市雅康精密机械有限公司	塘厦镇	电工机械专用设备制造
东莞市凯鹏复合材料有限公司	塘厦镇	石墨及碳素制品制造
东莞市亚通光电有限公司	塘厦镇	光电子器件及其他电子器件制造
东莞市纬迪实业有限公司	塘厦镇	电子元件及组件制造
广东星河生物科技股份有限公司	塘厦镇	食用菌种植
东莞市华世邦精密模具有限公司	塘厦镇	金属结构制造
广东升威电子制品有限公司	塘厦镇	电子元件及组件制造
东莞市力嘉电池有限公司	塘厦镇	锂离子电池制造
东莞市君凯电子有限公司	塘厦镇	风机、风扇制造
广东合科泰实业有限公司	塘厦镇	半导体分立器件制造
东莞丰裕电机有限公司	塘厦镇	其他通用设备制造业
广东志成冠军集团有限公司	塘厦镇	变压器、整流器和电感器制造
东莞市凯昶德电子科技股份有限公司	塘厦镇	电子元件及组件制造
东莞市锦润电子有限公司	塘厦镇	电子元件及组件制造
东莞市凯华电子有限公司	塘厦镇	电子元件及组件制造
东莞市澳星视听器材有限公司	塘厦镇	其他通用设备制造业
东莞启益电器机械有限公司	塘厦镇	变压器、整流器和电感器制造
东莞市冠佳电子设备有限公司	塘厦镇	其他电子设备制造
东莞市吉铼升电机有限公司	塘厦镇	微电机及其他电机制造
东莞永胜医疗制品有限公司	塘厦镇	医疗诊断、监护及治疗设备制造
东莞市鑫聚光电科技股份有限公司	塘厦镇	塑料零件制造
东莞立德电子有限公司	塘厦镇	变压器、整流器和电感器制造
东莞领航电子有限公司	塘厦镇	电子元件及组件制造

1-5 续表 27

(2016年)

企业名称	所在镇街	行业类别
东莞市宙辉电子科技有限公司	塘厦镇	其他电子设备制造
东莞阳天电子科技有限公司	塘厦镇	通信系统设备制造
东莞永湖复合材料有限公司	塘厦镇	体育器材及配件制造
广东坚朗五金制品股份有限公司	塘厦镇	建筑、家具用金属配件制造
广东力王新能源股份有限公司	塘厦镇	其他电池制造
东莞正阳电子有限公司	塘厦镇	电子元件及组件制造
东莞汉旭五金塑胶科技有限公司	塘厦镇	其他通用零部件制造
东莞华宏金属制品有限公司	塘厦镇	汽车零部件及配件制造
东莞勤德五金制品有限公司	塘厦镇	其他未列明金属制品制造
东莞市奥海电源科技有限公司	塘厦镇	其他电子设备制造
东莞市超日自动化设备科技有限公司	塘厦镇	其他金属加工机械制造
东莞市竞沃电子科技有限公司	塘厦镇	电子元件及组件制造
东莞市普尔信通讯器材有限公司	塘厦镇	通信系统设备制造
东莞市伟宏五金塑胶制品有限公司	塘厦镇	金属家具制造
东莞市易普达数码科技有限公司	塘厦镇	其他计算机制造
东莞市钰晟电子科技有限公司	塘厦镇	电子元件及组件制造
东莞特米勒电子科技有限公司	塘厦镇	电子元件及组件制造
东莞烨嘉电子科技有限公司	塘厦镇	模具制造
东莞以利沙五金制品有限公司	塘厦镇	其他未列明金属制品制造
宏腾电子科技（东莞）有限公司	塘厦镇	其他家用电力器具制造
东莞市高特电子有限公司	塘厦镇	电力电子元器件制造
东莞市善易机械科技有限公司	塘厦镇	其他通用设备制造业
爱鹏电子（东莞）有限公司	塘厦镇	集成电路制造
东莞华成环保包装科技股份有限公司	塘厦镇	机制纸及纸板制造
东莞兰域电器有限公司	塘厦镇	灯用电器附件及其他照明器具制造
东莞名翔电子有限公司	塘厦镇	电力电子元器件制造
东莞市贝特赛能源科技有限公司	塘厦镇	锂离子电池制造
东莞市德硕化工有限公司	塘厦镇	化学试剂和助剂制造
东莞市迪高电池科技有限公司	塘厦镇	其他电池制造
东莞市飞杰电脑针车有限公司	塘厦镇	纺织专用设备制造
东莞市高翔机械设备有限公司	塘厦镇	其他原动设备制造
东莞市冠顺实业有限公司	塘厦镇	其他未列明金属制品制造
东莞市海霖动画制作有限公司	塘厦镇	专业化设计服务
东莞市好美声电子有限公司	塘厦镇	其他电子设备制造
东莞市和域战士纳米科技有限公司	塘厦镇	金属表面处理及热处理加工
东莞市汇驰纸业有限公司	塘厦镇	其他纸制品制造
东莞市江涵电子有限公司	塘厦镇	计算机外围设备制造
东莞市康派皮具有限公司	塘厦镇	皮箱、包(袋)制造
东莞市利韬过滤材料有限公司	塘厦镇	非织造布制造
东莞市佩琦涂料有限公司	塘厦镇	涂料制造
东莞市普利星电子有限公司	塘厦镇	电子元件及组件制造
东莞市睿霖电子科技有限公司	塘厦镇	导航、气象及海洋专用仪器制造
东莞市伟升机械设备科技有限公司	塘厦镇	电子工业专用设备制造
东莞市新力光表面处理科技有限公司	塘厦镇	其他未列明电气机械及器材制造
东莞市鑫耀鹏五金制品有限公司	塘厦镇	金属结构制造
东莞市星火齿轮有限公司	塘厦镇	齿轮及齿轮减、变速箱制造
东莞市烨嘉光电科技有限公司	塘厦镇	模具制造
东莞市易都电子科技有限公司	塘厦镇	计算器及货币专用设备制造
东莞市逸音电子科技有限公司	塘厦镇	电子元件及组件制造
东莞市英思漫润滑科技有限公司	塘厦镇	炼油、化工生产专用设备制造
东莞市永邦新能源科技有限公司	塘厦镇	锂离子电池制造

1-5　续表 28

(2016年)

企业名称	所在镇街	行业类别
东莞市月宇电子有限公司	塘厦镇	锂离子电池制造
东莞市云帆电子科技有限公司	塘厦镇	锂离子电池制造
东莞市长讯精密技术有限公司	塘厦镇	电子元件及组件制造
东莞市中意厨房设备有限公司	塘厦镇	木质家具制造
东莞依利洋织物有限公司	塘厦镇	其他未列明制造业
东莞运宏模具有限公司	塘厦镇	模具制造
东莞方皓汽车配件有限公司	塘厦镇	其他非家用纺织制成品制造
东莞赛诺家居用品有限公司	塘厦镇	床上用品制造
东莞市般若电子科技有限公司	塘厦镇	计算机外围设备制造
东莞市菜鸟电子科技有限公司	塘厦镇	导航、气象及海洋专用仪器制造
东莞市尔必地机器人有限公司	塘厦镇	其他通用零部件制造
东莞市高晶电子科技有限公司	塘厦镇	电力电子元器件制造
东莞市和旺电器有限公司	塘厦镇	金属结构制造
东莞市恒丰换热器有限公司	塘厦镇	其他未列明制造业
东莞市宏联电子有限公司	塘厦镇	计算机零部件制造
东莞市华金电器有限公司	塘厦镇	集成电路制造
东莞市华鑫激光科技有限公司	塘厦镇	其他金属加工机械制造
东莞市杰发电子有限公司	塘厦镇	电容器及其配套设备制造
东莞市金都电子科技有限公司	塘厦镇	集成电路制造
东莞市巨星电池有限公司	塘厦镇	锂离子电池制造
东莞市零度导热材料有限公司	塘厦镇	其他合成材料制造
东莞市勤明士照明科技有限公司	塘厦镇	照明灯具制造
东莞市荣合电子有限公司	塘厦镇	计算机外围设备制造
东莞市三梯模具有限公司	塘厦镇	汽车零部件及配件制造
东莞市天蓝智能装备有限公司	塘厦镇	其他通用设备制造业
东莞市图强实业投资有限公司	塘厦镇	电子元件及组件制造
东莞市维迅机械科技有限公司	塘厦镇	其他专用设备制造
东莞市新贵电子科技有限公司	塘厦镇	计算机外围设备制造
东莞市雄驰电子有限公司	塘厦镇	其他橡胶制品制造
东莞市一品硅胶电子材料有限公司	塘厦镇	其他合成材料制造
东莞市长长昶达金属制品有限公司	塘厦镇	其他金属制日用品制造
东莞市正文机械有限公司	塘厦镇	其他专用设备制造
东莞照彰五金电器制品有限公司	塘厦镇	其他未列明金属制品制造
东莞市昱懋纳米科技有限公司	塘厦镇	变压器、整流器和电感器制造
东莞快裕达自动化设备有限公司	塘厦镇	其他机械和设备修理业
东莞市东勤电子有限公司	塘厦镇	其他电子设备制造
东莞市冬驭碳素科技控股有限公司	塘厦镇	石墨及碳素制品制造
东莞市发斯特精密五金有限公司	塘厦镇	其他未列明金属制品制造
东莞市海柯电子有限公司	塘厦镇	太阳能发电
东莞市泓旭五金制品有限公司	塘厦镇	金属结构制造
东莞市晶博光电有限公司	塘厦镇	平板玻璃制造
东莞市卡卡电子科技有限公司	塘厦镇	运输设备及生产用计数仪表制造
东莞市仁丰电子科技有限公司	塘厦镇	电子元件及组件制造
东莞市世翔精密机械制造有限公司	塘厦镇	其他金属加工机械制造
东莞市速普得电子科技股份有限公司	塘厦镇	通信系统设备制造
东莞市通豪实业投资有限公司	塘厦镇	技术玻璃制品制造
东莞市讯康实业有限公司	塘厦镇	其他电子设备制造
东莞市谊科数控科技有限公司	塘厦镇	金属成形机床制造
东莞市知音电子有限公司	塘厦镇	通信系统设备制造
东莞市庄正电子科技有限公司	塘厦镇	其他未列明电气机械及器材制造
东莞塘厦怡丰发泡胶有限公司	塘厦镇	其他制鞋业

1-5 续表 29

(2016年)

企业名称	所在镇街	行业类别
东星电声科技（东莞）有限公司	塘厦镇	音响设备制造
东莞铭基电子科技集团有限公司	塘厦镇	其他电子设备制造
东莞市誉铭新精密技术股份有限公司	塘厦镇	其他橡胶制品制造
中控智慧科技股份有限公司	塘厦镇	其他电子设备制造
东莞信柏结构陶瓷股份有限公司	塘厦镇	特种陶瓷制品制造
东莞轩朗实业有限公司	塘厦镇	光电子器件及其他电子器件制造
广东曙光自动化设备股份有限公司	塘厦镇	其他原动设备制造
广东新秀新材料股份有限公司	塘厦镇	其他合成材料制造
东莞康佳电子有限公司	凤岗镇	电视机制造
东莞市艺展电子有限公司	凤岗镇	汽车零部件及配件制造
东莞宇宙电路板设备有限公司	凤岗镇	其他通用设备制造业
东莞诚兴五金制品有限公司	凤岗镇	汽车零部件及配件制造
东莞奥美佳电子有限公司	凤岗镇	集成电路制造
东莞市海迪精机有限公司	凤岗镇	其他通用零部件制造
东莞永腾电子制品有限公司	凤岗镇	电子元件及组件制造
东莞联洲电子科技有限公司	凤岗镇	计算机外围设备制造
东莞市振华新能源科技有限公司	凤岗镇	锂离子电池制造
东莞市林积为实业投资有限公司	凤岗镇	电子元件及组件制造
东莞市旭通达模具塑胶有限公司	凤岗镇	模具制造
广东福聚多节能科技有限公司	凤岗镇	照明灯具制造
广东楚天龙智能卡有限公司	凤岗镇	集成电路制造
东莞康佳模具塑胶有限公司	凤岗镇	模具制造
东莞美驰图实业有限公司	凤岗镇	玩具制造
东莞勤百扬精密塑胶有限公司	凤岗镇	其他未列明制造业
东莞市福磁电子有限公司	凤岗镇	切削工具制造
东莞市恒生传感器有限公司	凤岗镇	其他电子设备制造
东莞市荣誉五金制品有限公司	凤岗镇	其他非金属矿物制品制造
东莞市台德实业有限公司	凤岗镇	音响设备制造
东莞市亿晶源光电科技有限公司	凤岗镇	照明灯具制造
嘉力时灯光设备（东莞）有限公司	凤岗镇	照明灯具制造
东莞标宝智能科技有限公司	凤岗镇	其他家用电力器具制造
东莞励国照明有限公司	凤岗镇	照明灯具制造
东莞市柏尔电子科技有限公司	凤岗镇	电力电子元器件制造
东莞市东立智能模具科技有限公司	凤岗镇	模具制造
东莞市丰润计算机有限公司	凤岗镇	计算机外围设备制造
东莞市浩阳五金科技有限公司	凤岗镇	金属结构制造
东莞市虹桥印刷有限公司	凤岗镇	包装装潢及其他印刷
东莞市鸿田精工科技股份有限公司	凤岗镇	其他塑料制品制造
东莞市华兴隆模具钢材有限公司	凤岗镇	钢压延加工
东莞市诺威新能源有限公司	凤岗镇	锂离子电池制造
东莞市容辰制罐有限公司	凤岗镇	金属包装容器制造
东莞市盛涵精密塑胶制品有限公司	凤岗镇	塑料零件制造
东莞市戍普电子科技有限公司	凤岗镇	电子元件及组件制造
东莞市数字印数码科技有限公司	凤岗镇	计算机整机制造
东莞市斯惠威电子科技有限公司	凤岗镇	音响设备制造
东莞市兄友模具塑胶有限公司	凤岗镇	模具制造
东莞市远鸿电子科技有限公司	凤岗镇	其他电子设备制造
东莞壹凌电子科技有限公司	凤岗镇	锂离子电池制造
东莞得利钟表有限公司	凤岗镇	钟表与计时仪器制造
东莞富亚电子有限公司	凤岗镇	光电子器件及其他电子器件制造
东莞晶石光学有限公司	凤岗镇	光学玻璃制造

1-5　续表 30

(2016年)

企业名称	所在镇街	行业类别
东莞精明五金科技有限公司	凤岗镇	其他未列明制造业
广东彩虹德记塑胶颜料股份有限公司	凤岗镇	颜料制造
东莞市东和电子制程有限公司	凤岗镇	电子工业专用设备制造
东莞市港大电子有限公司	凤岗镇	电力电子元器件制造
东莞市鸿展纸品有限公司	凤岗镇	纸和纸板容器制造
东莞市凯安机械配件有限公司	凤岗镇	金属结构制造
东莞市科隆实业有限公司	凤岗镇	切削工具制造
东莞市民兴电缆有限公司	凤岗镇	电线、电缆制造
东莞市奇为电机科技有限公司	凤岗镇	电工机械专用设备制造
东莞市万德数码印刷设备有限公司	凤岗镇	印刷专用设备制造
东莞市唯尔声视听设备有限公司	凤岗镇	音响设备制造
东莞市誉鑫塑胶模具有限公司	凤岗镇	其他未列明制造业
东莞市洲达电器有限公司	凤岗镇	家用厨房电器具制造
广东金霸智能科技股份有限公司	凤岗镇	微电机及其他电机制造
广东莱盛隆电子股份有限公司	凤岗镇	锂离子电池制造
东莞市湘将鑫五金制品有限公司	凤岗镇	其他未列明金属制品制造
东莞市沃泰家用电器有限公司	凤岗镇	其他家用电力器具制造
广东科维北斗电子股份有限公司	凤岗镇	其他电子设备制造
东莞市精伦实业有限公司	谢岗镇	其他塑料制品制造
东莞市南风塑料管材有限公司	谢岗镇	塑料板、管、型材制造
东莞首资宝电器制造有限公司	谢岗镇	其他未列明制造业
东莞市大兴化工有限公司	谢岗镇	涂料制造
东莞市东逸电气科技有限公司	谢岗镇	照明灯具制造
东莞市国鼎光电膜材科技有限公司	谢岗镇	塑料薄膜制造
美利龙餐厨具（东莞）有限公司	谢岗镇	其他非电力家用器具制造
台光五金制品（东莞）有限公司	谢岗镇	金属结构制造
东莞港重机械设备有限公司	谢岗镇	金属结构制造
东莞市鸿威精密五金制品有限公司	谢岗镇	模具制造
东莞市建昌实业有限公司	谢岗镇	其他有色金属压延加工
东莞市囗盛日用品有限公司	谢岗镇	日用塑料制品制造
东莞市文思顿五金塑胶有限公司	谢岗镇	其他未列明金属制品制造
东莞市优森电子有限公司	谢岗镇	印制电路板制造
广东四象智能制造股份有限公司	谢岗镇	其他电子设备制造
东莞富美康电器科技有限公司	谢岗镇	家用美容、保健电器具制造
东莞市凯盟表面处理技术开发有限公司	谢岗镇	专项化学用品制造
东莞市宇豪塑胶科技有限公司	谢岗镇	其他未列明制造业
广东润星科技股份有限公司	谢岗镇	金属切削机床制造
东莞英铭化工有限公司	常平镇	专项化学用品制造
迅得机械（东莞）有限公司	常平镇	其他专用仪器制造
东莞金杯印刷有限公司	常平镇	其他纸制品制造
东莞市天圣厨具实业有限公司	常平镇	家用厨房电器具制造
东莞市华立实业股份有限公司	常平镇	其他家具制造
东莞市麦蒂科技有限公司	常平镇	软件开发
广东嘉悦科技股份有限公司	常平镇	其他通用设备制造业
东莞运城制版有限公司	常平镇	包装装潢及其他印刷
东莞勤上光电股份有限公司	常平镇	照明灯具制造
东莞市星擎电子科技有限公司	常平镇	电子元件及组件制造
快捷达通信设备（东莞）有限公司	常平镇	通信系统设备制造
东莞市吉鑫高分子科技有限公司	常平镇	其他塑料制品制造
广东宏展科技有限公司	常平镇	制冷、空调设备制造
永泰电子（东莞）有限公司	常平镇	电子元件及组件制造

1-5 续表 31

(2016年)

企业名称	所在镇街	行业类别
东莞市瀛通电线有限公司	常平镇	电线、电缆制造
东莞市金鸿盛电器有限公司	常平镇	家用制冷电器具制造
东莞市宇洁新材料有限公司	常平镇	其他未列明制造业
东莞龙昌数码科技有限公司	常平镇	玩具制造
东莞欧达电子有限公司	常平镇	电子测量仪器制造
东莞丰卓机电设备有限公司	常平镇	其他专用设备制造
东莞集思工业设计有限公司	常平镇	其他电子设备制造
东莞市宝元通检测设备有限公司	常平镇	其他通用设备制造业
东莞市博思电子数码科技有限公司	常平镇	教学用模型及教具制造
东莞市卡尔文塑胶科技有限公司	常平镇	其他塑料制品制造
东莞市力与源电器设备有限公司	常平镇	其他通用设备制造业
东莞市明洁隧道建设材料有限公司	常平镇	其他专用化学产品制造
东莞市普万光电散热科技有限公司	常平镇	灯用电器附件及其他照明器具制造
东莞市途锐机械有限公司	常平镇	其他通用设备制造业
广东三奥动力设备有限公司	常平镇	发电机及发电机组制造
广东三木科技有限公司	常平镇	其他通用设备制造业
东莞市超逸建材有限公司	常平镇	其他建筑材料制造
东莞市杰伦塑胶灯饰有限公司	常平镇	照明灯具制造
东莞市乔锋机械有限公司	常平镇	金属切削机床制造
东莞市双俊电子科技有限公司	常平镇	汽车零部件及配件制造
东莞凡进工业模具有限公司	常平镇	其他塑料制品制造
东莞利铿电子有限公司	常平镇	电子元件及组件制造
东莞盛美塑胶机械有限公司	常平镇	塑料加工专用设备制造
东莞市百方建航机械配件有限公司	常平镇	其他金属加工机械制造
东莞市百富塑料科技有限公司	常平镇	初级形态塑料及合成树脂制造
东莞市龙谊电子科技有限公司	常平镇	电子元件及组件制造
东莞市青洋包装制品有限公司	常平镇	包装装潢及其他印刷
东莞市森泰玻璃制品有限公司	常平镇	其他玻璃制品制造
东莞市世通国际快件监管中心有限公司	常平镇	装卸搬运
东莞市索菲电子科技有限公司	常平镇	光电子器件及其他电子器件制造
东莞市万丰纳米材料有限公司	常平镇	塑料薄膜制造
东莞市威邦仪器设备有限公司	常平镇	实验分析仪器制造
东莞市映宁轩电子科技有限公司	常平镇	其他通用零部件制造
广东派迪茵体育股份有限公司	常平镇	其他体育用品制造
广东万恒通家居制品有限公司	常平镇	其他日用品生产专用设备制造
广东优科检测技术服务有限公司	常平镇	质检技术服务
广东智恒信息技术有限公司	常平镇	信息系统集成服务
东莞昶通精密五金有限公司	常平镇	电子元件及组件制造
东莞市承恩自动化设备有限公司	常平镇	电子工业专用设备制造
东莞市冠榕五金制品有限公司	常平镇	其他金属工具制造
东莞市国研电热材料有限公司	常平镇	其他未列明制造业
东莞市环宇文化科技有限公司	常平镇	其他文化艺术业
东莞市康茂电子有限公司	常平镇	计算机外围设备制造
东莞市林氏生物技术股份有限公司	常平镇	其他农业
东莞市美赛特自动化设备有限公司	常平镇	其他通用设备制造业
东莞市品冠检测科技有限公司	常平镇	其他通用设备制造业
东莞市深鹏电子有限公司	常平镇	泵及真空设备制造
东莞市沃顿橡塑新材料有限公司	常平镇	计算机外围设备制造
东莞市一辉油压机械有限公司	常平镇	其他金属加工机械制造
东莞市银燕电气科技有限公司	常平镇	微电机及其他电机制造
东莞市英耀灯饰有限公司	常平镇	照明灯具制造

1-5 续表 32

（2016年）

企业名称	所在镇街	行业类别
广东东莞市天润电子材料有限公司	常平镇	其他非金属矿物制品制造
广东弘擎电子材料科技有限公司	常平镇	塑料薄膜制造
东莞市安高瑞新材料科技有限公司	常平镇	其他基础化学原料制造
东莞市晟钫实业有限公司	常平镇	计算机外围设备制造
东莞市五全机械有限公司	常平镇	矿山机械制造
东莞市希锐自动化科技股份有限公司	常平镇	其他非金属加工专用设备制造
东莞市越铧电子科技有限公司	常平镇	试验机制造
广东维信智联科技有限公司	常平镇	信息系统集成服务
五川音响电子科技（东莞）有限公司	常平镇	音响设备制造
智嘉通讯科技（东莞）有限公司	常平镇	电子元件及组件制造
广东富林木业科技有限公司	常平镇	生态与环境
东莞市玖木通实业有限公司	桥头镇	其他电子设备制造
东莞市凯成环保科技有限公司	桥头镇	包装装潢及其他印刷
东莞市鑫诠光电技术有限公司	桥头镇	光电子器件及其他电子器件制造
东莞市吉之晟电子科技有限公司	桥头镇	电子元件及组件制造
东莞泰克威科技有限公司	桥头镇	其他电子设备制造
东莞市美盈森环保科技有限公司	桥头镇	纸和纸板容器制造
东莞市技塑塑胶科技有限公司	桥头镇	其他橡胶制品制造
东莞市井田自动化设备有限公司	桥头镇	其他通用设备制造业
东莞市托普莱斯光电技术有限公司	桥头镇	电视机制造
东莞市日新传导科技股份有限公司	桥头镇	电线、电缆制造
东莞新友智能科技有限公司	桥头镇	其他通用设备制造业
东莞市斯坦得电子材料有限公司	桥头镇	其他未列明制造业
东莞市富印胶粘科技有限公司	桥头镇	其他塑料制品制造
东莞市华星镀膜科技有限公司	桥头镇	通信终端设备制造
广东顺捷威玻璃机械有限公司	桥头镇	其他玻璃制品制造
东莞市美饰家窗帘制品有限公司	桥头镇	软木制品及其他木制品制造
东莞市耀弘光电有限公司	桥头镇	电光源制造
东莞兴博精密模具有限公司	桥头镇	模具制造
东莞大和化成汽车零配件有限公司	桥头镇	塑料零件制造
东莞市鼎力薄膜科技有限公司	桥头镇	塑料薄膜制造
东莞市峰沃光电有限公司	桥头镇	电视机制造
东莞市汇林包装有限公司	桥头镇	其他纸制品制造
东莞市龙天仪器设备有限公司	桥头镇	电子测量仪器制造
东莞市美芯龙物联网科技有限公司	桥头镇	电子元件及组件制造
东莞市睿泰涂布科技有限公司	桥头镇	塑料薄膜制造
广东宏工物料自动化系统有限公司	桥头镇	其他通用设备制造业
广东健润压铸科技有限公司	桥头镇	铝压延加工
广东太安伊侨气体设备有限公司	桥头镇	气体压缩机械制造
东莞市实优特电子有限公司	桥头镇	电子元件及组件制造
广东博识达科技股份有限公司	桥头镇	其他塑料制品制造
东莞市汉维科技股份有限公司	桥头镇	有机化学原料制造
东莞市西格玛自动化科技有限公司	桥头镇	其他通用设备制造业
广东金润和科技股份有限公司	桥头镇	其他电子设备制造
东莞缔奇智能股份有限公司	横沥镇	家用清洁卫生电器具制造
东莞市准光半导体照明有限公司	横沥镇	光电子器件及其他电子器件制造
东莞市鑫品模具有限公司	横沥镇	模具制造
东莞市万丰科技有限公司	横沥镇	电线、电缆制造
东莞虹日金属科技有限公司	横沥镇	其他金属加工机械制造
广东天誉飞歌电子科技有限公司	横沥镇	导航、气象及海洋专用仪器制造
东莞旭光五金氧化制品有限公司	横沥镇	金属表面处理及热处理加工

1-5 续表 33

(2016年)

企业名称	所在镇街	行业类别
东莞和汇电子有限公司	横沥镇	汽车零部件及配件制造
东莞市天倬模具有限公司	横沥镇	模具制造
东莞市久森新能源有限公司	横沥镇	锂离子电池制造
东莞市天倬电器有限公司	横沥镇	家用厨房电器具制造
东莞市恒和节能科技有限公司	横沥镇	其他水泥类似制品制造
东莞市森斯电子机械科技有限公司	横沥镇	工业自动控制系统装置制造
东莞市天桉硅胶科技有限公司	横沥镇	合成橡胶制造
广东正茂精机有限公司	横沥镇	塑料加工专用设备制造
东莞市和永包装有限公司	横沥镇	其他塑料制品制造
东莞雷笛克光学有限公司	横沥镇	其他未列明制造业
东莞巨扬电器有限公司	横沥镇	照明灯具制造
东莞市擎洲光电科技有限公司	横沥镇	照明灯具制造
东莞爱美达电子有限公司	横沥镇	其他通用零部件制造
东莞精恒电子有限公司	横沥镇	音响设备制造
东莞市中泰模具股份有限公司	横沥镇	模具制造
东莞台一盈拓科技股份有限公司	横沥镇	金属切削机床制造
东莞市孺子牛机器人有限公司	横沥镇	其他专用设备制造
东莞致嘉金属科技有限公司	横沥镇	模具制造
东莞市卓高电子科技有限公司	横沥镇	其他未列明制造业
意拉德电子（东莞）有限公司	横沥镇	其他未列明制造业
东莞市凯誉自动化设备有限公司	横沥镇	其他电子设备制造
东莞市兆科电子材料科技有限公司	横沥镇	其他未列明制造业
呈威电子（东莞）有限公司	横沥镇	集成电路制造
东莞市奥纳水务科技有限公司	横沥镇	其他专用仪器制造
东莞市博派电子科技有限公司	横沥镇	汽车零部件及配件制造
东莞市才立金属科技有限公司	横沥镇	其他专用设备制造
东莞市华庄电子有限公司	横沥镇	汽车零部件及配件制造
东莞市今隽机械有限公司	横沥镇	塑料加工专用设备制造
东莞市铭雷电子科技有限公司	横沥镇	其他医疗设备及器械制造
东莞市润丽华实业有限公司	横沥镇	油墨及类似产品制造
东莞市上运激光制版有限公司	横沥镇	印刷专用设备制造
东莞市永茂食品科技有限公司	横沥镇	豆制品制造
东莞市卓比塑胶制品有限公司	横沥镇	日用塑料制品制造
广东九佛新材料科技有限公司	横沥镇	其他合成材料制造
群智电子科技（东莞）有限公司	横沥镇	电力电子元器件制造
东莞骏屹精密模具有限公司	横沥镇	模具制造
东莞乔隆家具配件制品有限公司	横沥镇	其他家具制造
东莞市富士多实业投资有限公司	横沥镇	计算机外围设备制造
东莞市港奇电子有限公司	横沥镇	其他电子设备制造
东莞市高美光电照明有限公司	横沥镇	照明灯具制造
东莞市翰硕塑胶有限公司	横沥镇	计算机零部件制造
东莞市华越自动化设备有限公司	横沥镇	其他通用设备制造业
东莞市佳铠精密金属制品有限公司	横沥镇	弹簧制造
东莞市顺翼机械有限公司	横沥镇	其他专用设备制造
广东伟的新材料股份有限公司	横沥镇	其他塑料制品制造
东莞市优力普物联科技有限公司	横沥镇	通信终端设备制造
飞比达电子元器件（东莞）有限公司	横沥镇	电子元件及组件制造
广东壹豪新材料科技股份有限公司	横沥镇	其他塑料制品制造
广东智维立体成型科技有限公司	横沥镇	电子工业专用设备制造
东莞秦汉汽车模具技术有限公司	横沥镇	模具制造
东莞市鼎杰实业有限公司	横沥镇	其他塑料制品制造

1-5　续表 34

(2016年)

企业名称	所在镇街	行业类别
东莞市航达电子有限公司	横沥镇	绝缘制品制造
东莞市瑞凯环境检测仪器有限公司	横沥镇	环境监测专用仪器仪表制造
东莞市沃顿印刷有限公司	横沥镇	包装装潢及其他印刷
东莞市煜田新材料有限公司	横沥镇	特种陶瓷制品制造
东莞市元升光学有限公司	横沥镇	光学玻璃制造
博莱特光电科技（东莞）有限公司	横沥镇	照明灯具制造
东莞市尼的净化科技有限公司	横沥镇	其他合成材料制造
东莞市顺林模型礼品有限公司	横沥镇	玩具制造
广东明家联合移动科技股份有限公司	横沥镇	其他未列明电气机械及器材制造
鑫贺精密电子（东莞）有限公司	横沥镇	其他电子设备制造
广东泰晶新能源有限公司	横沥镇	太阳能发电
东莞市博恒达模具有限公司	横沥镇	模具制造
东莞市龙钢模胚钢材有限公司	横沥镇	先进制造业与装备
广东中德电缆有限公司	东坑镇	电线、电缆制造
东莞市康德威变压器有限公司	东坑镇	变压器、整流器和电感器制造
东莞市金禄电子科技有限公司	东坑镇	其他通用零部件制造
东莞市维美德电子材料有限公司	东坑镇	其他未列明金属制品制造
广东迅扬电脑科技股份有限公司	东坑镇	计算机外围设备制造
东莞城市装钉器材有限公司	东坑镇	其他通用设备制造业
东莞市赛德高树脂有限公司	东坑镇	其他合成材料制造
东莞市宝轮电脑刺绣机械有限公司	东坑镇	缝制机械制造
东莞明信电子有限公司	东坑镇	其他电子设备制造
东莞市博恩复合材料有限公司	东坑镇	其他橡胶制品制造
东莞市杰伟机械制造有限公司	东坑镇	其他通用设备制造业
东莞市迈安顿电子科技有限公司	东坑镇	其他电子设备制造
东莞市裕鸿傢具有限公司	东坑镇	其他家具制造
东莞市众盛硅橡胶制品有限公司	东坑镇	其他橡胶制品制造
广东宾豪科技股份有限公司	东坑镇	皮箱、包（袋）制造
广东华科检测技术服务有限公司	东坑镇	质检技术服务
东莞国亮电机有限公司	东坑镇	微电机及其他电机制造
东莞迈特通讯科技有限公司	东坑镇	通信系统设备制造
东莞市博通电气设备工程有限公司	东坑镇	制冷、空调设备制造
东莞市韩龙云数码科技有限公司	东坑镇	电视机制造
东莞新能德科技有限公司	东坑镇	锂离子电池制造
广东惠和硅制品有限公司	东坑镇	无机盐制造
东莞市艾炜特电子有限公司	东坑镇	集成电路及电子元器件
东莞市华胜展鸿电子科技有限公司	东坑镇	新能源照明灯具制造
广东泰卓光电科技股份有限公司	东坑镇	新能源电光源制造
东莞毓华电子科技有限公司	企石镇	电子元件及组件制造
东莞山多力汽车配件有限公司	企石镇	汽车零部件及配件制造
东莞市中镓半导体科技有限公司	企石镇	光电子器件及其他电子器件制造
广东美信科技股份有限公司	企石镇	其他通用零部件制造
东莞市台电环保科技有限公司	企石镇	塑料加工专用设备制造
东莞市新望包装机械有限公司	企石镇	包装专用设备制造
广东友通工业有限公司	企石镇	其他通用设备制造业
广东若天新材料科技有限公司	企石镇	其他基础化学原料制造
东莞联宝光电科技有限公司	企石镇	电子元件及组件制造
东莞健达照明有限公司	企石镇	电光源制造
东莞捷瑞精密硅胶科技有限公司	企石镇	其他橡胶制品制造
东莞仁海科技股份有限公司	企石镇	风机、风扇制造
东莞市美拉德食品有限公司	企石镇	其他未列明食品制造

1-5 续表 35

(2016年)

企业名称	所在镇街	行业类别
东莞市若美电子科技有限公司	企石镇	其他未列明制造业
东莞市博发光电科技有限公司	企石镇	照明灯具制造
东莞市恒丰高新技术开发有限公司	企石镇	日用塑料制品制造
东莞市慧勤光电科技有限公司	企石镇	光电子器件及其他电子器件制造
东莞市铁生辉制罐有限公司	企石镇	金属结构制造
东莞市享达光电科技有限公司	企石镇	照明灯具制造
广东鸿翔工程检测咨询有限公司	企石镇	其他未列明专业技术服务业
广东汇诚科技有限公司	企石镇	其他未列明信息技术服务业
广东绿源巢信息科技有限公司	企石镇	数据处理和存储服务
东莞市通日环保科技有限公司	企石镇	其他通用设备制造业
东莞市优特美工程塑料有限公司	企石镇	初级形态塑料及合成树脂制造
广东居峰环保科技有限公司	企石镇	环境保护专用设备制造
广东新光源电子科技有限公司	企石镇	电子元件及组件制造
广东伊普思实业有限公司	企石镇	泵及真空设备制造
东莞市思泉实业有限公司	企石镇	电力电子元器件制造
东莞市鑫晖达机械制造有限公司	企石镇	其他通用设备制造业
广东朝阳电子科技股份有限公司	企石镇	其他塑料制品制造
东莞乐域光电科技有限公司	石排镇	照明灯具制造
广东凯德能源科技有限公司	石排镇	锂离子电池制造
东莞市德颖光电有限公司	石排镇	其他电子设备制造
东莞铭普光磁股份有限公司	石排镇	光电子器件及其他电子器件制造
广东星弛光电科技有限公司	石排镇	平板玻璃制造
广东谷麦光电科技股份有限公司	石排镇	光电子器件及其他电子器件制造
广东旭业光电科技股份有限公司	石排镇	光电子器件及其他电子器件制造
东莞市悠悠美居家居制造有限公司	石排镇	日用塑料制品制造
东莞市智乐堡儿童玩具有限公司	石排镇	玩具制造
广东剑鑫科技股份有限公司	石排镇	化学试剂和助剂制造
东莞市盛旭电子科技有限公司	石排镇	电线、电缆制造
东莞市迈特运动用品有限公司	石排镇	运动防护用具制造
东莞市浩鑫电子有限公司	石排镇	电子元件及组件制造
东莞市鸿程机械有限公司	石排镇	印刷专用设备制造
东莞市立敏达电子科技有限公司	石排镇	电子元件及组件制造
东莞市励骏高分子材料有限公司	石排镇	日用塑料制品制造
东莞市启原实业有限公司	石排镇	其他塑料制品制造
东莞市双知艺坊洁具有限公司	石排镇	其他塑料制品制造
东莞市翔光光电科技有限公司	石排镇	电力电子元器件制造
东莞市长铭电子有限公司	石排镇	电线、电缆制造
东莞市港照照明科技有限公司	石排镇	光电子器件及其他电子器件制造
东莞市广督实业有限公司	石排镇	电子元件及组件制造
东莞市海威智能装备股份有限公司	石排镇	其他通用设备制造业
东莞市欣能电器有限公司	石排镇	家用厨房电器具制造
东莞市优拓汽车配件有限公司	石排镇	汽车零部件及配件制造
东莞市比迪电器有限公司	石排镇	光电子器件及其他电子器件制造
东莞市雅思机械设备有限公司	石排镇	包装专用设备制造
东莞市耐斯机械制造有限公司	茶山镇	其他未列明制造业
广东紫光电气有限公司	茶山镇	配电开关控制设备制造
东莞市闻誉实业有限公司	茶山镇	其他有色金属压延加工
广东悠派智能展示科技股份有限公司	茶山镇	其他家具制造
东莞市三肯电子制造有限公司	茶山镇	其他电子设备制造
东莞市英科水墨有限公司	茶山镇	油墨及类似产品制造
东莞森玛仕格里菲电路有限公司	茶山镇	印制电路板制造

1-5 续表 36

(2016年)

企业名称	所在镇街	行业类别
东莞市箭冠汽车配件制造有限公司	茶山镇	汽车零部件及配件制造
东莞市奥能工程塑料有限公司	茶山镇	其他塑料制品制造
东莞市思为客自动化科技股份有限公司	茶山镇	其他原动设备制造
东莞市欧科光电科技有限公司	茶山镇	其他塑料制品制造
东莞福哥电子有限公司	茶山镇	电子元件及组件制造
东莞市坚成电子科技有限公司	茶山镇	电工机械专用设备制造
东莞市拓展实业有限公司	茶山镇	涤纶纤维制造
东莞市沃森实业有限公司	茶山镇	其他金属加工机械制造
广东富本电梯有限公司	茶山镇	电梯、自动扶梯及升降机制造
东莞侨鼎弹簧机械有限公司	茶山镇	其他金属加工机械制造
东莞市特润电子科技有限公司	茶山镇	半导体分立器件制造
多摩电子（东莞）有限公司	茶山镇	其他电子设备制造
广东福美新材料科技有限公司	茶山镇	其他纸制品制造
广东新比克斯实业股份有限公司	茶山镇	五金产品批发
东莞联桥电子有限公司	茶山镇	印制电路板制造
东莞市昂力电池科技有限公司	茶山镇	其他电池制造
东莞市驰明电子科技有限公司	茶山镇	灯用电器附件及其他照明器具制造
东莞市汉和食品机械设备有限公司	茶山镇	其他通用设备制造业
东莞市可变电子有限公司	茶山镇	电子元件及组件制造
东莞市鹏驰净化科技有限公司	茶山镇	环境保护专用设备制造
东莞市腾信精密仪器有限公司	茶山镇	其他仪器仪表制造业
东莞翔国光电科技有限公司	茶山镇	印制电路板制造
东莞安力五金塑胶制品有限公司	茶山镇	其他未列明金属制品制造
东莞市宏诚光学制品有限公司	茶山镇	光学玻璃制造
东莞市鹏润化工产品有限公司	茶山镇	其他专用化学产品制造
东莞市耀宇塑胶五金制品有限公司	茶山镇	其他塑料制品制造
东莞市毅达电子有限公司	茶山镇	医疗诊断、监护及治疗设备制造
广东茵茵股份有限公司	茶山镇	其他纸制品制造
广东红珊瑚药业有限公司	松山湖	中成药生产
东莞市精研粉体科技有限公司	松山湖	锻件及粉末冶金制品制造
东莞市纳声电子设备科技有限公司	松山湖	其他专用设备制造
东莞市腾威电子材料技术有限公司	松山湖	其他电子设备制造
广东新球清洗科技股份有限公司	松山湖	肥皂及合成洗涤剂制造
东莞市风火轮热能科技有限公司	松山湖	其他原动设备制造
广东高标电子科技有限公司	松山湖	电力电子元器件制造
广东拓荒牛智能切割科技股份有限公司	松山湖	其他专用设备制造
广东康菱动力科技有限公司	松山湖	其他通用设备制造业
广东荣文能源科技集团有限公司	松山湖	其他未列明信息技术服务业
广东雨林木风计算机科技有限公司	松山湖	互联网信息服务
东莞中之光电股份有限公司	松山湖	光电子器件及其他电子器件制造
广东华南工业设计院	松山湖	专业化设计服务
广东大普通信技术有限公司	松山湖	电子元件及组件制造
东莞市万科建筑技术研究有限公司	松山湖	工程和技术研究和试验发展
东莞爱尚菇食品科技有限公司	松山湖	其他未列明食品制造
东莞市亚聚电子材料有限公司	松山湖	其他合成材料制造
东莞市天域半导体科技有限公司	松山湖	半导体分立器件制造
广东洛贝电子科技有限公司	松山湖	家用厨房电器具制造
广东正业科技股份有限公司	松山湖	实验分析仪器制造
广东生益科技股份有限公司	松山湖	电子元件及组件制造
华为终端（东莞）有限公司	松山湖	通信终端设备制造
东莞市凯欣电池材料有限公司	松山湖	锂离子电池制造

1-5 续表 37

(2016年)

企业名称	所在镇街	行业类别
广东阿尔派新材料股份有限公司	松山湖	其他输配电及控制设备制造
广东百圳君耀电子有限公司	松山湖	电子元件及组件制造
广东电子工业研究院有限公司	松山湖	信息技术咨询服务
广东中科遥感技术有限公司	松山湖	信息系统集成服务
领亚电子科技股份有限公司	松山湖	计算机外围设备制造
东莞瑞柯电子科技股份有限公司	松山湖	汽车零部件及配件制造
广东东阳光药业有限公司	松山湖	化学药品制剂制造
广东阿尔派电力科技股份有限公司	松山湖	其他输配电及控制设备制造
东莞市意普万尼龙科技股份有限公司	松山湖	初级形态塑料及合成树脂制造
东莞市百大新能源股份有限公司	松山湖	非金属废料和碎屑加工处理
东莞市贝特电子科技股份有限公司	松山湖	电子元件及组件制造
广东纳明新材料科技有限公司	松山湖	其他非金属矿物制品制造
广东威迪科技股份有限公司	松山湖	水资源专用机械制造
东莞市东思电子技术有限公司	松山湖	电子元件及组件制造
广东亨通光电科技有限公司	松山湖	光纤、光缆制造
广东科创工程技术有限公司	松山湖	其他水的处理、利用与分配
广东世纪网通信设备股份有限公司	松山湖	信息系统集成服务
广东科硕机械科技股份有限公司	松山湖	电子工业专用设备制造
东莞东石新材料开发有限公司	松山湖	玻璃纤维增强塑料制品制造
广东尚睿网络技术有限公司	松山湖	互联网信息服务
广东华盈光达科技有限公司	松山湖	信息系统集成服务
东莞市劲威智能冲压成套设备有限公司	松山湖	金属成形机床制造
东莞易步机器人有限公司	松山湖	助动自行车制造
广东三凯新材料股份有限公司	松山湖	其他橡胶制品制造
国云科技股份有限公司	松山湖	信息系统集成服务
东莞润赢电力科技有限公司	松山湖	信息系统集成服务
东莞市帕马智能停车服务有限公司	松山湖	其他未列明信息技术服务业
东莞市锐源仪器股份有限公司	松山湖	电子测量仪器制造
广东新东方光电有限公司	松山湖	光电子器件及其他电子器件制造
东莞市远峰科技有限公司	松山湖	其他电子设备制造
广东奥美格传导科技股份有限公司	松山湖	电线、电缆制造
广东泰通农业发展集团股份有限公司	松山湖	其他未列明农副食品加工
东莞新能源科技有限公司	松山湖	锂离子电池制造
东莞市科磊得数码光电科技有限公司	松山湖	照明灯具制造
广东中实金属有限公司	松山湖	其他常用有色金属冶炼
东莞温思帝寝具科技有限公司	松山湖	床上用品制造
广东国方医药科技有限公司	松山湖	中药材种植
广东长盈精密技术有限公司	松山湖	电子元件及组件制造
优利德科技（中国）有限公司	松山湖	电工仪器仪表制造
东莞成电精工自动化技术有限公司	松山湖	电工机械专用设备制造
东莞光谷茂和激光技术有限公司	松山湖	其他通用设备制造业
东莞精科自动化科技有限公司	松山湖	工业自动控制系统装置制造
东莞市创明电池技术有限公司	松山湖	锂离子电池制造
东莞市将为防伪科技有限公司	松山湖	其他纸制品制造
东莞市李群自动化技术有限公司	松山湖	其他专用设备制造
东莞市新弘高科智能仪表有限公司	松山湖	其他仪器仪表制造业
东莞市星火太阳能科技股份有限公司	松山湖	光伏设备及元器件制造
东莞市中鼎检测技术有限公司	松山湖	质检技术服务
广东维锐科技股份有限公司	松山湖	信息系统集成服务
广东艾力达动漫文化娱乐有限公司	松山湖	其他文化艺术业
广东博迈医疗器械有限公司	松山湖	医疗诊断、监护及治疗设备制造

1-5 续表 38

(2016年)

企业名称	所在镇街	行业类别
广东华灿电讯科技有限公司	松山湖	通信系统设备制造
广东凯宝机器人科技有限公司	松山湖	其他未列明制造业
广东睿超电子科技有限公司	松山湖	其他医疗设备及器械制造
广东万云信息科技有限公司	松山湖	信息系统集成服务
广东盈动高科自动化有限公司	松山湖	工业自动控制系统装置制造
东莞泛亚太生物科技有限公司	松山湖	食品及饲料添加剂制造
东莞三新电动汽车技术有限公司	松山湖	汽车整车制造
广东中道创意科技有限公司	松山湖	专业化设计服务
广东艾沃科技有限公司	松山湖	家用厨房电器具制造
广东丹邦科技有限公司	松山湖	印制电路板制造
东莞博捷生物科技有限公司	松山湖	其他医疗设备及器械制造
东莞固高自动化技术有限公司	松山湖	工业自动控制系统装置制造
东莞光韵达光电科技有限公司	松山湖	光电子器件及其他电子器件制造
东莞见达信息技术有限公司	松山湖	信息技术咨询服务
东莞帕姆蒂昊宇液态金属有限公司	松山湖	有色金属合金制造
东莞市百赛仪器有限公司	松山湖	工业自动控制系统装置制造
东莞市迪优门窗科技有限公司	松山湖	新材料技术推广服务
东莞市富卡信息科技有限公司	松山湖	互联网信息服务
东莞市杰诺软件科技有限公司	松山湖	计算机、软件及辅助设备零售
东莞市骏智机电科技有限公司	松山湖	工业自动控制系统装置制造
东莞市蓝姆材料科技有限公司	松山湖	绝缘制品制造
东莞市乐升电子有限公司	松山湖	集成电路设计
东莞市麦亘生物科技有限公司	松山湖	机械治疗及病房护理设备制造
东莞市泰创电子科技有限公司	松山湖	其他电子设备制造
东莞市腾宇龙机械能源科技股份有限公司	松山湖	其他橡胶制品制造
东莞市翔通光电技术有限公司	松山湖	光电子器件及其他电子器件制造
东莞市中图半导体科技有限公司	松山湖	光电子器件及其他电子器件制造
东莞斯富特检测技术服务有限公司	松山湖	质检技术服务
东莞松科信息科技有限公司	松山湖	信息技术咨询服务
东莞威耀数控设备有限公司	松山湖	其他专用设备制造
东莞熙隆电子科技有限公司	松山湖	其他互联网服务
东莞英华融泰医疗科技有限公司	松山湖	其他医疗设备及器械制造
东莞震坤软件有限公司	松山湖	软件开发
广东爱迪贝克软件科技有限公司	松山湖	计算机外围设备制造
广东酷乐互娱科技股份有限公司	松山湖	互联网信息服务
广东朗呈医疗器械科技有限公司	松山湖	口腔科用设备及器具制造
广东思派康电子科技有限公司	松山湖	其他电子设备制造
广东松湖动力技术有限公司	松山湖	锂离子电池制造
广东中硕能源科技有限公司	松山湖	其他科技推广和应用服务业
东莞爱乐电子科技有限公司	松山湖	音响设备制造
东莞成电金盘软件技术有限公司	松山湖	软件开发
东莞光智通讯科技有限公司	松山湖	光电子器件及其他电子器件制造
东莞华科东尼仪器有限公司	松山湖	供应用仪表及其他通用仪器制造
东莞日阵薄膜光伏技术有限公司	松山湖	其他专用仪器制造
东莞赛尔生物科技有限公司	松山湖	生物药品制造
东莞圣源环保科技有限公司	松山湖	水污染治理
东莞市安磁检测技术有限公司	松山湖	质检技术服务
东莞市大疆创新科技有限公司	松山湖	其他航空航天器制造
东莞市东铝铝业有限公司	松山湖	金属表面处理及热处理加工
东莞市方大新材料有限公司	松山湖	其他玻璃制造
东莞市光能新能源科技有限公司	松山湖	照明灯具制造

1-5 续表 39

(2016年)

企业名称	所在镇街	行业类别
东莞市升宇智能科技有限公司	松山湖	其他专用设备制造
东莞市松湖塑料机械股份有限公司	松山湖	塑料加工专用设备制造
东莞市新路标自动化设备技术有限公司	松山湖	电子工业专用设备制造
东莞市优超精密技术有限公司	松山湖	光电子器件及其他电子器件制造
东莞市珍葆电器科技有限公司	松山湖	家用厨房电器具制造
东莞市中科智恒新材料有限公司	松山湖	其他基础化学原料制造
东莞芯成电子科技有限公司	松山湖	电子元件及组件制造
东莞新吉凯氏测量技术有限公司	松山湖	质检技术服务
东莞展能信息科技有限公司	松山湖	互联网信息服务
广东东邦科技有限公司	松山湖	通信终端设备制造
广东合微集成电路技术有限公司	松山湖	集成电路设计
广东恒润光电有限公司	松山湖	照明灯具制造
广东葫芦堡文化科技股份有限公司	松山湖	木质家具制造
广东晶谷照明科技有限公司	松山湖	照明灯具制造
广东科明环境仪器工业有限公司	松山湖	供应用仪表及其他通用仪器制造
龙正环保股份有限公司	松山湖	热力生产和供应
广东全诚信息科技有限公司	松山湖	信息系统集成服务
广东思沃精密机械有限公司	松山湖	其他电子设备制造
广东微云科技股份有限公司	松山湖	软件开发
广东易凌科技股份有限公司	松山湖	软件开发
广东易能纳米科技有限公司	松山湖	工程和技术研究和试验发展
广东远峰汽车电子有限公司	松山湖	汽车零部件及配件制造
东莞赛微微电子有限公司	松山湖	集成电路设计
东莞市本润机器人科技股份有限公司	松山湖	其他原动设备制造
东莞市绿安奇生物工程有限公司	松山湖	保健食品制造
东莞市魔方新能源科技有限公司	松山湖	其他未列明制造业
东莞市清大曜嘉信息技术有限公司	松山湖	软件开发
东莞市微格能自动化设备有限公司	松山湖	其他专用设备制造
东莞市文轩五金制品有限公司	松山湖	金属结构制造
东莞市信腾机器人科技有限公司	松山湖	工业自动控制系统装置制造
广东新创华科环保股份有限公司	松山湖	环境保护监测
广东优尼德生物科技有限公司	松山湖	医疗诊断、监护及治疗设备制造
广东中贝能源科技有限公司	松山湖	配电开关控制设备制造
海洋王（东莞）照明科技有限公司	松山湖	照明灯具制造
广东巨细信息科技有限公司	松山湖	互联网接入及相关服务
东莞道汇环保科技股份有限公司	松山湖	环境保护专用设备制造
东莞东元环境科技股份有限公司	松山湖	水污染治理
东莞汉为智能技术有限公司	松山湖	机床附件制造
安美科技股份有限公司	松山湖	其他基础化学原料制造
东莞市科旺科技股份有限公司	松山湖	变压器、整流器和电感器制造
东莞市松庆智能自动化科技有限公司	松山湖	其他通用设备制造业
广东思谷智能技术有限公司	松山湖	其他未列明制造业
广东安尔发智能科技股份有限公司	松山湖	其他通用设备制造业
广东大族粤铭激光集团股份有限公司	松山湖	金属切削机床制造
佳禾智能科技股份有限公司	松山湖	集成电路制造
广东爱瓦力科技股份有限公司	松山湖	互联网信息服务
广东微模式软件股份有限公司	松山湖	软件开发
广东一一五科技股份有限公司	松山湖	互联网信息服务
易事特集团股份有限公司	松山湖	电子元件及组件制造
东莞市苏普尔电子科技有限公司	松山湖	通信电子设备
广东普赛特电子科技股份有限公司	松山湖	光电子器件及其他电子器件制造

中国统计出版社最新图书简目

（仅供参考，以实际出版为准）

统计资料

中国统计年鉴 中国统计摘要 中国发展报告
中国经济普查年鉴 国际统计年鉴 金砖国家联合统计手册
中国-东盟国家统计手册 中国农村统计年鉴 中国县域统计年鉴
中国城市统计年鉴 中国对外直接投资统计公报 中国地区经济监测报告
中国贸易外经统计年鉴 中国零售和餐饮连锁企业统计年鉴 中国商品交易市场统计年鉴
大中型批发零售和住宿餐饮企业统计年鉴 中国农产品价格调查年鉴 中国住户调查年鉴
中国价格统计年鉴 中国能源统计年鉴 全国农产品成本收益资料汇编
中国环境统计年鉴 中国建筑业统计年鉴 国外资源、能源和环境统计资料汇编
中国工业统计年鉴 中国城乡建设统计年鉴 中国县城建设统计年鉴
中国城市建设统计年鉴 中国科技统计年鉴 中国房地产统计年鉴
中国证券期货统计年鉴 中国劳动统计年鉴 中国第三产业统计年鉴
工业企业科技活动资料 中国社会统计年鉴 中国高技术产业统计年鉴
中国人才资源统计报告 中国教育统计年鉴 中国人口和就业统计年鉴
文化及相关产业统计概览 中国文化及相关产业统计年鉴 中国教育经费统计年鉴
中国民族统计年鉴 中国残疾人事业统计年鉴 中国民政统计年鉴
中国乡镇街道行政区域简册 中国基本单位统计年鉴 中国妇女儿童状况统计资料（英）

省级综合统计年鉴系列

北京 天津 河北 山西 内蒙古 辽宁 吉林 黑龙江 上海 江苏 浙江 安徽 福建 江西 山东 河南 湖北 湖南 广东 广西 海南 重庆 四川 贵州 云南 西藏 陕西 甘肃 青海 宁夏 新疆 新疆生产建设兵团

市(县)级综合统计年鉴系列

滨海新区 石家庄 唐山 邯郸 保定 沧州 邢台 廊坊 承德 衡水 秦皇岛 张家口 太原 大同 阳泉 长治 晋城 朔州 晋中 运城 忻州 临汾 吕梁 呼和浩特 呼和浩特新城区 鄂尔多斯 包头 沈阳 大连 长春 吉林 延吉 四平 通化 松原 哈尔滨 齐齐哈尔 黑龙江垦区 上海浦东新区 南京 无锡 徐州 常州 苏州 南通 连云港 淮安 盐城 扬州 镇江 泰州 宿迁 江阴 丹阳 海门 杭州 宁波 温州 嘉兴 湖州 绍兴 金华 衢州 舟山 台州 丽水 合肥 安庆 马鞍山 福州 厦门 宁德 漳州 龙岩 南昌 九江 上饶 新余 抚州 萍乡 赣州 吉安 景德镇 济南 青岛 潍坊 枣庄 日照 滕州 郑州 洛阳 平顶山 三门峡 商丘 信阳 济源 汝州 武汉 十堰 荆州 宜昌 荆门 咸宁 长沙 广州 深圳 惠州 东莞 汕尾 南宁 柳州 桂林 来宾 河池 防城港 海口 三亚 成都 贵阳 黔南 毕节 昆明 西安 咸阳 延安 宝鸡 安康 铜川 汉中 榆林 兰州 庆阳 银川 乌鲁木齐 兵团一师 兵团十师

调查年鉴系列

天津 山西 内蒙古 辽宁 吉林 上海 福建 江西 河南 湖北 湖南 广西 重庆 四川 云南 甘肃 宁夏 新疆

统计方法应用/实用手册

实用SAS统计分析教程 马克威统计分析与数据挖掘应用案例 统计公文知识问答
乡镇统计人员岗位知识培训系列教材：辅助调查员岗位基础知识 乡镇统计人员岗位基础知识
县级统计人员岗位知识培训系列教材：Excel在统计工作中的应用 简明统计分析
地市级统计人员岗位知识培训系列教材：统计报告与演示 Excel在统计工作中的应用

统计通俗读物/统计科普图书

国家统计局核心统计指标变迁 货架上的统计 账本里的统计

重点图书

砥砺奋进的五年——从十八大到十九大 新编英汉汉英统计大词典 中华医学统计百科全书
新常态下的中国服务业：理论与实践 新动能新产业发展报告-2017
挑大学选专业2018—考研择校指南 挑大学选专业2018—高考志愿填报指南